SUPERMAN YEAR ONE

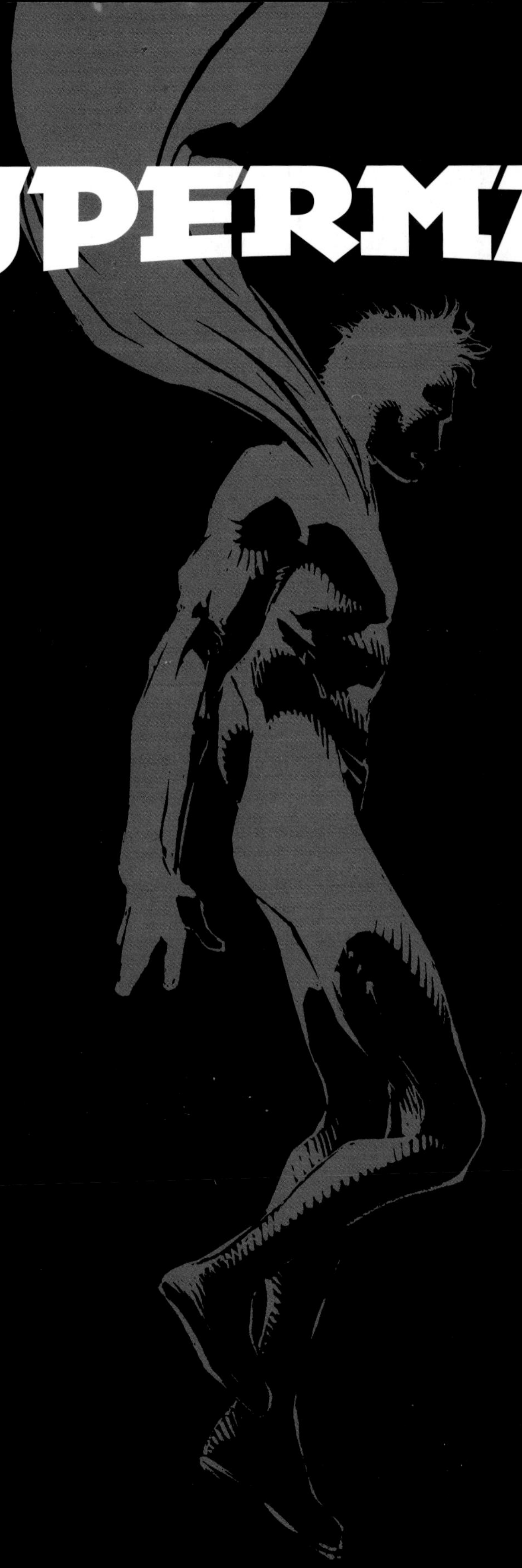

Story and Art by
FRANK MILLER and JOHN ROMITA JR.

Inks by
DANNY MIKI

Colors by
ALEX SINCLAIR

Letters by
JOHN WORKMAN

Dust Jacket Art and Original Series Cover Art by
JOHN ROMITA JR., DANNY MIKI, and ALEX SINCLAIR

Case Art by
FRANK MILLER and ALEX SINCLAIR

SUPERMAN created by JERRY SIEGEL and JOE SHUSTER
By special arrangement with the Jerry Siegel Family

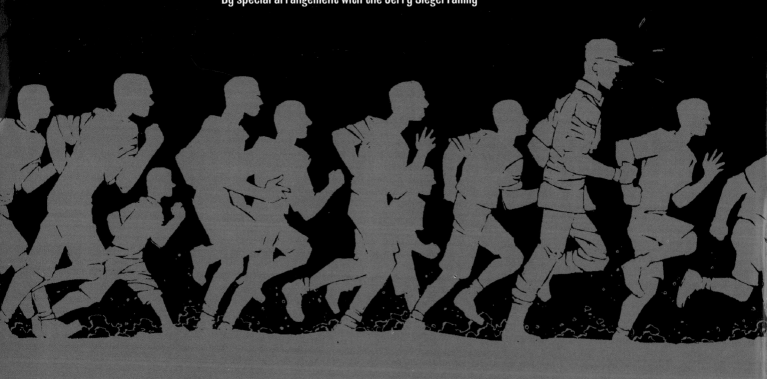

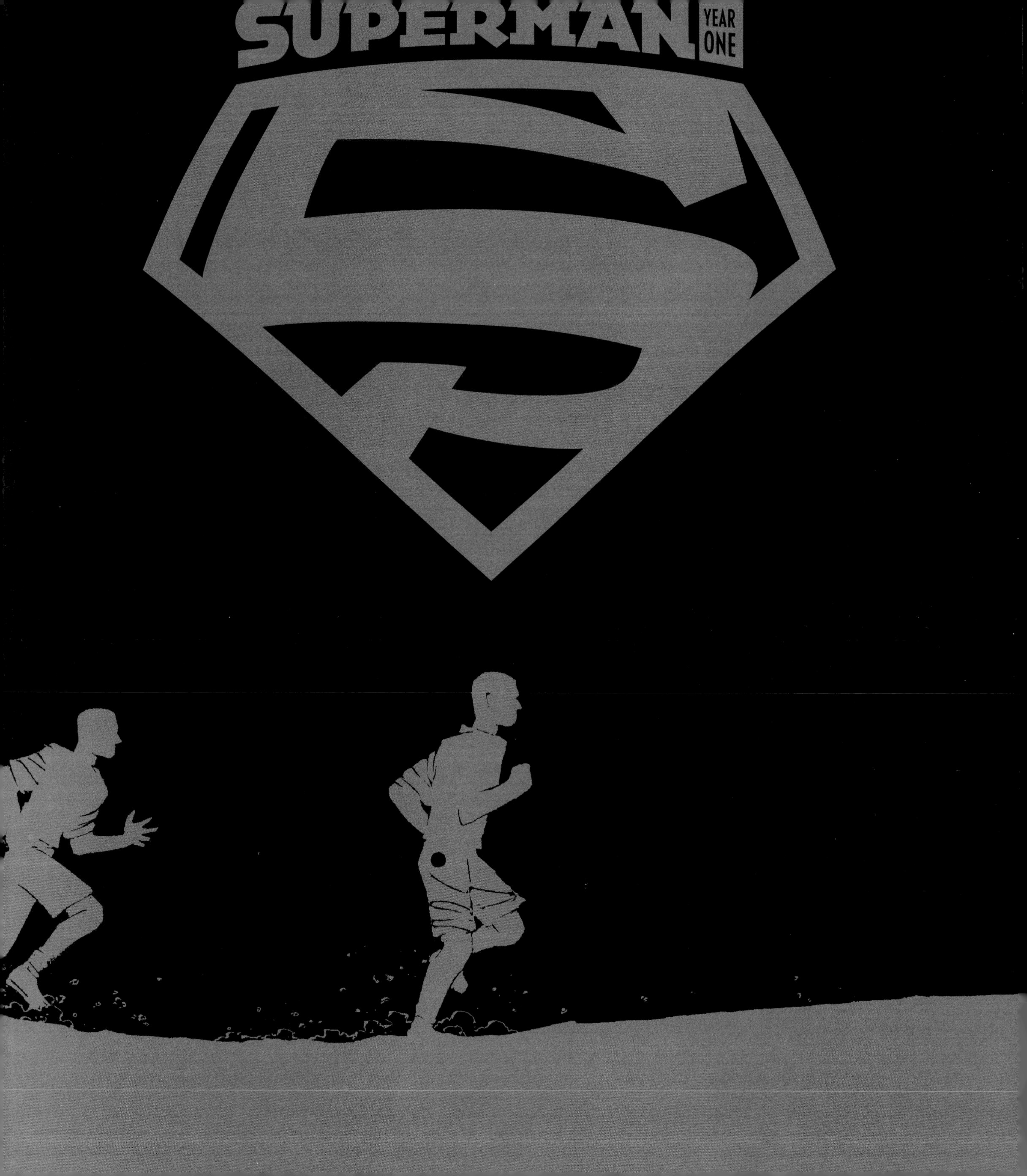
SUPERMAN
YEAR ONE

MARK DOYLE   Editor – Original Series
AMEDEO TURTURRO   Associate Editor – Original Series
JEB WOODARD   Group Editor – Collected Editions
SCOTT NYBAKKEN   Editor – Collected Edition
STEVE COOK   Design Director – Books
                            and Publication Design
KATE DURRÉ   Publication Production

BOB HARRAS   Senior VP – Editor-in-Chief, DC Comics

DAN DiDIO   Publisher
JIM LEE   Publisher & Chief Creative Officer
BOBBIE CHASE   VP – New Publishing Initiatives & Talent Development
DON FALLETTI   VP – Manufacturing Operations & Workflow Management
LAWRENCE GANEM   VP – Talent Services
ALISON GILL   Senior VP – Manufacturing & Operations
HANK KANALZ   Senior VP – Publishing Strategy & Support Services
DAN MIRON   VP – Publishing Operations
NICK J. NAPOLITANO   VP – Manufacturing Administration & Design
NANCY SPEARS   VP – Sales
MICHELE R. WELLS   VP & Executive Editor, Young Reader

Special Thanks To
SILENN THOMAS
STEVE MILLER
JEFF DANZIGER
NEAL ADAMS

SUPERMAN: YEAR ONE

DC Comics, 2900 West Alameda Ave., Burbank, CA 91505
Printed by Transcontinental Interglobe, Beauceville, QC, Canada. 10/4/19. First Printing.
ISBN: 978-1-4012-9137-2 • Barnes and Noble Exclusive Edition ISBN: 978-1-77950-238-4

Library of Congress Cataloging-in-Publication Data is available.

PEFC Certified
This product is
from sustainably
managed forests and
controlled sources

PEFC/01-31-106   www.pefc.org

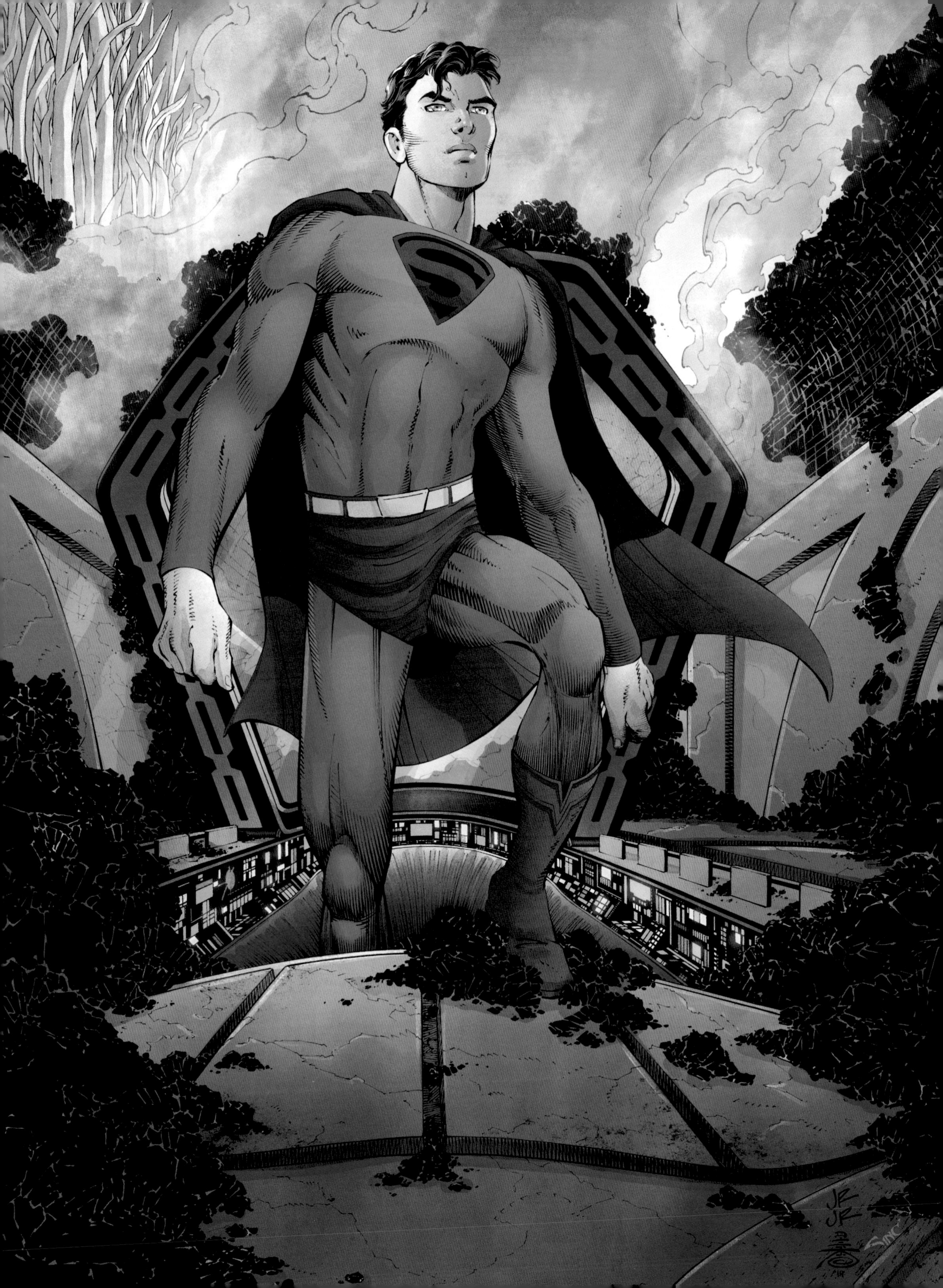

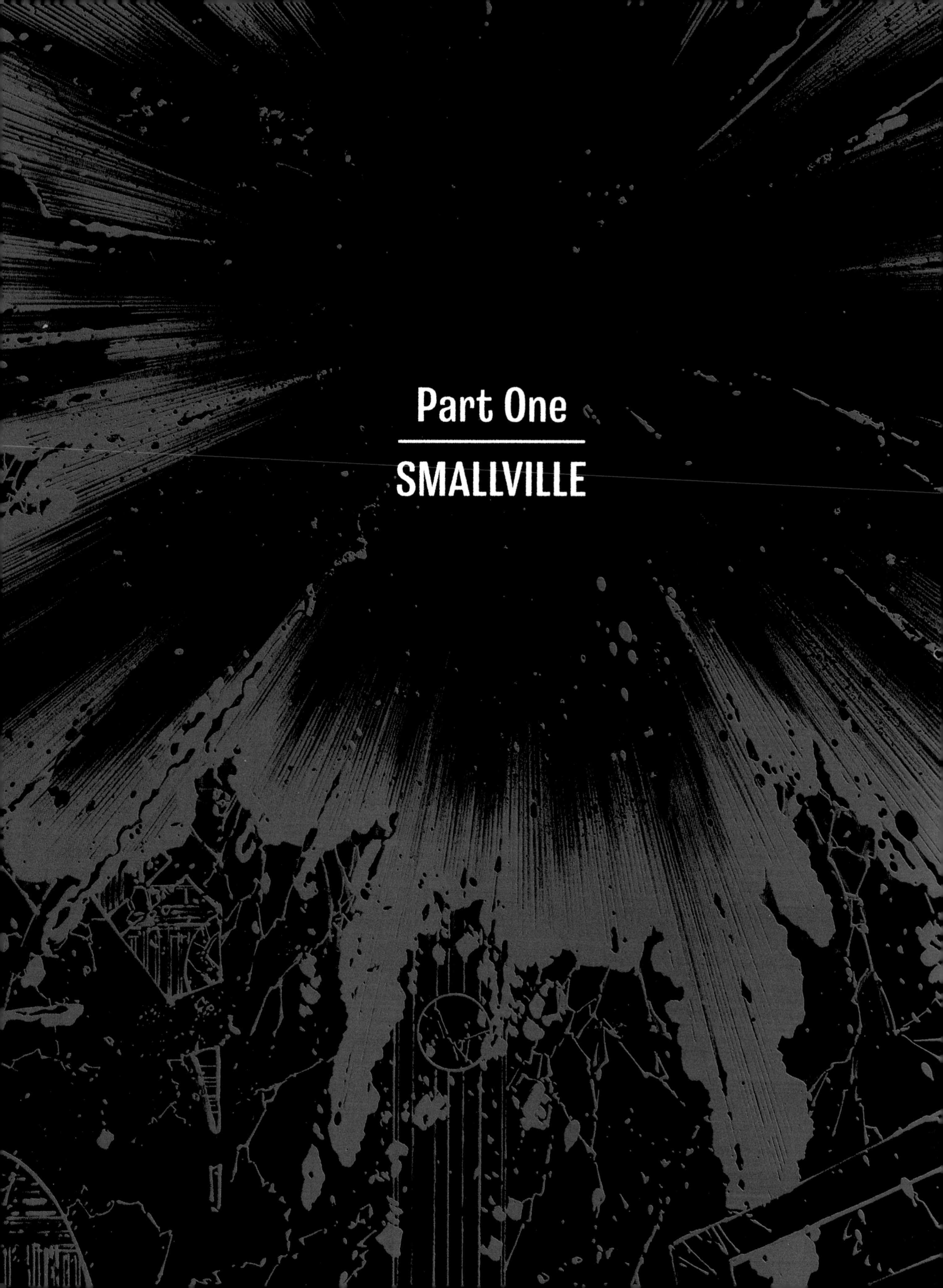

Part One

SMALLVILLE

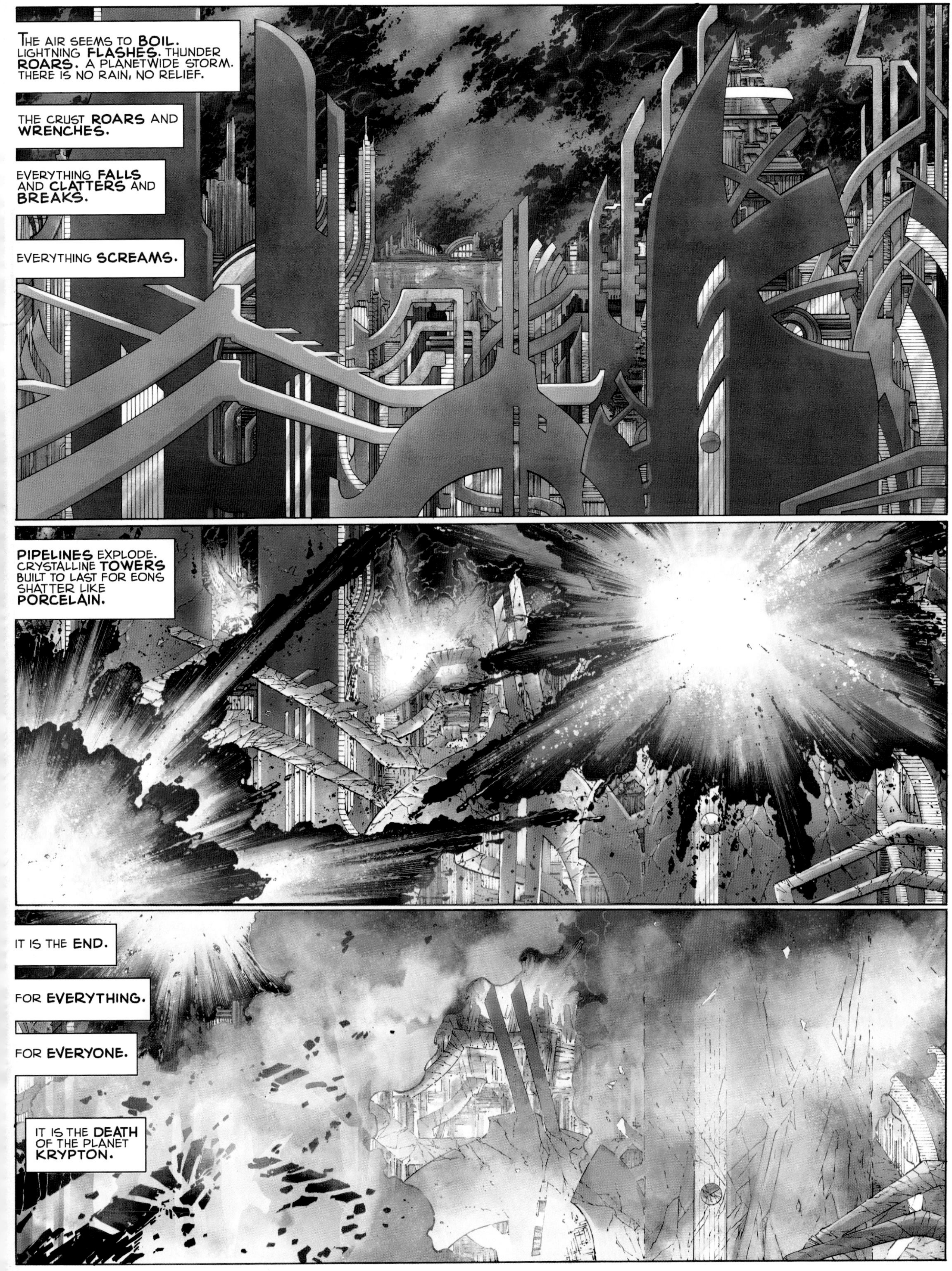
THE AIR SEEMS TO BOIL. LIGHTNING FLASHES. THUNDER ROARS. A PLANETWIDE STORM. THERE IS NO RAIN, NO RELIEF.
THE CRUST ROARS AND WRENCHES.
EVERYTHING FALLS AND CLATTERS AND BREAKS.
EVERYTHING SCREAMS.
PIPELINES EXPLODE. CRYSTALLINE TOWERS BUILT TO LAST FOR EONS SHATTER LIKE PORCELAIN.
IT IS THE END.
FOR EVERYTHING.
FOR EVERYONE.
IT IS THE DEATH OF THE PLANET KRYPTON.

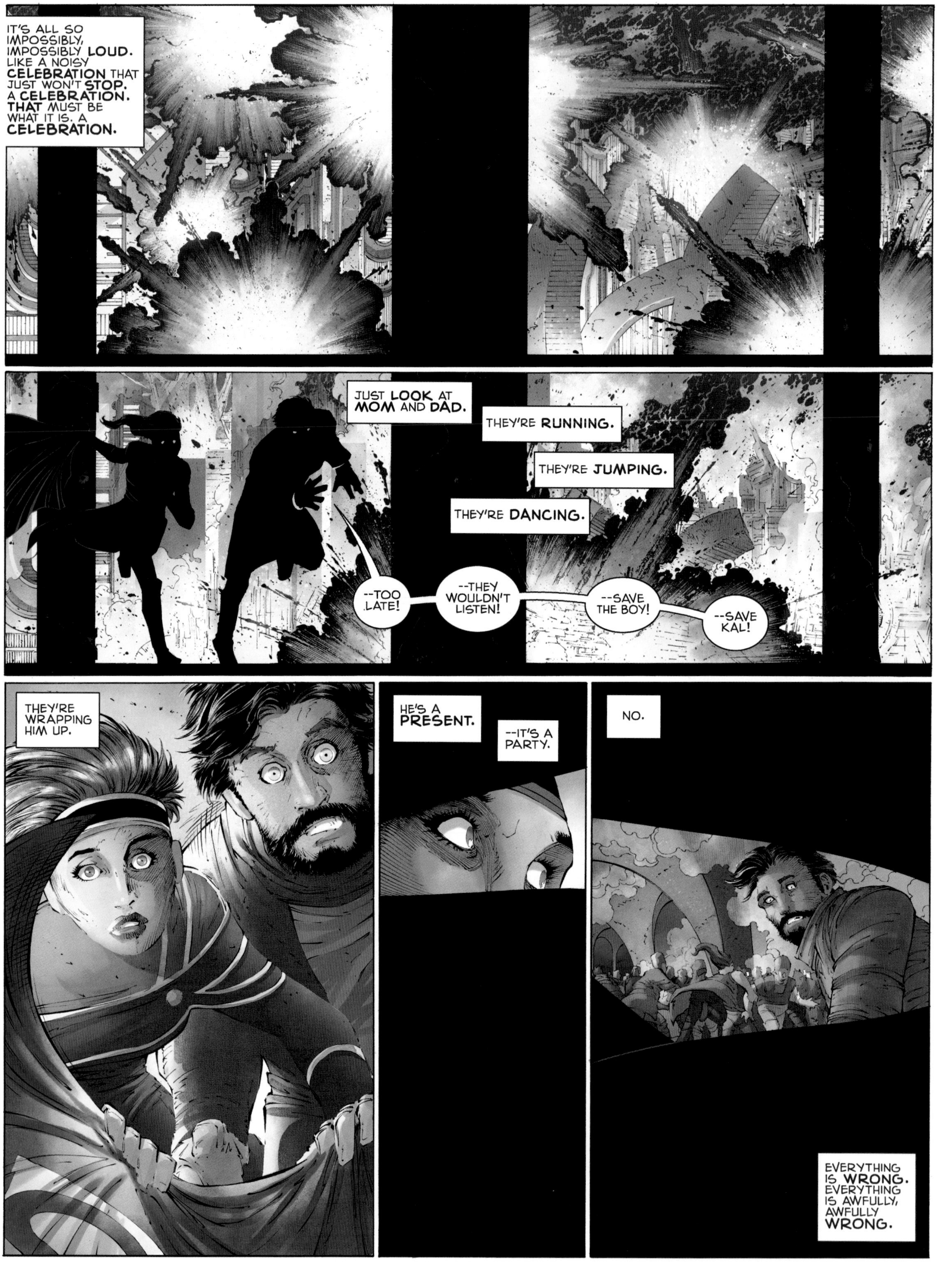

IT'S ALL SO IMPOSSIBLY, IMPOSSIBLY LOUD. LIKE A NOISY CELEBRATION THAT JUST WON'T STOP. A CELEBRATION. THAT MUST BE WHAT IT IS. A CELEBRATION.
JUST LOOK AT MOM AND DAD.
THEY'RE RUNNING.
THEY'RE JUMPING.
THEY'RE DANCING.
--TOO LATE!
--THEY WOULDN'T LISTEN!
--SAVE THE BOY!
--SAVE KAL!
THEY'RE WRAPPING HIM UP.
HE'S A PRESENT.
--IT'S A PARTY.
NO.
EVERYTHING IS WRONG. EVERYTHING IS AWFULLY, AWFULLY WRONG.

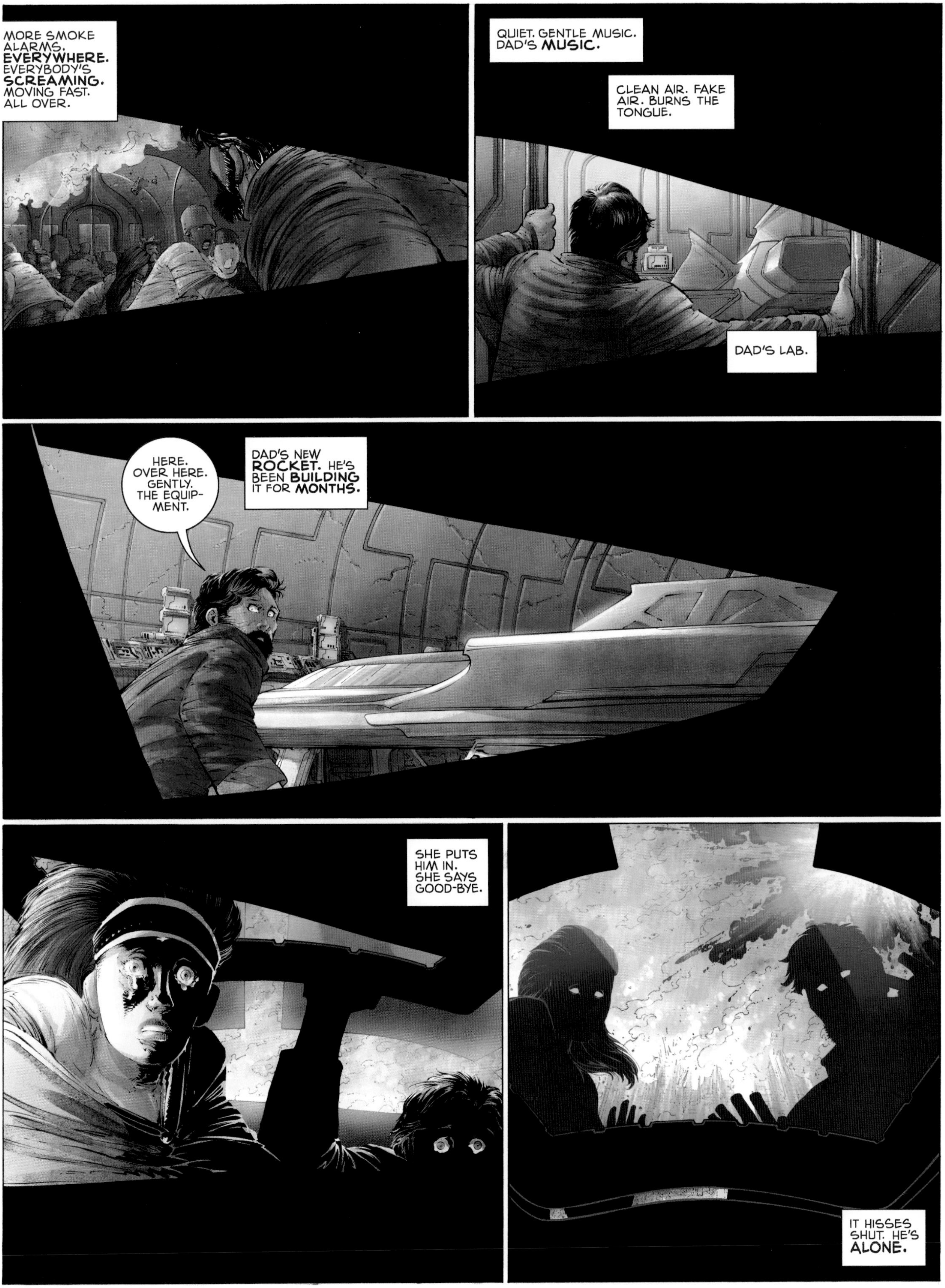
MORE SMOKE ALARMS. **EVERYWHERE.** EVERYBODY'S **SCREAMING.** MOVING FAST. ALL OVER.
QUIET. GENTLE MUSIC. DAD'S **MUSIC.**
CLEAN AIR. FAKE AIR. BURNS THE TONGUE.
DAD'S LAB.
HERE. OVER HERE. GENTLY. THE EQUIPMENT.
DAD'S NEW **ROCKET.** HE'S BEEN **BUILDING** IT FOR **MONTHS.**
SHE PUTS HIM IN. SHE SAYS GOOD-BYE.
IT HISSES SHUT. HE'S **ALONE.**

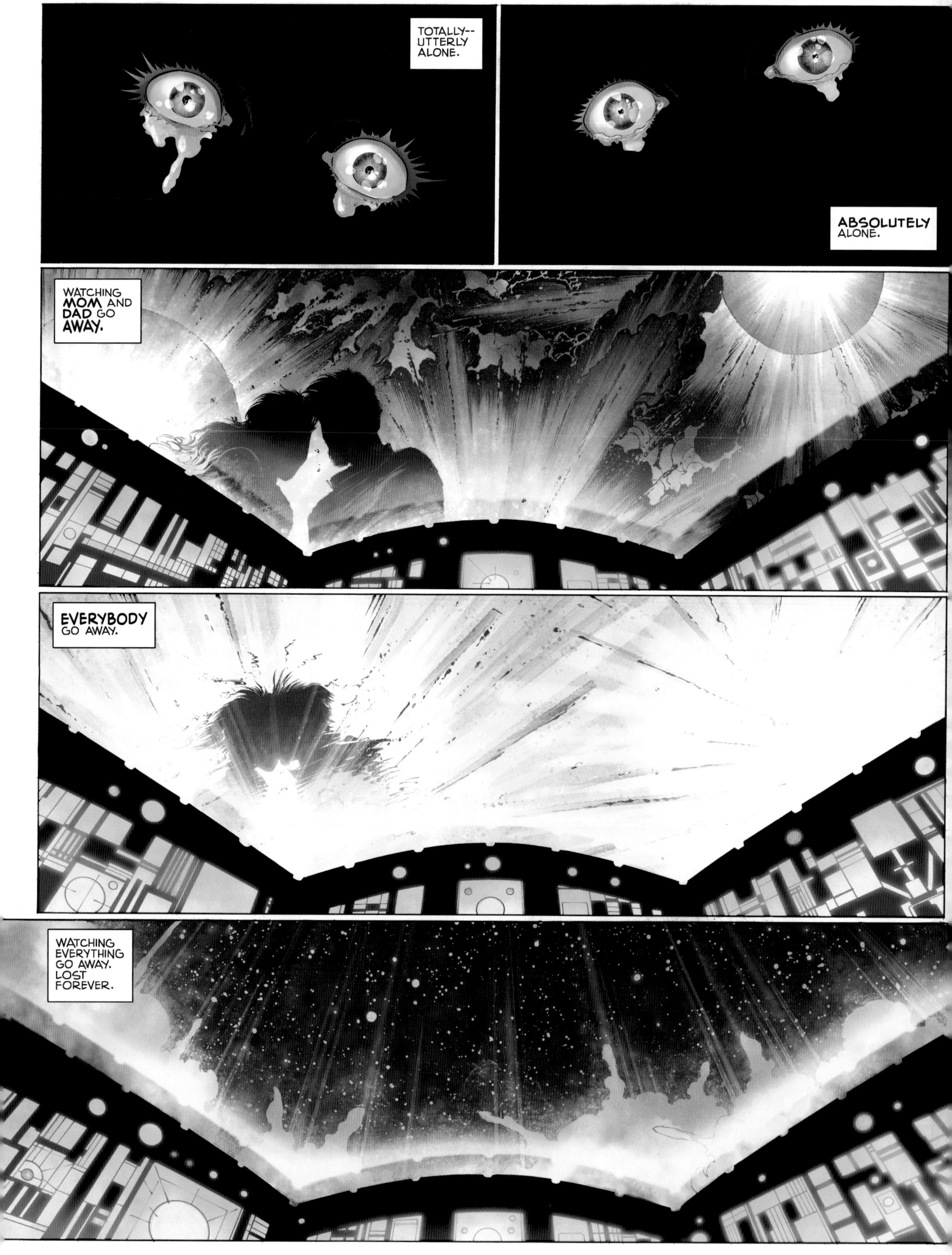
TOTALLY--
UTTERLY
ALONE.
ABSOLUTELY
ALONE.
WATCHING
MOM AND
DAD GO
AWAY.
EVERYBODY
GO AWAY.
WATCHING
EVERYTHING
GO AWAY.
LOST
FOREVER.

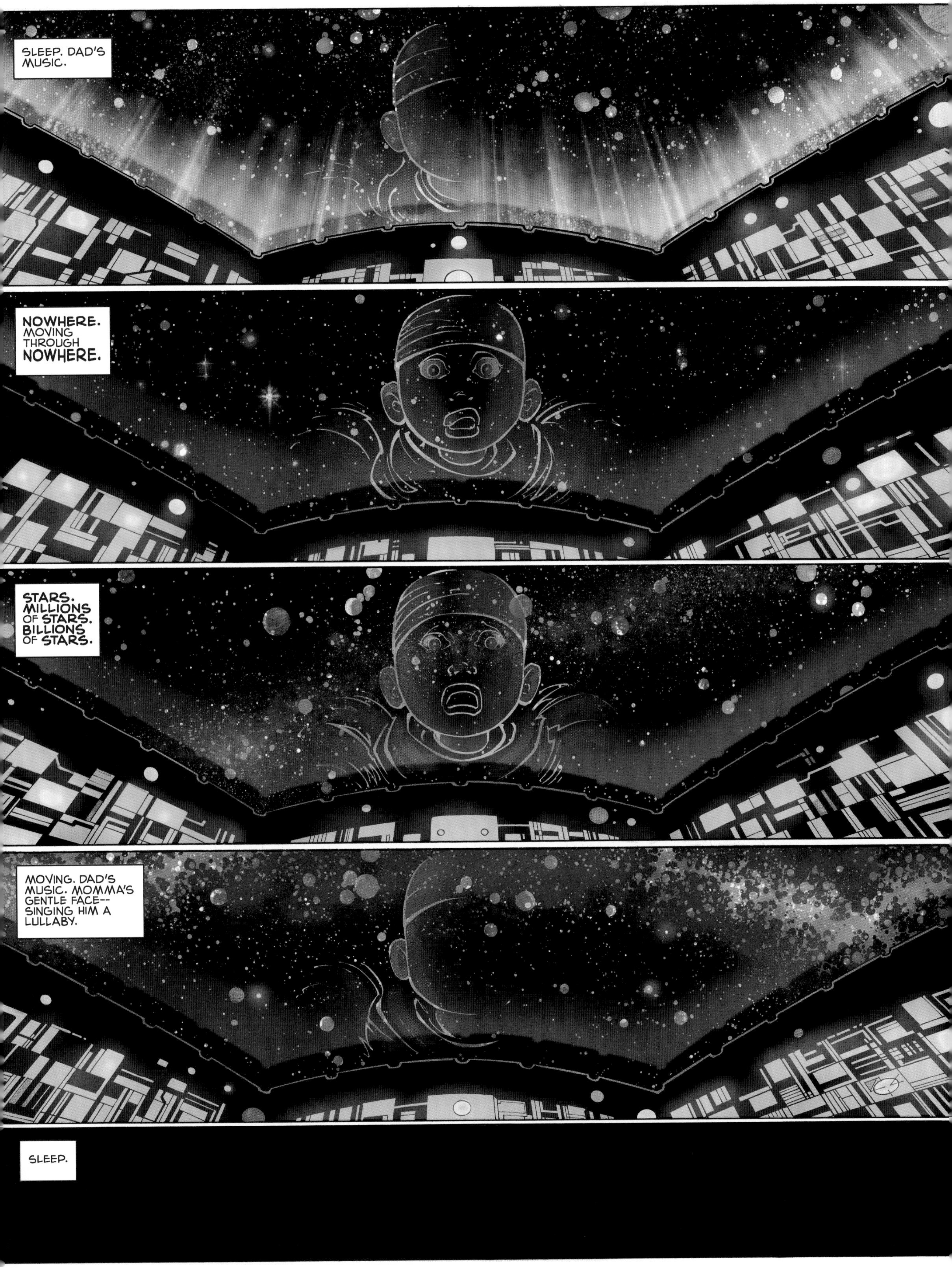
SLEEP. DAD'S MUSIC.
NOWHERE. MOVING THROUGH NOWHERE.
STARS. MILLIONS OF STARS. BILLIONS OF STARS.
MOVING. DAD'S MUSIC. MOMMA'S GENTLE FACE-- SINGING HIM A LULLABY.
SLEEP.

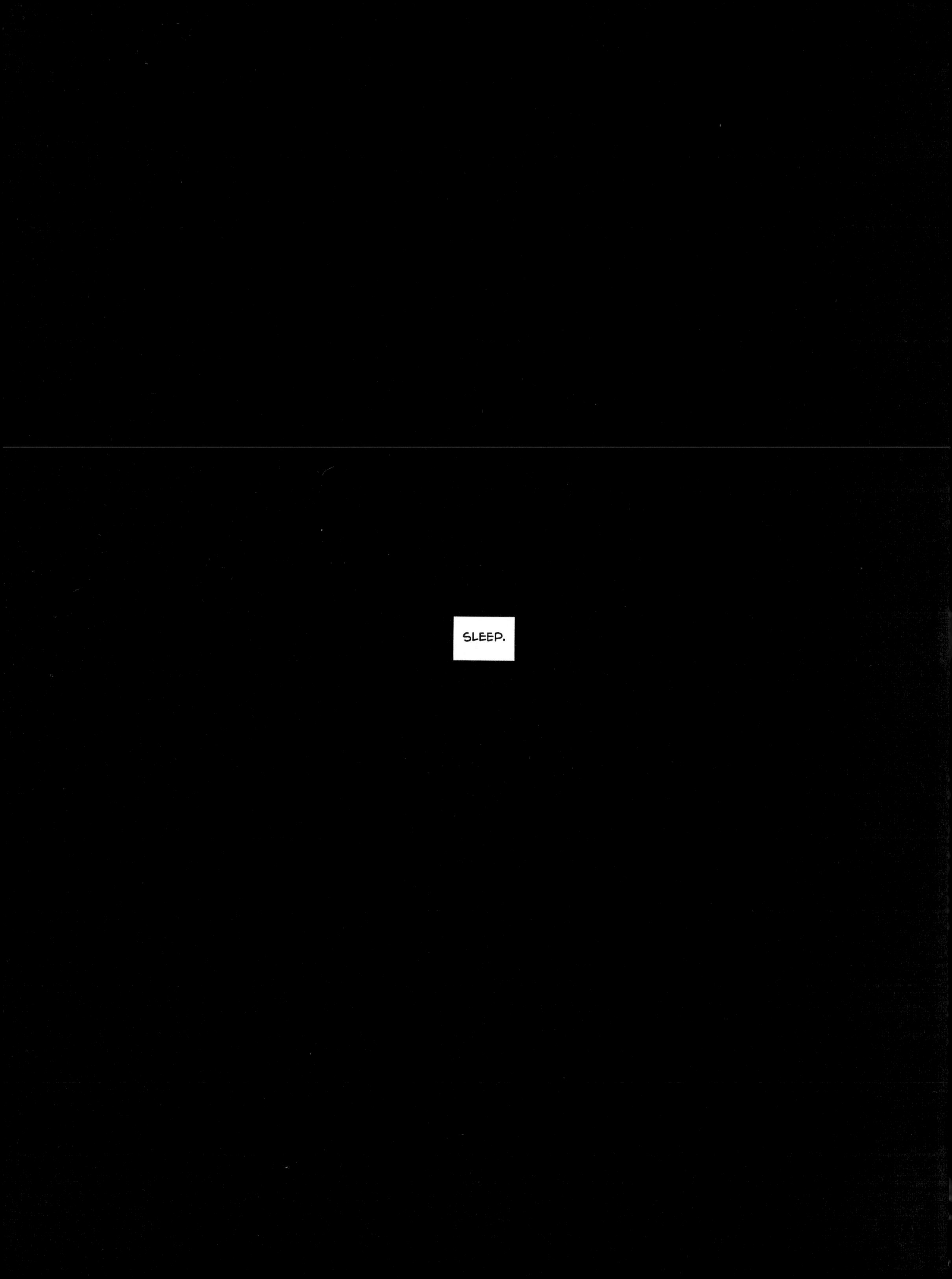
SLEEP.

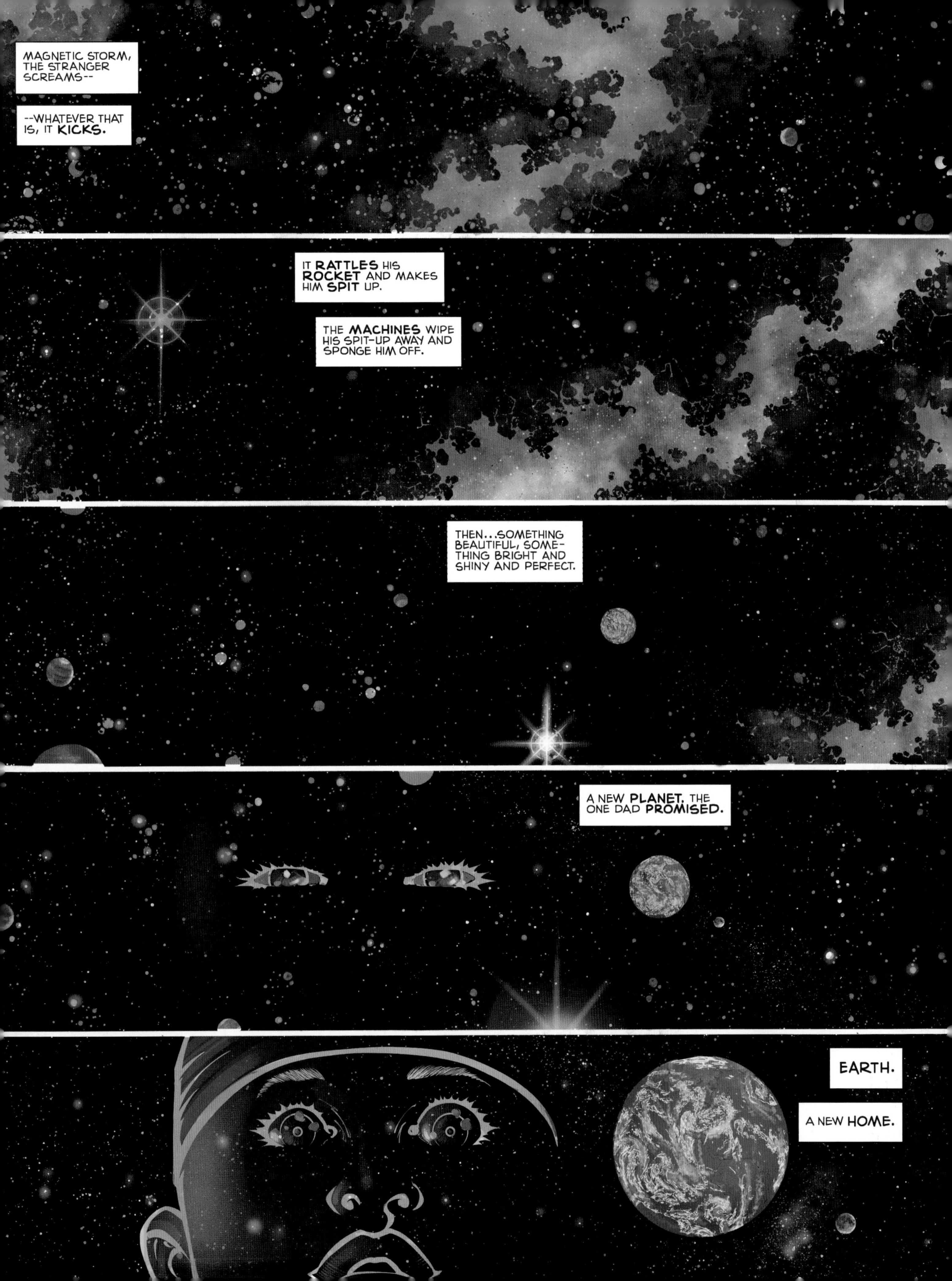
MAGNETIC STORM, THE STRANGER SCREAMS--
--WHATEVER THAT IS, IT KICKS.
IT RATTLES HIS ROCKET AND MAKES HIM SPIT UP.
THE MACHINES WIPE HIS SPIT-UP AWAY AND SPONGE HIM OFF.
THEN...SOMETHING BEAUTIFUL, SOMETHING BRIGHT AND SHINY AND PERFECT.
A NEW PLANET. THE ONE DAD PROMISED.
EARTH.
A NEW HOME.

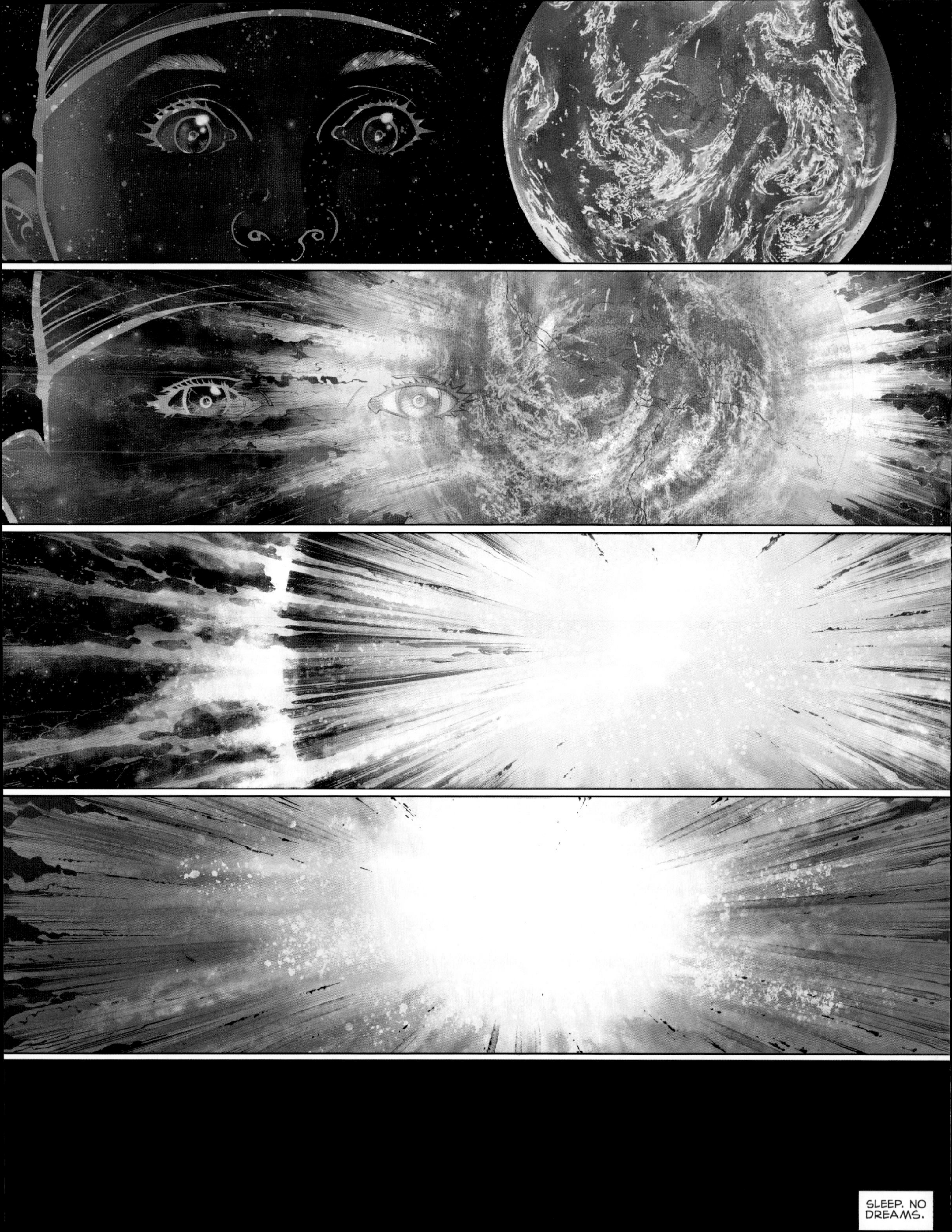
SLEEP. NO DREAMS.

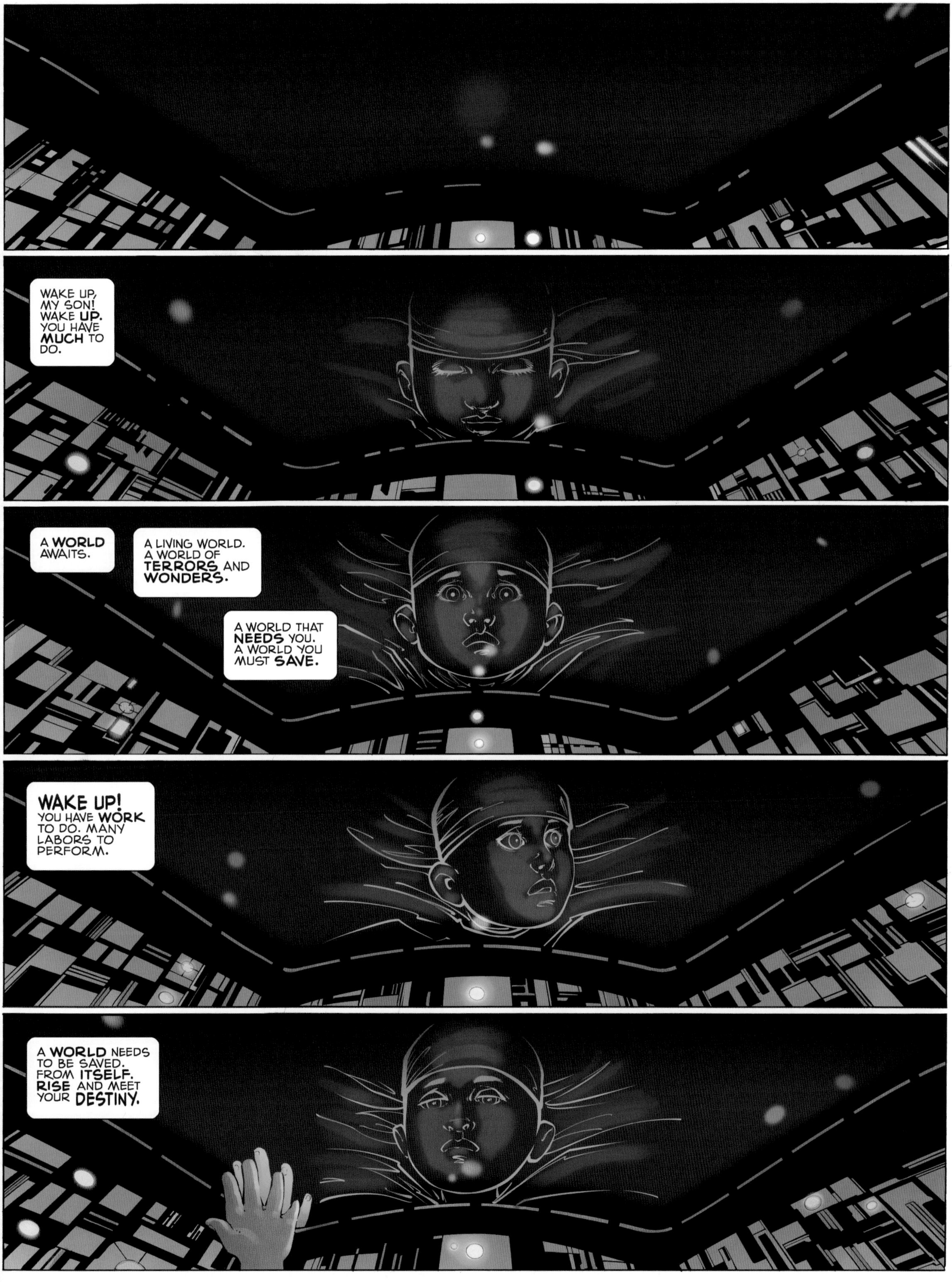
WAKE UP, MY SON! WAKE UP. YOU HAVE MUCH TO DO.
A WORLD AWAITS.
A LIVING WORLD. A WORLD OF TERRORS AND WONDERS.
A WORLD THAT NEEDS YOU. A WORLD YOU MUST SAVE.
WAKE UP! YOU HAVE WORK TO DO. MANY LABORS TO PERFORM.
A WORLD NEEDS TO BE SAVED. FROM ITSELF. RISE AND MEET YOUR DESTINY.

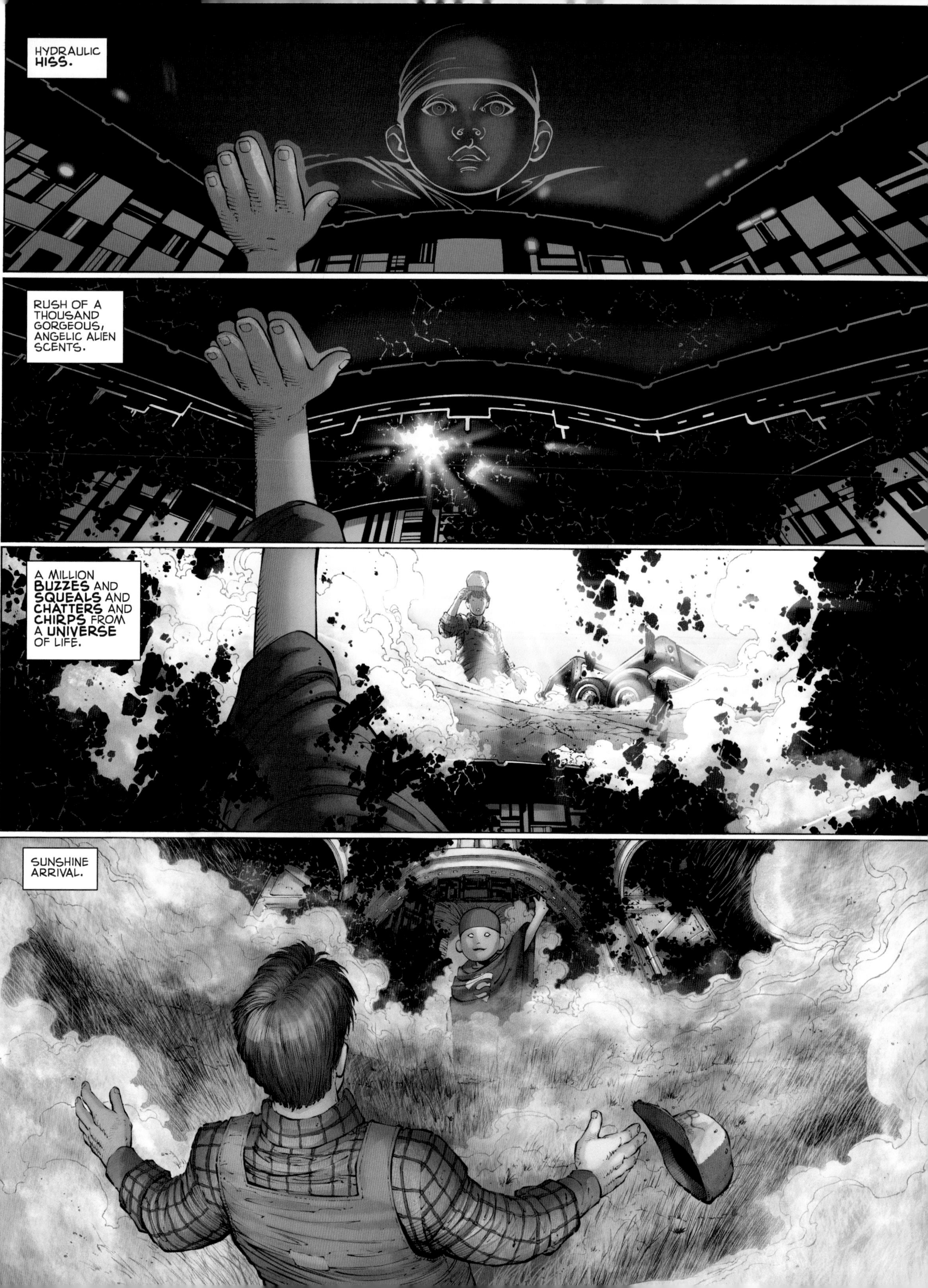
HYDRAULIC HISS.
RUSH OF A THOUSAND GORGEOUS, ANGELIC ALIEN SCENTS.
A MILLION BUZZES AND SQUEALS AND CHATTERS AND CHIRPS FROM A UNIVERSE OF LIFE.
SUNSHINE ARRIVAL.

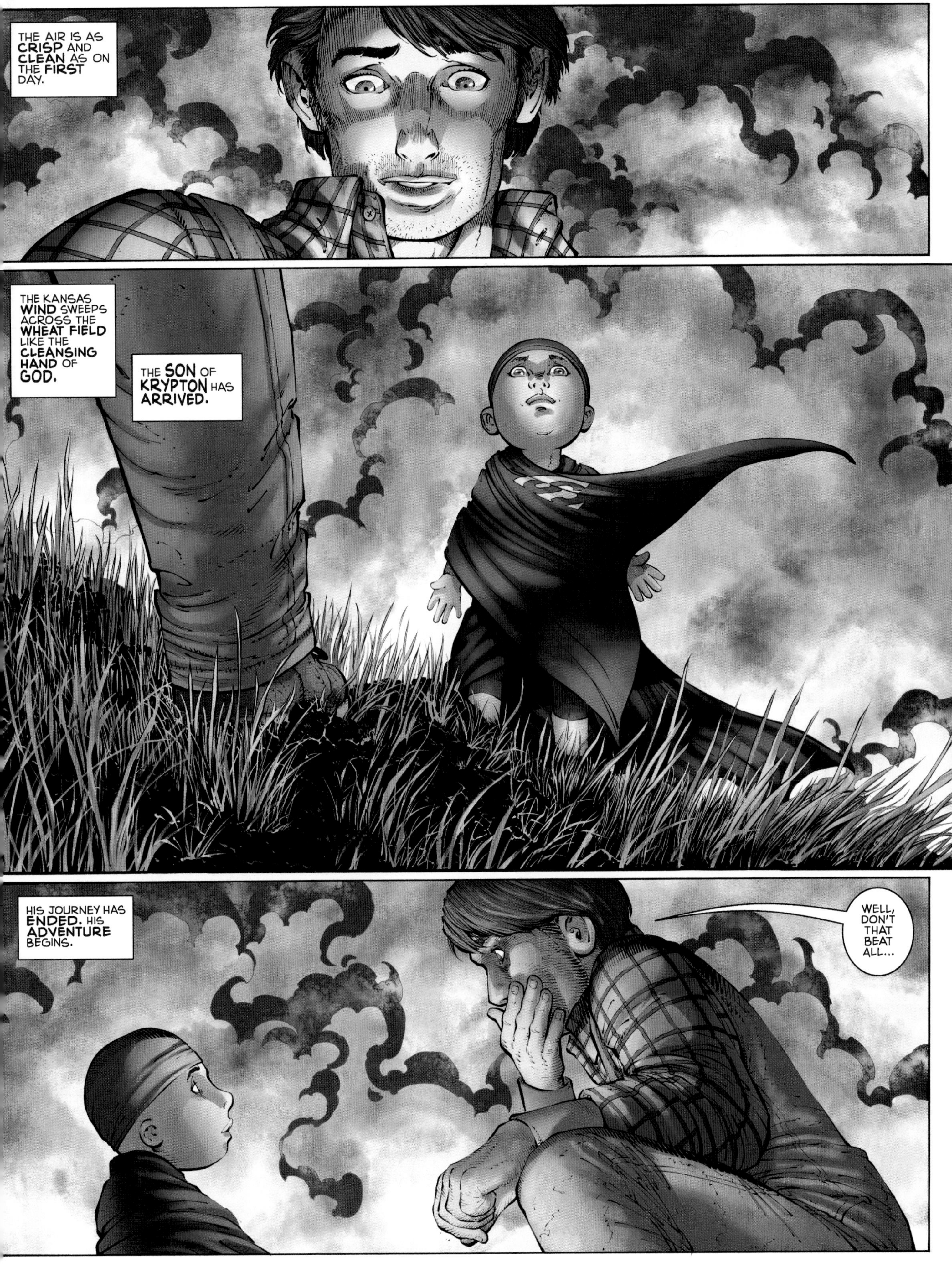
THE AIR IS AS CRISP AND CLEAN AS ON THE FIRST DAY.
THE KANSAS WIND SWEEPS ACROSS THE WHEAT FIELD LIKE THE CLEANSING HAND OF GOD.
THE SON OF KRYPTON HAS ARRIVED.
HIS JOURNEY HAS ENDED. HIS ADVENTURE BEGINS.
WELL, DON'T THAT BEAT ALL...

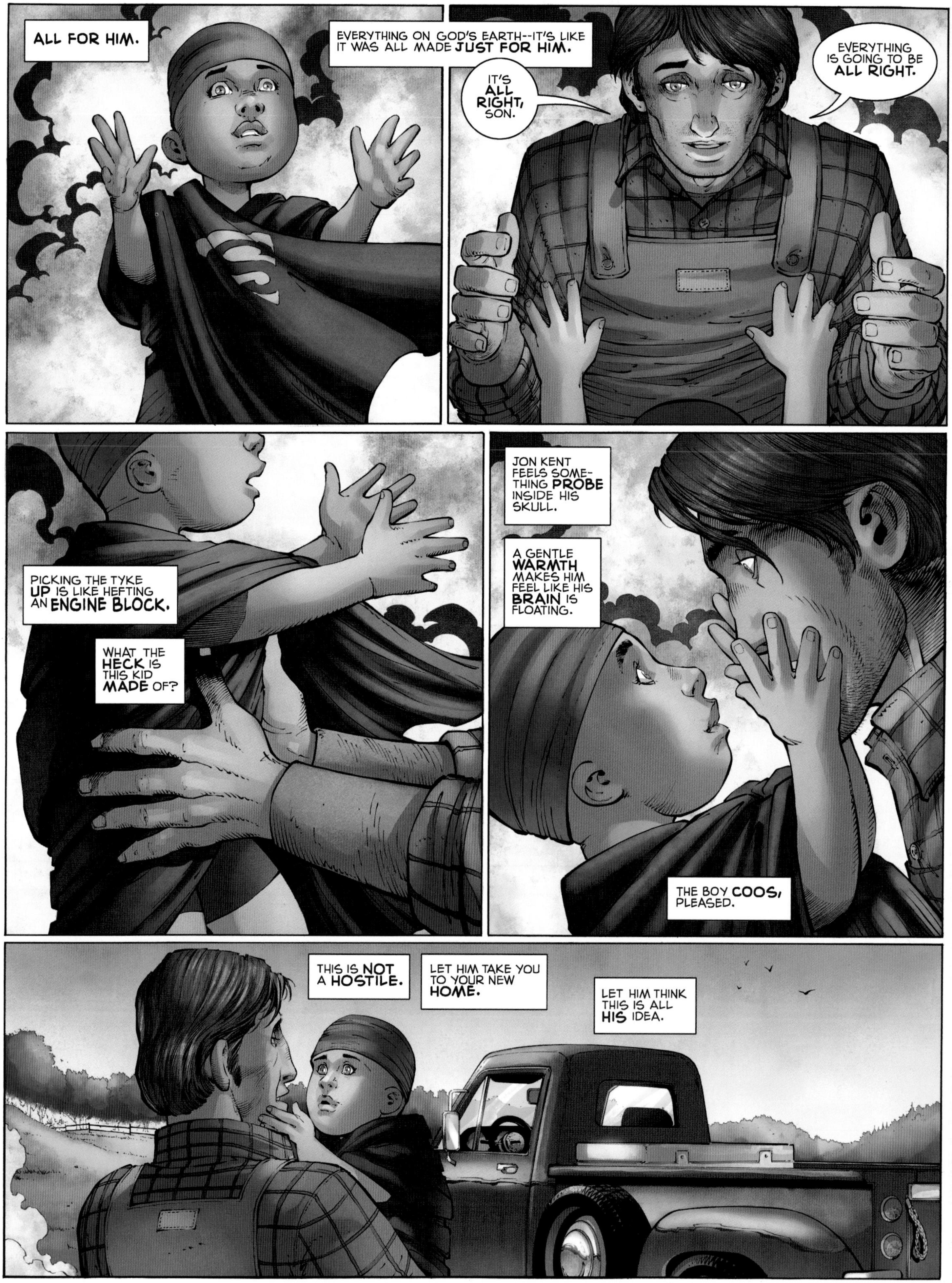
ALL FOR HIM.
EVERYTHING ON GOD'S EARTH--IT'S LIKE IT WAS ALL MADE JUST FOR HIM.
IT'S ALL RIGHT, SON.
EVERYTHING IS GOING TO BE ALL RIGHT.
PICKING THE TYKE UP IS LIKE HEFTING AN ENGINE BLOCK.
WHAT THE HECK IS THIS KID MADE OF?
JON KENT FEELS SOMETHING PROBE INSIDE HIS SKULL.
A GENTLE WARMTH MAKES HIM FEEL LIKE HIS BRAIN IS FLOATING.
THE BOY COOS, PLEASED.
THIS IS NOT A HOSTILE.
LET HIM TAKE YOU TO YOUR NEW HOME.
LET HIM THINK THIS IS ALL HIS IDEA.

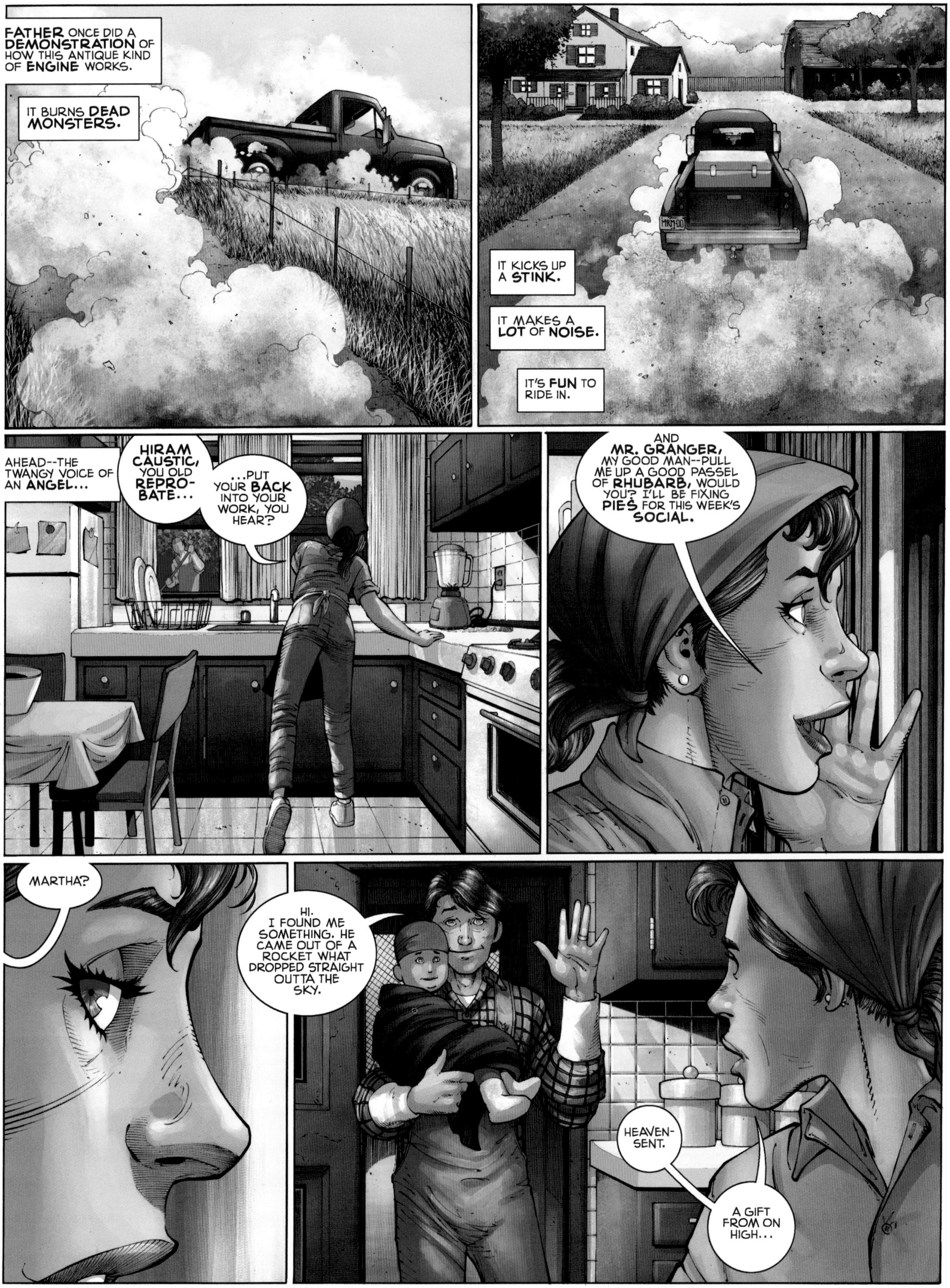
FATHER ONCE DID A DEMONSTRATION OF HOW THIS ANTIQUE KIND OF ENGINE WORKS.
IT BURNS DEAD MONSTERS.
IT KICKS UP A STINK.
IT MAKES A LOT OF NOISE.
IT'S FUN TO RIDE IN.
AHEAD--THE TWANGY VOICE OF AN ANGEL...
HIRAM CAUSTIC, YOU OLD REPRO-BATE...
...PUT YOUR BACK INTO YOUR WORK, YOU HEAR?
AND MR. GRANGER, MY GOOD MAN--PULL ME UP A GOOD PASSEL OF RHUBARB, WOULD YOU? I'LL BE FIXING PIES FOR THIS WEEK'S SOCIAL.
MARTHA?
HI. I FOUND ME SOMETHING. HE CAME OUT OF A ROCKET WHAT DROPPED STRAIGHT OUTTA THE SKY.
HEAVEN-SENT.
A GIFT FROM ON HIGH...

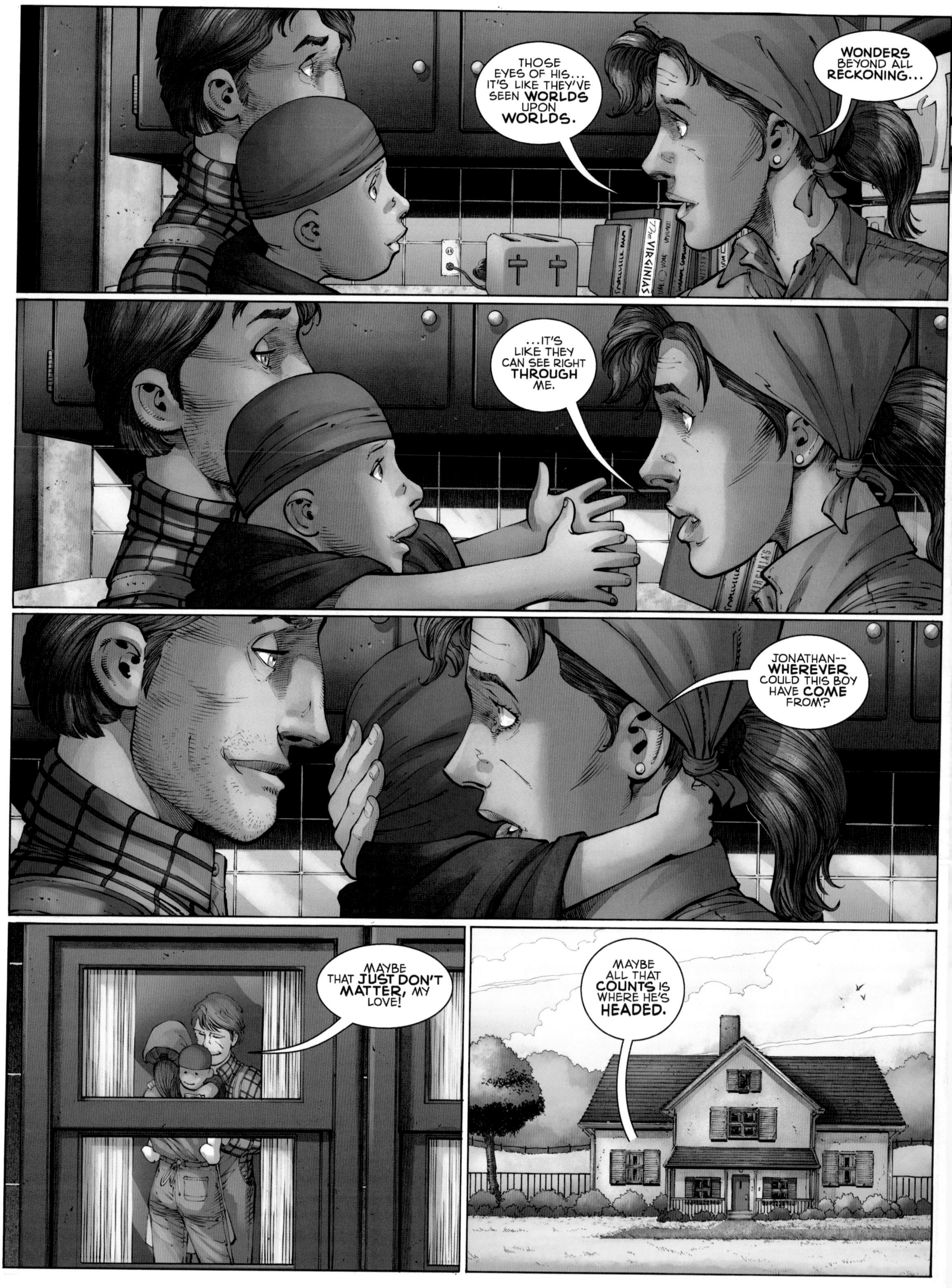
THOSE EYES OF HIS... IT'S LIKE THEY'VE SEEN WORLDS UPON WORLDS.
WONDERS BEYOND ALL RECKONING...
...IT'S LIKE THEY CAN SEE RIGHT THROUGH ME.
JONATHAN-- WHEREVER COULD THIS BOY HAVE COME FROM?
MAYBE THAT JUST DON'T MATTER, MY LOVE!
MAYBE ALL THAT COUNTS IS WHERE HE'S HEADED.

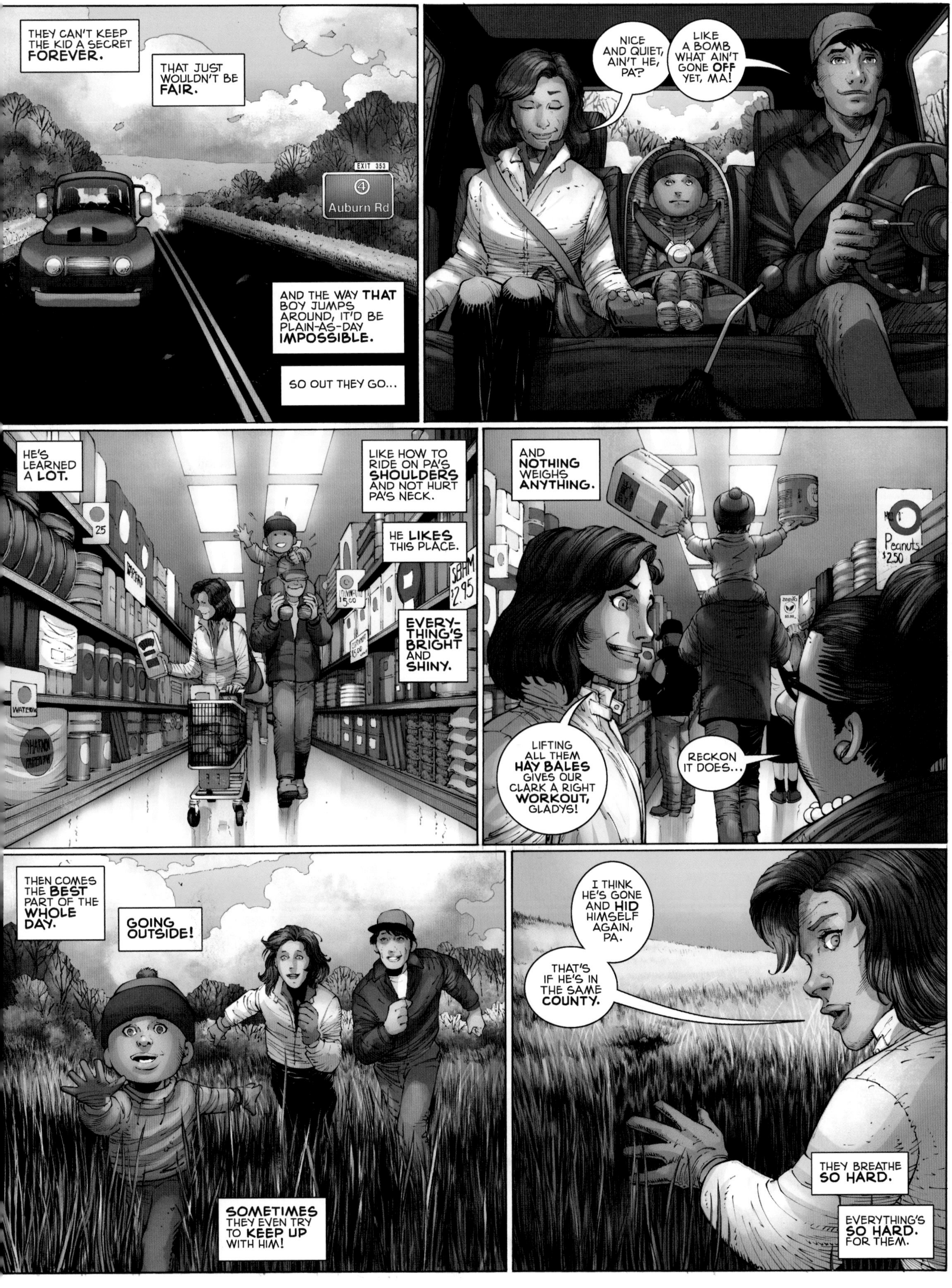
THEY CAN'T KEEP THE KID A SECRET FOREVER.
THAT JUST WOULDN'T BE FAIR.
EXIT 353
4
Auburn Rd
AND THE WAY THAT BOY JUMPS AROUND, IT'D BE PLAIN-AS-DAY IMPOSSIBLE.
SO OUT THEY GO...
NICE AND QUIET, AIN'T HE, PA?
LIKE A BOMB WHAT AIN'T GONE OFF YET, MA!
HE'S LEARNED A LOT.
LIKE HOW TO RIDE ON PA'S SHOULDERS AND NOT HURT PA'S NECK.
HE LIKES THIS PLACE.
EVERY-THING'S BRIGHT AND SHINY.
AND NOTHING WEIGHS ANYTHING.
Peanuts
$2.50
LIFTING ALL THEM HAY BALES GIVES OUR CLARK A RIGHT WORKOUT, GLADYS!
RECKON IT DOES...
THEN COMES THE BEST PART OF THE WHOLE DAY.
GOING OUTSIDE!
SOMETIMES THEY EVEN TRY TO KEEP UP WITH HIM!
I THINK HE'S GONE AND HID HIMSELF AGAIN, PA.
THAT'S IF HE'S IN THE SAME COUNTY.
THEY BREATHE SO HARD.
EVERYTHING'S SO HARD. FOR THEM.

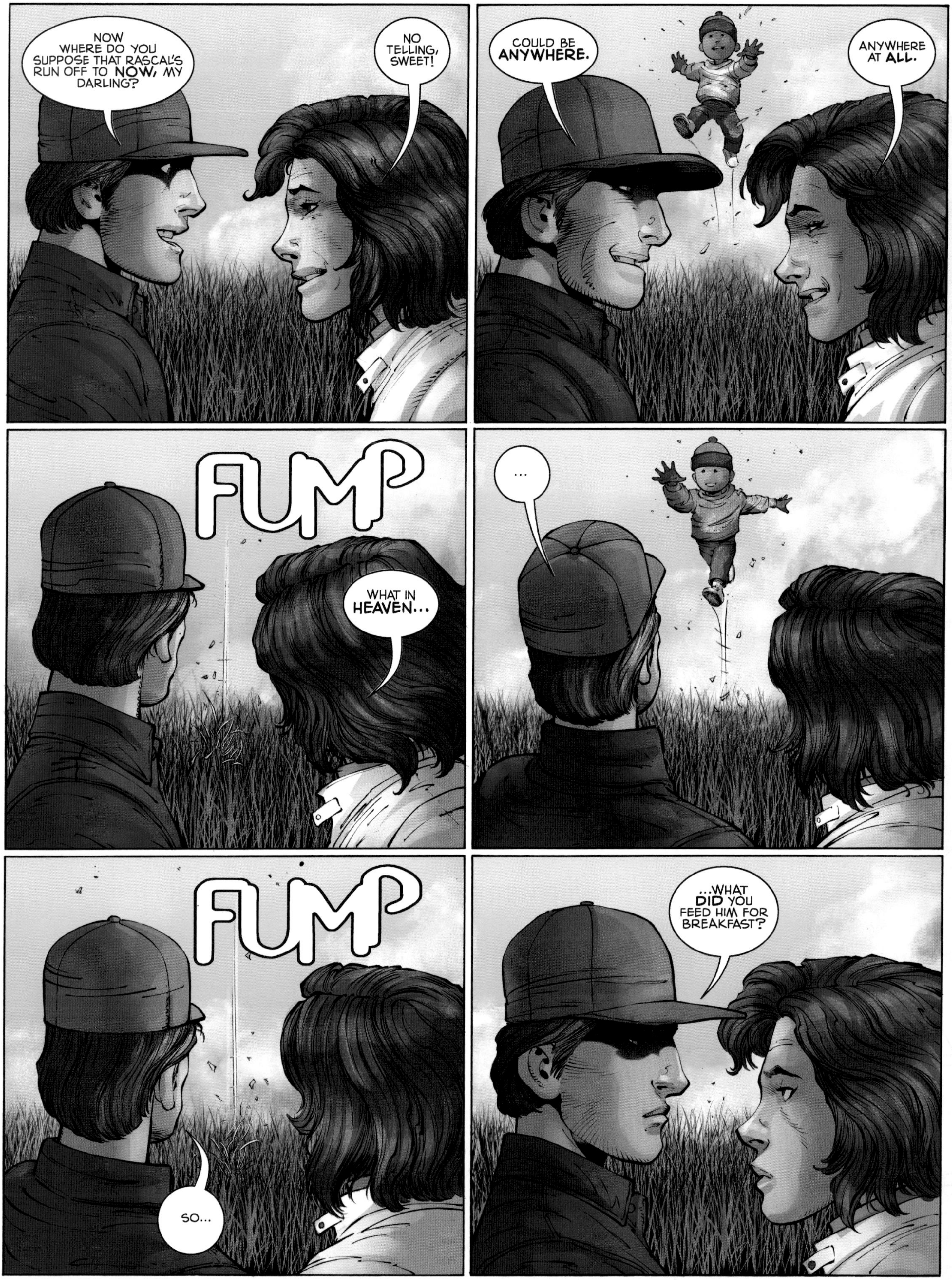
NOW WHERE DO YOU SUPPOSE THAT RASCAL'S RUN OFF TO NOW, MY DARLING?
NO TELLING, SWEET!
COULD BE ANYWHERE.
ANYWHERE AT ALL.
FUMP
WHAT IN HEAVEN...
...
FUMP
SO...
...WHAT DID YOU FEED HIM FOR BREAKFAST?

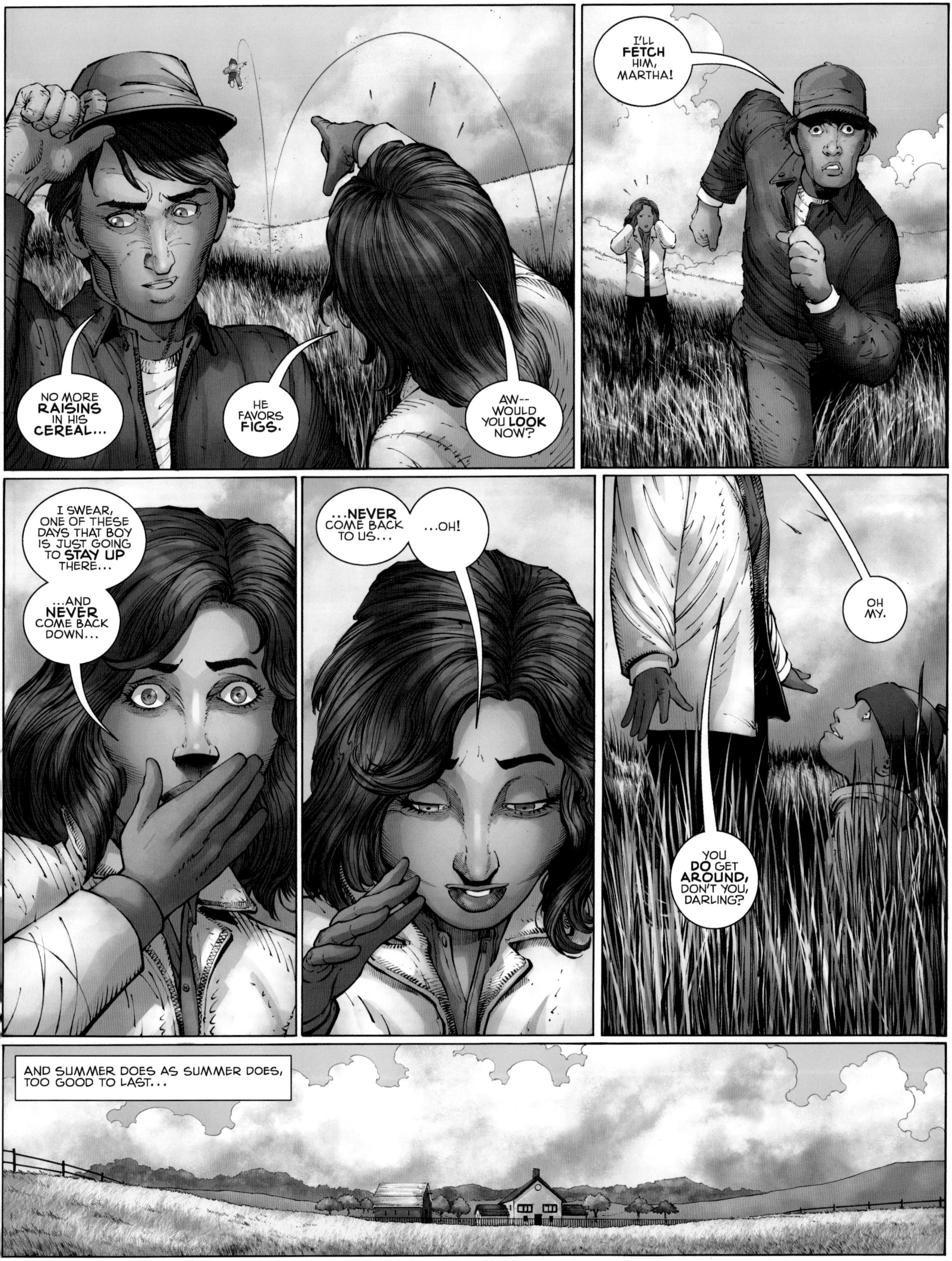
NO MORE RAISINS IN HIS CEREAL...
HE FAVORS FIGS.
AW-- WOULD YOU LOOK NOW?
I'LL FETCH HIM, MARTHA!
I SWEAR, ONE OF THESE DAYS THAT BOY IS JUST GOING TO STAY UP THERE...
...AND NEVER COME BACK DOWN...
...NEVER COME BACK TO US...
...OH!
OH MY.
YOU DO GET AROUND, DON'T YOU, DARLING?
AND SUMMER DOES AS SUMMER DOES, TOO GOOD TO LAST...

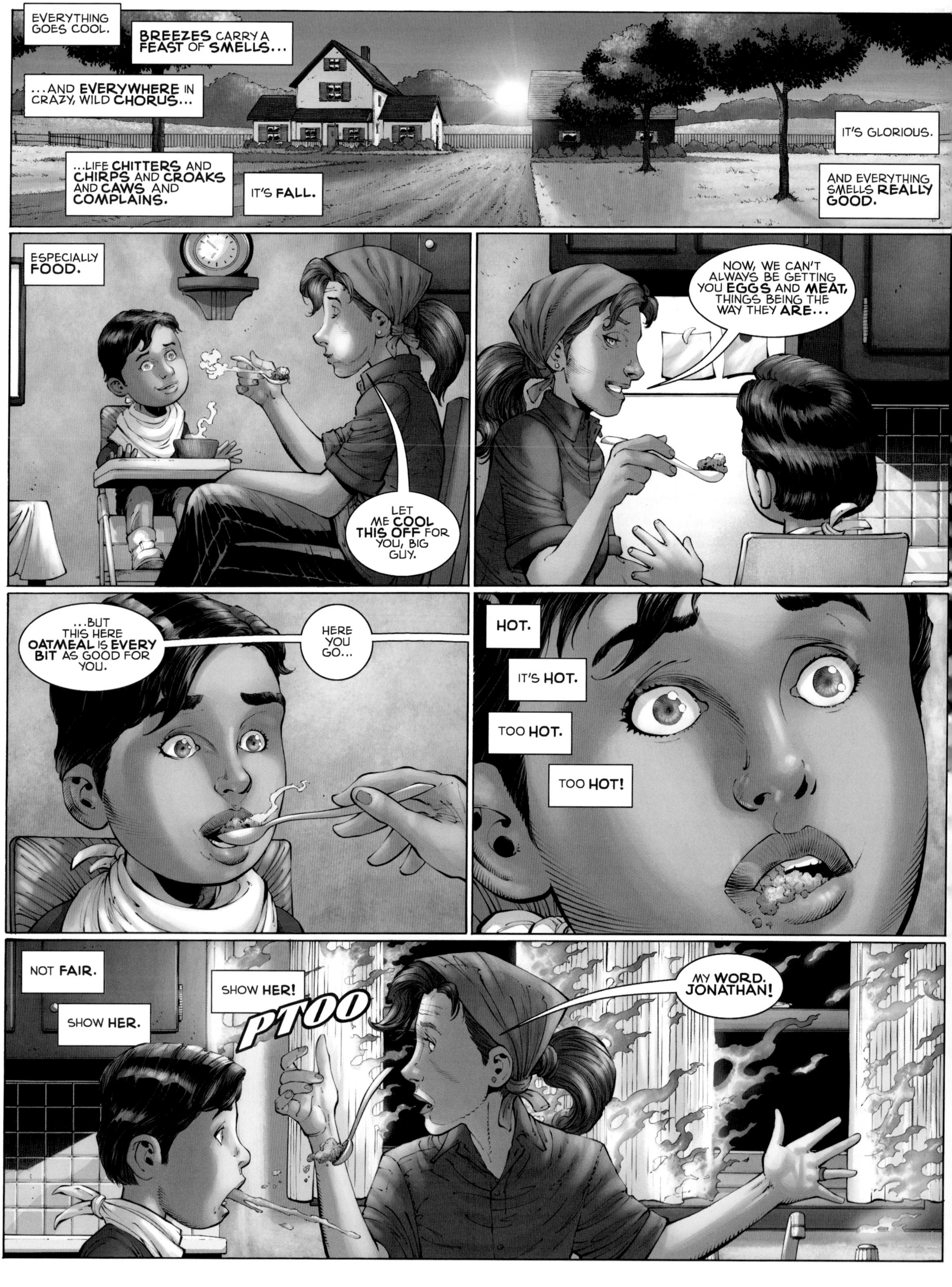
EVERYTHING GOES COOL.
BREEZES CARRY A FEAST OF SMELLS...
...AND EVERYWHERE IN CRAZY, WILD CHORUS...
...LIFE CHITTERS AND CHIRPS AND CROAKS AND CAWS AND COMPLAINS.
IT'S FALL.
IT'S GLORIOUS.
AND EVERYTHING SMELLS REALLY GOOD.
ESPECIALLY FOOD.
LET ME COOL THIS OFF FOR YOU, BIG GUY.
NOW, WE CAN'T ALWAYS BE GETTING YOU EGGS AND MEAT, THINGS BEING THE WAY THEY ARE...
...BUT THIS HERE OATMEAL IS EVERY BIT AS GOOD FOR YOU.
HERE YOU GO...
HOT.
IT'S HOT.
TOO HOT.
TOO HOT!
NOT FAIR.
SHOW HER.
SHOW HER!
PTOO
MY WORD. JONATHAN!

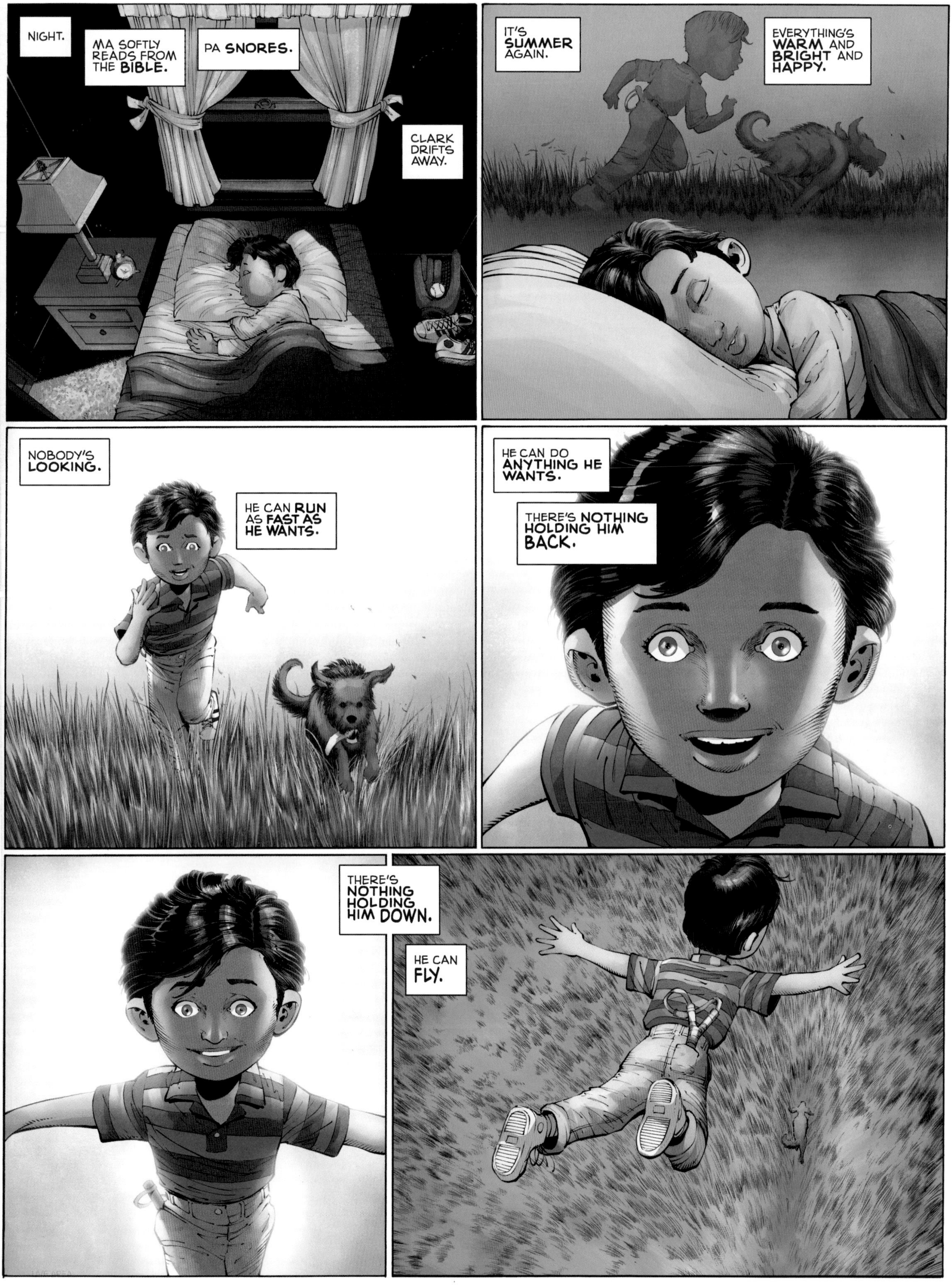
NIGHT.
MA SOFTLY READS FROM THE BIBLE.
PA SNORES.
CLARK DRIFTS AWAY.
IT'S SUMMER AGAIN.
EVERYTHING'S WARM AND BRIGHT AND HAPPY.
NOBODY'S LOOKING.
HE CAN RUN AS FAST AS HE WANTS.
HE CAN DO ANYTHING HE WANTS.
THERE'S NOTHING HOLDING HIM BACK.
THERE'S NOTHING HOLDING HIM DOWN.
HE CAN FLY.

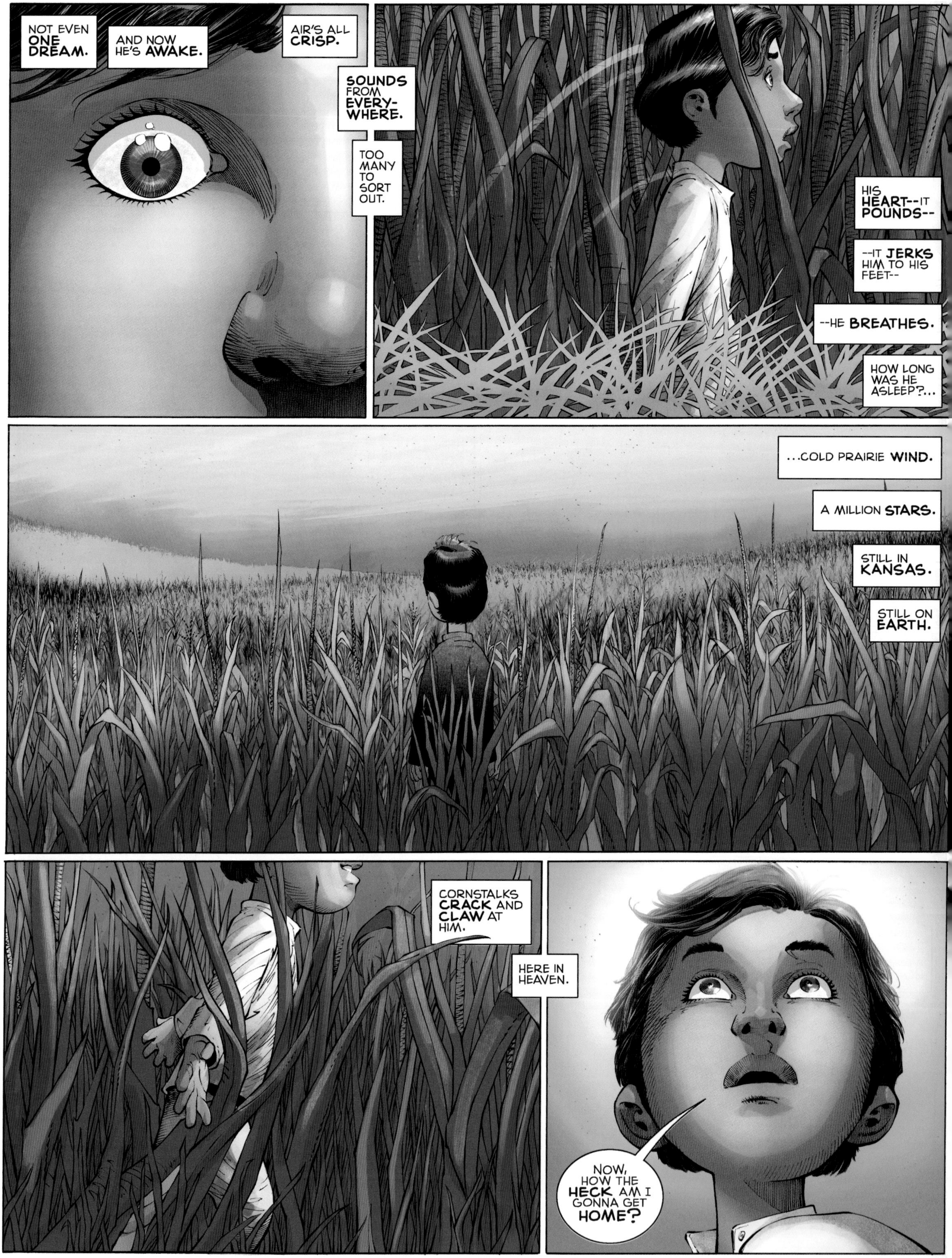
NOT EVEN ONE DREAM.
AND NOW HE'S AWAKE.
AIR'S ALL CRISP.
SOUNDS FROM EVERY-WHERE.
TOO MANY TO SORT OUT.
HIS HEART--IT POUNDS--
--IT JERKS HIM TO HIS FEET--
--HE BREATHES.
HOW LONG WAS HE ASLEEP?...
...COLD PRAIRIE WIND.
A MILLION STARS.
STILL IN KANSAS.
STILL ON EARTH.
CORNSTALKS CRACK AND CLAW AT HIM.
HERE IN HEAVEN.
NOW, HOW THE HECK AM I GONNA GET HOME?

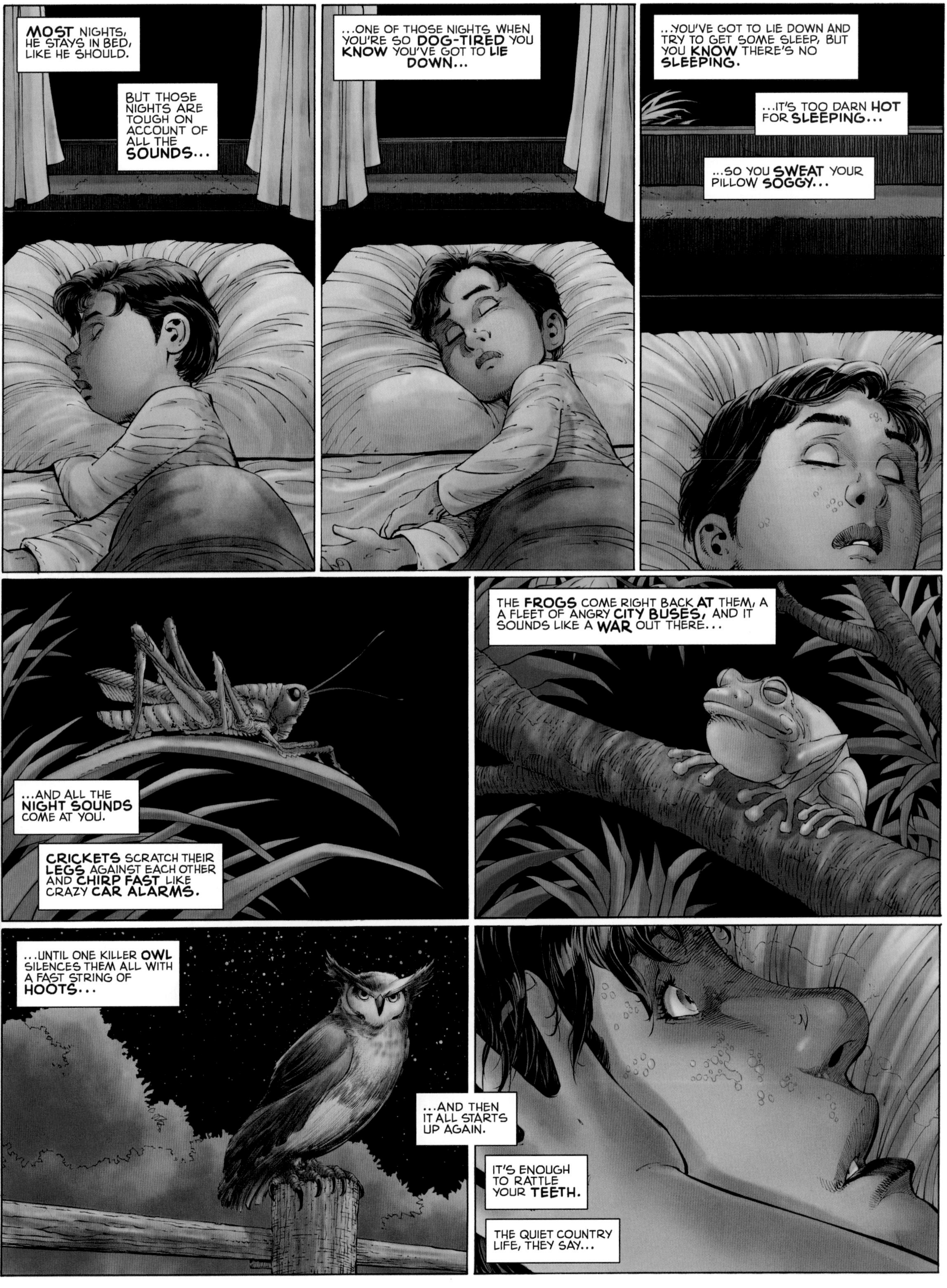
MOST NIGHTS, HE STAYS IN BED, LIKE HE SHOULD.
BUT THOSE NIGHTS ARE TOUGH ON ACCOUNT OF ALL THE SOUNDS...
...ONE OF THOSE NIGHTS WHEN YOU'RE SO DOG-TIRED YOU KNOW YOU'VE GOT TO LIE DOWN...
...YOU'VE GOT TO LIE DOWN AND TRY TO GET SOME SLEEP, BUT YOU KNOW THERE'S NO SLEEPING.
...IT'S TOO DARN HOT FOR SLEEPING...
...SO YOU SWEAT YOUR PILLOW SOGGY...
...AND ALL THE NIGHT SOUNDS COME AT YOU.
CRICKETS SCRATCH THEIR LEGS AGAINST EACH OTHER AND CHIRP FAST LIKE CRAZY CAR ALARMS.
THE FROGS COME RIGHT BACK AT THEM, A A FLEET OF ANGRY CITY BUSES, AND IT SOUNDS LIKE A WAR OUT THERE...
...UNTIL ONE KILLER OWL SILENCES THEM ALL WITH A FAST STRING OF HOOTS...
...AND THEN IT ALL STARTS UP AGAIN.
IT'S ENOUGH TO RATTLE YOUR TEETH.
THE QUIET COUNTRY LIFE, THEY SAY...

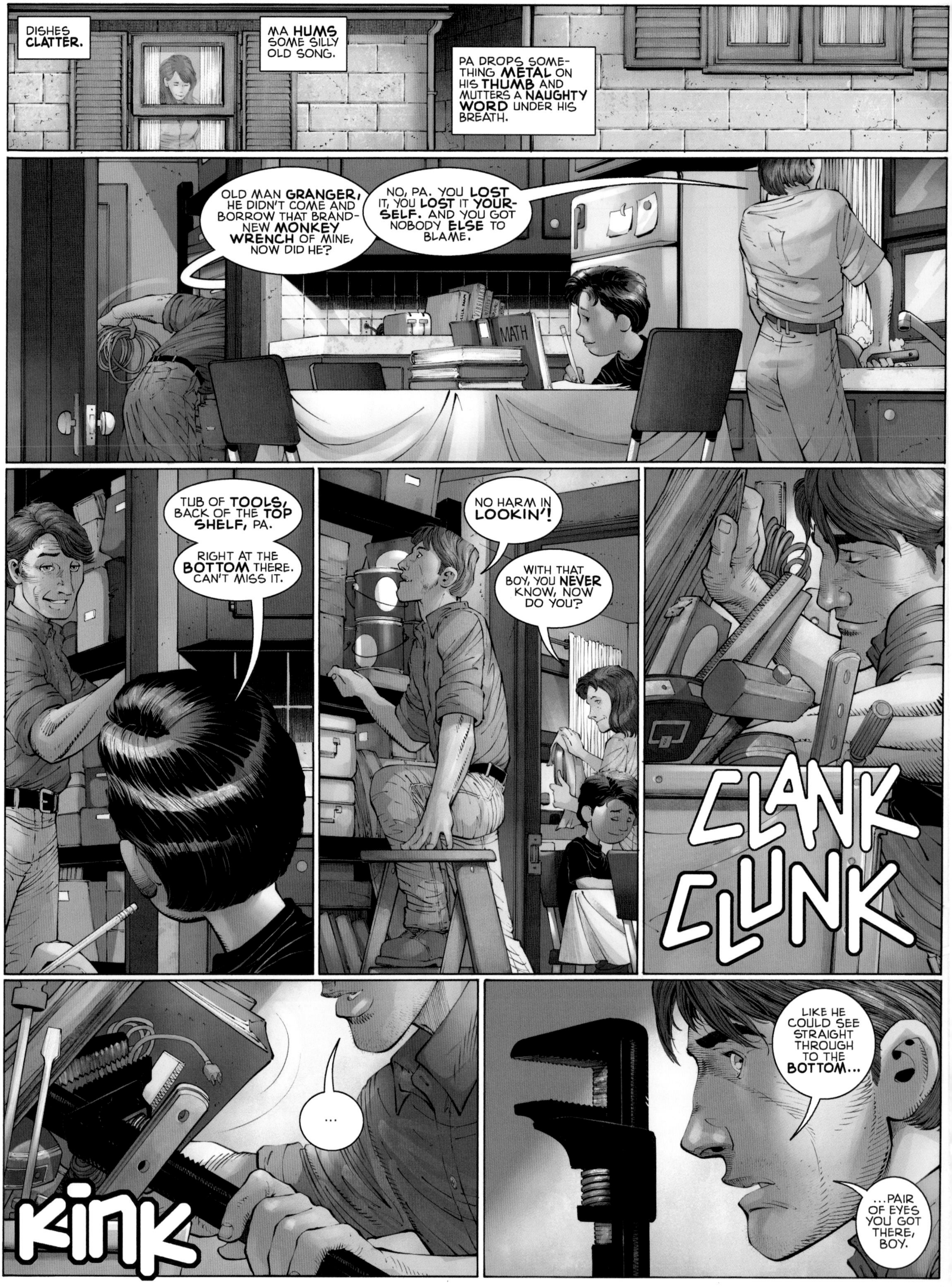
DISHES CLATTER.
MA HUMS SOME SILLY OLD SONG.
PA DROPS SOMETHING METAL ON HIS THUMB AND MUTTERS A NAUGHTY WORD UNDER HIS BREATH.
OLD MAN GRANGER, HE DIDN'T COME AND BORROW THAT BRAND-NEW MONKEY WRENCH OF MINE, NOW DID HE?
NO, PA. YOU LOST IT, YOU LOST IT YOURSELF. AND YOU GOT NOBODY ELSE TO BLAME.
MATH
TUB OF TOOLS, BACK OF THE TOP SHELF, PA.
RIGHT AT THE BOTTOM THERE. CAN'T MISS IT.
NO HARM IN LOOKIN'!
WITH THAT BOY, YOU NEVER KNOW, NOW DO YOU?
CLANK
CLUNK
KINK
...
LIKE HE COULD SEE STRAIGHT THROUGH TO THE BOTTOM...
...PAIR OF EYES YOU GOT THERE, BOY.

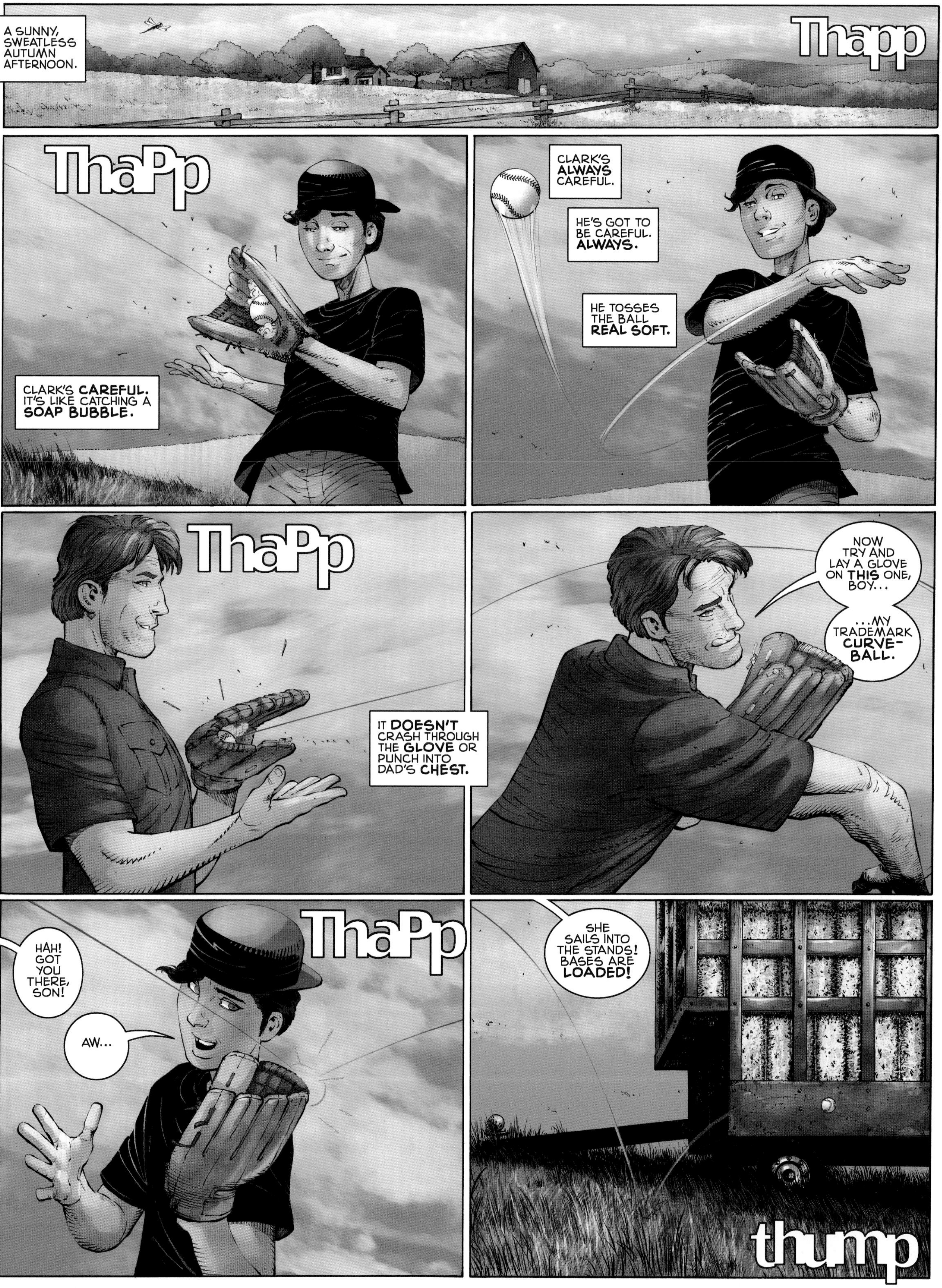
A SUNNY, SWEATLESS AUTUMN AFTERNOON.
Thapp
ThaPp
CLARK'S CAREFUL. IT'S LIKE CATCHING A SOAP BUBBLE.
CLARK'S ALWAYS CAREFUL.
HE'S GOT TO BE CAREFUL. ALWAYS.
HE TOSSES THE BALL REAL SOFT.
ThaPp
IT DOESN'T CRASH THROUGH THE GLOVE OR PUNCH INTO DAD'S CHEST.
NOW TRY AND LAY A GLOVE ON THIS ONE, BOY...
...MY TRADEMARK CURVE-BALL.
ThaPp
HAH! GOT YOU THERE, SON!
AW...
SHE SAILS INTO THE STANDS! BASES ARE LOADED!
thump

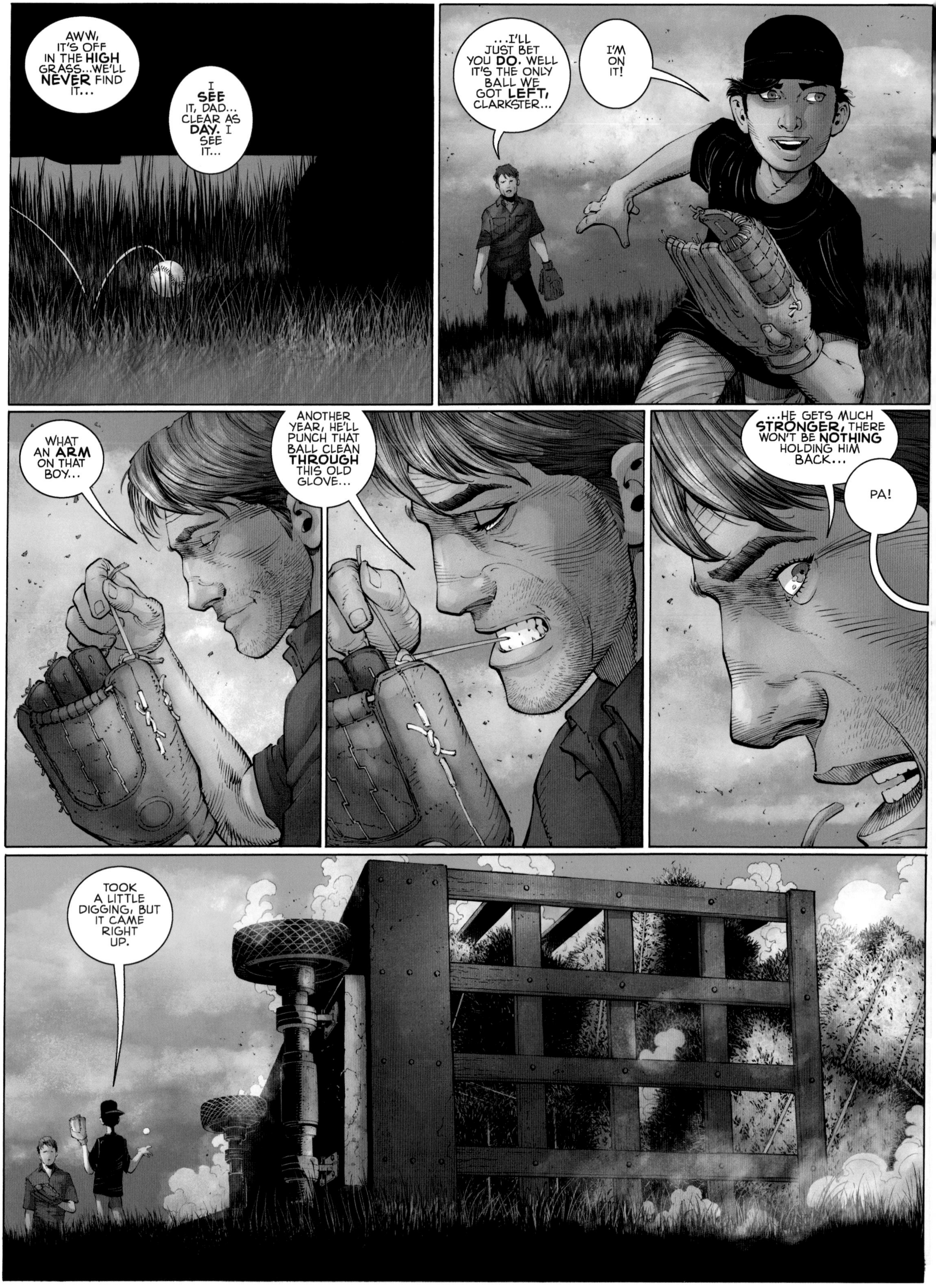
AWW, IT'S OFF IN THE HIGH GRASS...WE'LL NEVER FIND IT...
I SEE IT, DAD... CLEAR AS DAY. I SEE IT...
...I'LL JUST BET YOU DO. WELL IT'S THE ONLY BALL WE GOT LEFT, CLARKSTER...
I'M ON IT!
WHAT AN ARM ON THAT BOY...
ANOTHER YEAR, HE'LL PUNCH THAT BALL CLEAN THROUGH THIS OLD GLOVE...
...HE GETS MUCH STRONGER, THERE WON'T BE NOTHING HOLDING HIM BACK...
PA!
TOOK A LITTLE DIGGING, BUT IT CAME RIGHT UP.

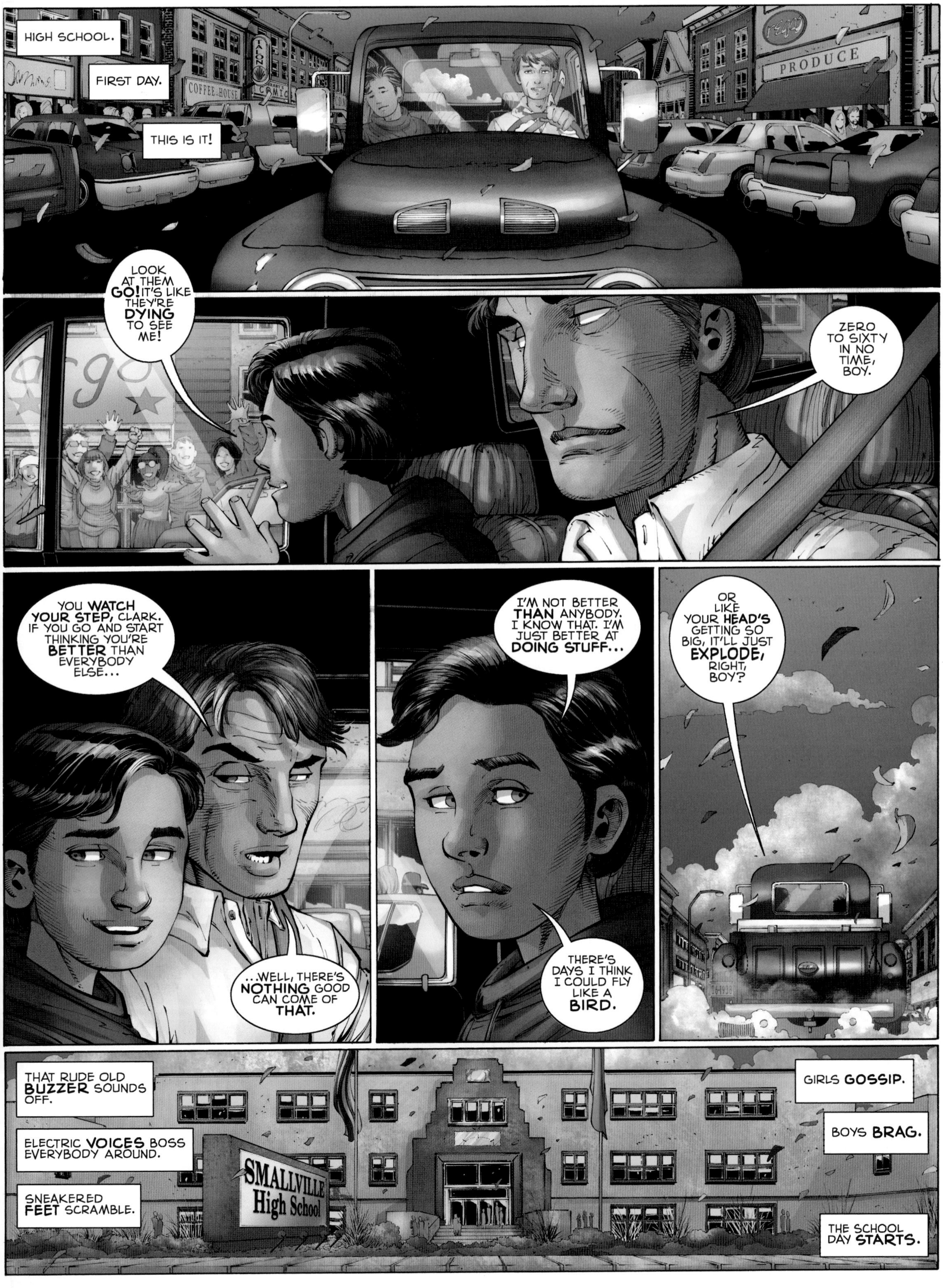
HIGH SCHOOL.
FIRST DAY.
THIS IS IT!
LOOK AT THEM **GO!** IT'S LIKE THEY'RE **DYING** TO SEE ME!
ZERO TO SIXTY IN NO TIME, BOY.
YOU **WATCH YOUR STEP,** CLARK. IF YOU GO AND START THINKING YOU'RE **BETTER** THAN EVERYBODY ELSE...
...WELL, THERE'S **NOTHING** GOOD CAN COME OF **THAT.**
I'M NOT BETTER **THAN** ANYBODY. I KNOW THAT. I'M JUST BETTER AT **DOING STUFF...**
THERE'S DAYS I THINK I COULD FLY LIKE A **BIRD.**
OR LIKE YOUR **HEAD'S** GETTING SO BIG, IT'LL JUST **EXPLODE,** RIGHT, BOY?
THAT RUDE OLD **BUZZER** SOUNDS OFF.
ELECTRIC **VOICES** BOSS EVERYBODY AROUND.
SNEAKERED **FEET** SCRAMBLE.
SMALLVILLE High School
GIRLS **GOSSIP.**
BOYS **BRAG.**
THE SCHOOL DAY **STARTS.**

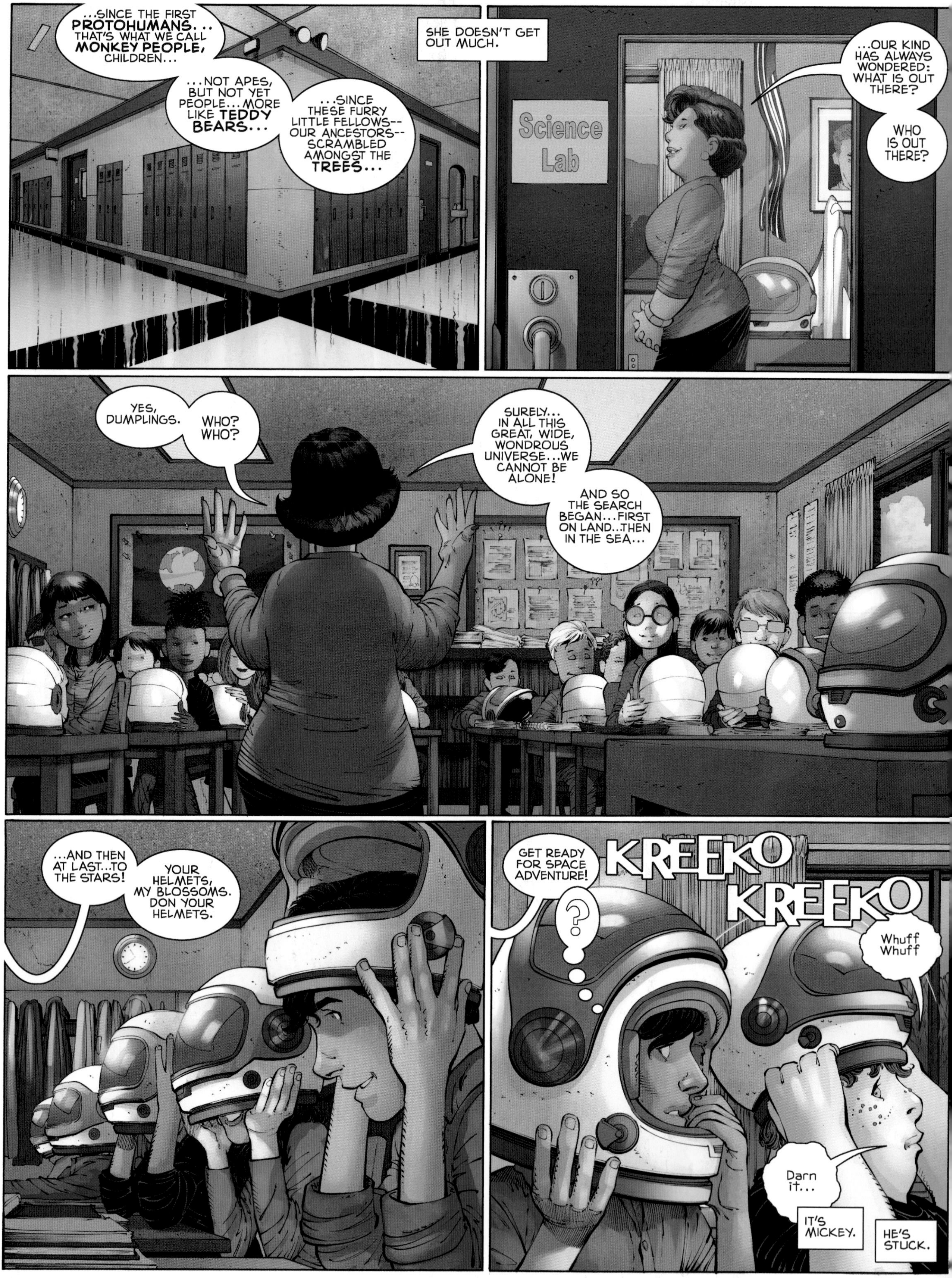
...SINCE THE FIRST **PROTOHUMANS**... THAT'S WHAT WE CALL **MONKEY PEOPLE,** CHILDREN...
...NOT APES, BUT NOT YET PEOPLE...MORE LIKE **TEDDY BEARS**...
...SINCE THESE FURRY LITTLE FELLOWS-- OUR ANCESTORS-- SCRAMBLED AMONGST THE **TREES**...
SHE DOESN'T GET OUT MUCH.
Science Lab
...OUR KIND HAS ALWAYS WONDERED: WHAT IS OUT THERE?
WHO IS OUT THERE?
YES, DUMPLINGS.
WHO? WHO?
SURELY... IN ALL THIS GREAT, WIDE, WONDROUS UNIVERSE...WE CANNOT BE ALONE!
AND SO THE SEARCH BEGAN...FIRST ON LAND...THEN IN THE SEA...
...AND THEN AT LAST...TO THE STARS!
YOUR HELMETS, MY BLOSSOMS. DON YOUR HELMETS.
GET READY FOR SPACE ADVENTURE!
KREEKO
KREEKO
?
Whuff Whuff
Darn it...
IT'S MICKEY.
HE'S STUCK.

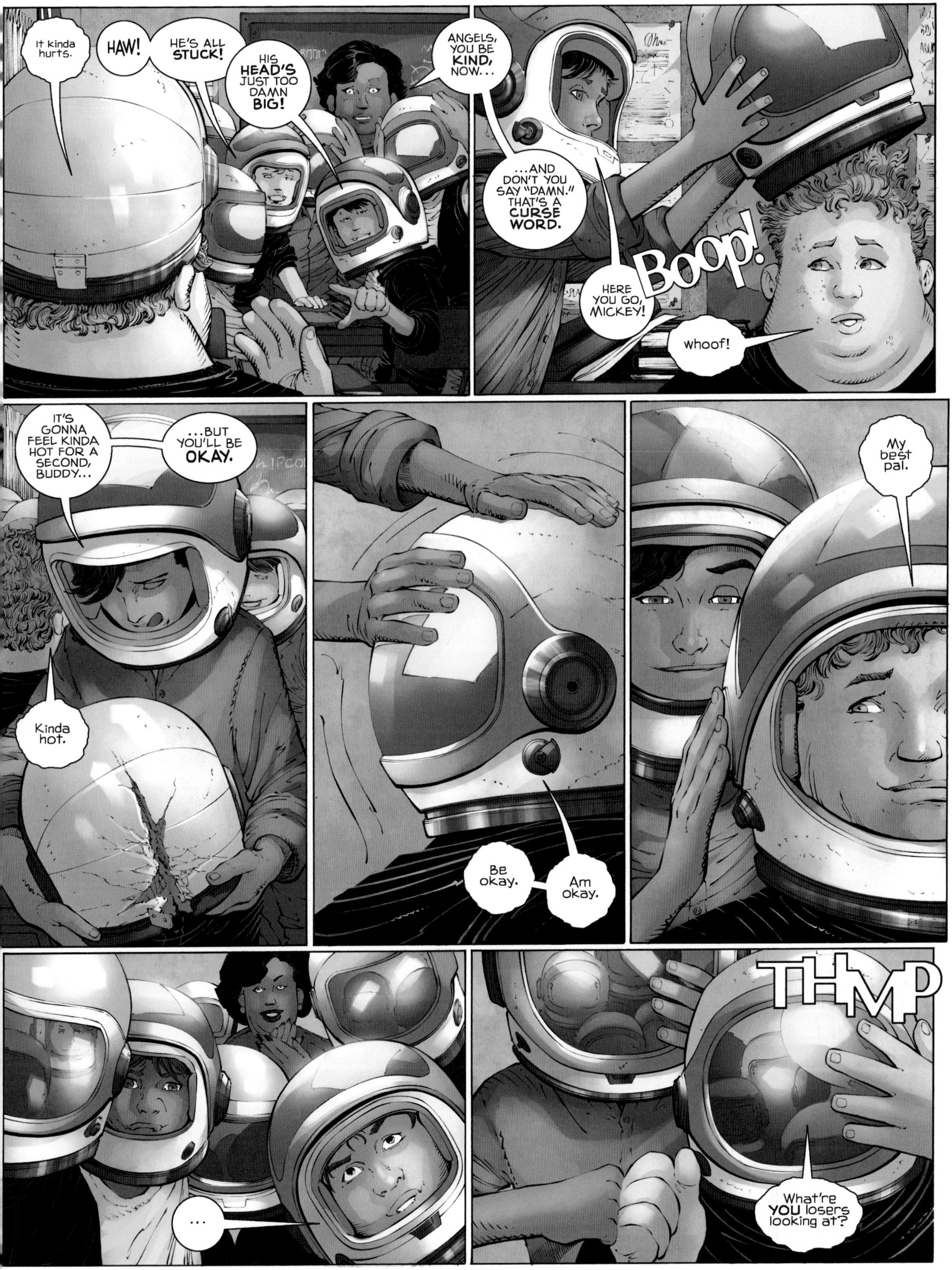

It kinda hurts.
HAW!
HE'S ALL STUCK!
HIS HEAD'S JUST TOO DAMN BIG!
ANGELS, YOU BE KIND, NOW...
...AND DON'T YOU SAY "DAMN." THAT'S A CURSE WORD.
HERE YOU GO, MICKEY!
BOOP!
whoof!
IT'S GONNA FEEL KINDA HOT FOR A SECOND, BUDDY...
...BUT YOU'LL BE OKAY.
Kinda hot.
Be okay.
Am okay.
My best pal.
...
THMP
What're YOU losers looking at?

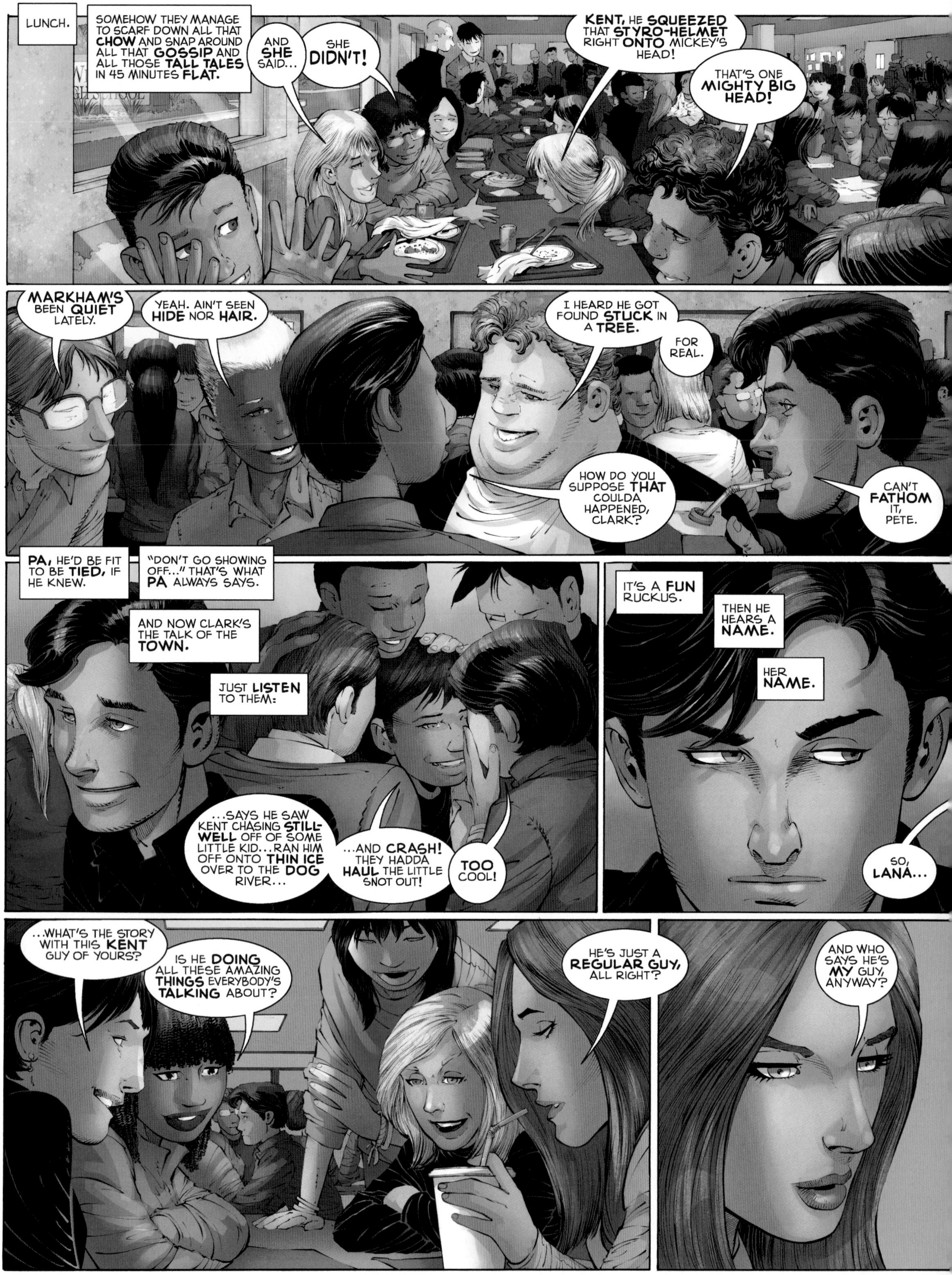
LUNCH.
SOMEHOW THEY MANAGE TO SCARF DOWN ALL THAT CHOW AND SNAP AROUND ALL THAT GOSSIP AND ALL THOSE TALL TALES IN 45 MINUTES FLAT.
AND SHE SAID...
SHE DIDN'T!
KENT, HE SQUEEZED THAT STYRO-HELMET RIGHT ONTO MICKEY'S HEAD!
THAT'S ONE MIGHTY BIG HEAD!
MARKHAM'S BEEN QUIET LATELY.
YEAH. AIN'T SEEN HIDE NOR HAIR.
I HEARD HE GOT FOUND STUCK IN A TREE.
FOR REAL.
HOW DO YOU SUPPOSE THAT COULDA HAPPENED, CLARK?
CAN'T FATHOM IT, PETE.
PA, HE'D BE FIT TO BE TIED, IF HE KNEW.
"DON'T GO SHOWING OFF..." THAT'S WHAT PA ALWAYS SAYS.
AND NOW CLARK'S THE TALK OF THE TOWN.
JUST LISTEN TO THEM:
...SAYS HE SAW KENT CHASING STILL-WELL OFF OF SOME LITTLE KID...RAN HIM OFF ONTO THIN ICE OVER TO THE DOG RIVER...
...AND CRASH! THEY HADDA HAUL THE LITTLE SNOT OUT!
TOO COOL!
IT'S A FUN RUCKUS.
THEN HE HEARS A NAME.
HER NAME.
SO, LANA...
...WHAT'S THE STORY WITH THIS KENT GUY OF YOURS?
IS HE DOING ALL THESE AMAZING THINGS EVERYBODY'S TALKING ABOUT?
HE'S JUST A REGULAR GUY, ALL RIGHT?
AND WHO SAYS HE'S MY GUY, ANYWAY?

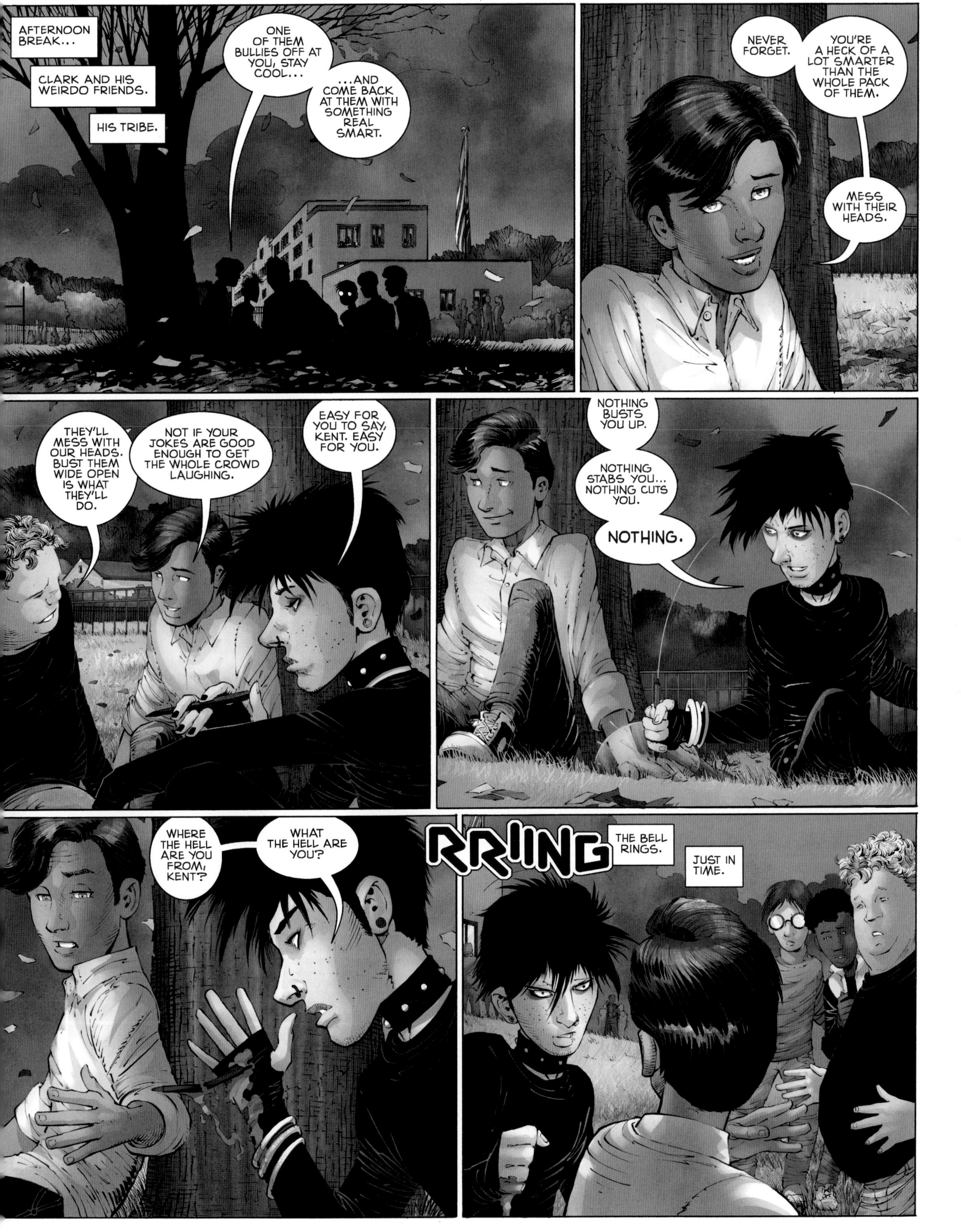
AFTERNOON BREAK...
CLARK AND HIS WEIRDO FRIENDS.
HIS TRIBE.
ONE OF THEM BULLIES OFF AT YOU, STAY COOL...
...AND COME BACK AT THEM WITH SOMETHING REAL SMART.
NEVER FORGET.
YOU'RE A HECK OF A LOT SMARTER THAN THE WHOLE PACK OF THEM.
MESS WITH THEIR HEADS.
THEY'LL MESS WITH OUR HEADS. BUST THEM WIDE OPEN IS WHAT THEY'LL DO.
NOT IF YOUR JOKES ARE GOOD ENOUGH TO GET THE WHOLE CROWD LAUGHING.
EASY FOR YOU TO SAY, KENT. EASY FOR YOU.
NOTHING BUSTS YOU UP.
NOTHING STABS YOU... NOTHING CUTS YOU.
NOTHING.
WHERE THE HELL ARE YOU FROM, KENT?
WHAT THE HELL ARE YOU?
RRING
THE BELL RINGS.
JUST IN TIME.

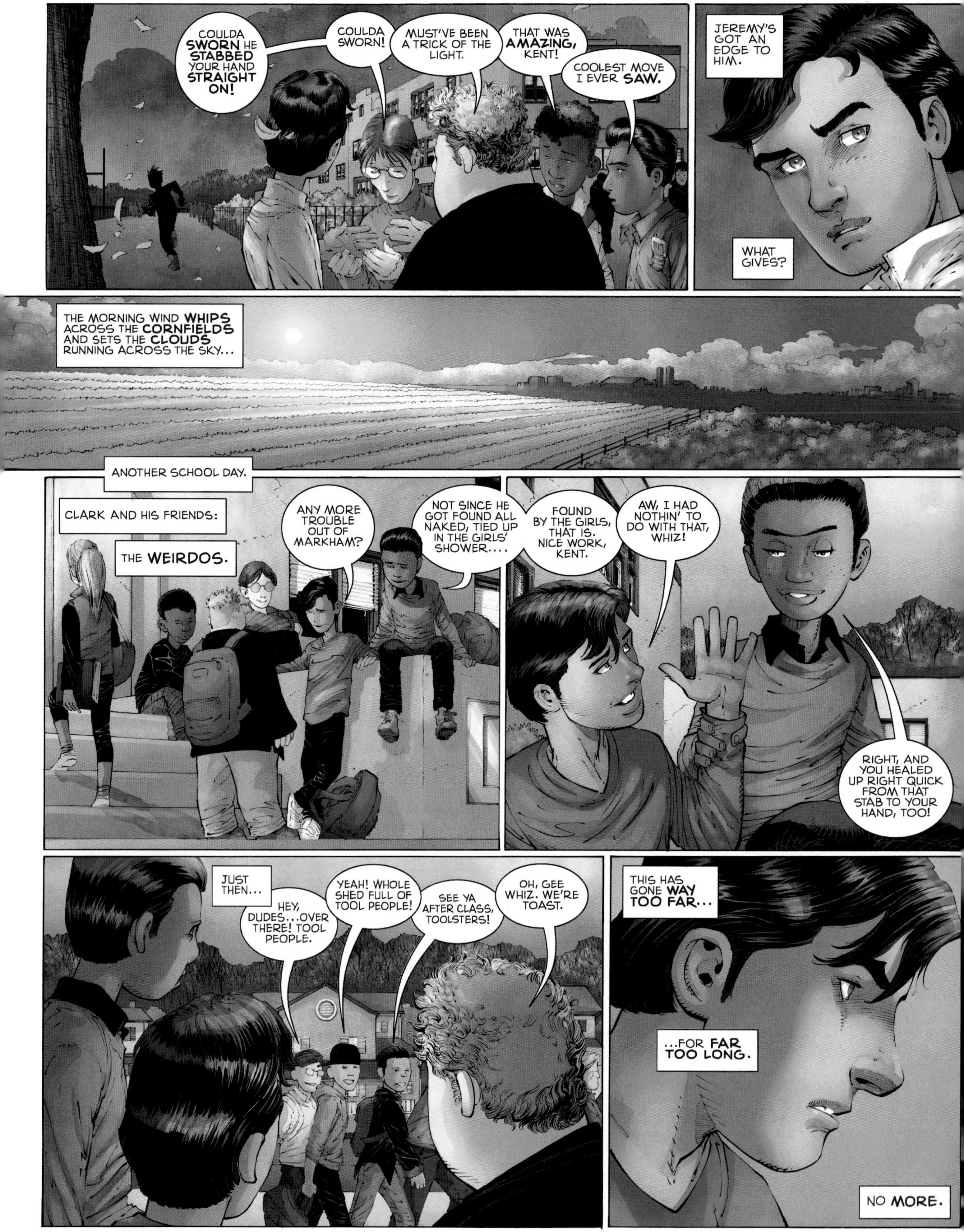
COULDA SWORN HE STABBED YOUR HAND STRAIGHT ON!
COULDA SWORN!
MUST'VE BEEN A TRICK OF THE LIGHT.
THAT WAS AMAZING, KENT!
COOLEST MOVE I EVER SAW.
JEREMY'S GOT AN EDGE TO HIM.
WHAT GIVES?
THE MORNING WIND WHIPS ACROSS THE CORNFIELDS AND SETS THE CLOUDS RUNNING ACROSS THE SKY...
ANOTHER SCHOOL DAY.
CLARK AND HIS FRIENDS:
THE WEIRDOS.
ANY MORE TROUBLE OUT OF MARKHAM?
NOT SINCE HE GOT FOUND ALL NAKED, TIED UP IN THE GIRLS' SHOWER....
FOUND BY THE GIRLS, THAT IS. NICE WORK, KENT.
AW, I HAD NOTHIN' TO DO WITH THAT, WHIZ!
RIGHT, AND YOU HEALED UP RIGHT QUICK FROM THAT STAB TO YOUR HAND, TOO!
JUST THEN...
HEY, DUDES...OVER THERE! TOOL PEOPLE.
YEAH! WHOLE SHED FULL OF TOOL PEOPLE!
SEE YA AFTER CLASS, TOOLSTERS!
OH, GEE WHIZ. WE'RE TOAST.
THIS HAS GONE WAY TOO FAR...
...FOR FAR TOO LONG.
NO MORE.

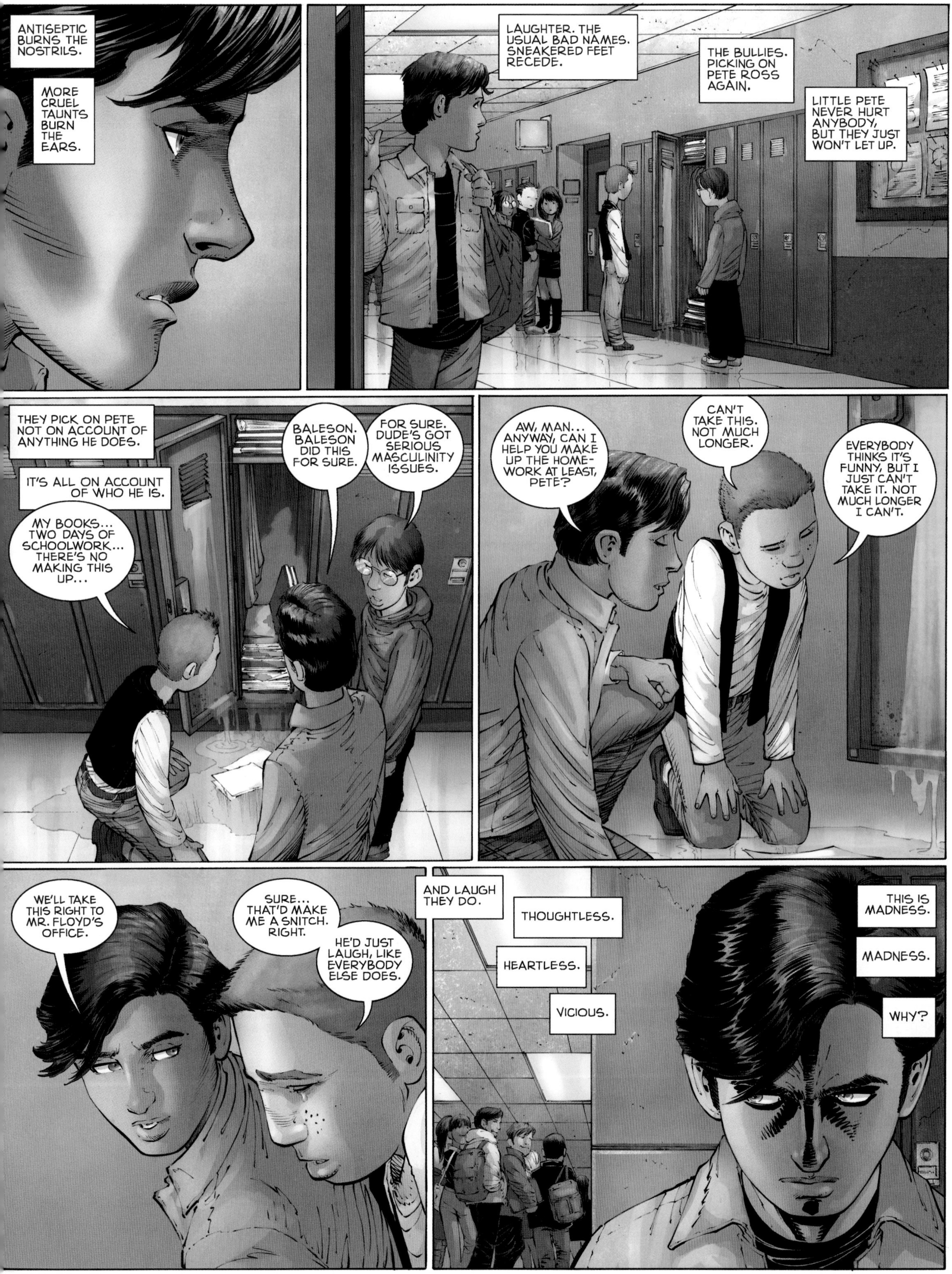
ANTISEPTIC BURNS THE NOSTRILS.
MORE CRUEL TAUNTS BURN THE EARS.
LAUGHTER. THE USUAL BAD NAMES. SNEAKERED FEET RECEDE.
THE BULLIES. PICKING ON PETE ROSS AGAIN.
LITTLE PETE NEVER HURT ANYBODY, BUT THEY JUST WON'T LET UP.
THEY PICK ON PETE NOT ON ACCOUNT OF ANYTHING HE DOES.
IT'S ALL ON ACCOUNT OF WHO HE IS.
MY BOOKS... TWO DAYS OF SCHOOLWORK... THERE'S NO MAKING THIS UP...
BALESON. BALESON DID THIS FOR SURE.
FOR SURE. DUDE'S GOT SERIOUS MASCULINITY ISSUES.
AW, MAN... ANYWAY, CAN I HELP YOU MAKE UP THE HOME-WORK AT LEAST, PETE?
CAN'T TAKE THIS. NOT MUCH LONGER.
EVERYBODY THINKS IT'S FUNNY, BUT I JUST CAN'T TAKE IT. NOT MUCH LONGER I CAN'T.
WE'LL TAKE THIS RIGHT TO MR. FLOYD'S OFFICE.
SURE... THAT'D MAKE ME A SNITCH. RIGHT.
HE'D JUST LAUGH, LIKE EVERYBODY ELSE DOES.
AND LAUGH THEY DO.
THOUGHTLESS.
HEARTLESS.
VICIOUS.
THIS IS MADNESS.
MADNESS.
WHY?

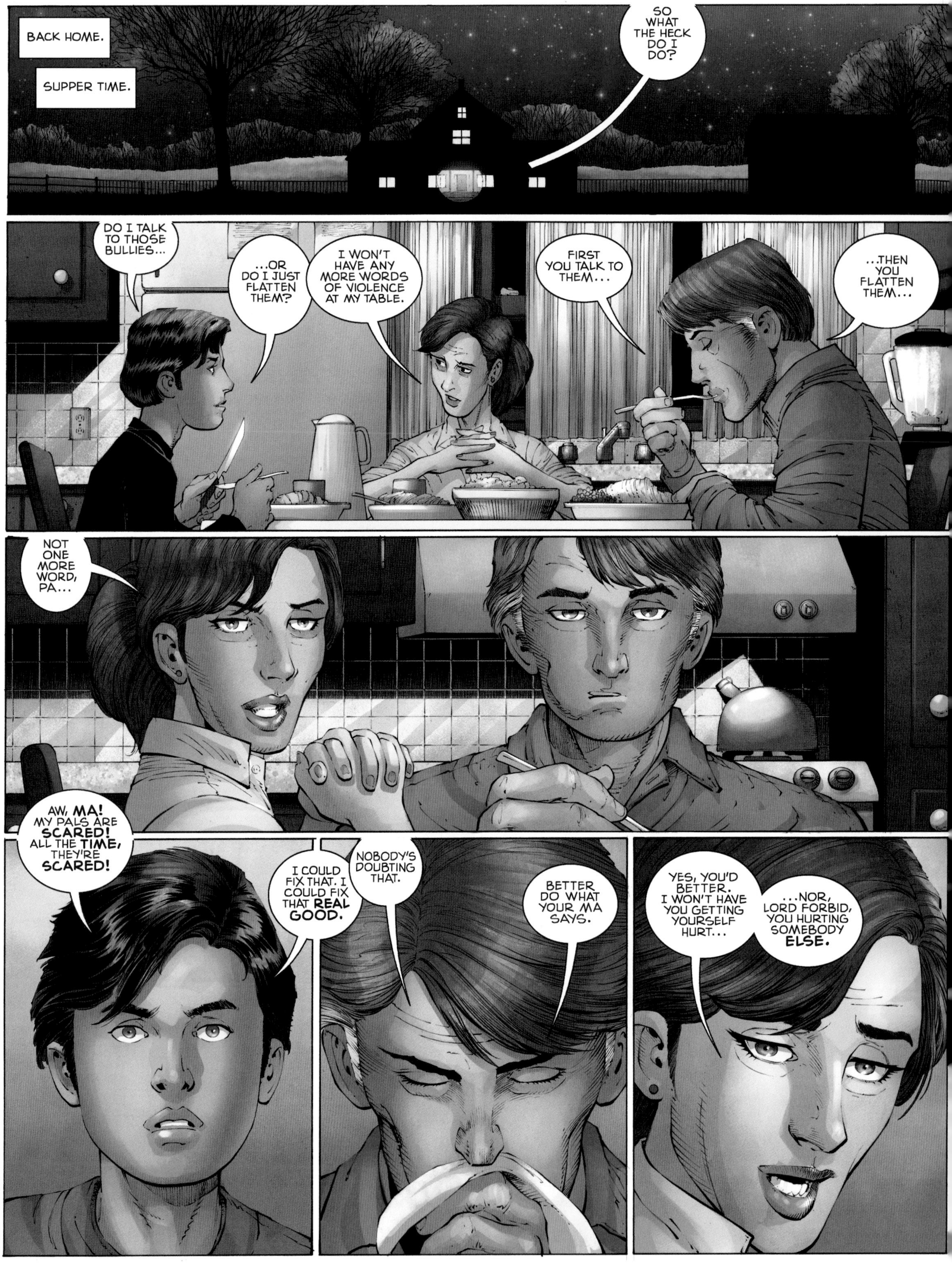
BACK HOME.
SUPPER TIME.
SO WHAT THE HECK DO I DO?
DO I TALK TO THOSE BULLIES...
...OR DO I JUST FLATTEN THEM?
I WON'T HAVE ANY MORE WORDS OF VIOLENCE AT MY TABLE.
FIRST YOU TALK TO THEM...
...THEN YOU FLATTEN THEM...
NOT ONE MORE WORD, PA...
AW, MA! MY PALS ARE SCARED! ALL THE TIME, THEY'RE SCARED!
I COULD FIX THAT. I COULD FIX THAT REAL GOOD.
NOBODY'S DOUBTING THAT.
BETTER DO WHAT YOUR MA SAYS.
YES, YOU'D BETTER. I WON'T HAVE YOU GETTING YOURSELF HURT...
...NOR, LORD FORBID, YOU HURTING SOMEBODY ELSE.

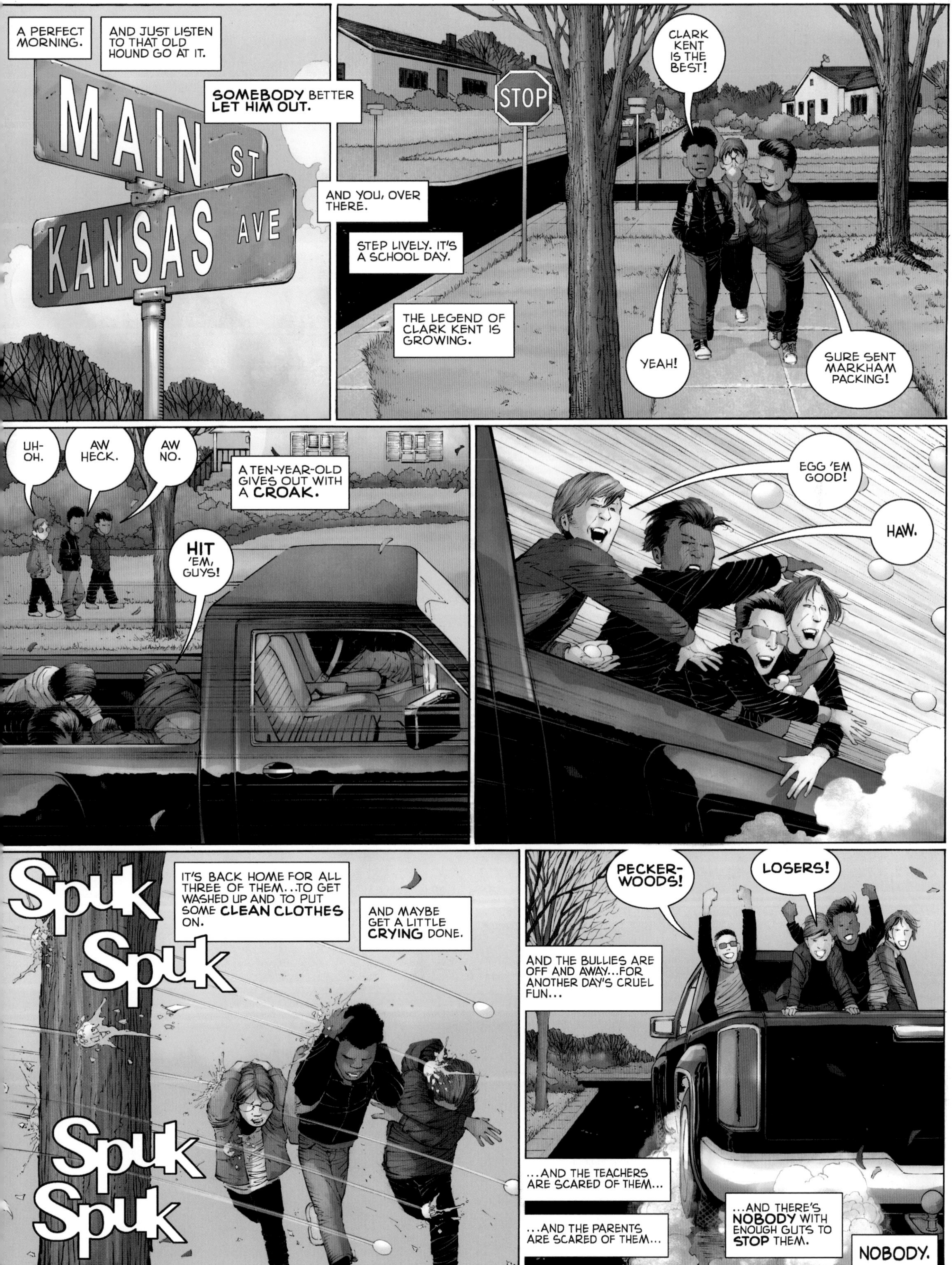

A PERFECT MORNING.
AND JUST LISTEN TO THAT OLD HOUND GO AT IT.
MAIN ST
KANSAS AVE
SOMEBODY BETTER LET HIM OUT.
STOP
AND YOU, OVER THERE.
STEP LIVELY. IT'S A SCHOOL DAY.
THE LEGEND OF CLARK KENT IS GROWING.
CLARK KENT IS THE BEST!
YEAH!
SURE SENT MARKHAM PACKING!
UH-OH.
AW HECK.
AW NO.
A TEN-YEAR-OLD GIVES OUT WITH A CROAK.
HIT 'EM, GUYS!
EGG 'EM GOOD!
HAW.
Spuk
Spuk
Spuk
Spuk
IT'S BACK HOME FOR ALL THREE OF THEM...TO GET WASHED UP AND TO PUT SOME CLEAN CLOTHES ON.
AND MAYBE GET A LITTLE CRYING DONE.
PECKER-WOODS!
LOSERS!
AND THE BULLIES ARE OFF AND AWAY...FOR ANOTHER DAY'S CRUEL FUN...
...AND THE TEACHERS ARE SCARED OF THEM...
...AND THE PARENTS ARE SCARED OF THEM...
...AND THERE'S NOBODY WITH ENOUGH GUTS TO STOP THEM.
NOBODY.

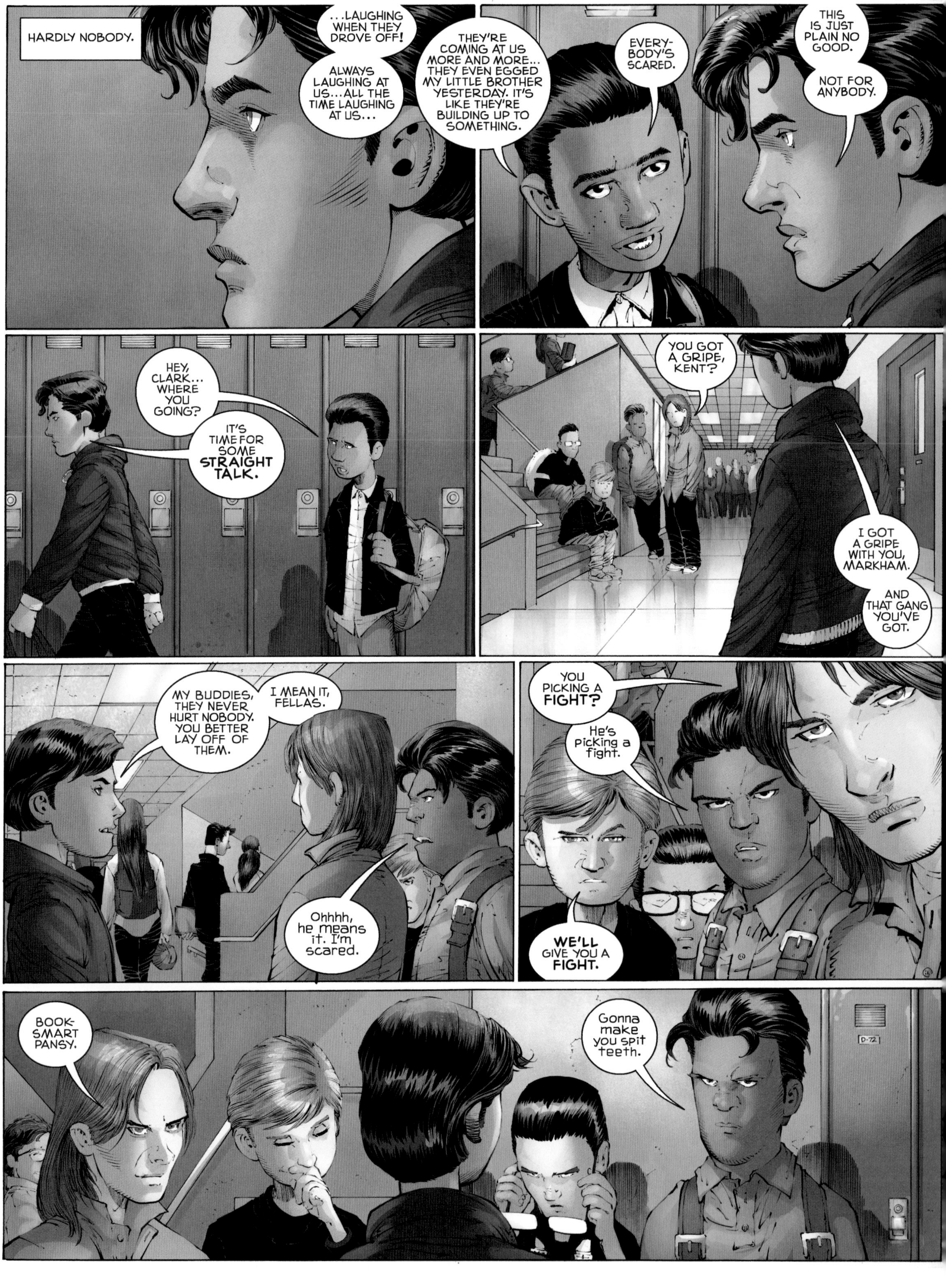
HARDLY NOBODY.
...LAUGHING WHEN THEY DROVE OFF!
ALWAYS LAUGHING AT US...ALL THE TIME LAUGHING AT US...
THEY'RE COMING AT US MORE AND MORE... THEY EVEN EGGED MY LITTLE BROTHER YESTERDAY. IT'S LIKE THEY'RE BUILDING UP TO SOMETHING.
EVERY-BODY'S SCARED.
THIS IS JUST PLAIN NO GOOD.
NOT FOR ANYBODY.
HEY, CLARK... WHERE YOU GOING?
IT'S TIME FOR SOME STRAIGHT TALK.
YOU GOT A GRIPE, KENT?
I GOT A GRIPE WITH YOU, MARKHAM.
AND THAT GANG YOU'VE GOT.
MY BUDDIES, THEY NEVER HURT NOBODY. YOU BETTER LAY OFF OF THEM.
I MEAN IT, FELLAS.
Ohhhh, he means it. I'm scared.
YOU PICKING A FIGHT?
He's picking a fight.
WE'LL GIVE YOU A FIGHT.
BOOK-SMART PANSY.
Gonna make you spit teeth.
D-72

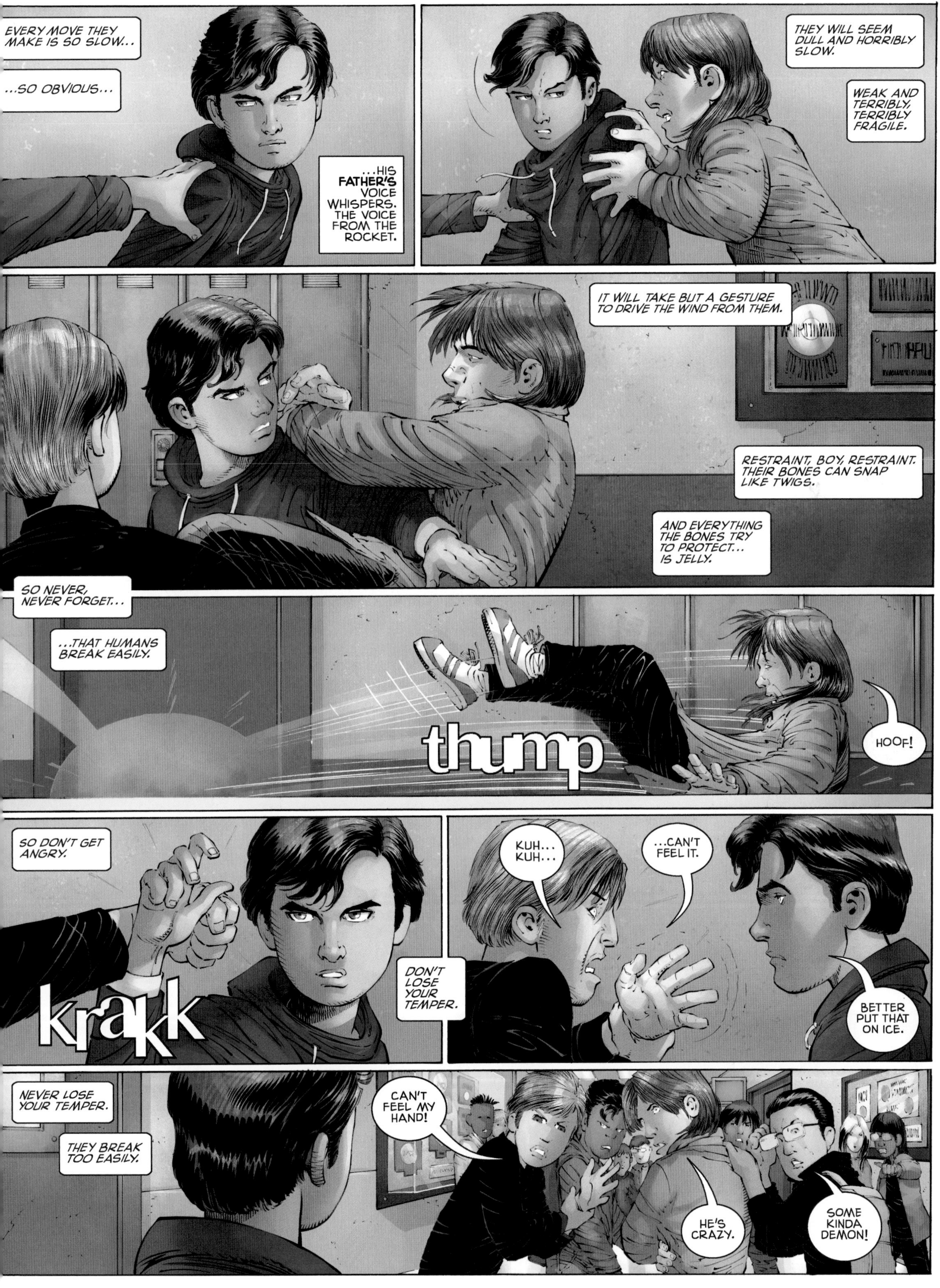
EVERY MOVE THEY MAKE IS SO SLOW...
...SO OBVIOUS...
...HIS FATHER'S VOICE WHISPERS. THE VOICE FROM THE ROCKET.
THEY WILL SEEM DULL AND HORRIBLY SLOW.
WEAK AND TERRIBLY, TERRIBLY FRAGILE.
IT WILL TAKE BUT A GESTURE TO DRIVE THE WIND FROM THEM.
RESTRAINT, BOY, RESTRAINT. THEIR BONES CAN SNAP LIKE TWIGS.
AND EVERYTHING THE BONES TRY TO PROTECT... IS JELLY.
SO NEVER, NEVER FORGET...
...THAT HUMANS BREAK EASILY.
thump
HOOF!
SO DON'T GET ANGRY.
krakk
DON'T LOSE YOUR TEMPER.
KUH... KUH...
...CAN'T FEEL IT.
BETTER PUT THAT ON ICE.
NEVER LOSE YOUR TEMPER.
THEY BREAK TOO EASILY.
CAN'T FEEL MY HAND!
HE'S CRAZY.
SOME KINDA DEMON!

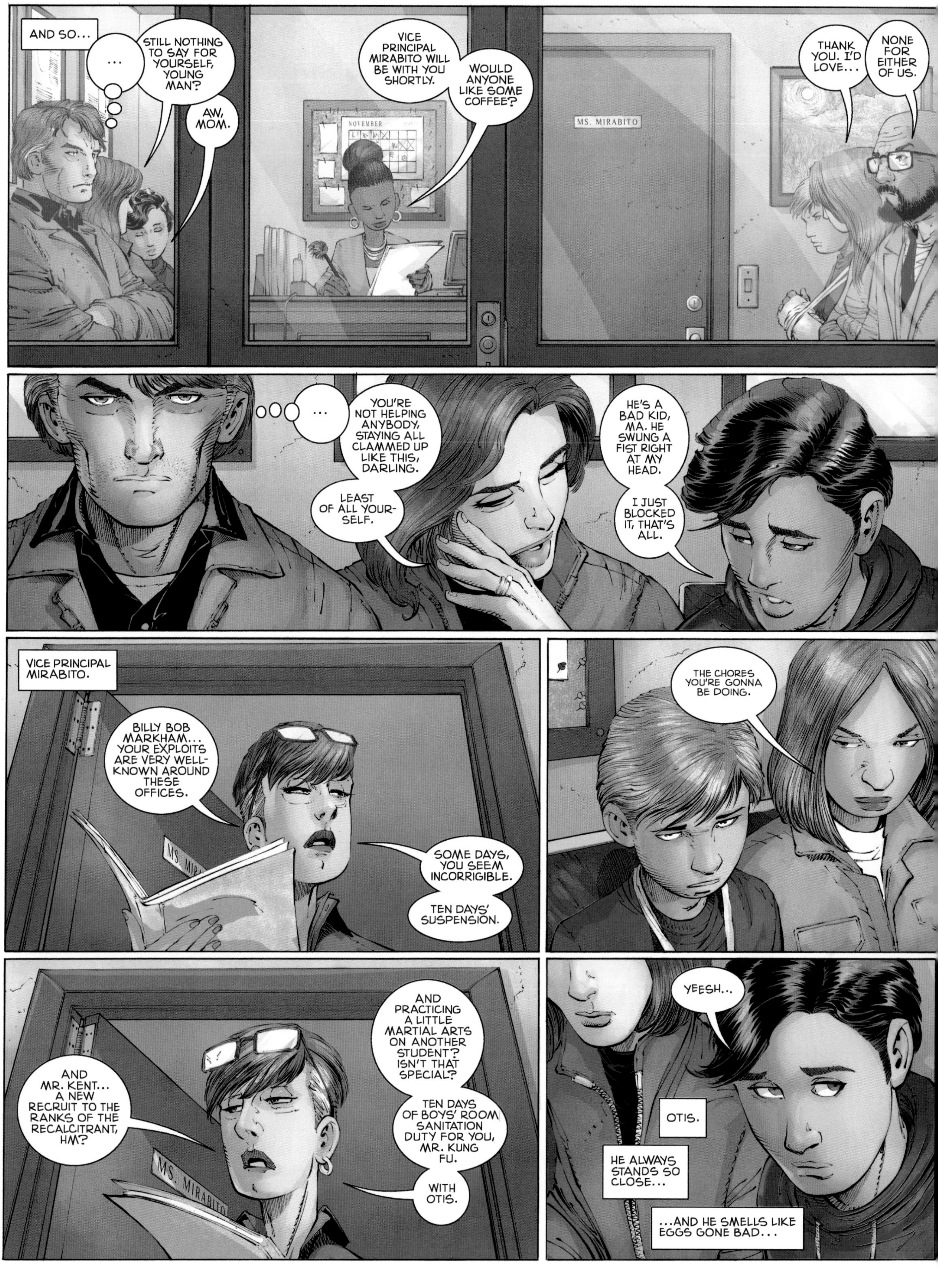
AND SO...
...
STILL NOTHING TO SAY FOR YOURSELF, YOUNG MAN?
AW, MOM.
VICE PRINCIPAL MIRABITO WILL BE WITH YOU SHORTLY.
WOULD ANYONE LIKE SOME COFFEE?
NOVEMBER
MS. MIRABITO
THANK YOU. I'D LOVE...
NONE FOR EITHER OF US.
...
YOU'RE NOT HELPING ANYBODY, STAYING ALL CLAMMED UP LIKE THIS, DARLING.
LEAST OF ALL YOURSELF.
HE'S A BAD KID, MA. HE SWUNG A FIST RIGHT AT MY HEAD.
I JUST BLOCKED IT, THAT'S ALL.
VICE PRINCIPAL MIRABITO.
BILLY BOB MARKHAM... YOUR EXPLOITS ARE VERY WELL-KNOWN AROUND THESE OFFICES.
SOME DAYS, YOU SEEM INCORRIGIBLE.
TEN DAYS' SUSPENSION.
THE CHORES YOU'RE GONNA BE DOING.
AND MR. KENT... A NEW RECRUIT TO THE RANKS OF THE RECALCITRANT, HM?
AND PRACTICING A LITTLE MARTIAL ARTS ON ANOTHER STUDENT? ISN'T THAT SPECIAL?
TEN DAYS OF BOYS' ROOM SANITATION DUTY FOR YOU, MR. KUNG FU.
WITH OTIS.
MS. MIRABITO
YEESH...
OTIS.
HE ALWAYS STANDS SO CLOSE...
...AND HE SMELLS LIKE EGGS GONE BAD...

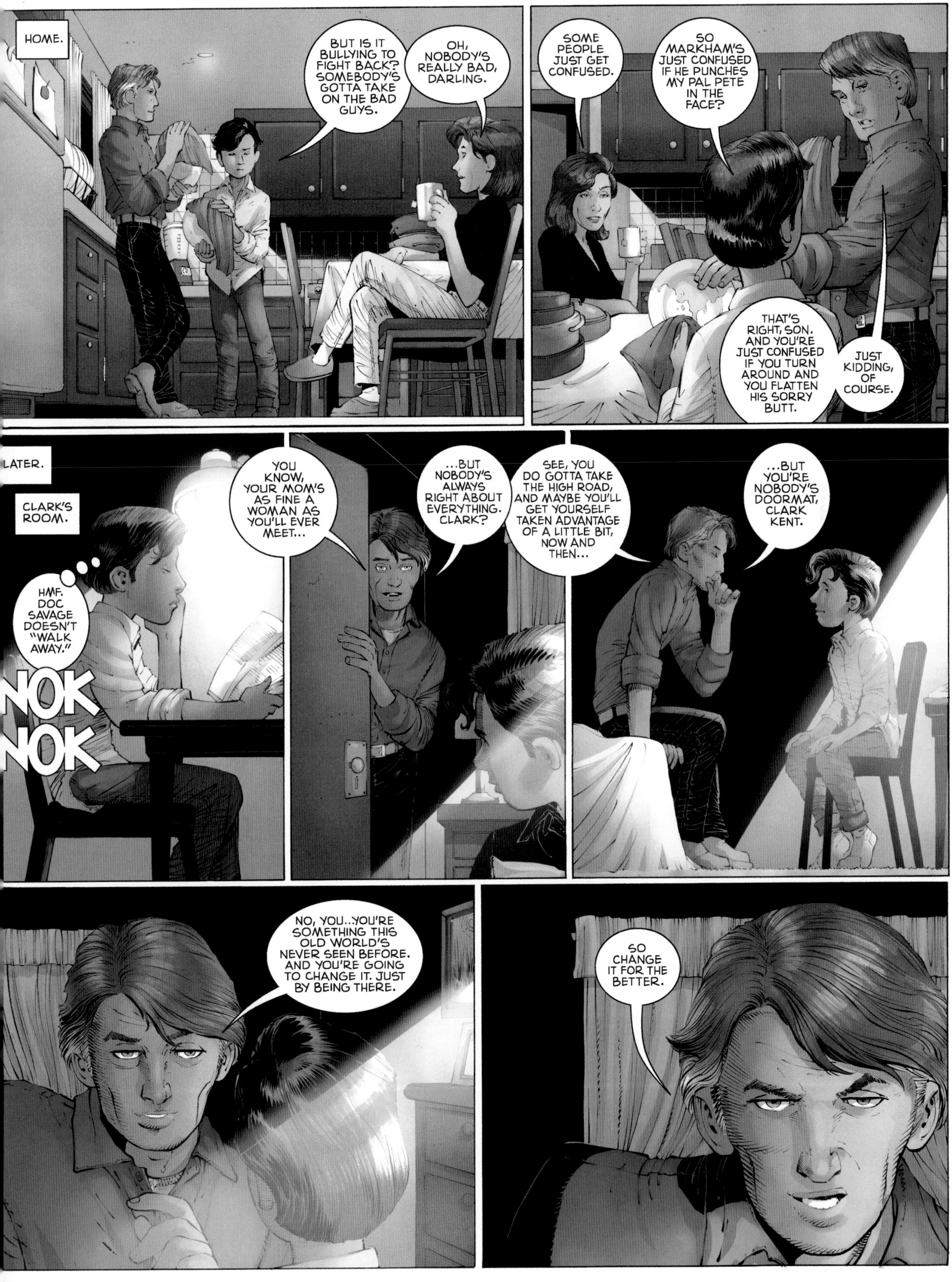
HOME.
BUT IS IT BULLYING TO FIGHT BACK? SOMEBODY'S GOTTA TAKE ON THE BAD GUYS.
OH, NOBODY'S REALLY BAD, DARLING.
SOME PEOPLE JUST GET CONFUSED.
SO MARKHAM'S JUST CONFUSED IF HE PUNCHES MY PAL PETE IN THE FACE?
THAT'S RIGHT, SON. AND YOU'RE JUST CONFUSED IF YOU TURN AROUND AND YOU FLATTEN HIS SORRY BUTT.
JUST KIDDING, OF COURSE.
LATER.
CLARK'S ROOM.
HMF. DOC SAVAGE DOESN'T "WALK AWAY."
NOK NOK
YOU KNOW, YOUR MOM'S AS FINE A WOMAN AS YOU'LL EVER MEET...
...BUT NOBODY'S ALWAYS RIGHT ABOUT EVERYTHING. CLARK?
SEE, YOU DO GOTTA TAKE THE HIGH ROAD, AND MAYBE YOU'LL GET YOURSELF TAKEN ADVANTAGE OF A LITTLE BIT, NOW AND THEN...
...BUT YOU'RE NOBODY'S DOORMAT, CLARK KENT.
NO, YOU...YOU'RE SOMETHING THIS OLD WORLD'S NEVER SEEN BEFORE. AND YOU'RE GOING TO CHANGE IT. JUST BY BEING THERE.
SO CHANGE IT FOR THE BETTER.

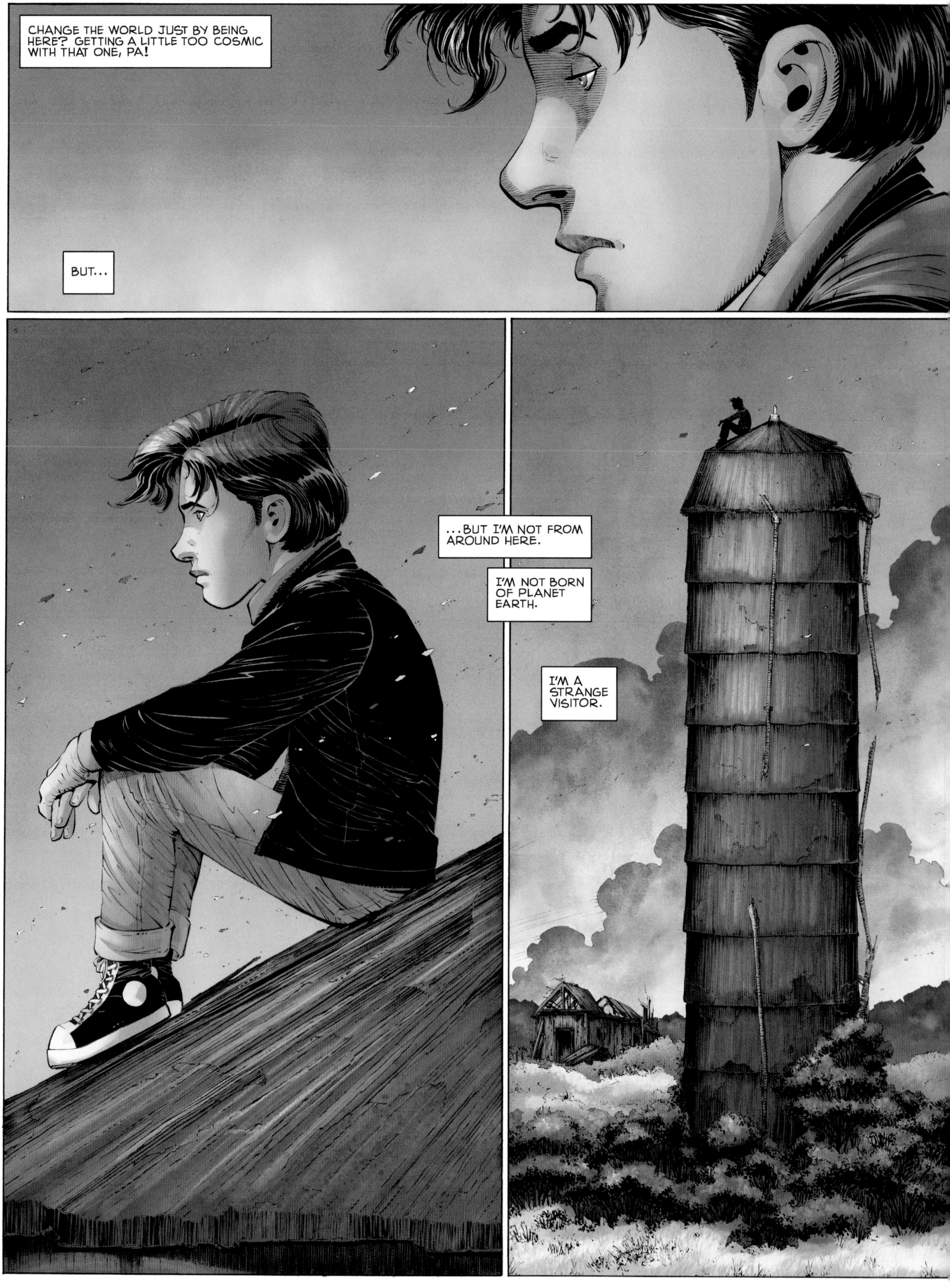
CHANGE THE WORLD JUST BY BEING HERE? GETTING A LITTLE TOO COSMIC WITH THAT ONE, PA!
BUT...
...BUT I'M NOT FROM AROUND HERE.
I'M NOT BORN OF PLANET EARTH.
I'M A STRANGE VISITOR.

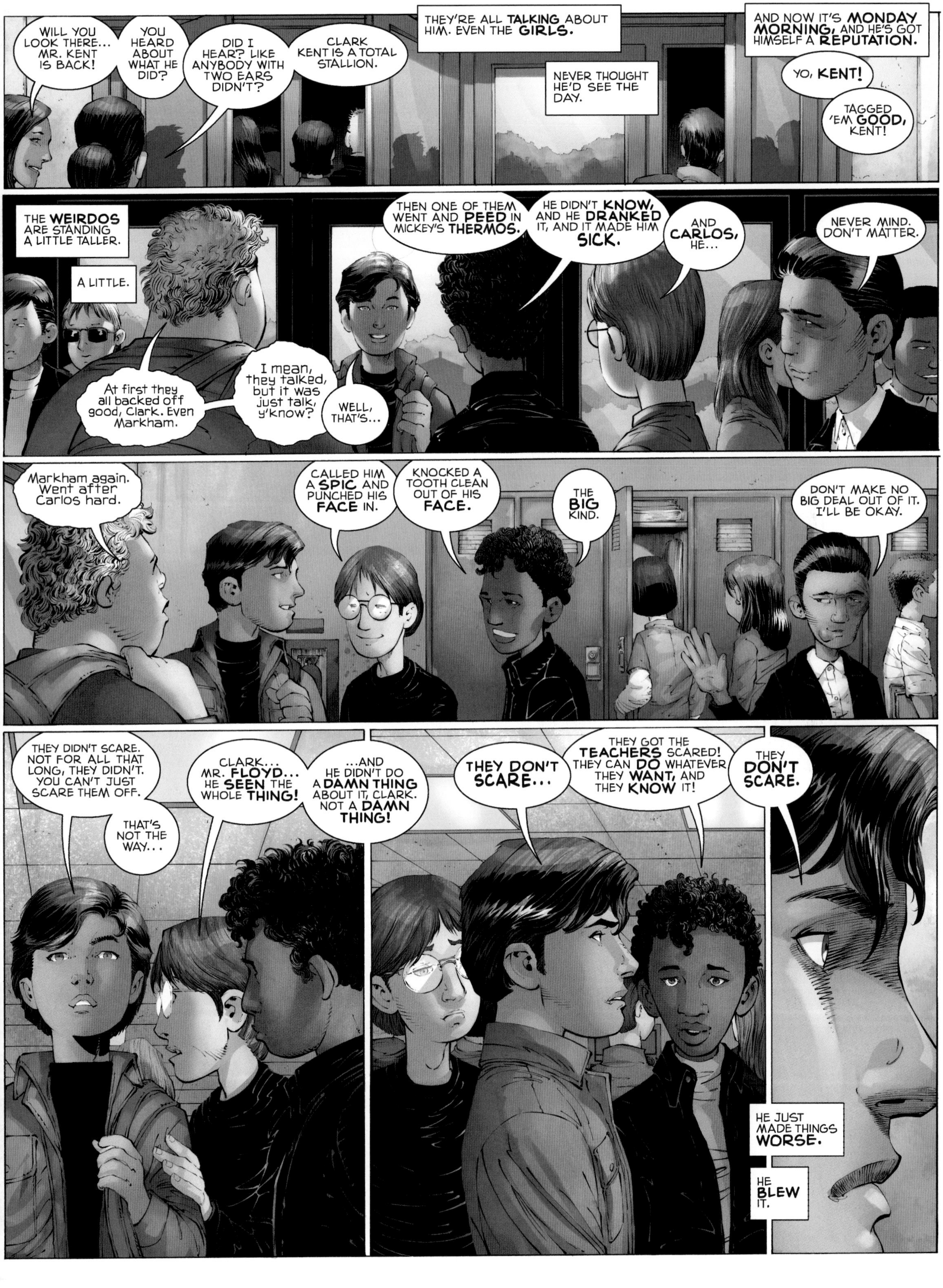
WILL YOU LOOK THERE... MR. KENT IS BACK!
YOU HEARD ABOUT WHAT HE DID?
DID I HEAR? LIKE ANYBODY WITH TWO EARS DIDN'T?
CLARK KENT IS A TOTAL STALLION.
THEY'RE ALL TALKING ABOUT HIM. EVEN THE GIRLS.
NEVER THOUGHT HE'D SEE THE DAY.
AND NOW IT'S MONDAY MORNING, AND HE'S GOT HIMSELF A REPUTATION.
YO, KENT!
TAGGED 'EM GOOD, KENT!
THE WEIRDOS ARE STANDING A LITTLE TALLER.
A LITTLE.
At first they all backed off good, Clark. Even Markham.
I mean, they talked, but it was just talk, y'know?
WELL, THAT'S...
THEN ONE OF THEM WENT AND PEED IN MICKEY'S THERMOS.
HE DIDN'T KNOW, AND HE DRANKED IT, AND IT MADE HIM SICK.
AND CARLOS, HE...
NEVER MIND. DON'T MATTER.
Markham again. Went after Carlos hard.
CALLED HIM A SPIC AND PUNCHED HIS FACE IN.
KNOCKED A TOOTH CLEAN OUT OF HIS FACE.
THE BIG KIND.
DON'T MAKE NO BIG DEAL OUT OF IT. I'LL BE OKAY.
THEY DIDN'T SCARE. NOT FOR ALL THAT LONG, THEY DIDN'T. YOU CAN'T JUST SCARE THEM OFF.
THAT'S NOT THE WAY...
CLARK... MR. FLOYD... HE SEEN THE WHOLE THING!
...AND HE DIDN'T DO A DAMN THING ABOUT IT, CLARK. NOT A DAMN THING!
THEY DON'T SCARE...
THEY GOT THE TEACHERS SCARED! THEY CAN DO WHATEVER THEY WANT, AND THEY KNOW IT!
THEY DON'T SCARE.
HE JUST MADE THINGS WORSE.
HE BLEW IT.

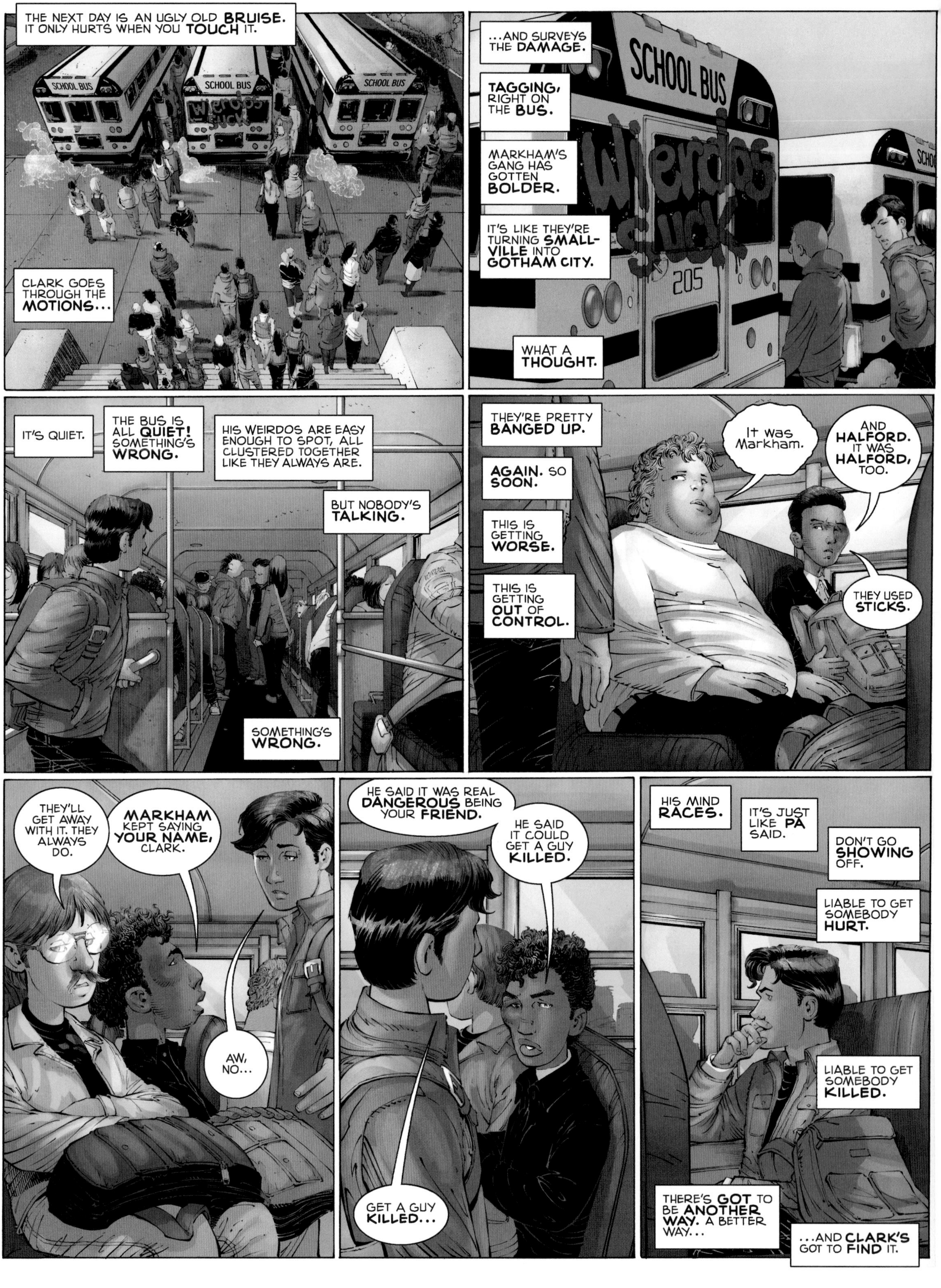
THE NEXT DAY IS AN UGLY OLD BRUISE. IT ONLY HURTS WHEN YOU TOUCH IT.
SCHOOL BUS
SCHOOL BUS
SCHOOL BUS
CLARK GOES THROUGH THE MOTIONS...
...AND SURVEYS THE DAMAGE.
SCHOOL BUS
TAGGING, RIGHT ON THE BUS.
MARKHAM'S GANG HAS GOTTEN BOLDER.
IT'S LIKE THEY'RE TURNING SMALLVILLE INTO GOTHAM CITY.
205
WHAT A THOUGHT.
IT'S QUIET.
THE BUS IS ALL QUIET! SOMETHING'S WRONG.
HIS WEIRDOS ARE EASY ENOUGH TO SPOT, ALL CLUSTERED TOGETHER LIKE THEY ALWAYS ARE.
BUT NOBODY'S TALKING.
SOMETHING'S WRONG.
THEY'RE PRETTY BANGED UP.
AGAIN. SO SOON.
THIS IS GETTING WORSE.
THIS IS GETTING OUT OF CONTROL.
It was Markham.
AND HALFORD. IT WAS HALFORD, TOO.
THEY USED STICKS.
THEY'LL GET AWAY WITH IT. THEY ALWAYS DO.
MARKHAM KEPT SAYING YOUR NAME, CLARK.
AW, NO...
HE SAID IT WAS REAL DANGEROUS BEING YOUR FRIEND.
HE SAID IT COULD GET A GUY KILLED.
GET A GUY KILLED...
HIS MIND RACES.
IT'S JUST LIKE PA SAID.
DON'T GO SHOWING OFF.
LIABLE TO GET SOMEBODY HURT.
LIABLE TO GET SOMEBODY KILLED.
THERE'S GOT TO BE ANOTHER WAY. A BETTER WAY...
...AND CLARK'S GOT TO FIND IT.

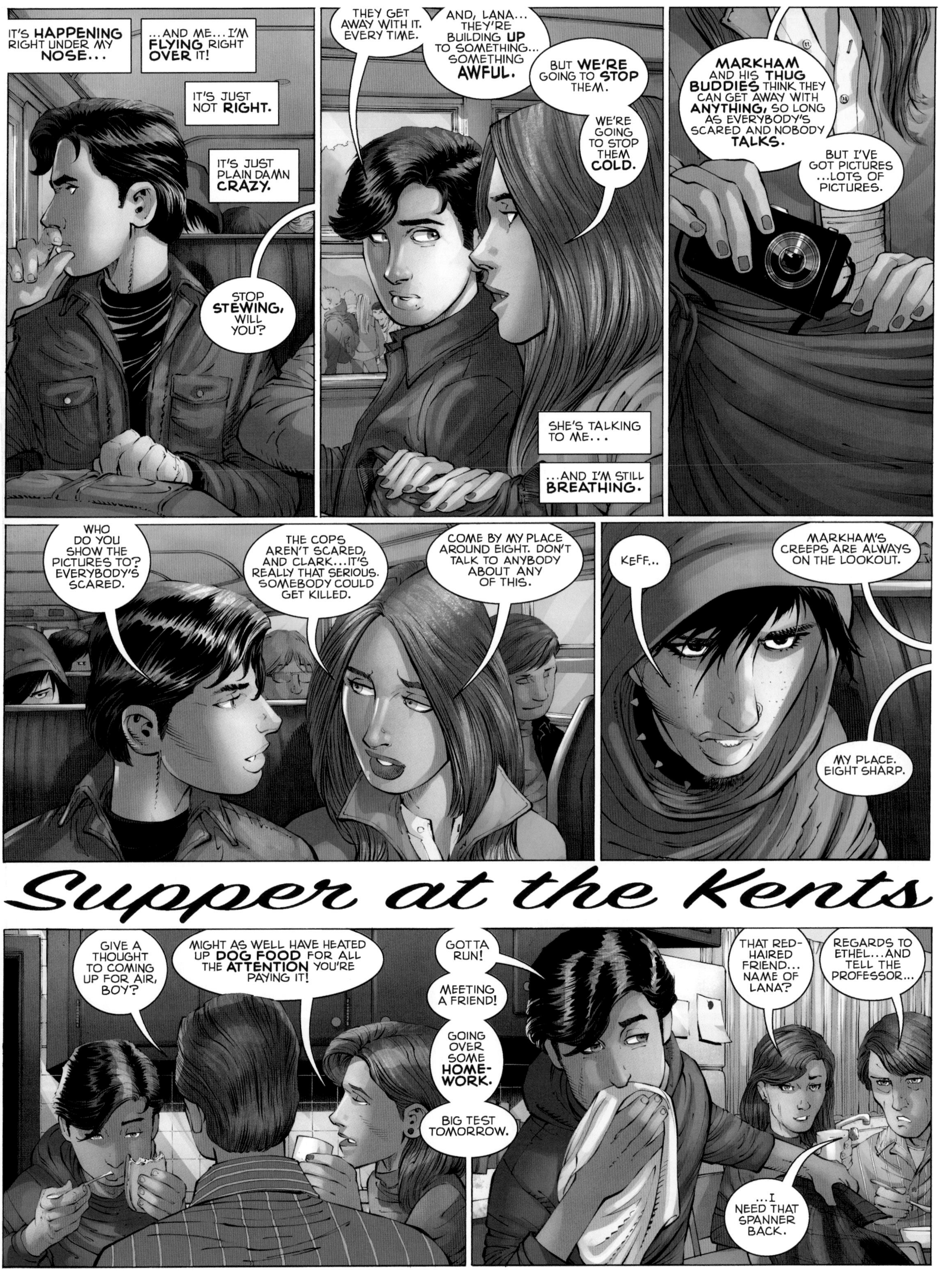
IT'S HAPPENING RIGHT UNDER MY NOSE...
...AND ME... I'M FLYING RIGHT OVER IT!
IT'S JUST NOT RIGHT.
IT'S JUST PLAIN DAMN CRAZY.
STOP STEWING, WILL YOU?
THEY GET AWAY WITH IT. EVERY TIME.
AND, LANA... THEY'RE BUILDING UP TO SOMETHING... SOMETHING AWFUL.
BUT WE'RE GOING TO STOP THEM.
WE'RE GOING TO STOP THEM COLD.
SHE'S TALKING TO ME...
...AND I'M STILL BREATHING.
MARKHAM AND HIS THUG BUDDIES THINK THEY CAN GET AWAY WITH ANYTHING, SO LONG AS EVERYBODY'S SCARED AND NOBODY TALKS.
BUT I'VE GOT PICTURES ...LOTS OF PICTURES.
WHO DO YOU SHOW THE PICTURES TO? EVERYBODY'S SCARED.
THE COPS AREN'T SCARED, AND CLARK... IT'S REALLY THAT SERIOUS. SOMEBODY COULD GET KILLED.
COME BY MY PLACE AROUND EIGHT. DON'T TALK TO ANYBODY ABOUT ANY OF THIS.
KEFF...
MARKHAM'S CREEPS ARE ALWAYS ON THE LOOKOUT.
MY PLACE. EIGHT SHARP.
Supper at the Kents
GIVE A THOUGHT TO COMING UP FOR AIR, BOY?
MIGHT AS WELL HAVE HEATED UP DOG FOOD FOR ALL THE ATTENTION YOU'RE PAYING IT!
GOTTA RUN!
MEETING A FRIEND!
GOING OVER SOME HOME-WORK.
BIG TEST TOMORROW.
THAT RED-HAIRED FRIEND... NAME OF LANA?
REGARDS TO ETHEL... AND TELL THE PROFESSOR...
...I NEED THAT SPANNER BACK.

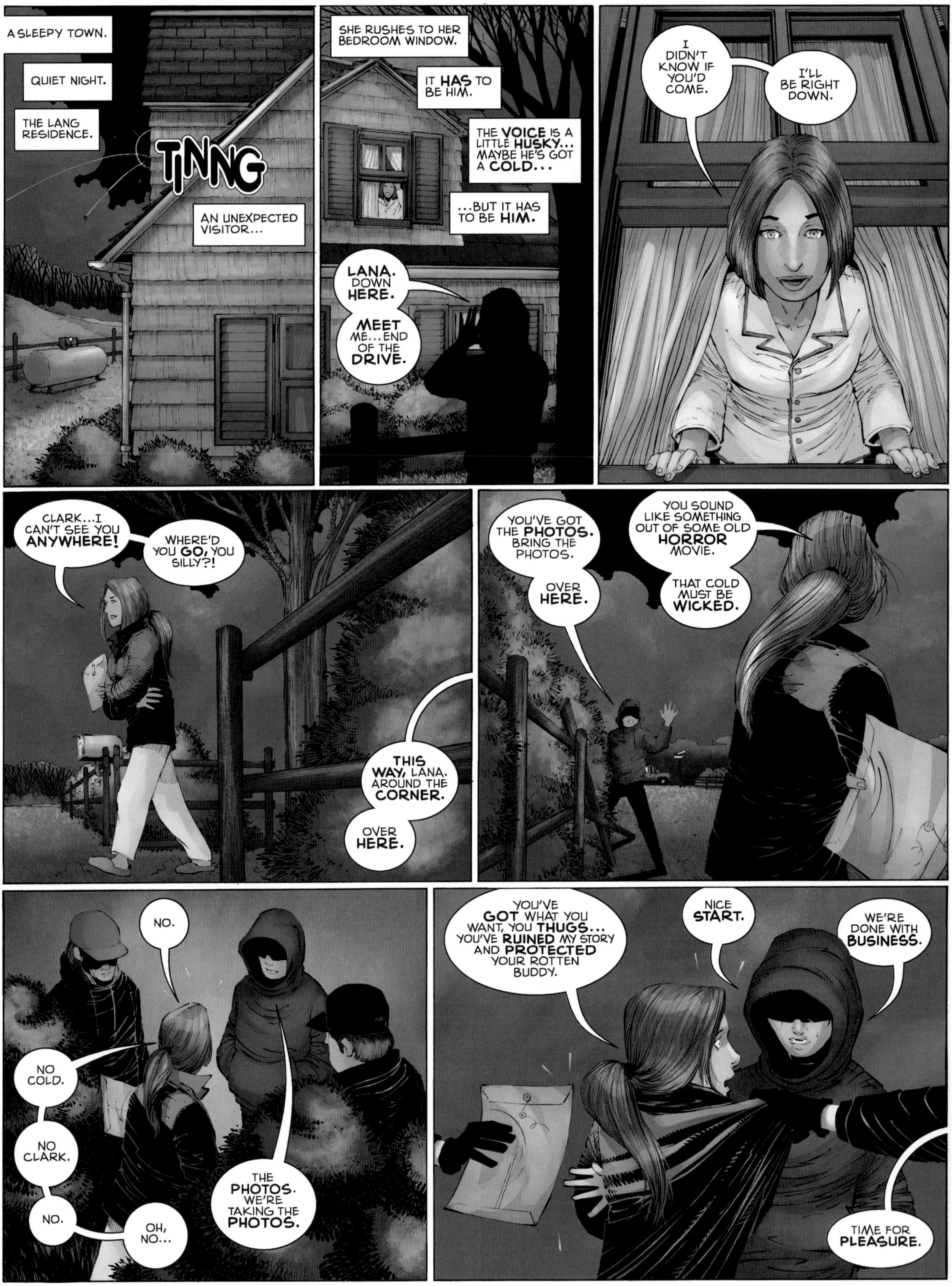
A SLEEPY TOWN.
QUIET NIGHT.
THE LANG RESIDENCE.
TINNG
AN UNEXPECTED VISITOR...
SHE RUSHES TO HER BEDROOM WINDOW.
IT HAS TO BE HIM.
THE VOICE IS A LITTLE HUSKY... MAYBE HE'S GOT A COLD...
...BUT IT HAS TO BE HIM.
LANA. DOWN HERE.
MEET ME...END OF THE DRIVE.
I DIDN'T KNOW IF YOU'D COME.
I'LL BE RIGHT DOWN.
CLARK...I CAN'T SEE YOU ANYWHERE!
WHERE'D YOU GO, YOU SILLY?!
THIS WAY, LANA. AROUND THE CORNER.
OVER HERE.
YOU'VE GOT THE PHOTOS. BRING THE PHOTOS.
OVER HERE.
YOU SOUND LIKE SOMETHING OUT OF SOME OLD HORROR MOVIE.
THAT COLD MUST BE WICKED.
NO.
NO COLD.
NO CLARK.
NO.
OH, NO...
THE PHOTOS. WE'RE TAKING THE PHOTOS.
YOU'VE GOT WHAT YOU WANT, YOU THUGS... YOU'VE RUINED MY STORY AND PROTECTED YOUR ROTTEN BUDDY.
NICE START.
WE'RE DONE WITH BUSINESS.
TIME FOR PLEASURE.

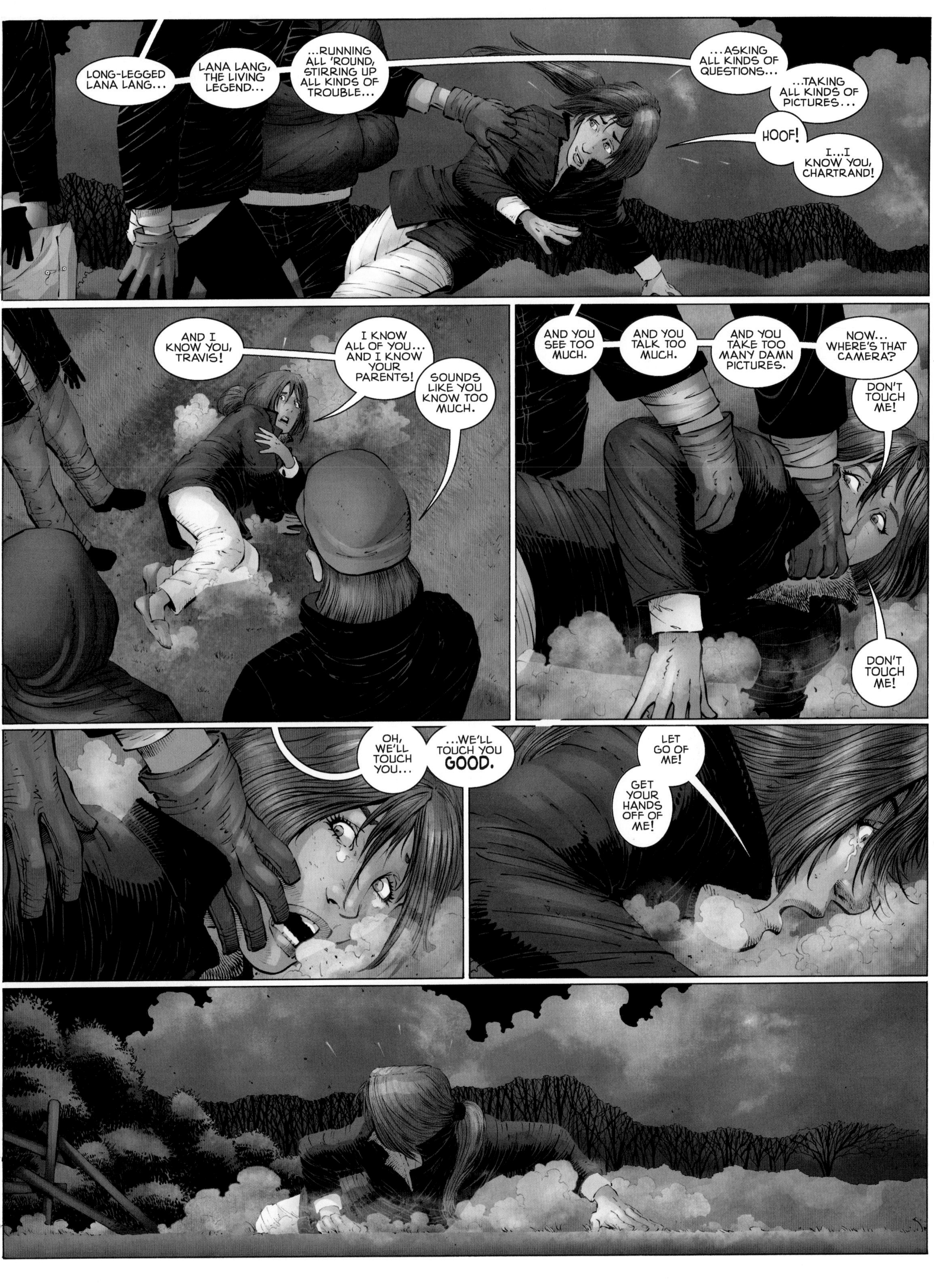
LONG-LEGGED LANA LANG...
LANA LANG, THE LIVING LEGEND...
...RUNNING ALL 'ROUND, STIRRING UP ALL KINDS OF TROUBLE...
...ASKING ALL KINDS OF QUESTIONS...
...TAKING ALL KINDS OF PICTURES...
HOOF!
I...I KNOW YOU, CHARTRAND!
AND I KNOW YOU, TRAVIS!
I KNOW ALL OF YOU... AND I KNOW YOUR PARENTS!
SOUNDS LIKE YOU KNOW TOO MUCH.
AND YOU SEE TOO MUCH.
AND YOU TALK TOO MUCH.
AND YOU TAKE TOO MANY DAMN PICTURES.
NOW... WHERE'S THAT CAMERA?
DON'T TOUCH ME!
DON'T TOUCH ME!
OH, WE'LL TOUCH YOU...
...WE'LL TOUCH YOU GOOD.
LET GO OF ME!
GET YOUR HANDS OFF OF ME!

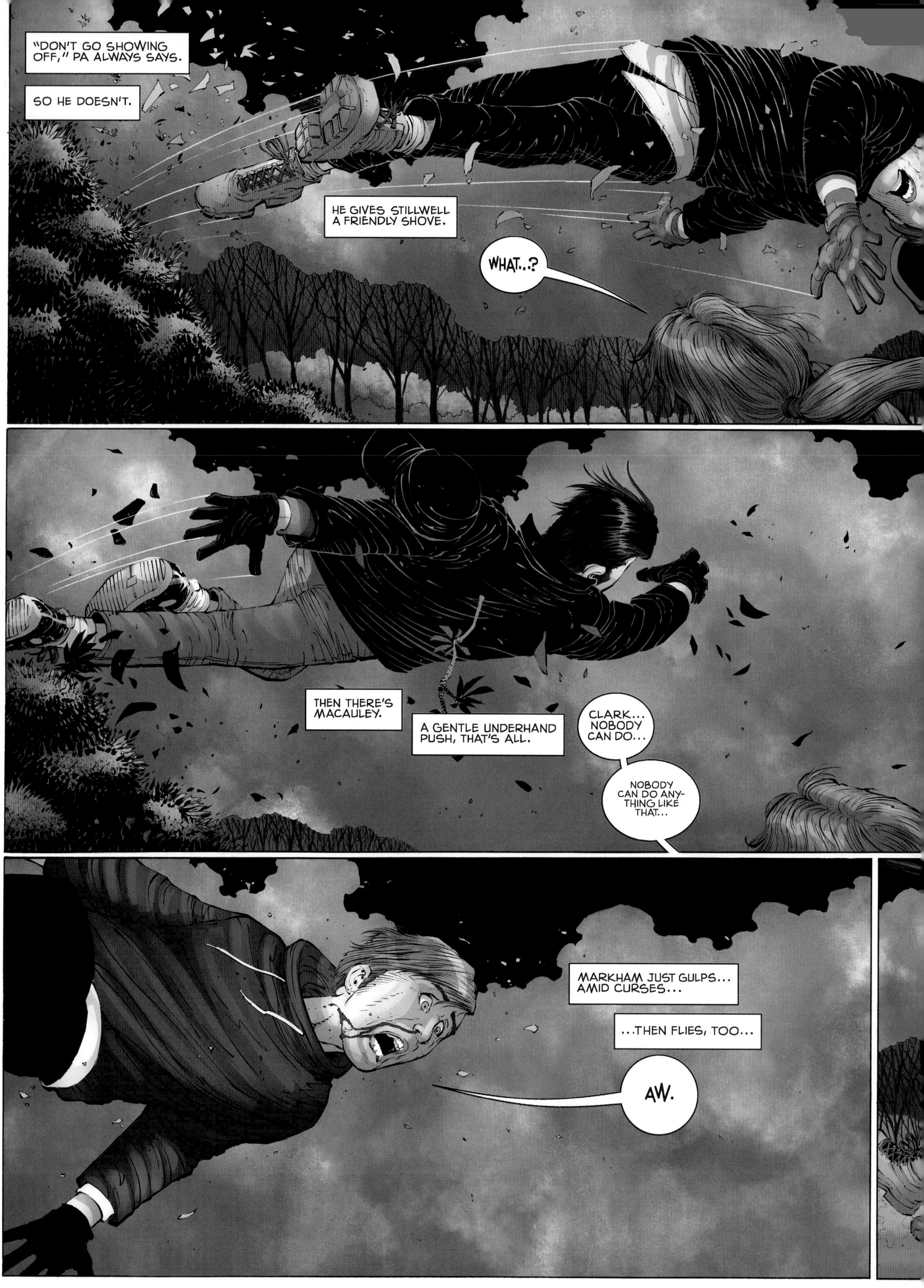
"DON'T GO SHOWING OFF," PA ALWAYS SAYS.
SO HE DOESN'T.
HE GIVES STILLWELL A FRIENDLY SHOVE.
WHAT..?
THEN THERE'S MACAULEY.
A GENTLE UNDERHAND PUSH, THAT'S ALL.
CLARK... NOBODY CAN DO...
NOBODY CAN DO ANY-THING LIKE THAT...
MARKHAM JUST GULPS... AMID CURSES...
...THEN FLIES, TOO...
AW.

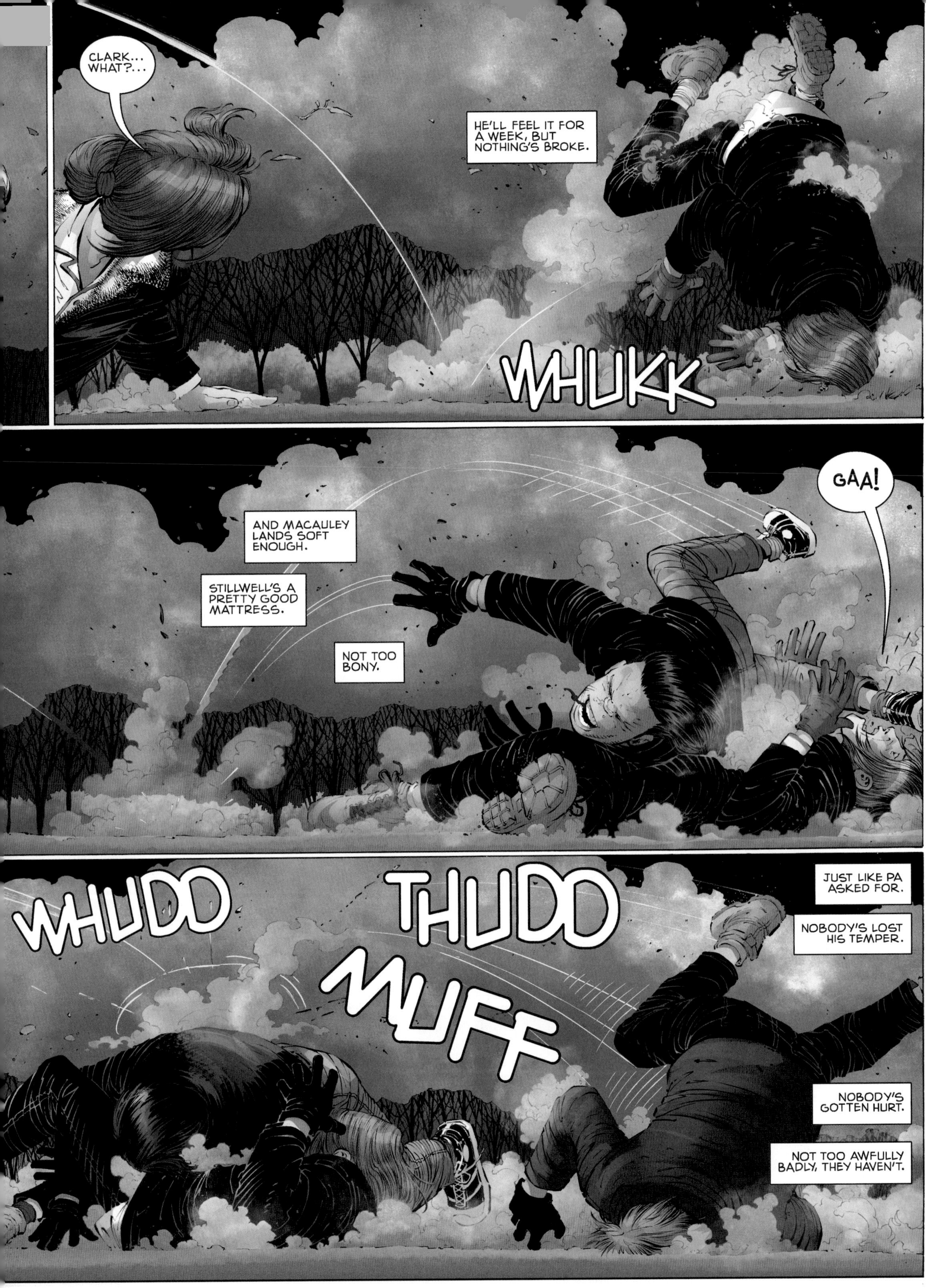
CLARK... WHAT?...
HE'LL FEEL IT FOR A WEEK, BUT NOTHING'S BROKE.
WHUKK
AND MACAULEY LANDS SOFT ENOUGH.
STILLWELL'S A PRETTY GOOD MATTRESS.
NOT TOO BONY.
GAA!
WHUDD
THUDD
MUFF
JUST LIKE PA ASKED FOR.
NOBODY'S LOST HIS TEMPER.
NOBODY'S GOTTEN HURT.
NOT TOO AWFULLY BADLY, THEY HAVEN'T.

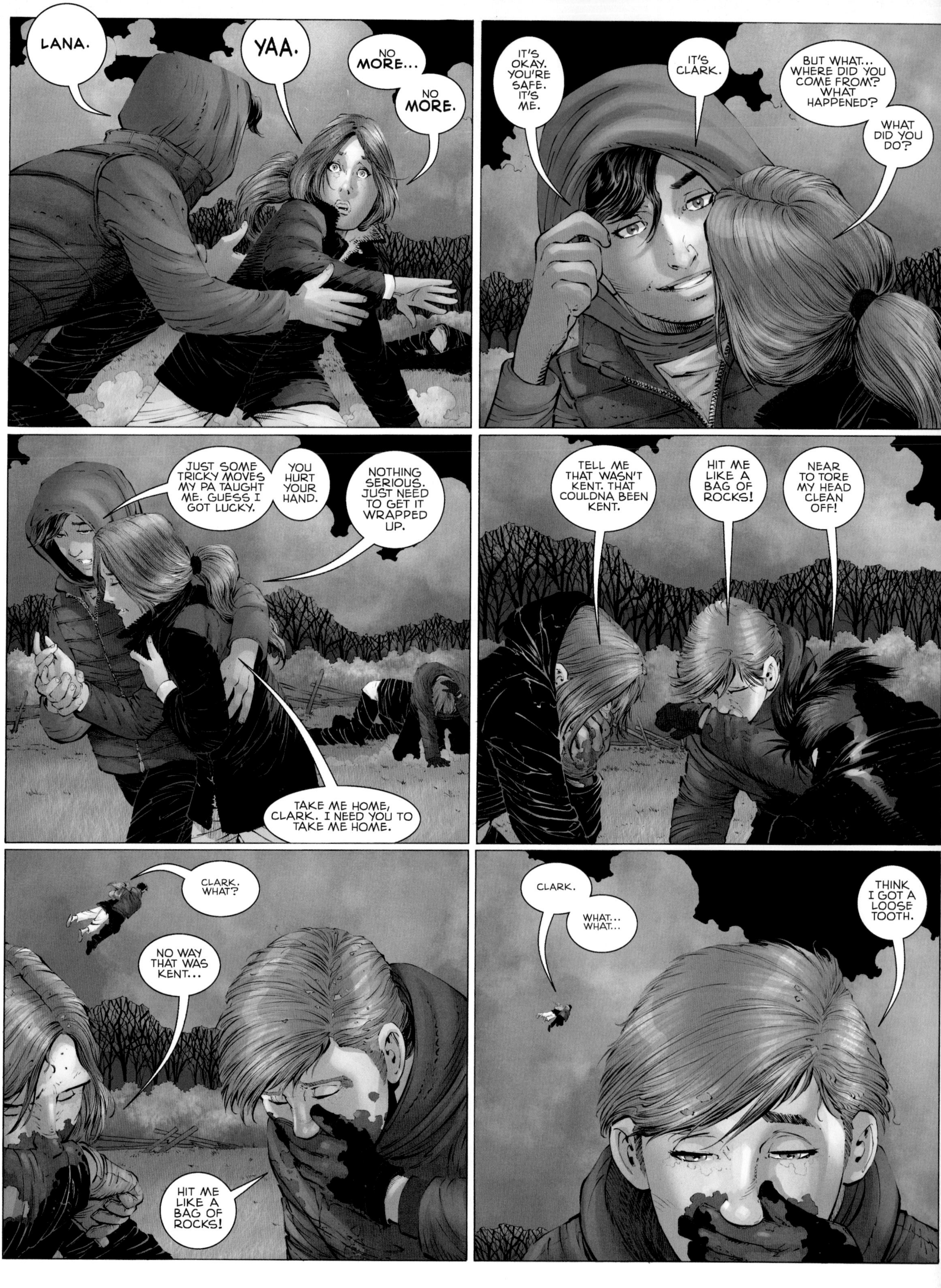
LANA.
YAA.
NO MORE...
NO MORE.
IT'S OKAY. YOU'RE SAFE. IT'S ME.
IT'S CLARK.
BUT WHAT... WHERE DID YOU COME FROM? WHAT HAPPENED?
WHAT DID YOU DO?
JUST SOME TRICKY MOVES MY PA TAUGHT ME. GUESS I GOT LUCKY.
YOU HURT YOUR HAND.
NOTHING SERIOUS. JUST NEED TO GET IT WRAPPED UP.
TAKE ME HOME, CLARK. I NEED YOU TO TAKE ME HOME.
TELL ME THAT WASN'T KENT. THAT COULDNA BEEN KENT.
HIT ME LIKE A BAG OF ROCKS!
NEAR TO TORE MY HEAD CLEAN OFF!
CLARK. WHAT?
NO WAY THAT WAS KENT...
HIT ME LIKE A BAG OF ROCKS!
CLARK.
WHAT... WHAT...
THINK I GOT A LOOSE TOOTH.

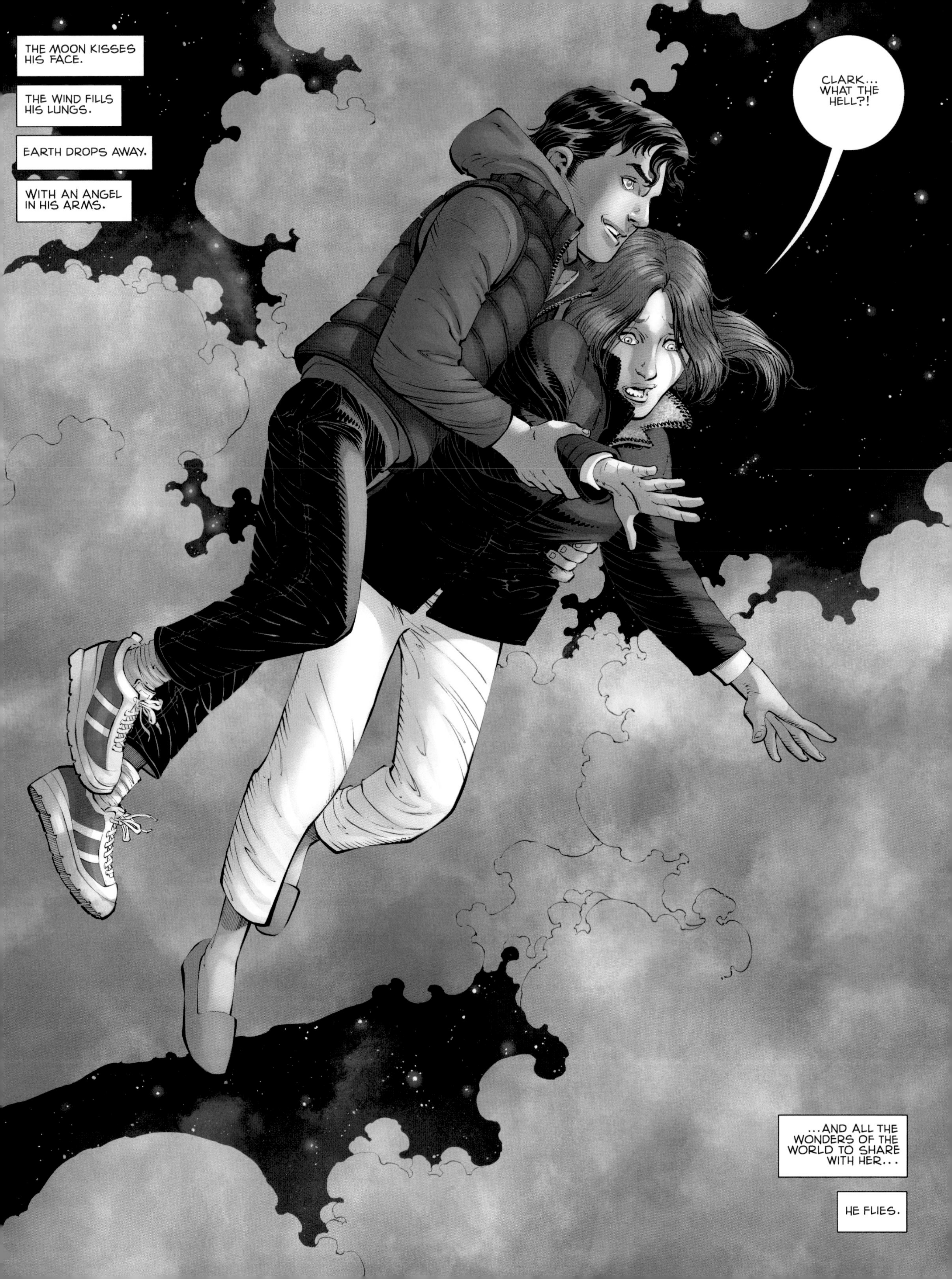
THE MOON KISSES HIS FACE.
THE WIND FILLS HIS LUNGS.
EARTH DROPS AWAY.
WITH AN ANGEL IN HIS ARMS.
CLARK... WHAT THE HELL?!
...AND ALL THE WONDERS OF THE WORLD TO SHARE WITH HER...
HE FLIES.

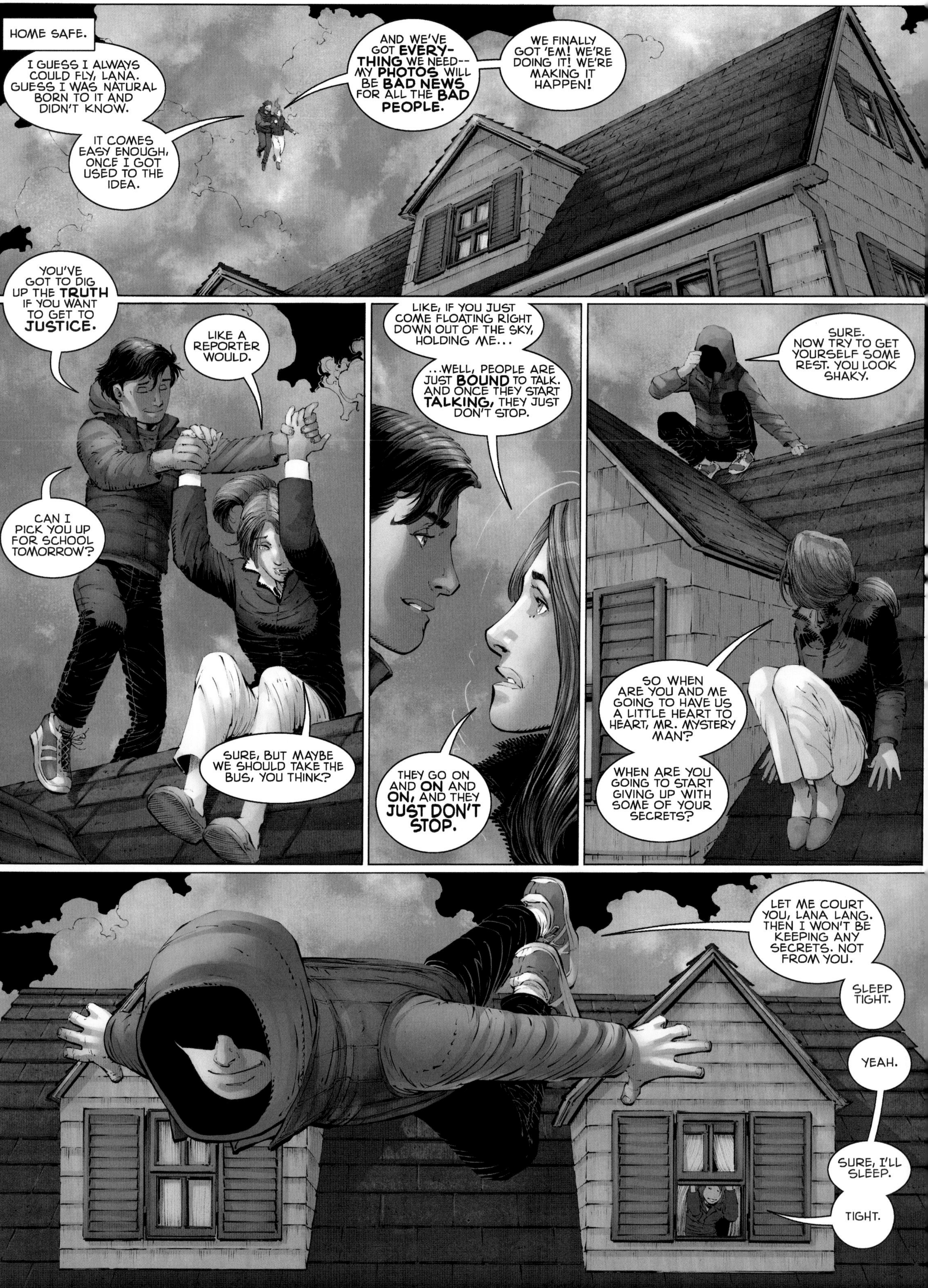
HOME SAFE.
I GUESS I ALWAYS COULD FLY, LANA. GUESS I WAS NATURAL BORN TO IT AND DIDN'T KNOW.
IT COMES EASY ENOUGH, ONCE I GOT USED TO THE IDEA.
AND WE'VE GOT EVERYTHING WE NEED-- MY PHOTOS WILL BE BAD NEWS FOR ALL THE BAD PEOPLE.
WE FINALLY GOT 'EM! WE'RE DOING IT! WE'RE MAKING IT HAPPEN!
YOU'VE GOT TO DIG UP THE TRUTH IF YOU WANT TO GET TO JUSTICE.
LIKE A REPORTER WOULD.
CAN I PICK YOU UP FOR SCHOOL TOMORROW?
SURE, BUT MAYBE WE SHOULD TAKE THE BUS, YOU THINK?
LIKE, IF YOU JUST COME FLOATING RIGHT DOWN OUT OF THE SKY, HOLDING ME...
...WELL, PEOPLE ARE JUST BOUND TO TALK. AND ONCE THEY START TALKING, THEY JUST DON'T STOP.
THEY GO ON AND ON AND ON, AND THEY JUST DON'T STOP.
SURE. NOW TRY TO GET YOURSELF SOME REST. YOU LOOK SHAKY.
SO WHEN ARE YOU AND ME GOING TO HAVE US A LITTLE HEART TO HEART, MR. MYSTERY MAN?
WHEN ARE YOU GOING TO START GIVING UP WITH SOME OF YOUR SECRETS?
LET ME COURT YOU, LANA LANG. THEN I WON'T BE KEEPING ANY SECRETS. NOT FROM YOU.
SLEEP TIGHT.
YEAH.
SURE, I'LL SLEEP.
TIGHT.

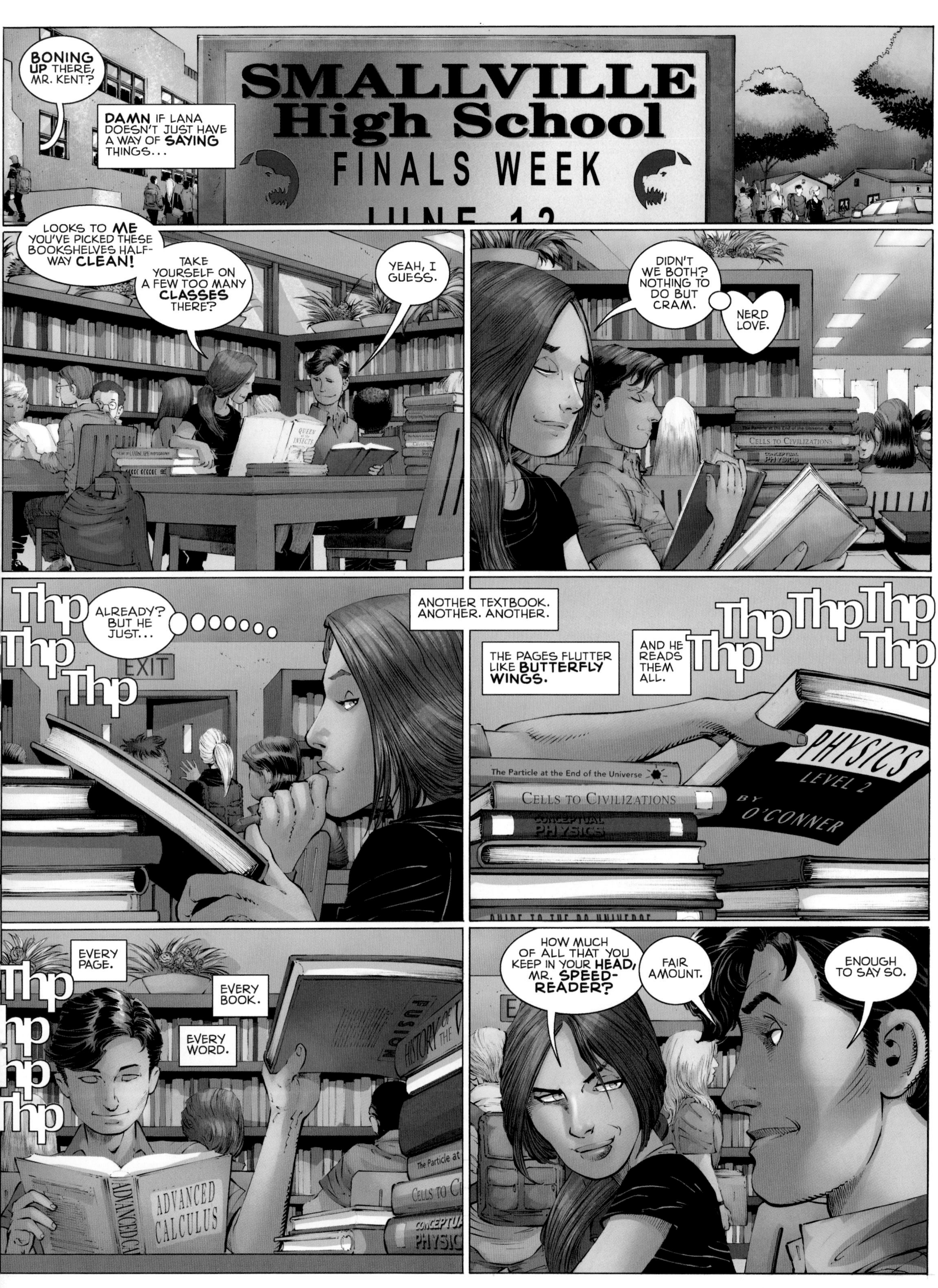
BONING UP THERE, MR. KENT?
DAMN IF LANA DOESN'T JUST HAVE A WAY OF SAYING THINGS...
SMALLVILLE High School
FINALS WEEK
LOOKS TO ME YOU'VE PICKED THESE BOOKSHELVES HALF-WAY CLEAN!
TAKE YOURSELF ON A FEW TOO MANY CLASSES THERE?
YEAH, I GUESS.
QUEEN of the INSECTS
DIDN'T WE BOTH? NOTHING TO DO BUT CRAM.
NERD LOVE.
The Particle at the End of the Universe
CELLS TO CIVILIZATIONS
CONCEPTUAL PHYSICS
Thp Thp Thp
ALREADY? BUT HE JUST...
ANOTHER TEXTBOOK. ANOTHER. ANOTHER.
EXIT
THE PAGES FLUTTER LIKE BUTTERFLY WINGS.
AND HE READS THEM ALL.
Thp Thp Thp Thp Thp
PHYSICS LEVEL 2 BY O'CONNER
The Particle at the End of the Universe
CELLS TO CIVILIZATIONS
CONCEPTUAL PHYSICS
Thp
EVERY PAGE.
EVERY BOOK.
EVERY WORD.
FUSION
HISTORY OF THE
ADVANCED CALCULUS
HOW MUCH OF ALL THAT YOU KEEP IN YOUR HEAD, MR. SPEED-READER?
FAIR AMOUNT.
ENOUGH TO SAY SO.

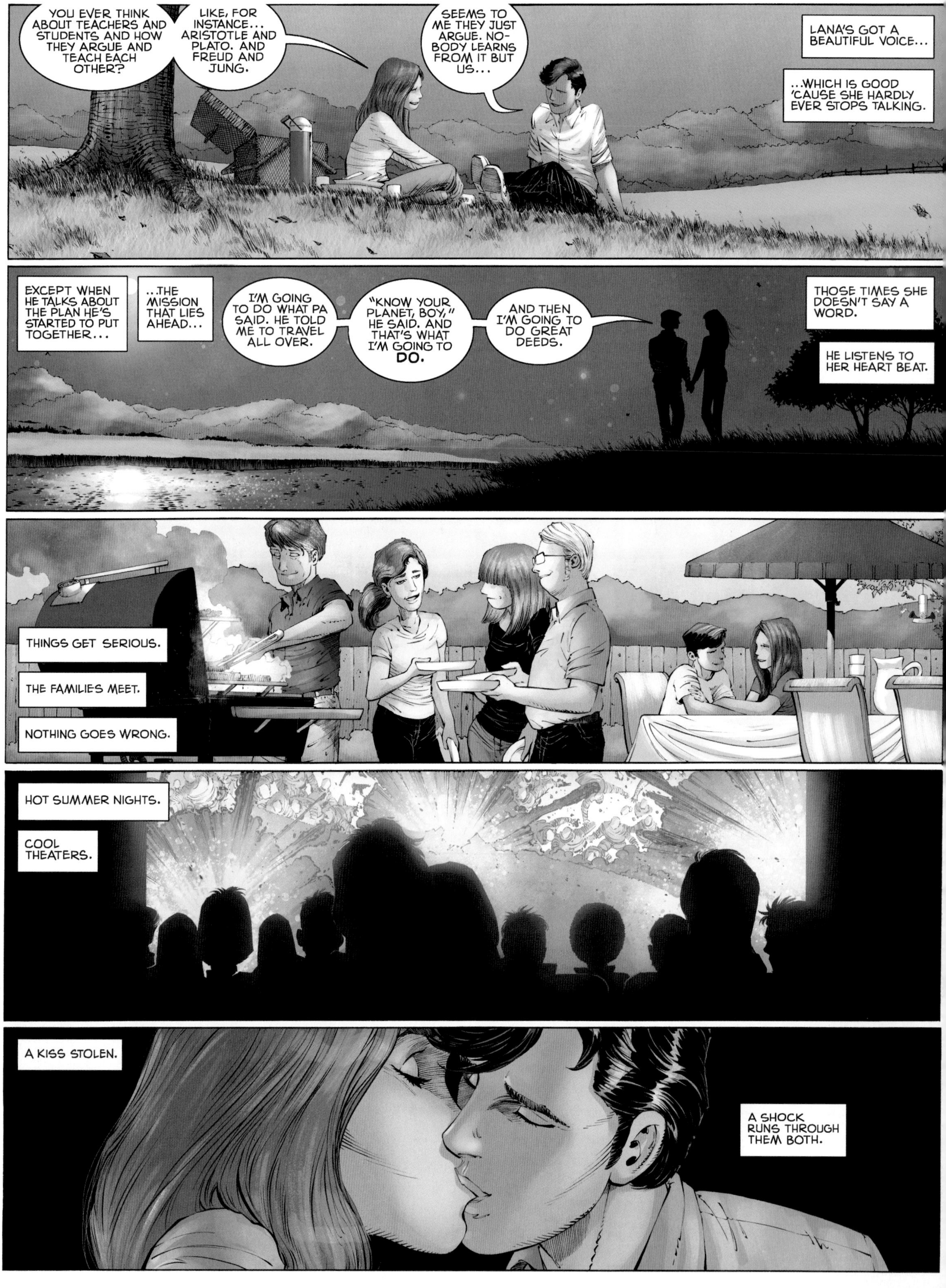
YOU EVER THINK ABOUT TEACHERS AND STUDENTS AND HOW THEY ARGUE AND TEACH EACH OTHER?
LIKE, FOR INSTANCE... ARISTOTLE AND PLATO. AND FREUD AND JUNG.
SEEMS TO ME THEY JUST ARGUE. NO-BODY LEARNS FROM IT BUT US...
LANA'S GOT A BEAUTIFUL VOICE...
...WHICH IS GOOD 'CAUSE SHE HARDLY EVER STOPS TALKING.
EXCEPT WHEN HE TALKS ABOUT THE PLAN HE'S STARTED TO PUT TOGETHER...
...THE MISSION THAT LIES AHEAD...
I'M GOING TO DO WHAT PA SAID. HE TOLD ME TO TRAVEL ALL OVER.
"KNOW YOUR PLANET, BOY," HE SAID. AND THAT'S WHAT I'M GOING TO DO.
AND THEN I'M GOING TO DO GREAT DEEDS.
THOSE TIMES SHE DOESN'T SAY A WORD.
HE LISTENS TO HER HEART BEAT.
THINGS GET SERIOUS.
THE FAMILIES MEET.
NOTHING GOES WRONG.
HOT SUMMER NIGHTS.
COOL THEATERS.
A KISS STOLEN.
A SHOCK RUNS THROUGH THEM BOTH.

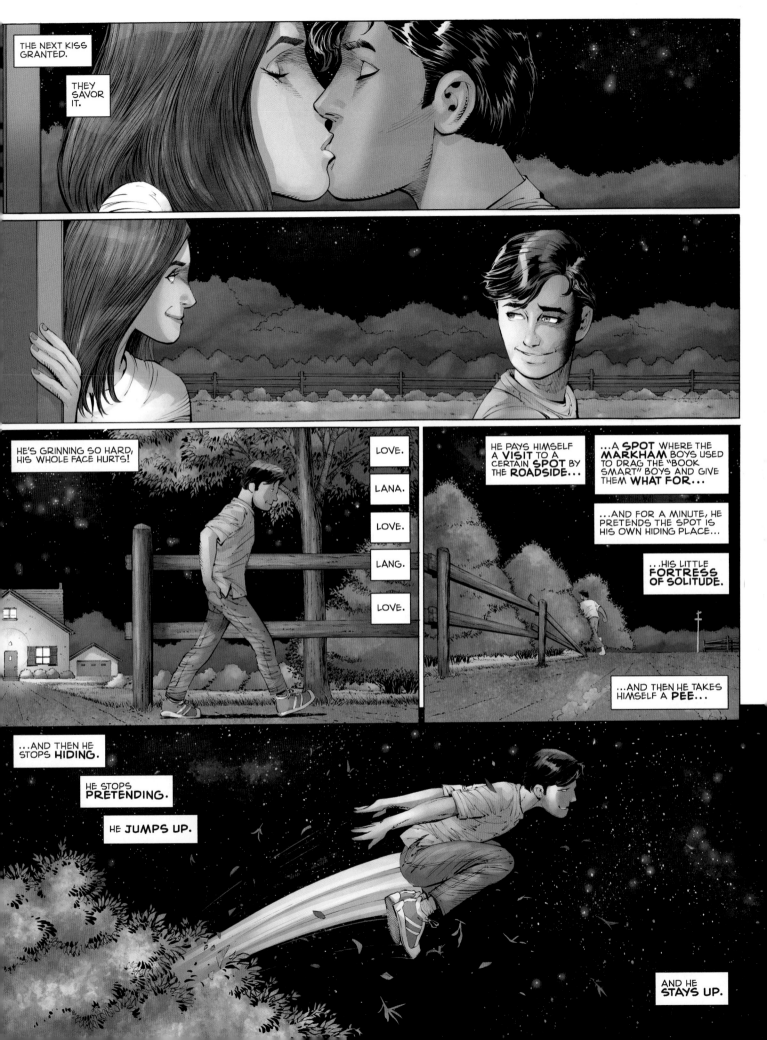

THE NEXT KISS GRANTED.

THEY SAVOR IT.

HE'S GRINNING SO HARD, HIS WHOLE FACE HURTS!

LOVE.

LANA.

LOVE.

LANG.

LOVE.

HE PAYS HIMSELF A VISIT TO A CERTAIN SPOT BY THE ROADSIDE...

...A SPOT WHERE THE MARKHAM BOYS USED TO DRAG THE "BOOK SMART" BOYS AND GIVE THEM WHAT FOR...

...AND FOR A MINUTE, HE PRETENDS THE SPOT IS HIS OWN HIDING PLACE...

...HIS LITTLE FORTRESS OF SOLITUDE.

...AND THEN HE TAKES HIMSELF A PEE...

...AND THEN HE STOPS HIDING.

HE STOPS PRETENDING.

HE JUMPS UP.

AND HE STAYS UP.

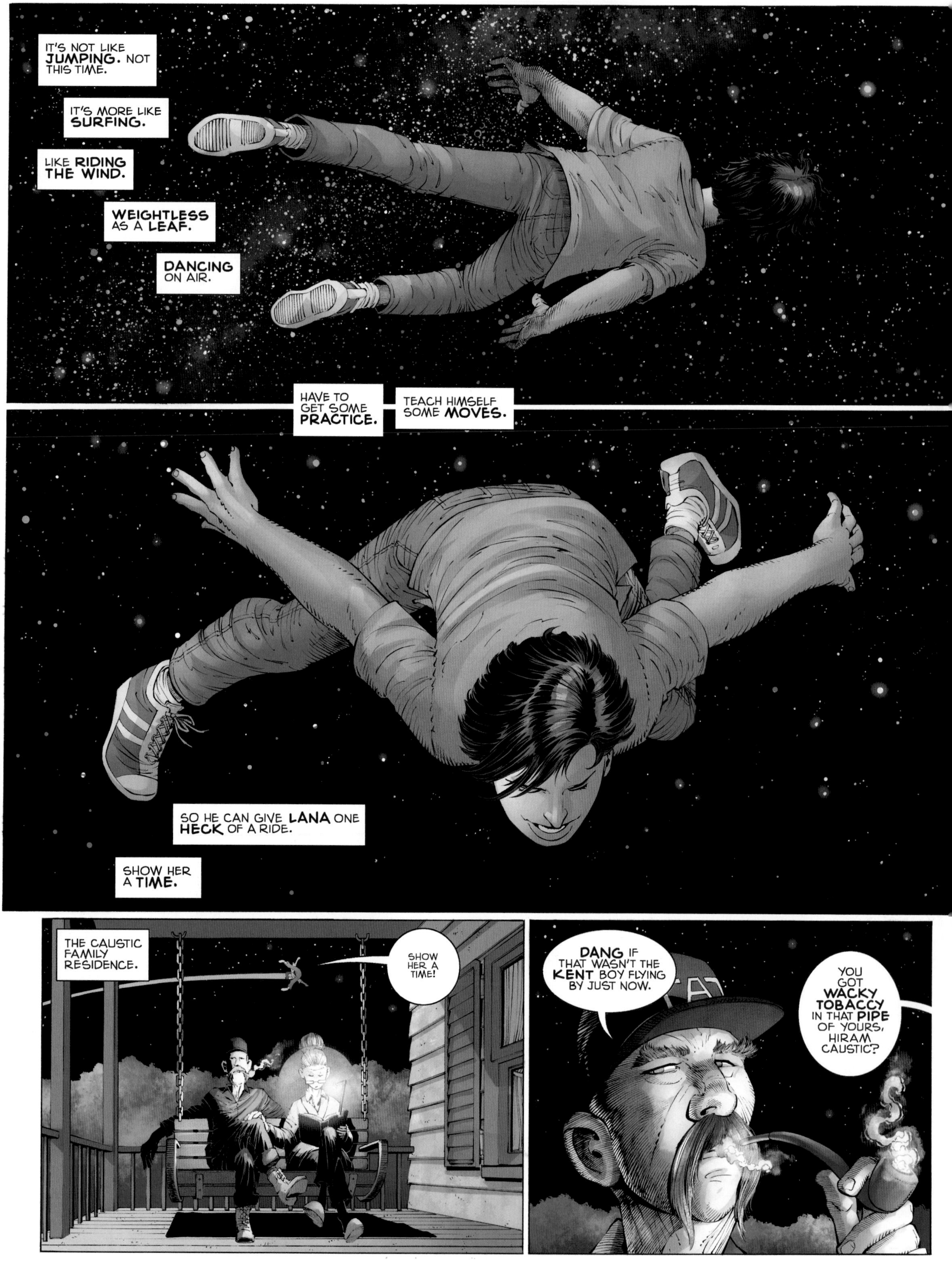

IT'S NOT LIKE JUMPING. NOT THIS TIME.
IT'S MORE LIKE SURFING.
LIKE RIDING THE WIND.
WEIGHTLESS AS A LEAF.
DANCING ON AIR.
HAVE TO GET SOME PRACTICE.
TEACH HIMSELF SOME MOVES.
SO HE CAN GIVE LANA ONE HECK OF A RIDE.
SHOW HER A TIME.
THE CAUSTIC FAMILY RESIDENCE.
SHOW HER A TIME!
DANG IF THAT WASN'T THE KENT BOY FLYING BY JUST NOW.
YOU GOT WACKY TOBACCY IN THAT PIPE OF YOURS, HIRAM CAUSTIC?

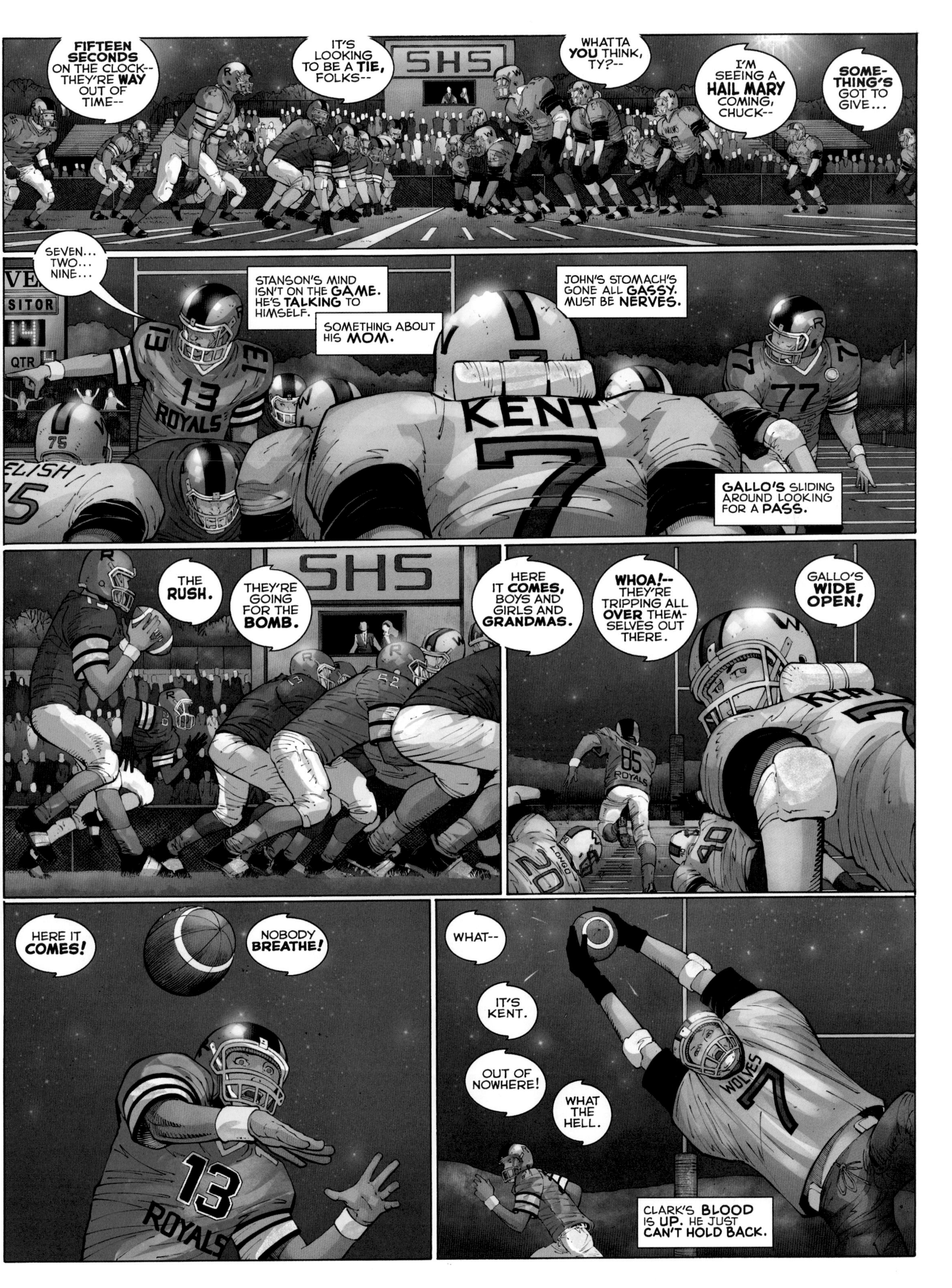
FIFTEEN SECONDS ON THE CLOCK-- THEY'RE WAY OUT OF TIME--
IT'S LOOKING TO BE A TIE, FOLKS--
SHS
WHATTA YOU THINK, TY?--
I'M SEEING A HAIL MARY COMING, CHUCK--
SOME-THING'S GOT TO GIVE...
SEVEN... TWO... NINE...
STANSON'S MIND ISN'T ON THE GAME. HE'S TALKING TO HIMSELF.
SOMETHING ABOUT HIS MOM.
JOHN'S STOMACH'S GONE ALL GASSY. MUST BE NERVES.
KENT 7
13 ROYALS
77
GALLO'S SLIDING AROUND LOOKING FOR A PASS.
SHS
THE RUSH.
THEY'RE GOING FOR THE BOMB.
HERE IT COMES, BOYS AND GIRLS AND GRANDMAS.
WHOA!-- THEY'RE TRIPPING ALL OVER THEM-SELVES OUT THERE.
GALLO'S WIDE OPEN!
85 ROYALS
HERE IT COMES!
NOBODY BREATHE!
13 ROYALS
WHAT--
IT'S KENT.
OUT OF NOWHERE!
WHAT THE HELL.
WOLVES 7
CLARK'S BLOOD IS UP. HE JUST CAN'T HOLD BACK.

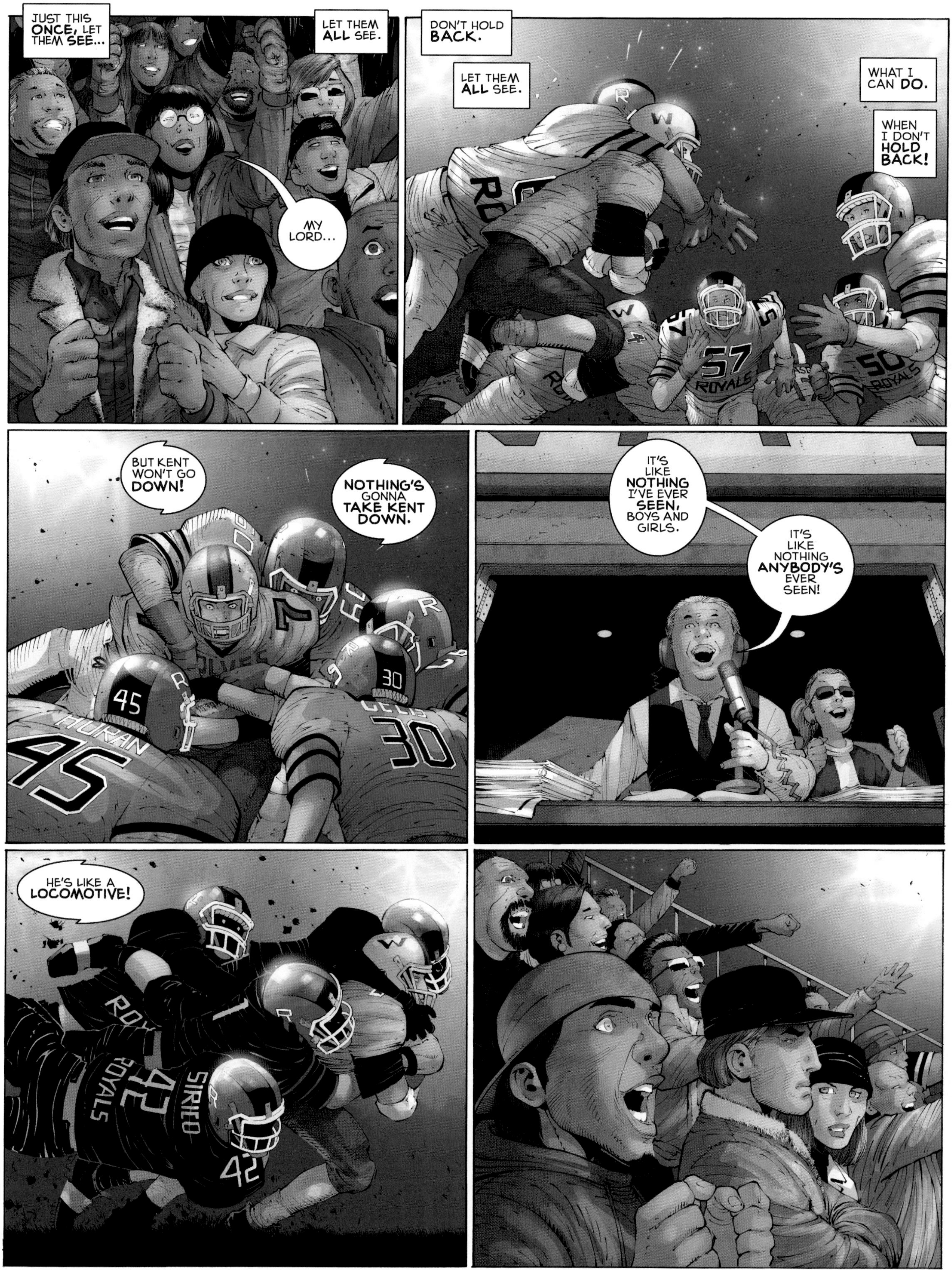
JUST THIS ONCE, LET THEM SEE...
LET THEM ALL SEE.
MY LORD...
DON'T HOLD BACK.
LET THEM ALL SEE.
WHAT I CAN DO.
WHEN I DON'T HOLD BACK!
BUT KENT WON'T GO DOWN!
NOTHING'S GONNA TAKE KENT DOWN.
IT'S LIKE NOTHING I'VE EVER SEEN, BOYS AND GIRLS.
IT'S LIKE NOTHING ANYBODY'S EVER SEEN!
HE'S LIKE A LOCOMOTIVE!

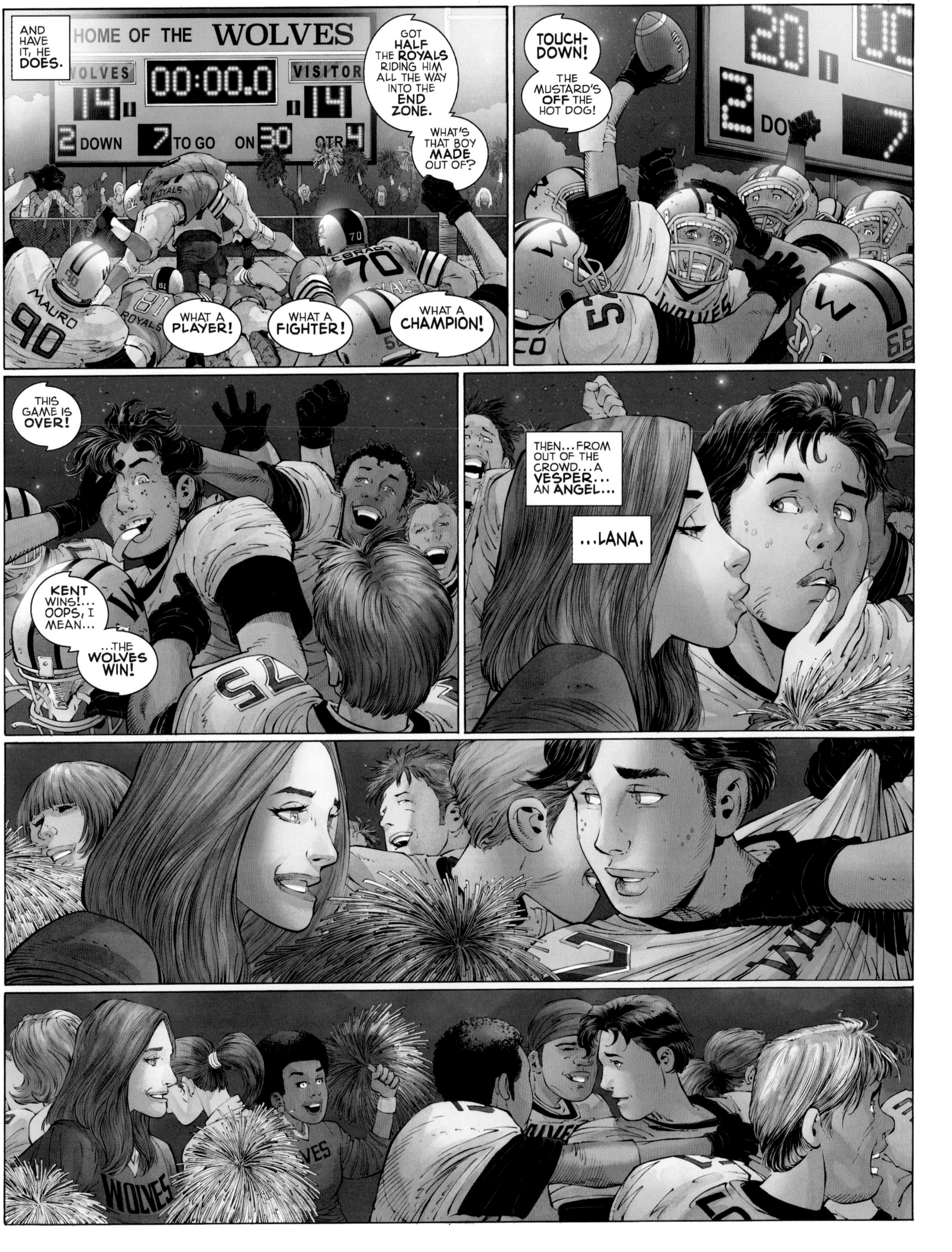

AND HAVE IT, HE DOES.
HOME OF THE WOLVES
WOLVES 14 00:00.0 VISITOR 14
2 DOWN 7 TO GO ON 30 QTR 4
GOT HALF THE ROYALS RIDING HIM ALL THE WAY INTO THE END ZONE.
WHAT'S THAT BOY MADE OUT OF?
WHAT A PLAYER!
WHAT A FIGHTER!
WHAT A CHAMPION!
TOUCH-DOWN!
THE MUSTARD'S OFF THE HOT DOG!
THIS GAME IS OVER!
KENT WINS!... OOPS, I MEAN...
...THE WOLVES WIN!
THEN...FROM OUT OF THE CROWD...A VESPER... AN ANGEL...
...LANA.

THE WORKDAY WINDS ON DOWN.

THEIR BACKS ARE SLICK WITH SWEAT.

NOT MUCH CHANGES, NOT OUT HERE ON THE PRAIRIE.

EXCEPT NOW AND THEN...

WHAT'S THAT, PA?

I SAID, SCHOOL'S ALMOST DONE, CLARK. WHAT'S NEXT FOR MY BOY? YOU GONNA BE A CIRCUS ACT OR A MALE MODEL?

MALE MODEL. SOMETIMES I JUST BUST MYSELF UP.

I FIGURE I'M GONNA GO AND TAKE THAT ADVICE YOU'RE SO FOND OF GIVING ME.

I'M GONNA GET OUT AND AROUND... I'M GONNA GO OUT AND KNOW MY PLANET.

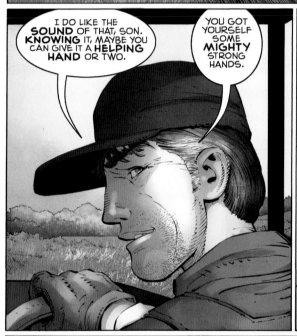

I DO LIKE THE SOUND OF THAT, SON. KNOWING IT, MAYBE YOU CAN GIVE IT A HELPING HAND OR TWO.

YOU GOT YOURSELF SOME MIGHTY STRONG HANDS.

HOOF.

I'LL START WITH THE WATER... THE OCEANS. THERE'S MORE WATER THAN THERE IS LAND...JUST LOOK AT A GLOBE.

AND THAT'S WHERE THE MOST LIFE IS.

YOU'VE GIVEN THIS A FEW BUCKETS OF THOUGHT.

GUESS YOU COULD PUT IT THAT WAY.

SCHOOL'S JUST ABOUT DONE. CROPS ARE IN...

...IT'S TIME FOR ME TO GO SOON.

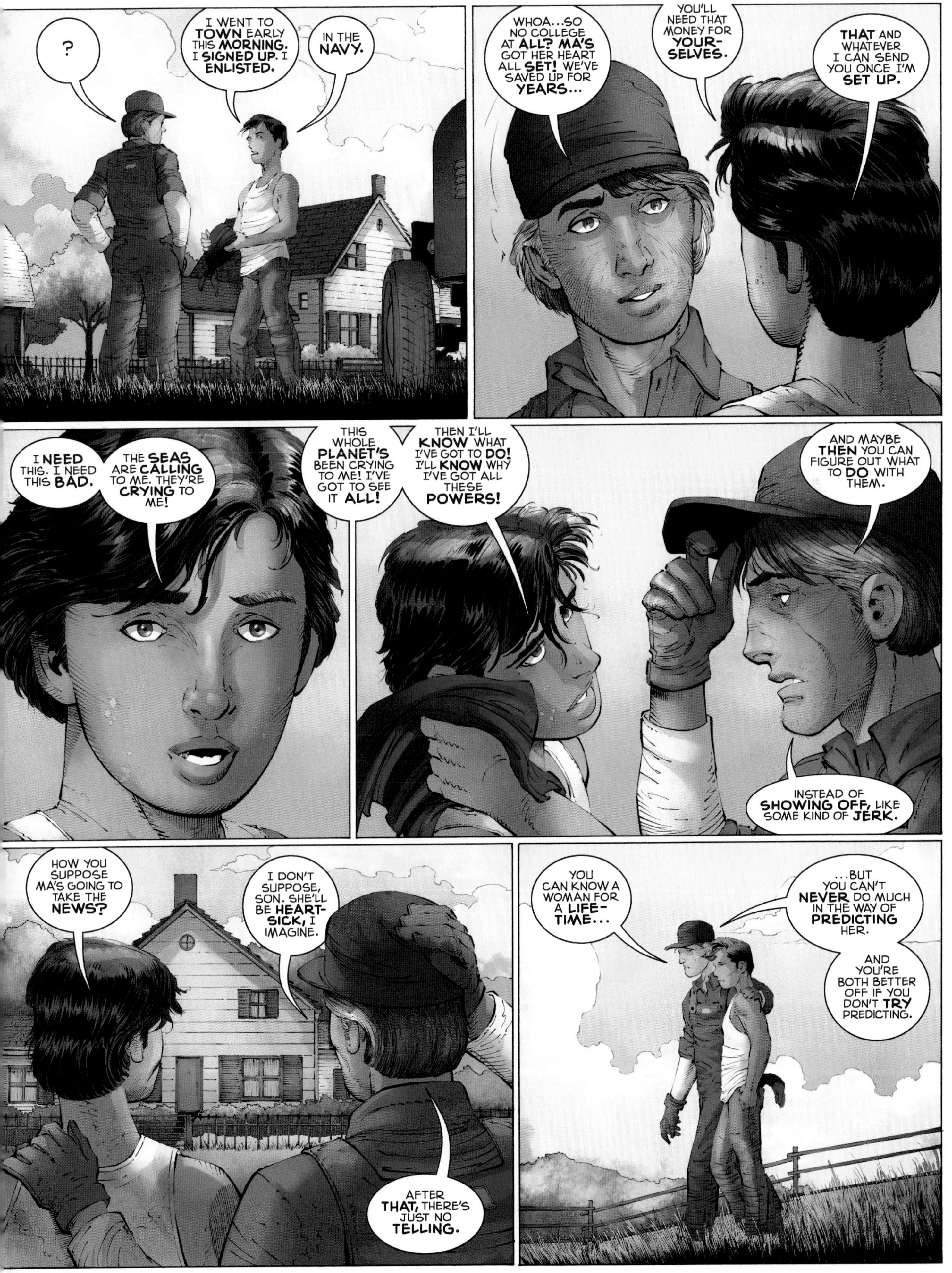
?
I WENT TO TOWN EARLY THIS MORNING. I SIGNED UP. I ENLISTED.
IN THE NAVY.
WHOA...SO NO COLLEGE AT ALL? MA'S GOT HER HEART ALL SET! WE'VE SAVED UP FOR YEARS...
YOU'LL NEED THAT MONEY FOR YOURSELVES.
THAT AND WHATEVER I CAN SEND YOU ONCE I'M SET UP.
I NEED THIS. I NEED THIS BAD.
THE SEAS ARE CALLING TO ME. THEY'RE CRYING TO ME!
THIS WHOLE PLANET'S BEEN CRYING TO ME! I'VE GOT TO SEE IT ALL!
THEN I'LL KNOW WHAT I'VE GOT TO DO! I'LL KNOW WHY I'VE GOT ALL THESE POWERS!
AND MAYBE THEN YOU CAN FIGURE OUT WHAT TO DO WITH THEM.
INSTEAD OF SHOWING OFF, LIKE SOME KIND OF JERK.
HOW YOU SUPPOSE MA'S GOING TO TAKE THE NEWS?
I DON'T SUPPOSE, SON. SHE'LL BE HEART-SICK, I IMAGINE.
AFTER THAT, THERE'S JUST NO TELLING.
YOU CAN KNOW A WOMAN FOR A LIFE-TIME...
...BUT YOU CAN'T NEVER DO MUCH IN THE WAY OF PREDICTING HER.
AND YOU'RE BOTH BETTER OFF IF YOU DON'T TRY PREDICTING.

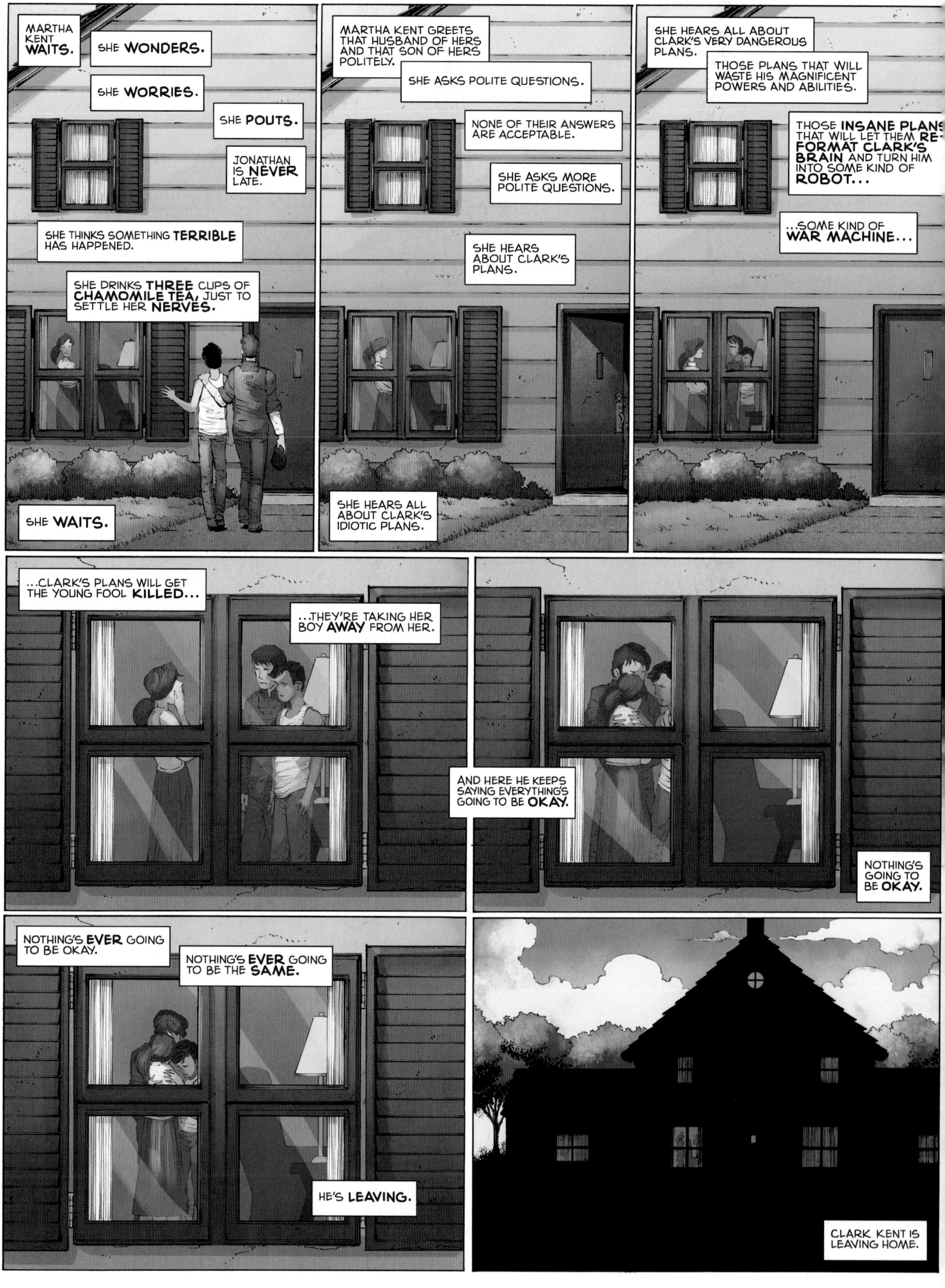
MARTHA KENT WAITS.
SHE WONDERS.
SHE WORRIES.
SHE POUTS.
JONATHAN IS NEVER LATE.
SHE THINKS SOMETHING TERRIBLE HAS HAPPENED.
SHE DRINKS THREE CUPS OF CHAMOMILE TEA, JUST TO SETTLE HER NERVES.
SHE WAITS.
MARTHA KENT GREETS THAT HUSBAND OF HERS AND THAT SON OF HERS POLITELY.
SHE ASKS POLITE QUESTIONS.
NONE OF THEIR ANSWERS ARE ACCEPTABLE.
SHE ASKS MORE POLITE QUESTIONS.
SHE HEARS ABOUT CLARK'S PLANS.
SHE HEARS ALL ABOUT CLARK'S IDIOTIC PLANS.
SHE HEARS ALL ABOUT CLARK'S VERY DANGEROUS PLANS.
THOSE PLANS THAT WILL WASTE HIS MAGNIFICENT POWERS AND ABILITIES.
THOSE INSANE PLANS THAT WILL LET THEM RE-FORMAT CLARK'S BRAIN AND TURN HIM INTO SOME KIND OF ROBOT...
...SOME KIND OF WAR MACHINE...
...CLARK'S PLANS WILL GET THE YOUNG FOOL KILLED...
...THEY'RE TAKING HER BOY AWAY FROM HER.
AND HERE HE KEEPS SAYING EVERYTHING'S GOING TO BE OKAY.
NOTHING'S GOING TO BE OKAY.
NOTHING'S EVER GOING TO BE OKAY.
NOTHING'S EVER GOING TO BE THE SAME.
HE'S LEAVING.
CLARK KENT IS LEAVING HOME.

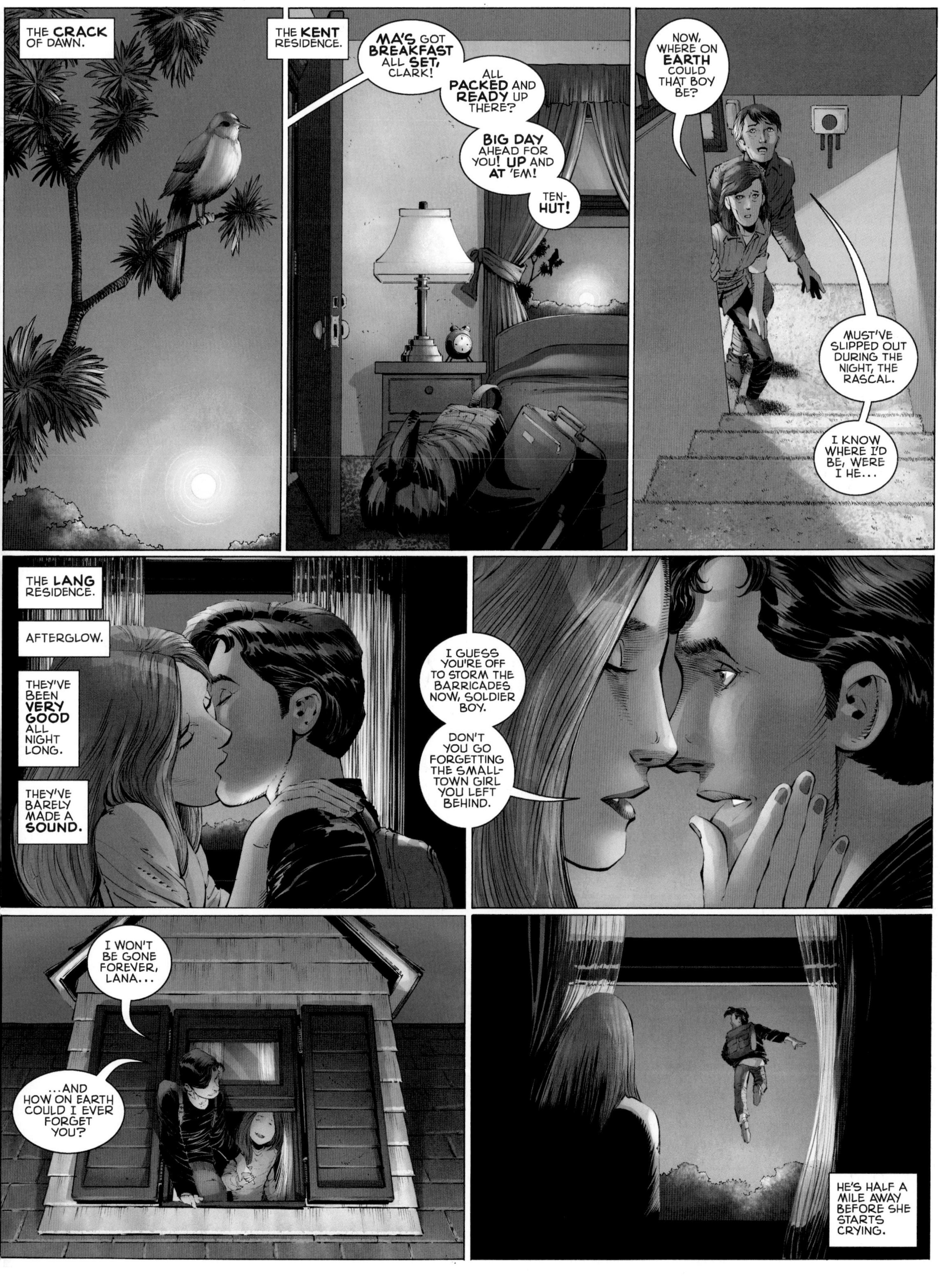
THE CRACK OF DAWN.
THE KENT RESIDENCE.
MA'S GOT BREAKFAST ALL SET, CLARK!
ALL PACKED AND READY UP THERE?
BIG DAY AHEAD FOR YOU! UP AND AT 'EM!
TEN-HUT!
NOW, WHERE ON EARTH COULD THAT BOY BE?
MUST'VE SLIPPED OUT DURING THE NIGHT, THE RASCAL.
I KNOW WHERE I'D BE, WERE I HE...
THE LANG RESIDENCE.
AFTERGLOW.
THEY'VE BEEN VERY GOOD ALL NIGHT LONG.
THEY'VE BARELY MADE A SOUND.
I GUESS YOU'RE OFF TO STORM THE BARRICADES NOW, SOLDIER BOY.
DON'T YOU GO FORGETTING THE SMALL-TOWN GIRL YOU LEFT BEHIND.
I WON'T BE GONE FOREVER, LANA...
...AND HOW ON EARTH COULD I EVER FORGET YOU?
HE'S HALF A MILE AWAY BEFORE SHE STARTS CRYING.

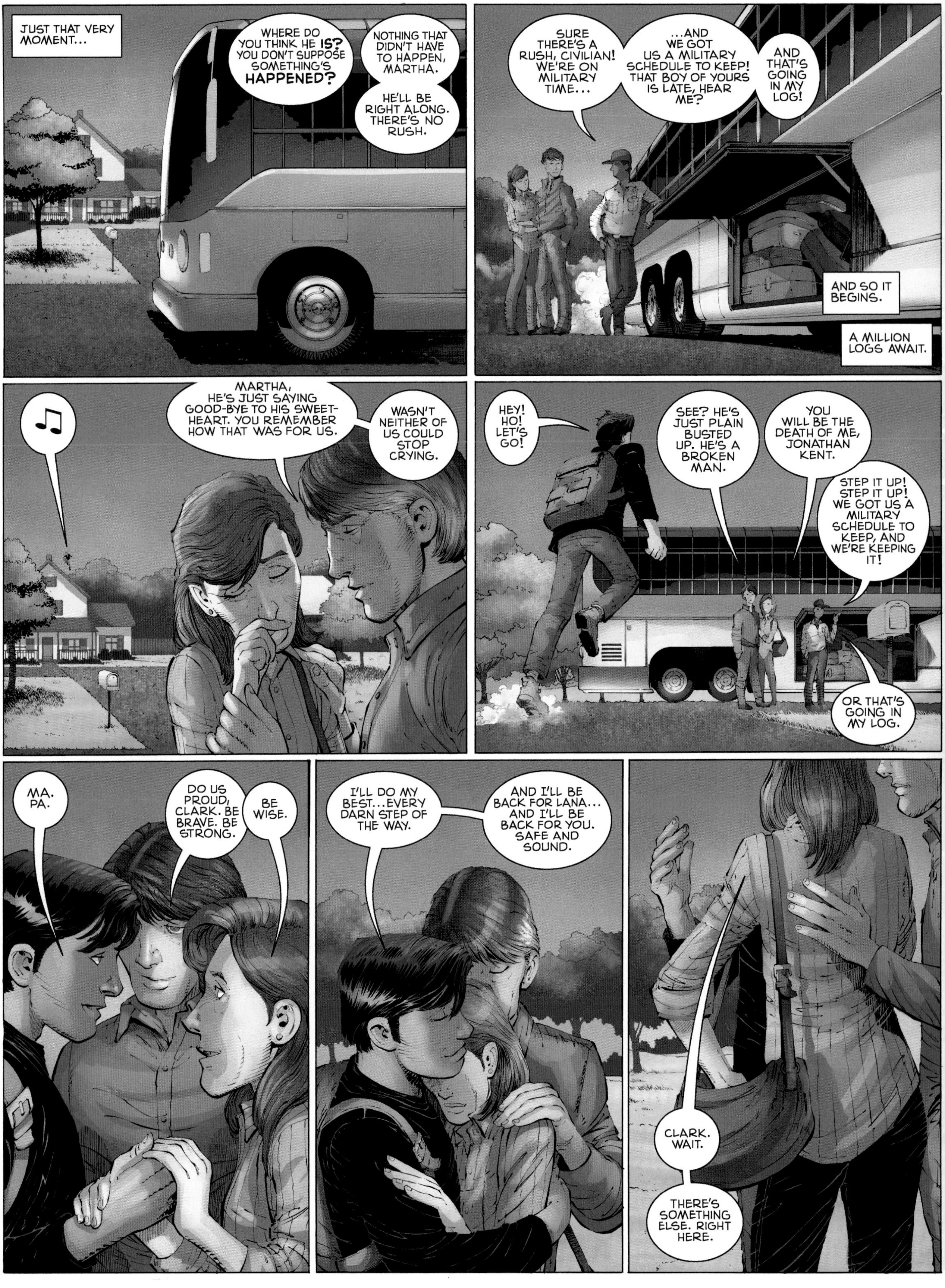
JUST THAT VERY MOMENT...
WHERE DO YOU THINK HE IS? YOU DON'T SUPPOSE SOMETHING'S HAPPENED?
NOTHING THAT DIDN'T HAVE TO HAPPEN, MARTHA.
HE'LL BE RIGHT ALONG. THERE'S NO RUSH.
SURE THERE'S A RUSH, CIVILIAN! WE'RE ON MILITARY TIME...
...AND WE GOT US A MILITARY SCHEDULE TO KEEP! THAT BOY OF YOURS IS LATE, HEAR ME?
AND THAT'S GOING IN MY LOG!
AND SO IT BEGINS.
A MILLION LOGS AWAIT.
♫
MARTHA, HE'S JUST SAYING GOOD-BYE TO HIS SWEETHEART. YOU REMEMBER HOW THAT WAS FOR US.
WASN'T NEITHER OF US COULD STOP CRYING.
HEY! HO! LET'S GO!
SEE? HE'S JUST PLAIN BUSTED UP. HE'S A BROKEN MAN.
YOU WILL BE THE DEATH OF ME, JONATHAN KENT.
STEP IT UP! STEP IT UP! WE GOT US A MILITARY SCHEDULE TO KEEP, AND WE'RE KEEPING IT!
OR THAT'S GOING IN MY LOG.
MA. PA.
DO US PROUD, CLARK. BE BRAVE. BE STRONG.
BE WISE.
I'LL DO MY BEST...EVERY DARN STEP OF THE WAY.
AND I'LL BE BACK FOR LANA... AND I'LL BE BACK FOR YOU. SAFE AND SOUND.
CLARK. WAIT.
THERE'S SOMETHING ELSE. RIGHT HERE.

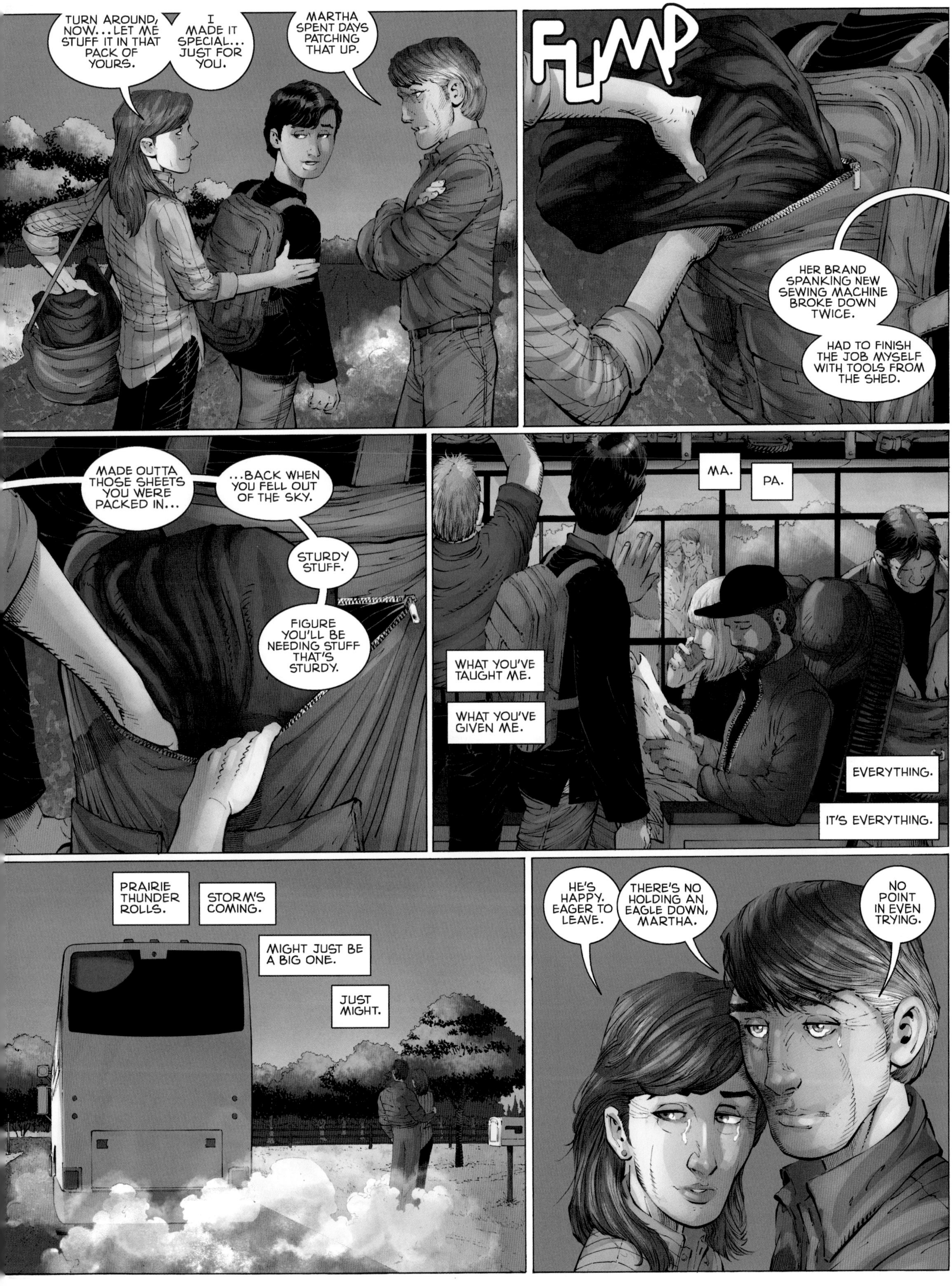
TURN AROUND, NOW...LET ME STUFF IT IN THAT PACK OF YOURS.
I MADE IT SPECIAL... JUST FOR YOU.
MARTHA SPENT DAYS PATCHING THAT UP.
FLUMP
HER BRAND SPANKING NEW SEWING MACHINE BROKE DOWN TWICE.
HAD TO FINISH THE JOB MYSELF WITH TOOLS FROM THE SHED.
MADE OUTTA THOSE SHEETS YOU WERE PACKED IN...
...BACK WHEN YOU FELL OUT OF THE SKY.
STURDY STUFF.
FIGURE YOU'LL BE NEEDING STUFF THAT'S STURDY.
MA.
PA.
WHAT YOU'VE TAUGHT ME.
WHAT YOU'VE GIVEN ME.
EVERYTHING.
IT'S EVERYTHING.
PRAIRIE THUNDER ROLLS.
STORM'S COMING.
MIGHT JUST BE A BIG ONE.
JUST MIGHT.
HE'S HAPPY. EAGER TO LEAVE.
THERE'S NO HOLDING AN EAGLE DOWN, MARTHA.
NO POINT IN EVEN TRYING.

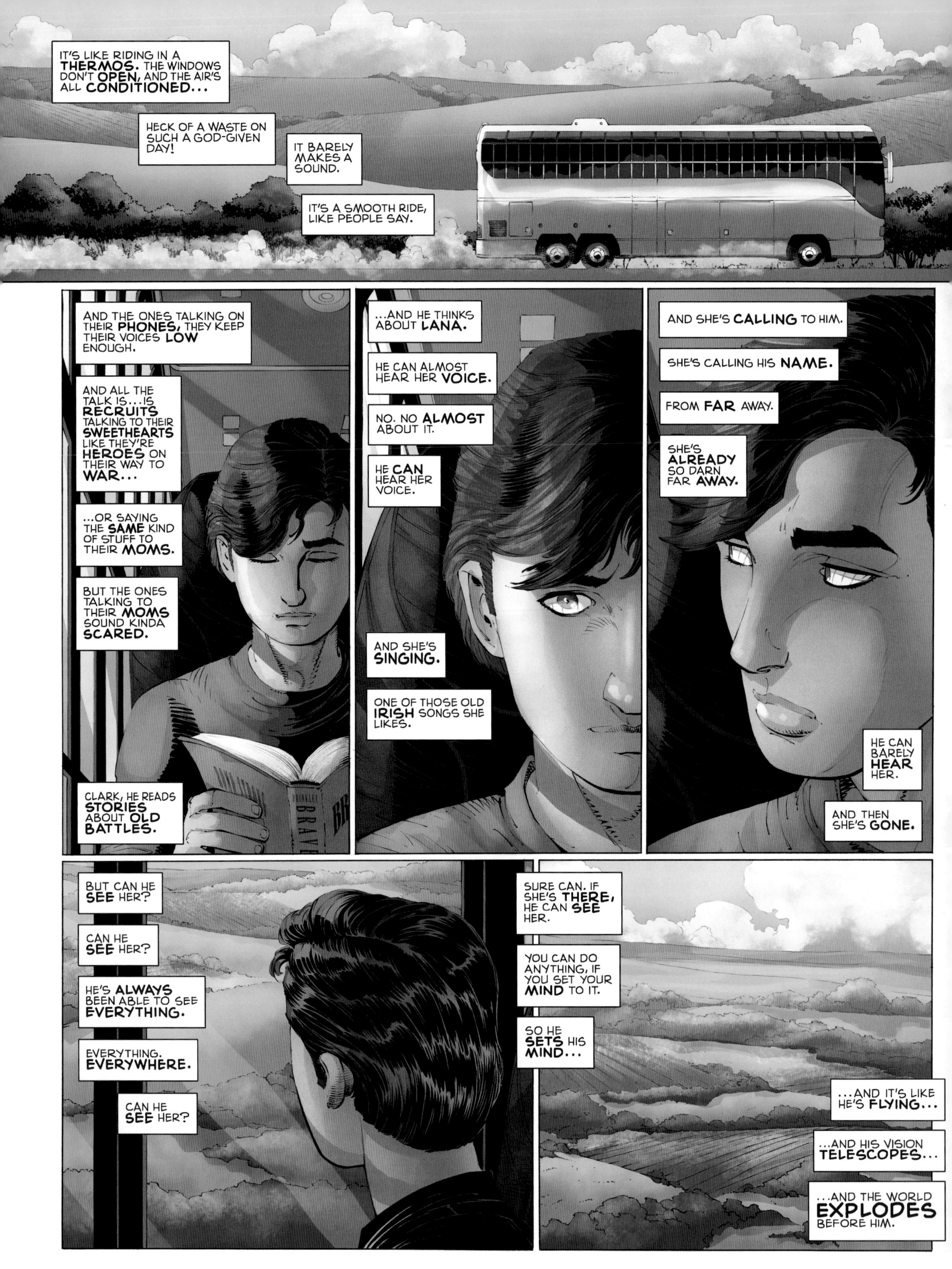
IT'S LIKE RIDING IN A THERMOS. THE WINDOWS DON'T OPEN, AND THE AIR'S ALL CONDITIONED...
HECK OF A WASTE ON SUCH A GOD-GIVEN DAY!
IT BARELY MAKES A SOUND.
IT'S A SMOOTH RIDE, LIKE PEOPLE SAY.
AND THE ONES TALKING ON THEIR PHONES, THEY KEEP THEIR VOICES LOW ENOUGH.
AND ALL THE TALK IS...IS RECRUITS TALKING TO THEIR SWEETHEARTS LIKE THEY'RE HEROES ON THEIR WAY TO WAR...
...OR SAYING THE SAME KIND OF STUFF TO THEIR MOMS.
BUT THE ONES TALKING TO THEIR MOMS SOUND KINDA SCARED.
CLARK, HE READS STORIES ABOUT OLD BATTLES.
...AND HE THINKS ABOUT LANA.
HE CAN ALMOST HEAR HER VOICE.
NO. NO ALMOST ABOUT IT.
HE CAN HEAR HER VOICE.
AND SHE'S SINGING.
ONE OF THOSE OLD IRISH SONGS SHE LIKES.
AND SHE'S CALLING TO HIM.
SHE'S CALLING HIS NAME.
FROM FAR AWAY.
SHE'S ALREADY SO DARN FAR AWAY.
HE CAN BARELY HEAR HER.
AND THEN SHE'S GONE.
BUT CAN HE SEE HER?
CAN HE SEE HER?
HE'S ALWAYS BEEN ABLE TO SEE EVERYTHING.
EVERYTHING. EVERYWHERE.
CAN HE SEE HER?
SURE CAN. IF SHE'S THERE, HE CAN SEE HER.
YOU CAN DO ANYTHING, IF YOU SET YOUR MIND TO IT.
SO HE SETS HIS MIND...
...AND IT'S LIKE HE'S FLYING...
...AND HIS VISION TELESCOPES...
...AND THE WORLD EXPLODES BEFORE HIM.

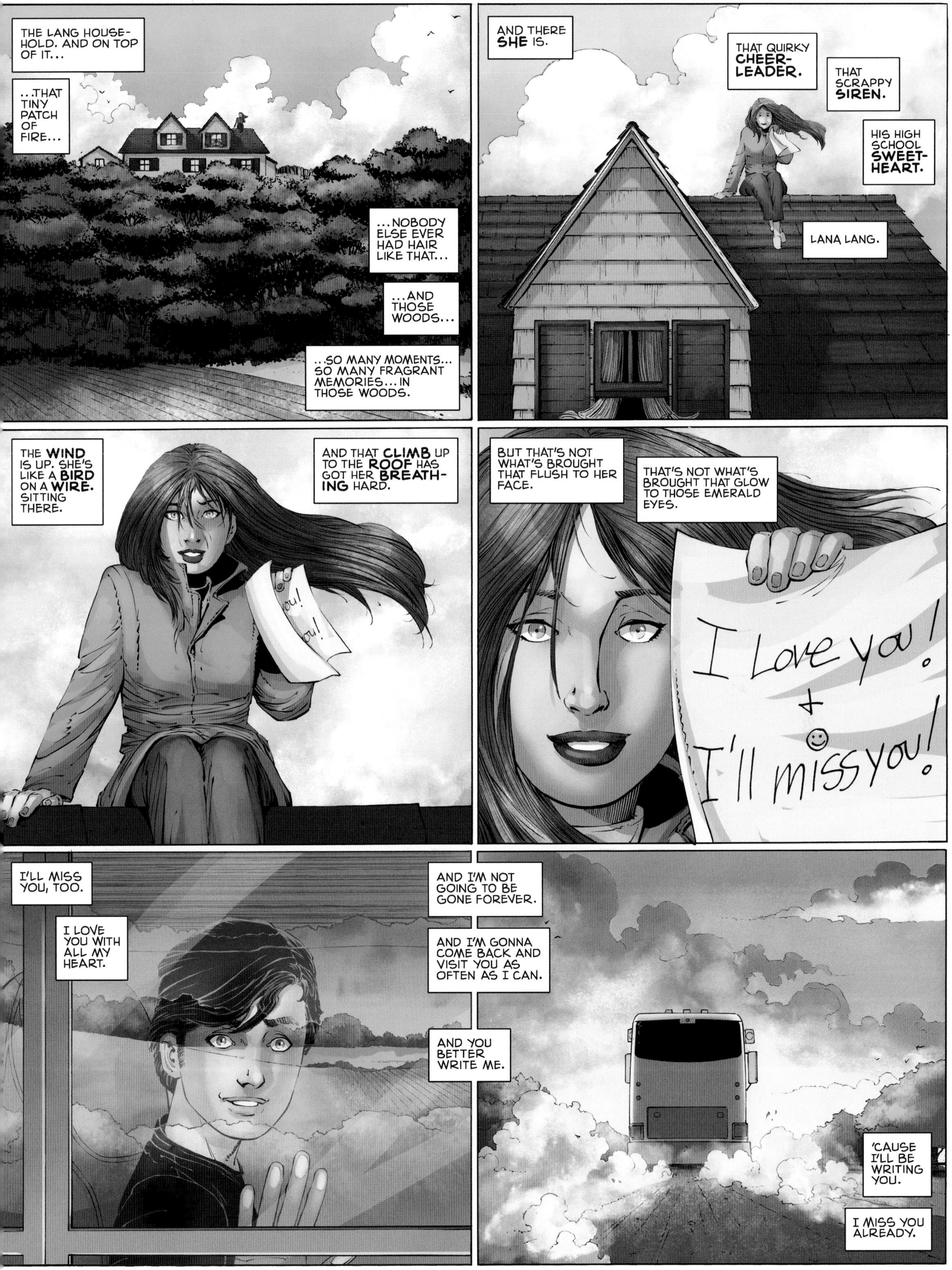
THE LANG HOUSE-HOLD. AND ON TOP OF IT...
...THAT TINY PATCH OF FIRE...
...NOBODY ELSE EVER HAD HAIR LIKE THAT...
...AND THOSE WOODS...
...SO MANY MOMENTS... SO MANY FRAGRANT MEMORIES... IN THOSE WOODS.
AND THERE SHE IS.
THAT QUIRKY CHEER-LEADER.
THAT SCRAPPY SIREN.
HIS HIGH SCHOOL SWEET-HEART.
LANA LANG.
THE WIND IS UP. SHE'S LIKE A BIRD ON A WIRE. SITTING THERE.
AND THAT CLIMB UP TO THE ROOF HAS GOT HER BREATH-ING HARD.
BUT THAT'S NOT WHAT'S BROUGHT THAT FLUSH TO HER FACE.
THAT'S NOT WHAT'S BROUGHT THAT GLOW TO THOSE EMERALD EYES.
I Love you! + I'll miss you!
I'LL MISS YOU, TOO.
I LOVE YOU WITH ALL MY HEART.
AND I'M NOT GOING TO BE GONE FOREVER.
AND I'M GONNA COME BACK AND VISIT YOU AS OFTEN AS I CAN.
AND YOU BETTER WRITE ME.
'CAUSE I'LL BE WRITING YOU.
I MISS YOU ALREADY.

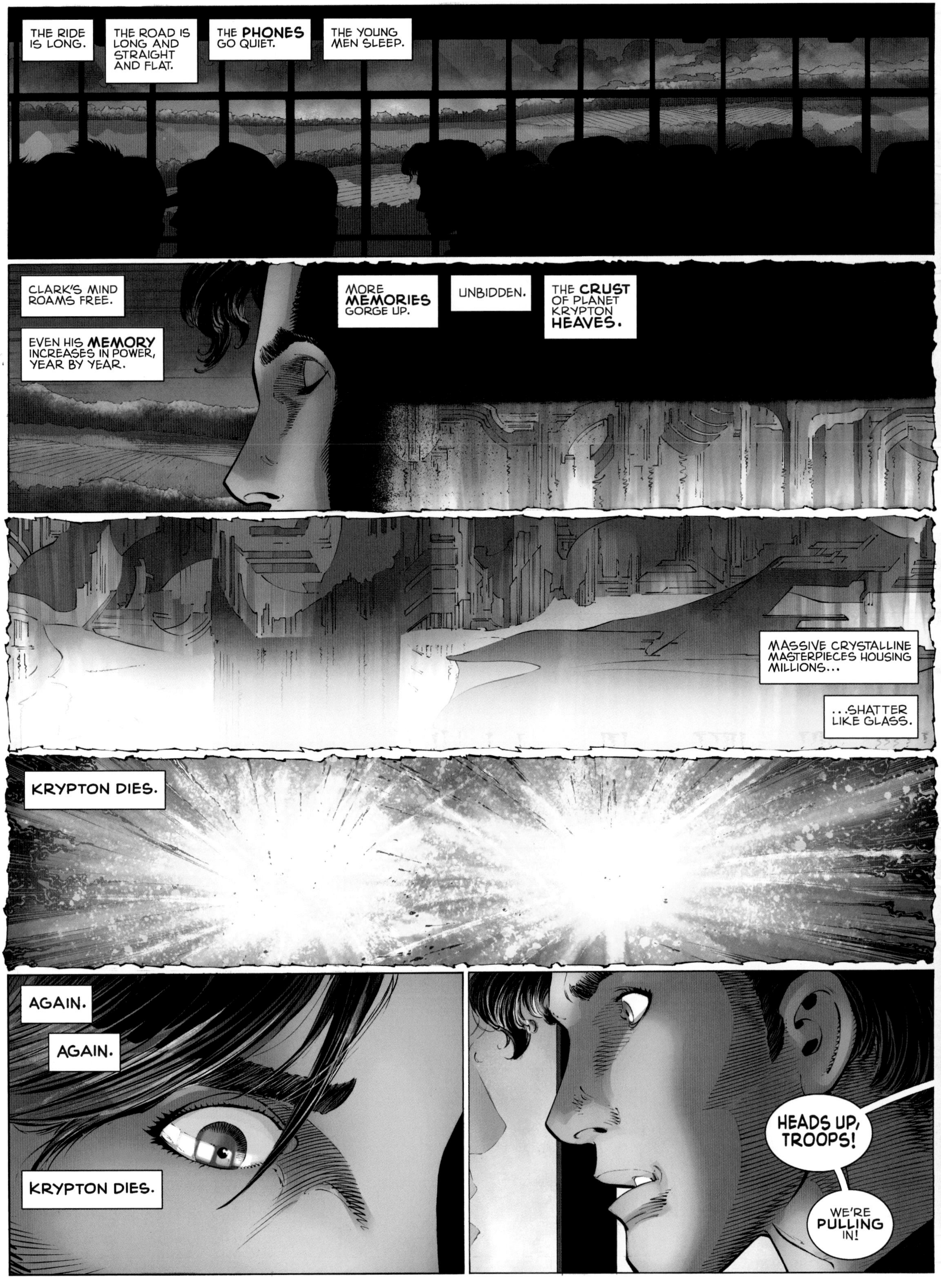
THE RIDE IS LONG.
THE ROAD IS LONG AND STRAIGHT AND FLAT.
THE PHONES GO QUIET.
THE YOUNG MEN SLEEP.
CLARK'S MIND ROAMS FREE.
EVEN HIS MEMORY INCREASES IN POWER, YEAR BY YEAR.
MORE MEMORIES GORGE UP.
UNBIDDEN.
THE CRUST OF PLANET KRYPTON HEAVES.
MASSIVE CRYSTALLINE MASTERPIECES HOUSING MILLIONS...
...SHATTER LIKE GLASS.
KRYPTON DIES.
AGAIN.
AGAIN.
KRYPTON DIES.
HEADS UP, TROOPS!
WE'RE PULLING IN!

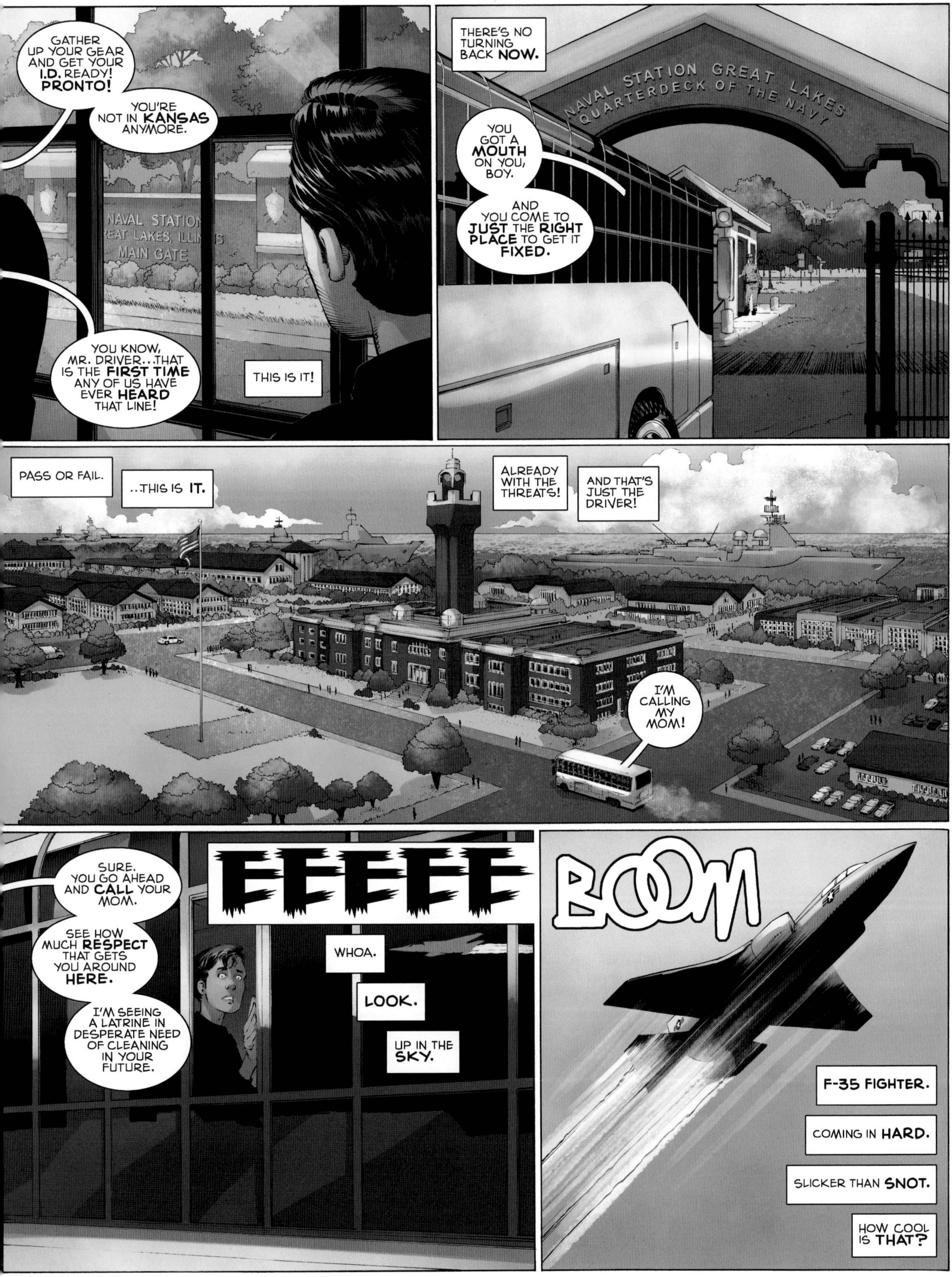
GATHER UP YOUR GEAR AND GET YOUR I.D. READY! PRONTO!
YOU'RE NOT IN KANSAS ANYMORE.
NAVAL STATION GREAT LAKES, ILLINOIS MAIN GATE
YOU KNOW, MR. DRIVER...THAT IS THE FIRST TIME ANY OF US HAVE EVER HEARD THAT LINE!
THIS IS IT!
THERE'S NO TURNING BACK NOW.
NAVAL STATION GREAT LAKES
QUARTERDECK OF THE NAVY
YOU GOT A MOUTH ON YOU, BOY.
AND YOU COME TO JUST THE RIGHT PLACE TO GET IT FIXED.
PASS OR FAIL.
...THIS IS IT.
ALREADY WITH THE THREATS!
AND THAT'S JUST THE DRIVER!
I'M CALLING MY MOM!
SURE. YOU GO AHEAD AND CALL YOUR MOM.
SEE HOW MUCH RESPECT THAT GETS YOU AROUND HERE.
I'M SEEING A LATRINE IN DESPERATE NEED OF CLEANING IN YOUR FUTURE.
EEEEE
WHOA.
LOOK.
UP IN THE SKY.
BOOM
F-35 FIGHTER.
COMING IN HARD.
SLICKER THAN SNOT.
HOW COOL IS THAT?

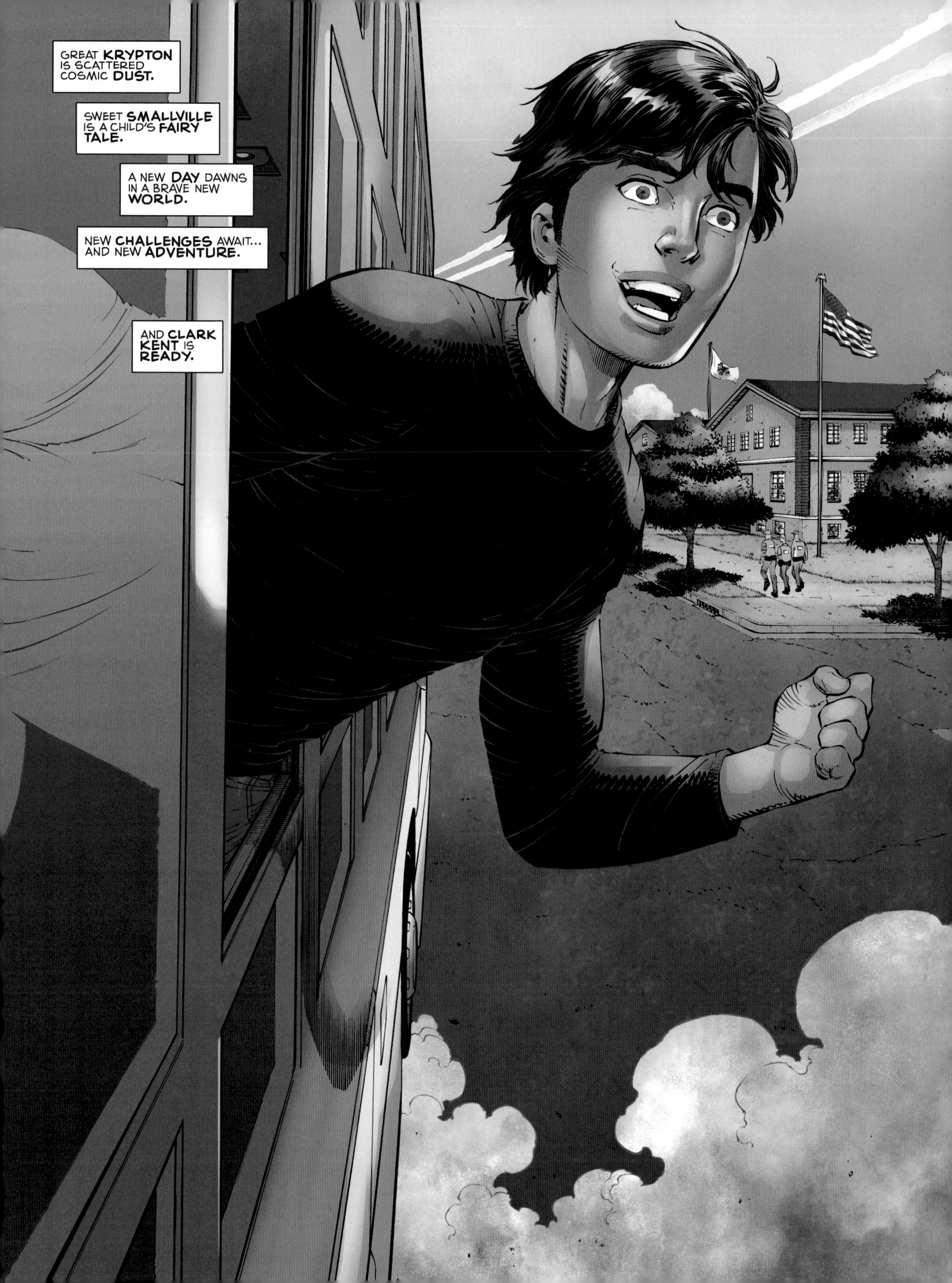
GREAT KRYPTON IS SCATTERED COSMIC DUST.
SWEET SMALLVILLE IS A CHILD'S FAIRY TALE.
A NEW DAY DAWNS IN A BRAVE NEW WORLD.
NEW CHALLENGES AWAIT... AND NEW ADVENTURE.
AND CLARK KENT IS READY.

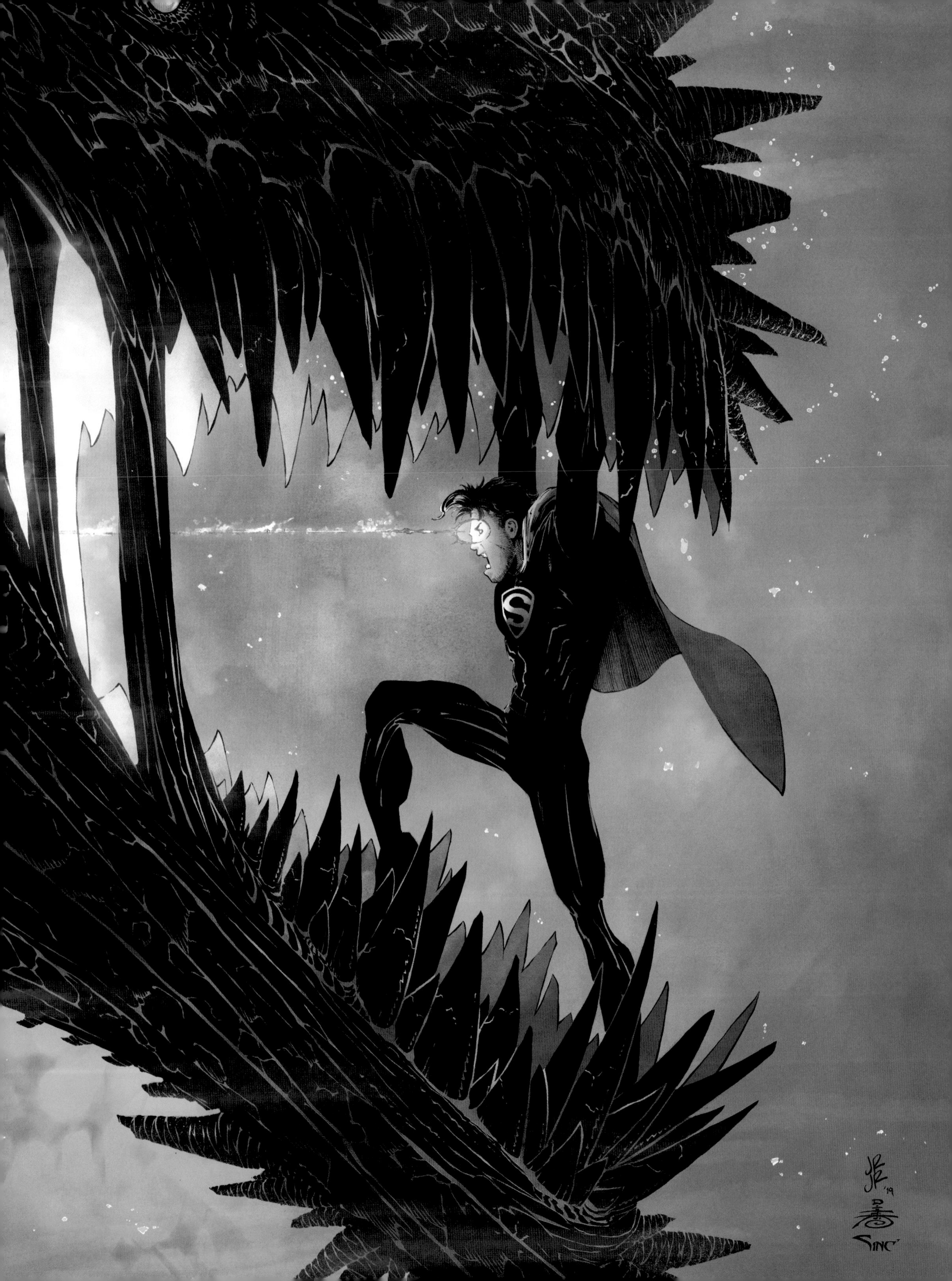

Part Two

ATLANTIS

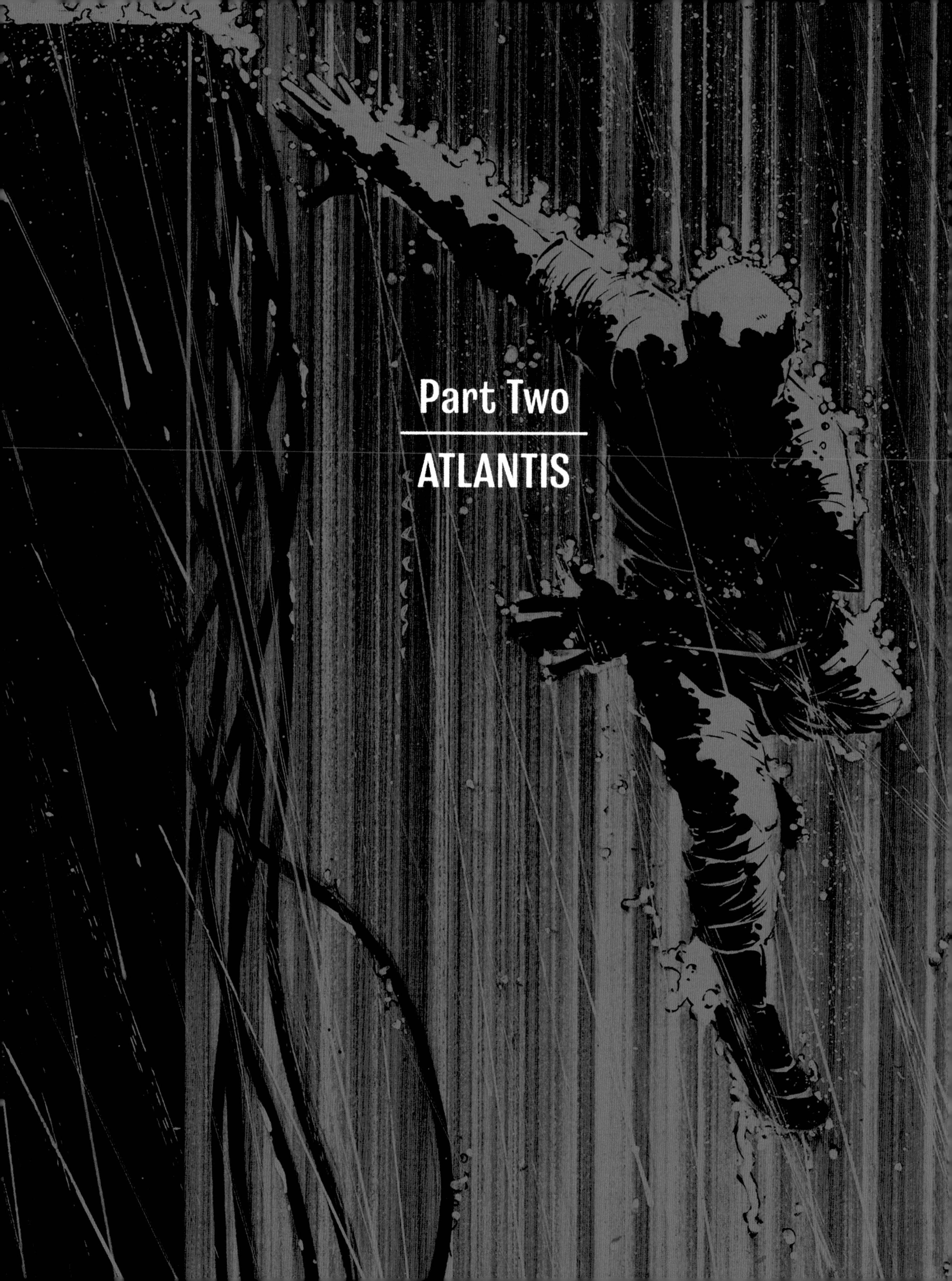

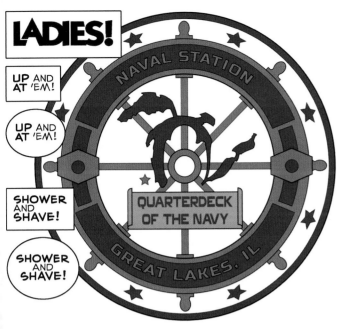

LADIES!

UP AND AT 'EM!

UP AND AT 'EM!

SHOWER AND SHAVE!

SHOWER AND SHAVE!

NAVAL STATION

QUARTERDECK OF THE NAVY

GREAT LAKES, IL

SUCK THAT GUT IN!

SUCK THAT GUT IN!

CHIN UP!

CHIN UP!

PARTY'S OVER!

PARTY'S OVER!

NO MORE PRETTY BOY!

NO MORE PRETTY BOY!

TOUGH HAIR YOU GOT THERE, PAL. THREE BLADES ALREADY. COME STRAIGHT OUTTA YOUR PAY.

UH-HUH, UH-HUH...

SHAVE IT OFF!

SHAVE IT OFF!

SLAP IT CLEAN!

HUT!

HUT!

HUT!

STEP LIVELY, THERE! TIME'S A-WASTIN'!

STEP LIVELY, THERE!

LIKE A PACK OF SHAKY-LEGGED BABY MULES, WE DRAG OUR GEAR INSIDE.

INTO SOME NEW LIFE THAT'S LOOKING TO BE SOME KIND OF STRANGE.

FRONT AND CENTER!

FRONT AND CENTER!

SOME KIND OF STRANGE... AND SOME KIND OF LOUD.

HUT!

HUT!

HUT!

253

TOMORROW'S GONNA HURT!

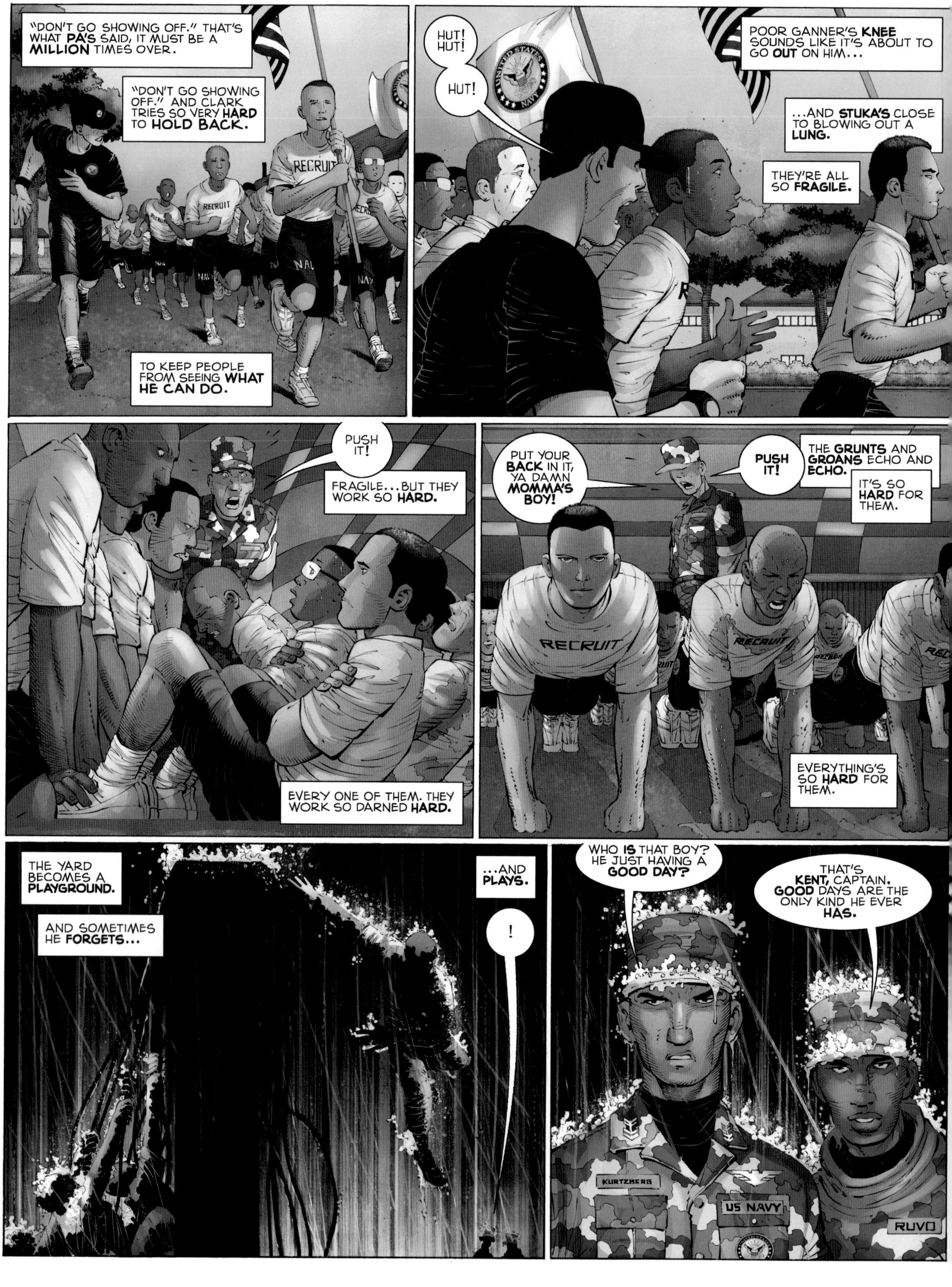

"DON'T GO SHOWING OFF." THAT'S WHAT PA'S SAID, IT MUST BE A MILLION TIMES OVER.
"DON'T GO SHOWING OFF." AND CLARK TRIES SO VERY HARD TO HOLD BACK.
RECRUIT
RECRUIT
TO KEEP PEOPLE FROM SEEING WHAT HE CAN DO.
HUT! HUT!
HUT!
POOR GANNER'S KNEE SOUNDS LIKE IT'S ABOUT TO GO OUT ON HIM...
...AND STUKA'S CLOSE TO BLOWING OUT A LUNG.
THEY'RE ALL SO FRAGILE.
PUSH IT!
FRAGILE...BUT THEY WORK SO HARD.
EVERY ONE OF THEM. THEY WORK SO DARNED HARD.
PUT YOUR BACK IN IT, YA DAMN MOMMA'S BOY!
PUSH IT!
THE GRUNTS AND GROANS ECHO AND ECHO.
IT'S SO HARD FOR THEM.
RECRUIT
RECRUIT
EVERYTHING'S SO HARD FOR THEM.
THE YARD BECOMES A PLAYGROUND.
AND SOMETIMES HE FORGETS...
...AND PLAYS.
!
WHO IS THAT BOY? HE JUST HAVING A GOOD DAY?
THAT'S KENT, CAPTAIN. GOOD DAYS ARE THE ONLY KIND HE EVER HAS.
KURTZBERG
US NAVY
RUVO

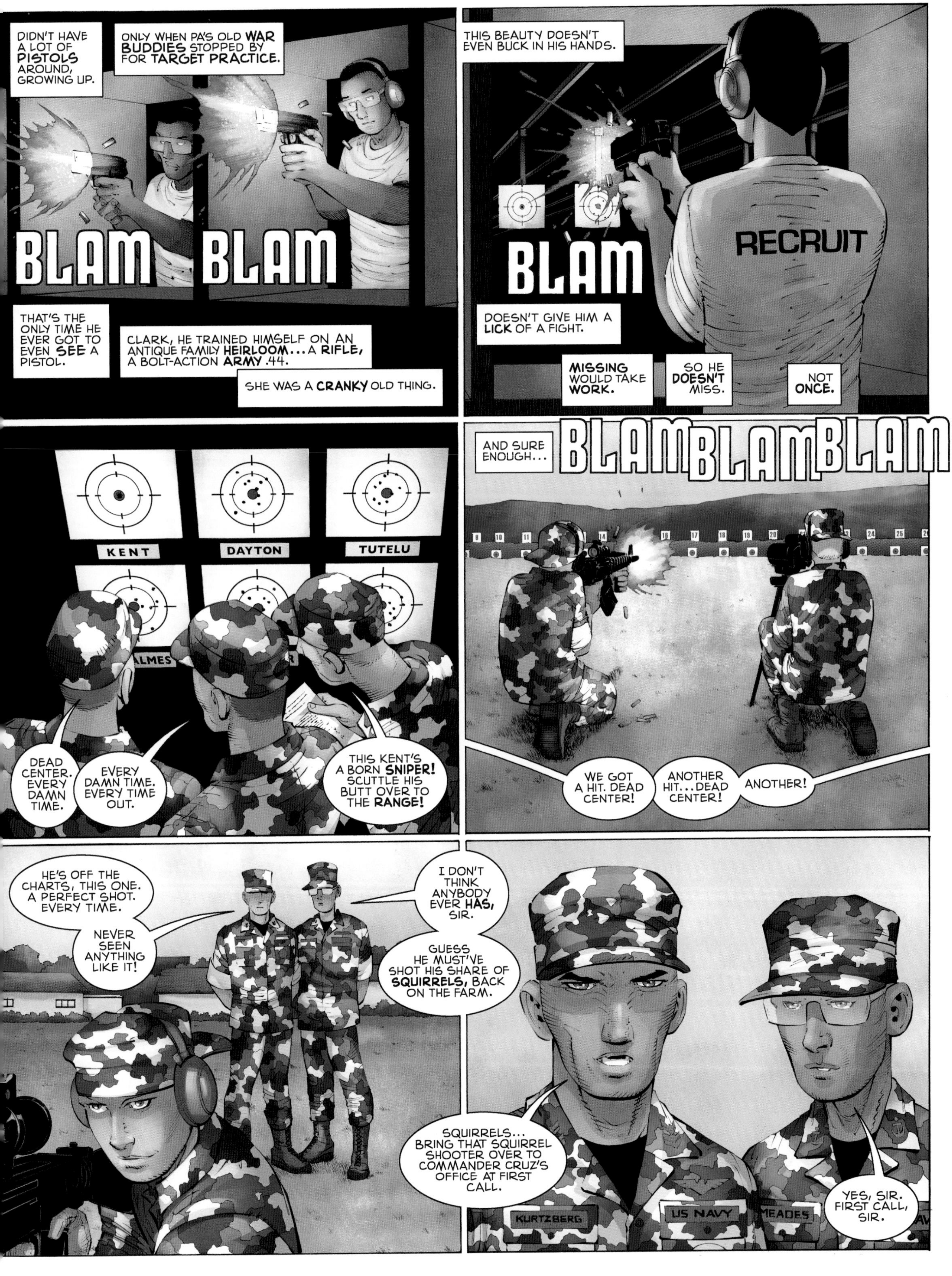
DIDN'T HAVE A LOT OF PISTOLS AROUND, GROWING UP.
ONLY WHEN PA'S OLD WAR BUDDIES STOPPED BY FOR TARGET PRACTICE.
BLAM
BLAM
THAT'S THE ONLY TIME HE EVER GOT TO EVEN SEE A PISTOL.
CLARK, HE TRAINED HIMSELF ON AN ANTIQUE FAMILY HEIRLOOM... A RIFLE, A BOLT-ACTION ARMY .44.
SHE WAS A CRANKY OLD THING.
THIS BEAUTY DOESN'T EVEN BUCK IN HIS HANDS.
BLAM
RECRUIT
DOESN'T GIVE HIM A LICK OF A FIGHT.
MISSING WOULD TAKE WORK.
SO HE DOESN'T MISS.
NOT ONCE.
KENT
DAYTON
TUTELU
DEAD CENTER. EVERY DAMN TIME.
EVERY DAMN TIME. EVERY TIME OUT.
THIS KENT'S A BORN SNIPER! SCUTTLE HIS BUTT OVER TO THE RANGE!
AND SURE ENOUGH...
BLAMBLAMBLAM
WE GOT A HIT. DEAD CENTER!
ANOTHER HIT... DEAD CENTER!
ANOTHER!
HE'S OFF THE CHARTS, THIS ONE. A PERFECT SHOT. EVERY TIME.
NEVER SEEN ANYTHING LIKE IT!
I DON'T THINK ANYBODY EVER HAS, SIR.
GUESS HE MUST'VE SHOT HIS SHARE OF SQUIRRELS, BACK ON THE FARM.
SQUIRRELS... BRING THAT SQUIRREL SHOOTER OVER TO COMMANDER CRUZ'S OFFICE AT FIRST CALL.
KURTZBERG
US NAVY
MEADES
YES, SIR. FIRST CALL, SIR.

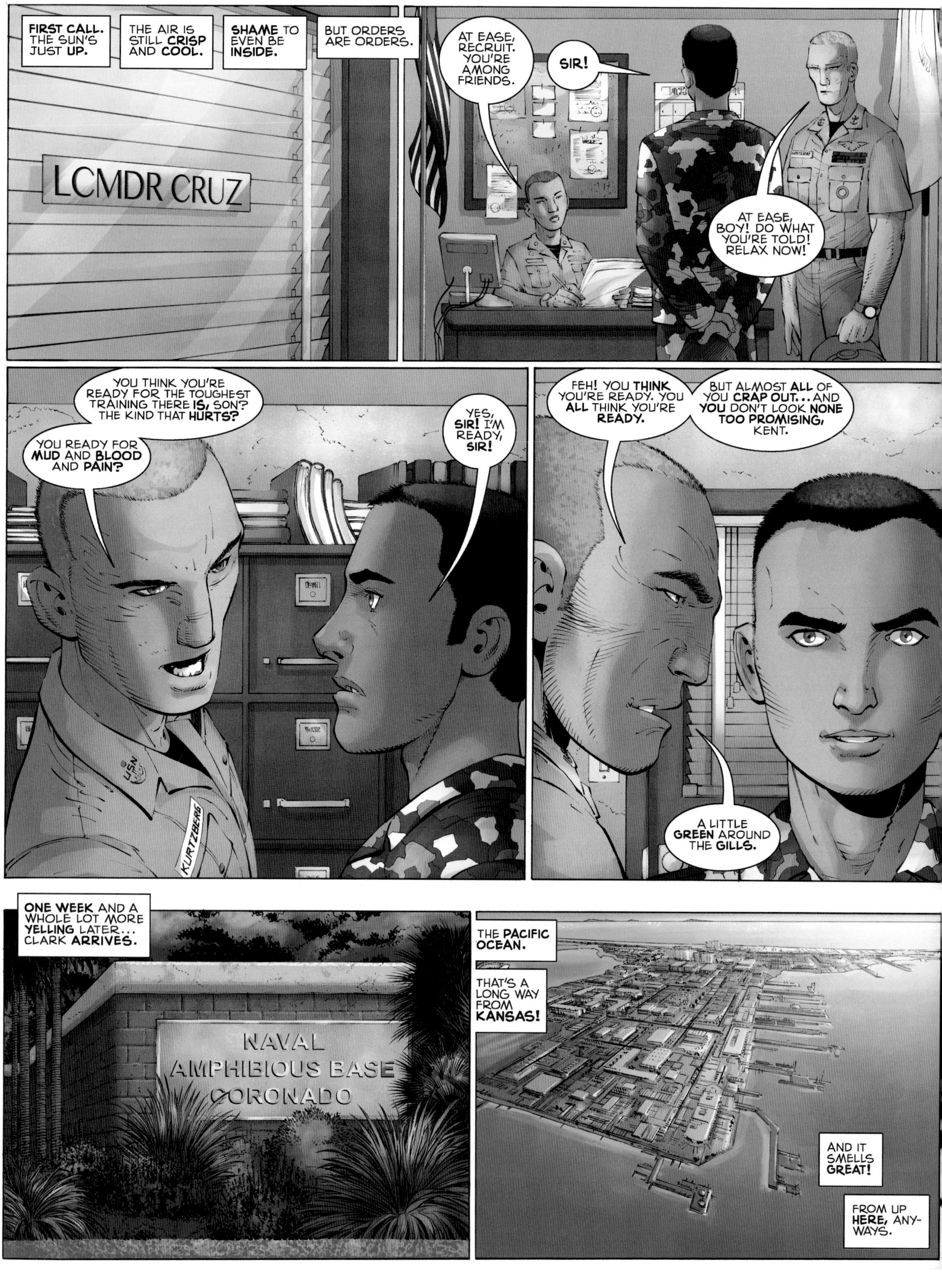
FIRST CALL. THE SUN'S JUST UP.
THE AIR IS STILL CRISP AND COOL.
SHAME TO EVEN BE INSIDE.
BUT ORDERS ARE ORDERS.
LCMDR CRUZ
AT EASE, RECRUIT. YOU'RE AMONG FRIENDS.
SIR!
AT EASE, BOY! DO WHAT YOU'RE TOLD! RELAX NOW!
YOU THINK YOU'RE READY FOR THE TOUGHEST TRAINING THERE IS, SON? THE KIND THAT HURTS?
YOU READY FOR MUD AND BLOOD AND PAIN?
YES, SIR! I'M READY, SIR!
KURTZBERG
FEH! YOU THINK YOU'RE READY. YOU ALL THINK YOU'RE READY.
BUT ALMOST ALL OF YOU CRAP OUT... AND YOU DON'T LOOK NONE TOO PROMISING, KENT.
A LITTLE GREEN AROUND THE GILLS.
ONE WEEK AND A WHOLE LOT MORE YELLING LATER... CLARK ARRIVES.
NAVAL AMPHIBIOUS BASE CORONADO
THE PACIFIC OCEAN.
THAT'S A LONG WAY FROM KANSAS!
AND IT SMELLS GREAT!
FROM UP HERE, ANY-WAYS.

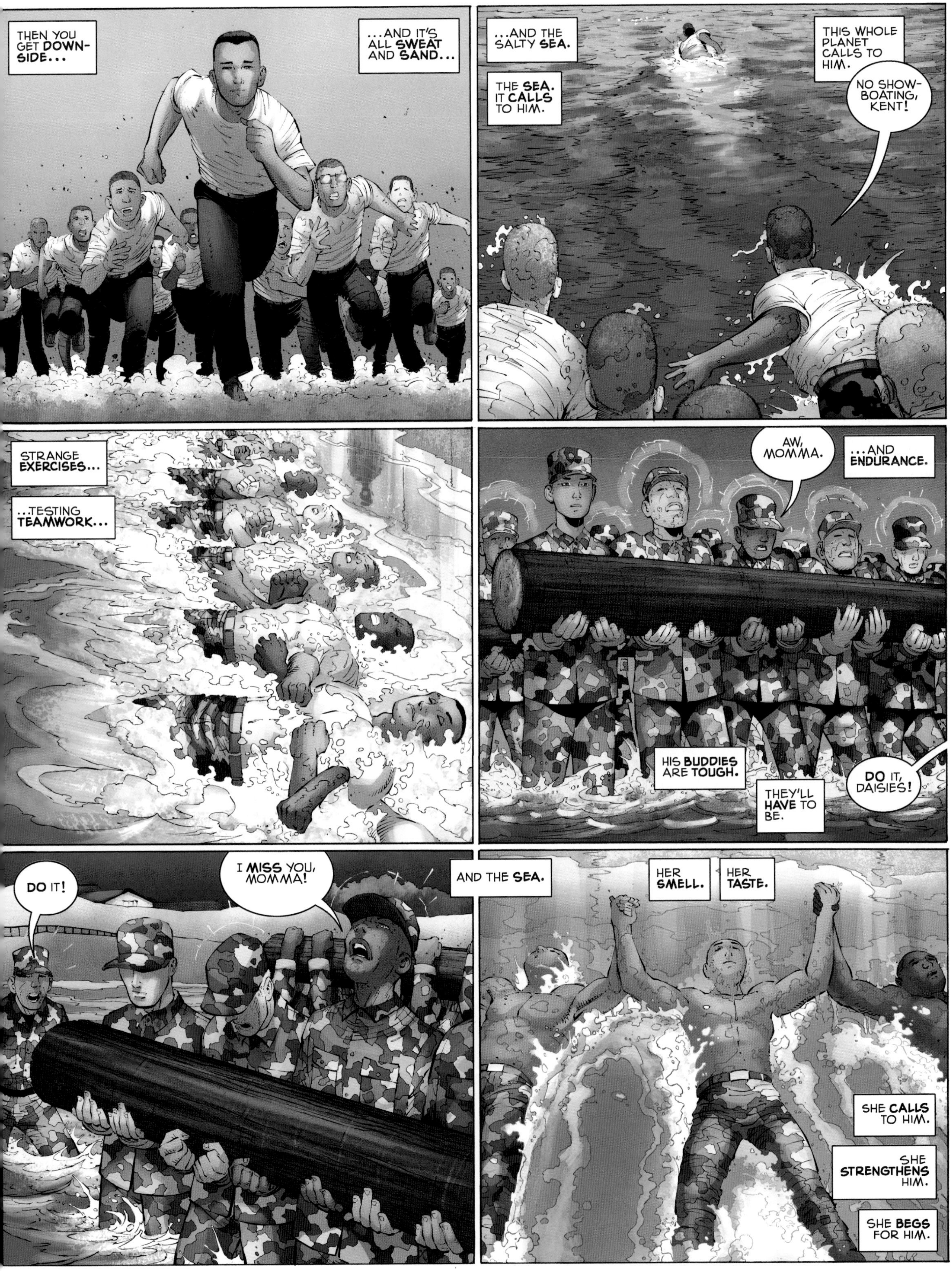
THEN YOU GET DOWN-SIDE...
...AND IT'S ALL SWEAT AND SAND...
...AND THE SALTY SEA.
THE SEA. IT CALLS TO HIM.
THIS WHOLE PLANET CALLS TO HIM.
NO SHOW-BOATING, KENT!
STRANGE EXERCISES...
...TESTING TEAMWORK...
AW, MOMMA.
...AND ENDURANCE.
HIS BUDDIES ARE TOUGH.
THEY'LL HAVE TO BE.
DO IT, DAISIES!
DO IT!
I MISS YOU, MOMMA!
AND THE SEA.
HER SMELL.
HER TASTE.
SHE CALLS TO HIM.
SHE STRENGTHENS HIM.
SHE BEGS FOR HIM.

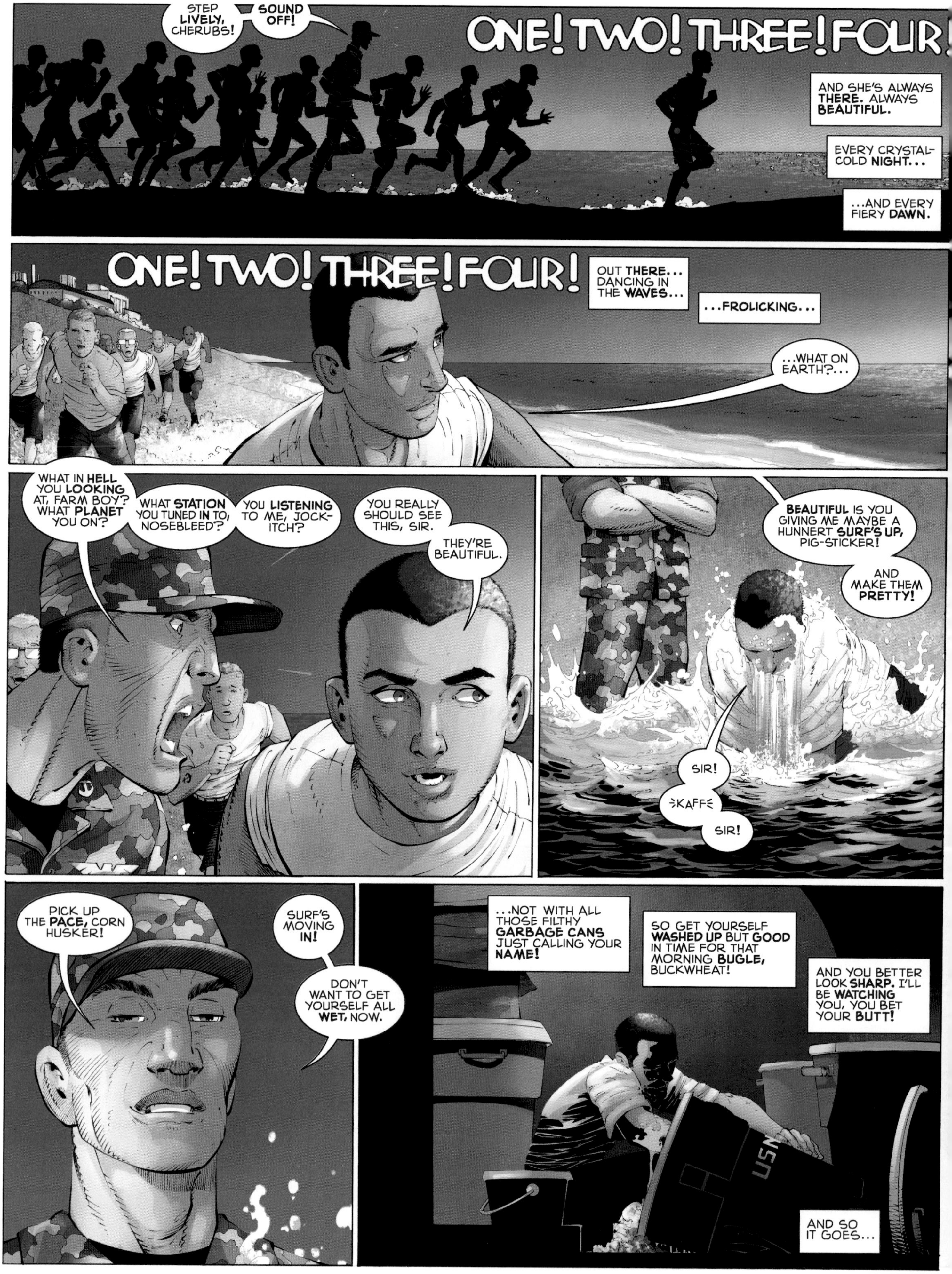
STEP LIVELY, CHERUBS!
SOUND OFF!
ONE! TWO! THREE! FOUR!
AND SHE'S ALWAYS THERE. ALWAYS BEAUTIFUL.
EVERY CRYSTAL-COLD NIGHT...
...AND EVERY FIERY DAWN.
ONE! TWO! THREE! FOUR!
OUT THERE... DANCING IN THE WAVES...
...FROLICKING...
...WHAT ON EARTH?...
WHAT IN HELL YOU LOOKING AT, FARM BOY? WHAT PLANET YOU ON?
WHAT STATION YOU TUNED IN TO, NOSEBLEED?
YOU LISTENING TO ME, JOCK-ITCH?
YOU REALLY SHOULD SEE THIS, SIR.
THEY'RE BEAUTIFUL.
BEAUTIFUL IS YOU GIVING ME MAYBE A HUNNERT SURF'S UP, PIG-STICKER!
AND MAKE THEM PRETTY!
SIR!
KAFF
SIR!
PICK UP THE PACE, CORN HUSKER!
SURF'S MOVING IN!
DON'T WANT TO GET YOURSELF ALL WET, NOW.
...NOT WITH ALL THOSE FILTHY GARBAGE CANS JUST CALLING YOUR NAME!
SO GET YOURSELF WASHED UP BUT GOOD IN TIME FOR THAT MORNING BUGLE, BUCKWHEAT!
AND YOU BETTER LOOK SHARP. I'LL BE WATCHING YOU, YOU BET YOUR BUTT!
AND SO IT GOES...

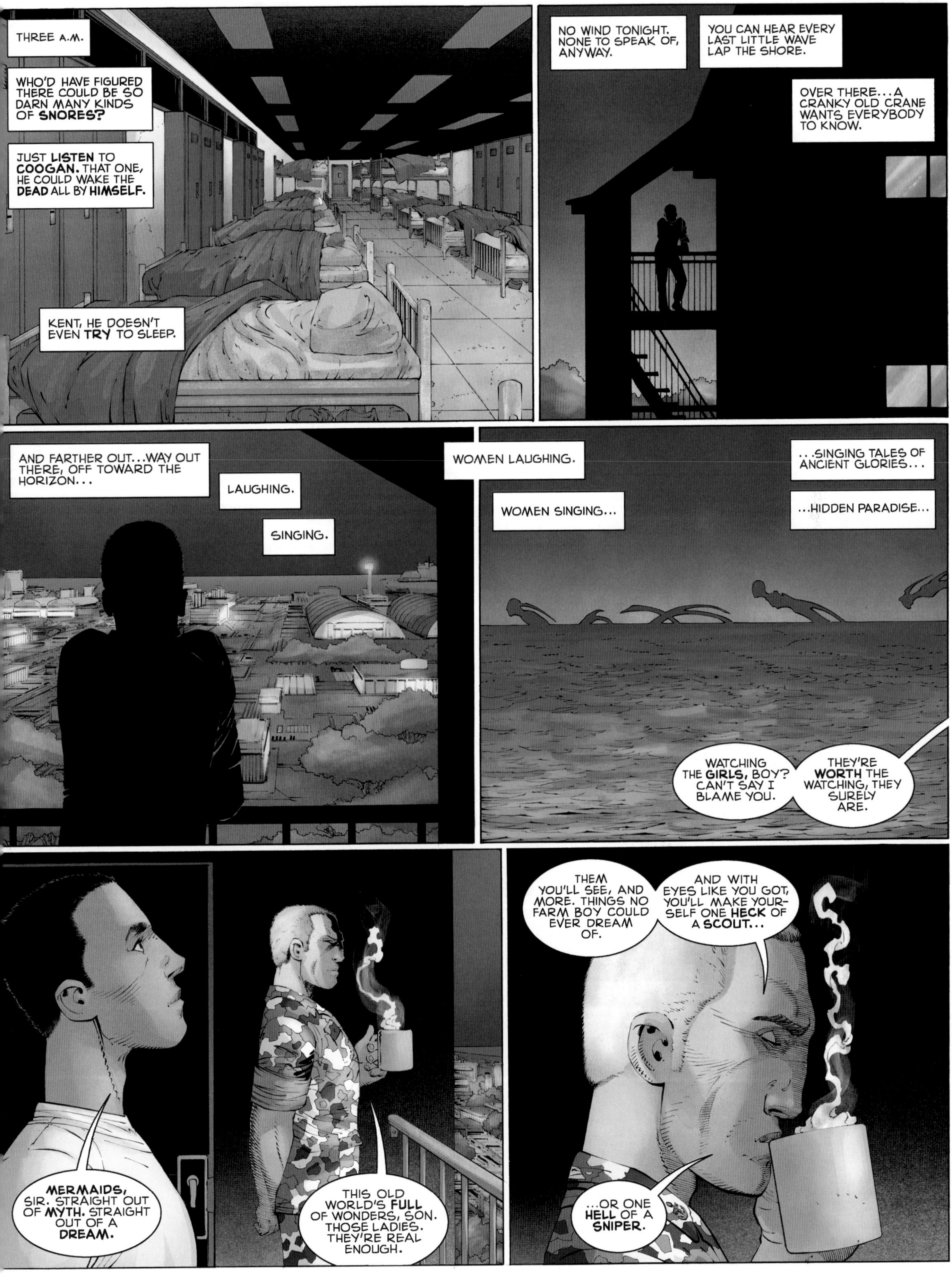

THREE A.M.
WHO'D HAVE FIGURED THERE COULD BE SO DARN MANY KINDS OF SNORES?
JUST LISTEN TO COOGAN. THAT ONE, HE COULD WAKE THE DEAD ALL BY HIMSELF.
KENT, HE DOESN'T EVEN TRY TO SLEEP.
NO WIND TONIGHT. NONE TO SPEAK OF, ANYWAY.
YOU CAN HEAR EVERY LAST LITTLE WAVE LAP THE SHORE.
OVER THERE... A CRANKY OLD CRANE WANTS EVERYBODY TO KNOW.
AND FARTHER OUT... WAY OUT THERE, OFF TOWARD THE HORIZON...
LAUGHING.
SINGING.
WOMEN LAUGHING.
WOMEN SINGING...
...SINGING TALES OF ANCIENT GLORIES...
...HIDDEN PARADISE...
WATCHING THE GIRLS, BOY? CAN'T SAY I BLAME YOU.
THEY'RE WORTH THE WATCHING, THEY SURELY ARE.
MERMAIDS, SIR. STRAIGHT OUT OF MYTH. STRAIGHT OUT OF A DREAM.
THIS OLD WORLD'S FULL OF WONDERS, SON. THOSE LADIES. THEY'RE REAL ENOUGH.
THEM YOU'LL SEE, AND MORE. THINGS NO FARM BOY COULD EVER DREAM OF.
AND WITH EYES LIKE YOU GOT, YOU'LL MAKE YOURSELF ONE HECK OF A SCOUT...
...OR ONE HELL OF A SNIPER.

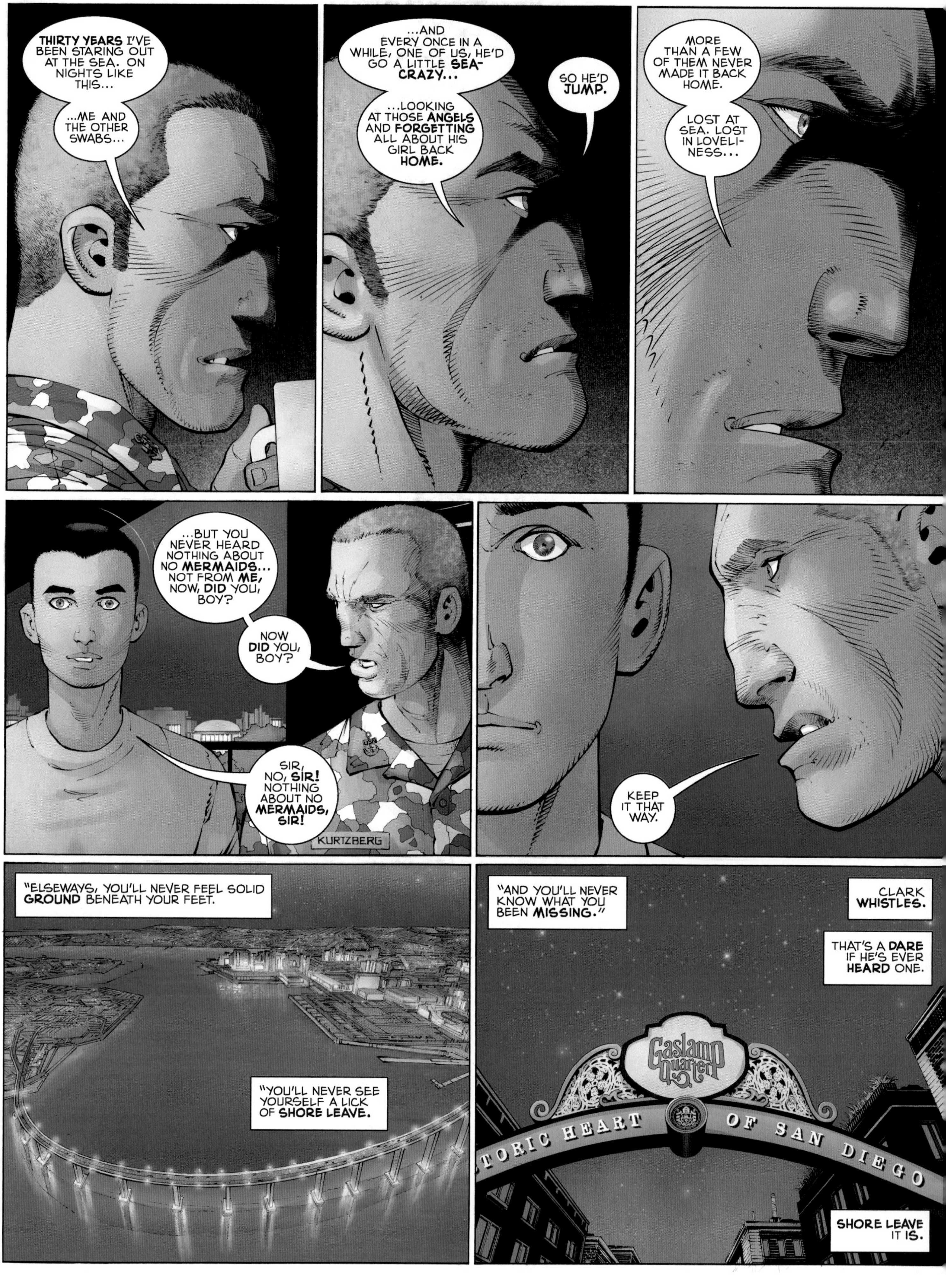

THIRTY YEARS I'VE BEEN STARING OUT AT THE SEA. ON NIGHTS LIKE THIS...
...ME AND THE OTHER SWABS...
...AND EVERY ONCE IN A WHILE, ONE OF US, HE'D GO A LITTLE SEA-CRAZY...
...LOOKING AT THOSE ANGELS AND FORGETTING ALL ABOUT HIS GIRL BACK HOME.
SO HE'D JUMP.
MORE THAN A FEW OF THEM NEVER MADE IT BACK HOME.
LOST AT SEA. LOST IN LOVELINESS...
...BUT YOU NEVER HEARD NOTHING ABOUT NO MERMAIDS... NOT FROM ME, NOW, DID YOU, BOY?
NOW DID YOU, BOY?
SIR, NO, SIR! NOTHING ABOUT NO MERMAIDS, SIR!
KURTZBERG
KEEP IT THAT WAY.
"ELSEWAYS, YOU'LL NEVER FEEL SOLID GROUND BENEATH YOUR FEET.
"YOU'LL NEVER SEE YOURSELF A LICK OF SHORE LEAVE.
"AND YOU'LL NEVER KNOW WHAT YOU BEEN MISSING."
CLARK WHISTLES.
THAT'S A DARE IF HE'S EVER HEARD ONE.
Gaslamp Quarter
TORIC HEART OF SAN DIEGO
SHORE LEAVE IT IS.

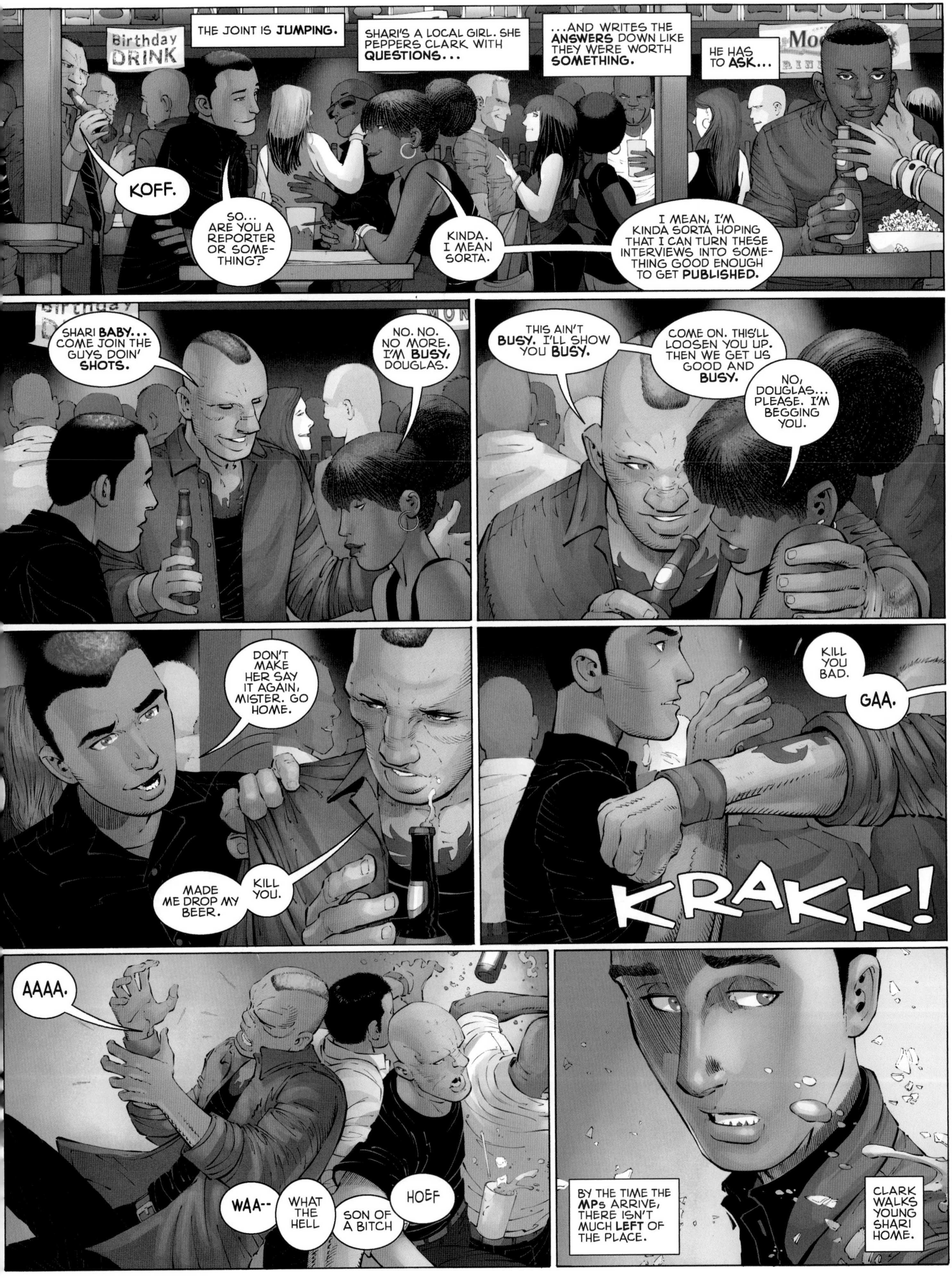
Birthday DRINK
THE JOINT IS JUMPING.
SHARI'S A LOCAL GIRL. SHE PEPPERS CLARK WITH QUESTIONS...
...AND WRITES THE ANSWERS DOWN LIKE THEY WERE WORTH SOMETHING.
HE HAS TO ASK...
KOFF.
SO... ARE YOU A REPORTER OR SOME-THING?
KINDA. I MEAN SORTA.
I MEAN, I'M KINDA SORTA HOPING THAT I CAN TURN THESE INTERVIEWS INTO SOME-THING GOOD ENOUGH TO GET PUBLISHED.
SHARI BABY... COME JOIN THE GUYS DOIN' SHOTS.
NO. NO. NO MORE. I'M BUSY, DOUGLAS.
THIS AIN'T BUSY. I'LL SHOW YOU BUSY.
COME ON. THIS'LL LOOSEN YOU UP. THEN WE GET US GOOD AND BUSY.
NO, DOUGLAS... PLEASE. I'M BEGGING YOU.
DON'T MAKE HER SAY IT AGAIN, MISTER. GO HOME.
MADE ME DROP MY BEER.
KILL YOU.
KILL YOU BAD.
GAA.
KRAKK!
AAAA.
WAA--
WHAT THE HELL
SON OF A BITCH
HOEF
BY THE TIME THE MPs ARRIVE, THERE ISN'T MUCH LEFT OF THE PLACE.
CLARK WALKS YOUNG SHARI HOME.

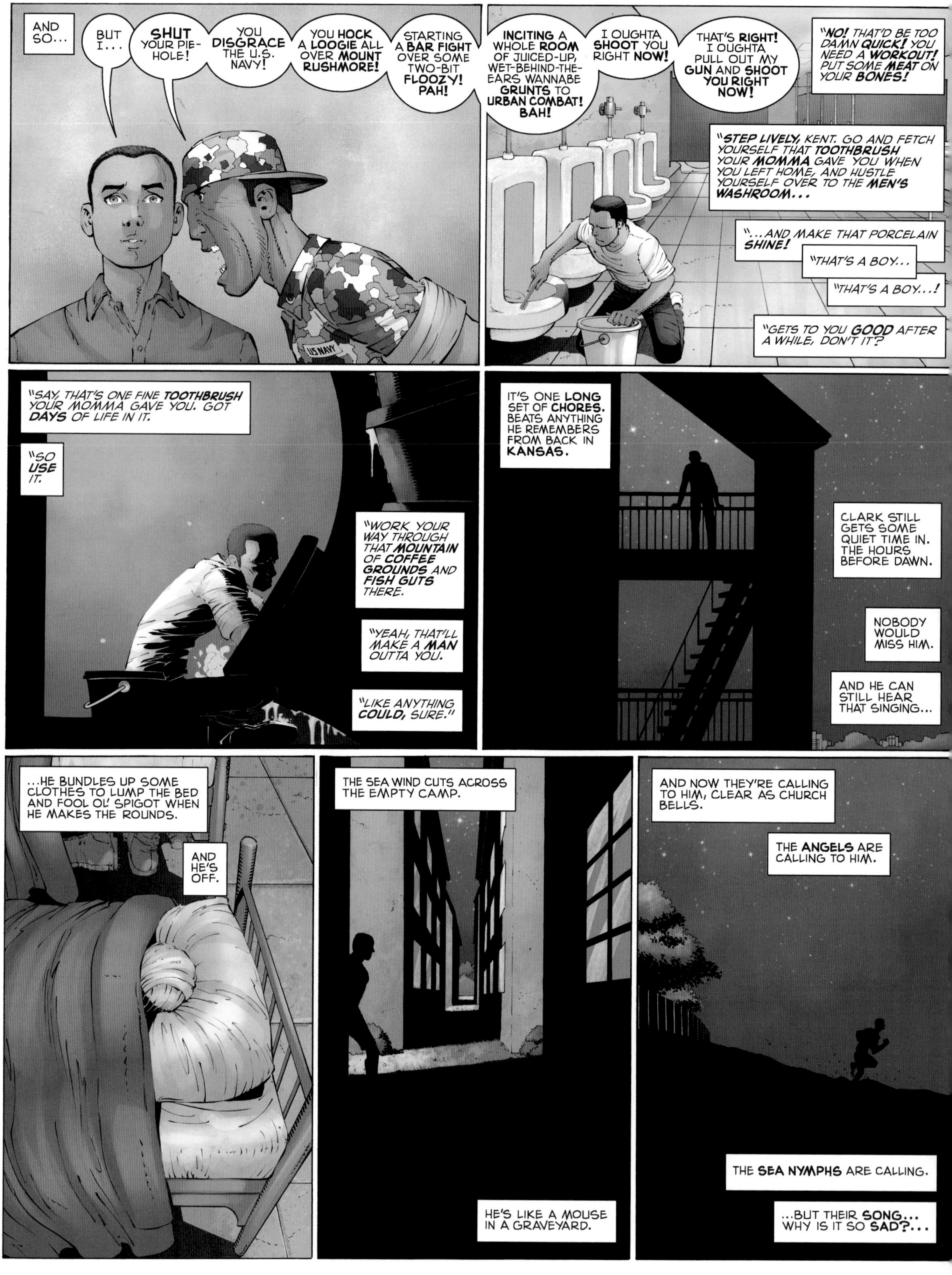
AND SO...
BUT I...
SHUT YOUR PIE-HOLE!
YOU DISGRACE THE U.S. NAVY!
YOU HOCK A LOOGIE ALL OVER MOUNT RUSHMORE!
STARTING A BAR FIGHT OVER SOME TWO-BIT FLOOZY! PAH!
INCITING A WHOLE ROOM OF JUICED-UP, WET-BEHIND-THE-EARS WANNABE GRUNTS TO URBAN COMBAT! BAH!
I OUGHTA SHOOT YOU RIGHT NOW!
THAT'S RIGHT! I OUGHTA PULL OUT MY GUN AND SHOOT YOU RIGHT NOW!
U.S. NAVY
"NO! THAT'D BE TOO DAMN QUICK! YOU NEED A WORKOUT! PUT SOME MEAT ON YOUR BONES!
"STEP LIVELY, KENT. GO AND FETCH YOURSELF THAT TOOTHBRUSH YOUR MOMMA GAVE YOU WHEN YOU LEFT HOME, AND HUSTLE YOURSELF OVER TO THE MEN'S WASHROOM...
"...AND MAKE THAT PORCELAIN SHINE!
"THAT'S A BOY...
"THAT'S A BOY...!
"GETS TO YOU GOOD AFTER A WHILE, DON'T IT?
"SAY, THAT'S ONE FINE TOOTHBRUSH YOUR MOMMA GAVE YOU. GOT DAYS OF LIFE IN IT.
"SO USE IT.
"WORK YOUR WAY THROUGH THAT MOUNTAIN OF COFFEE GROUNDS AND FISH GUTS THERE.
"YEAH, THAT'LL MAKE A MAN OUTTA YOU.
"LIKE ANYTHING COULD, SURE."
IT'S ONE LONG SET OF CHORES. BEATS ANYTHING HE REMEMBERS FROM BACK IN KANSAS.
CLARK STILL GETS SOME QUIET TIME IN. THE HOURS BEFORE DAWN.
NOBODY WOULD MISS HIM.
AND HE CAN STILL HEAR THAT SINGING...
...HE BUNDLES UP SOME CLOTHES TO LUMP THE BED AND FOOL OL' SPIGOT WHEN HE MAKES THE ROUNDS.
AND HE'S OFF.
THE SEA WIND CUTS ACROSS THE EMPTY CAMP.
HE'S LIKE A MOUSE IN A GRAVEYARD.
AND NOW THEY'RE CALLING TO HIM, CLEAR AS CHURCH BELLS.
THE ANGELS ARE CALLING TO HIM.
THE SEA NYMPHS ARE CALLING.
...BUT THEIR SONG... WHY IS IT SO SAD?...

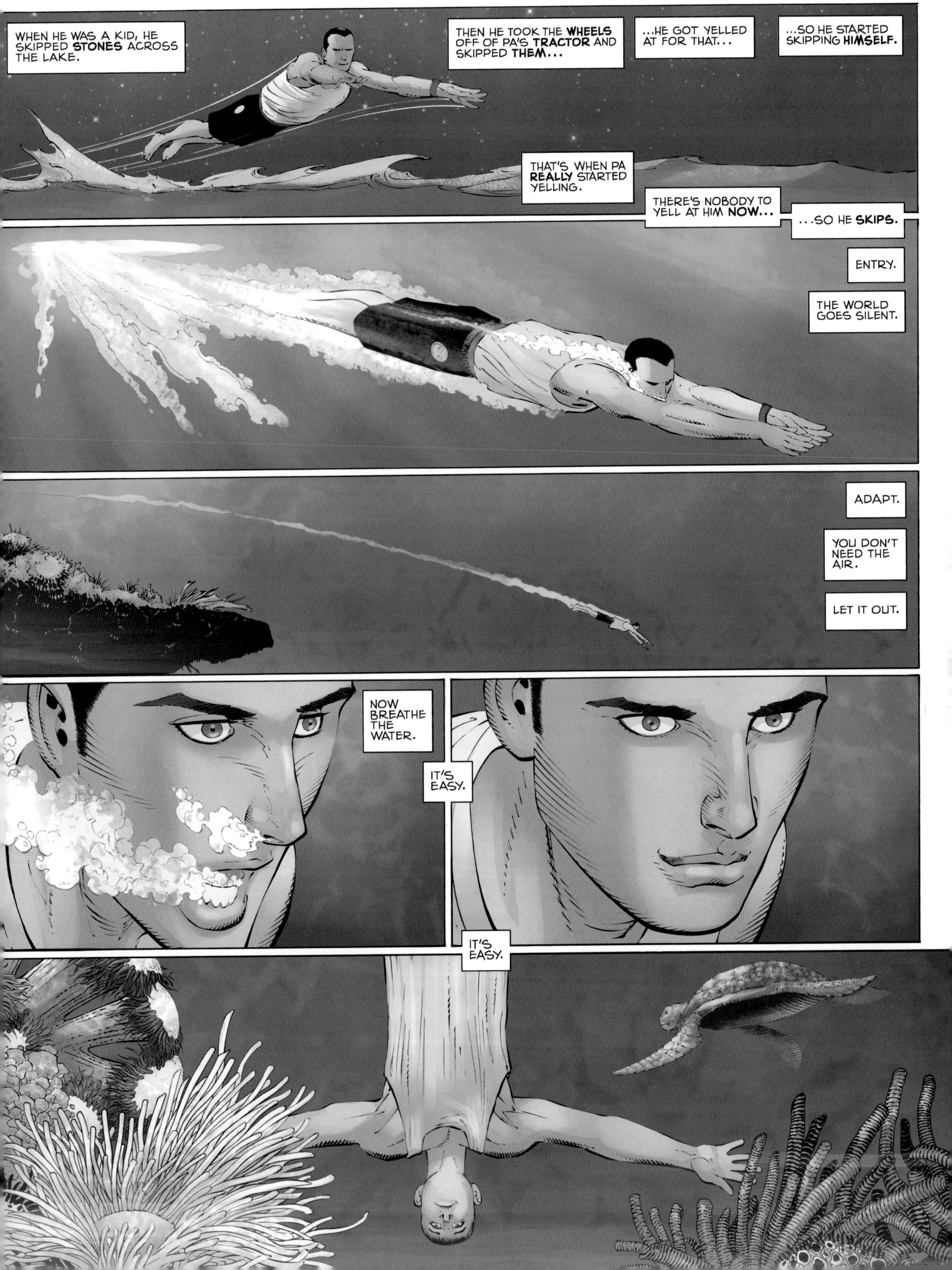
WHEN HE WAS A KID, HE SKIPPED **STONES** ACROSS THE LAKE.
THEN HE TOOK THE **WHEELS** OFF OF PA'S **TRACTOR** AND SKIPPED **THEM...**
...HE GOT YELLED AT FOR THAT...
...SO HE STARTED SKIPPING **HIMSELF.**
THAT'S WHEN PA **REALLY** STARTED YELLING.
THERE'S NOBODY TO YELL AT HIM **NOW...**
...SO HE **SKIPS.**
ENTRY.
THE WORLD GOES SILENT.
ADAPT.
YOU DON'T NEED THE AIR.
LET IT OUT.
NOW BREATHE THE WATER.
IT'S EASY.
IT'S EASY.

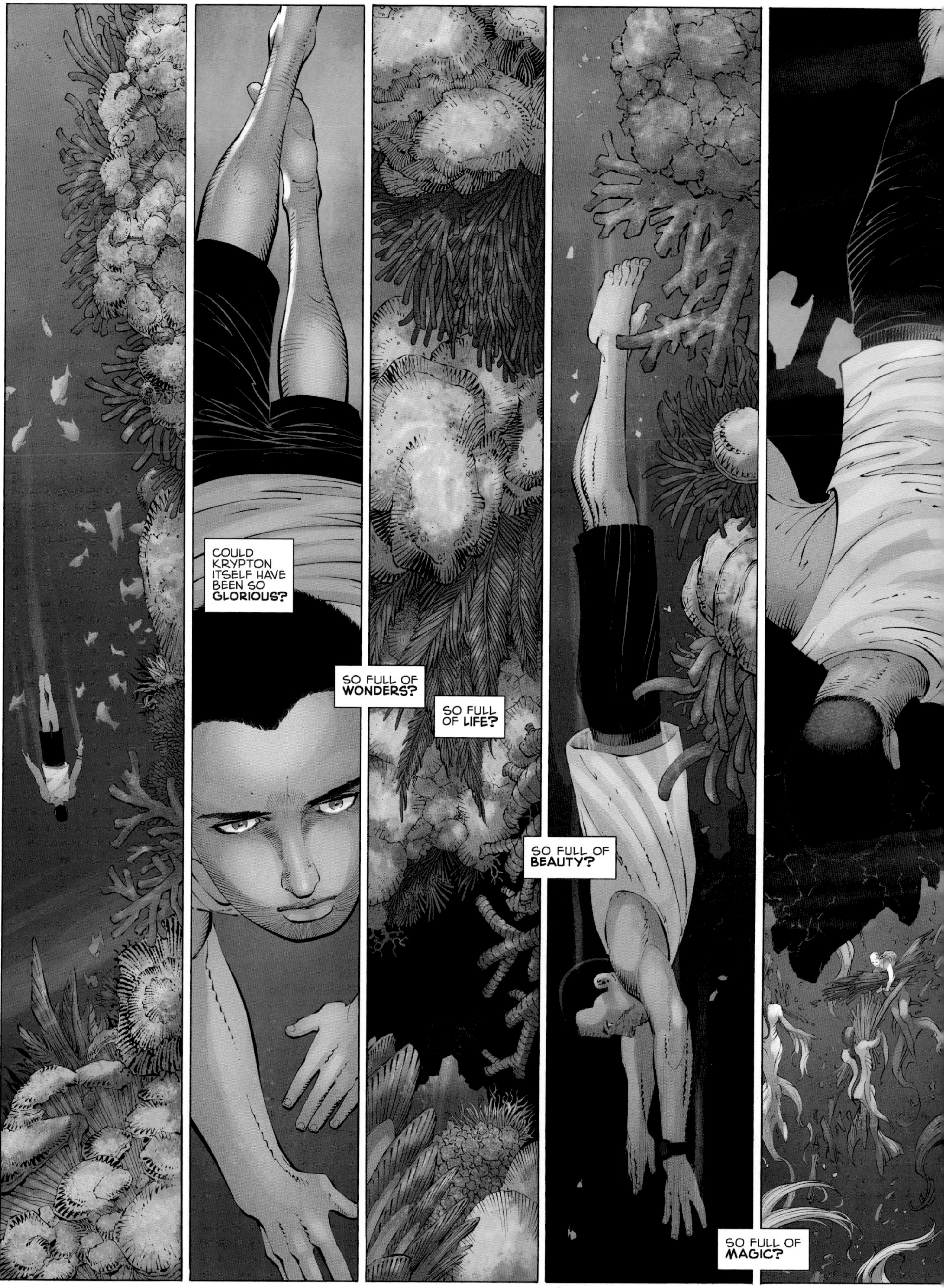
COULD KRYPTON ITSELF HAVE BEEN SO **GLORIOUS?**
SO FULL OF **WONDERS?**
SO FULL OF **LIFE?**
SO FULL OF **BEAUTY?**
SO FULL OF **MAGIC?**

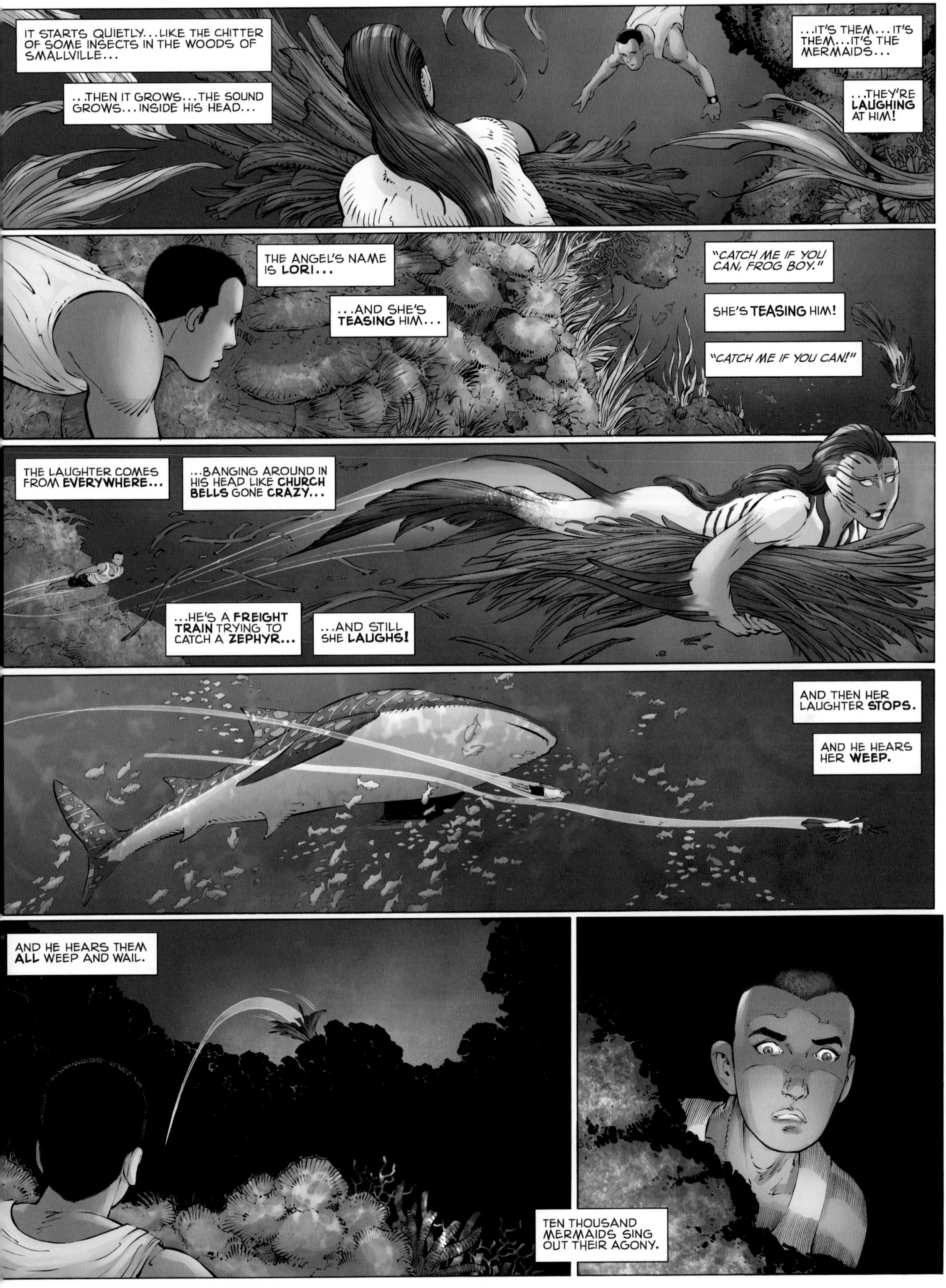
IT STARTS QUIETLY...LIKE THE CHITTER OF SOME INSECTS IN THE WOODS OF SMALLVILLE...
...THEN IT GROWS...THE SOUND GROWS...INSIDE HIS HEAD...
...IT'S THEM...IT'S THEM...IT'S THE MERMAIDS...
...THEY'RE **LAUGHING** AT HIM!
THE ANGEL'S NAME IS **LORI**...
...AND SHE'S **TEASING** HIM...
"CATCH ME IF YOU CAN, FROG BOY."
SHE'S **TEASING** HIM!
"CATCH ME IF YOU CAN!"
THE LAUGHTER COMES FROM **EVERYWHERE**...
...BANGING AROUND IN HIS HEAD LIKE **CHURCH BELLS** GONE **CRAZY**...
...HE'S A **FREIGHT TRAIN** TRYING TO CATCH A **ZEPHYR**...
...AND STILL SHE **LAUGHS!**
AND THEN HER LAUGHTER **STOPS.**
AND HE HEARS HER **WEEP.**
AND HE HEARS THEM **ALL** WEEP AND WAIL.
TEN THOUSAND MERMAIDS SING OUT THEIR AGONY.

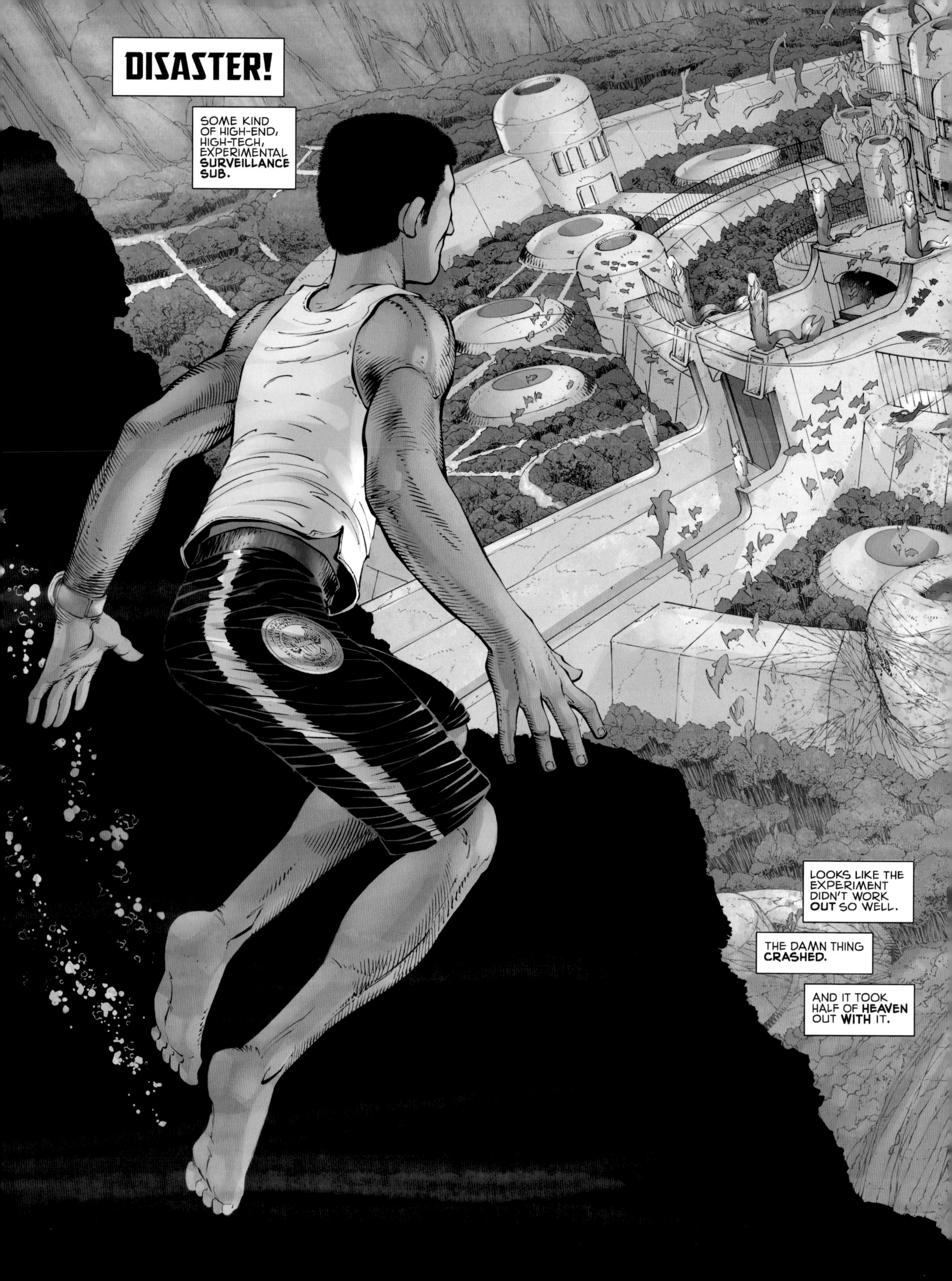
DISASTER!
SOME KIND OF HIGH-END, HIGH-TECH, EXPERIMENTAL **SURVEILLANCE SUB.**
LOOKS LIKE THE EXPERIMENT DIDN'T WORK **OUT** SO WELL.
THE DAMN THING **CRASHED.**
AND IT TOOK HALF OF **HEAVEN** OUT **WITH** IT.

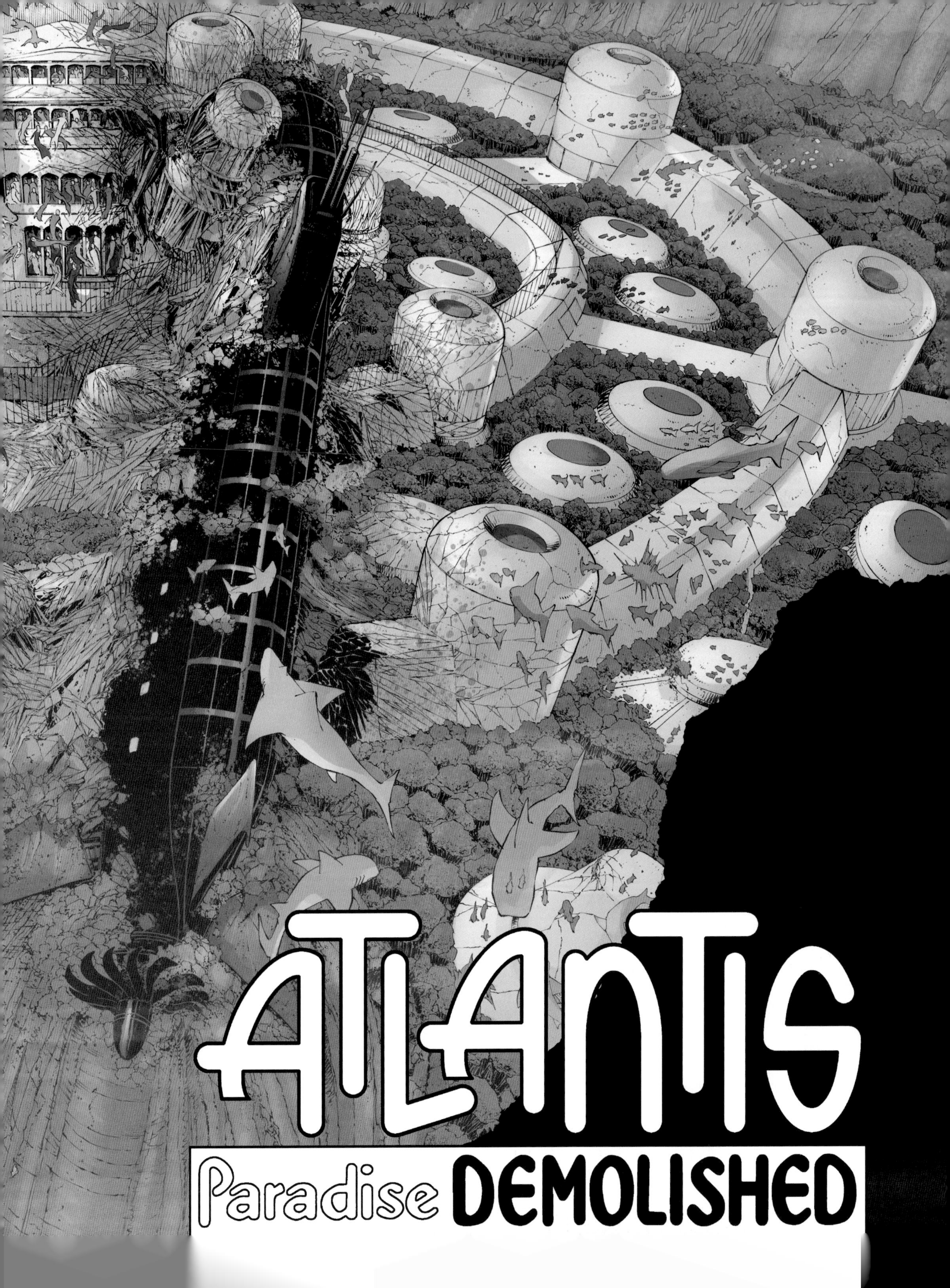
ATLANTIS
Paradise DEMOLISHED

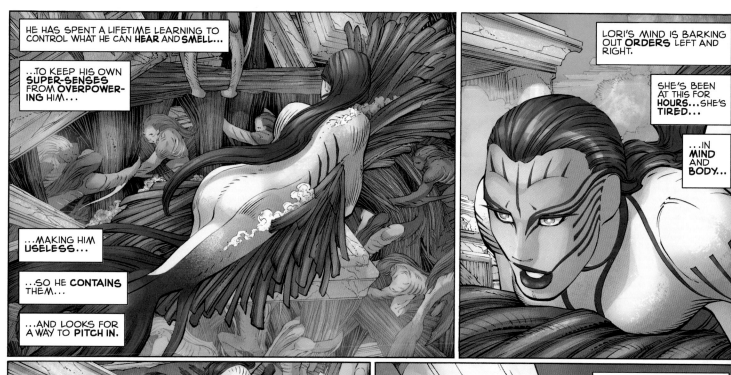

HE HAS SPENT A LIFETIME LEARNING TO CONTROL WHAT HE CAN **HEAR** AND **SMELL**...

...TO KEEP HIS OWN **SUPER-SENSES** FROM **OVERPOWER-ING** HIM...

...MAKING HIM **USELESS**...

...SO HE **CONTAINS** THEM...

...AND LOOKS FOR A WAY TO **PITCH IN**.

LORI'S MIND IS BARKING OUT **ORDERS** LEFT AND RIGHT.

SHE'S BEEN AT THIS FOR **HOURS**...SHE'S **TIRED**...

...IN **MIND** AND **BODY**...

...**COMMANDING** SCARED **CIVILIANS**...

...AND USING SEA **MUSH** AS MAKESHIFT **MORTAR**.

STILL GOT A FEW HOURS. MAYBE I CAN HELP GET THINGS STABLE BEFORE BUGLE.

OR MAYBE I'LL JUST STAY ALL DAY AND LET MYSELF GET YELLED AT.

KURTZBERG COULD USE THE **EXERCISE**.

RIGHT NOW, THESE FOLKS NEED **HELP**.

THAT'S ALL THAT MATTERS.

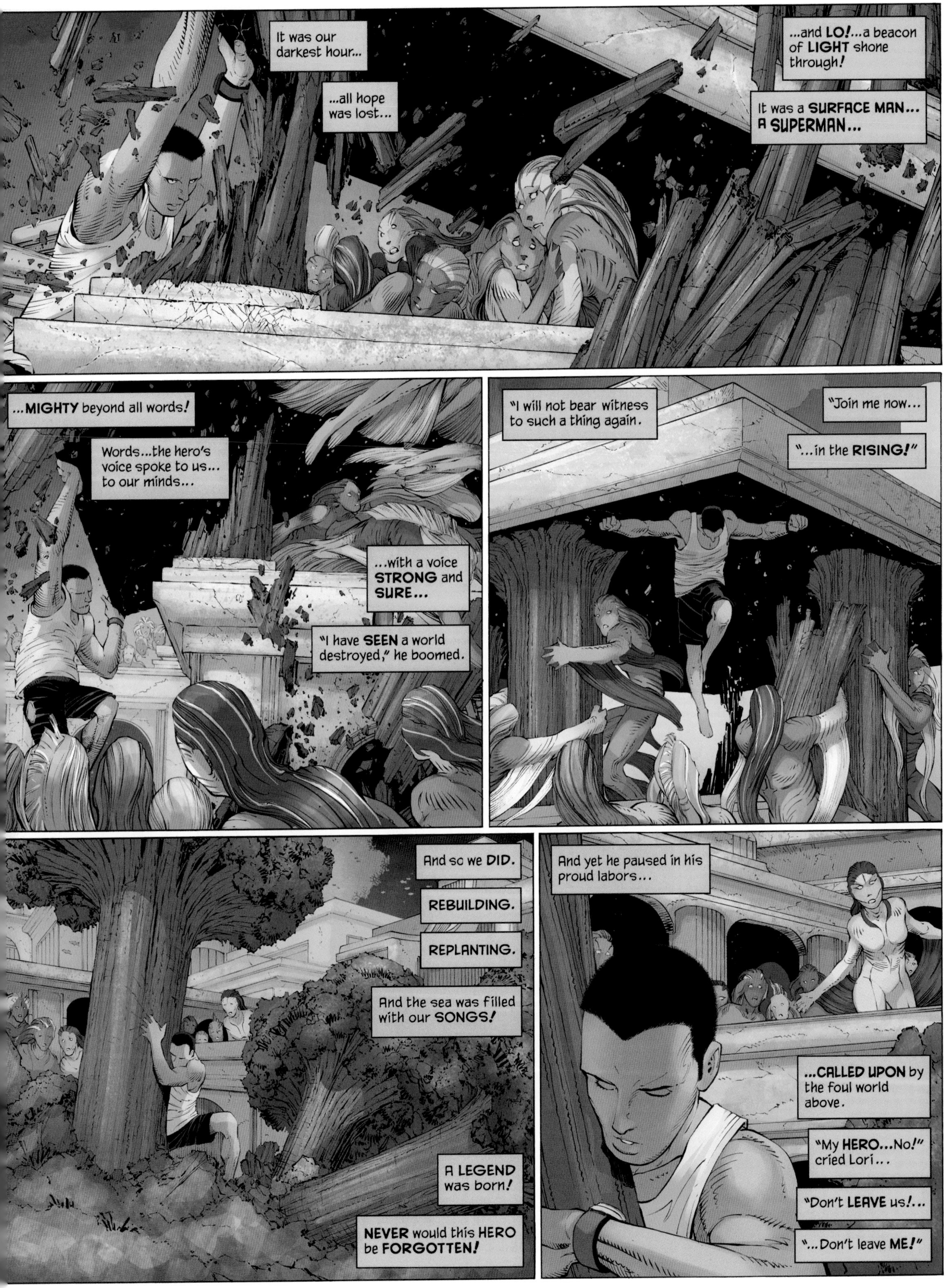
It was our darkest hour...
...all hope was lost...
...and LO!...a beacon of LIGHT shone through!
It was a SURFACE MAN... A SUPERMAN...
...MIGHTY beyond all words!
Words...the hero's voice spoke to us... to our minds...
...with a voice STRONG and SURE...
"I have SEEN a world destroyed," he boomed.
"I will not bear witness to such a thing again.
"Join me now...
"...in the RISING!"
And so we DID.
REBUILDING.
REPLANTING.
And the sea was filled with our SONGS!
A LEGEND was born!
NEVER would this HERO be FORGOTTEN!
And yet he paused in his proud labors...
...CALLED UPON by the foul world above.
"My HERO...No!" cried Lori...
"Don't LEAVE us!...
"...Don't leave ME!"

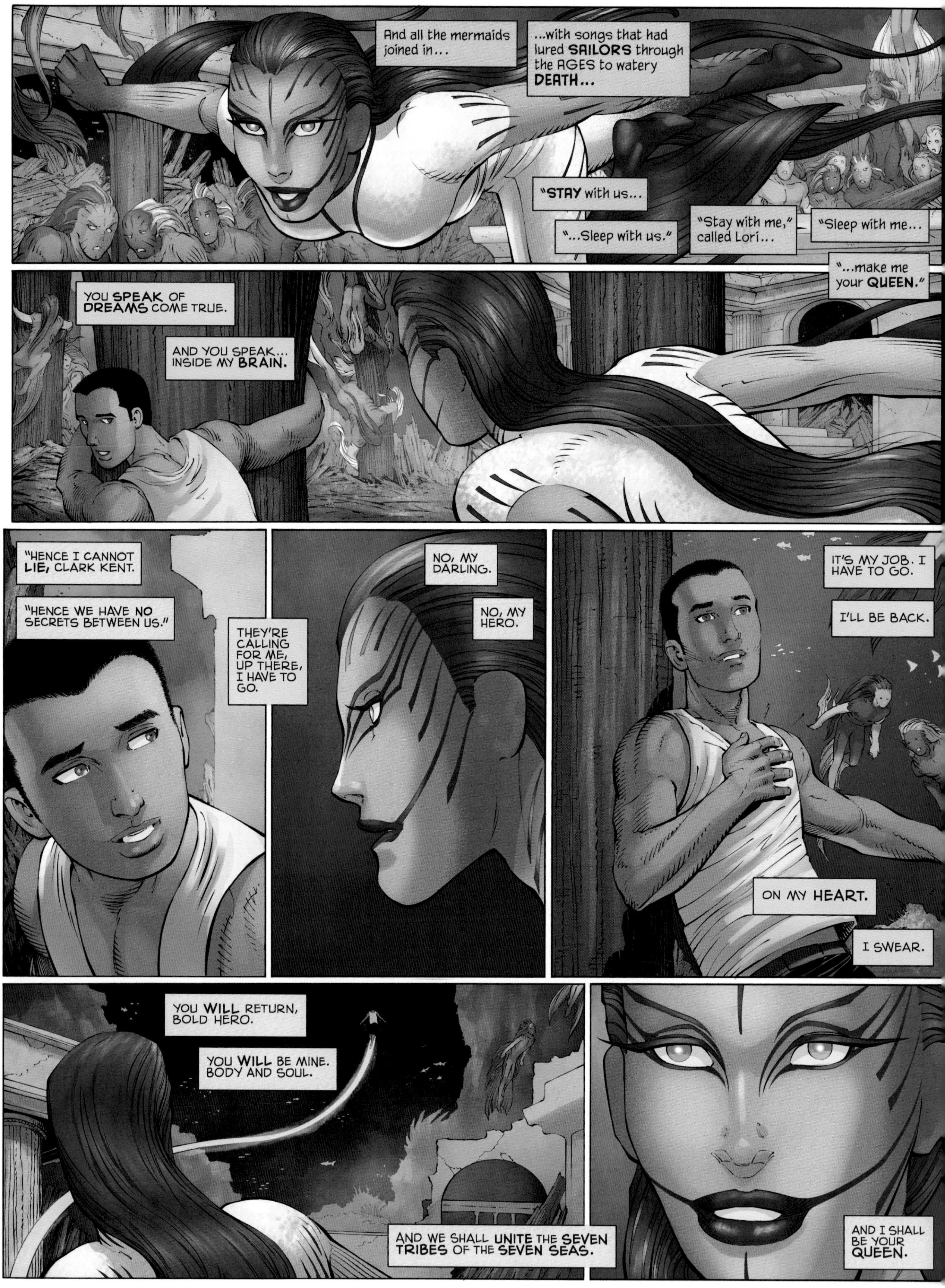
And all the mermaids joined in…
…with songs that had lured SAILORS through the AGES to watery DEATH…
"STAY with us…
"…Sleep with us."
"Stay with me," called Lori…
"Sleep with me…
"…make me your QUEEN."
YOU SPEAK OF DREAMS COME TRUE.
AND YOU SPEAK… INSIDE MY BRAIN.
"HENCE I CANNOT LIE, CLARK KENT.
"HENCE WE HAVE NO SECRETS BETWEEN US."
THEY'RE CALLING FOR ME, UP THERE, I HAVE TO GO.
NO, MY DARLING.
NO, MY HERO.
IT'S MY JOB. I HAVE TO GO.
I'LL BE BACK.
ON MY HEART.
I SWEAR.
YOU WILL RETURN, BOLD HERO.
YOU WILL BE MINE. BODY AND SOUL.
AND WE SHALL UNITE THE SEVEN TRIBES OF THE SEVEN SEAS.
AND I SHALL BE YOUR QUEEN.

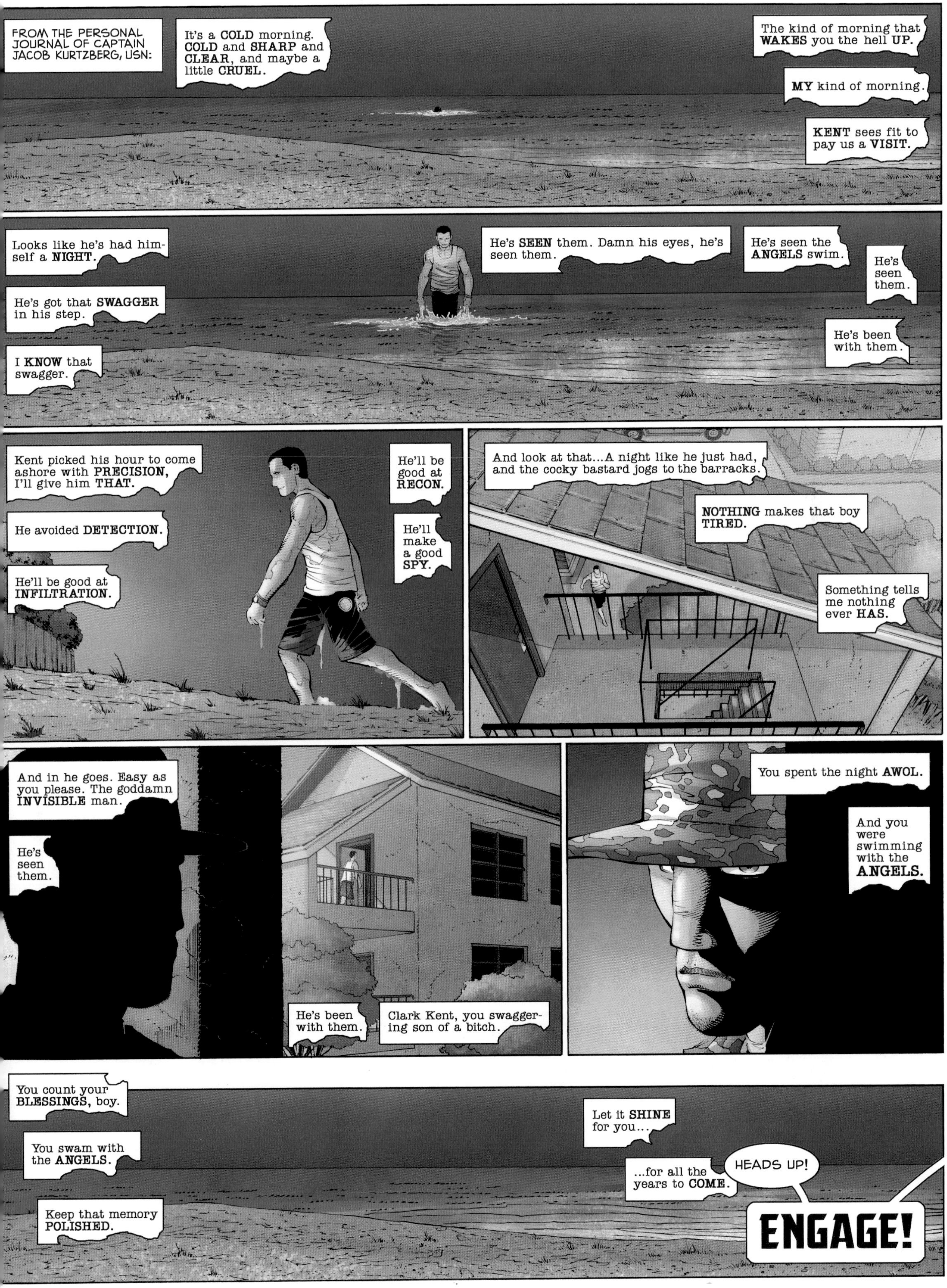
FROM THE PERSONAL JOURNAL OF CAPTAIN JACOB KURTZBERG, USN:
It's a COLD morning. COLD and SHARP and CLEAR, and maybe a little CRUEL.
The kind of morning that WAKES you the hell UP.
MY kind of morning.
KENT sees fit to pay us a VISIT.
Looks like he's had himself a NIGHT.
He's got that SWAGGER in his step.
I KNOW that swagger.
He's SEEN them. Damn his eyes, he's seen them.
He's seen the ANGELS swim.
He's seen them.
He's been with them.
Kent picked his hour to come ashore with PRECISION, I'll give him THAT.
He avoided DETECTION.
He'll be good at INFILTRATION.
He'll be good at RECON.
He'll make a good SPY.
And look at that... A night like he just had, and the cocky bastard jogs to the barracks.
NOTHING makes that boy TIRED.
Something tells me nothing ever HAS.
And in he goes. Easy as you please. The goddamn INVISIBLE man.
He's seen them.
He's been with them.
Clark Kent, you swaggering son of a bitch.
You spent the night AWOL.
And you were swimming with the ANGELS.
You count your BLESSINGS, boy.
You swam with the ANGELS.
Keep that memory POLISHED.
Let it SHINE for you...
...for all the years to COME.
HEADS UP!
ENGAGE!

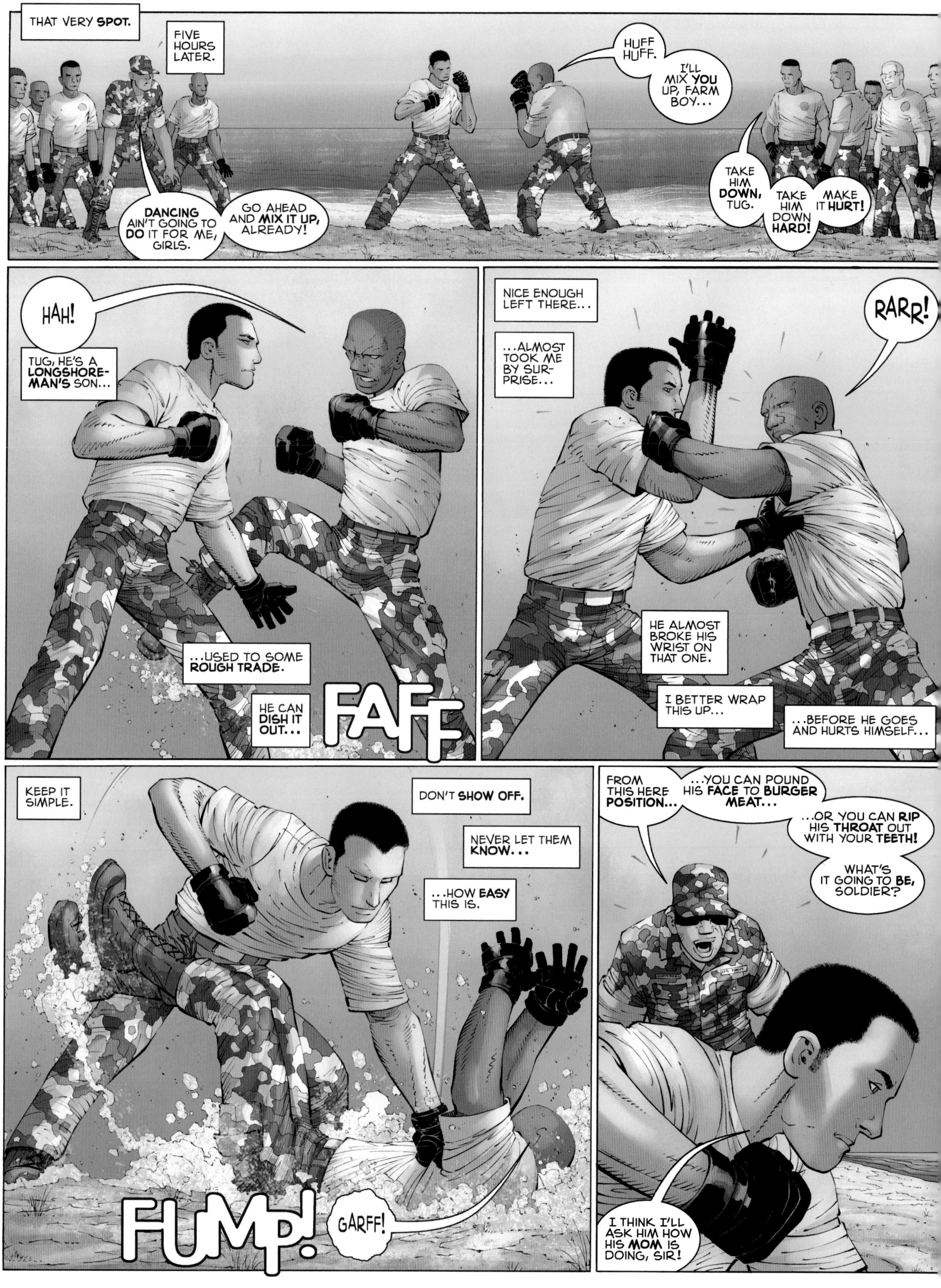
THAT VERY **SPOT**.
FIVE HOURS LATER.
HUFF HUFF.
I'LL MIX **YOU** UP, FARM BOY...
DANCING AIN'T GOING TO **DO** IT FOR ME, GIRLS.
GO AHEAD AND **MIX IT UP,** ALREADY!
TAKE HIM **DOWN,** TUG.
TAKE HIM DOWN **HARD!**
MAKE IT **HURT!**
HAH!
TUG, HE'S A **LONGSHORE-MAN'S** SON...
...USED TO SOME **ROUGH TRADE.**
HE CAN **DISH IT OUT...**
FAFF
NICE ENOUGH LEFT THERE...
...ALMOST TOOK ME BY SUR-PRISE...
RARR!
HE ALMOST BROKE HIS WRIST ON THAT ONE.
I BETTER WRAP THIS UP...
...BEFORE HE GOES AND HURTS HIMSELF...
KEEP IT SIMPLE.
DON'T **SHOW OFF.**
NEVER LET THEM **KNOW...**
...HOW **EASY** THIS IS.
FUMP!
GARFF!
FROM THIS HERE **POSITION...**
...YOU CAN POUND HIS **FACE** TO **BURGER MEAT...**
...OR YOU CAN **RIP** HIS **THROAT** OUT WITH YOUR **TEETH!**
WHAT'S IT GOING TO **BE,** SOLDIER?
I THINK I'LL ASK HIM HOW HIS **MOM** IS DOING, SIR!

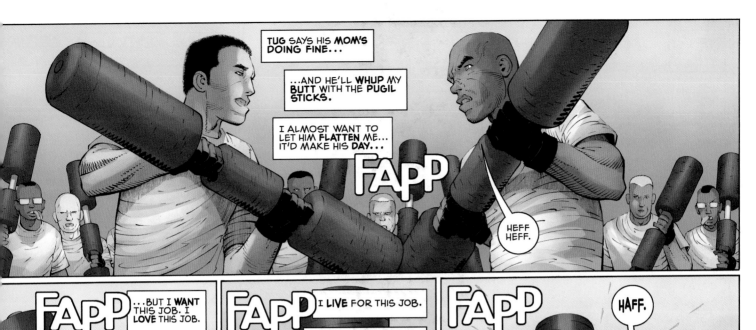

TUG SAYS HIS **MOM'S** DOING FINE...

...AND HE'LL **WHUP** MY **BUTT** WITH THE **PUGIL** STICKS.

I ALMOST WANT TO LET HIM **FLATTEN** ME... IT'D MAKE HIS **DAY**...

FAPP

HEFF HEFF.

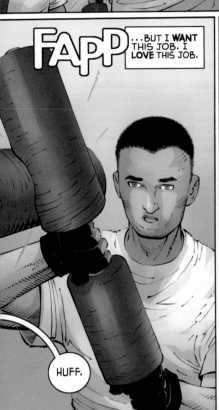

FAPP ...BUT I **WANT** THIS JOB. I **LOVE** THIS JOB.

HUFF.

FAPP I **LIVE** FOR THIS JOB.

I **WANT** TO BE A **SEAL.**

HUFF.

FAPP

HAFF.

I WANT THE **ACTION.**

I WANT THE **DANGER.**

WHUDD

AND I WANT THE **FUN.**

BLAGG.

FEEL IT, BOY. FEEL THE **POWER.** A MAN'S **LIFE.** RIGHT IN YOUR **HANDS!**

...HIS **EYES**... **BEGGING**...

...AND IT'S ALL UP TO **YOU**...HE'S **ALL YOURS**...

..YOURS TO **KILL**...

...ALL **YOURS,** AND YOURS TO **KILL**...

THIS IS GETTING VERY **WEIRD**...

...ALL AROUND ME...

...AND INSIDE ME...

...I'M **INTO** THIS...

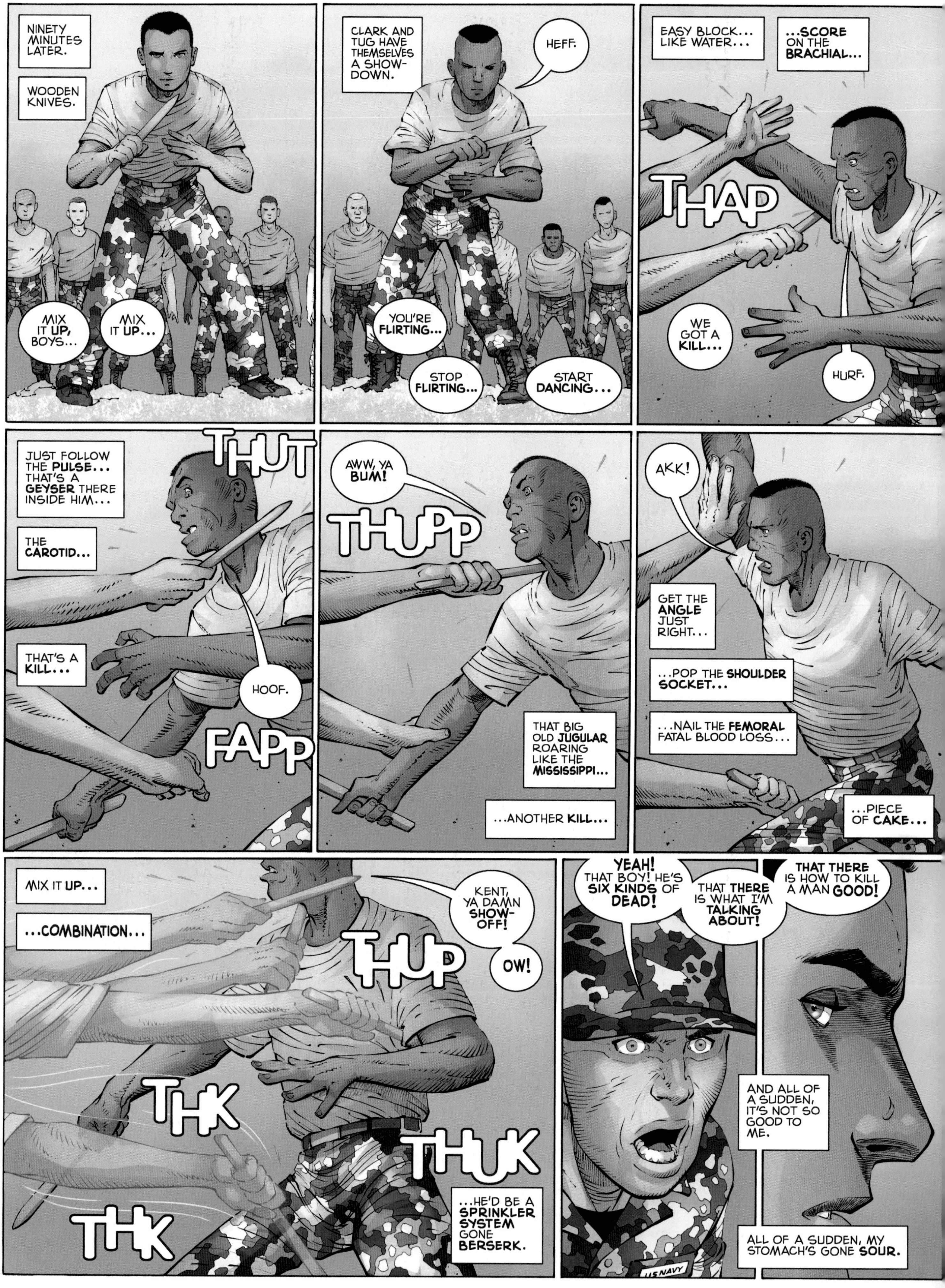
NINETY MINUTES LATER.
WOODEN KNIVES.
MIX IT UP, BOYS...
MIX IT UP...
CLARK AND TUG HAVE THEMSELVES A SHOW-DOWN.
HEFF.
YOU'RE FLIRTING...
STOP FLIRTING...
START DANCING...
EASY BLOCK... LIKE WATER...
...SCORE ON THE BRACHIAL...
THAP
WE GOT A KILL...
HURF.
JUST FOLLOW THE PULSE... THAT'S A GEYSER THERE INSIDE HIM...
THUT
THE CAROTID...
THAT'S A KILL...
HOOF.
FAPP
AWW, YA BUM!
THUPP
THAT BIG OLD JUGULAR ROARING LIKE THE MISSISSIPPI...
...ANOTHER KILL...
AKK!
GET THE ANGLE JUST RIGHT...
...POP THE SHOULDER SOCKET...
...NAIL THE FEMORAL FATAL BLOOD LOSS...
...PIECE OF CAKE...
MIX IT UP...
...COMBINATION...
KENT, YA DAMN SHOW-OFF!
THUP
OW!
THK
THUK
THK
...HE'D BE A SPRINKLER SYSTEM GONE BERSERK.
YEAH! THAT BOY! HE'S SIX KINDS OF DEAD!
THAT THERE IS WHAT I'M TALKING ABOUT!
THAT THERE IS HOW TO KILL A MAN GOOD!
U.S. NAVY
AND ALL OF A SUDDEN, IT'S NOT SO GOOD TO ME.
ALL OF A SUDDEN, MY STOMACH'S GONE SOUR.

THREE A.M.

BACK HOME, IT'D BE CRICKETS CHIRPING IN CHORUS AND FROGS GOING OFF LIKE CAR ALARMS AFTER AN EARTHQUAKE.

HERE, IT'S JUST FAT COOGAN'S SNORING HIS SMOKER'S SNORE.

ZZZSNORT.

NO WONDER CLARK CAN'T SLEEP. ALL THIS NOISE...

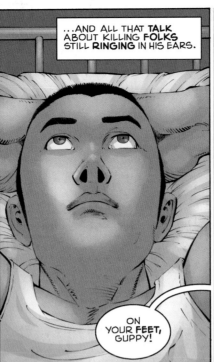

...AND ALL THAT TALK ABOUT KILLING FOLKS STILL RINGING IN HIS EARS.

ON YOUR FEET, GUPPY!

NO REST FOR THE WICKED, KID! STEP LIVELY!

HUSTLE THE BOYS TO BRIEFING ROOM ALPHA!

SIR YES SIR!

RIGHT AWAY, SIR!

BRIEFING ROOM ALPHA!

GOT US A MAYDAY CALL... SHE'S AN OIL TANKER OFF FORTY WEST...

...DRONES SHOW PIRATE ACTION.

IT'S LOOKING LIKE A COMBAT DIVE.

SOUNDS LIKE FUN!

YOU BOYS AIN'T READY...BUT YOU'RE THE ONLY ONES NEAR ENOUGH.

FUN IT WON'T BE, SAILOR. THAT MOMMA, SHE'S HAULING HERSELF ONE HOT LOAD OF CRUDE ...AND JET FUEL. ENOUGH TO TORCH NEWARK!

WE GO IN FIFTEEN, AND WE GO IN WET! GET MOVING!

FIFTEEN.

WE GET MOVING.

WE GO IN WET.

IT'S FUN ANYWAY.

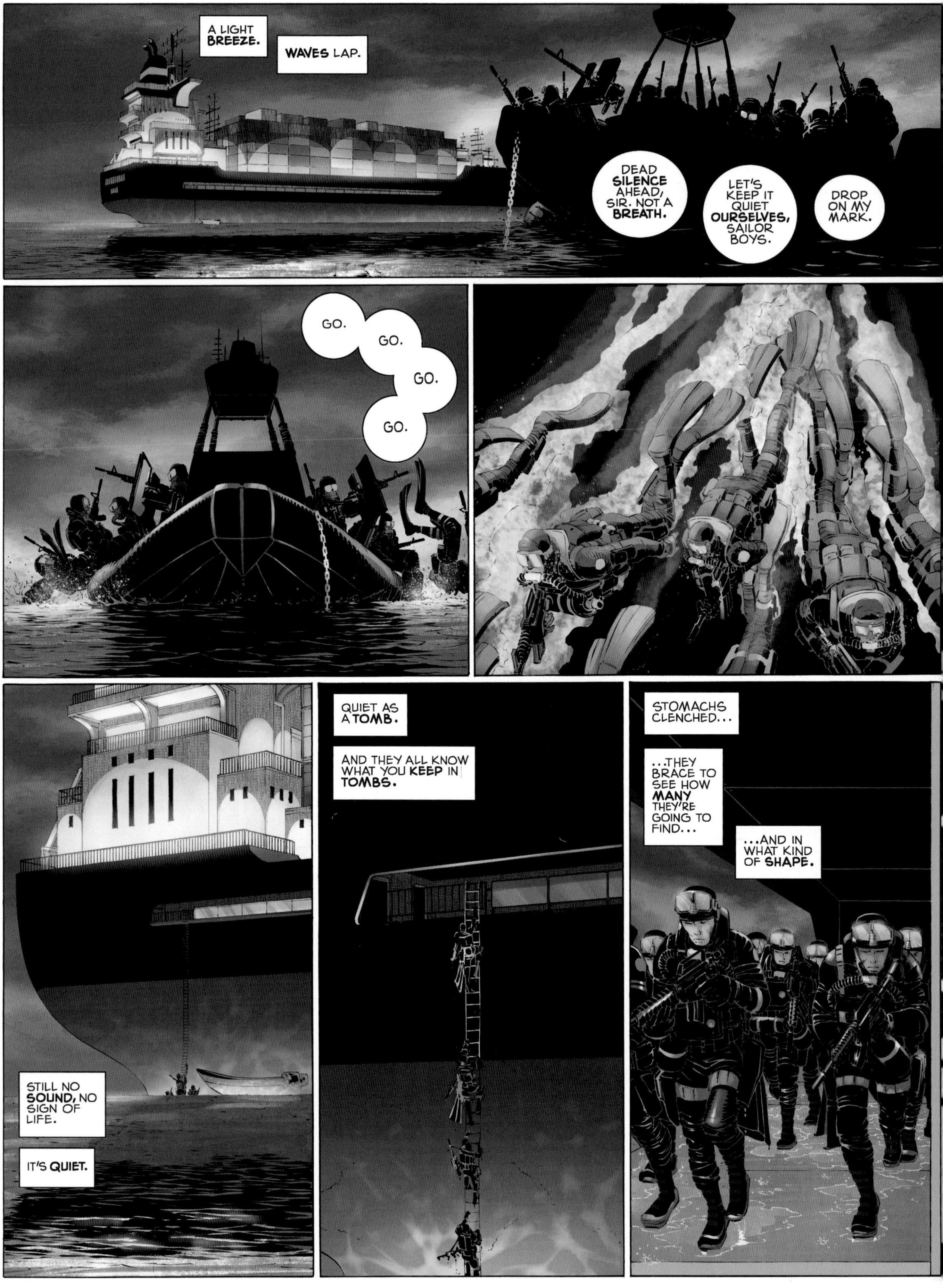
A LIGHT **BREEZE.**
WAVES LAP.
DEAD **SILENCE** AHEAD, SIR. NOT A **BREATH.**
LET'S KEEP IT QUIET **OURSELVES,** SAILOR BOYS.
DROP ON MY MARK.
GO.
GO.
GO.
GO.
STILL NO **SOUND,** NO SIGN OF LIFE.
IT'S **QUIET.**
QUIET AS A **TOMB.**
AND THEY ALL KNOW WHAT YOU **KEEP** IN **TOMBS.**
STOMACHS CLENCHED...
...THEY BRACE TO SEE HOW **MANY** THEY'RE GOING TO FIND...
...AND IN WHAT KIND OF **SHAPE.**

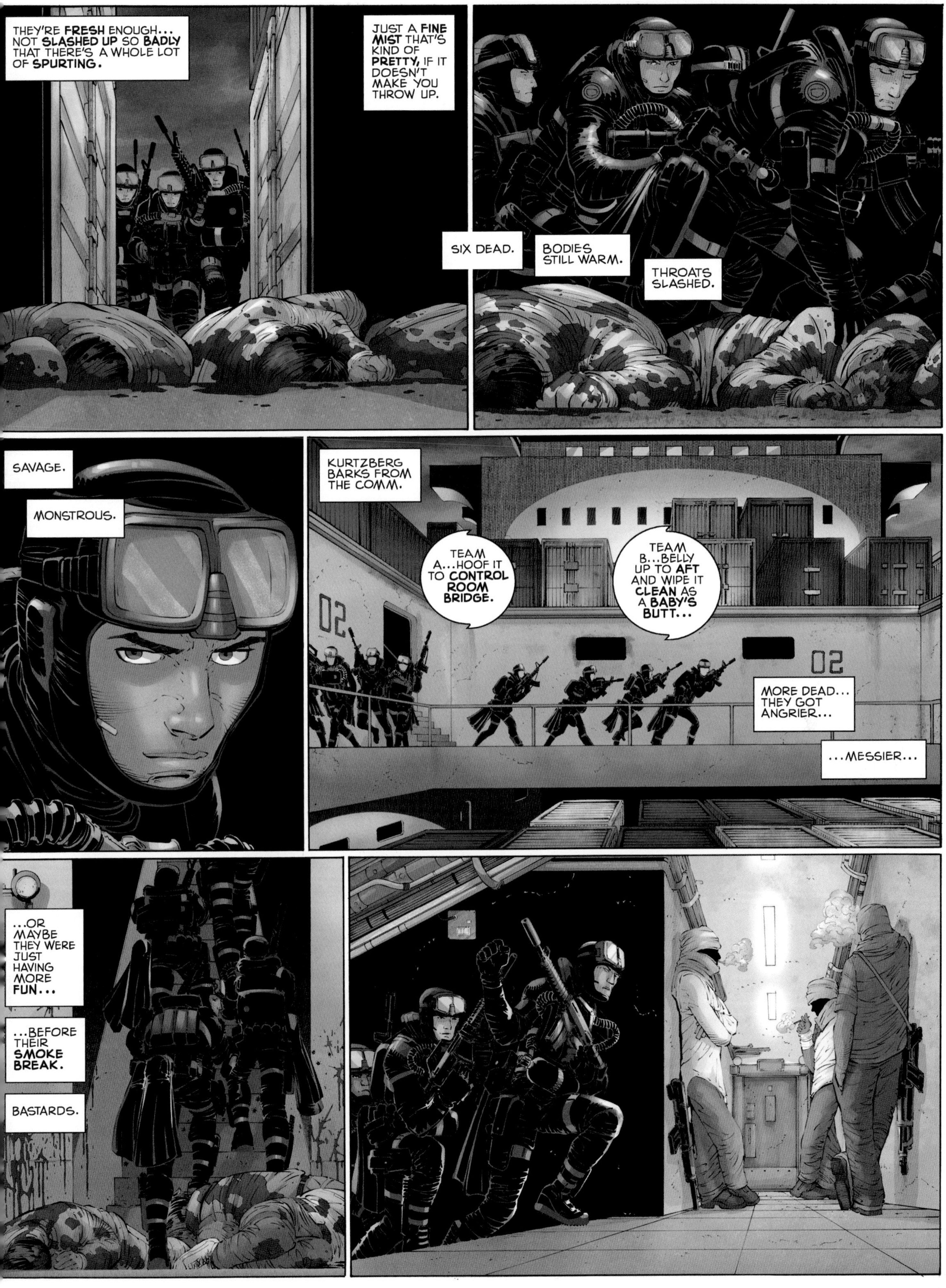
THEY'RE FRESH ENOUGH... NOT SLASHED UP SO BADLY THAT THERE'S A WHOLE LOT OF SPURTING.
JUST A FINE MIST THAT'S KIND OF PRETTY, IF IT DOESN'T MAKE YOU THROW UP.
SIX DEAD.
BODIES STILL WARM.
THROATS SLASHED.
SAVAGE.
MONSTROUS.
KURTZBERG BARKS FROM THE COMM.
TEAM A...HOOF IT TO CONTROL ROOM BRIDGE.
TEAM B...BELLY UP TO AFT AND WIPE IT CLEAN AS A BABY'S BUTT...
02
02
MORE DEAD... THEY GOT ANGRIER...
...MESSIER...
...OR MAYBE THEY WERE JUST HAVING MORE FUN...
...BEFORE THEIR SMOKE BREAK.
BASTARDS.

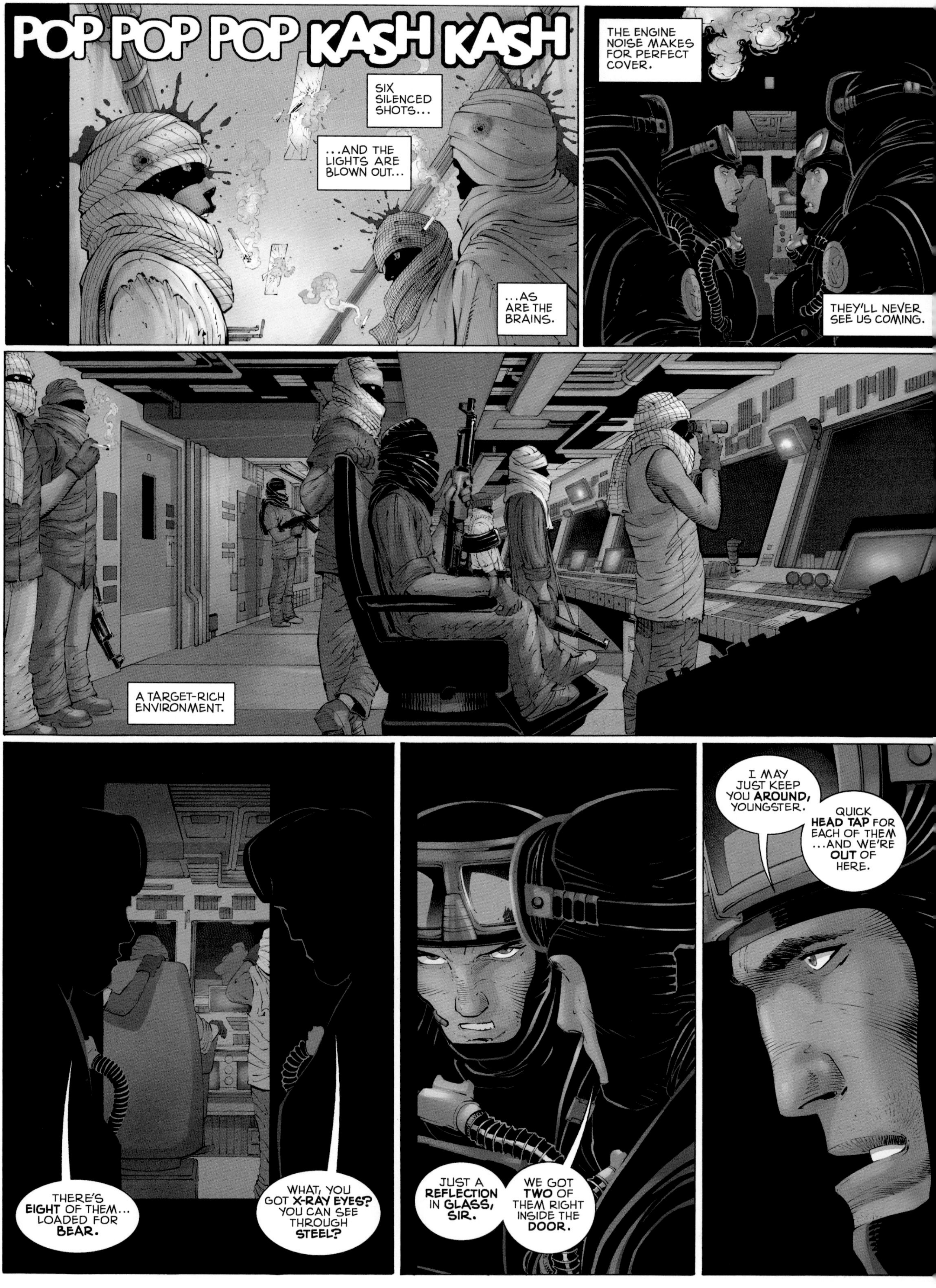
POP POP POP KASH KASH
SIX SILENCED SHOTS...
...AND THE LIGHTS ARE BLOWN OUT...
...AS ARE THE BRAINS.
THE ENGINE NOISE MAKES FOR PERFECT COVER.
THEY'LL NEVER SEE US COMING.
A TARGET-RICH ENVIRONMENT.
THERE'S EIGHT OF THEM... LOADED FOR BEAR.
WHAT, YOU GOT X-RAY EYES? YOU CAN SEE THROUGH STEEL?
JUST A REFLECTION IN GLASS, SIR.
WE GOT TWO OF THEM RIGHT INSIDE THE DOOR.
I MAY JUST KEEP YOU AROUND, YOUNGSTER.
QUICK HEAD TAP FOR EACH OF THEM ...AND WE'RE OUT OF HERE.

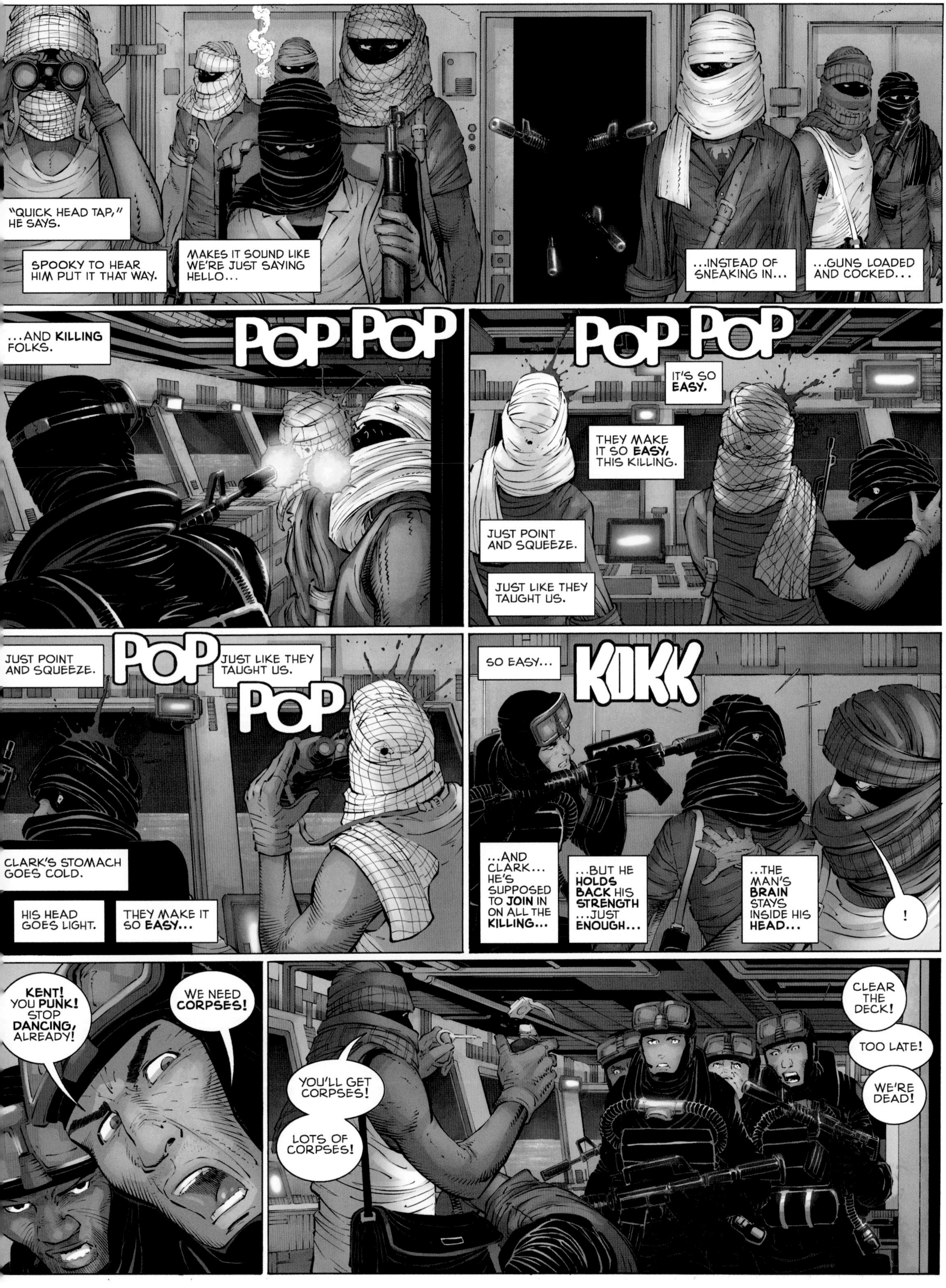
"QUICK HEAD TAP," HE SAYS.
SPOOKY TO HEAR HIM PUT IT THAT WAY.
MAKES IT SOUND LIKE WE'RE JUST SAYING HELLO...
...INSTEAD OF SNEAKING IN...
...GUNS LOADED AND COCKED...
...AND KILLING FOLKS.
POP POP
POP POP
IT'S SO EASY.
THEY MAKE IT SO EASY, THIS KILLING.
JUST POINT AND SQUEEZE.
JUST LIKE THEY TAUGHT US.
JUST POINT AND SQUEEZE.
POP
JUST LIKE THEY TAUGHT US.
POP
CLARK'S STOMACH GOES COLD.
HIS HEAD GOES LIGHT.
THEY MAKE IT SO EASY...
SO EASY...
KOKK
...AND CLARK... HE'S SUPPOSED TO JOIN IN ON ALL THE KILLING...
...BUT HE HOLDS BACK HIS STRENGTH ...JUST ENOUGH...
...THE MAN'S BRAIN STAYS INSIDE HIS HEAD...
!
KENT! YOU PUNK! STOP DANCING, ALREADY!
WE NEED CORPSES!
YOU'LL GET CORPSES!
LOTS OF CORPSES!
CLEAR THE DECK!
TOO LATE!
WE'RE DEAD!

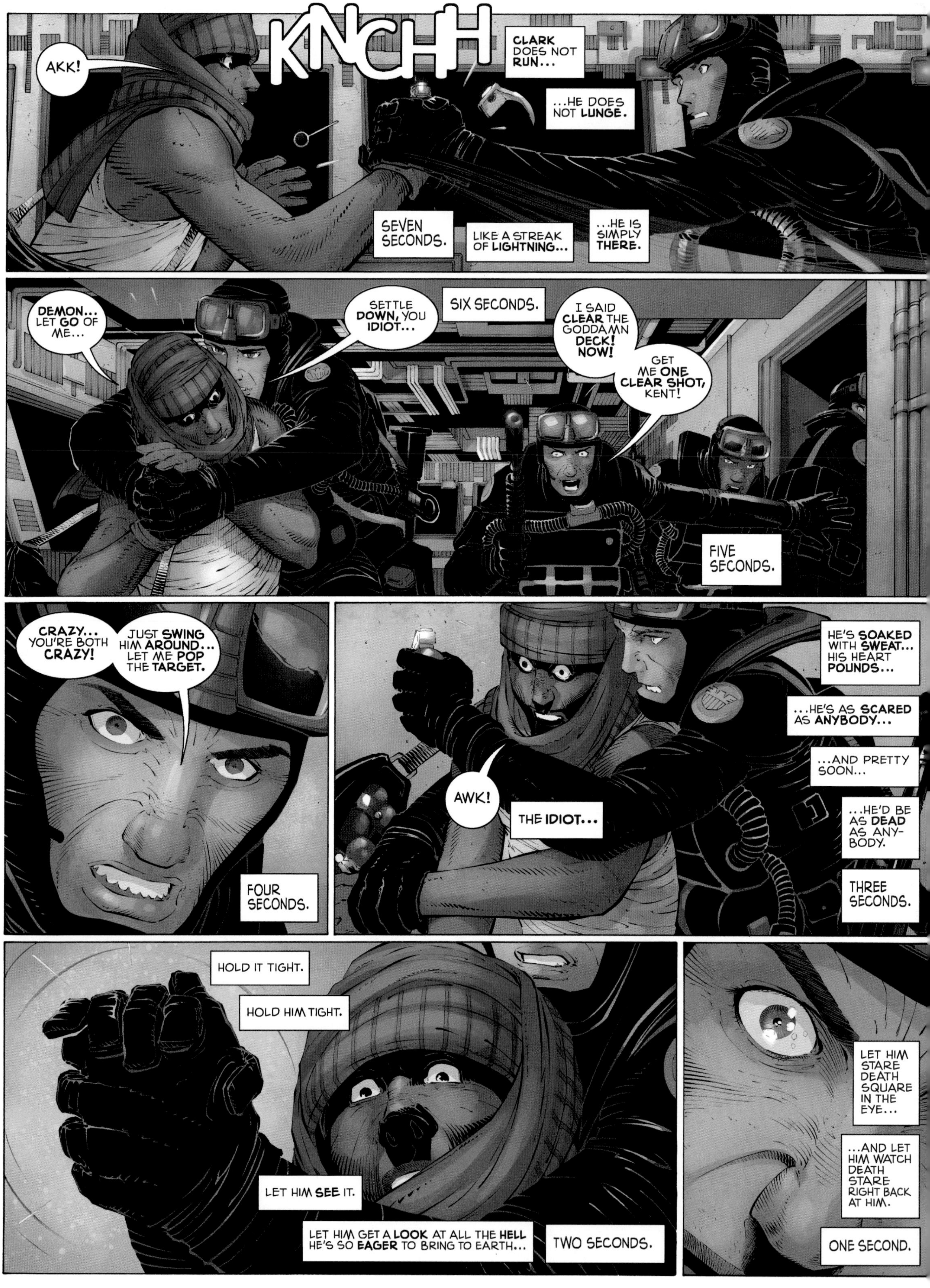
KNCHH
AKK!
CLARK DOES NOT RUN...
...HE DOES NOT LUNGE.
SEVEN SECONDS.
LIKE A STREAK OF LIGHTNING...
...HE IS SIMPLY THERE.
DEMON... LET GO OF ME...
SETTLE DOWN, YOU IDIOT...
SIX SECONDS.
I SAID CLEAR THE GODDAMN DECK! NOW!
GET ME ONE CLEAR SHOT, KENT!
FIVE SECONDS.
CRAZY... YOU'RE BOTH CRAZY!
JUST SWING HIM AROUND... LET ME POP THE TARGET.
FOUR SECONDS.
HE'S SOAKED WITH SWEAT... HIS HEART POUNDS...
...HE'S AS SCARED AS ANYBODY...
...AND PRETTY SOON...
AWK!
THE IDIOT...
...HE'D BE AS DEAD AS ANY-BODY.
THREE SECONDS.
HOLD IT TIGHT.
HOLD HIM TIGHT.
LET HIM SEE IT.
LET HIM GET A LOOK AT ALL THE HELL HE'S SO EAGER TO BRING TO EARTH...
TWO SECONDS.
LET HIM STARE DEATH SQUARE IN THE EYE...
...AND LET HIM WATCH DEATH STARE RIGHT BACK AT HIM.
ONE SECOND.

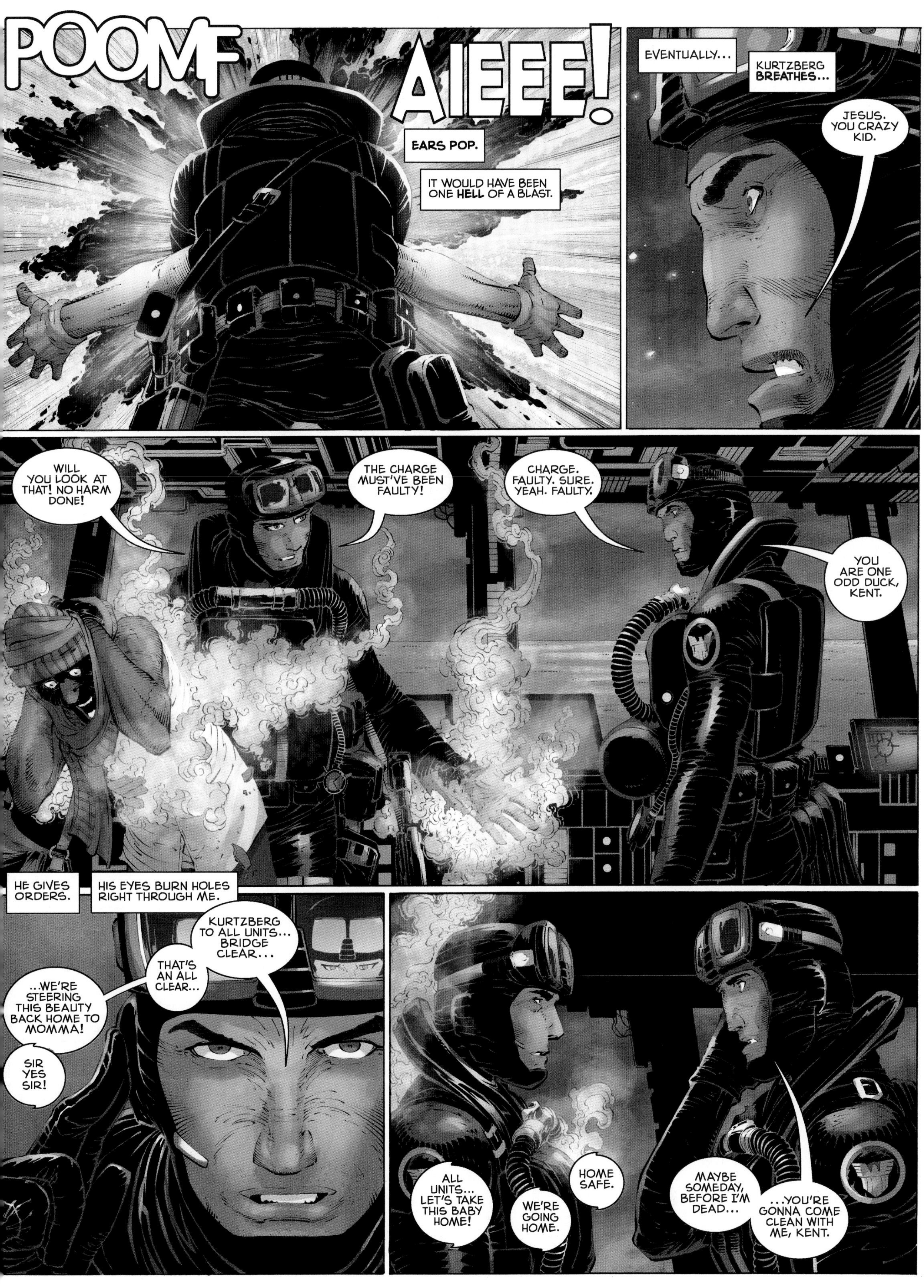
POOMF
AIEEE!
EARS POP.
IT WOULD HAVE BEEN ONE HELL OF A BLAST.
EVENTUALLY...
KURTZBERG BREATHES...
JESUS. YOU CRAZY KID.
WILL YOU LOOK AT THAT! NO HARM DONE!
THE CHARGE MUST'VE BEEN FAULTY!
CHARGE. FAULTY. SURE. YEAH. FAULTY.
YOU ARE ONE ODD DUCK, KENT.
HE GIVES ORDERS.
HIS EYES BURN HOLES RIGHT THROUGH ME.
KURTZBERG TO ALL UNITS... BRIDGE CLEAR...
THAT'S AN ALL CLEAR...
...WE'RE STEERING THIS BEAUTY BACK HOME TO MOMMA!
SIR YES SIR!
ALL UNITS... LET'S TAKE THIS BABY HOME!
WE'RE GOING HOME.
HOME SAFE.
MAYBE SOMEDAY, BEFORE I'M DEAD...
...YOU'RE GONNA COME CLEAN WITH ME, KENT.

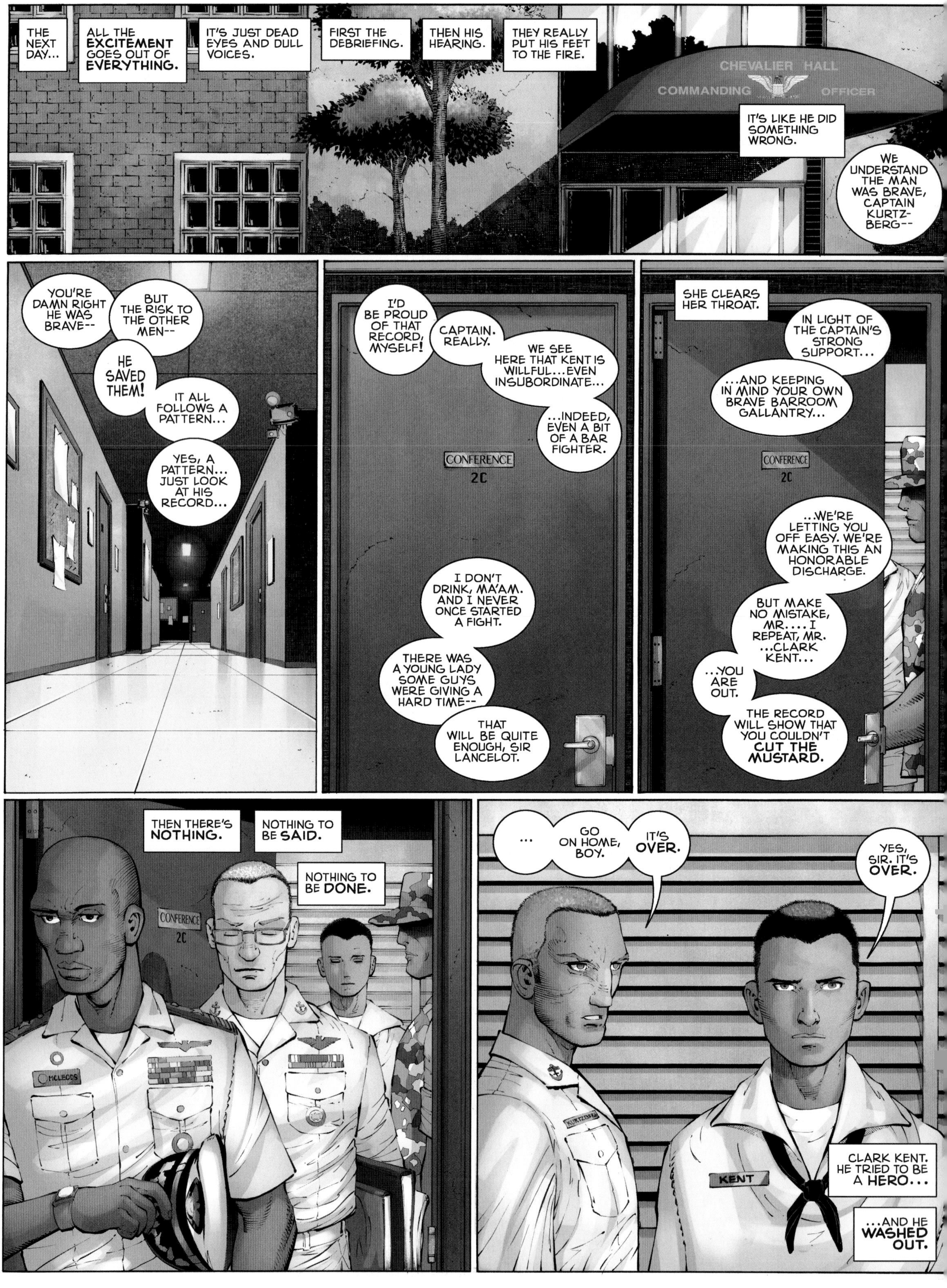
THE NEXT DAY...
ALL THE EXCITEMENT GOES OUT OF EVERYTHING.
IT'S JUST DEAD EYES AND DULL VOICES.
FIRST THE DEBRIEFING.
THEN HIS HEARING.
THEY REALLY PUT HIS FEET TO THE FIRE.
CHEVALIER HALL
COMMANDING OFFICER
IT'S LIKE HE DID SOMETHING WRONG.
WE UNDERSTAND THE MAN WAS BRAVE, CAPTAIN KURTZ-BERG--
YOU'RE DAMN RIGHT HE WAS BRAVE--
BUT THE RISK TO THE OTHER MEN--
HE SAVED THEM!
IT ALL FOLLOWS A PATTERN...
YES, A PATTERN... JUST LOOK AT HIS RECORD...
I'D BE PROUD OF THAT RECORD, MYSELF!
CAPTAIN. REALLY.
WE SEE HERE THAT KENT IS WILLFUL... EVEN INSUBORDINATE...
...INDEED, EVEN A BIT OF A BAR FIGHTER.
CONFERENCE
2C
I DON'T DRINK, MA'AM. AND I NEVER ONCE STARTED A FIGHT.
THERE WAS A YOUNG LADY SOME GUYS WERE GIVING A HARD TIME--
THAT WILL BE QUITE ENOUGH, SIR LANCELOT.
SHE CLEARS HER THROAT.
IN LIGHT OF THE CAPTAIN'S STRONG SUPPORT...
...AND KEEPING IN MIND YOUR OWN BRAVE BARROOM GALLANTRY...
CONFERENCE
2C
...WE'RE LETTING YOU OFF EASY. WE'RE MAKING THIS AN HONORABLE DISCHARGE.
BUT MAKE NO MISTAKE, MR.... I REPEAT, MR. ...CLARK KENT...
...YOU ARE OUT.
THE RECORD WILL SHOW THAT YOU COULDN'T CUT THE MUSTARD.
THEN THERE'S NOTHING.
NOTHING TO BE SAID.
NOTHING TO BE DONE.
CONFERENCE
2C
MCLEODS
...
GO ON HOME, BOY.
IT'S OVER.
YES, SIR. IT'S OVER.
KURTZBERG
KENT
CLARK KENT. HE TRIED TO BE A HERO...
...AND HE WASHED OUT.

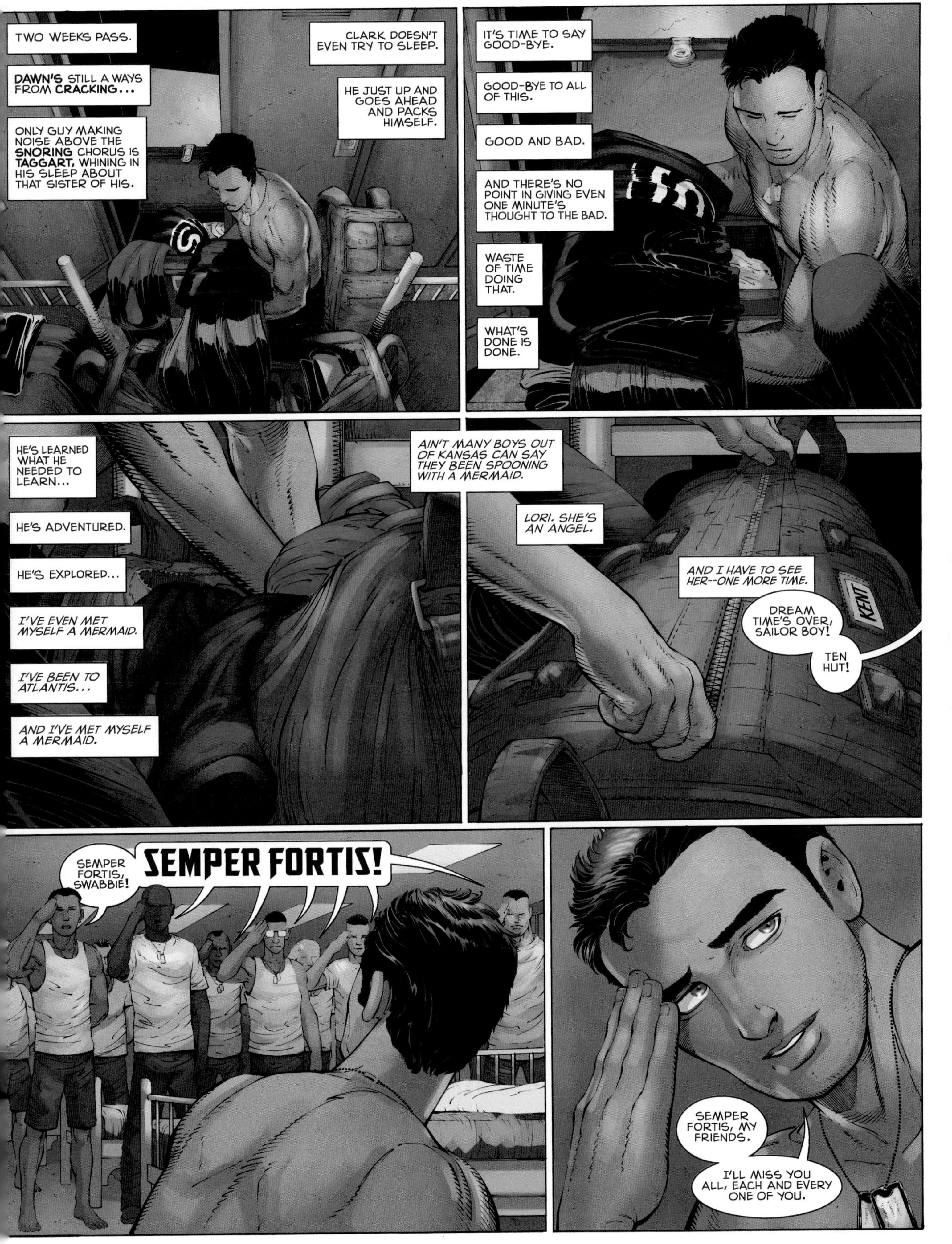
TWO WEEKS PASS.
DAWN'S STILL A WAYS FROM CRACKING...
ONLY GUY MAKING NOISE ABOVE THE SNORING CHORUS IS TAGGART, WHINING IN HIS SLEEP ABOUT THAT SISTER OF HIS.
CLARK DOESN'T EVEN TRY TO SLEEP.
HE JUST UP AND GOES AHEAD AND PACKS HIMSELF.
IT'S TIME TO SAY GOOD-BYE.
GOOD-BYE TO ALL OF THIS.
GOOD AND BAD.
AND THERE'S NO POINT IN GIVING EVEN ONE MINUTE'S THOUGHT TO THE BAD.
WASTE OF TIME DOING THAT.
WHAT'S DONE IS DONE.
HE'S LEARNED WHAT HE NEEDED TO LEARN...
HE'S ADVENTURED.
HE'S EXPLORED...
I'VE EVEN MET MYSELF A MERMAID.
I'VE BEEN TO ATLANTIS...
AND I'VE MET MYSELF A MERMAID.
AIN'T MANY BOYS OUT OF KANSAS CAN SAY THEY BEEN SPOONING WITH A MERMAID.
LORI. SHE'S AN ANGEL.
AND I HAVE TO SEE HER--ONE MORE TIME.
KENT
DREAM TIME'S OVER, SAILOR BOY!
TEN HUT!
SEMPER FORTIS, SWABBIE!
SEMPER FORTIS!
SEMPER FORTIS, MY FRIENDS.
I'LL MISS YOU ALL, EACH AND EVERY ONE OF YOU.

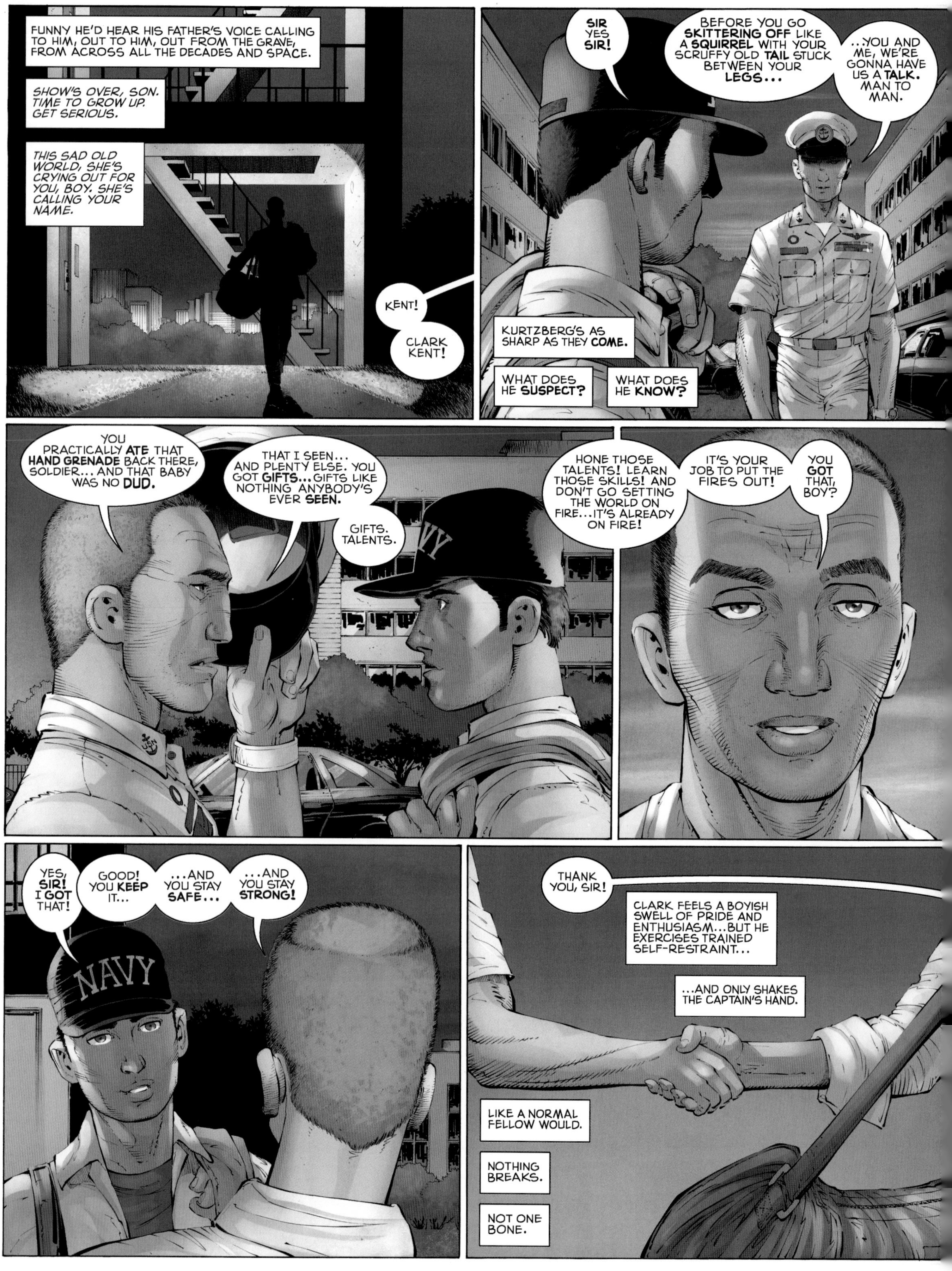
FUNNY HE'D HEAR HIS FATHER'S VOICE CALLING TO HIM, OUT TO HIM, OUT FROM THE GRAVE, FROM ACROSS ALL THE DECADES AND SPACE.
SHOW'S OVER, SON. TIME TO GROW UP. GET SERIOUS.
THIS SAD OLD WORLD, SHE'S CRYING OUT FOR YOU, BOY. SHE'S CALLING YOUR NAME.
KENT!
CLARK KENT!
SIR YES SIR!
BEFORE YOU GO SKITTERING OFF LIKE A SQUIRREL WITH YOUR SCRUFFY OLD TAIL STUCK BETWEEN YOUR LEGS...
...YOU AND ME, WE'RE GONNA HAVE US A TALK. MAN TO MAN.
KURTZBERG'S AS SHARP AS THEY COME.
WHAT DOES HE SUSPECT?
WHAT DOES HE KNOW?
YOU PRACTICALLY ATE THAT HAND GRENADE BACK THERE, SOLDIER... AND THAT BABY WAS NO DUD.
THAT I SEEN... AND PLENTY ELSE. YOU GOT GIFTS... GIFTS LIKE NOTHING ANYBODY'S EVER SEEN.
GIFTS. TALENTS.
HONE THOSE TALENTS! LEARN THOSE SKILLS! AND DON'T GO SETTING THE WORLD ON FIRE... IT'S ALREADY ON FIRE!
IT'S YOUR JOB TO PUT THE FIRES OUT!
YOU GOT THAT, BOY?
YES, SIR! I GOT THAT!
GOOD! YOU KEEP IT...
...AND YOU STAY SAFE...
...AND YOU STAY STRONG!
NAVY
THANK YOU, SIR!
CLARK FEELS A BOYISH SWELL OF PRIDE AND ENTHUSIASM... BUT HE EXERCISES TRAINED SELF-RESTRAINT...
...AND ONLY SHAKES THE CAPTAIN'S HAND.
LIKE A NORMAL FELLOW WOULD.
NOTHING BREAKS.
NOT ONE BONE.

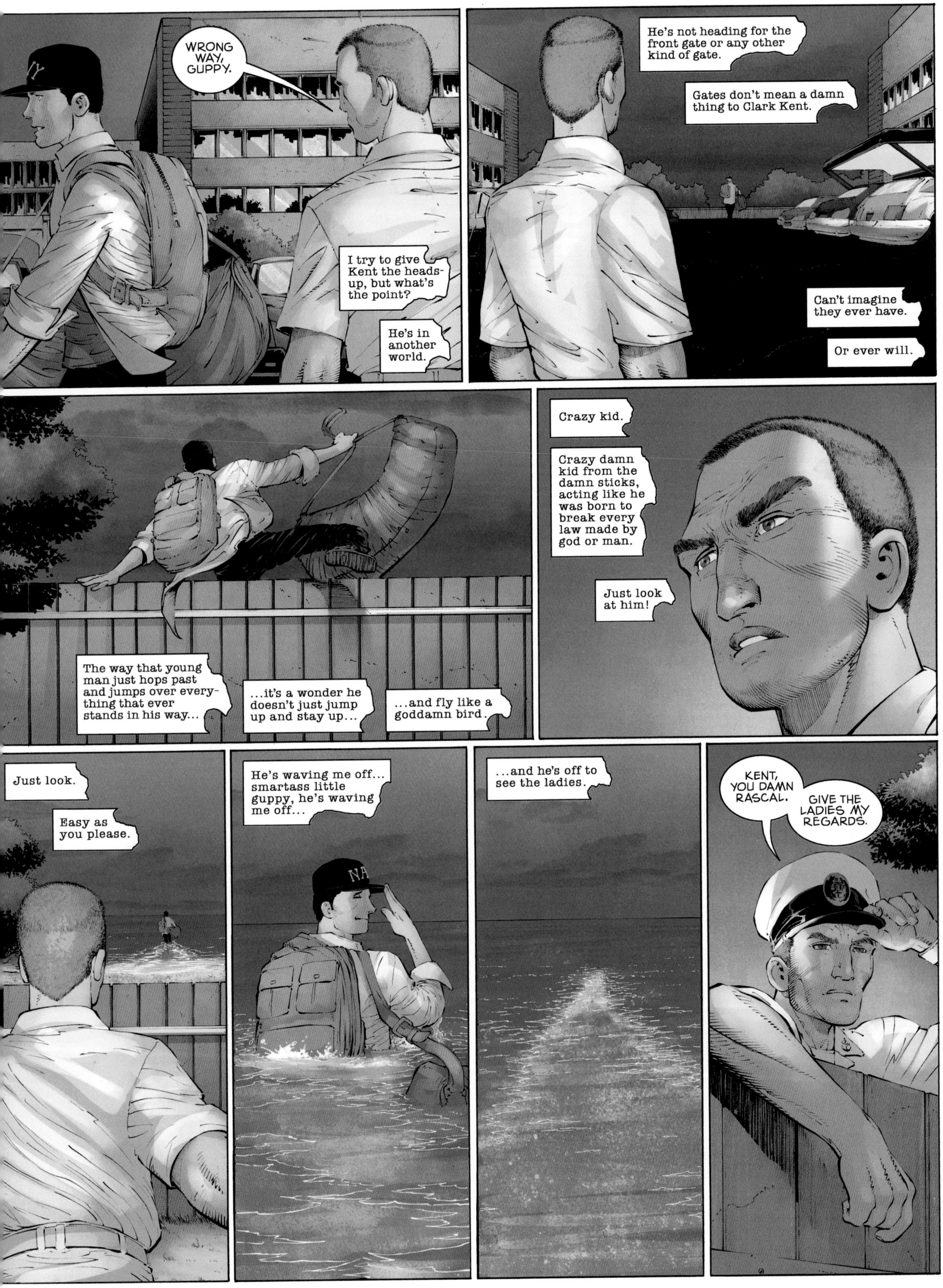
WRONG WAY, GUPPY.
I try to give Kent the heads-up, but what's the point?
He's in another world.
He's not heading for the front gate or any other kind of gate.
Gates don't mean a damn thing to Clark Kent.
Can't imagine they ever have.
Or ever will.
The way that young man just hops past and jumps over everything that ever stands in his way...
...it's a wonder he doesn't just jump up and stay up...
...and fly like a goddamn bird.
Crazy kid.
Crazy damn kid from the damn sticks, acting like he was born to break every law made by god or man.
Just look at him!
Just look.
Easy as you please.
He's waving me off... smartass little guppy, he's waving me off...
...and he's off to see the ladies.
KENT, YOU DAMN RASCAL.
GIVE THE LADIES MY REGARDS.

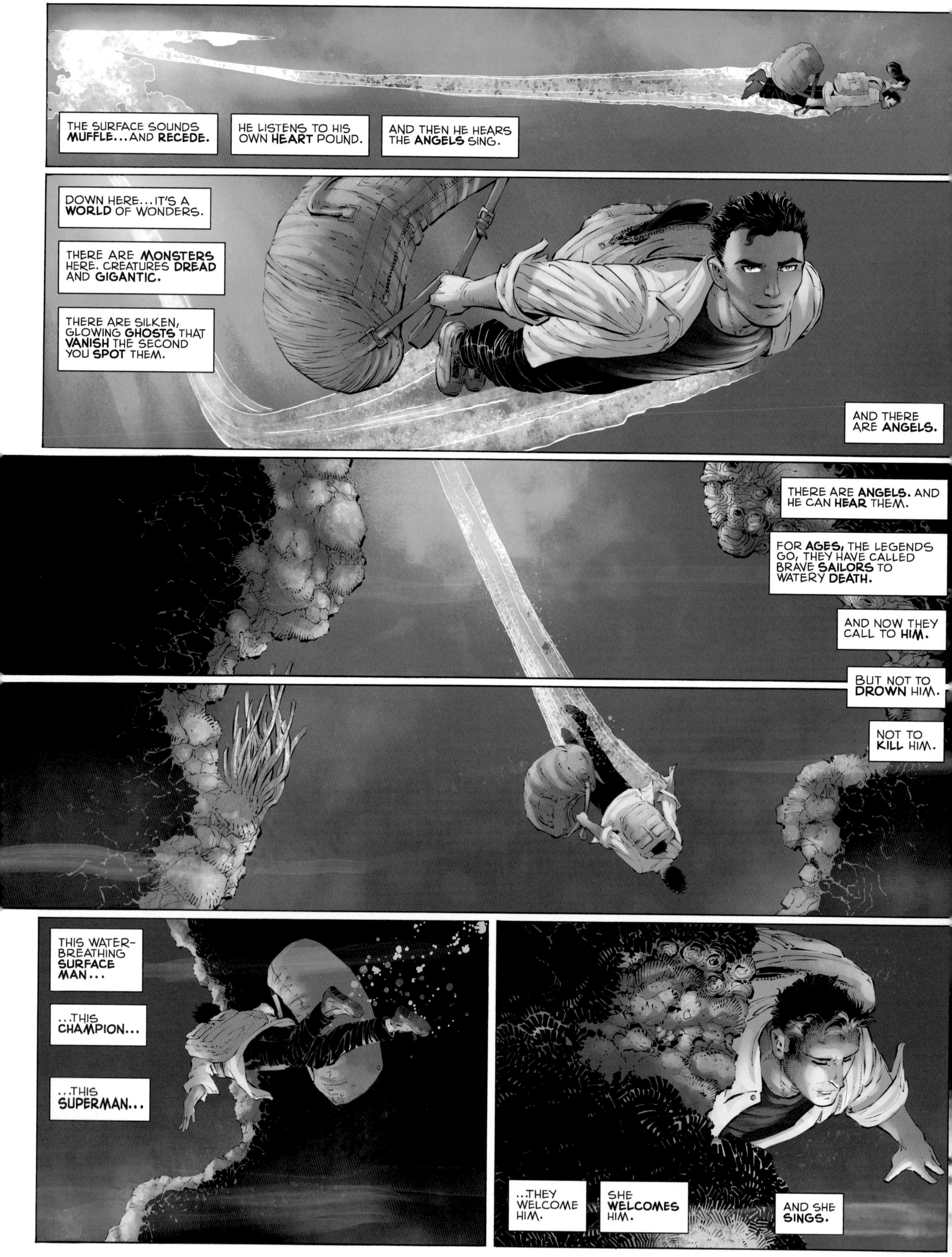
THE SURFACE SOUNDS MUFFLE...AND RECEDE.
HE LISTENS TO HIS OWN HEART POUND.
AND THEN HE HEARS THE ANGELS SING.
DOWN HERE...IT'S A WORLD OF WONDERS.
THERE ARE MONSTERS HERE. CREATURES DREAD AND GIGANTIC.
THERE ARE SILKEN, GLOWING GHOSTS THAT VANISH THE SECOND YOU SPOT THEM.
AND THERE ARE ANGELS.
THERE ARE ANGELS. AND HE CAN HEAR THEM.
FOR AGES, THE LEGENDS GO, THEY HAVE CALLED BRAVE SAILORS TO WATERY DEATH.
AND NOW THEY CALL TO HIM.
BUT NOT TO DROWN HIM.
NOT TO KILL HIM.
THIS WATER-BREATHING SURFACE MAN...
...THIS CHAMPION...
...THIS SUPERMAN...
...THEY WELCOME HIM.
SHE WELCOMES HIM.
AND SHE SINGS.

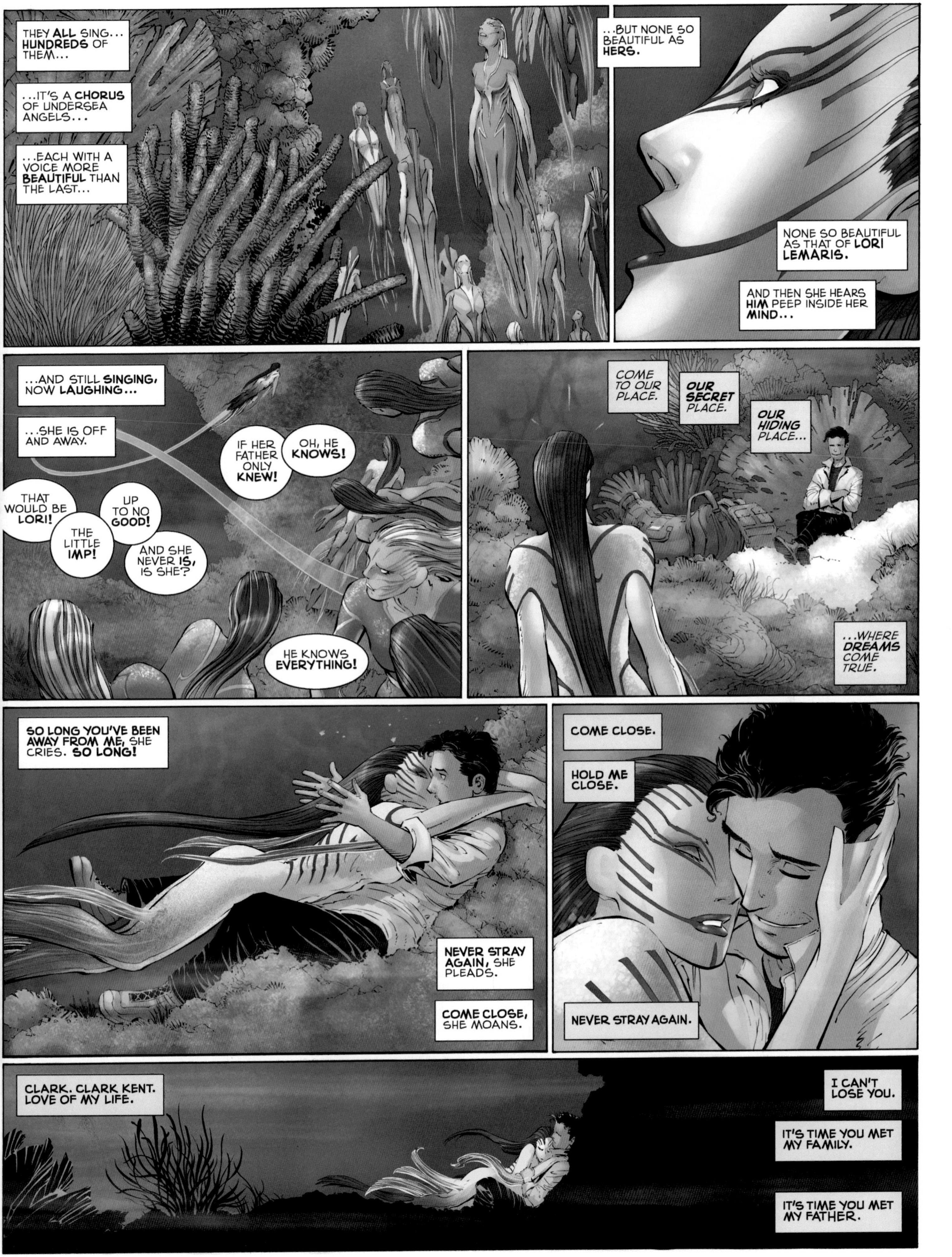
THEY ALL SING... HUNDREDS OF THEM...
...IT'S A CHORUS OF UNDERSEA ANGELS...
...EACH WITH A VOICE MORE BEAUTIFUL THAN THE LAST...
...BUT NONE SO BEAUTIFUL AS HERS.
NONE SO BEAUTIFUL AS THAT OF LORI LEMARIS.
AND THEN SHE HEARS HIM PEEP INSIDE HER MIND...
...AND STILL SINGING, NOW LAUGHING...
...SHE IS OFF AND AWAY.
IF HER FATHER ONLY KNEW!
OH, HE KNOWS!
THAT WOULD BE LORI!
UP TO NO GOOD!
THE LITTLE IMP!
AND SHE NEVER IS, IS SHE?
HE KNOWS EVERYTHING!
COME TO OUR PLACE.
OUR SECRET PLACE.
OUR HIDING PLACE...
...WHERE DREAMS COME TRUE.
SO LONG YOU'VE BEEN AWAY FROM ME, SHE CRIES. SO LONG!
NEVER STRAY AGAIN, SHE PLEADS.
COME CLOSE, SHE MOANS.
COME CLOSE.
HOLD ME CLOSE.
NEVER STRAY AGAIN.
CLARK. CLARK KENT. LOVE OF MY LIFE.
I CAN'T LOSE YOU.
IT'S TIME YOU MET MY FAMILY.
IT'S TIME YOU MET MY FATHER.

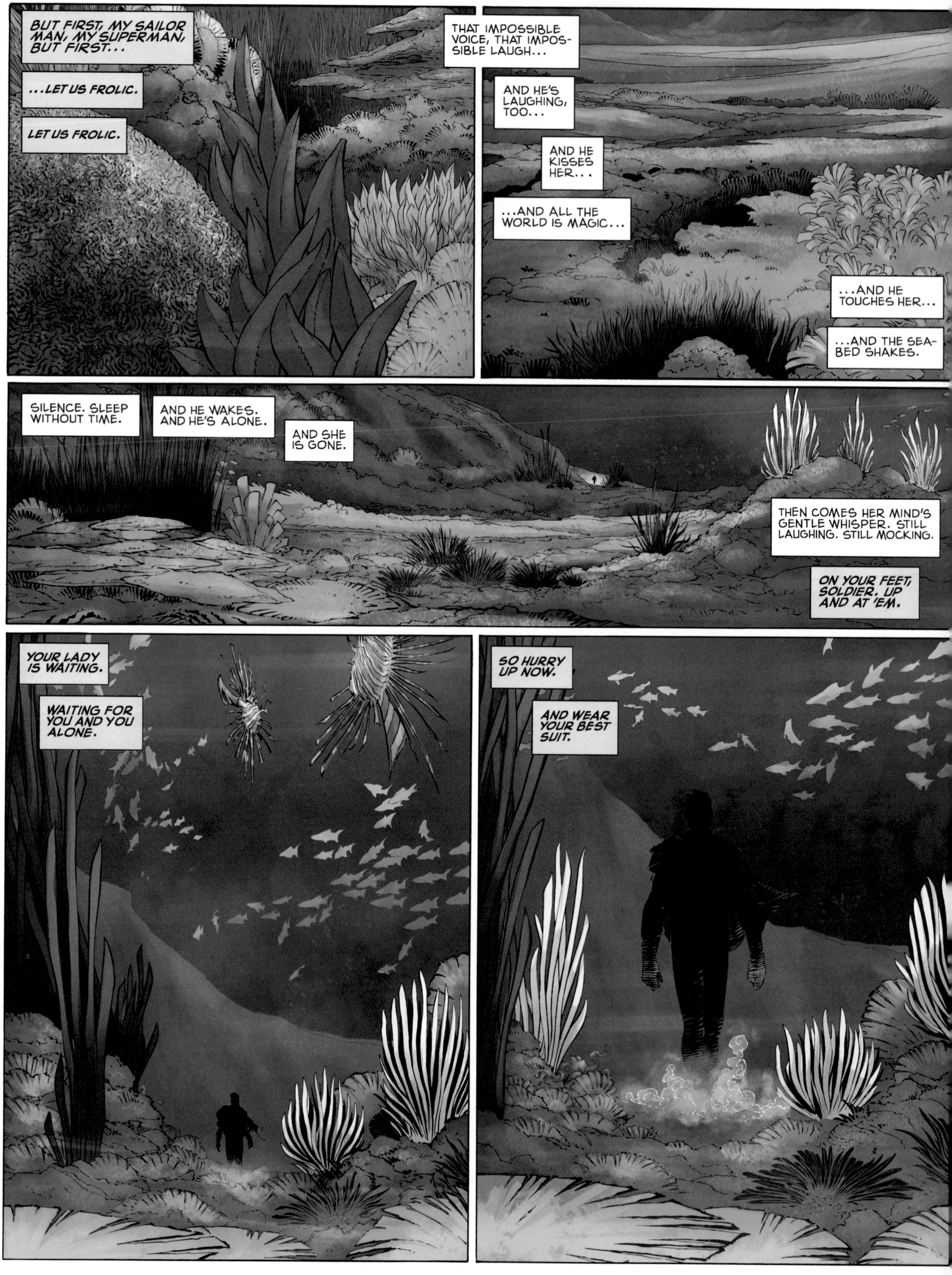
BUT FIRST, MY SAILOR MAN, MY SUPERMAN, BUT FIRST...
...LET US FROLIC.
LET US FROLIC.
THAT IMPOSSIBLE VOICE, THAT IMPOSSIBLE LAUGH...
AND HE'S LAUGHING, TOO...
AND HE KISSES HER...
...AND ALL THE WORLD IS MAGIC...
...AND HE TOUCHES HER...
...AND THE SEABED SHAKES.
SILENCE. SLEEP WITHOUT TIME.
AND HE WAKES. AND HE'S ALONE.
AND SHE IS GONE.
THEN COMES HER MIND'S GENTLE WHISPER. STILL LAUGHING. STILL MOCKING.
ON YOUR FEET, SOLDIER. UP AND AT 'EM.
YOUR LADY IS WAITING.
WAITING FOR YOU AND YOU ALONE.
SO HURRY UP NOW.
AND WEAR YOUR BEST SUIT.

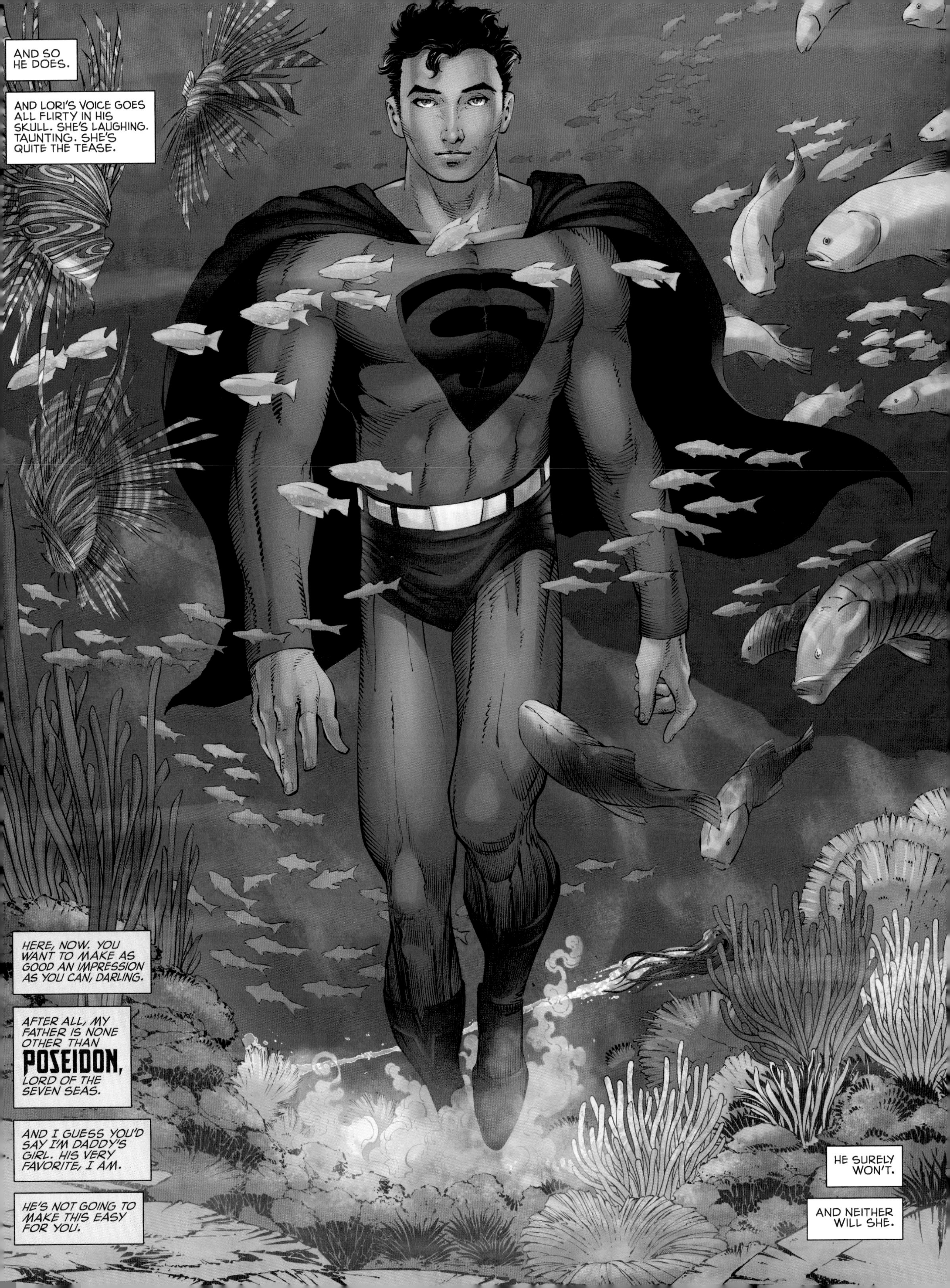
AND SO HE DOES.
AND LORI'S VOICE GOES ALL FLIRTY IN HIS SKULL. SHE'S LAUGHING. TAUNTING. SHE'S QUITE THE TEASE.
HERE, NOW. YOU WANT TO MAKE AS GOOD AN IMPRESSION AS YOU CAN, DARLING.
AFTER ALL, MY FATHER IS NONE OTHER THAN POSEIDON, LORD OF THE SEVEN SEAS.
AND I GUESS YOU'D SAY I'M DADDY'S GIRL. HIS VERY FAVORITE, I AM.
HE'S NOT GOING TO MAKE THIS EASY FOR YOU.
HE SURELY WON'T.
AND NEITHER WILL SHE.

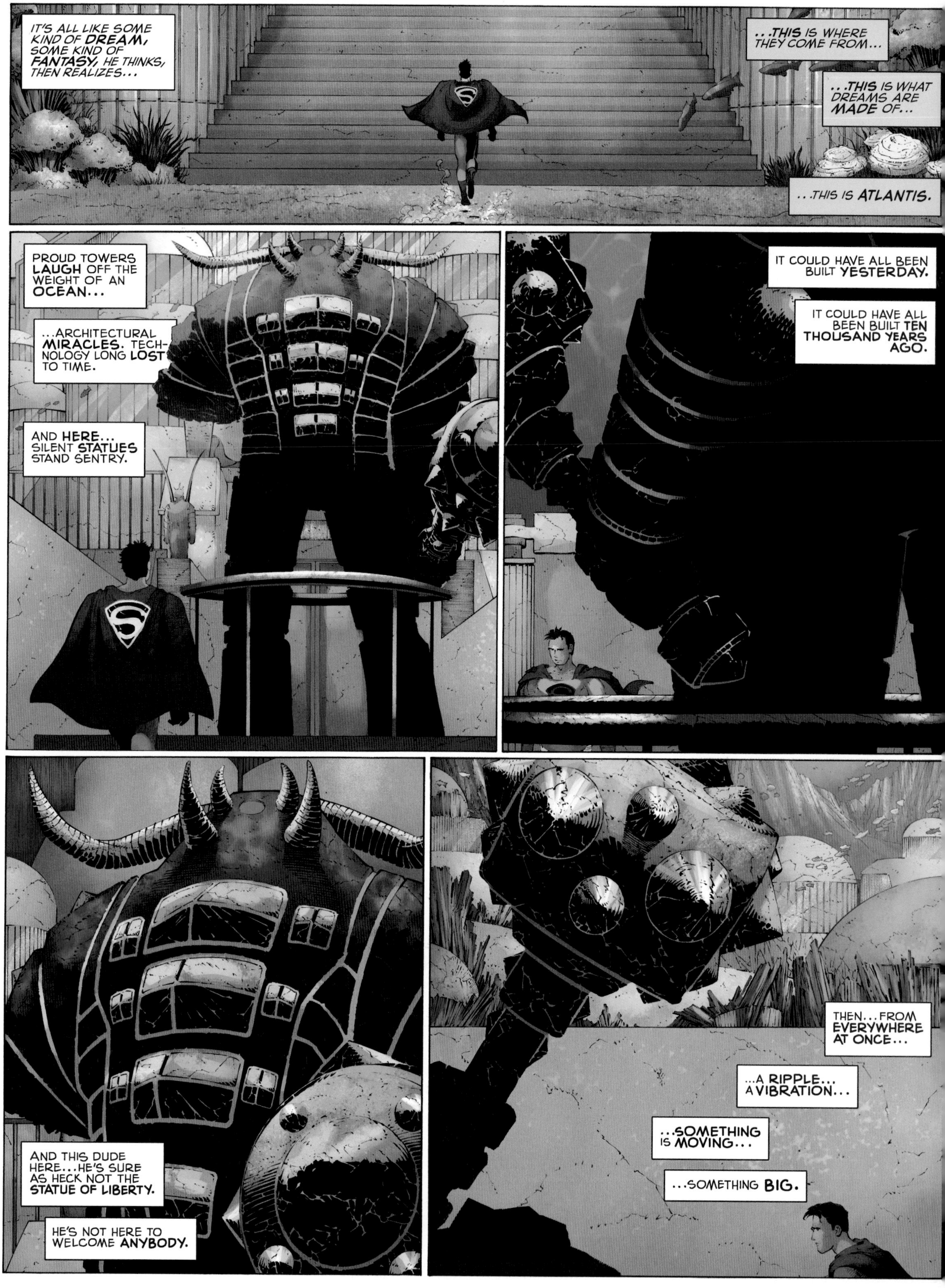
IT'S ALL LIKE SOME KIND OF DREAM, SOME KIND OF FANTASY, HE THINKS, THEN REALIZES...
...THIS IS WHERE THEY COME FROM...
...THIS IS WHAT DREAMS ARE MADE OF...
...THIS IS ATLANTIS.
PROUD TOWERS LAUGH OFF THE WEIGHT OF AN OCEAN...
...ARCHITECTURAL MIRACLES. TECH-NOLOGY LONG LOST TO TIME.
AND HERE... SILENT STATUES STAND SENTRY.
IT COULD HAVE ALL BEEN BUILT YESTERDAY.
IT COULD HAVE ALL BEEN BUILT TEN THOUSAND YEARS AGO.
AND THIS DUDE HERE... HE'S SURE AS HECK NOT THE STATUE OF LIBERTY.
HE'S NOT HERE TO WELCOME ANYBODY.
THEN... FROM EVERYWHERE AT ONCE...
...A RIPPLE... A VIBRATION...
...SOMETHING IS MOVING...
...SOMETHING BIG.

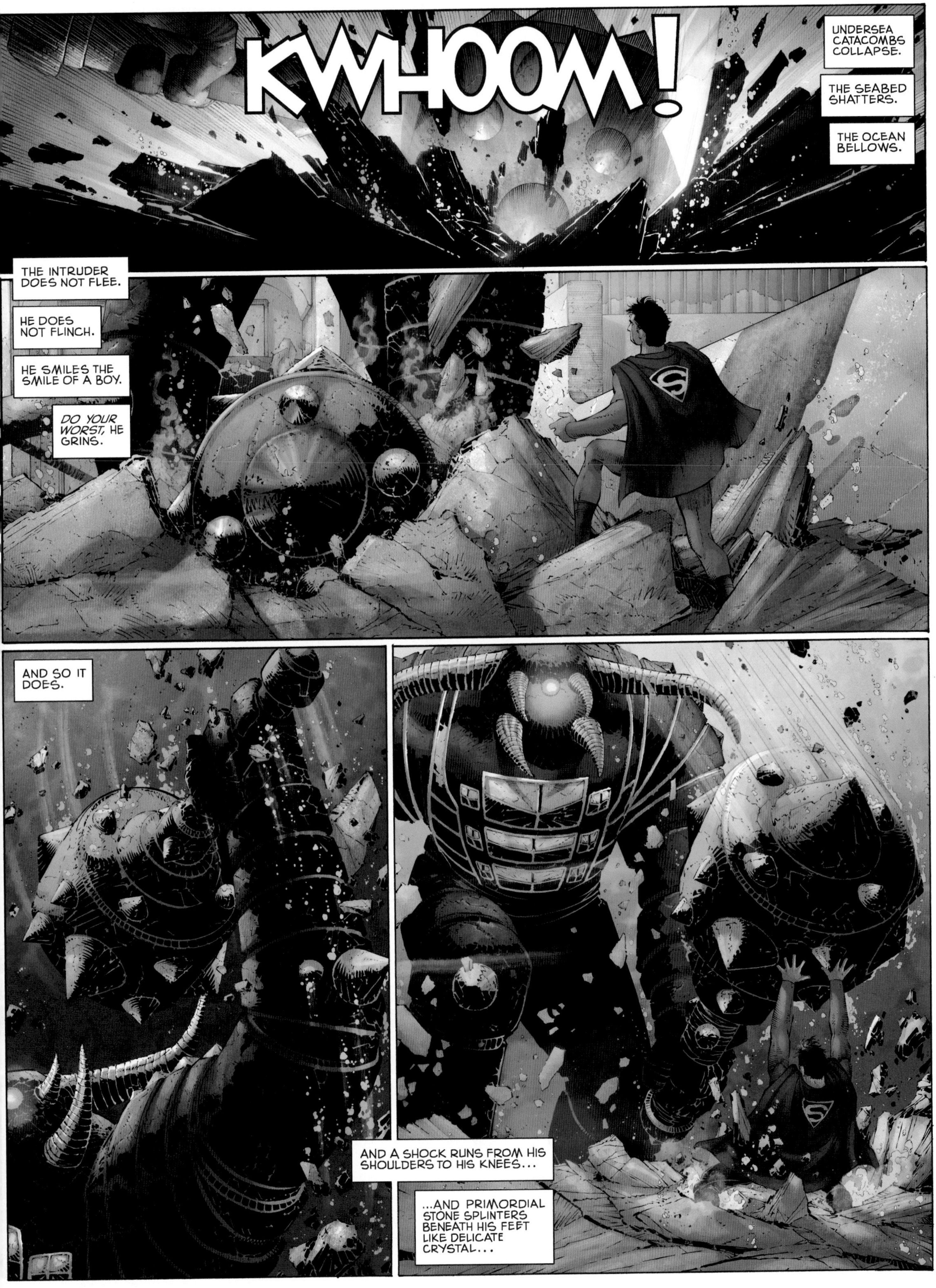
KWHOOM!
UNDERSEA CATACOMBS COLLAPSE.
THE SEABED SHATTERS.
THE OCEAN BELLOWS.
THE INTRUDER DOES NOT FLEE.
HE DOES NOT FLINCH.
HE SMILES THE SMILE OF A BOY.
DO YOUR WORST, HE GRINS.
AND SO IT DOES.
AND A SHOCK RUNS FROM HIS SHOULDERS TO HIS KNEES...
...AND PRIMORDIAL STONE SPLINTERS BENEATH HIS FEET LIKE DELICATE CRYSTAL...

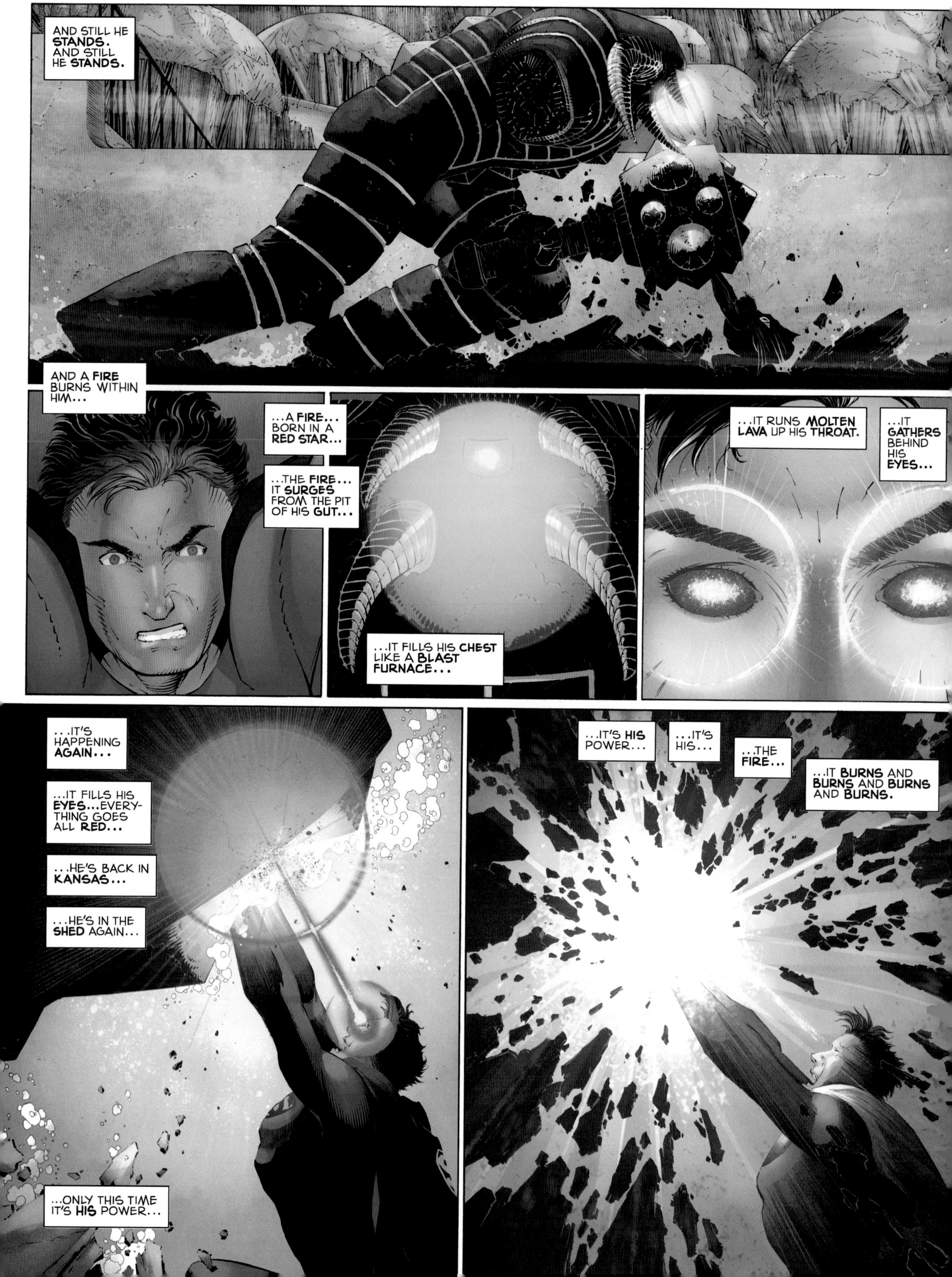

AND STILL HE STANDS. AND STILL HE STANDS.
AND A FIRE BURNS WITHIN HIM...
...A FIRE... BORN IN A RED STAR...
...THE FIRE... IT SURGES FROM THE PIT OF HIS GUT...
...IT FILLS HIS CHEST LIKE A BLAST FURNACE...
...IT RUNS MOLTEN LAVA UP HIS THROAT.
...IT GATHERS BEHIND HIS EYES...
...IT'S HAPPENING AGAIN...
...IT FILLS HIS EYES...EVERY-THING GOES ALL RED...
...HE'S BACK IN KANSAS...
...HE'S IN THE SHED AGAIN...
...ONLY THIS TIME IT'S HIS POWER...
...IT'S HIS POWER...
...IT'S HIS...
...THE FIRE...
...IT BURNS AND BURNS AND BURNS AND BURNS.

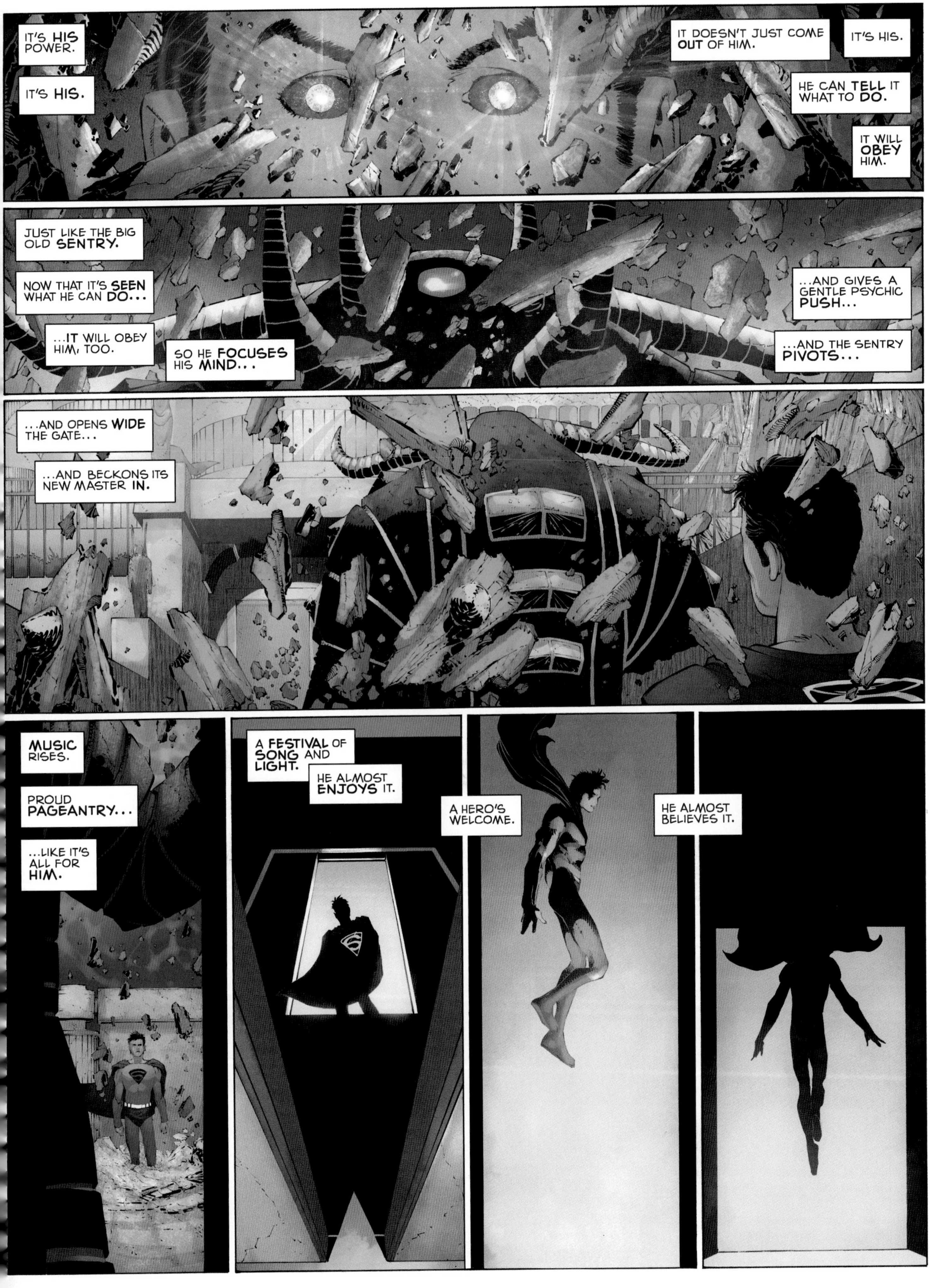
IT'S HIS POWER.
IT'S HIS.
IT DOESN'T JUST COME OUT OF HIM.
IT'S HIS.
HE CAN TELL IT WHAT TO DO.
IT WILL OBEY HIM.
JUST LIKE THE BIG OLD SENTRY.
NOW THAT IT'S SEEN WHAT HE CAN DO...
...IT WILL OBEY HIM, TOO.
SO HE FOCUSES HIS MIND...
...AND GIVES A GENTLE PSYCHIC PUSH...
...AND THE SENTRY PIVOTS...
...AND OPENS WIDE THE GATE...
...AND BECKONS ITS NEW MASTER IN.
MUSIC RISES.
PROUD PAGEANTRY...
...LIKE IT'S ALL FOR HIM.
A FESTIVAL OF SONG AND LIGHT.
HE ALMOST ENJOYS IT.
A HERO'S WELCOME.
HE ALMOST BELIEVES IT.

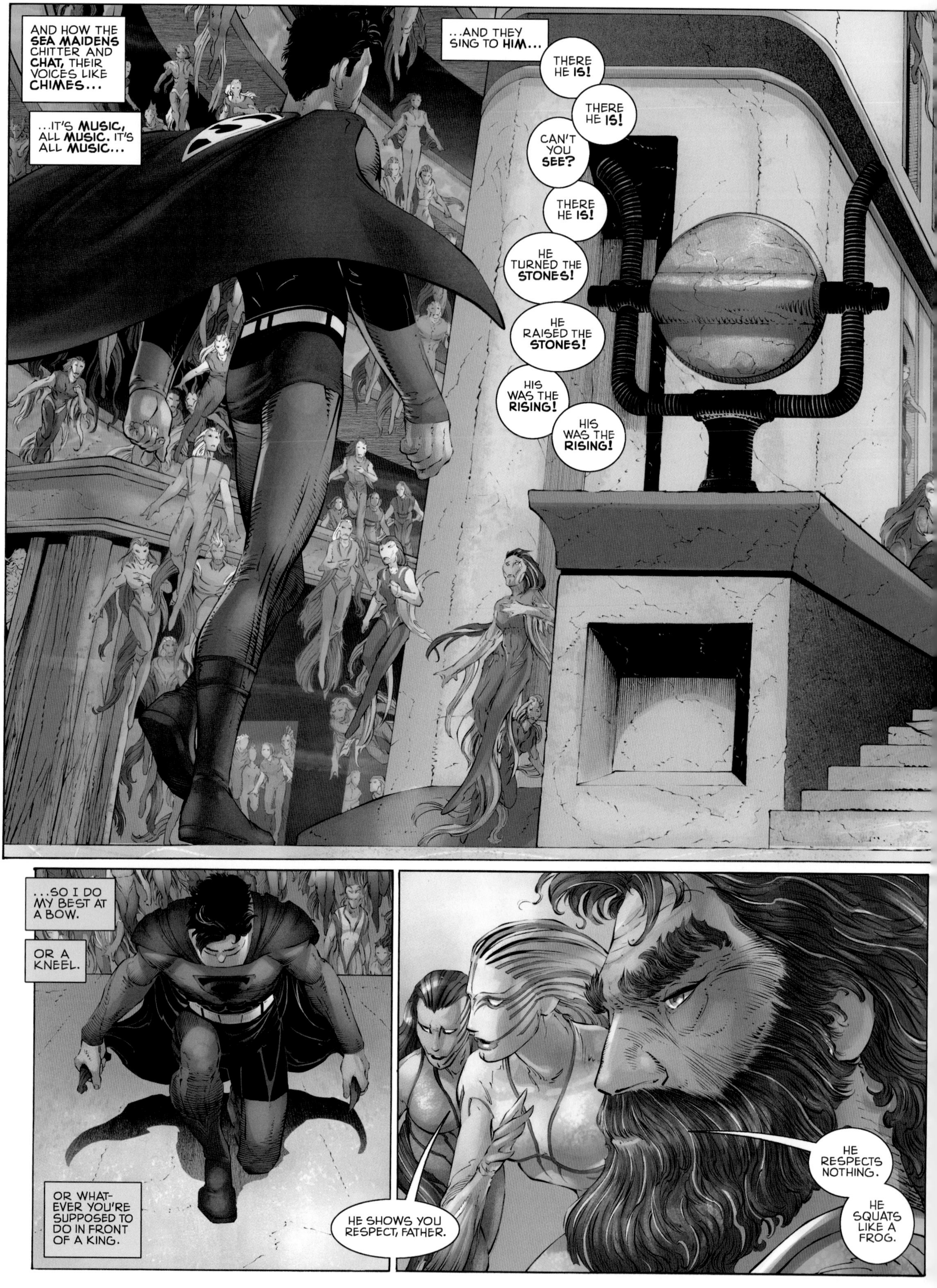

AND HOW THE **SEA MAIDENS** CHITTER AND **CHAT,** THEIR VOICES LIKE **CHIMES...**
...IT'S **MUSIC,** ALL **MUSIC.** IT'S ALL **MUSIC...**
...AND THEY SING TO **HIM...**
THERE HE **IS!**
THERE HE **IS!**
CAN'T YOU **SEE?**
THERE HE **IS!**
HE TURNED THE **STONES!**
HE RAISED THE **STONES!**
HIS WAS THE **RISING!**
HIS WAS THE **RISING!**
...SO I DO MY BEST AT A BOW.
OR A KNEEL.
OR WHATEVER YOU'RE SUPPOSED TO DO IN FRONT OF A KING.
HE SHOWS YOU RESPECT, FATHER.
HE RESPECTS NOTHING.
HE SQUATS LIKE A FROG.

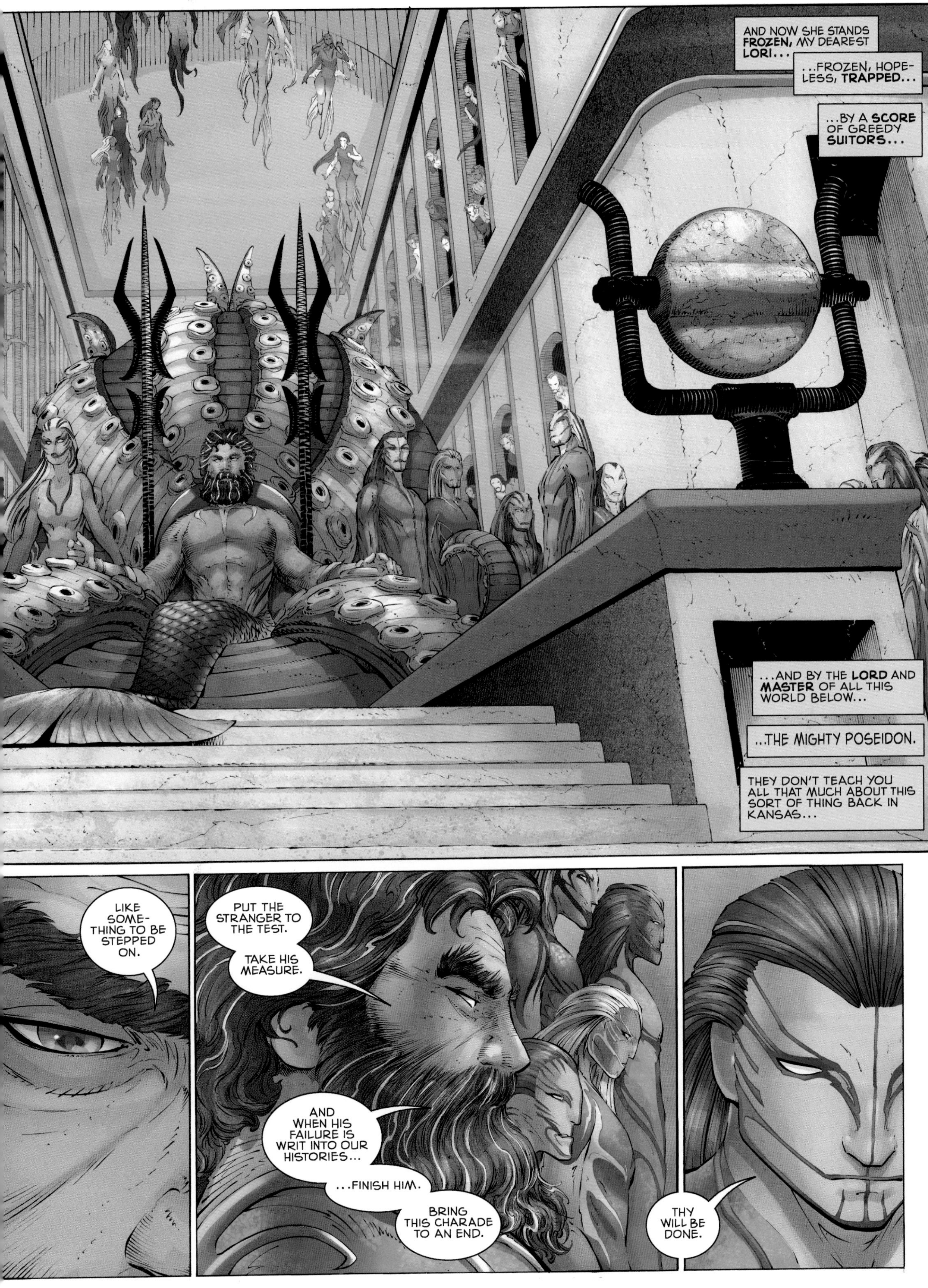
AND NOW SHE STANDS FROZEN, MY DEAREST LORI...
...FROZEN, HOPE-LESS, TRAPPED...
...BY A SCORE OF GREEDY SUITORS...
...AND BY THE LORD AND MASTER OF ALL THIS WORLD BELOW...
...THE MIGHTY POSEIDON.
THEY DON'T TEACH YOU ALL THAT MUCH ABOUT THIS SORT OF THING BACK IN KANSAS...
LIKE SOME-THING TO BE STEPPED ON.
PUT THE STRANGER TO THE TEST.
TAKE HIS MEASURE.
AND WHEN HIS FAILURE IS WRIT INTO OUR HISTORIES...
...FINISH HIM.
BRING THIS CHARADE TO AN END.
THY WILL BE DONE.

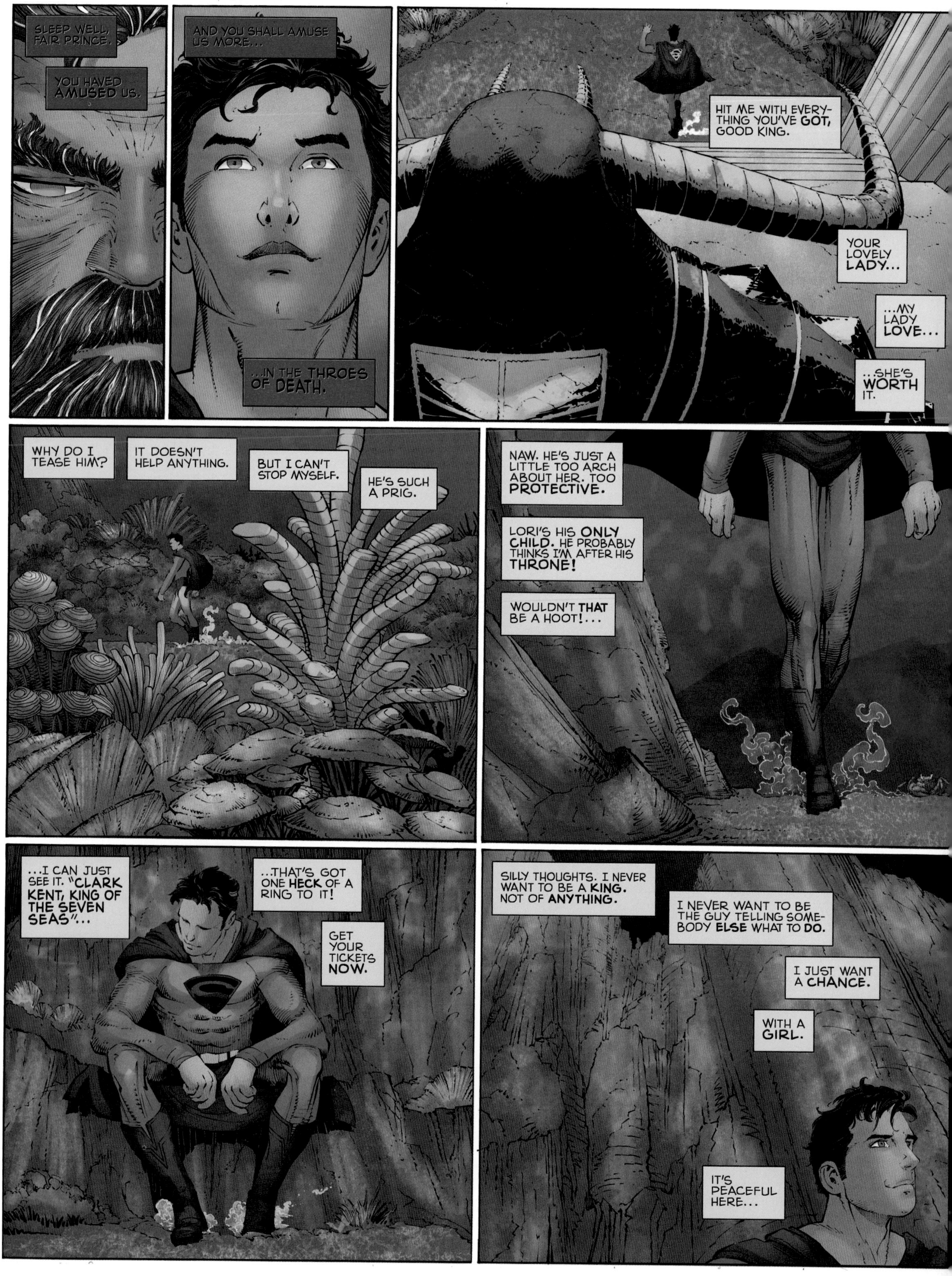
SLEEP WELL, FAIR PRINCE.
YOU HAVED AMUSED US.
AND YOU SHALL AMUSE US MORE...
...IN THE THROES OF DEATH.
HIT ME WITH EVERY-THING YOU'VE GOT, GOOD KING.
YOUR LOVELY LADY...
...MY LADY LOVE...
...SHE'S WORTH IT.
WHY DO I TEASE HIM?
IT DOESN'T HELP ANYTHING.
BUT I CAN'T STOP MYSELF.
HE'S SUCH A PRIG.
NAW. HE'S JUST A LITTLE TOO ARCH ABOUT HER. TOO PROTECTIVE.
LORI'S HIS ONLY CHILD. HE PROBABLY THINKS I'M AFTER HIS THRONE!
WOULDN'T THAT BE A HOOT!...
...I CAN JUST SEE IT. "CLARK KENT, KING OF THE SEVEN SEAS"...
...THAT'S GOT ONE HECK OF A RING TO IT!
GET YOUR TICKETS NOW.
SILLY THOUGHTS. I NEVER WANT TO BE A KING. NOT OF ANYTHING.
I NEVER WANT TO BE THE GUY TELLING SOME-BODY ELSE WHAT TO DO.
I JUST WANT A CHANCE.
WITH A GIRL.
IT'S PEACEFUL HERE...

LOOK AT ME...I'M **SHAKING**...

...**SHAKING**...HEY... NO...THAT'S NOT **ME**...

...**EVERYTHING'S** SHAKING...

...UNDERSEA **QUAKE**...

...**NO**...

...NOT A **QUAKE**...

...**NOT** FROM **BELOW**...

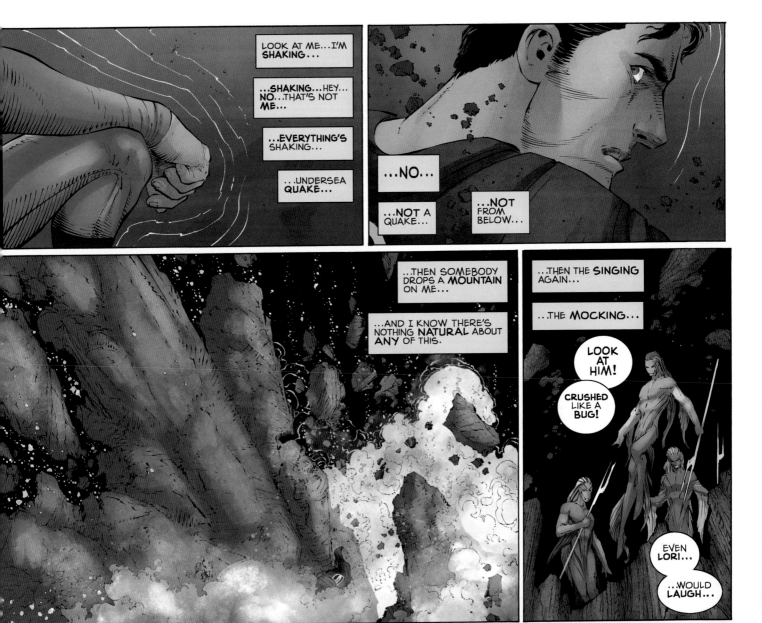

...THEN SOMEBODY DROPS A **MOUNTAIN** ON ME...

...AND I KNOW THERE'S NOTHING **NATURAL** ABOUT **ANY** OF THIS.

...THEN THE **SINGING** AGAIN...

...THE **MOCKING**...

LOOK AT **HIM**!

CRUSHED LIKE A **BUG**!

EVEN **LORI**...

...WOULD **LAUGH**...

THESE GUYS ARE STARTING TO **HONK** ME OFF.

IT'S **HIGH TIME** I GAVE THEM **WHAT** FOR.

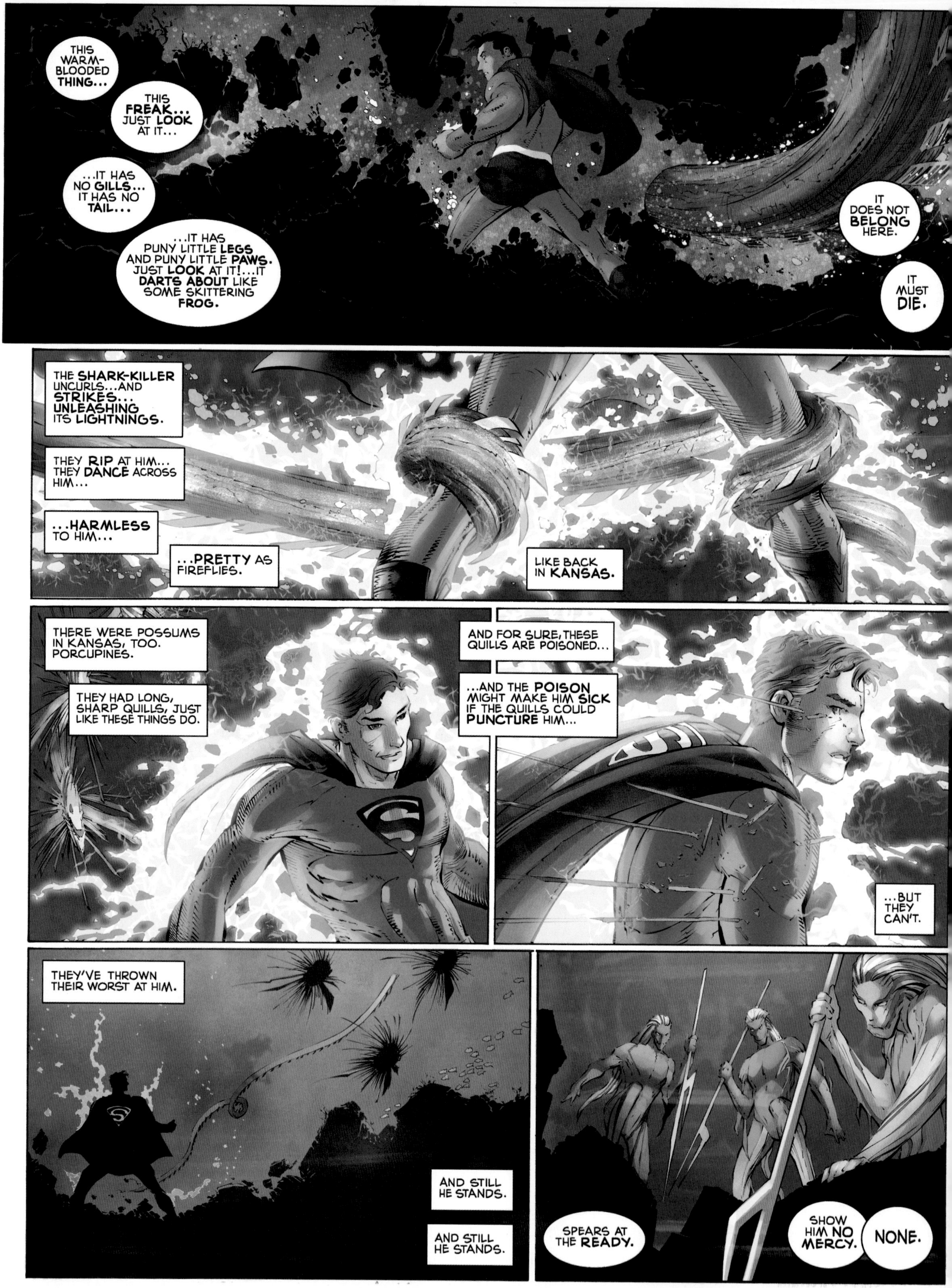
THIS WARM-BLOODED THING...
THIS FREAK... JUST LOOK AT IT...
...IT HAS NO GILLS... IT HAS NO TAIL...
...IT HAS PUNY LITTLE LEGS AND PUNY LITTLE PAWS. JUST LOOK AT IT!...IT DARTS ABOUT LIKE SOME SKITTERING FROG.
IT DOES NOT BELONG HERE.
IT MUST DIE.
THE SHARK-KILLER UNCURLS...AND STRIKES... UNLEASHING ITS LIGHTNINGS.
THEY RIP AT HIM... THEY DANCE ACROSS HIM...
...HARMLESS TO HIM...
...PRETTY AS FIREFLIES.
LIKE BACK IN KANSAS.
THERE WERE POSSUMS IN KANSAS, TOO. PORCUPINES.
THEY HAD LONG, SHARP QUILLS, JUST LIKE THESE THINGS DO.
AND FOR SURE, THESE QUILLS ARE POISONED...
...AND THE POISON MIGHT MAKE HIM SICK IF THE QUILLS COULD PUNCTURE HIM...
...BUT THEY CAN'T.
THEY'VE THROWN THEIR WORST AT HIM.
AND STILL HE STANDS.
AND STILL HE STANDS.
SPEARS AT THE READY.
SHOW HIM NO MERCY.
NONE.

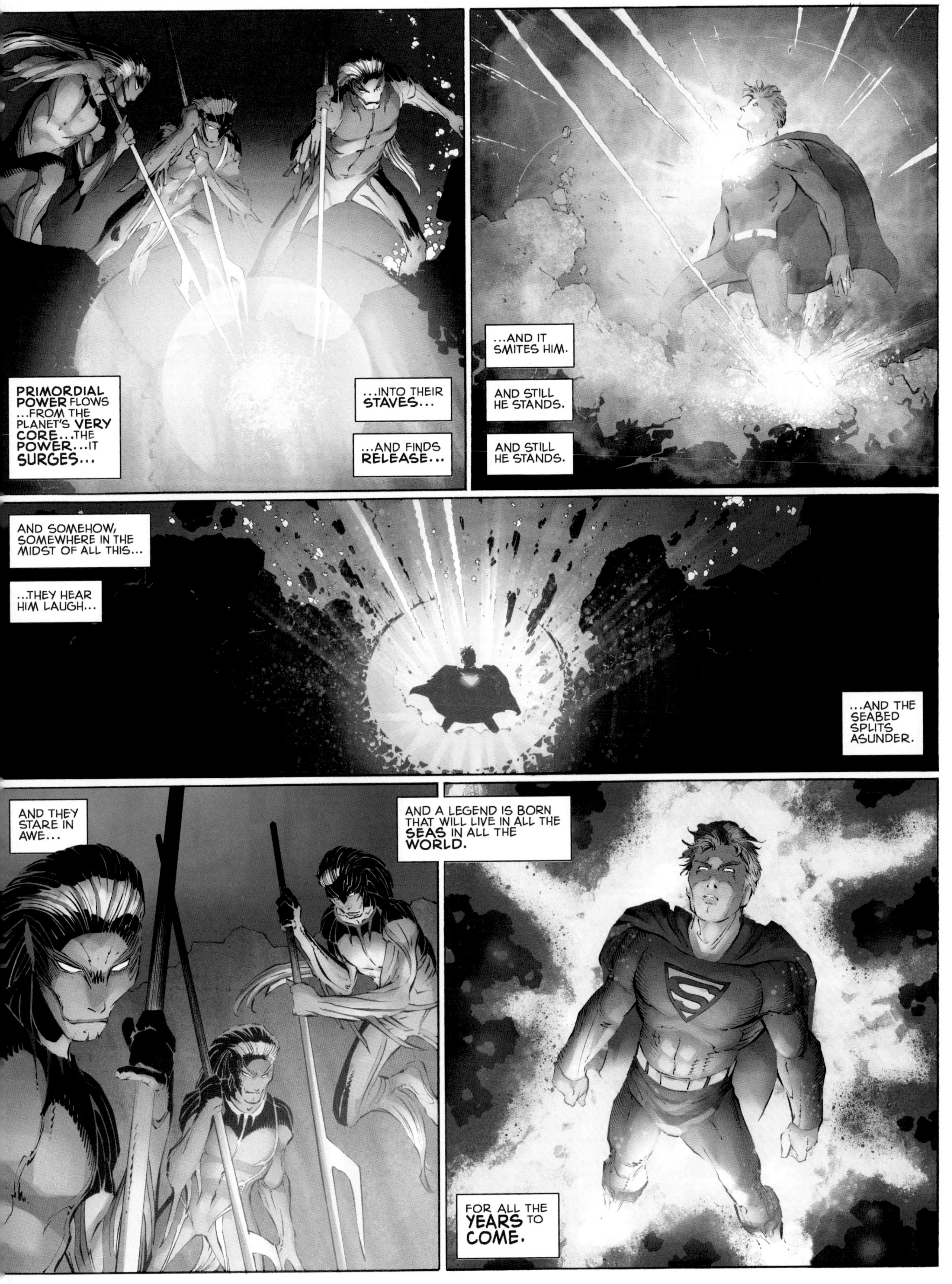
PRIMORDIAL POWER FLOWS ...FROM THE PLANET'S VERY CORE...THE POWER...IT SURGES...
...INTO THEIR STAVES...
...AND FINDS RELEASE...
...AND IT SMITES HIM.
AND STILL HE STANDS.
AND STILL HE STANDS.
AND SOMEHOW, SOMEWHERE IN THE MIDST OF ALL THIS...
...THEY HEAR HIM LAUGH...
...AND THE SEABED SPLITS ASUNDER.
AND THEY STARE IN AWE...
AND A LEGEND IS BORN THAT WILL LIVE IN ALL THE SEAS IN ALL THE WORLD.
FOR ALL THE YEARS TO COME.

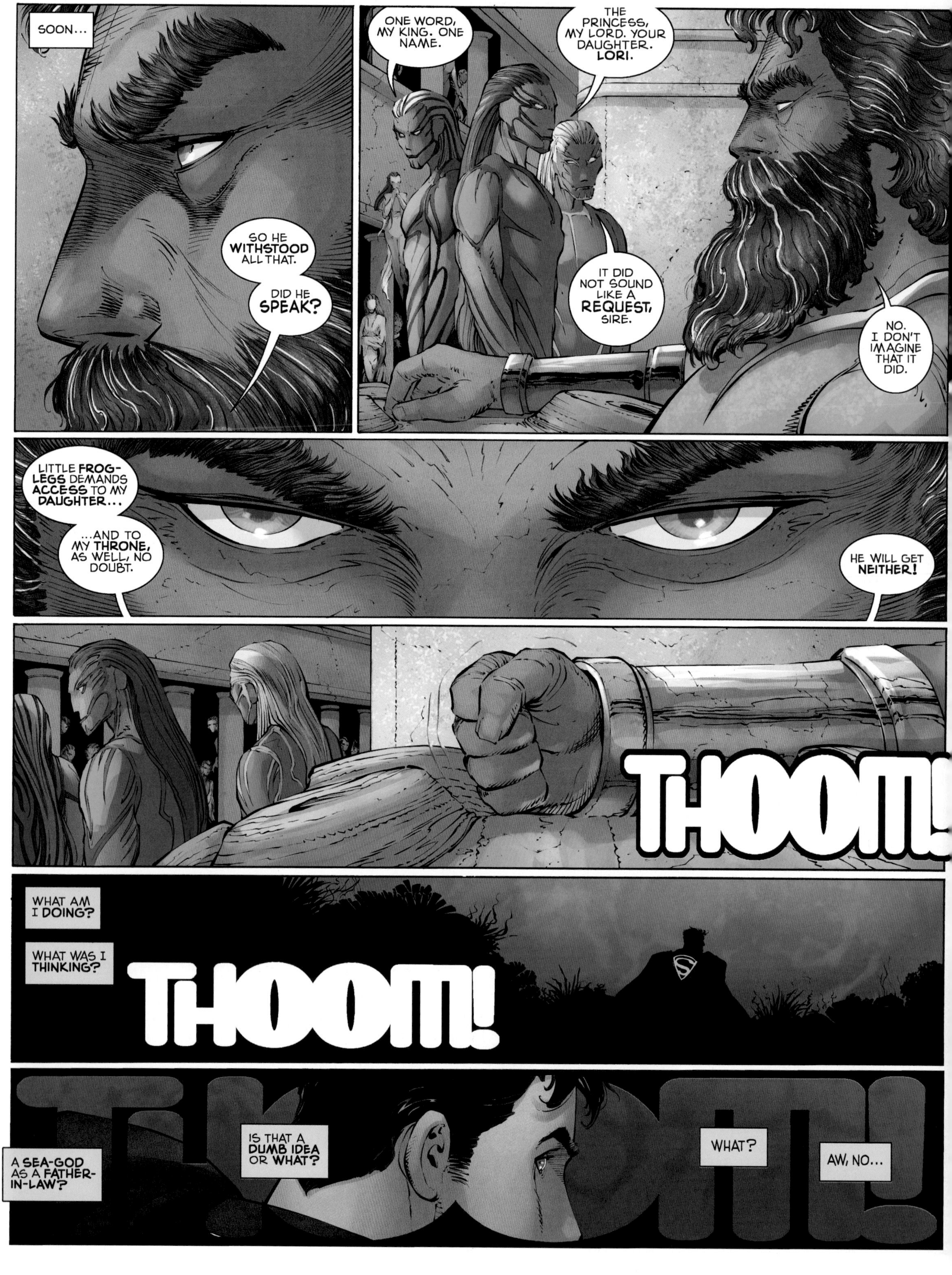
SOON...
SO HE **WITHSTOOD** ALL THAT.
DID HE **SPEAK?**
ONE WORD, MY KING. ONE NAME.
THE PRINCESS, MY LORD. YOUR DAUGHTER. **LORI.**
IT DID NOT SOUND LIKE A **REQUEST,** SIRE.
NO. I DON'T IMAGINE THAT IT DID.
LITTLE **FROG-LEGS** DEMANDS **ACCESS** TO MY **DAUGHTER...**
...AND TO MY **THRONE,** AS WELL, NO DOUBT.
HE WILL GET **NEITHER!**
THOOM!
WHAT AM I **DOING?**
WHAT WAS I **THINKING?**
THOOM!
A **SEA-GOD** AS A **FATHER-IN-LAW?**
IS THAT A **DUMB IDEA** OR **WHAT?**
WHAT?
AW, NO...

POOM!

HE REMEMBERS A DAY FROM LONG AGO. FROM BEFORE HE WAS OLD ENOUGH TO STAND UP.

THE DAY HIS WORLD EXPLODED.

KOFF!

BUT HE DOESN'T BLAST AWAY IN A ROCKET SHIP FROM THIS WORLD, NO.

IT LANDS ON **HIM.**

IT LANDS ON HIM.

IT **SHOVES** HIM **DEEP** INTO THE OCEAN **FLOOR...**

...AND THE EARTH **DEVOURS** HIM.

IT **EATS** HIM **ALIVE.**

PLANET EARTH HAS **CAPTURED** HIM.

AND IT HAS **EATEN** HIM ALIVE.

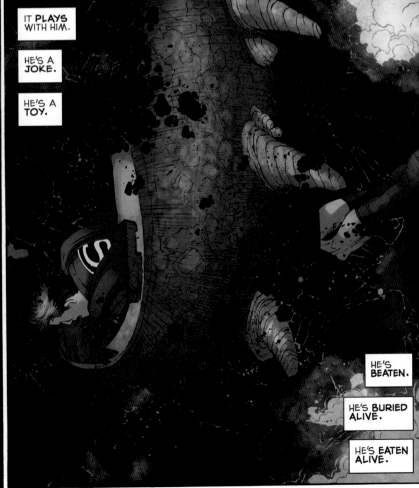

IT **PLAYS** WITH HIM.

HE'S A **JOKE.**

HE'S A **TOY.**

HE'S **BEATEN.**

HE'S **BURIED ALIVE.**

HE'S **EATEN ALIVE.**

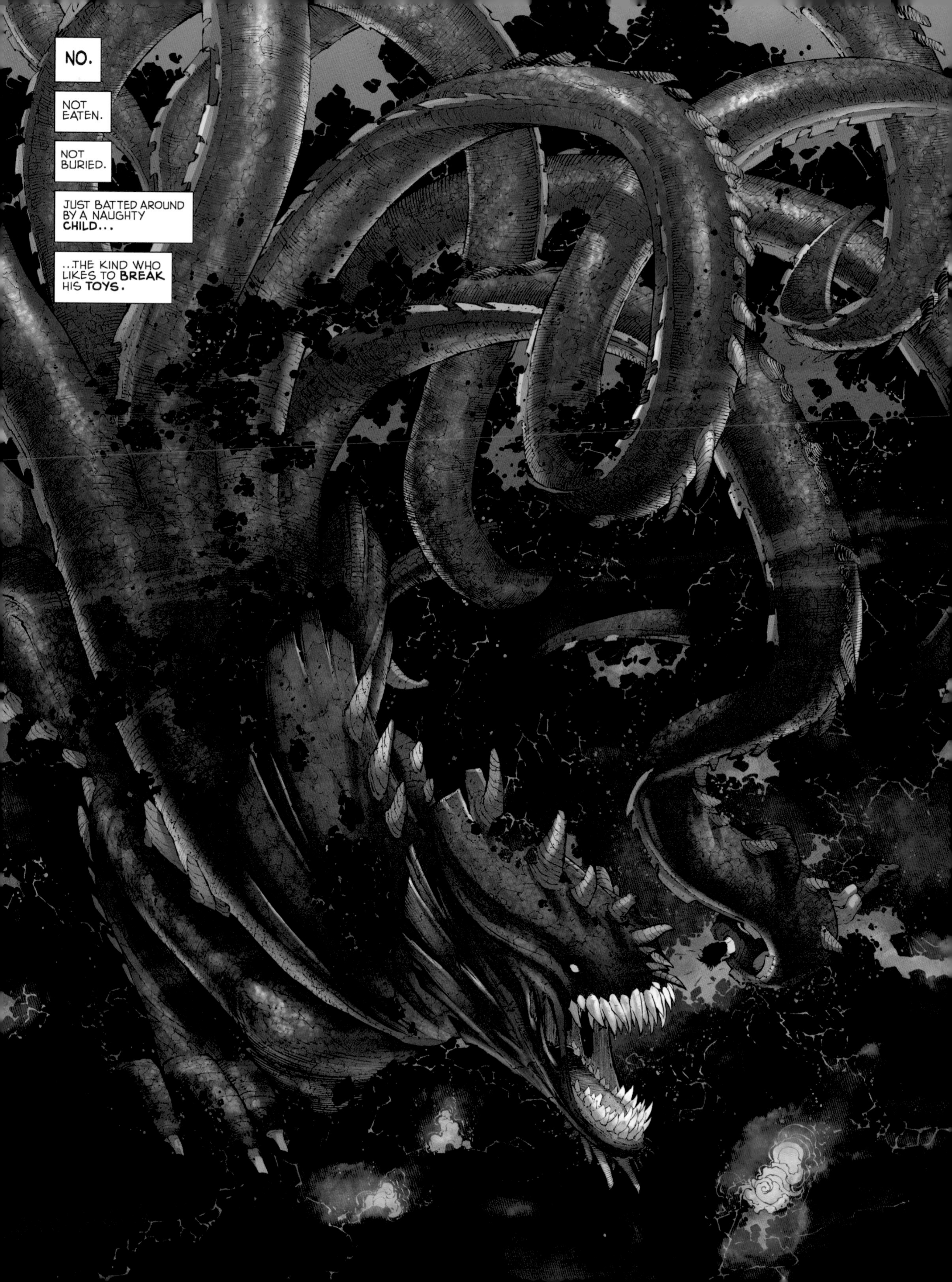
NO.
NOT EATEN.
NOT BURIED.
JUST BATTED AROUND BY A NAUGHTY **CHILD...**
...THE KIND WHO LIKES TO **BREAK** HIS **TOYS.**

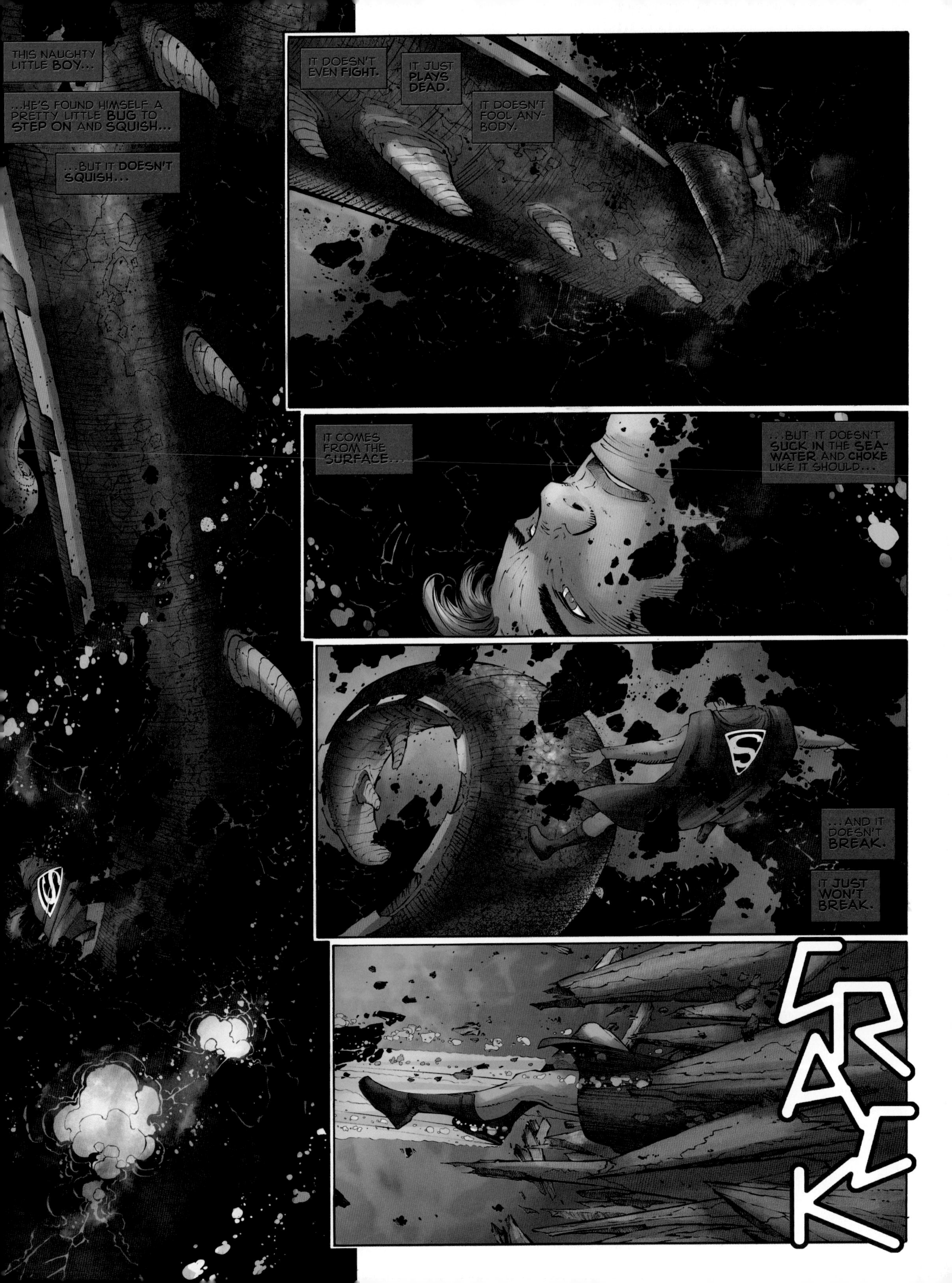
THIS NAUGHTY LITTLE BOY...
...HE'S FOUND HIMSELF A PRETTY LITTLE BUG TO STEP ON AND SQUISH...
...BUT IT DOESN'T SQUISH...
IT DOESN'T EVEN FIGHT.
IT JUST PLAYS DEAD.
IT DOESN'T FOOL ANYBODY.
IT COMES FROM THE SURFACE...
...BUT IT DOESN'T SUCK IN THE SEAWATER AND CHOKE LIKE IT SHOULD...
...AND IT DOESN'T BREAK.
IT JUST WON'T BREAK.
CRAKK

NASTY LITTLE MOSQUITO.

DEFIANT LITTLE LAND-FROG. JUST LOOK AT IT.

IT'S MOCKING ME.

IT'S MAKING FUN OF ME.

NOT FOR LONG, IT ISN'T.

NOT FOR LONG.

DON'T BREAK ANY TEETH ON IT.

JUST SWALLOW IT WHOLE.

CHOW IT DOWN.

THAT'LL SHOW IT.

THAT'LL SHOW IT.

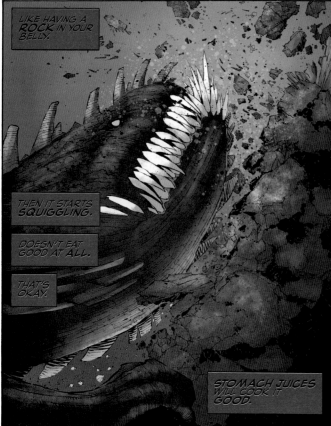

LIKE HAVING A ROCK IN YOUR BELLY.

THEN IT STARTS SQUIGGLING.

DOESN'T EAT GOOD AT ALL.

THAT'S OKAY.

STOMACH JUICES WILL COOK IT GOOD.

FEEL KIND OF SICK.

GO HOME.

TAKE A REST.

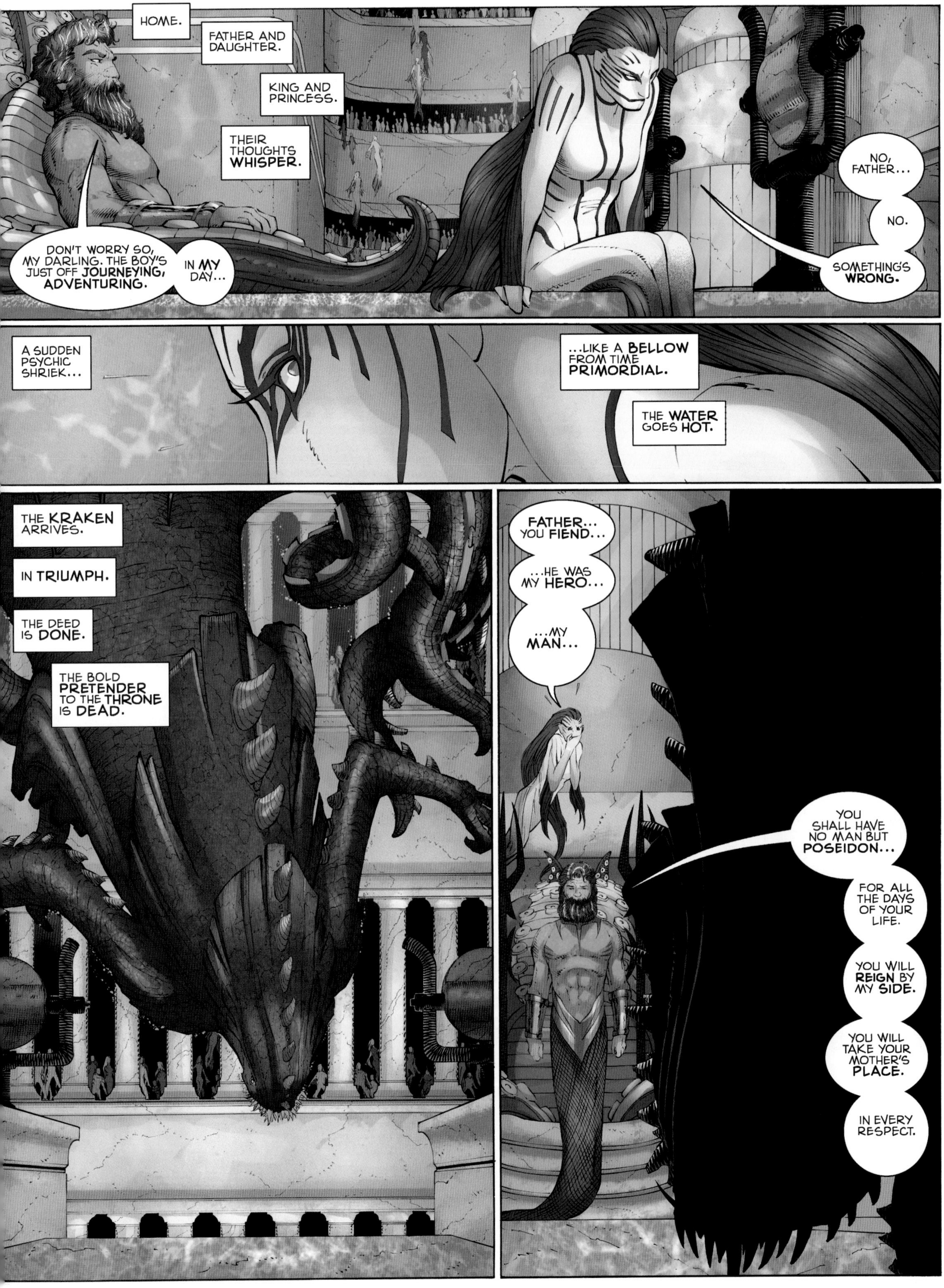
HOME.
FATHER AND DAUGHTER.
KING AND PRINCESS.
THEIR THOUGHTS WHISPER.
NO, FATHER...
NO.
SOMETHING'S WRONG.
DON'T WORRY SO, MY DARLING. THE BOY'S JUST OFF JOURNEYING, ADVENTURING.
IN MY DAY...
A SUDDEN PSYCHIC SHRIEK...
...LIKE A BELLOW FROM TIME PRIMORDIAL.
THE WATER GOES HOT.
THE KRAKEN ARRIVES.
IN TRIUMPH.
THE DEED IS DONE.
THE BOLD PRETENDER TO THE THRONE IS DEAD.
FATHER... YOU FIEND...
...HE WAS MY HERO...
...MY MAN...
YOU SHALL HAVE NO MAN BUT POSEIDON...
FOR ALL THE DAYS OF YOUR LIFE.
YOU WILL REIGN BY MY SIDE.
YOU WILL TAKE YOUR MOTHER'S PLACE.
IN EVERY RESPECT.

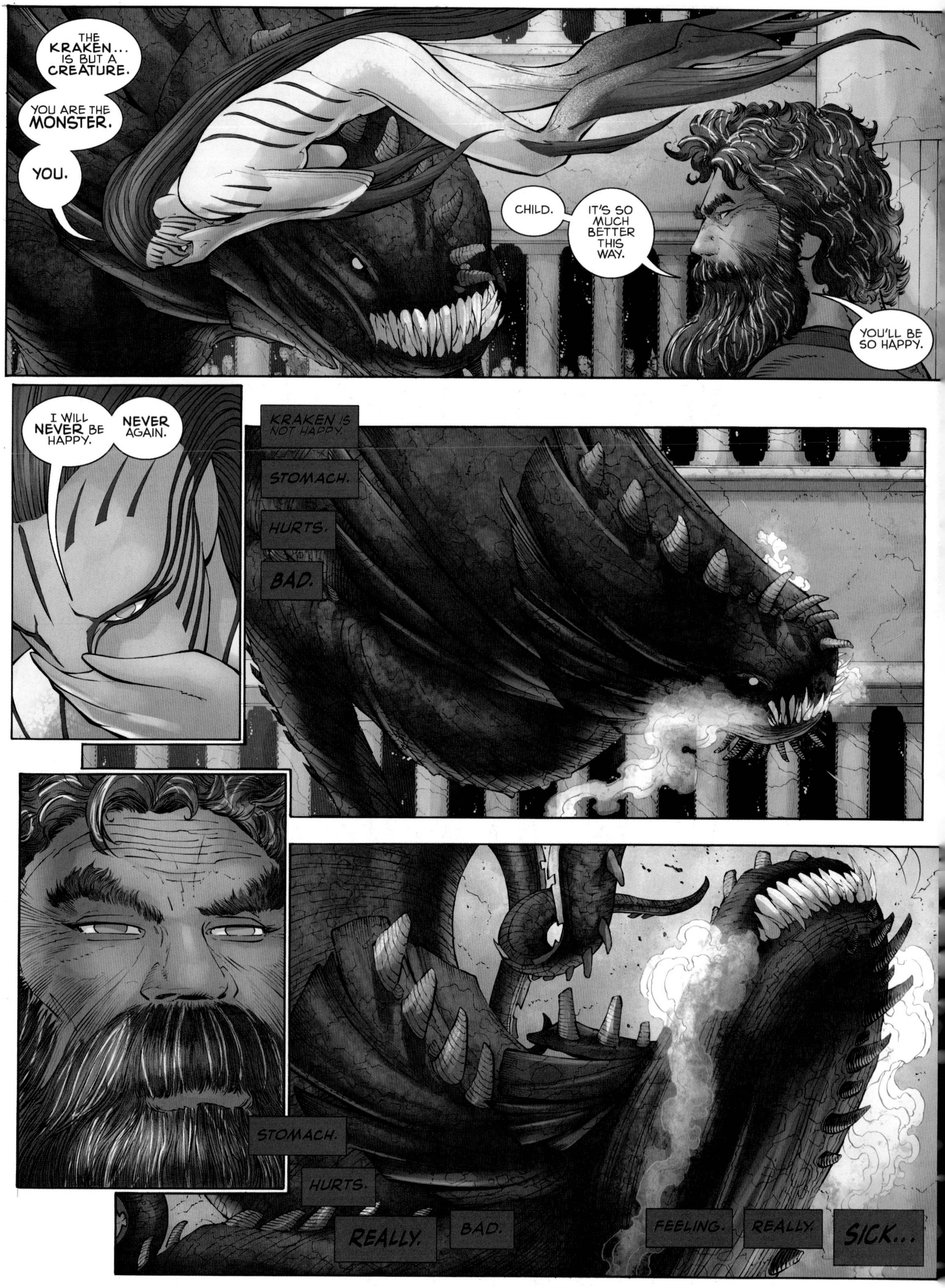
THE KRAKEN... IS BUT A CREATURE.
YOU ARE THE MONSTER.
YOU.
CHILD.
IT'S SO MUCH BETTER THIS WAY.
YOU'LL BE SO HAPPY.
I WILL NEVER BE HAPPY.
NEVER AGAIN.
KRAKEN IS NOT HAPPY.
STOMACH.
HURTS.
BAD.
STOMACH.
HURTS.
REALLY.
BAD.
FEELING.
REALLY.
SICK...

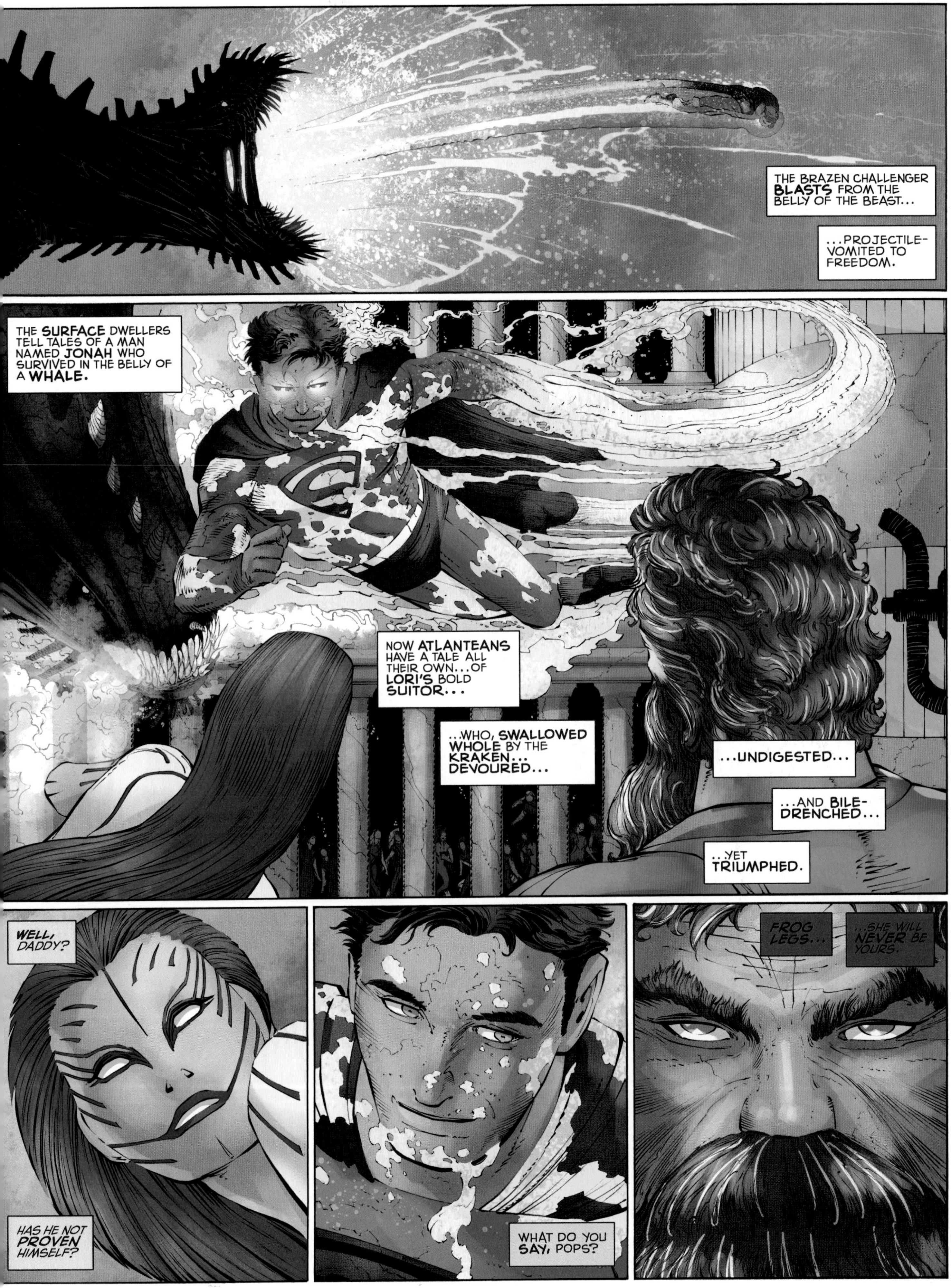
THE BRAZEN CHALLENGER BLASTS FROM THE BELLY OF THE BEAST...
...PROJECTILE-VOMITED TO FREEDOM.
THE SURFACE DWELLERS TELL TALES OF A MAN NAMED JONAH WHO SURVIVED IN THE BELLY OF A WHALE.
NOW ATLANTEANS HAVE A TALE ALL THEIR OWN...OF LORI'S BOLD SUITOR...
...WHO, SWALLOWED WHOLE BY THE KRAKEN... DEVOURED...
...UNDIGESTED...
...AND BILE-DRENCHED...
...YET TRIUMPHED.
WELL, DADDY?
HAS HE NOT PROVEN HIMSELF?
WHAT DO YOU SAY, POPS?
FROG LEGS...
...SHE WILL NEVER BE YOURS.

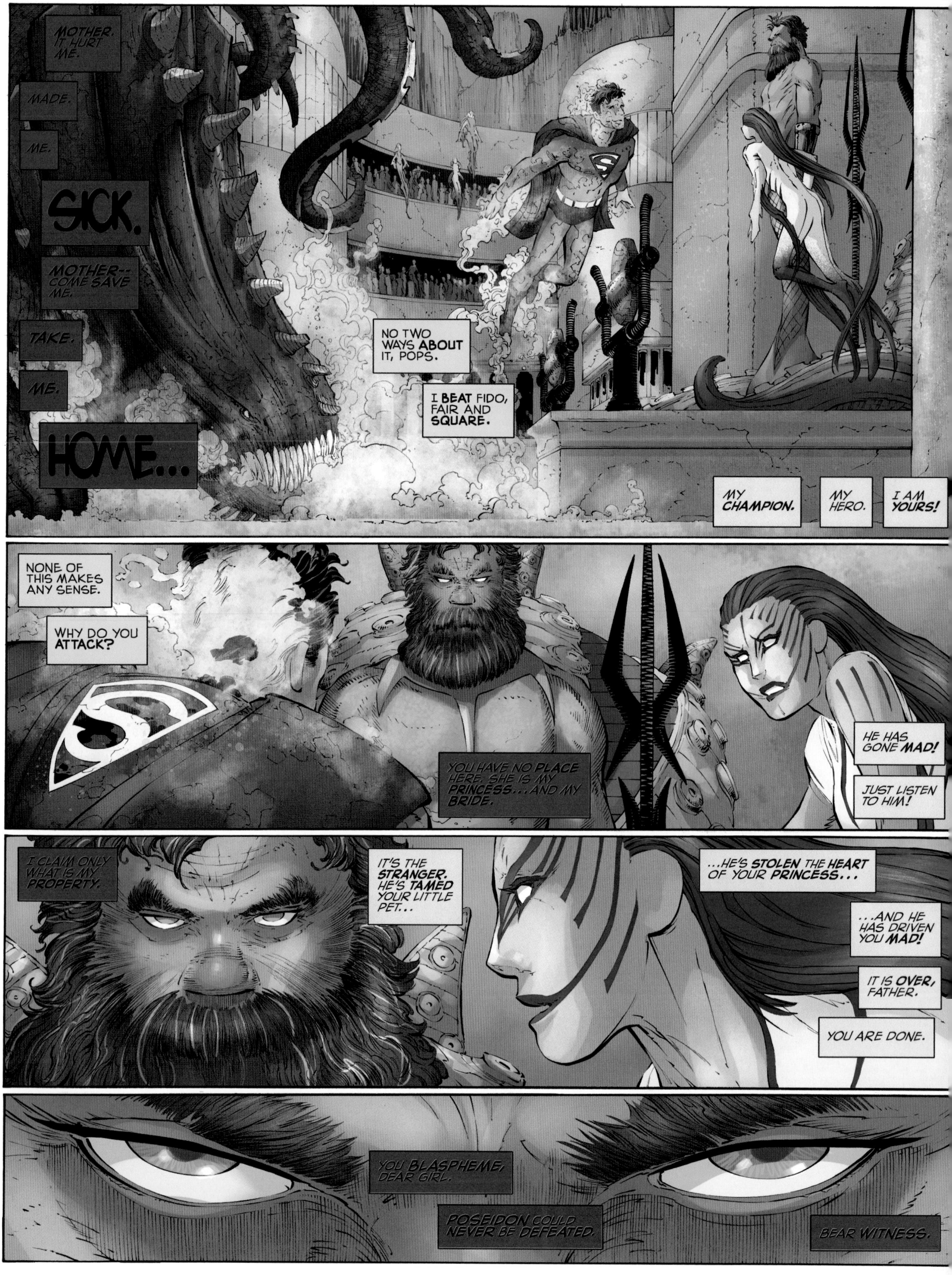
MOTHER. IT HURT ME.
MADE.
ME.
SICK.
MOTHER-- COME SAVE ME.
TAKE.
ME.
HOME...
NO TWO WAYS ABOUT IT, POPS.
I BEAT FIDO, FAIR AND SQUARE.
MY CHAMPION.
MY HERO.
I AM YOURS!
NONE OF THIS MAKES ANY SENSE.
WHY DO YOU ATTACK?
YOU HAVE NO PLACE HERE. SHE IS MY PRINCESS... AND MY BRIDE.
HE HAS GONE MAD!
JUST LISTEN TO HIM!
I CLAIM ONLY WHAT IS MY PROPERTY.
IT'S THE STRANGER. HE'S TAMED YOUR LITTLE PET...
...HE'S STOLEN THE HEART OF YOUR PRINCESS...
...AND HE HAS DRIVEN YOU MAD!
IT IS OVER, FATHER.
YOU ARE DONE.
YOU BLASPHEME, DEAR GIRL.
POSEIDON COULD NEVER BE DEFEATED.
BEAR WITNESS.

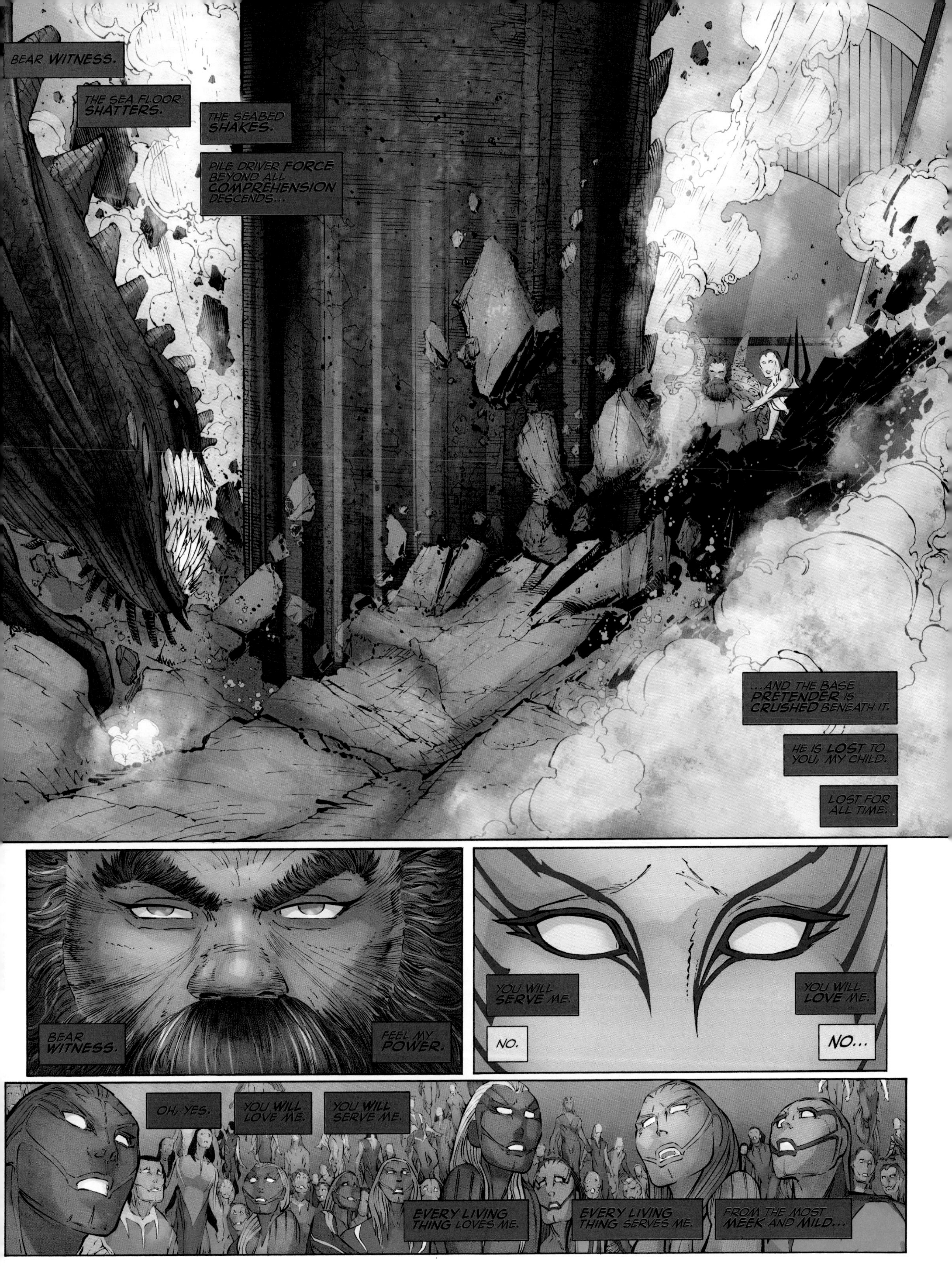
BEAR WITNESS.
THE SEA FLOOR SHATTERS.
THE SEABED SHAKES.
PILE DRIVER FORCE BEYOND ALL COMPREHENSION DESCENDS...
...AND THE BASE PRETENDER IS CRUSHED BENEATH IT.
HE IS LOST TO YOU, MY CHILD.
LOST FOR ALL TIME.
BEAR WITNESS.
FEEL MY POWER.
YOU WILL SERVE ME.
NO.
YOU WILL LOVE ME.
NO...
OH, YES.
YOU WILL LOVE ME.
YOU WILL SERVE ME.
EVERY LIVING THING LOVES ME.
EVERY LIVING THING SERVES ME.
FROM THE MOST MEEK AND MILD...

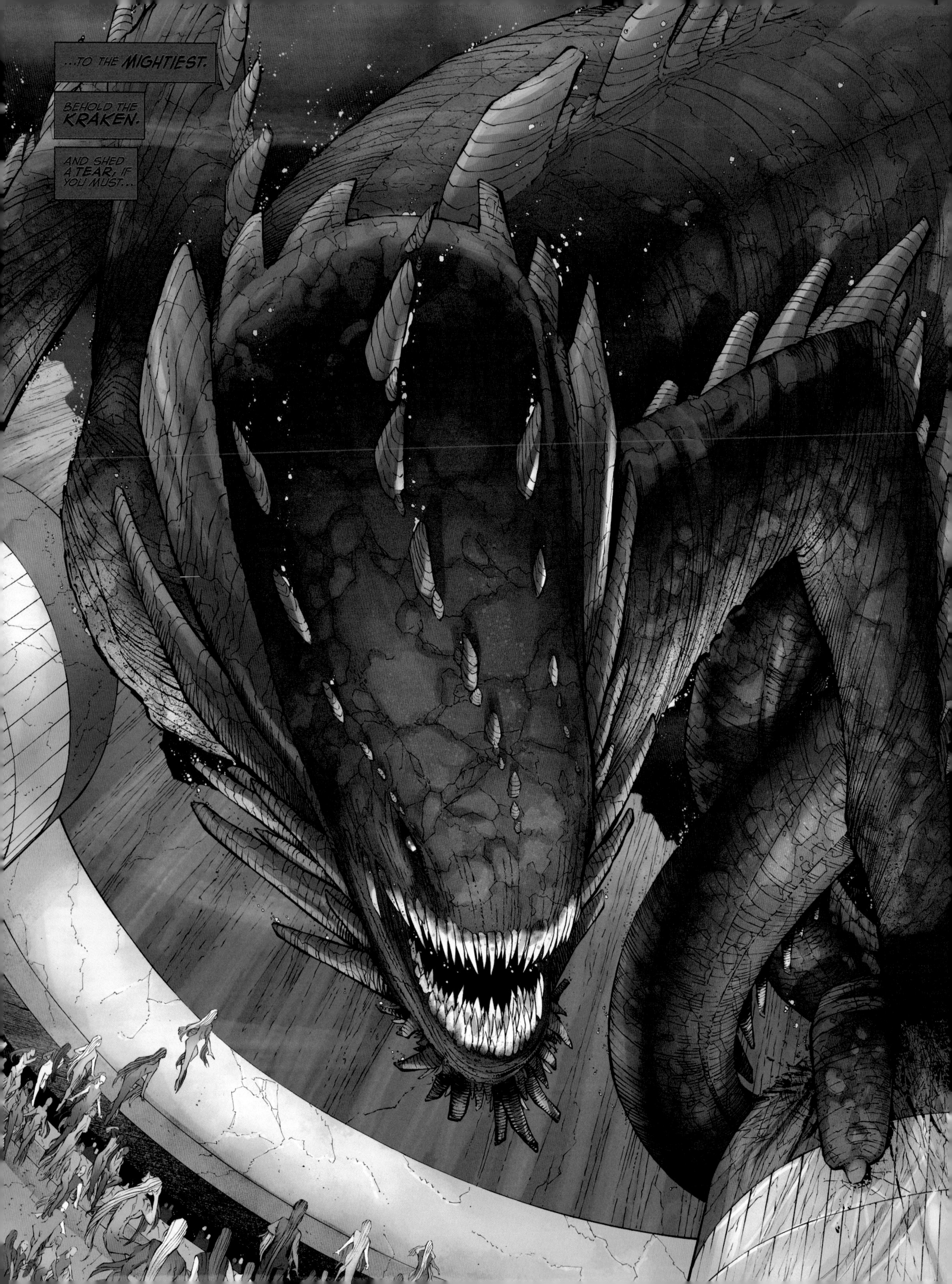
...TO THE MIGHTIEST.
BEHOLD THE KRAKEN.
AND SHED A TEAR, IF YOU MUST...

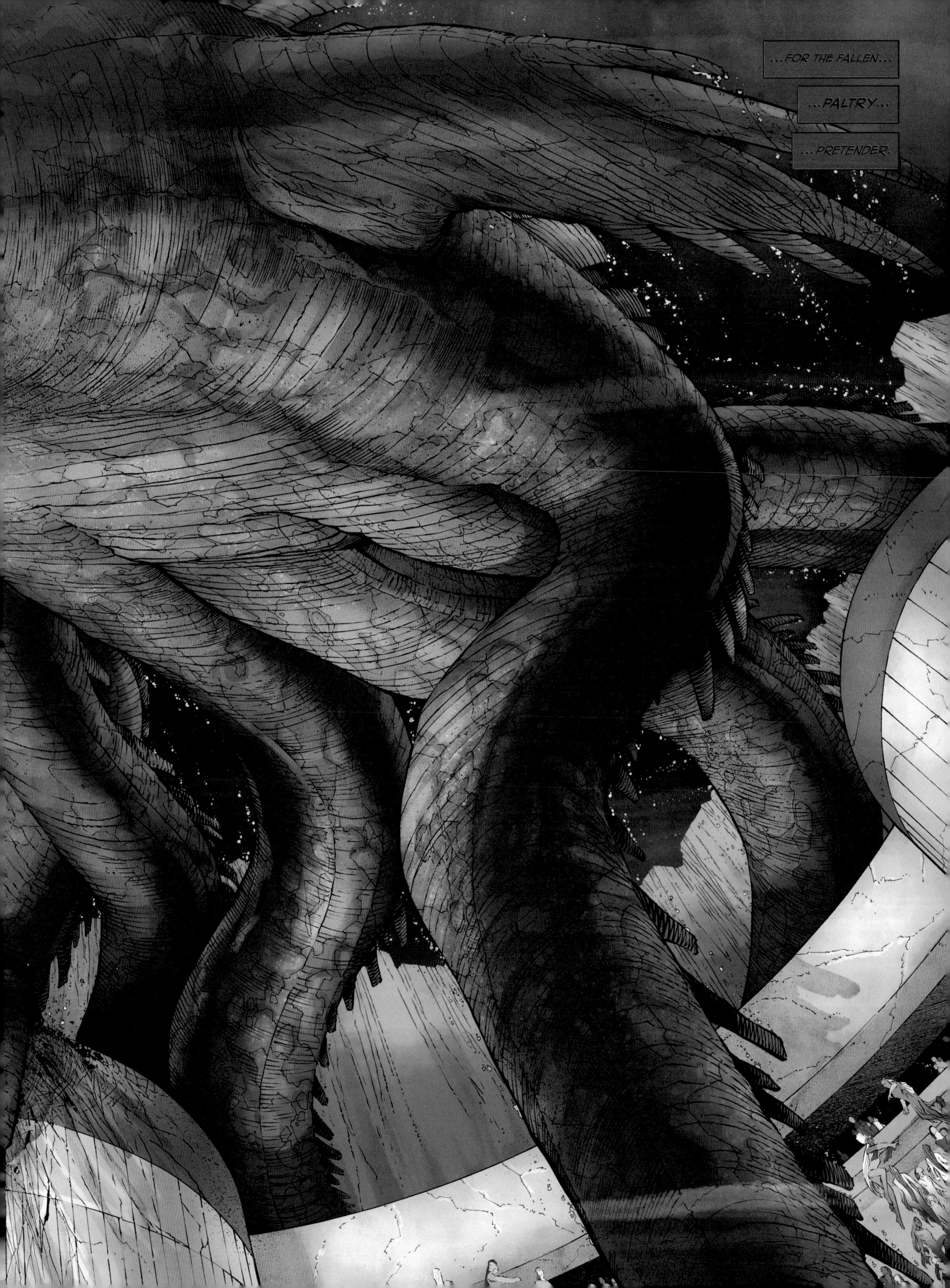
...FOR THE FALLEN...
...PALTRY...
...PRETENDER.

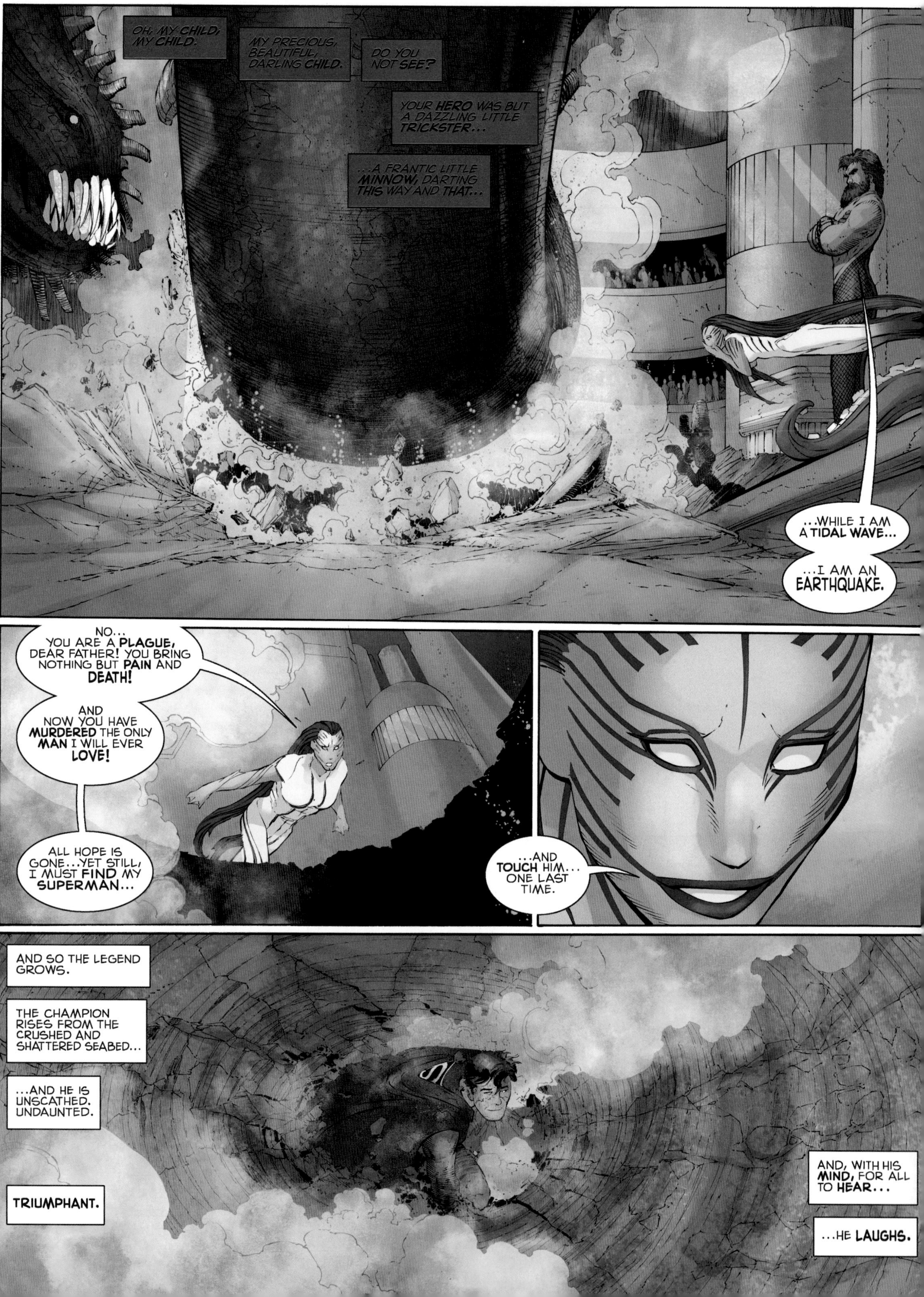
OH, MY CHILD, MY CHILD.
MY PRECIOUS, BEAUTIFUL, DARLING CHILD.
DO YOU NOT SEE?
YOUR HERO WAS BUT A DAZZLING LITTLE TRICKSTER...
...A FRANTIC LITTLE MINNOW, DARTING THIS WAY AND THAT...
...WHILE I AM A TIDAL WAVE...
...I AM AN EARTHQUAKE.
NO... YOU ARE A PLAGUE, DEAR FATHER! YOU BRING NOTHING BUT PAIN AND DEATH!
AND NOW YOU HAVE MURDERED THE ONLY MAN I WILL EVER LOVE!
ALL HOPE IS GONE...YET STILL, I MUST FIND MY SUPERMAN...
...AND TOUCH HIM... ONE LAST TIME.
AND SO THE LEGEND GROWS.
THE CHAMPION RISES FROM THE CRUSHED AND SHATTERED SEABED...
...AND HE IS UNSCATHED. UNDAUNTED.
TRIUMPHANT.
AND, WITH HIS MIND, FOR ALL TO HEAR...
...HE LAUGHS.

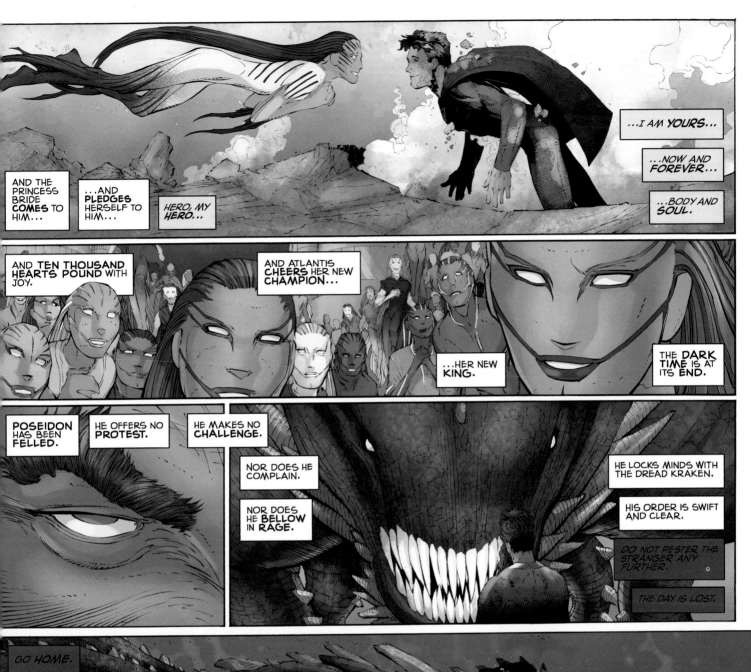

...I AM YOURS...

...NOW AND FOREVER...

...BODY AND SOUL.

AND THE PRINCESS BRIDE **COMES** TO HIM...

...AND **PLEDGES** HERSELF TO HIM...

HERO, MY **HERO**...

AND **TEN THOUSAND HEARTS** POUND WITH JOY.

AND ATLANTIS **CHEERS** HER NEW **CHAMPION**...

...HER NEW **KING**.

THE **DARK TIME** IS AT ITS **END**.

POSEIDON HAS BEEN **FELLED**.

HE OFFERS NO **PROTEST**.

HE MAKES NO **CHALLENGE**.

NOR DOES HE **COMPLAIN**.

NOR DOES HE **BELLOW** IN RAGE.

HE LOCKS MINDS WITH THE **DREAD KRAKEN**.

HIS ORDER IS **SWIFT** AND **CLEAR**.

DO NOT PESTER THE STRANGER ANY FURTHER.

THE DAY IS LOST.

GO HOME.

NURSE YOUR WOUNDS.

COME WHEN CALLED.

THE DAY IS LOST.

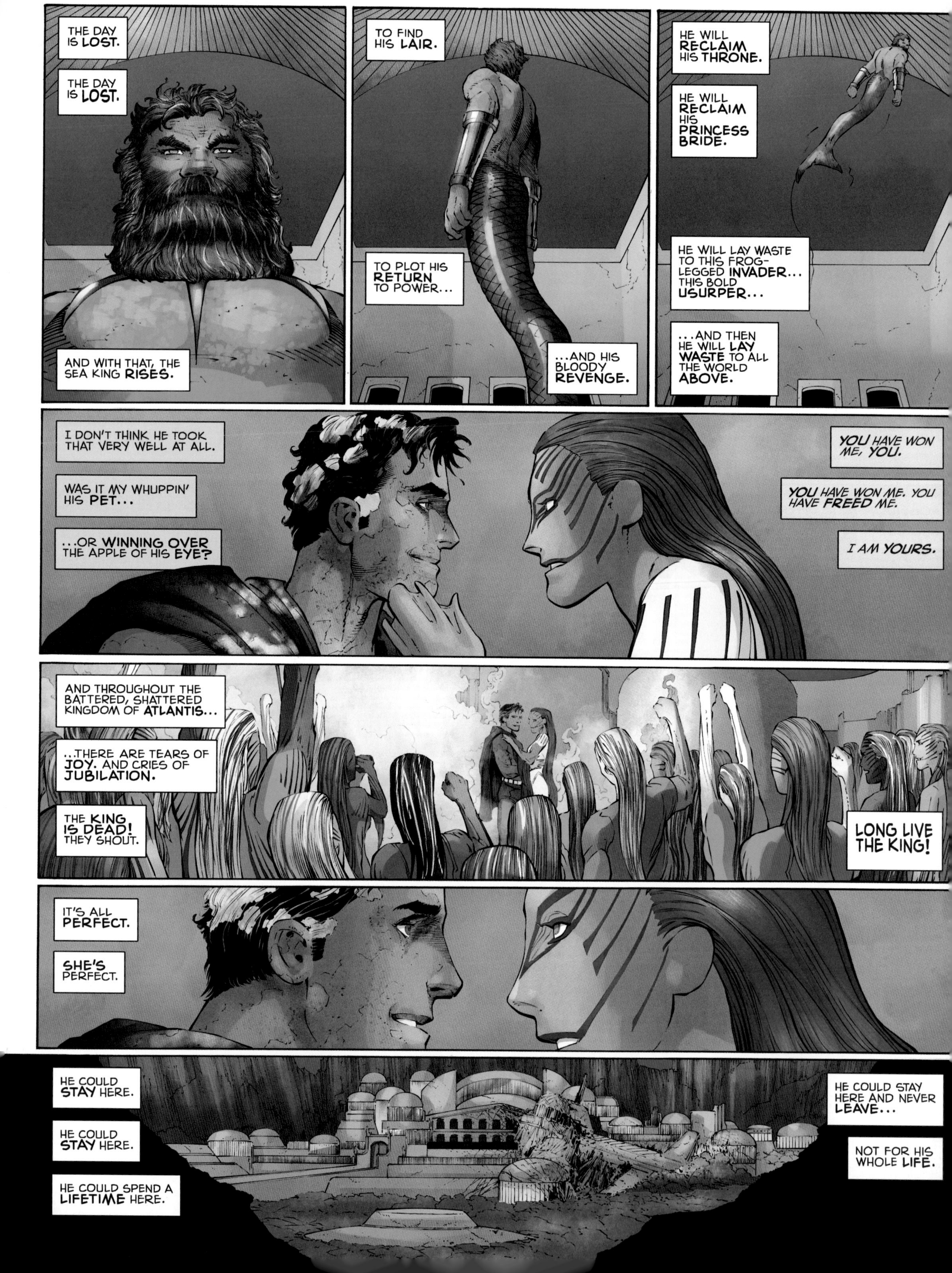
THE DAY IS LOST.
THE DAY IS LOST.
AND WITH THAT, THE SEA KING RISES.
TO FIND HIS LAIR.
TO PLOT HIS RETURN TO POWER...
...AND HIS BLOODY REVENGE.
HE WILL RECLAIM HIS THRONE.
HE WILL RECLAIM HIS PRINCESS BRIDE.
HE WILL LAY WASTE TO THIS FROG-LEGGED INVADER... THIS BOLD USURPER...
...AND THEN HE WILL LAY WASTE TO ALL THE WORLD ABOVE.
I DON'T THINK HE TOOK THAT VERY WELL AT ALL.
WAS IT MY WHUPPIN' HIS PET...
...OR WINNING OVER THE APPLE OF HIS EYE?
YOU HAVE WON ME, YOU.
YOU HAVE WON ME. YOU HAVE FREED ME.
I AM YOURS.
AND THROUGHOUT THE BATTERED, SHATTERED KINGDOM OF ATLANTIS...
...THERE ARE TEARS OF JOY. AND CRIES OF JUBILATION.
THE KING IS DEAD! THEY SHOUT.
LONG LIVE THE KING!
IT'S ALL PERFECT.
SHE'S PERFECT.
HE COULD STAY HERE.
HE COULD STAY HERE.
HE COULD SPEND A LIFETIME HERE.
HE COULD STAY HERE AND NEVER LEAVE...
NOT FOR HIS WHOLE LIFE.

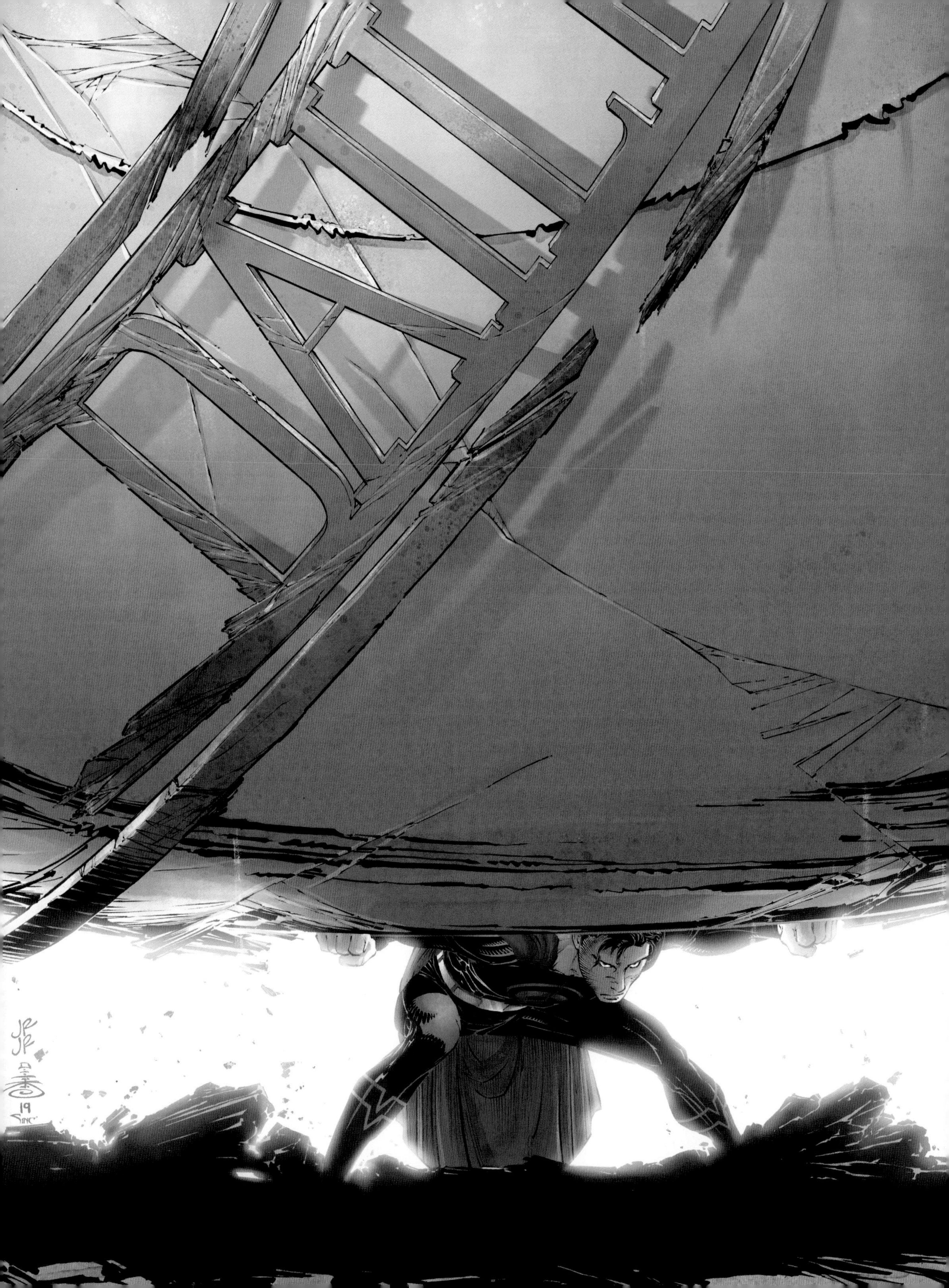

Part Three

METROPOLIS

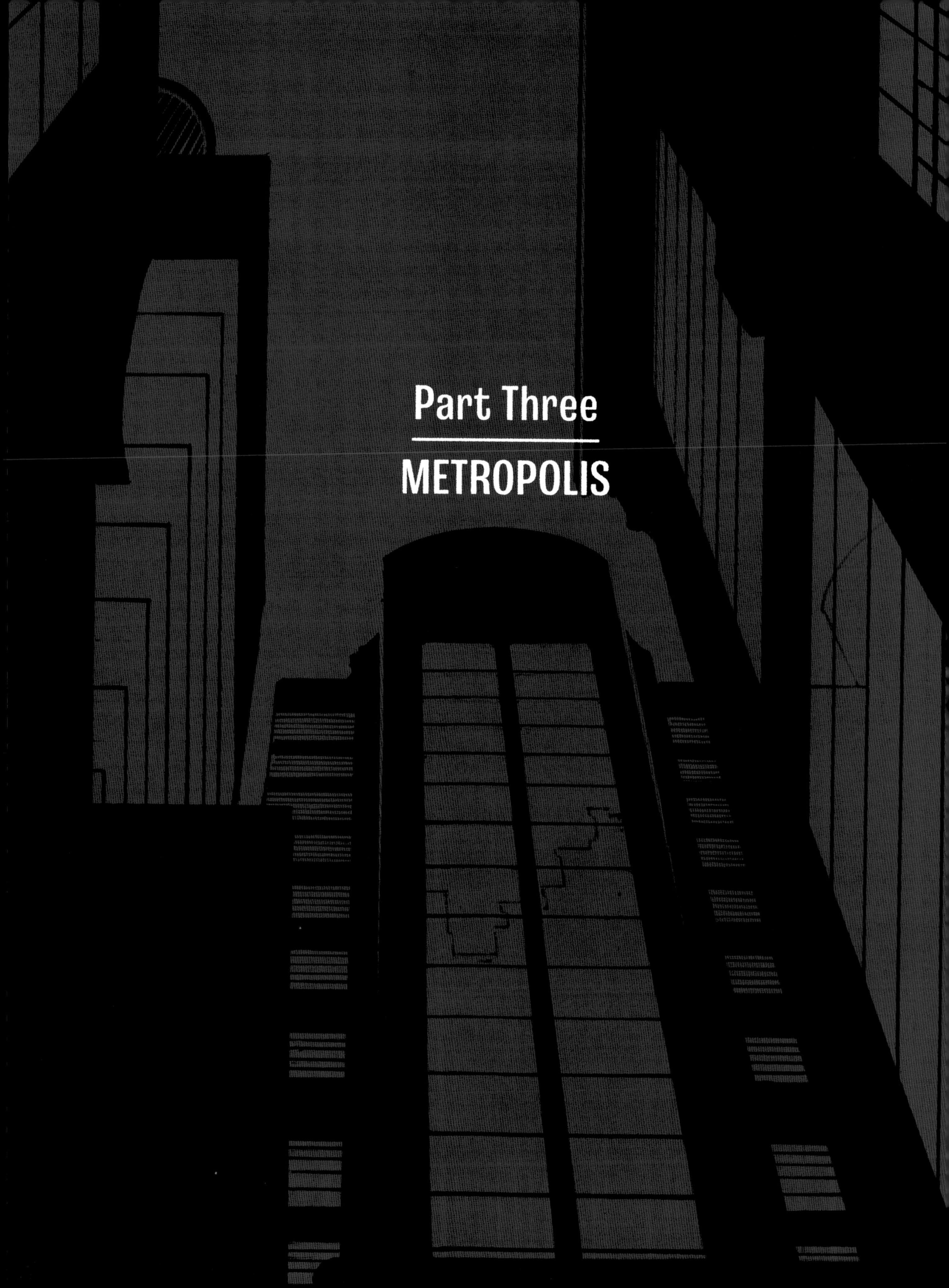

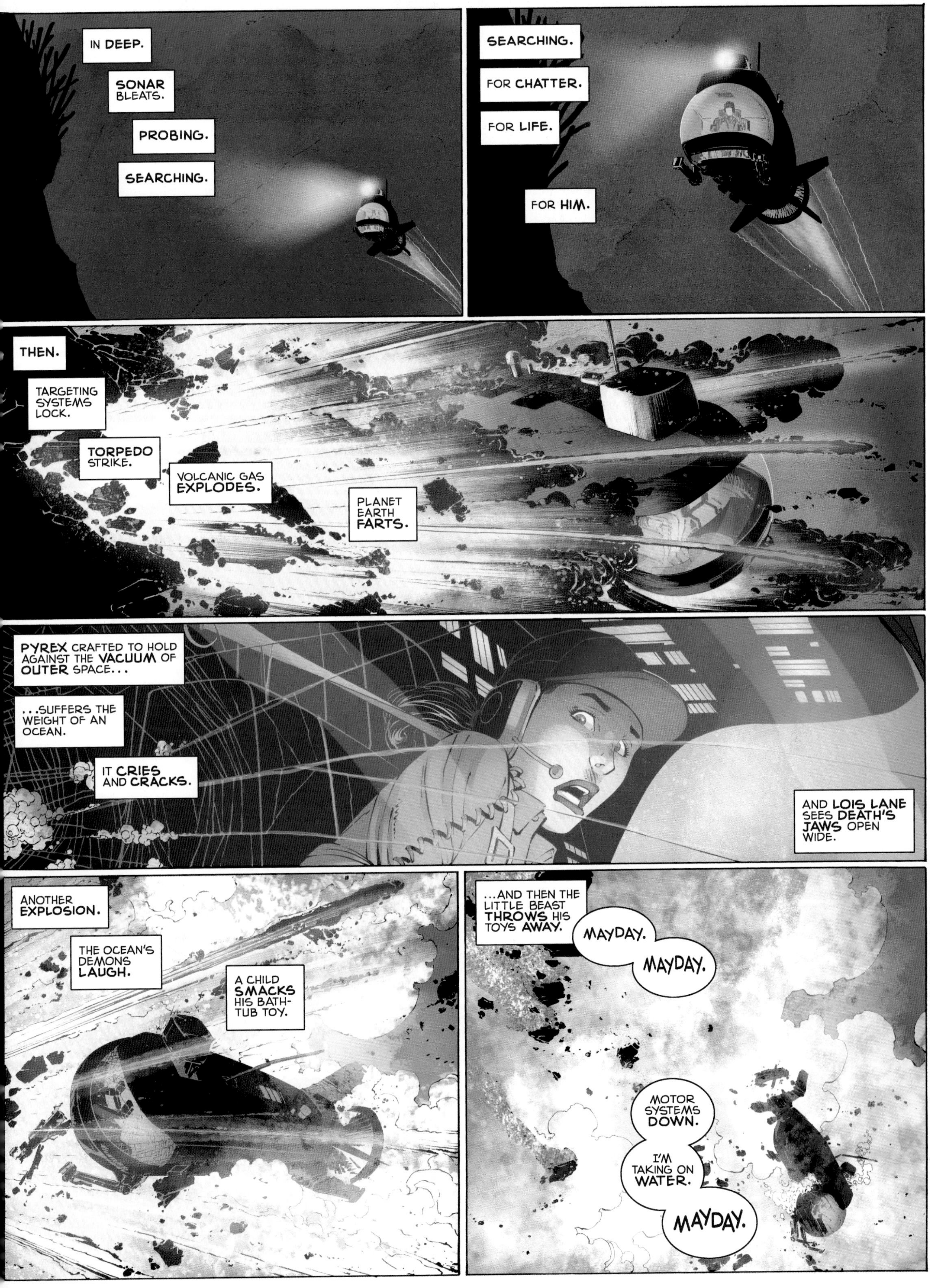

IN DEEP.
SONAR BLEATS.
PROBING.
SEARCHING.
SEARCHING.
FOR CHATTER.
FOR LIFE.
FOR HIM.
THEN.
TARGETING SYSTEMS LOCK.
TORPEDO STRIKE.
VOLCANIC GAS EXPLODES.
PLANET EARTH FARTS.
PYREX CRAFTED TO HOLD AGAINST THE VACUUM OF OUTER SPACE...
...SUFFERS THE WEIGHT OF AN OCEAN.
IT CRIES AND CRACKS.
AND LOIS LANE SEES DEATH'S JAWS OPEN WIDE.
ANOTHER EXPLOSION.
THE OCEAN'S DEMONS LAUGH.
A CHILD SMACKS HIS BATH-TUB TOY.
...AND THEN THE LITTLE BEAST THROWS HIS TOYS AWAY.
MAYDAY.
MAYDAY.
MOTOR SYSTEMS DOWN.
I'M TAKING ON WATER.
MAYDAY.

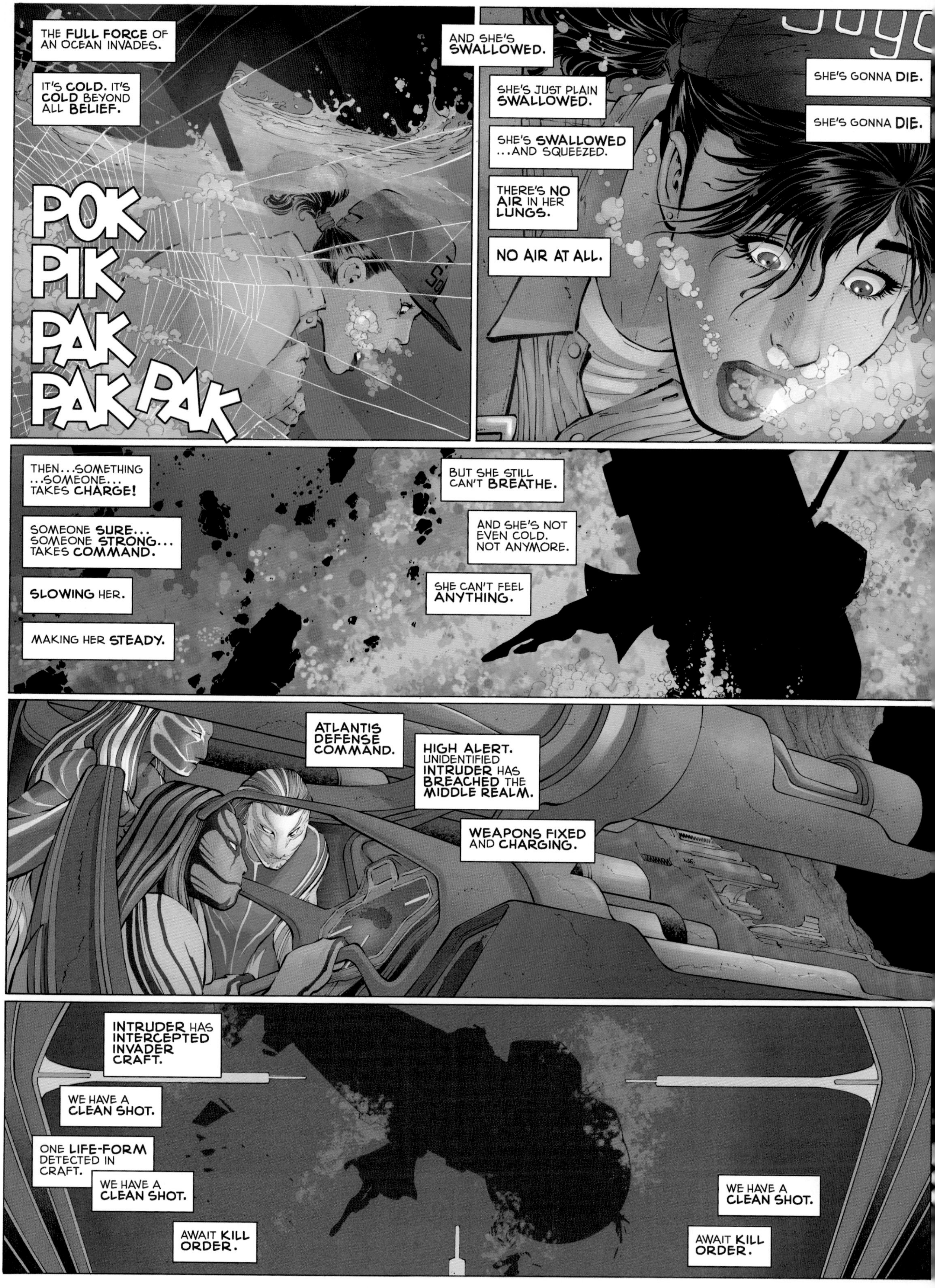
THE FULL FORCE OF AN OCEAN INVADES.
IT'S COLD. IT'S COLD BEYOND ALL BELIEF.
POK
PIK
PAK
PAK PAK
AND SHE'S SWALLOWED.
SHE'S JUST PLAIN SWALLOWED.
SHE'S SWALLOWED ...AND SQUEEZED.
THERE'S NO AIR IN HER LUNGS.
NO AIR AT ALL.
SHE'S GONNA DIE.
SHE'S GONNA DIE.
THEN...SOMETHING ...SOMEONE... TAKES CHARGE!
SOMEONE SURE... SOMEONE STRONG... TAKES COMMAND.
SLOWING HER.
MAKING HER STEADY.
BUT SHE STILL CAN'T BREATHE.
AND SHE'S NOT EVEN COLD. NOT ANYMORE.
SHE CAN'T FEEL ANYTHING.
ATLANTIS DEFENSE COMMAND.
HIGH ALERT. UNIDENTIFIED INTRUDER HAS BREACHED THE MIDDLE REALM.
WEAPONS FIXED AND CHARGING.
INTRUDER HAS INTERCEPTED INVADER CRAFT.
WE HAVE A CLEAN SHOT.
ONE LIFE-FORM DETECTED IN CRAFT.
WE HAVE A CLEAN SHOT.
AWAIT KILL ORDER.
WE HAVE A CLEAN SHOT.
AWAIT KILL ORDER.

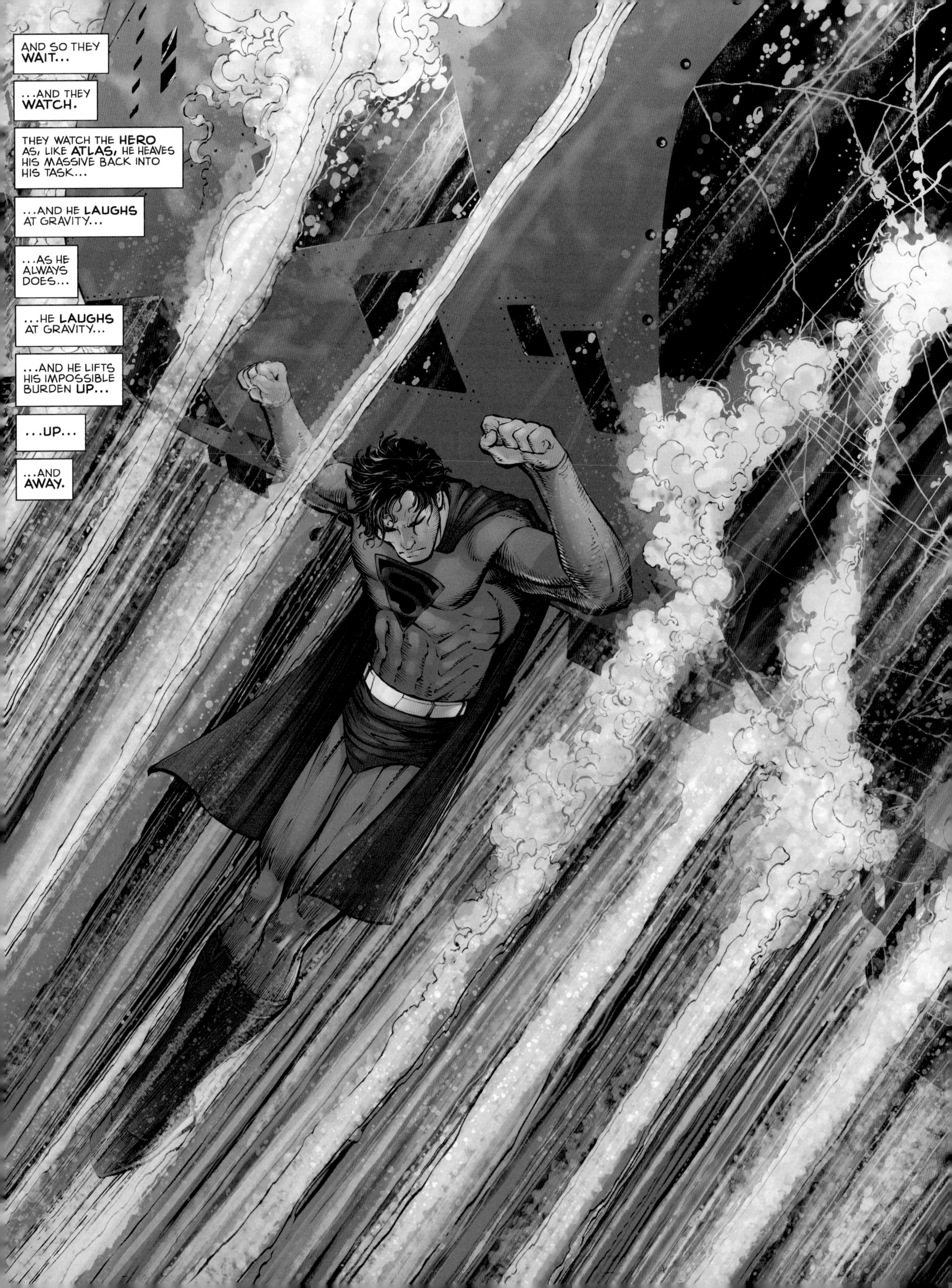
AND SO THEY WAIT...
...AND THEY WATCH.
THEY WATCH THE HERO AS, LIKE ATLAS, HE HEAVES HIS MASSIVE BACK INTO HIS TASK...
...AND HE LAUGHS AT GRAVITY...
...AS HE ALWAYS DOES...
...HE LAUGHS AT GRAVITY...
...AND HE LIFTS HIS IMPOSSIBLE BURDEN UP...
...UP...
...AND AWAY.

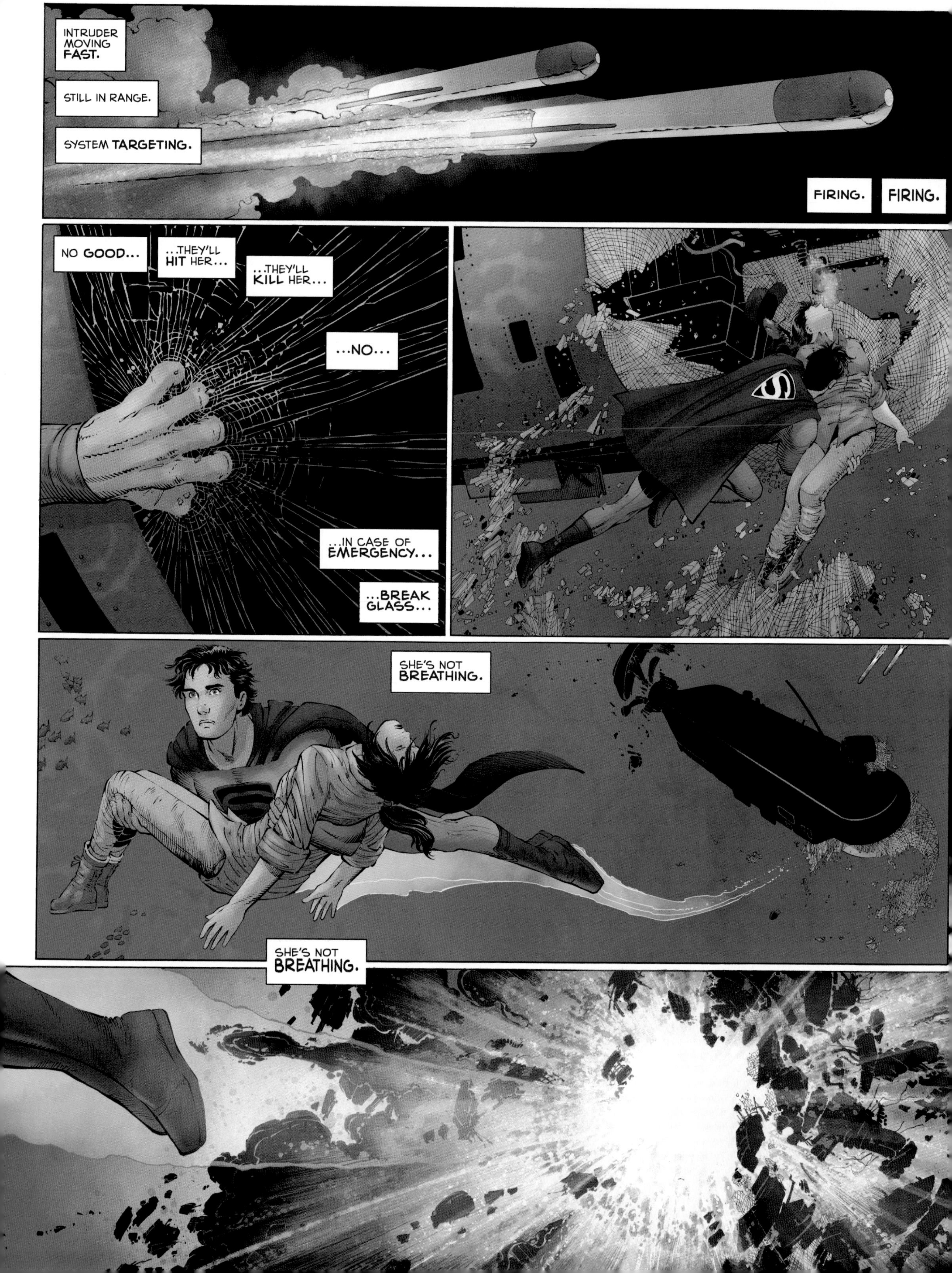
INTRUDER MOVING FAST.
STILL IN RANGE.
SYSTEM TARGETING.
FIRING.
FIRING.
NO GOOD...
...THEY'LL HIT HER...
...THEY'LL KILL HER...
...NO...
...IN CASE OF EMERGENCY...
...BREAK GLASS...
SHE'S NOT BREATHING.
SHE'S NOT BREATHING.

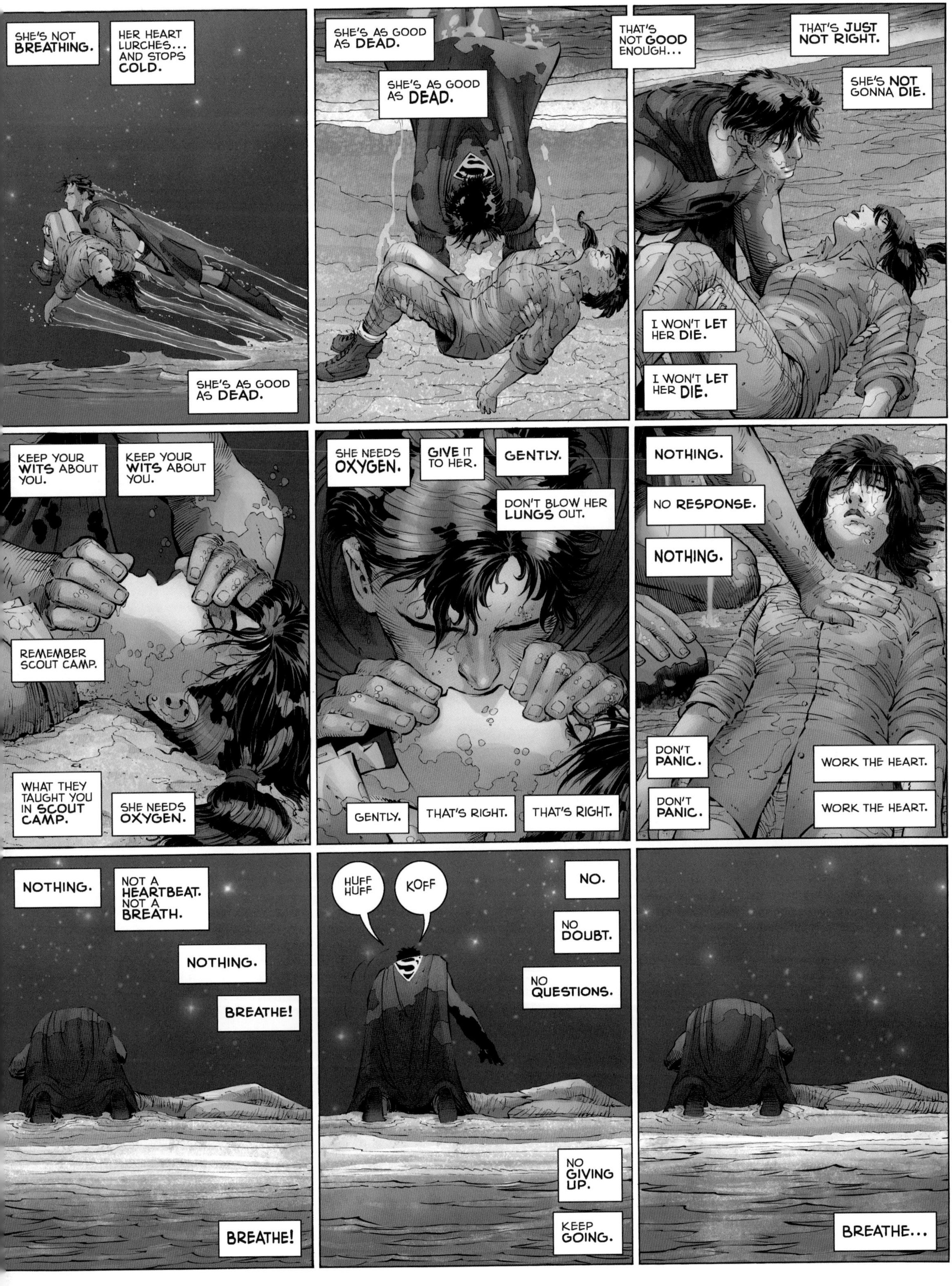
SHE'S NOT BREATHING.
HER HEART LURCHES... AND STOPS COLD.
SHE'S AS GOOD AS DEAD.
SHE'S AS GOOD AS DEAD.
SHE'S AS GOOD AS DEAD.
THAT'S NOT GOOD ENOUGH...
THAT'S JUST NOT RIGHT.
SHE'S NOT GONNA DIE.
I WON'T LET HER DIE.
I WON'T LET HER DIE.
KEEP YOUR WITS ABOUT YOU.
KEEP YOUR WITS ABOUT YOU.
REMEMBER SCOUT CAMP.
WHAT THEY TAUGHT YOU IN SCOUT CAMP.
SHE NEEDS OXYGEN.
SHE NEEDS OXYGEN.
GIVE IT TO HER.
GENTLY.
DON'T BLOW HER LUNGS OUT.
GENTLY.
THAT'S RIGHT.
THAT'S RIGHT.
NOTHING.
NO RESPONSE.
NOTHING.
DON'T PANIC.
DON'T PANIC.
WORK THE HEART.
WORK THE HEART.
NOTHING.
NOT A HEARTBEAT. NOT A BREATH.
NOTHING.
BREATHE!
BREATHE!
HUFF HUFF
KOFF
NO.
NO DOUBT.
NO QUESTIONS.
NO GIVING UP.
KEEP GOING.
BREATHE...

AND IT **HURTS** LIKE **HELL**.

GHARKKK

...BUT BREATHE SHE DOES.

WHAT FEELS LIKE HALF AN **OCEAN** GORGES UP AND **OUT** OF HER.

KAFF

AND IT **HURTS** EVEN **MORE**.

AND STILL HER STOMACH WANTS TO THROW UP...

HUKK HUKK OH GOD.

...BUT THERE IS NOTHING LEFT TO THROW UP...

...AND SHE STARES STRAIGHT INTO HIS GOD-BLUE EYES.

AND SHE WANTS TO **SING** LIKE A **BIRD**...

...BUT HER DAMN **VOICE** COMES OUT LIKE **WET GRAVEL**.

THANK... MY NAME IS LOIS.

PLEASE DON'T **STRAIN** YOURSELF. YOU'VE BEEN THROUGH A LOT.

YOU'RE GOING TO BE FINE.

YOU'RE SAFE WITH ME.

"YOU'RE SAFE WITH ME."

IT SOUNDS SO **SIMPLE** WHEN HE SAYS IT.

SO SIMPLE...AND SO UTTERLY **TRUE**.

LIKE SHE'D **ALWAYS** BE SAFE IN HIS ARMS.

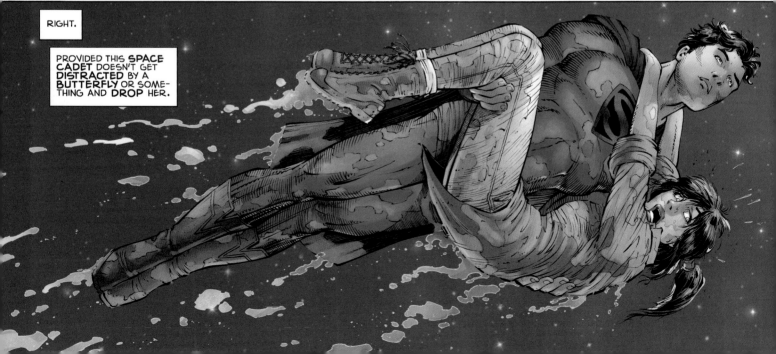

RIGHT.

PROVIDED THIS **SPACE CADET** DOESN'T GET **DISTRACTED** BY A **BUTTERFLY** OR SOMETHING AND **DROP** HER.

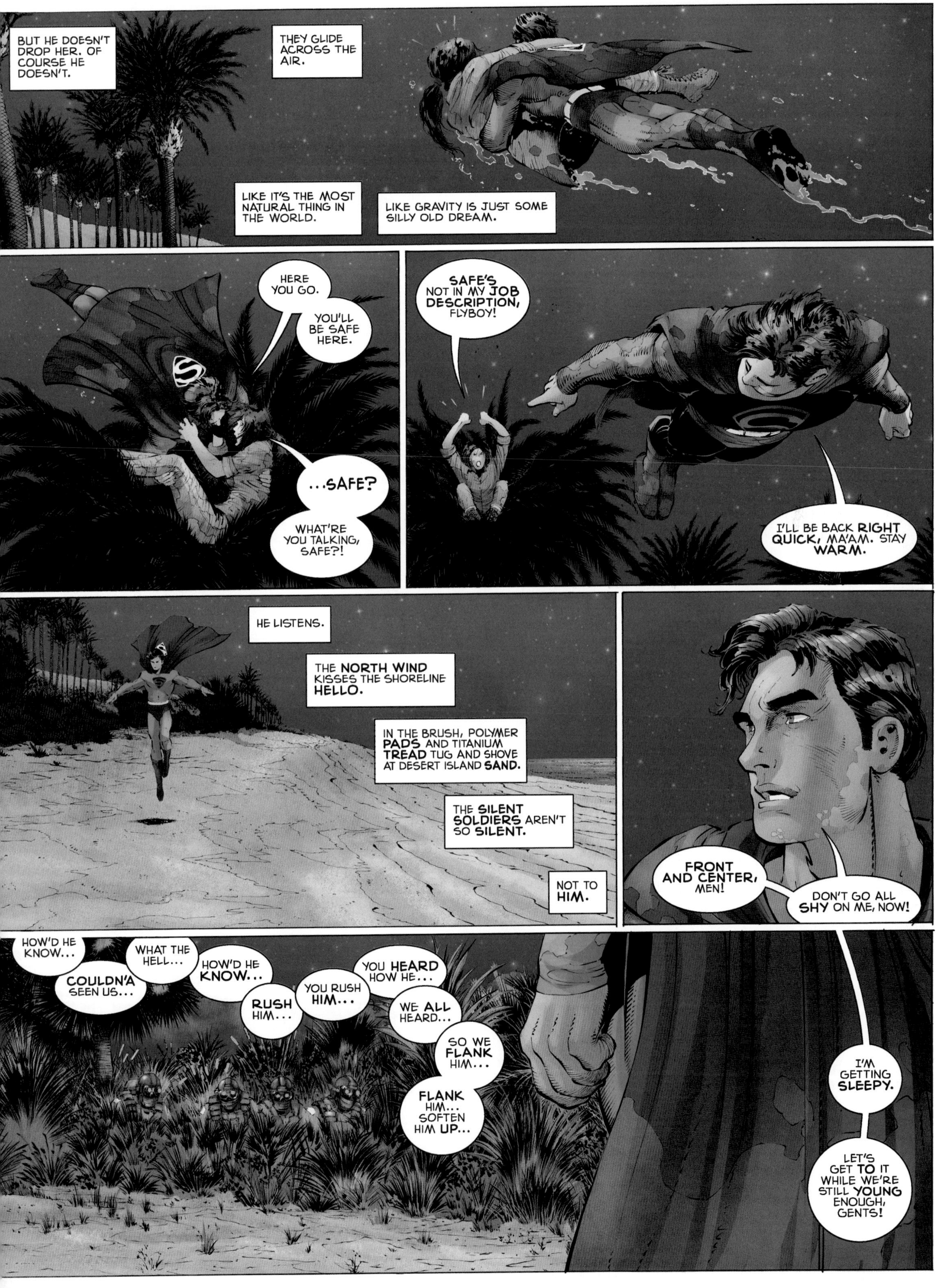

BUT HE DOESN'T DROP HER. OF COURSE HE DOESN'T.
THEY GLIDE ACROSS THE AIR.
LIKE IT'S THE MOST NATURAL THING IN THE WORLD.
LIKE GRAVITY IS JUST SOME SILLY OLD DREAM.
HERE YOU GO.
YOU'LL BE SAFE HERE.
...SAFE?
WHAT'RE YOU TALKING, SAFE?!
SAFE'S NOT IN MY JOB DESCRIPTION, FLYBOY!
I'LL BE BACK RIGHT QUICK, MA'AM. STAY WARM.
HE LISTENS.
THE NORTH WIND KISSES THE SHORELINE HELLO.
IN THE BRUSH, POLYMER PADS AND TITANIUM TREAD TUG AND SHOVE AT DESERT ISLAND SAND.
THE SILENT SOLDIERS AREN'T SO SILENT.
NOT TO HIM.
FRONT AND CENTER, MEN!
DON'T GO ALL SHY ON ME, NOW!
HOW'D HE KNOW...
COULDN'A SEEN US...
WHAT THE HELL...
HOW'D HE KNOW...
RUSH HIM...
YOU RUSH HIM...
YOU HEARD HOW HE...
WE ALL HEARD...
SO WE FLANK HIM...
FLANK HIM... SOFTEN HIM UP...
I'M GETTING SLEEPY.
LET'S GET TO IT WHILE WE'RE STILL YOUNG ENOUGH, GENTS!

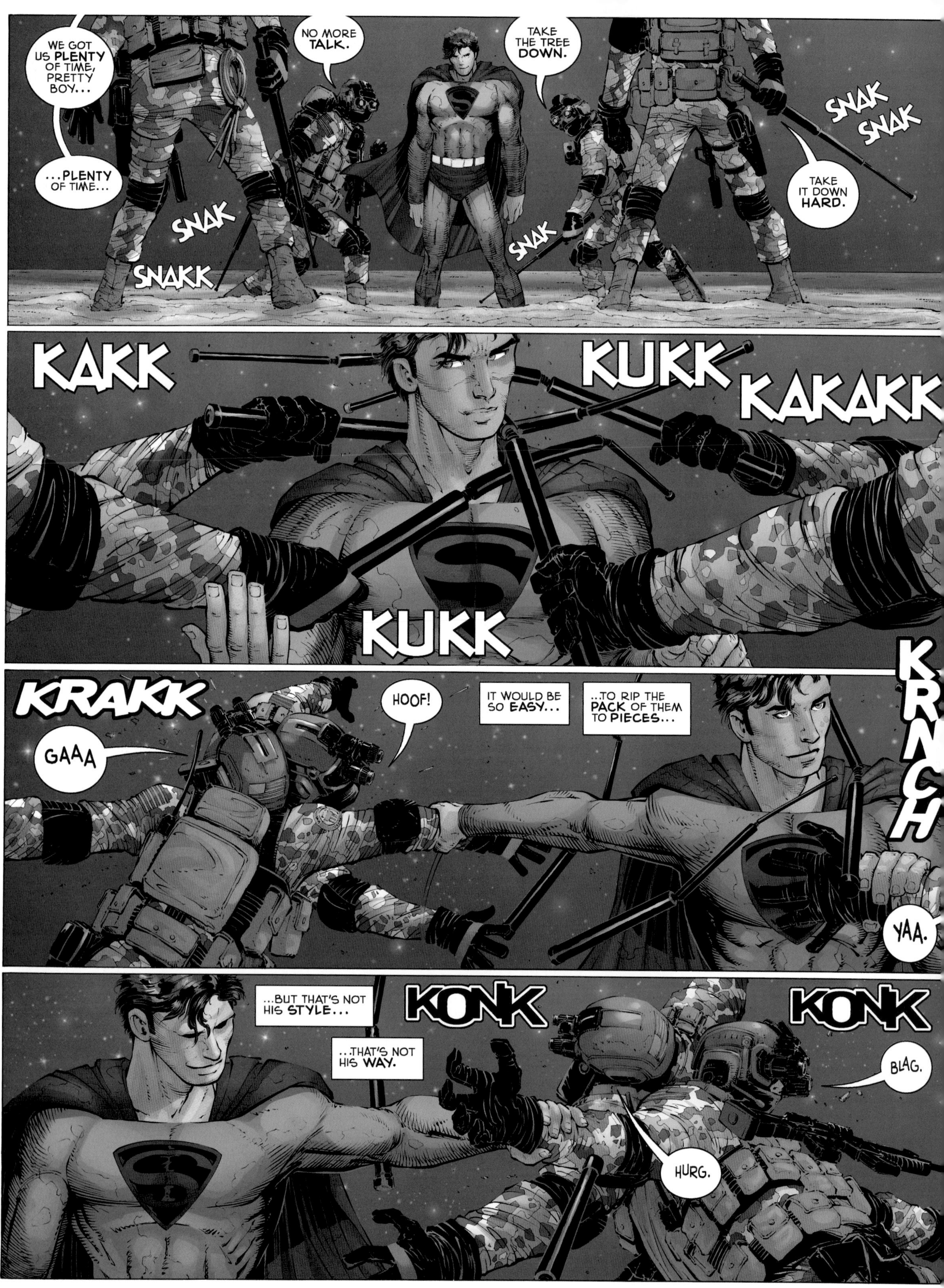
WE GOT US PLENTY OF TIME, PRETTY BOY...
...PLENTY OF TIME...
NO MORE TALK.
TAKE THE TREE DOWN.
SNAK SNAK
TAKE IT DOWN HARD.
SNAK
SNAKK
SNAK
KAKK
KUKK
KAKAKK
KUKK
KRAKK
GAAA
HOOF!
IT WOULD BE SO EASY...
..TO RIP THE PACK OF THEM TO PIECES...
KRNCH
YAA.
...BUT THAT'S NOT HIS STYLE...
..THAT'S NOT HIS WAY.
KONK
KONK
BLAG.
HURG.

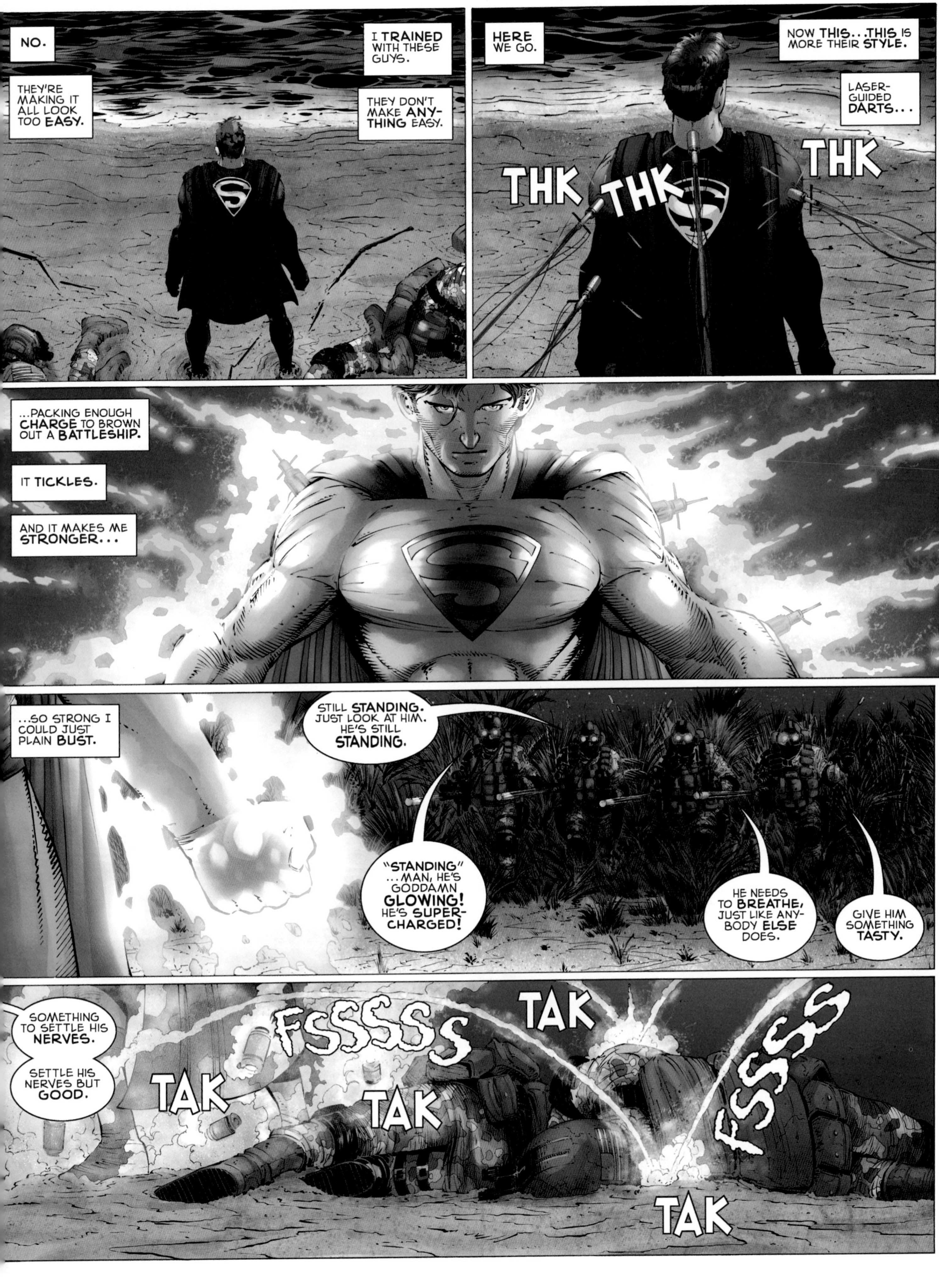
NO.
THEY'RE MAKING IT ALL LOOK TOO EASY.
I TRAINED WITH THESE GUYS.
THEY DON'T MAKE ANYTHING EASY.
HERE WE GO.
NOW THIS... THIS IS MORE THEIR STYLE.
LASER-GUIDED DARTS...
THK
THK
THK
...PACKING ENOUGH CHARGE TO BROWN OUT A BATTLESHIP.
IT TICKLES.
AND IT MAKES ME STRONGER...
...SO STRONG I COULD JUST PLAIN BUST.
STILL STANDING. JUST LOOK AT HIM. HE'S STILL STANDING.
"STANDING" ...MAN, HE'S GODDAMN GLOWING! HE'S SUPER-CHARGED!
HE NEEDS TO BREATHE, JUST LIKE ANYBODY ELSE DOES.
GIVE HIM SOMETHING TASTY.
SOMETHING TO SETTLE HIS NERVES.
SETTLE HIS NERVES BUT GOOD.
FSSSSS
TAK
TAK
TAK
FSSSS
TAK

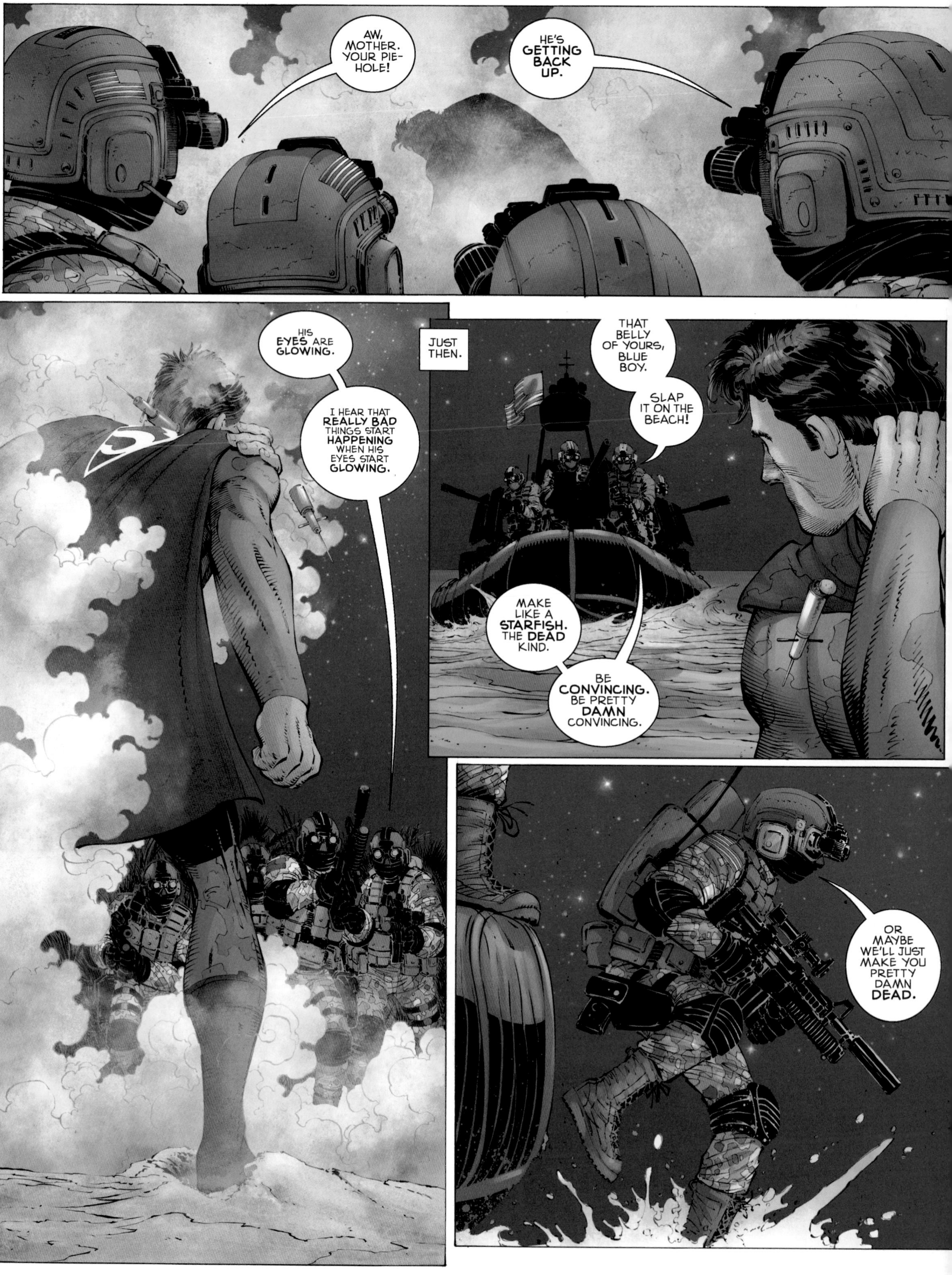

AW, MOTHER. YOUR PIE-HOLE!
HE'S GETTING BACK UP.
HIS EYES ARE GLOWING.
I HEAR THAT REALLY BAD THINGS START HAPPENING WHEN HIS EYES START GLOWING.
JUST THEN.
THAT BELLY OF YOURS, BLUE BOY.
SLAP IT ON THE BEACH!
MAKE LIKE A STARFISH. THE DEAD KIND.
BE CONVINCING. BE PRETTY DAMN CONVINCING.
OR MAYBE WE'LL JUST MAKE YOU PRETTY DAMN DEAD.

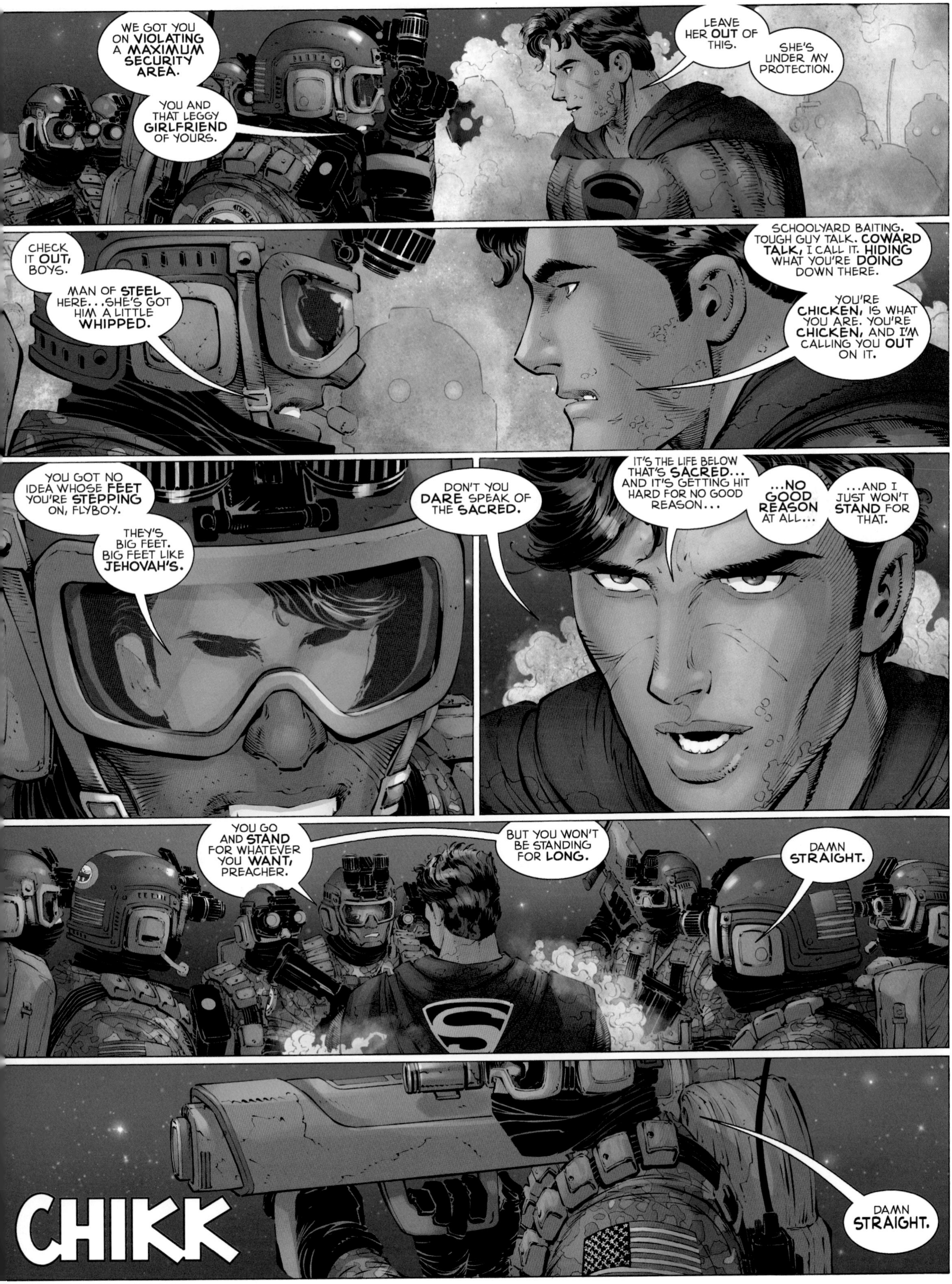
WE GOT YOU ON VIOLATING A MAXIMUM SECURITY AREA.
YOU AND THAT LEGGY GIRLFRIEND OF YOURS.
LEAVE HER OUT OF THIS.
SHE'S UNDER MY PROTECTION.
CHECK IT OUT, BOYS.
MAN OF STEEL HERE... SHE'S GOT HIM A LITTLE WHIPPED.
SCHOOLYARD BAITING. TOUGH GUY TALK. COWARD TALK, I CALL IT. HIDING WHAT YOU'RE DOING DOWN THERE.
YOU'RE CHICKEN, IS WHAT YOU ARE. YOU'RE CHICKEN, AND I'M CALLING YOU OUT ON IT.
YOU GOT NO IDEA WHOSE FEET YOU'RE STEPPING ON, FLYBOY.
THEY'S BIG FEET. BIG FEET LIKE JEHOVAH'S.
DON'T YOU DARE SPEAK OF THE SACRED.
IT'S THE LIFE BELOW THAT'S SACRED... AND IT'S GETTING HIT HARD FOR NO GOOD REASON...
...NO GOOD REASON AT ALL...
...AND I JUST WON'T STAND FOR THAT.
YOU GO AND STAND FOR WHATEVER YOU WANT, PREACHER.
BUT YOU WON'T BE STANDING FOR LONG.
DAMN STRAIGHT.
CHIKK
DAMN STRAIGHT.

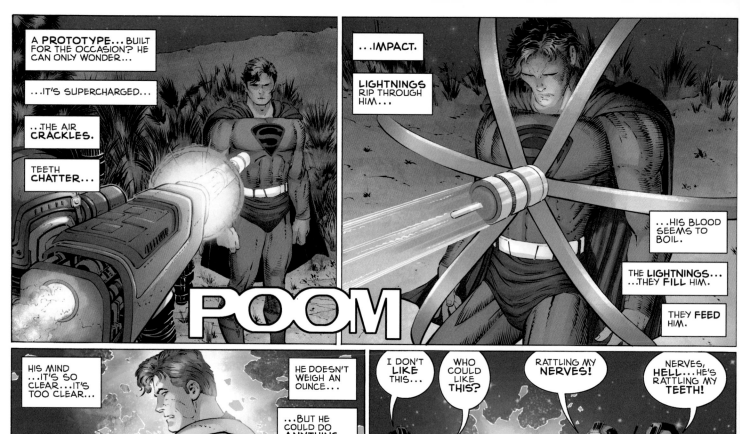

A PROTOTYPE... BUILT FOR THE OCCASION? HE CAN ONLY WONDER...

...IT'S SUPERCHARGED...

...THE AIR CRACKLES.

TEETH CHATTER...

POOM

...IMPACT.

LIGHTNINGS RIP THROUGH HIM...

...HIS BLOOD SEEMS TO BOIL.

THE LIGHTNINGS... ...THEY FILL HIM.

THEY FEED HIM.

HIS MIND ...IT'S SO CLEAR...IT'S TOO CLEAR...

HE DOESN'T WEIGH AN OUNCE...

...BUT HE COULD DO ANYTHING...

...ANYTHING.

THIS IS PLAIN

DAMN

WEIRD.

I DON'T LIKE THIS...

WHO COULD LIKE THIS?

RATTLING MY NERVES!

NERVES, HELL...HE'S RATTLING MY TEETH!

SCRAMBLE THE PARTICLE BEAM!

"PARTICLE BEAM"...?

HE DOESN'T WANT TO KNOW.

YAA

LET THEM EAT SHRAPNEL.

GARR.

HUGG.

SHRAKK

THEY'LL LIVE.

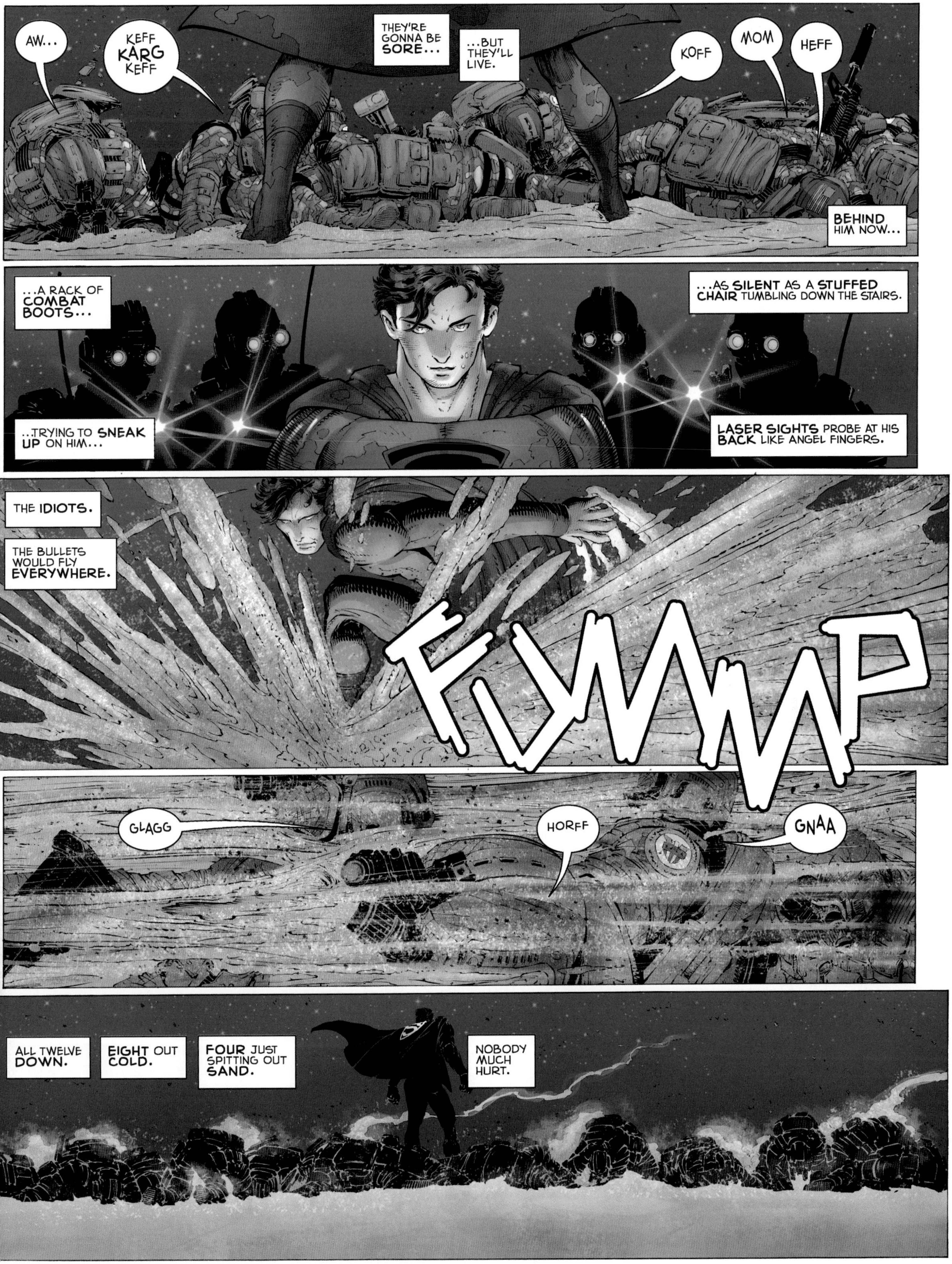
AW...
KEFF KARG KEFF
THEY'RE GONNA BE SORE...
...BUT THEY'LL LIVE.
KOFF
MOM
HEFF
BEHIND HIM NOW...
...A RACK OF COMBAT BOOTS...
...TRYING TO SNEAK UP ON HIM...
...AS SILENT AS A STUFFED CHAIR TUMBLING DOWN THE STAIRS.
LASER SIGHTS PROBE AT HIS BACK LIKE ANGEL FINGERS.
THE IDIOTS.
THE BULLETS WOULD FLY EVERYWHERE.
FLYMMP
GLAGG
HORFF
GNAA
ALL TWELVE DOWN.
EIGHT OUT COLD.
FOUR JUST SPITTING OUT SAND.
NOBODY MUCH HURT.

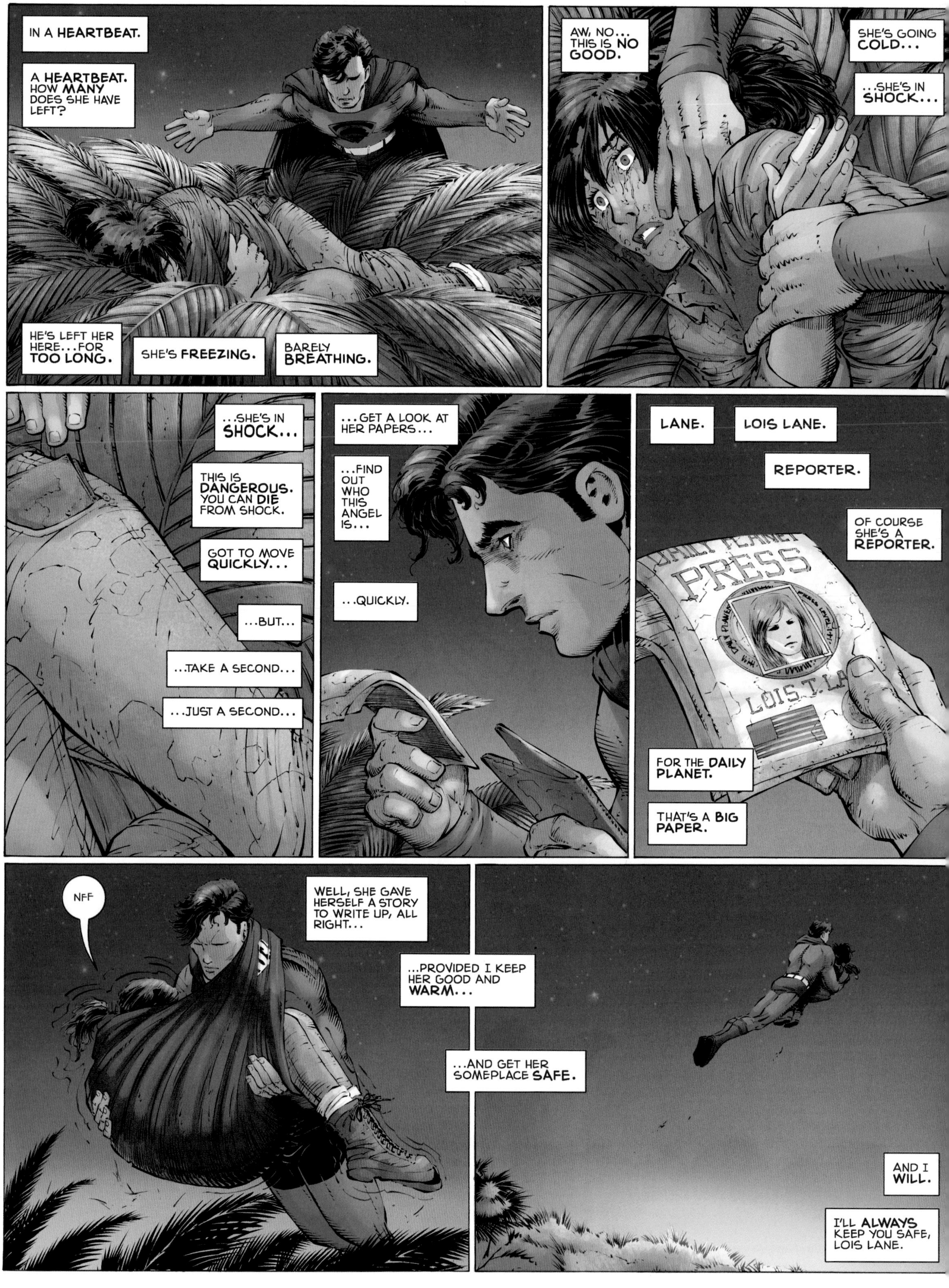
IN A HEARTBEAT.
A HEARTBEAT. HOW MANY DOES SHE HAVE LEFT?
HE'S LEFT HER HERE...FOR TOO LONG.
SHE'S FREEZING.
BARELY BREATHING.
AW, NO... THIS IS NO GOOD.
SHE'S GOING COLD...
...SHE'S IN SHOCK...
...SHE'S IN SHOCK...
THIS IS DANGEROUS. YOU CAN DIE FROM SHOCK.
GOT TO MOVE QUICKLY...
...BUT...
...TAKE A SECOND...
...JUST A SECOND...
...GET A LOOK AT HER PAPERS...
...FIND OUT WHO THIS ANGEL IS...
...QUICKLY.
LANE.
LOIS LANE.
REPORTER.
OF COURSE SHE'S A REPORTER.
PRESS
FOR THE DAILY PLANET.
THAT'S A BIG PAPER.
NFF
WELL, SHE GAVE HERSELF A STORY TO WRITE UP, ALL RIGHT...
...PROVIDED I KEEP HER GOOD AND WARM...
...AND GET HER SOMEPLACE SAFE.
AND I WILL.
I'LL ALWAYS KEEP YOU SAFE, LOIS LANE.

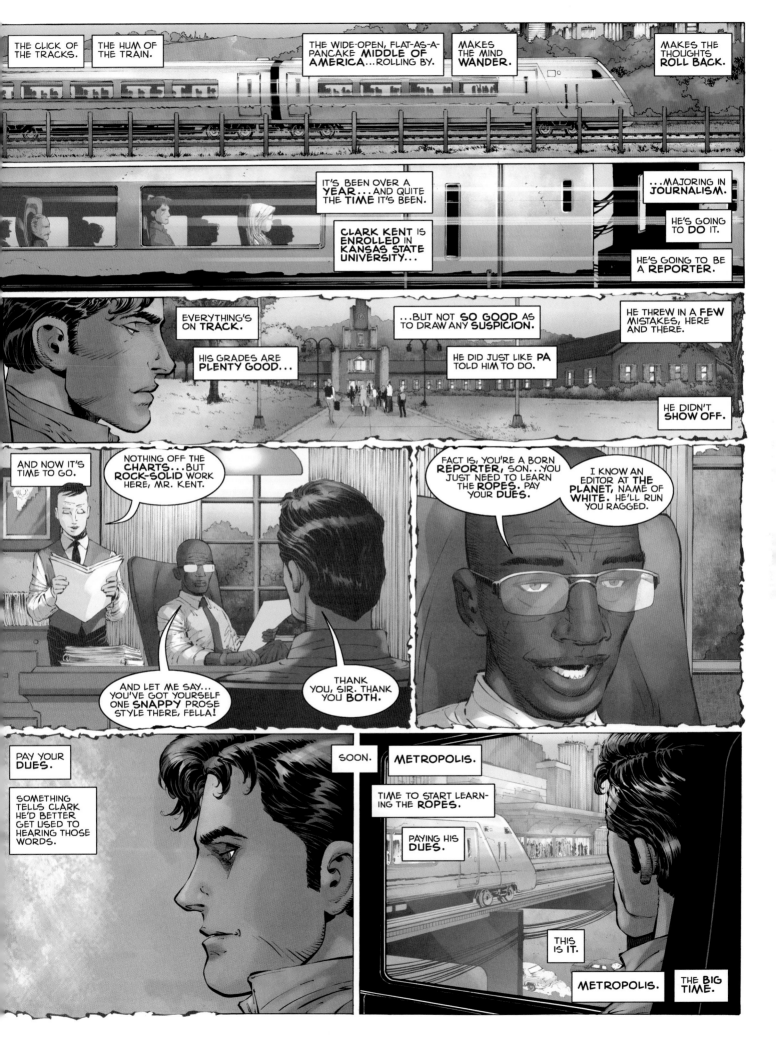

THE CLICK OF THE TRACKS.

THE HUM OF THE TRAIN.

THE WIDE-OPEN, FLAT-AS-A-PANCAKE **MIDDLE OF AMERICA**...ROLLING BY.

MAKES THE MIND **WANDER.**

MAKES THE THOUGHTS **ROLL BACK.**

IT'S BEEN OVER A **YEAR**...AND QUITE THE **TIME** IT'S BEEN.

CLARK KENT IS ENROLLED IN KANSAS STATE UNIVERSITY...

...MAJORING IN **JOURNALISM.**

HE'S GOING TO **DO** IT.

HE'S GOING TO BE A **REPORTER.**

EVERYTHING'S ON **TRACK.**

HIS GRADES ARE PLENTY GOOD...

...BUT NOT **SO GOOD** AS TO DRAW ANY **SUSPICION.**

HE DID JUST LIKE **PA** TOLD HIM TO DO.

HE THREW IN A **FEW** MISTAKES, HERE AND THERE.

HE DIDN'T SHOW OFF.

AND NOW IT'S TIME TO GO.

NOTHING OFF THE **CHARTS**...BUT **ROCK-SOLID** WORK HERE, MR. KENT.

AND LET ME SAY... YOU'VE GOT YOURSELF ONE **SNAPPY** PROSE STYLE THERE, FELLA!

THANK YOU, SIR. THANK YOU **BOTH.**

FACT IS, YOU'RE A BORN **REPORTER,** SON...YOU JUST NEED TO LEARN THE **ROPES.** PAY YOUR **DUES.**

I KNOW AN EDITOR AT **THE PLANET,** NAME OF **WHITE.** HE'LL RUN YOU RAGGED.

PAY YOUR **DUES.**

SOMETHING TELLS CLARK HE'D BETTER GET USED TO HEARING THOSE WORDS.

SOON.

METROPOLIS.

TIME TO START LEARNING THE **ROPES.**

PAYING HIS **DUES.**

THIS IS IT.

METROPOLIS.

THE **BIG TIME.**

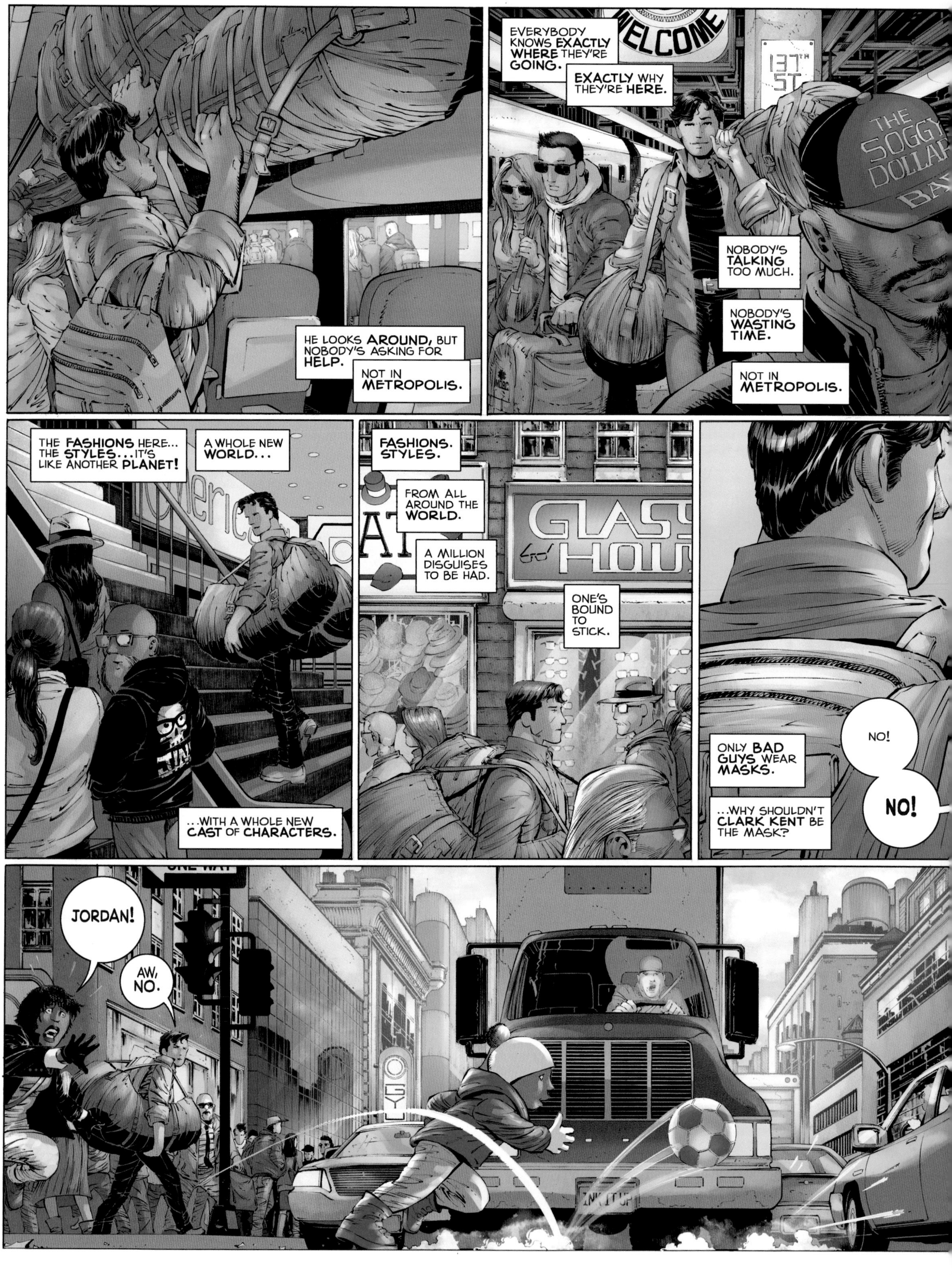
HE LOOKS AROUND, BUT NOBODY'S ASKING FOR HELP.
NOT IN METROPOLIS.
WELCOME
137TH ST
EVERYBODY KNOWS EXACTLY WHERE THEY'RE GOING.
EXACTLY WHY THEY'RE HERE.
THE SOGGY DOLLAR
NOBODY'S TALKING TOO MUCH.
NOBODY'S WASTING TIME.
NOT IN METROPOLIS.
THE FASHIONS HERE... THE STYLES... IT'S LIKE ANOTHER PLANET!
A WHOLE NEW WORLD...
...WITH A WHOLE NEW CAST OF CHARACTERS.
FASHIONS. STYLES.
FROM ALL AROUND THE WORLD.
A MILLION DISGUISES TO BE HAD.
GLASS HOU
ONE'S BOUND TO STICK.
ONLY BAD GUYS WEAR MASKS.
...WHY SHOULDN'T CLARK KENT BE THE MASK?
NO!
NO!
JORDAN!
AW, NO.

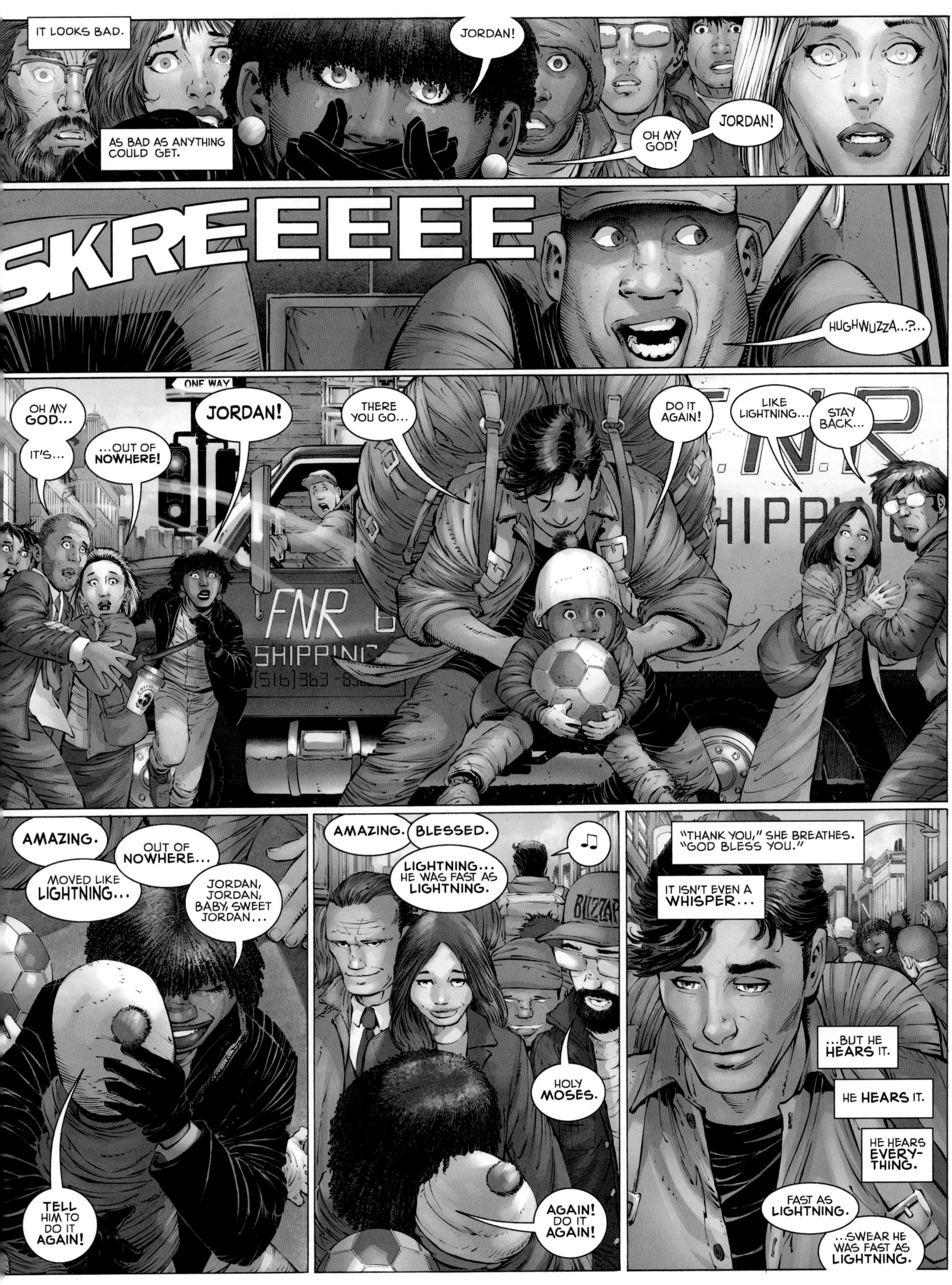
IT LOOKS BAD.
AS BAD AS ANYTHING COULD GET.
JORDAN!
OH MY GOD!
JORDAN!
SKREEEEEE
HUGHWUZZA...?...
ONE WAY
OH MY GOD...
IT'S...
JORDAN!
...OUT OF NOWHERE!
THERE YOU GO...
DO IT AGAIN!
LIKE LIGHTNING...
STAY BACK...
FNR
SHIPPING
AMAZING.
OUT OF NOWHERE...
MOVED LIKE LIGHTNING...
JORDAN, JORDAN, BABY, SWEET JORDAN...
TELL HIM TO DO IT AGAIN!
AMAZING.
BLESSED.
LIGHTNING... HE WAS FAST AS LIGHTNING.
HOLY MOSES.
AGAIN! DO IT AGAIN!
"THANK YOU," SHE BREATHES. "GOD BLESS YOU."
IT ISN'T EVEN A WHISPER...
...BUT HE HEARS IT.
HE HEARS IT.
HE HEARS EVERY-THING.
FAST AS LIGHTNING.
...SWEAR HE WAS FAST AS LIGHTNING.

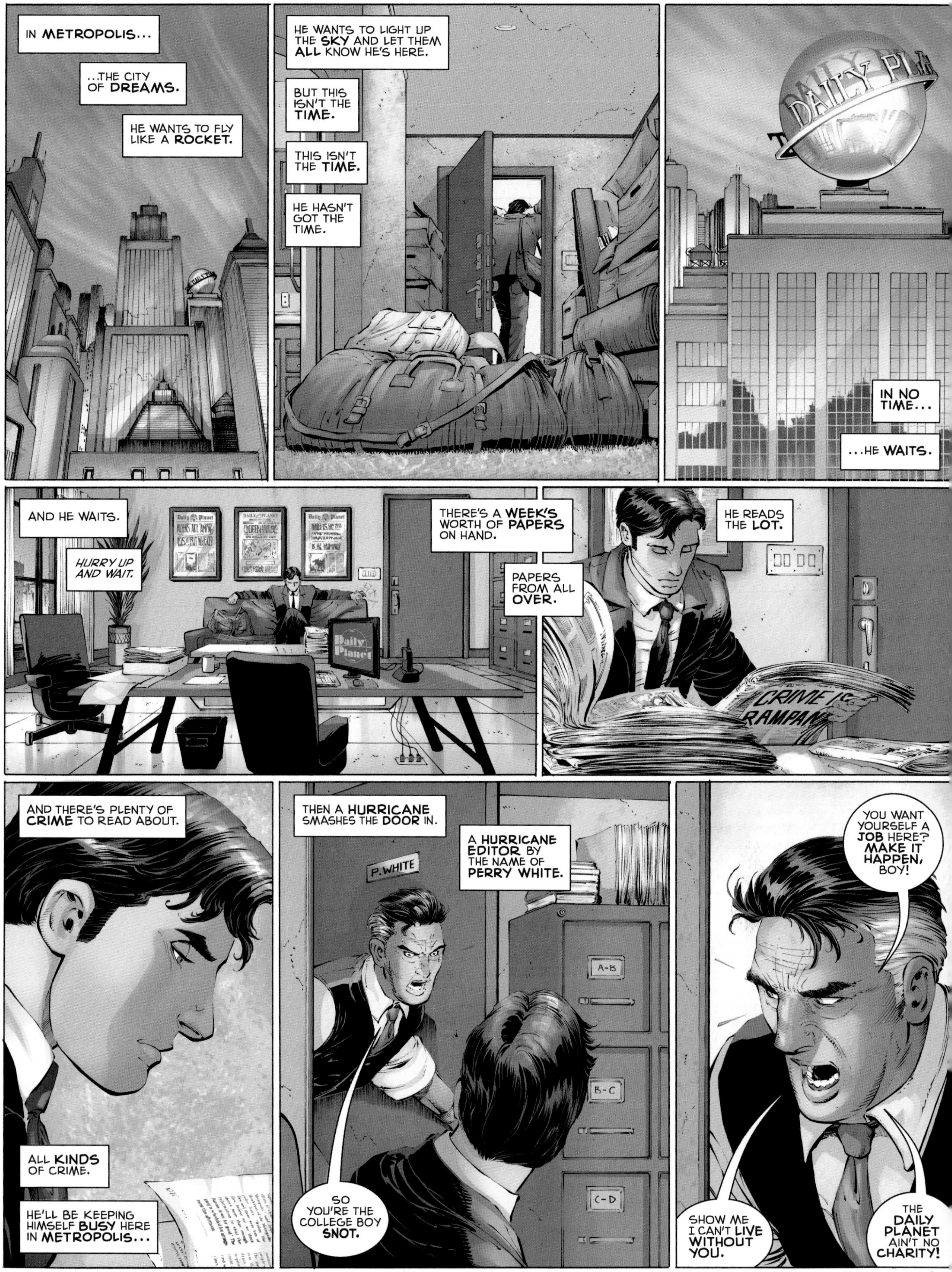
IN METROPOLIS...
...THE CITY OF DREAMS.
HE WANTS TO FLY LIKE A ROCKET.
HE WANTS TO LIGHT UP THE SKY AND LET THEM ALL KNOW HE'S HERE.
BUT THIS ISN'T THE TIME.
THIS ISN'T THE TIME.
HE HASN'T GOT THE TIME.
IN NO TIME...
...HE WAITS.
AND HE WAITS.
HURRY UP AND WAIT.
THERE'S A WEEK'S WORTH OF PAPERS ON HAND.
PAPERS FROM ALL OVER.
HE READS THE LOT.
AND THERE'S PLENTY OF CRIME TO READ ABOUT.
ALL KINDS OF CRIME.
HE'LL BE KEEPING HIMSELF BUSY HERE IN METROPOLIS...
THEN A HURRICANE SMASHES THE DOOR IN.
A HURRICANE EDITOR BY THE NAME OF PERRY WHITE.
P. WHITE
SO YOU'RE THE COLLEGE BOY SNOT.
YOU WANT YOURSELF A JOB HERE? MAKE IT HAPPEN, BOY!
SHOW ME I CAN'T LIVE WITHOUT YOU.
THE DAILY PLANET AIN'T NO CHARITY!

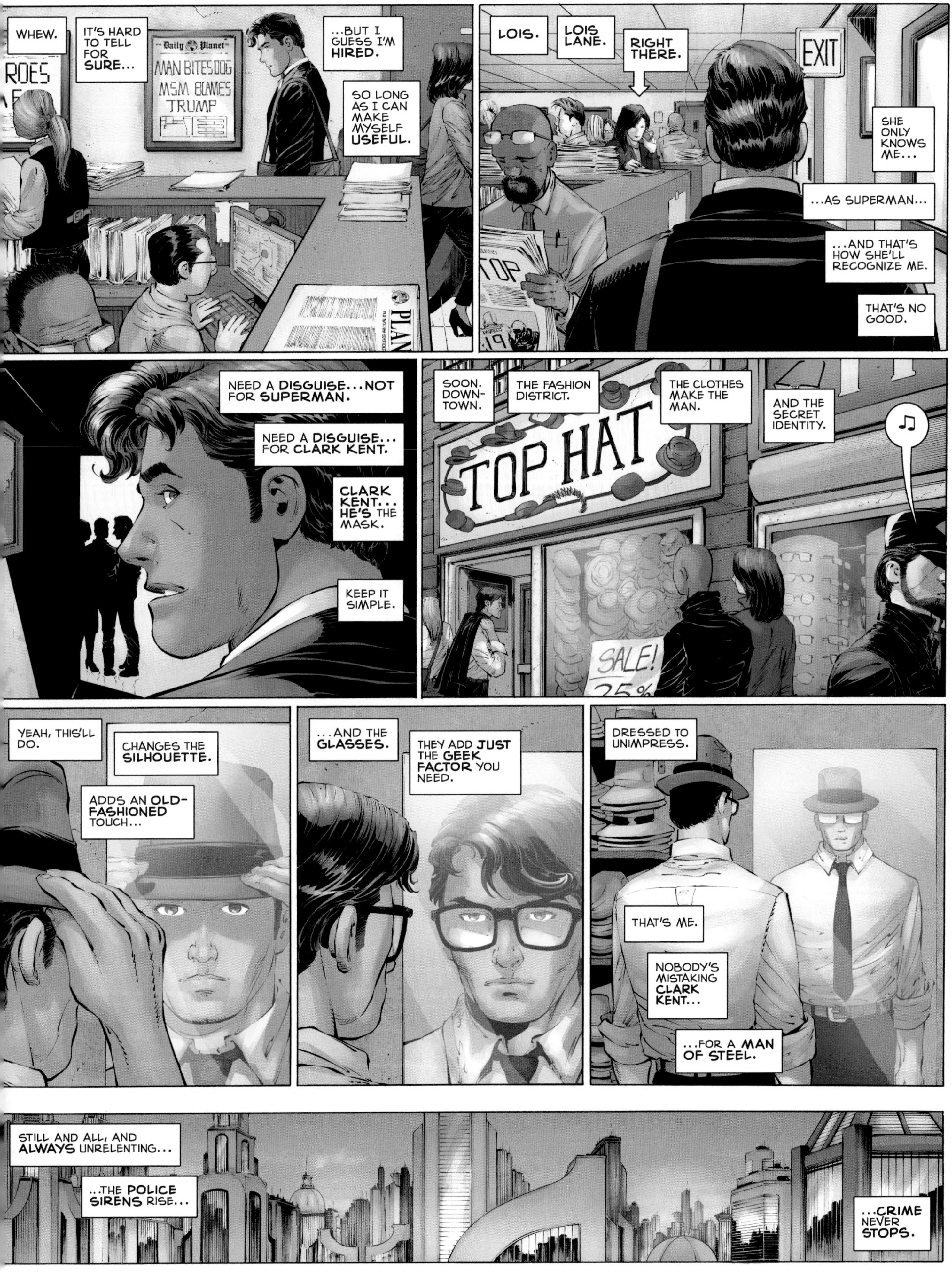
WHEW.
IT'S HARD TO TELL FOR SURE...
...BUT I GUESS I'M HIRED.
SO LONG AS I CAN MAKE MYSELF USEFUL.
Daily Planet
MAN BITES DOG
MSM BLAMES TRUMP
LOIS.
LOIS LANE.
RIGHT THERE.
EXIT
SHE ONLY KNOWS ME...
...AS SUPERMAN...
...AND THAT'S HOW SHE'LL RECOGNIZE ME.
THAT'S NO GOOD.
NEED A DISGUISE...NOT FOR SUPERMAN.
NEED A DISGUISE... FOR CLARK KENT.
CLARK KENT... HE'S THE MASK.
KEEP IT SIMPLE.
SOON. DOWNTOWN.
THE FASHION DISTRICT.
THE CLOTHES MAKE THE MAN.
AND THE SECRET IDENTITY.
♫
TOP HAT
SALE!
YEAH, THIS'LL DO.
CHANGES THE SILHOUETTE.
ADDS AN OLD-FASHIONED TOUCH...
...AND THE GLASSES.
THEY ADD JUST THE GEEK FACTOR YOU NEED.
DRESSED TO UNIMPRESS.
THAT'S ME.
NOBODY'S MISTAKING CLARK KENT...
...FOR A MAN OF STEEL.
STILL AND ALL, AND ALWAYS UNRELENTING...
...THE POLICE SIRENS RISE...
...CRIME NEVER STOPS.

FROM A **HIGH PERCH**, HE LETS THE CITY'S **WHITE NOISE** WASH ACROSS HIM...

...THEN HE CHERRY-PICKS THROUGH ALL THE **HONKS** AND **SQUABBLES**...

...**ZEROING IN** ON **FLASH POINTS** OF **TROUBLE**.

SORTING THROUGH THEM...

...SO **MANY**!

SO **MANY**...AND, **SUPERMAN** OR **NOT**...

...THERE'S ONLY **ONE** OF HIM.

WHERE TO **START**?

ORGANIZE YOUR THOUGHTS, **KENT**!

PRIORITIZE!

START WHERE IT **STARTS**.

CRIME **STARTS** ON THE STREETS.

SO WHAT DO CROOKS **WANT**? THEY WANT **MONEY**.

WHERE DO THEY **FIND** IT?

BANKS.

NEVER MIND THE THIRD-RATE **MUGGERS** AND STREET **SWINDLERS**.

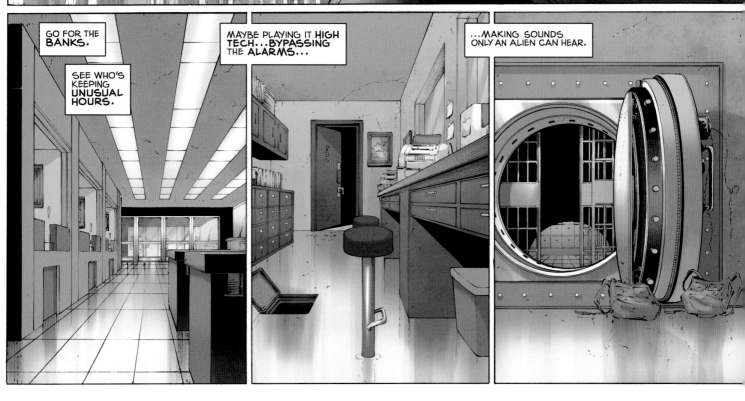

GO FOR THE **BANKS**.

SEE WHO'S KEEPING **UNUSUAL HOURS**.

MAYBE PLAYING IT **HIGH TECH**...BYPASSING THE **ALARMS**...

...MAKING SOUNDS ONLY AN **ALIEN** CAN HEAR.

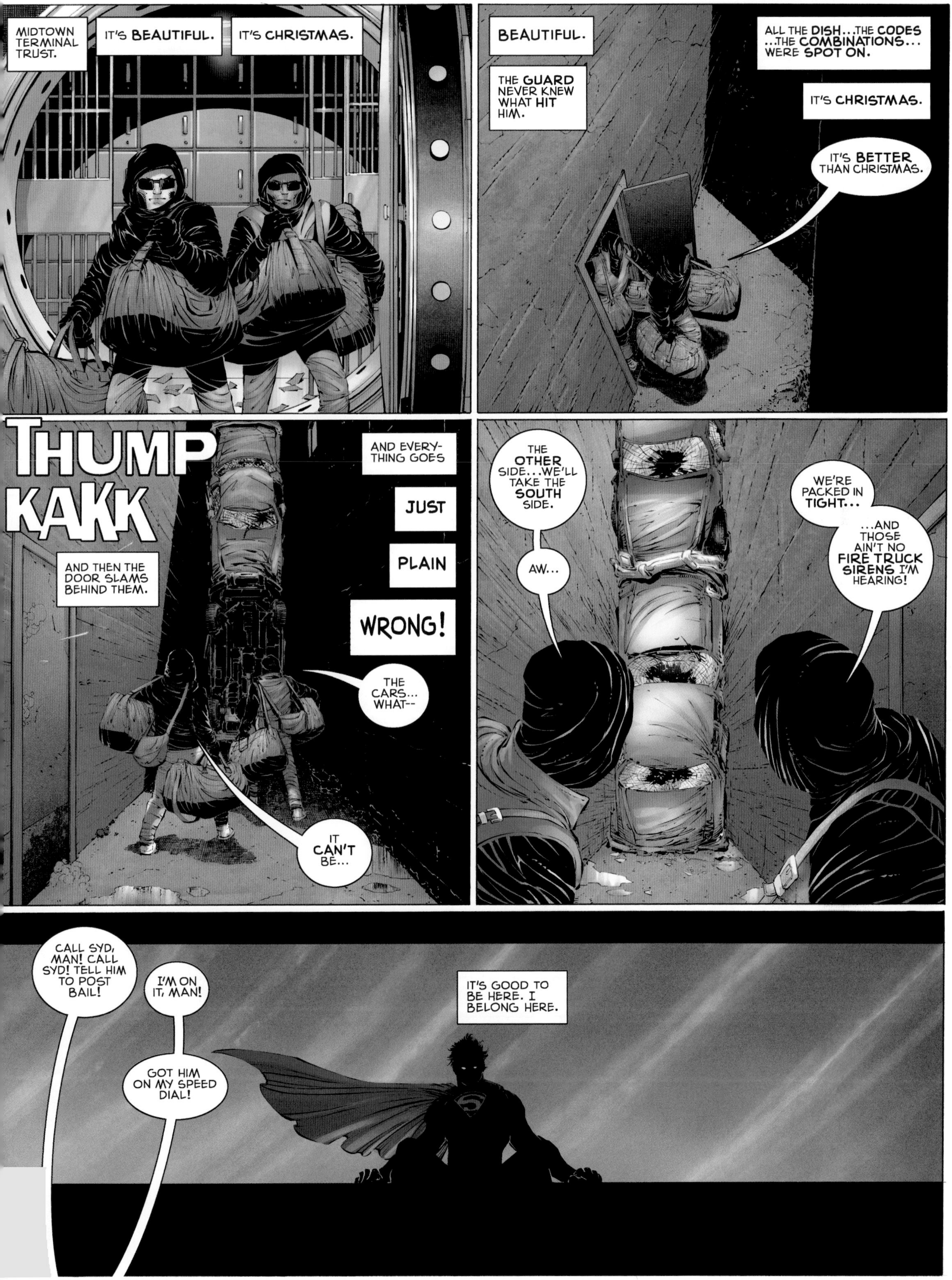
MIDTOWN TERMINAL TRUST.
IT'S BEAUTIFUL.
IT'S CHRISTMAS.
BEAUTIFUL.
THE GUARD NEVER KNEW WHAT HIT HIM.
ALL THE DISH... THE CODES ...THE COMBINATIONS... WERE SPOT ON.
IT'S CHRISTMAS.
IT'S BETTER THAN CHRISTMAS.
THUMP
KAKK
AND THEN THE DOOR SLAMS BEHIND THEM.
AND EVERY-THING GOES
JUST
PLAIN
WRONG!
THE CARS... WHAT--
IT CAN'T BE...
THE OTHER SIDE... WE'LL TAKE THE SOUTH SIDE.
AW...
WE'RE PACKED IN TIGHT...
...AND THOSE AIN'T NO FIRE TRUCK SIRENS I'M HEARING!
CALL SYD, MAN! CALL SYD! TELL HIM TO POST BAIL!
I'M ON IT, MAN!
GOT HIM ON MY SPEED DIAL!
IT'S GOOD TO BE HERE. I BELONG HERE.

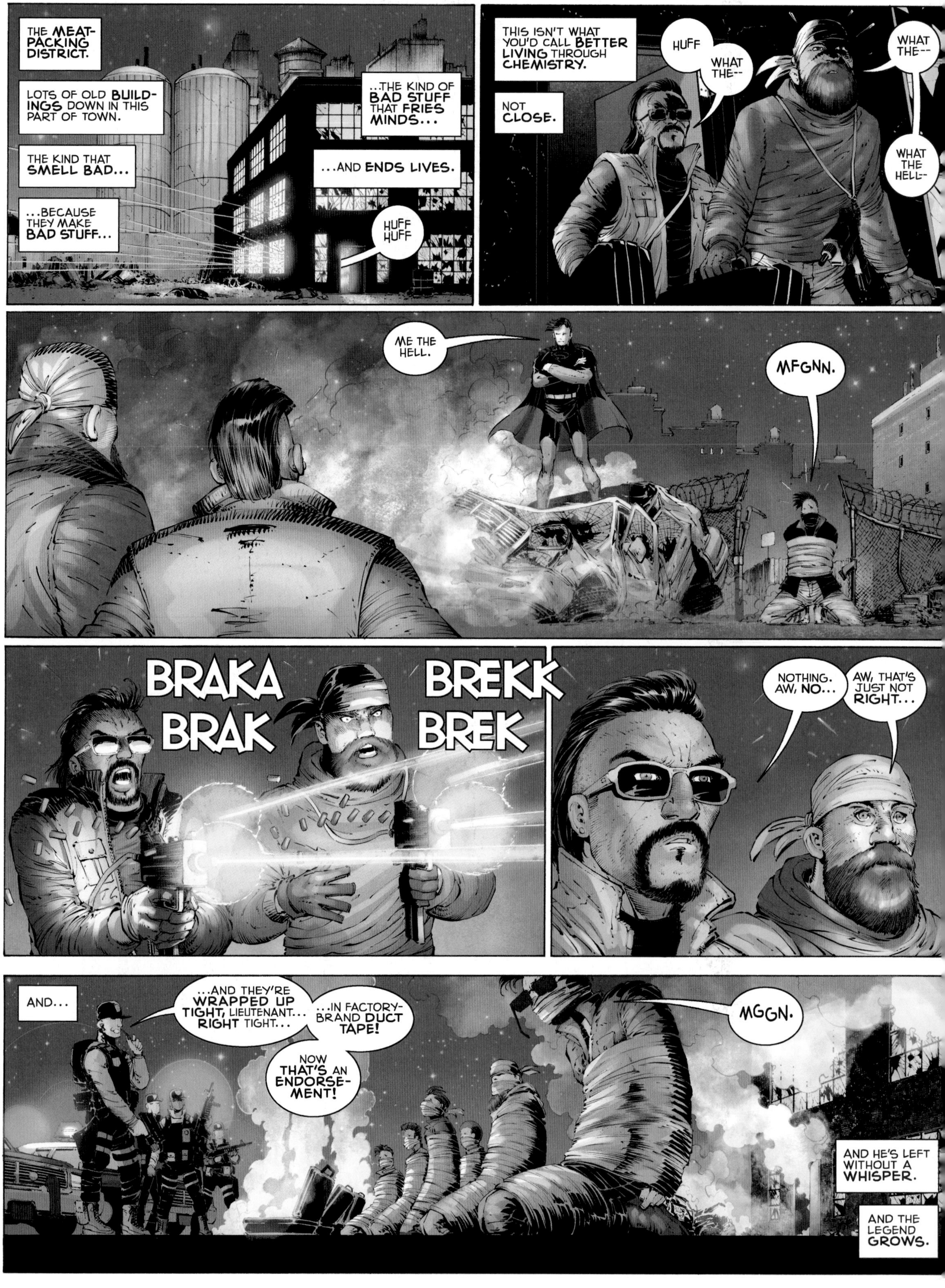
THE MEAT-PACKING DISTRICT.
LOTS OF OLD BUILDINGS DOWN IN THIS PART OF TOWN.
THE KIND THAT SMELL BAD...
...BECAUSE THEY MAKE BAD STUFF...
...THE KIND OF BAD STUFF THAT FRIES MINDS...
...AND ENDS LIVES.
HUFF HUFF
THIS ISN'T WHAT YOU'D CALL BETTER LIVING THROUGH CHEMISTRY.
NOT CLOSE.
HUFF
WHAT THE--
WHAT THE--
WHAT THE HELL--
ME THE HELL.
MFGNN.
BRAKA BRAK
BREKK BREK
NOTHING. AW, NO...
AW, THAT'S JUST NOT RIGHT...
AND...
...AND THEY'RE WRAPPED UP TIGHT, LIEUTENANT... RIGHT TIGHT...
...IN FACTORY-BRAND DUCT TAPE!
NOW THAT'S AN ENDORSE-MENT!
MGGN.
AND HE'S LEFT WITHOUT A WHISPER.
AND THE LEGEND GROWS.

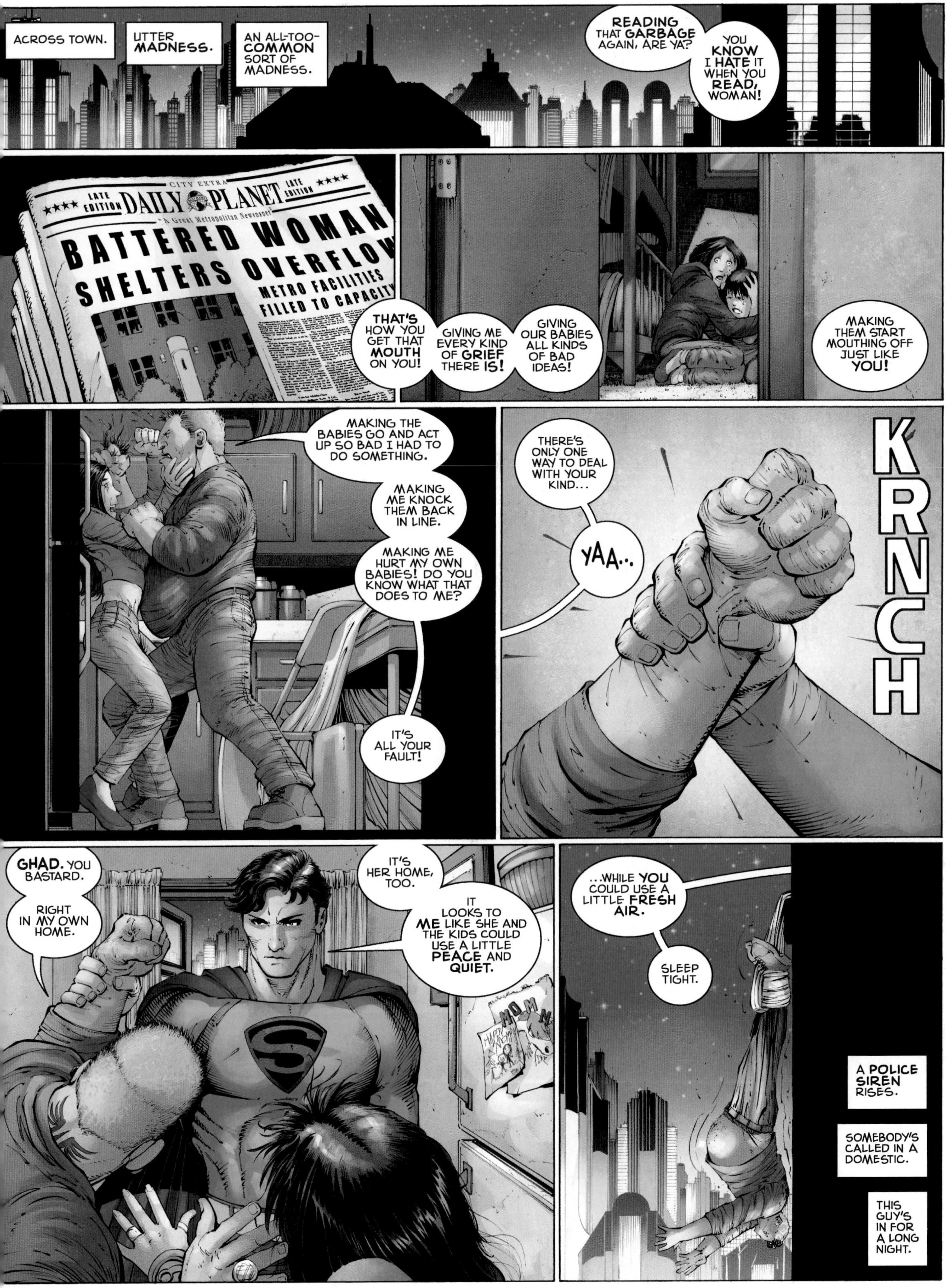

ACROSS TOWN.
UTTER MADNESS.
AN ALL-TOO-COMMON SORT OF MADNESS.
READING THAT GARBAGE AGAIN, ARE YA?
YOU KNOW I HATE IT WHEN YOU READ, WOMAN!
CITY EXTRA
LATE EDITION DAILY PLANET LATE EDITION
"A Great Metropolitan Newspaper"
BATTERED WOMAN SHELTERS OVERFLOW
METRO FACILITIES FILLED TO CAPACITY
THAT'S HOW YOU GET THAT MOUTH ON YOU!
GIVING ME EVERY KIND OF GRIEF THERE IS!
GIVING OUR BABIES ALL KINDS OF BAD IDEAS!
MAKING THEM START MOUTHING OFF JUST LIKE YOU!
MAKING THE BABIES GO AND ACT UP SO BAD I HAD TO DO SOMETHING.
MAKING ME KNOCK THEM BACK IN LINE.
MAKING ME HURT MY OWN BABIES! DO YOU KNOW WHAT THAT DOES TO ME?
IT'S ALL YOUR FAULT!
THERE'S ONLY ONE WAY TO DEAL WITH YOUR KIND...
YAA...
KRNCH
GHAD. YOU BASTARD.
RIGHT IN MY OWN HOME.
IT'S HER HOME, TOO.
IT LOOKS TO ME LIKE SHE AND THE KIDS COULD USE A LITTLE PEACE AND QUIET.
...WHILE YOU COULD USE A LITTLE FRESH AIR.
SLEEP TIGHT.
A POLICE SIREN RISES.
SOMEBODY'S CALLED IN A DOMESTIC.
THIS GUY'S IN FOR A LONG NIGHT.

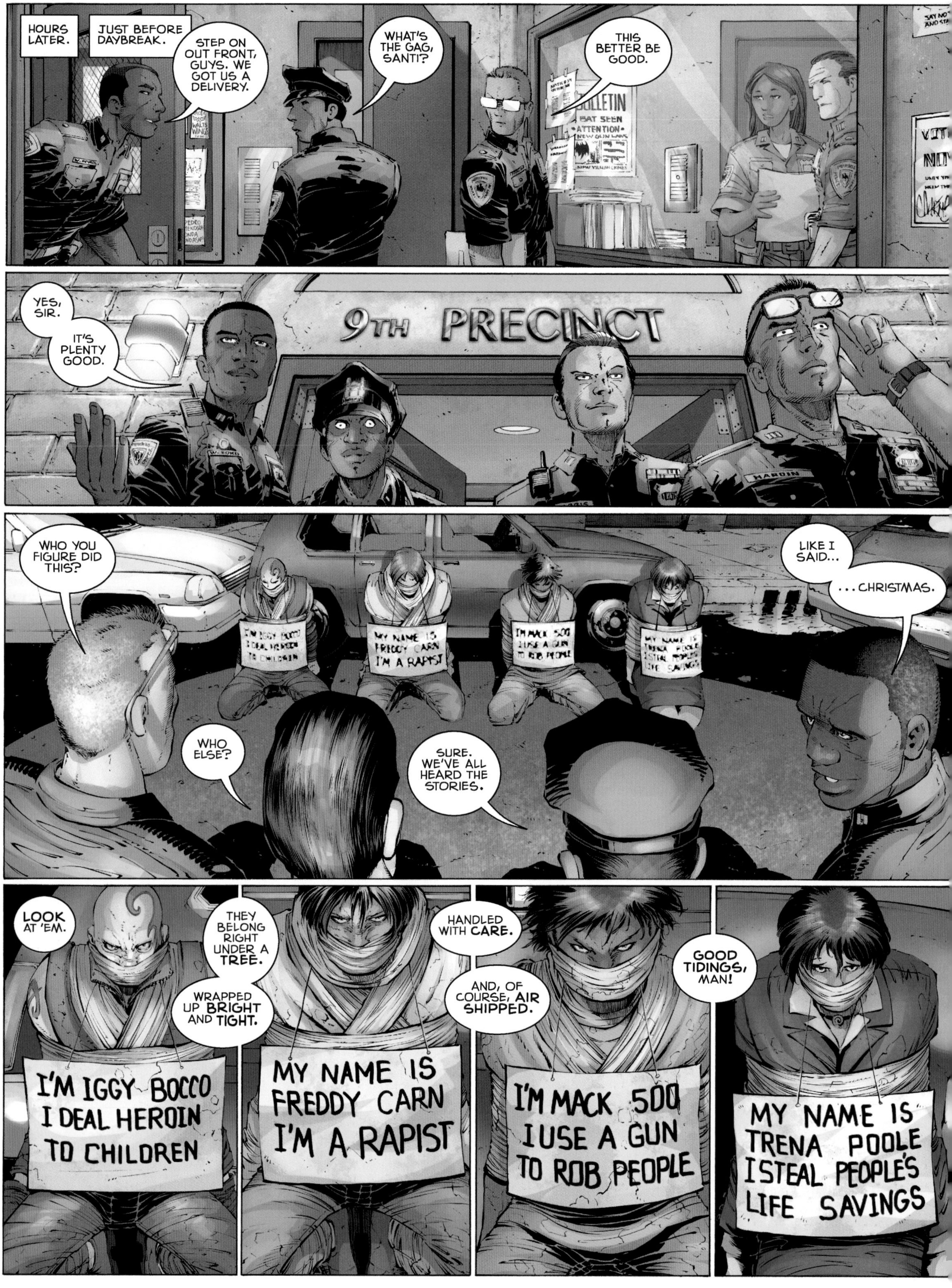

HOURS LATER.
JUST BEFORE DAYBREAK.
STEP ON OUT FRONT, GUYS. WE GOT US A DELIVERY.
WHAT'S THE GAG, SANTI?
THIS BETTER BE GOOD.
BULLETIN
BAT SEEN
ATTENTION
NEW GUN LAWS
9TH PRECINCT
YES, SIR.
IT'S PLENTY GOOD.
WHO YOU FIGURE DID THIS?
WHO ELSE?
SURE. WE'VE ALL HEARD THE STORIES.
LIKE I SAID...
...CHRISTMAS.
LOOK AT 'EM.
THEY BELONG RIGHT UNDER A TREE.
WRAPPED UP BRIGHT AND TIGHT.
HANDLED WITH CARE.
AND, OF COURSE, AIR SHIPPED.
GOOD TIDINGS, MAN!
I'M IGGY BOCCO I DEAL HEROIN TO CHILDREN
MY NAME IS FREDDY CARN I'M A RAPIST
I'M MACK 500 I USE A GUN TO ROB PEOPLE
MY NAME IS TRENA POOLE I STEAL PEOPLE'S LIFE SAVINGS

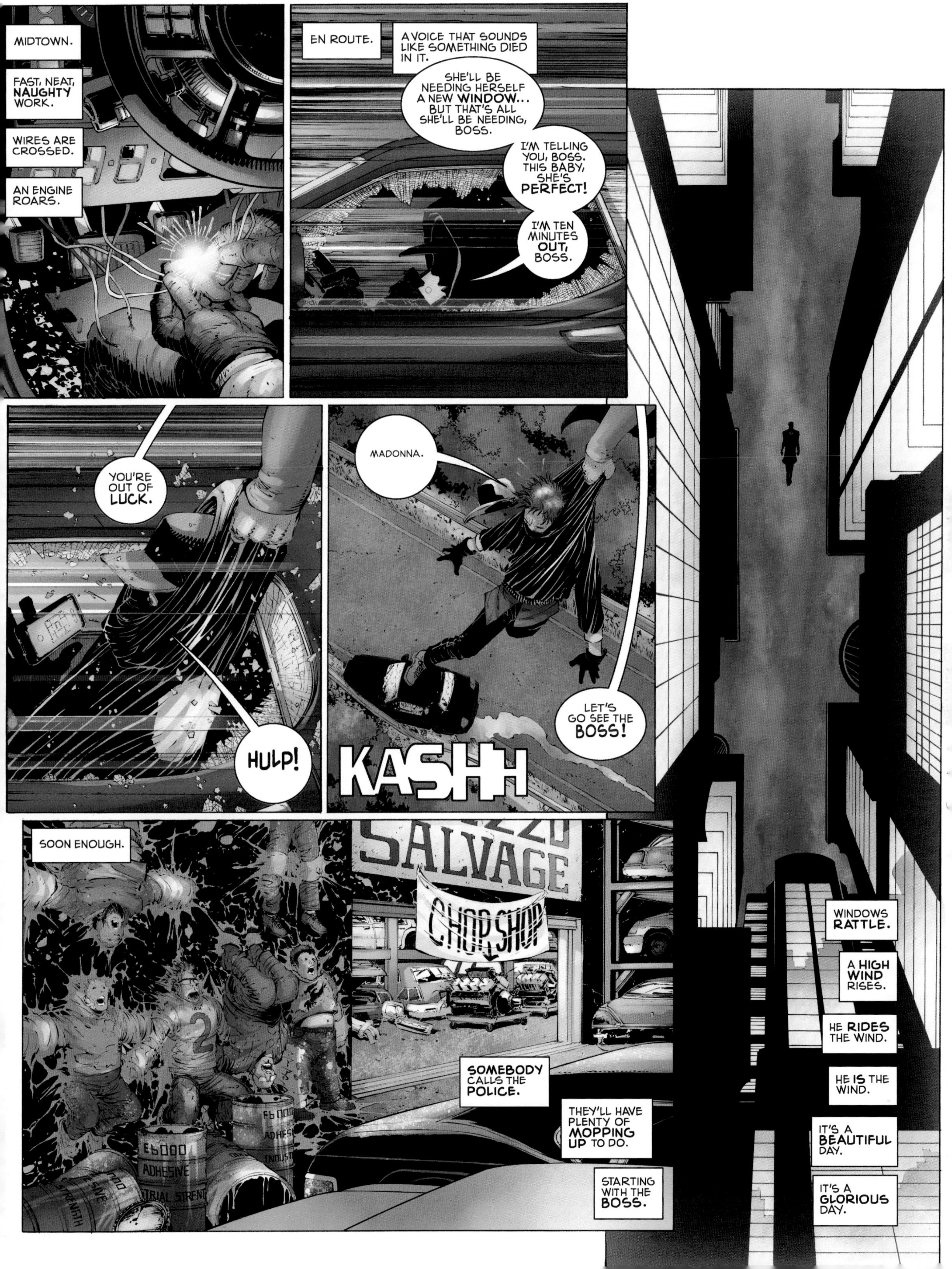

MIDTOWN.
FAST, NEAT, NAUGHTY WORK.
WIRES ARE CROSSED.
AN ENGINE ROARS.
EN ROUTE.
A VOICE THAT SOUNDS LIKE SOMETHING DIED IN IT.
SHE'LL BE NEEDING HERSELF A NEW WINDOW... BUT THAT'S ALL SHE'LL BE NEEDING, BOSS.
I'M TELLING YOU, BOSS. THIS BABY, SHE'S PERFECT!
I'M TEN MINUTES OUT, BOSS.
YOU'RE OUT OF LUCK.
HULP!
MADONNA.
LET'S GO SEE THE BOSS!
KASHH
SOON ENOUGH.
SALVAGE
CHOP SHOP
E6000
ADHESIVE
SOMEBODY CALLS THE POLICE.
THEY'LL HAVE PLENTY OF MOPPING UP TO DO.
STARTING WITH THE BOSS.
WINDOWS RATTLE.
A HIGH WIND RISES.
HE RIDES THE WIND.
HE IS THE WIND.
IT'S A BEAUTIFUL DAY.
IT'S A GLORIOUS DAY.

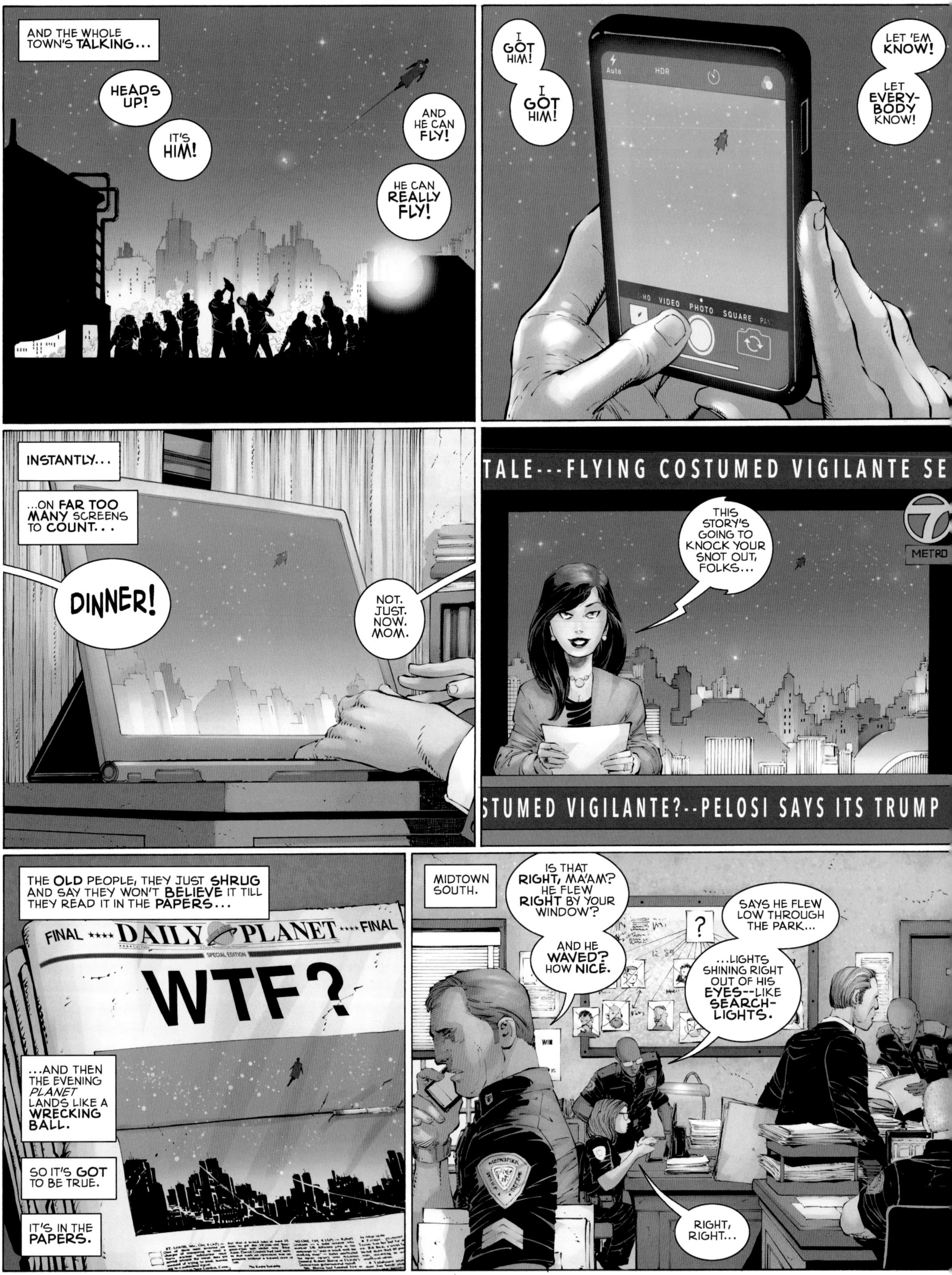

AND THE WHOLE TOWN'S TALKING...
HEADS UP!
IT'S HIM!
AND HE CAN FLY!
HE CAN REALLY FLY!
I GOT HIM!
I GOT HIM!
LET 'EM KNOW!
LET EVERY-BODY KNOW!
Auto
HDR
VIDEO
PHOTO
SQUARE
INSTANTLY...
...ON FAR TOO MANY SCREENS TO COUNT...
DINNER!
NOT. JUST. NOW. MOM.
TALE---FLYING COSTUMED VIGILANTE SE
THIS STORY'S GOING TO KNOCK YOUR SNOT OUT, FOLKS...
7
METRO
STUMED VIGILANTE?--PELOSI SAYS ITS TRUMP
THE OLD PEOPLE, THEY JUST SHRUG AND SAY THEY WON'T BELIEVE IT TILL THEY READ IT IN THE PAPERS...
FINAL ★★★★ DAILY PLANET ★★★★ FINAL
SPECIAL EDITION
WTF?
...AND THEN THE EVENING PLANET LANDS LIKE A WRECKING BALL.
SO IT'S GOT TO BE TRUE.
IT'S IN THE PAPERS.
MIDTOWN SOUTH.
IS THAT RIGHT, MA'AM? HE FLEW RIGHT BY YOUR WINDOW?
AND HE WAVED? HOW NICE.
SAYS HE FLEW LOW THROUGH THE PARK...
...LIGHTS SHINING RIGHT OUT OF HIS EYES--LIKE SEARCH-LIGHTS.
RIGHT, RIGHT...

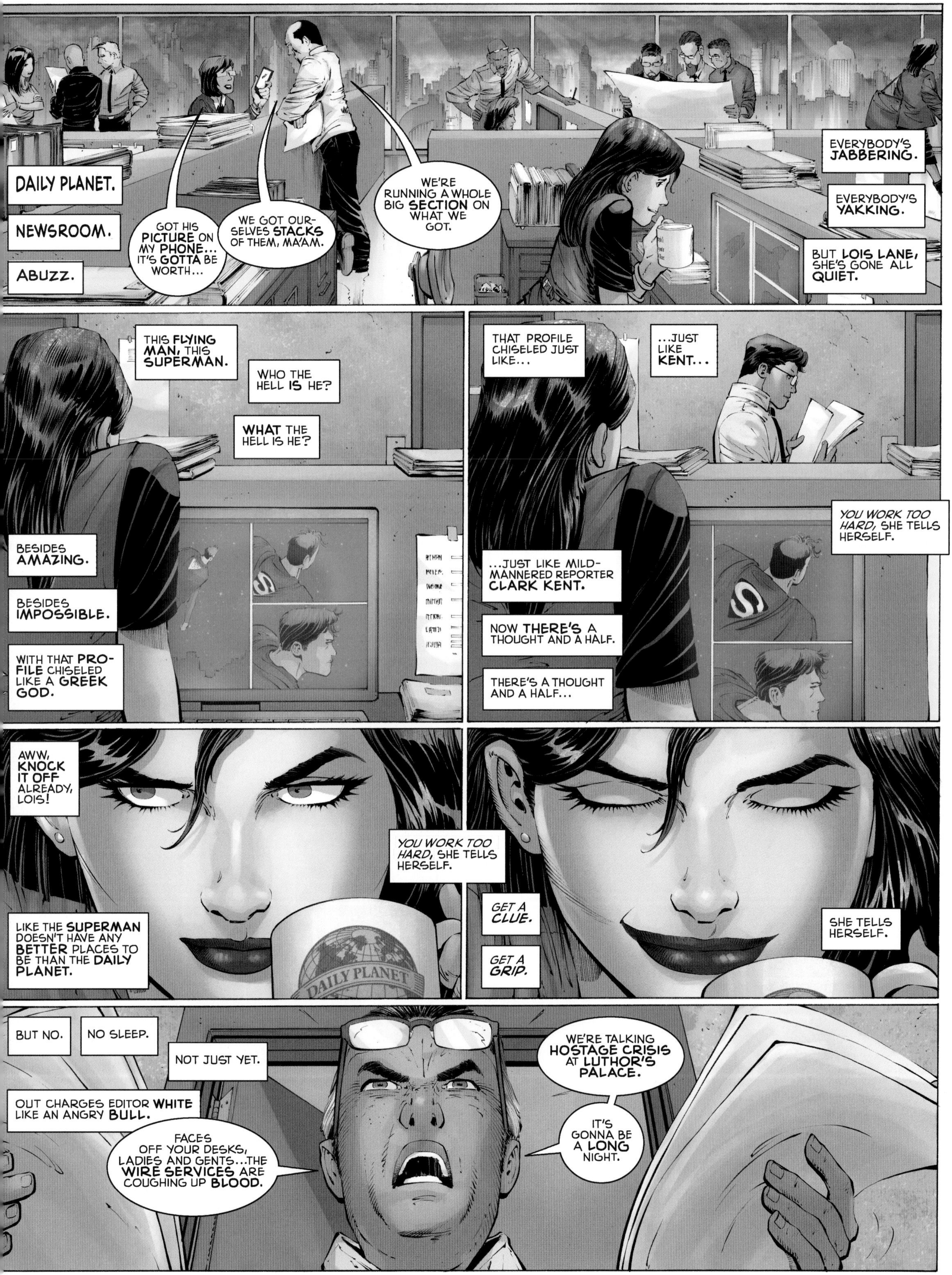

DAILY PLANET.
NEWSROOM.
ABUZZ.
GOT HIS PICTURE ON MY PHONE... IT'S GOTTA BE WORTH...
WE GOT OURSELVES STACKS OF THEM, MA'AM.
WE'RE RUNNING A WHOLE BIG SECTION ON WHAT WE GOT.
EVERYBODY'S JABBERING.
EVERYBODY'S YAKKING.
BUT LOIS LANE, SHE'S GONE ALL QUIET.
THIS FLYING MAN, THIS SUPERMAN.
WHO THE HELL IS HE?
WHAT THE HELL IS HE?
BESIDES AMAZING.
BESIDES IMPOSSIBLE.
WITH THAT PROFILE CHISELED LIKE A GREEK GOD.
THAT PROFILE CHISELED JUST LIKE...
...JUST LIKE KENT...
...JUST LIKE MILD-MANNERED REPORTER CLARK KENT.
NOW THERE'S A THOUGHT AND A HALF.
THERE'S A THOUGHT AND A HALF...
YOU WORK TOO HARD, SHE TELLS HERSELF.
AWW, KNOCK IT OFF ALREADY, LOIS!
LIKE THE SUPERMAN DOESN'T HAVE ANY BETTER PLACES TO BE THAN THE DAILY PLANET.
DAILY PLANET
YOU WORK TOO HARD, SHE TELLS HERSELF.
GET A CLUE.
GET A GRIP.
SHE TELLS HERSELF.
BUT NO.
NO SLEEP.
NOT JUST YET.
OUT CHARGES EDITOR WHITE LIKE AN ANGRY BULL.
FACES OFF YOUR DESKS, LADIES AND GENTS...THE WIRE SERVICES ARE COUGHING UP BLOOD.
WE'RE TALKING HOSTAGE CRISIS AT LUTHOR'S PALACE.
IT'S GONNA BE A LONG NIGHT.

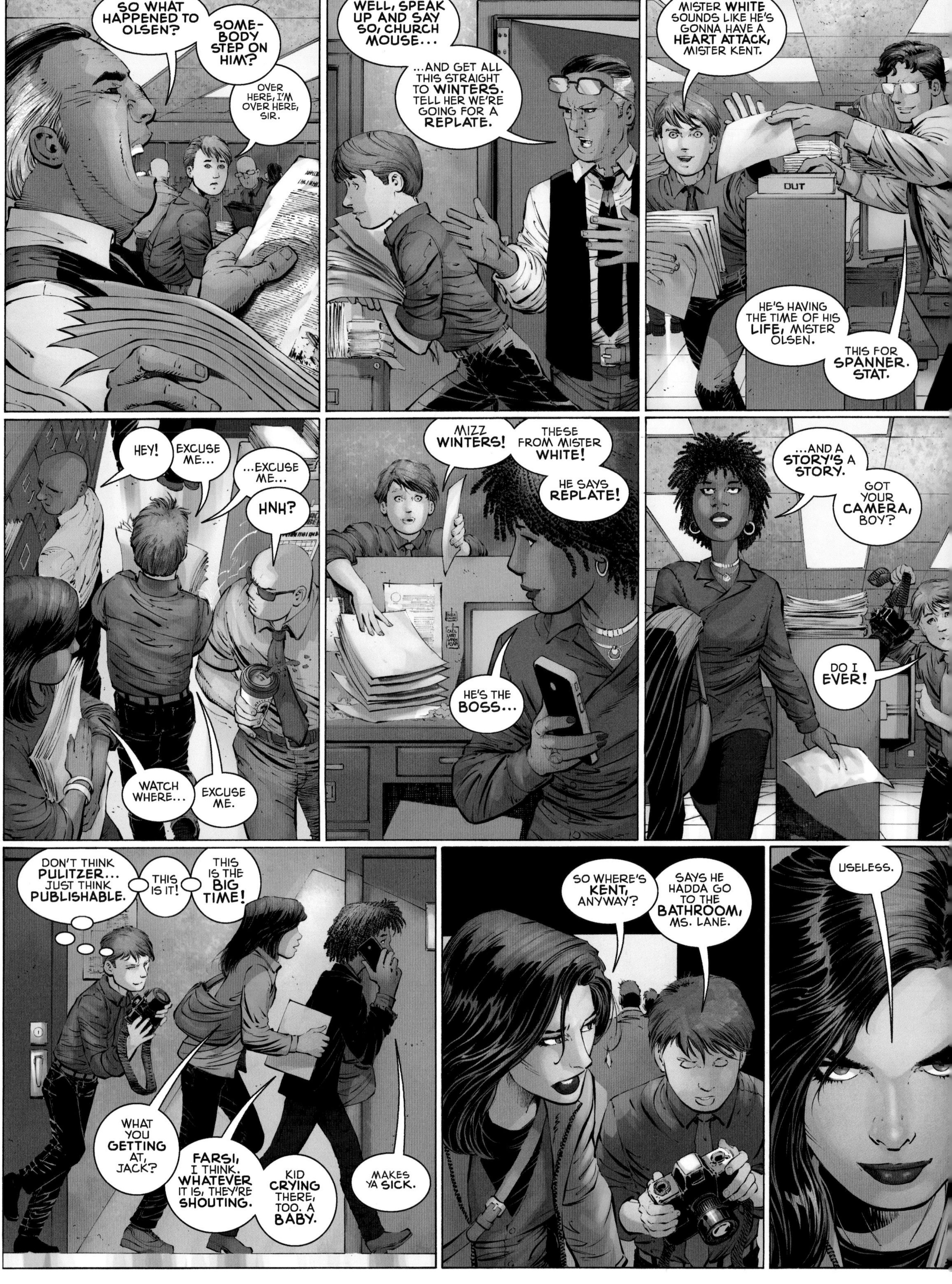
SO WHAT HAPPENED TO OLSEN?
SOME-BODY STEP ON HIM?
OVER HERE, I'M OVER HERE, SIR.
WELL, SPEAK UP AND SAY SO, CHURCH MOUSE...
...AND GET ALL THIS STRAIGHT TO WINTERS. TELL HER WE'RE GOING FOR A REPLATE.
MISTER WHITE SOUNDS LIKE HE'S GONNA HAVE A HEART ATTACK, MISTER KENT.
HE'S HAVING THE TIME OF HIS LIFE, MISTER OLSEN.
THIS FOR SPANNER. STAT.
OUT
HEY!
EXCUSE ME...
...EXCUSE ME...
HNH?
WATCH WHERE...
EXCUSE ME.
MIZZ WINTERS!
THESE FROM MISTER WHITE!
HE SAYS REPLATE!
HE'S THE BOSS...
...AND A STORY'S A STORY.
GOT YOUR CAMERA, BOY?
DO I EVER!
DON'T THINK PULITZER... JUST THINK PUBLISHABLE.
THIS IS IT!
THIS IS THE BIG TIME!
WHAT YOU GETTING AT, JACK?
FARSI, I THINK. WHATEVER IT IS, THEY'RE SHOUTING.
KID CRYING THERE, TOO. A BABY.
MAKES YA SICK.
SO WHERE'S KENT, ANYWAY?
SAYS HE HADDA GO TO THE BATHROOM, MS. LANE.
USELESS.

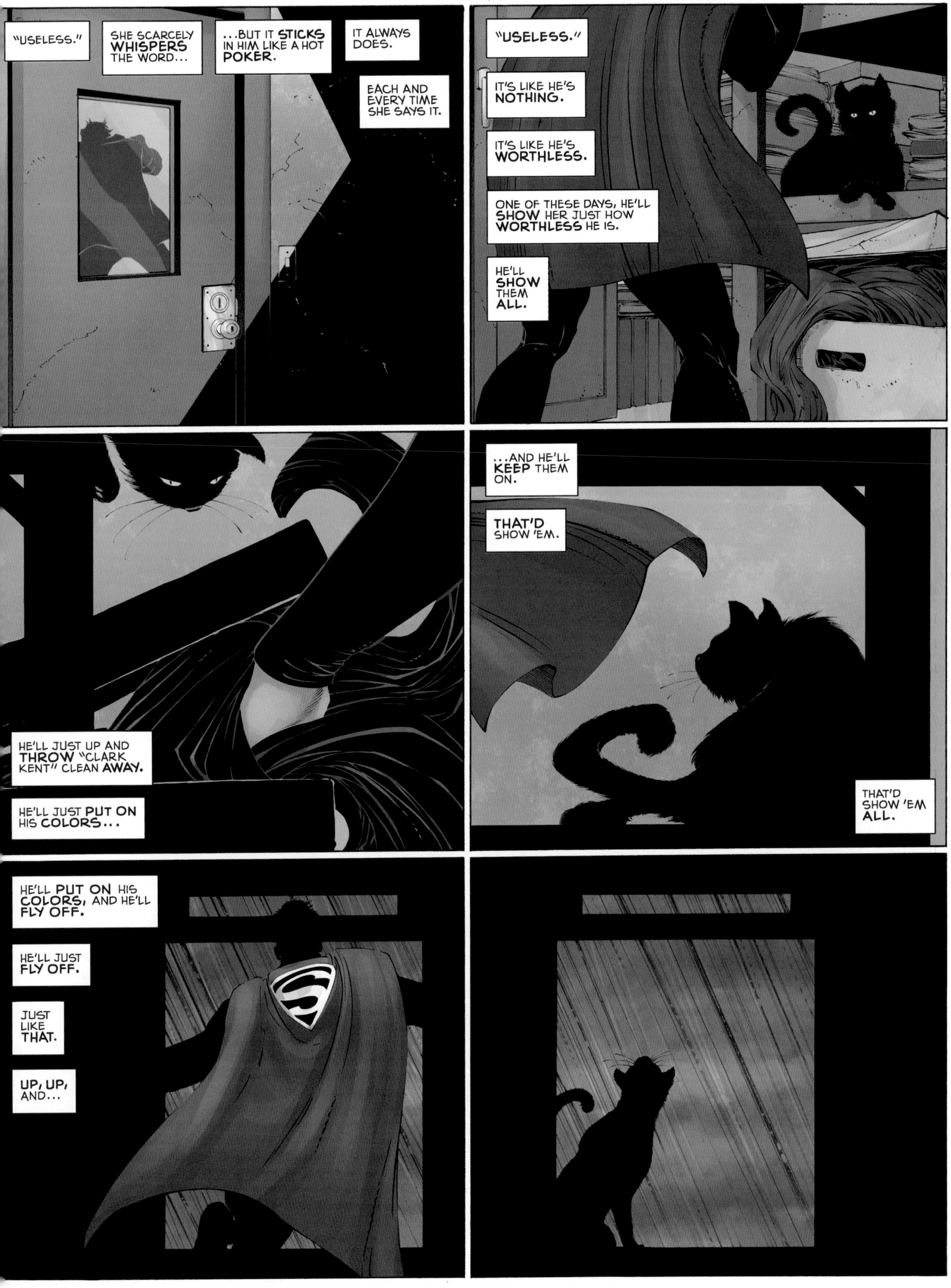
"USELESS."
SHE SCARCELY WHISPERS THE WORD...
...BUT IT STICKS IN HIM LIKE A HOT POKER.
IT ALWAYS DOES.
EACH AND EVERY TIME SHE SAYS IT.
"USELESS."
IT'S LIKE HE'S NOTHING.
IT'S LIKE HE'S WORTHLESS.
ONE OF THESE DAYS, HE'LL SHOW HER JUST HOW WORTHLESS HE IS.
HE'LL SHOW THEM ALL.
HE'LL JUST UP AND THROW "CLARK KENT" CLEAN AWAY.
HE'LL JUST PUT ON HIS COLORS...
...AND HE'LL KEEP THEM ON.
THAT'D SHOW 'EM.
THAT'D SHOW 'EM ALL.
HE'LL PUT ON HIS COLORS, AND HE'LL FLY OFF.
HE'LL JUST FLY OFF.
JUST LIKE THAT.
UP, UP, AND...

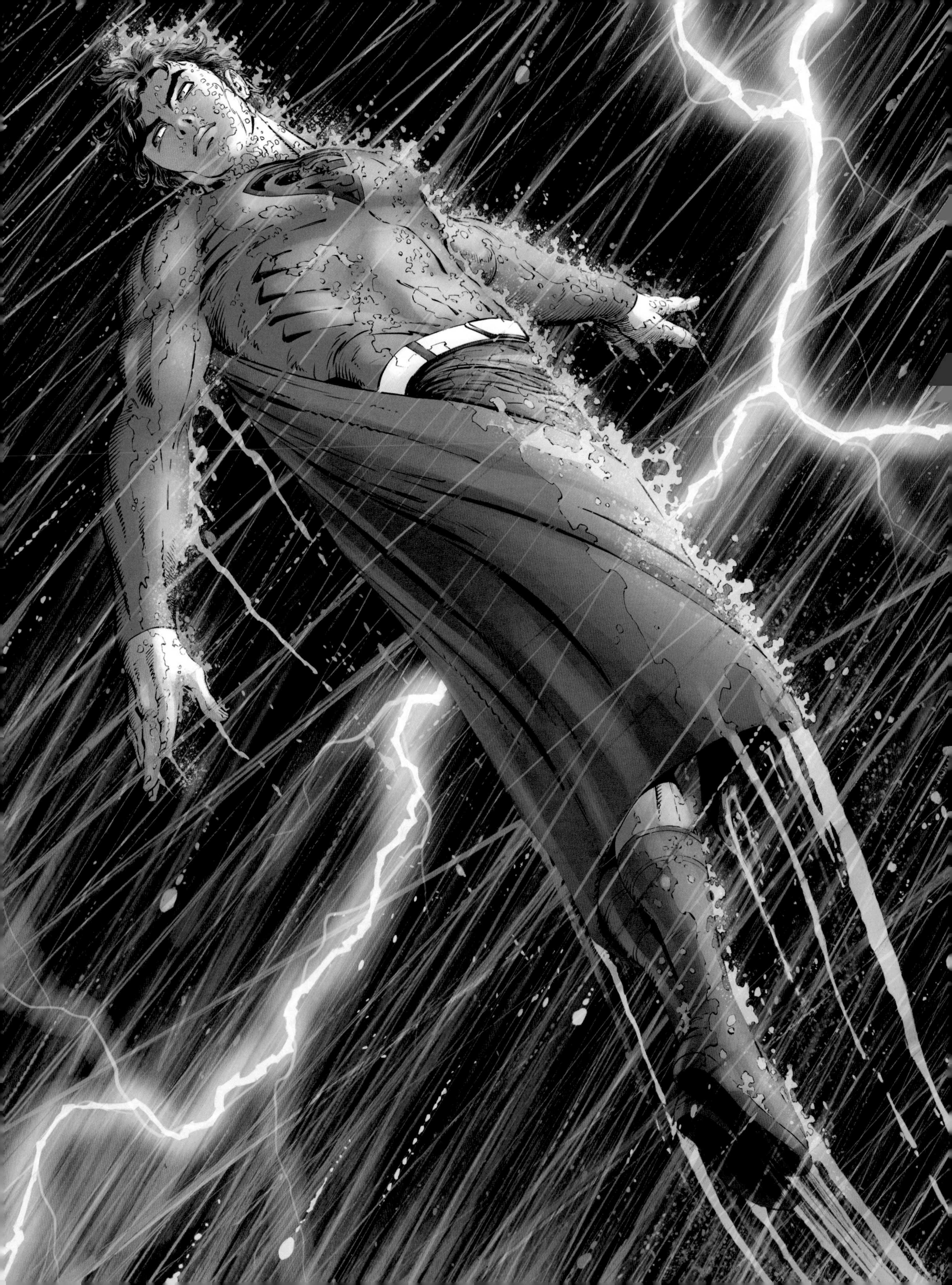

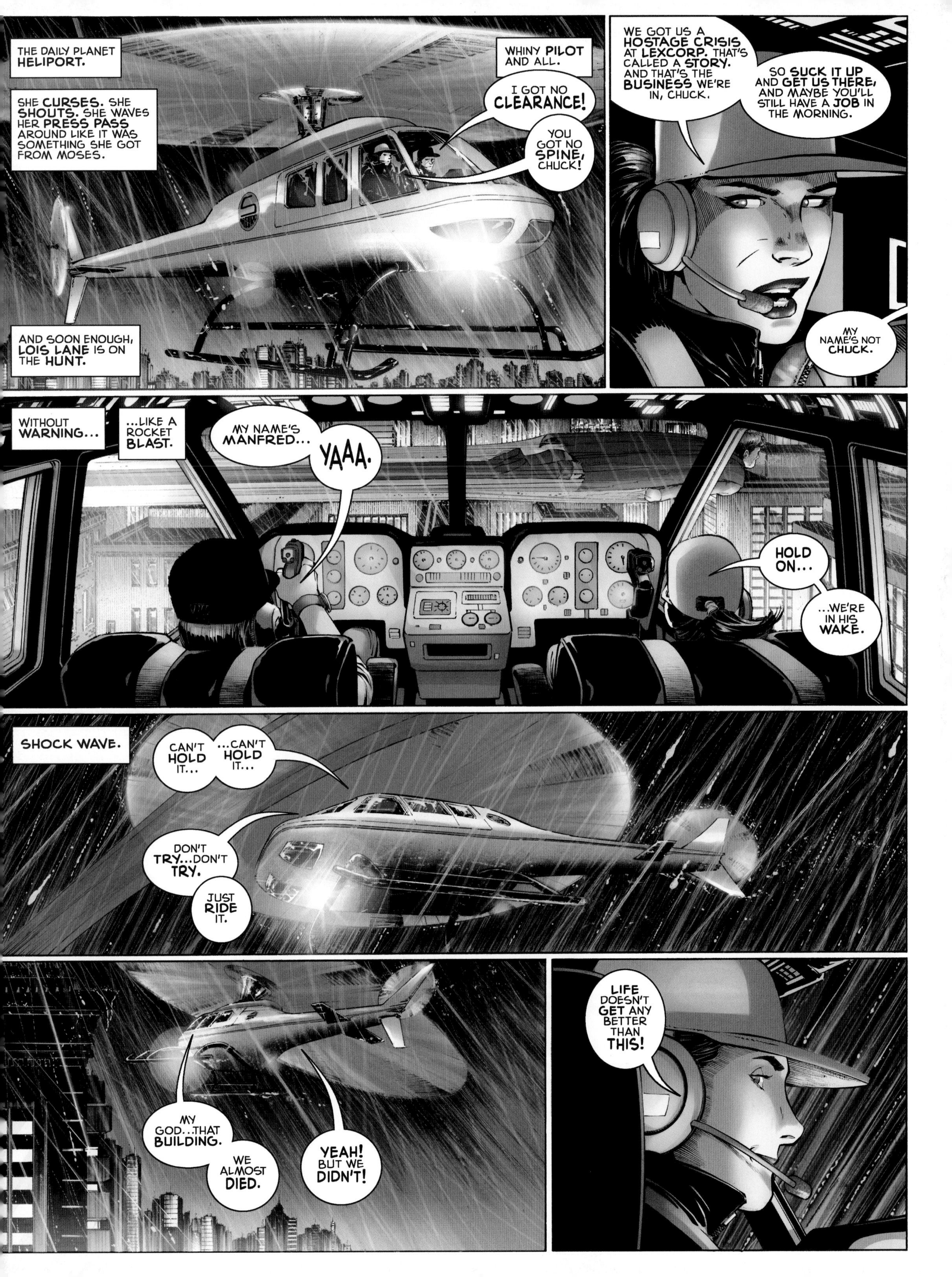

THE DAILY PLANET HELIPORT.
SHE CURSES. SHE SHOUTS. SHE WAVES HER PRESS PASS AROUND LIKE IT WAS SOMETHING SHE GOT FROM MOSES.
WHINY PILOT AND ALL.
I GOT NO CLEARANCE!
YOU GOT NO SPINE, CHUCK!
AND SOON ENOUGH, LOIS LANE IS ON THE HUNT.
WE GOT US A HOSTAGE CRISIS AT LEXCORP. THAT'S CALLED A STORY. AND THAT'S THE BUSINESS WE'RE IN, CHUCK.
SO SUCK IT UP AND GET US THERE, AND MAYBE YOU'LL STILL HAVE A JOB IN THE MORNING.
MY NAME'S NOT CHUCK.
WITHOUT WARNING...
...LIKE A ROCKET BLAST.
MY NAME'S MANFRED...
YAAA.
HOLD ON...
...WE'RE IN HIS WAKE.
SHOCK WAVE.
CAN'T HOLD IT...
...CAN'T HOLD IT...
DON'T TRY...DON'T TRY.
JUST RIDE IT.
MY GOD...THAT BUILDING.
WE ALMOST DIED.
YEAH! BUT WE DIDN'T!
LIFE DOESN'T GET ANY BETTER THAN THIS!

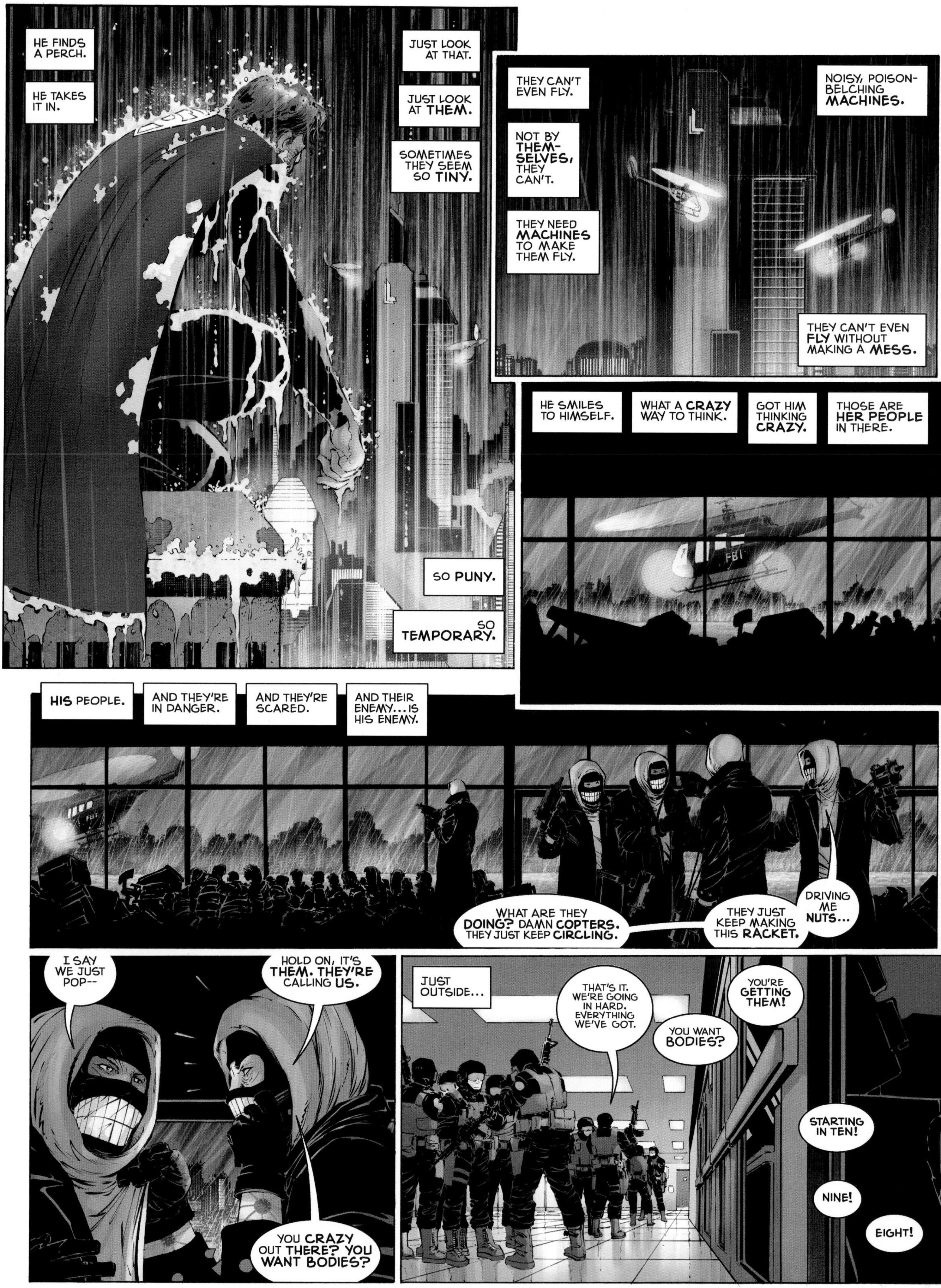
HE FINDS A PERCH.
HE TAKES IT IN.
JUST LOOK AT THAT.
JUST LOOK AT THEM.
SOMETIMES THEY SEEM SO TINY.
SO PUNY.
SO TEMPORARY.
THEY CAN'T EVEN FLY.
NOT BY THEM-SELVES, THEY CAN'T.
THEY NEED MACHINES TO MAKE THEM FLY.
NOISY, POISON-BELCHING MACHINES.
THEY CAN'T EVEN FLY WITHOUT MAKING A MESS.
HE SMILES TO HIMSELF.
WHAT A CRAZY WAY TO THINK.
GOT HIM THINKING CRAZY.
THOSE ARE HER PEOPLE IN THERE.
FBI
HIS PEOPLE.
AND THEY'RE IN DANGER.
AND THEY'RE SCARED.
AND THEIR ENEMY... IS HIS ENEMY.
WHAT ARE THEY DOING? DAMN COPTERS. THEY JUST KEEP CIRCLING.
THEY JUST KEEP MAKING THIS RACKET.
DRIVING ME NUTS...
I SAY WE JUST POP--
HOLD ON, IT'S THEM. THEY'RE CALLING US.
YOU CRAZY OUT THERE? YOU WANT BODIES?
JUST OUTSIDE...
THAT'S IT. WE'RE GOING IN HARD. EVERYTHING WE'VE GOT.
YOU WANT BODIES?
YOU'RE GETTING THEM!
STARTING IN TEN!
NINE!
EIGHT!

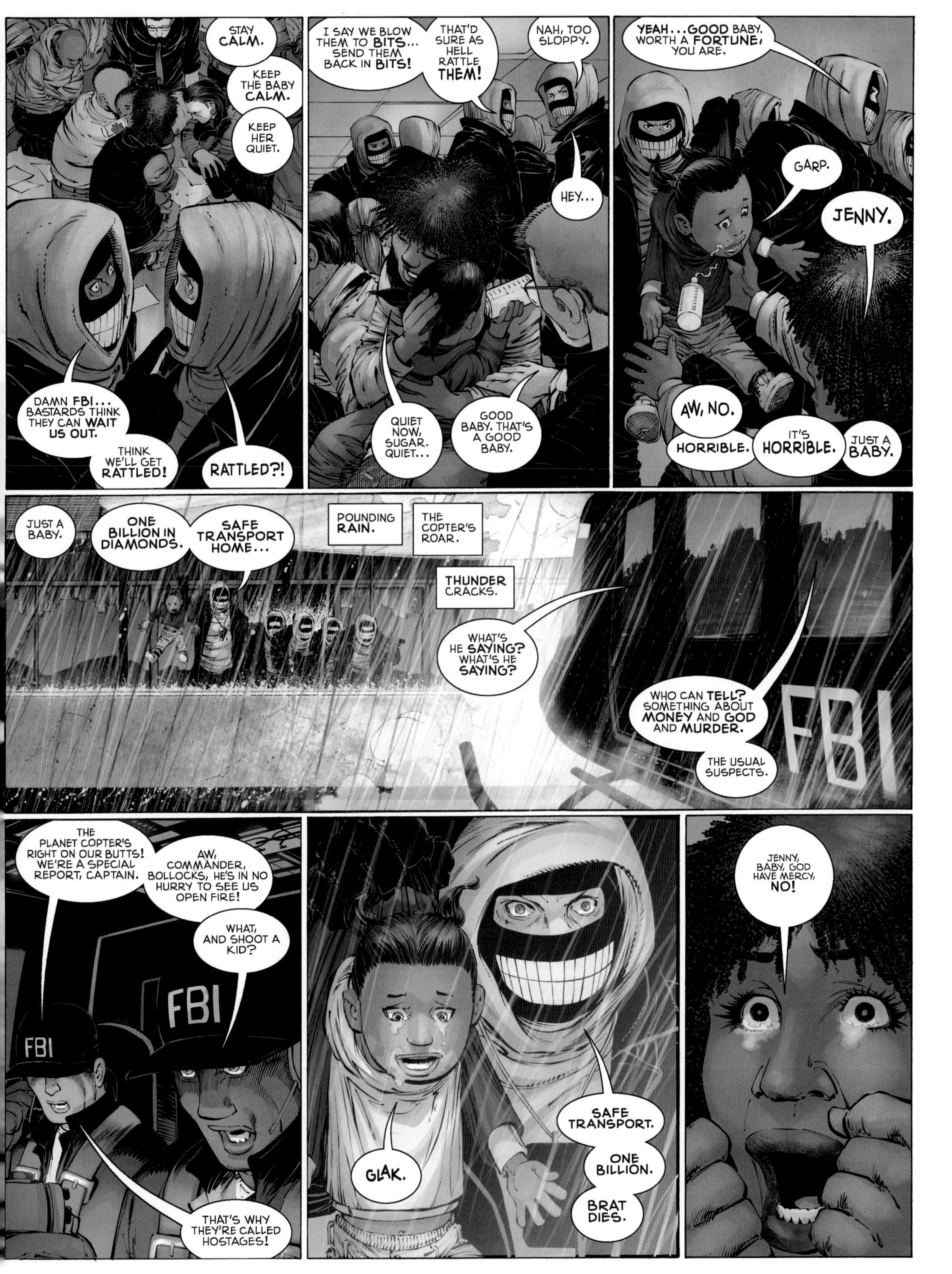
STAY CALM.
KEEP THE BABY CALM.
KEEP HER QUIET.
DAMN FBI... BASTARDS THINK THEY CAN WAIT US OUT.
THINK WE'LL GET RATTLED!
RATTLED?!
I SAY WE BLOW THEM TO BITS... SEND THEM BACK IN BITS!
THAT'D SURE AS HELL RATTLE THEM!
NAH, TOO SLOPPY.
HEY...
QUIET NOW, SUGAR. QUIET...
GOOD BABY. THAT'S A GOOD BABY.
YEAH...GOOD BABY. WORTH A FORTUNE, YOU ARE.
GARP.
JENNY.
AW, NO.
HORRIBLE.
IT'S HORRIBLE.
JUST A BABY.
JUST A BABY.
ONE BILLION IN DIAMONDS.
SAFE TRANSPORT HOME...
POUNDING RAIN.
THE COPTER'S ROAR.
THUNDER CRACKS.
WHAT'S HE SAYING? WHAT'S HE SAYING?
WHO CAN TELL? SOMETHING ABOUT MONEY AND GOD AND MURDER.
THE USUAL SUSPECTS.
FBI
THE PLANET COPTER'S RIGHT ON OUR BUTTS! WE'RE A SPECIAL REPORT, CAPTAIN.
AW, COMMANDER, BOLLOCKS, HE'S IN NO HURRY TO SEE US OPEN FIRE!
WHAT, AND SHOOT A KID?
THAT'S WHY THEY'RE CALLED HOSTAGES!
FBI
FBI
GLAK.
SAFE TRANSPORT.
ONE BILLION.
BRAT DIES.
JENNY, BABY, GOD HAVE MERCY, NO!

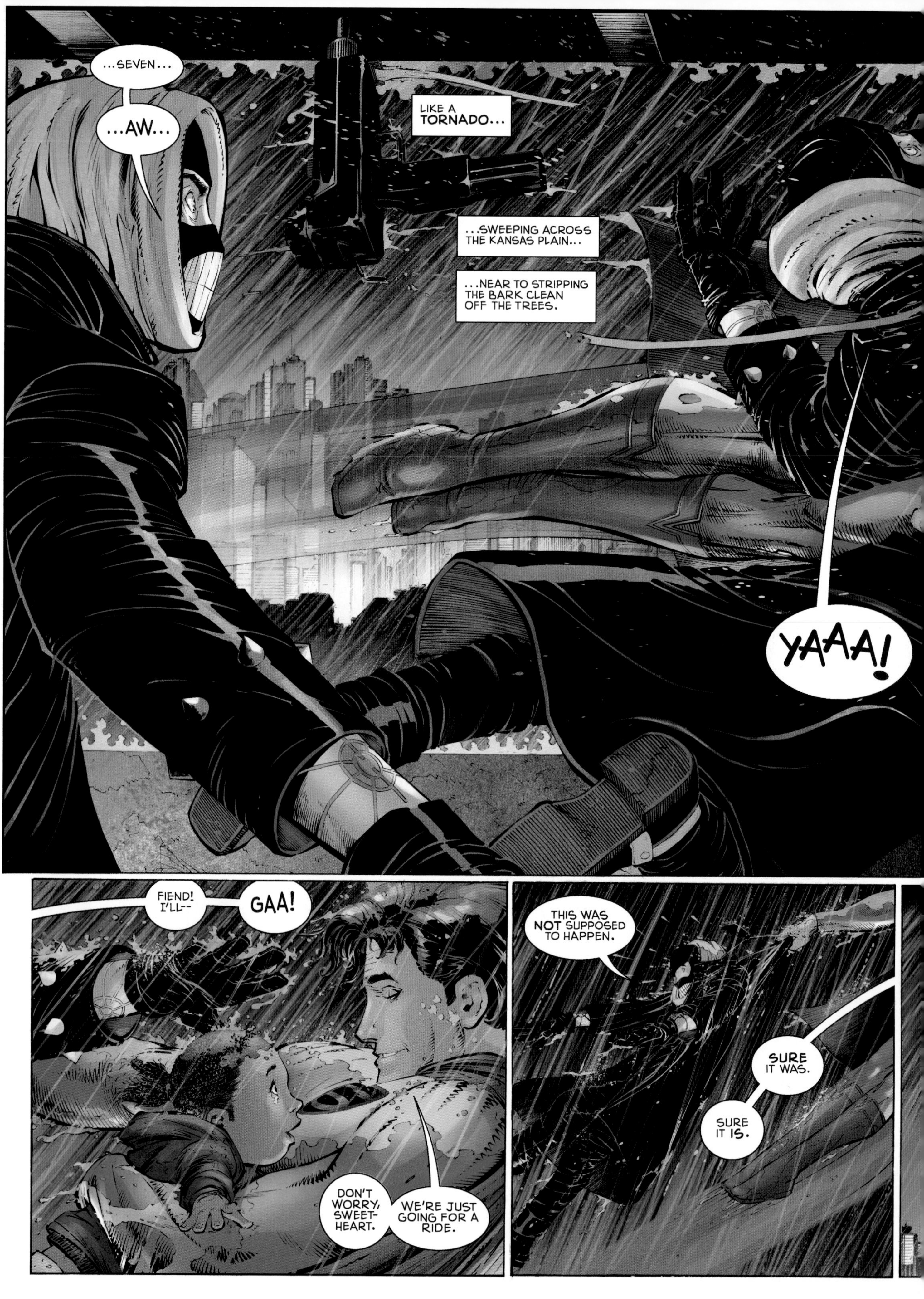
...SEVEN...
...AW...
LIKE A TORNADO...
...SWEEPING ACROSS THE KANSAS PLAIN...
...NEAR TO STRIPPING THE BARK CLEAN OFF THE TREES.
YAAA!
FIEND! I'LL--
GAA!
DON'T WORRY, SWEET-HEART.
WE'RE JUST GOING FOR A RIDE.
THIS WAS NOT SUPPOSED TO HAPPEN.
SURE IT WAS.
SURE IT IS.

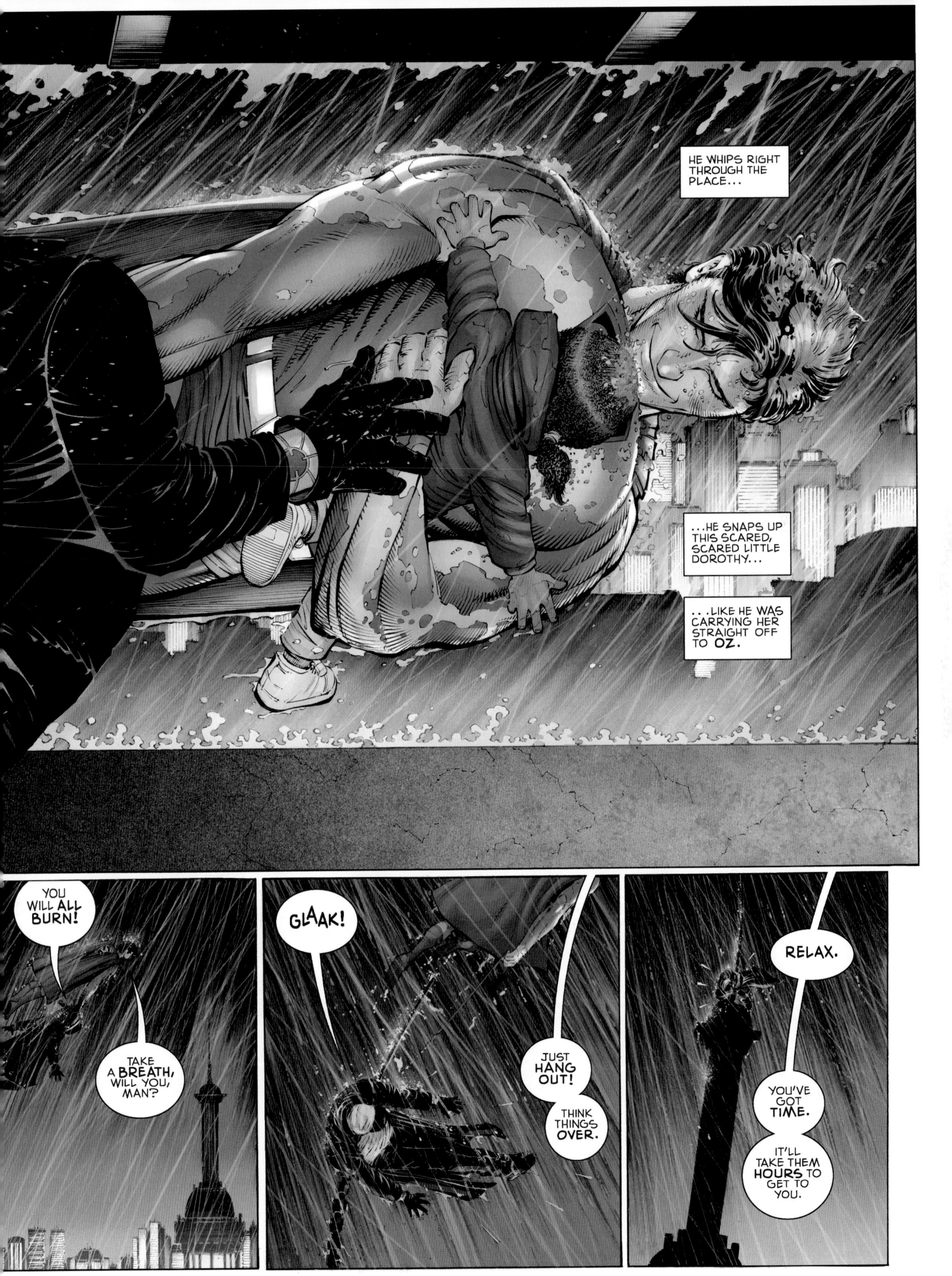
HE WHIPS RIGHT THROUGH THE PLACE...
...HE SNAPS UP THIS SCARED, SCARED LITTLE DOROTHY...
...LIKE HE WAS CARRYING HER STRAIGHT OFF TO OZ.
YOU WILL ALL BURN!
TAKE A BREATH, WILL YOU, MAN?
GLAAK!
JUST HANG OUT!
THINK THINGS OVER.
RELAX.
YOU'VE GOT TIME.
IT'LL TAKE THEM HOURS TO GET TO YOU.

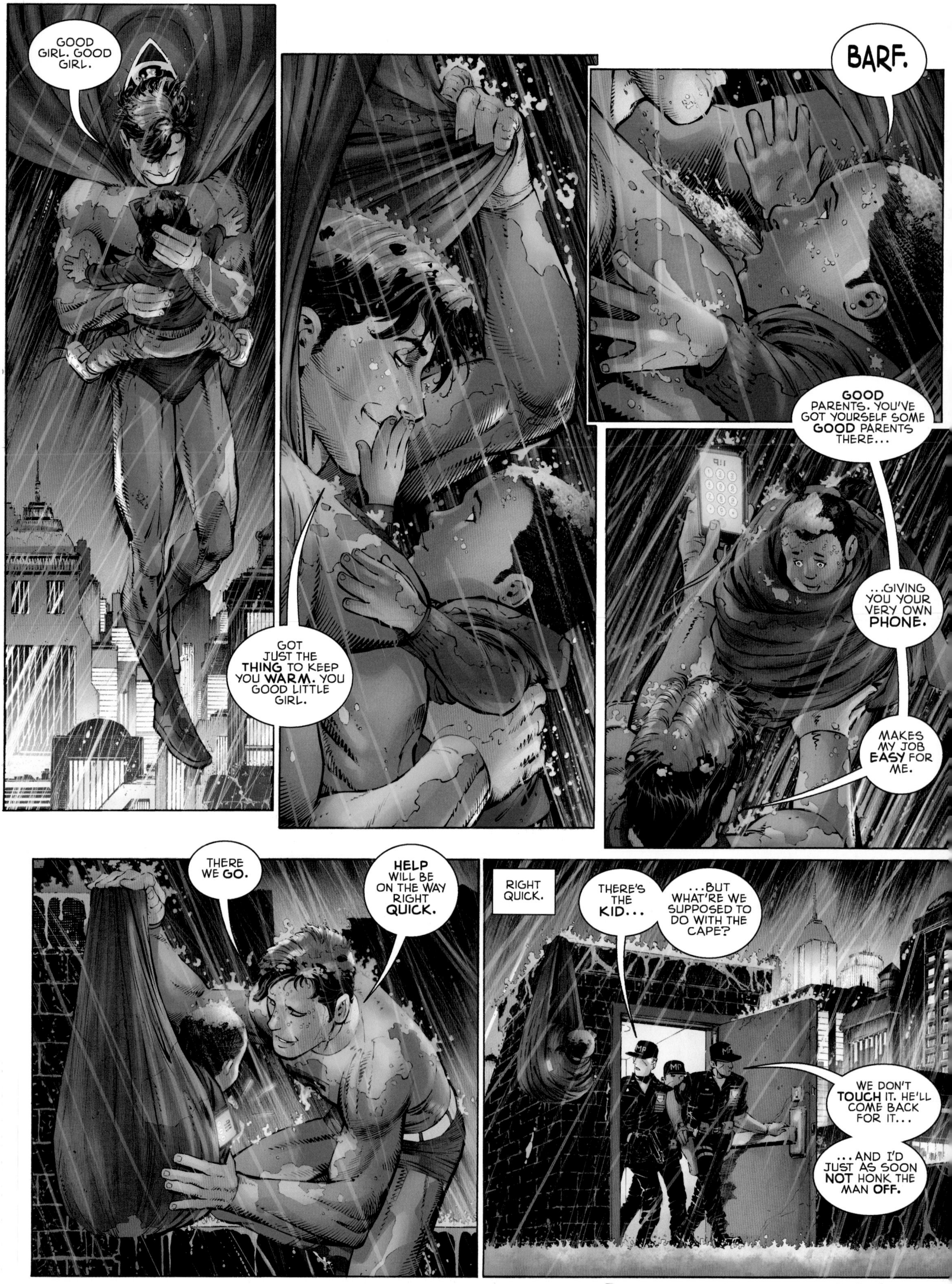
GOOD GIRL. GOOD GIRL.
GOT JUST THE THING TO KEEP YOU WARM. YOU GOOD LITTLE GIRL.
BARF.
GOOD PARENTS. YOU'VE GOT YOURSELF SOME GOOD PARENTS THERE...
...GIVING YOU YOUR VERY OWN PHONE.
MAKES MY JOB EASY FOR ME.
911
THERE WE GO.
HELP WILL BE ON THE WAY RIGHT QUICK.
RIGHT QUICK.
THERE'S THE KID...
...BUT WHAT'RE WE SUPPOSED TO DO WITH THE CAPE?
WE DON'T TOUCH IT. HE'LL COME BACK FOR IT...
...AND I'D JUST AS SOON NOT HONK THE MAN OFF.

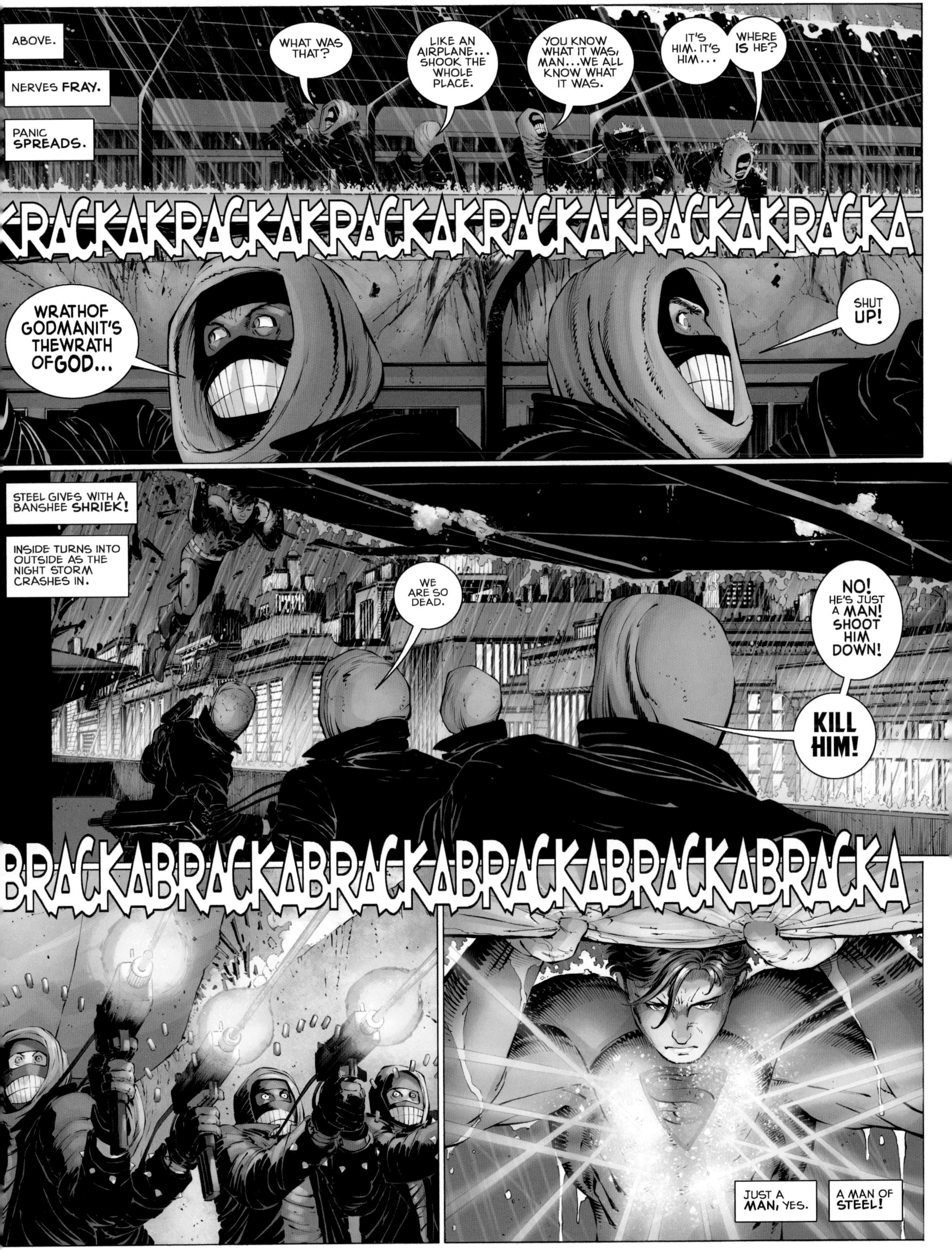

ABOVE.
NERVES FRAY.
PANIC SPREADS.
WHAT WAS THAT?
LIKE AN AIRPLANE... SHOOK THE WHOLE PLACE.
YOU KNOW WHAT IT WAS, MAN... WE ALL KNOW WHAT IT WAS.
IT'S HIM. IT'S HIM...
WHERE IS HE?
KRACKAKRACKAKRACKAKRACKAKRACKAKRACKA
WRATHOF GODMANIT'S THEWRATH OFGOD...
SHUT UP!
STEEL GIVES WITH A BANSHEE SHRIEK!
INSIDE TURNS INTO OUTSIDE AS THE NIGHT STORM CRASHES IN.
WE ARE SO DEAD.
NO! HE'S JUST A MAN! SHOOT HIM DOWN!
KILL HIM!
BRACKABRACKABRACKABRACKABRACKABRACKA
JUST A MAN, YES.
A MAN OF STEEL!

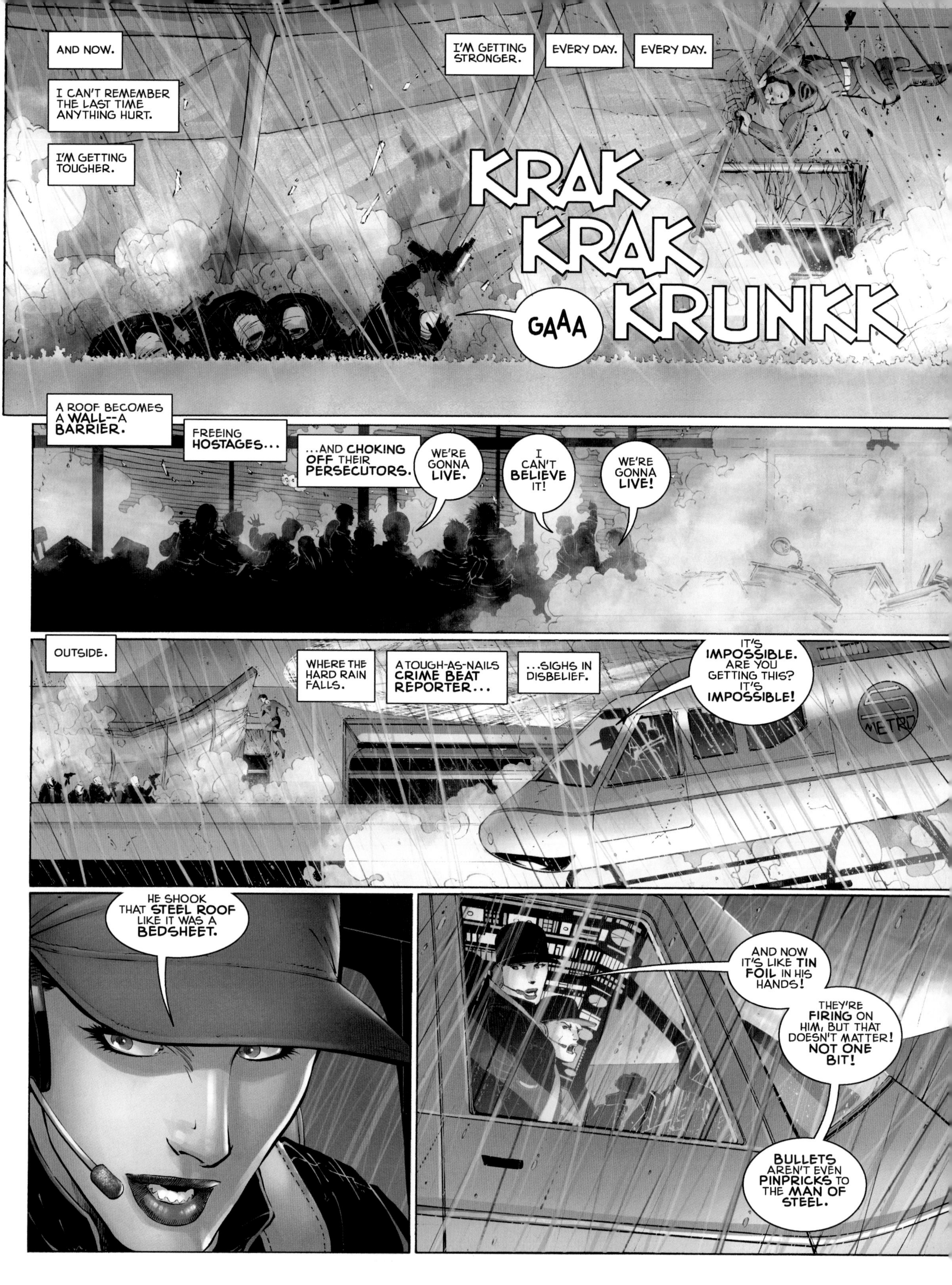
AND NOW.
I CAN'T REMEMBER THE LAST TIME ANYTHING HURT.
I'M GETTING TOUGHER.
I'M GETTING STRONGER.
EVERY DAY.
EVERY DAY.
KRAK
KRAK
GAAA
KRUNKK
A ROOF BECOMES A WALL--A BARRIER.
FREEING HOSTAGES...
...AND CHOKING OFF THEIR PERSECUTORS.
WE'RE GONNA LIVE.
I CAN'T BELIEVE IT!
WE'RE GONNA LIVE!
OUTSIDE.
WHERE THE HARD RAIN FALLS.
A TOUGH-AS-NAILS CRIME BEAT REPORTER...
...SIGHS IN DISBELIEF.
IT'S IMPOSSIBLE. ARE YOU GETTING THIS? IT'S IMPOSSIBLE!
HE SHOOK THAT STEEL ROOF LIKE IT WAS A BEDSHEET.
AND NOW IT'S LIKE TIN FOIL IN HIS HANDS!
THEY'RE FIRING ON HIM, BUT THAT DOESN'T MATTER! NOT ONE BIT!
BULLETS AREN'T EVEN PINPRICKS TO THE MAN OF STEEL.

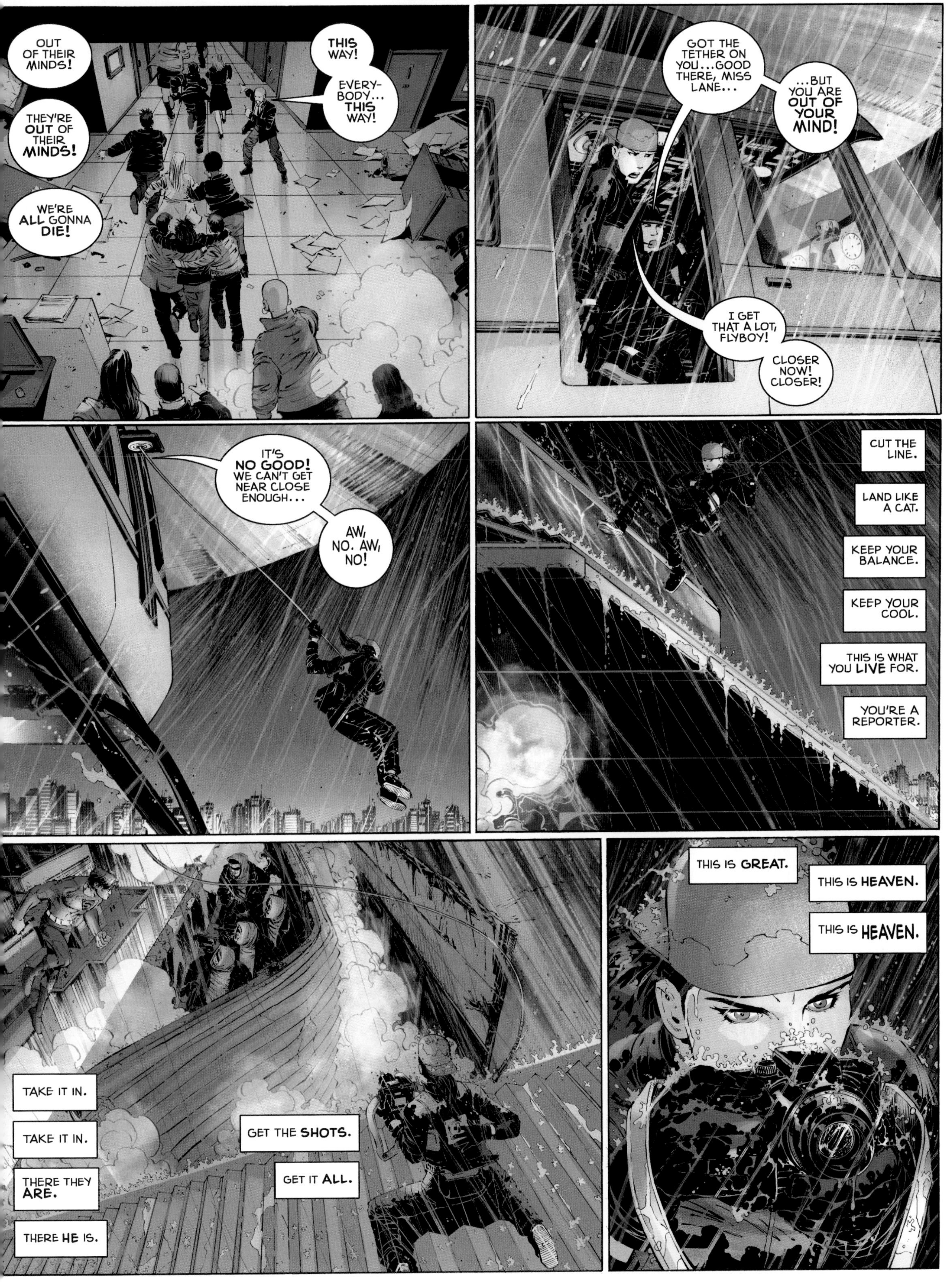

OUT OF THEIR MINDS!
THEY'RE OUT OF THEIR MINDS!
WE'RE ALL GONNA DIE!
THIS WAY!
EVERYBODY... THIS WAY!
GOT THE TETHER ON YOU...GOOD THERE, MISS LANE...
...BUT YOU ARE OUT OF YOUR MIND!
I GET THAT A LOT, FLYBOY!
CLOSER NOW! CLOSER!
IT'S NO GOOD! WE CAN'T GET NEAR CLOSE ENOUGH...
AW, NO. AW, NO!
CUT THE LINE.
LAND LIKE A CAT.
KEEP YOUR BALANCE.
KEEP YOUR COOL.
THIS IS WHAT YOU LIVE FOR.
YOU'RE A REPORTER.
TAKE IT IN.
TAKE IT IN.
THERE THEY ARE.
THERE HE IS.
GET THE SHOTS.
GET IT ALL.
THIS IS GREAT.
THIS IS HEAVEN.
THIS IS HEAVEN.

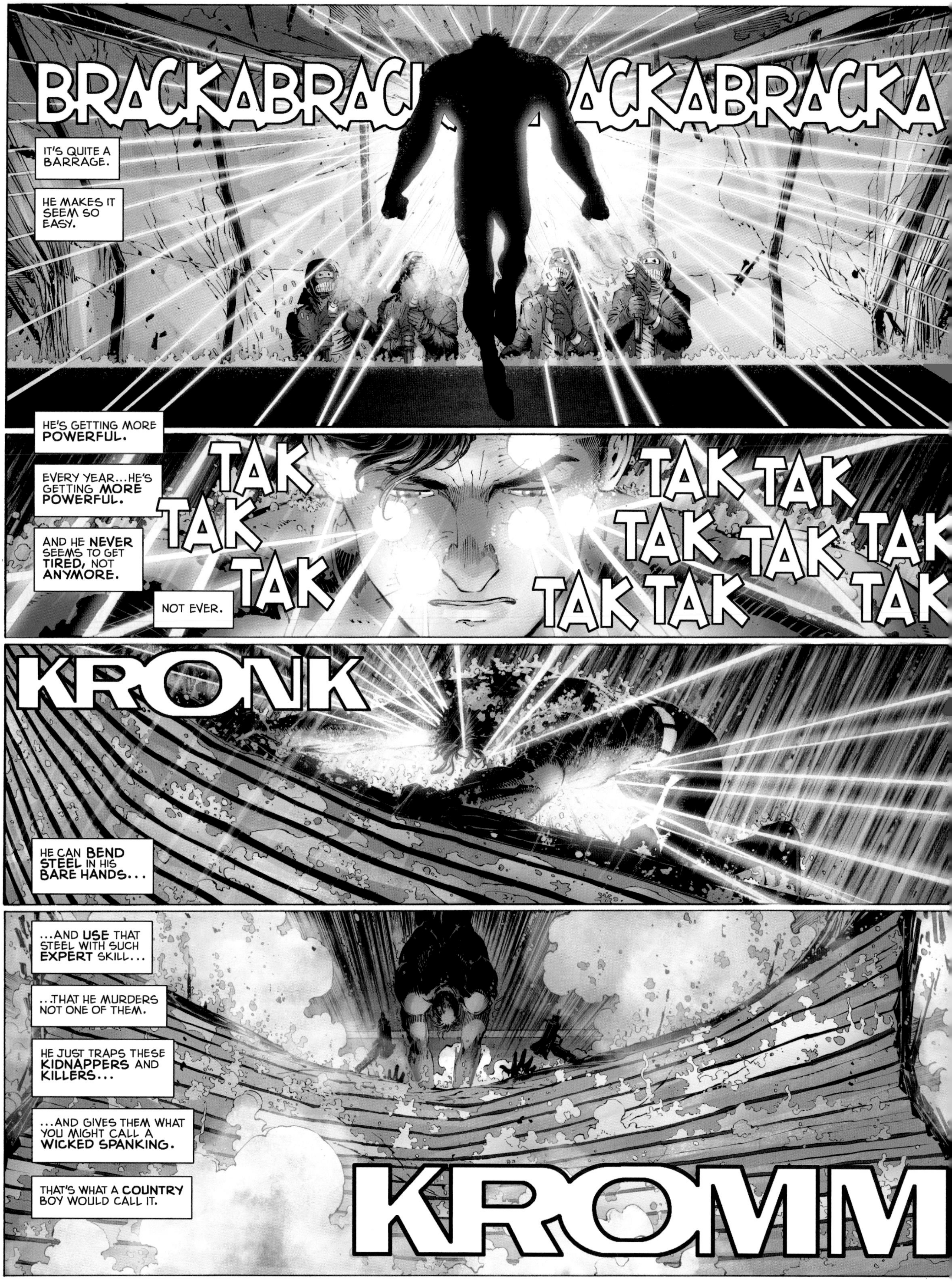
BRACKABRACK
RACKABRACKA
IT'S QUITE A BARRAGE.
HE MAKES IT SEEM SO EASY.
HE'S GETTING MORE POWERFUL.
EVERY YEAR...HE'S GETTING MORE POWERFUL.
AND HE NEVER SEEMS TO GET TIRED, NOT ANYMORE.
NOT EVER.
TAK TAK TAK
TAK TAK TAK TAK TAK TAK TAK TAK TAK
KRONK
HE CAN BEND STEEL IN HIS BARE HANDS...
...AND USE THAT STEEL WITH SUCH EXPERT SKILL...
...THAT HE MURDERS NOT ONE OF THEM.
HE JUST TRAPS THESE KIDNAPPERS AND KILLERS...
...AND GIVES THEM WHAT YOU MIGHT CALL A WICKED SPANKING.
THAT'S WHAT A COUNTRY BOY WOULD CALL IT.
KROMM

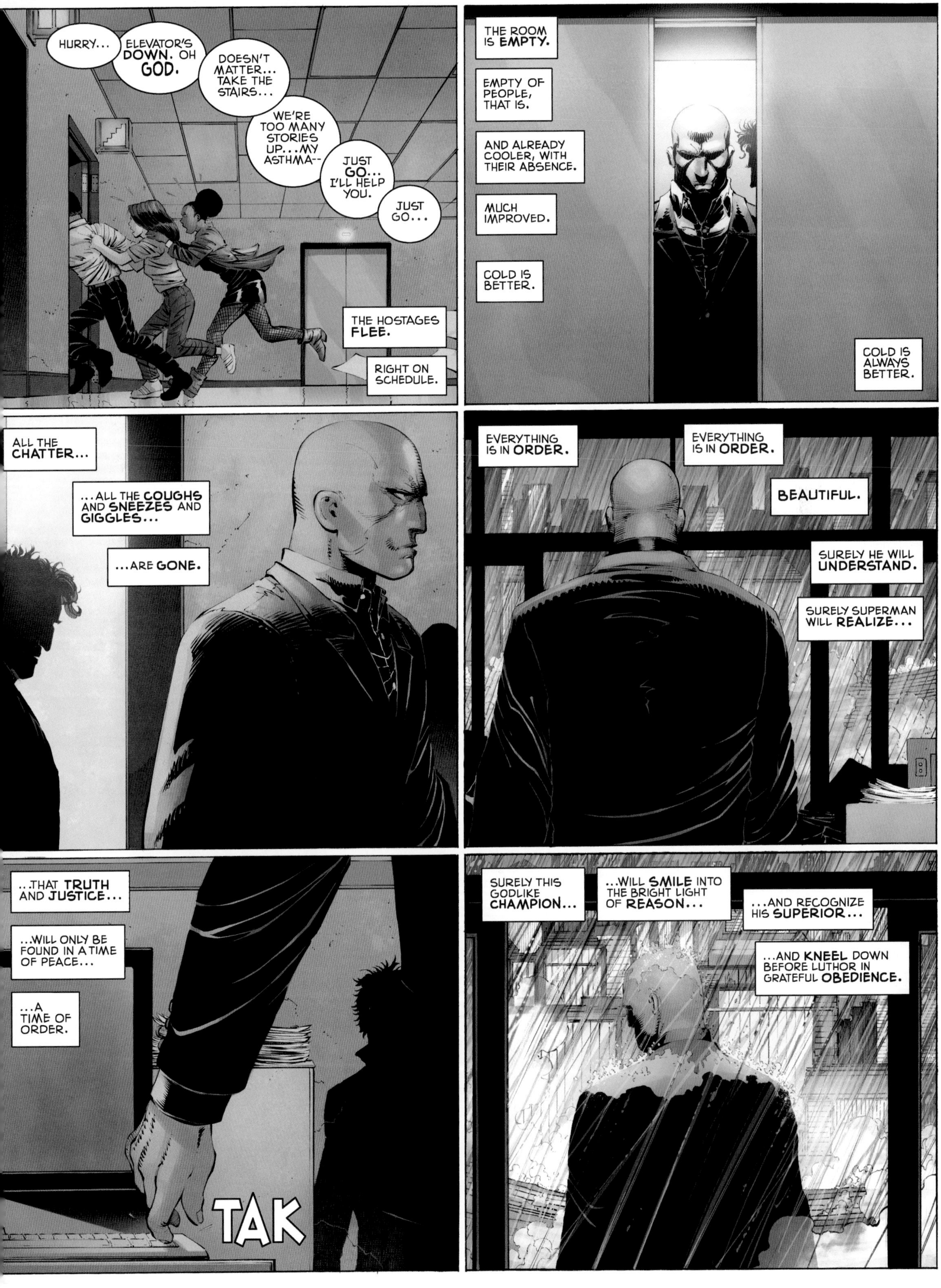
HURRY...
ELEVATOR'S DOWN. OH GOD.
DOESN'T MATTER... TAKE THE STAIRS...
WE'RE TOO MANY STORIES UP... MY ASTHMA--
JUST GO... I'LL HELP YOU.
JUST GO...
THE HOSTAGES FLEE.
RIGHT ON SCHEDULE.
THE ROOM IS EMPTY.
EMPTY OF PEOPLE, THAT IS.
AND ALREADY COOLER, WITH THEIR ABSENCE.
MUCH IMPROVED.
COLD IS BETTER.
COLD IS ALWAYS BETTER.
ALL THE CHATTER...
...ALL THE COUGHS AND SNEEZES AND GIGGLES...
...ARE GONE.
EVERYTHING IS IN ORDER.
EVERYTHING IS IN ORDER.
BEAUTIFUL.
SURELY HE WILL UNDERSTAND.
SURELY SUPERMAN WILL REALIZE...
...THAT TRUTH AND JUSTICE...
...WILL ONLY BE FOUND IN A TIME OF PEACE...
...A TIME OF ORDER.
TAK
SURELY THIS GODLIKE CHAMPION...
...WILL SMILE INTO THE BRIGHT LIGHT OF REASON...
...AND RECOGNIZE HIS SUPERIOR...
...AND KNEEL DOWN BEFORE LUTHOR IN GRATEFUL OBEDIENCE.

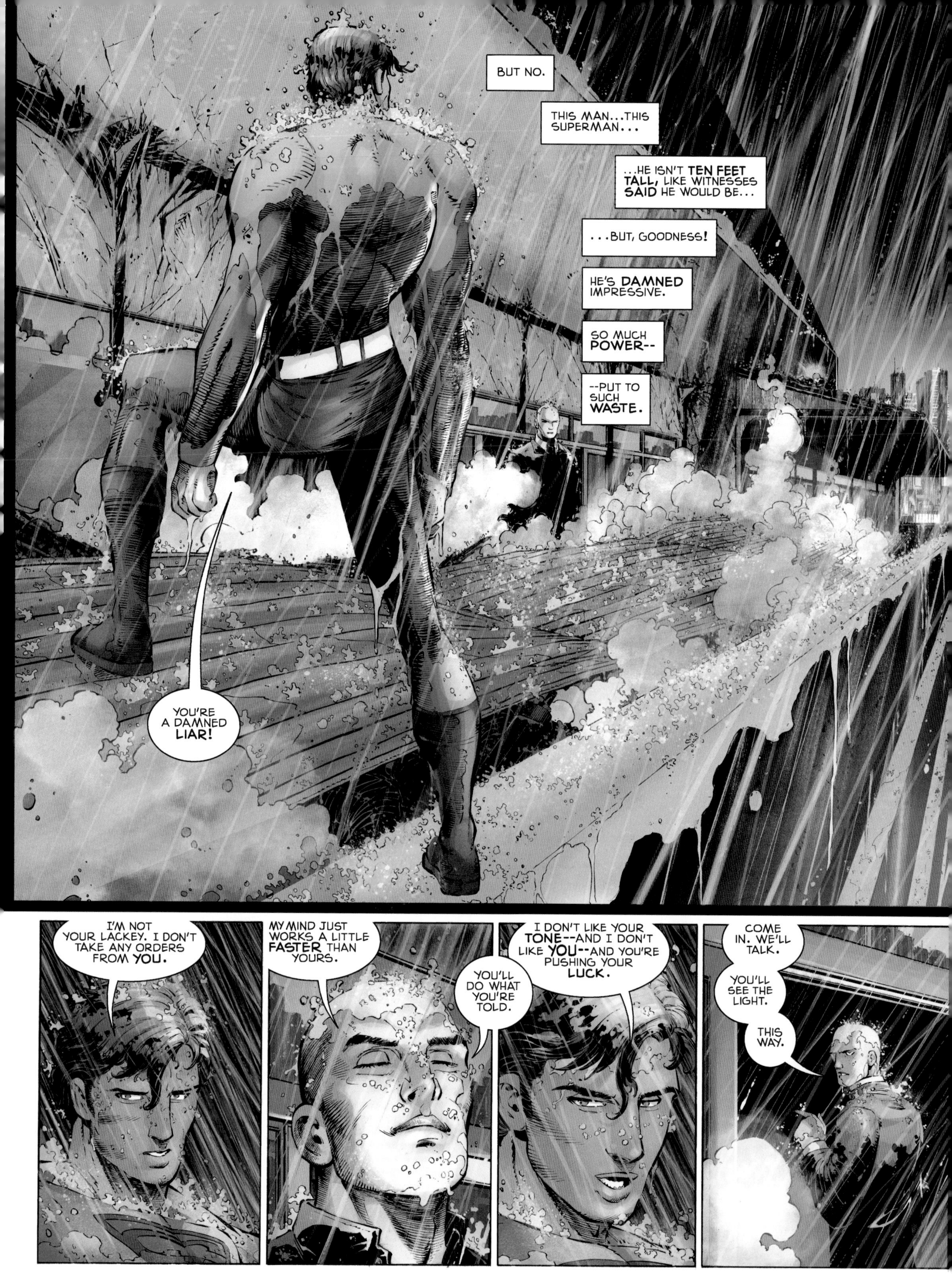

BUT NO.
THIS MAN...THIS SUPERMAN...
...HE ISN'T TEN FEET TALL, LIKE WITNESSES SAID HE WOULD BE...
...BUT, GOODNESS!
HE'S DAMNED IMPRESSIVE.
SO MUCH POWER--
--PUT TO SUCH WASTE.
YOU'RE A DAMNED LIAR!
I'M NOT YOUR LACKEY. I DON'T TAKE ANY ORDERS FROM YOU.
MY MIND JUST WORKS A LITTLE FASTER THAN YOURS.
YOU'LL DO WHAT YOU'RE TOLD.
I DON'T LIKE YOUR TONE--AND I DON'T LIKE YOU--AND YOU'RE PUSHING YOUR LUCK.
COME IN. WE'LL TALK.
YOU'LL SEE THE LIGHT.
THIS WAY.

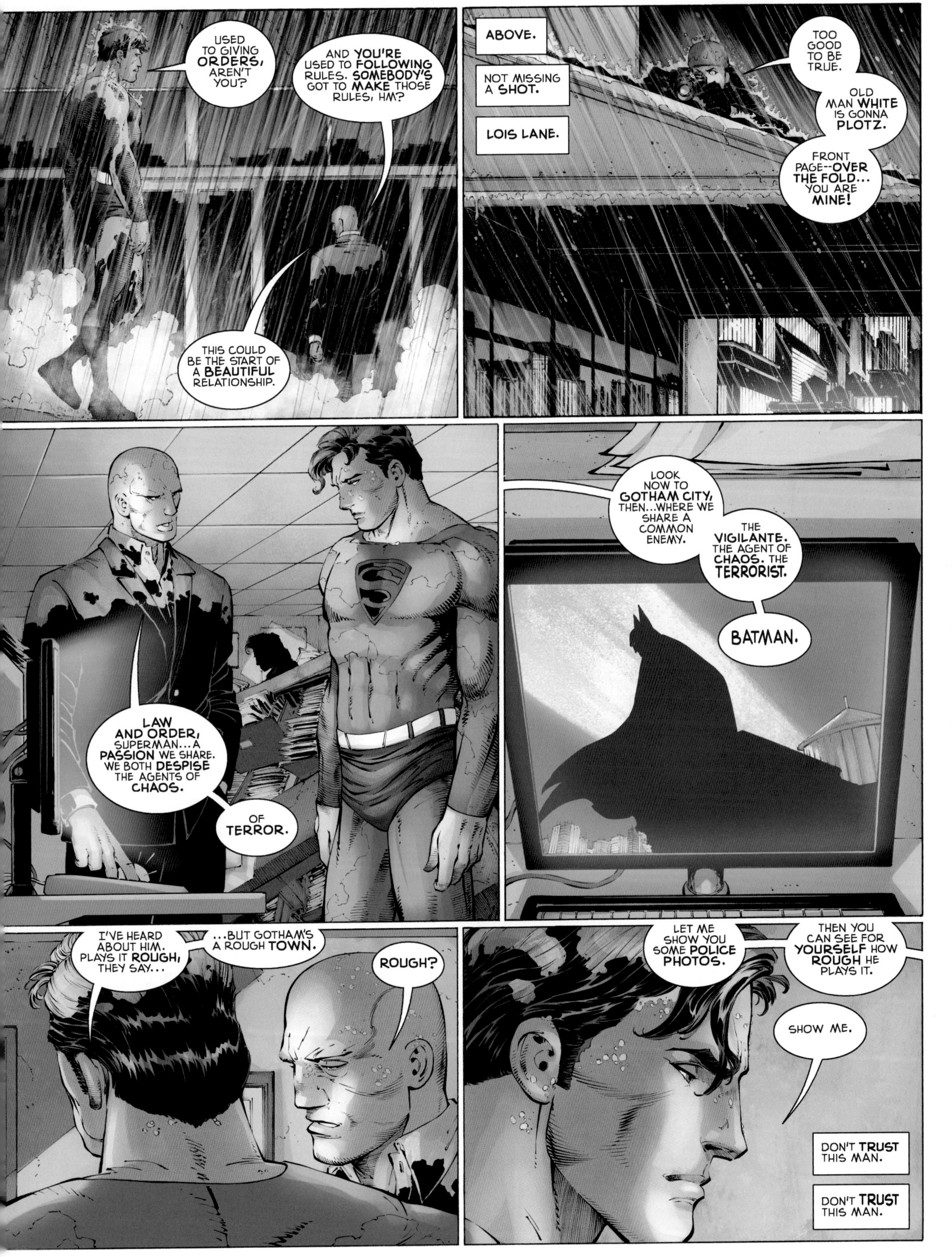

USED TO GIVING ORDERS, AREN'T YOU?
AND YOU'RE USED TO FOLLOWING RULES. SOMEBODY'S GOT TO MAKE THOSE RULES, HM?
THIS COULD BE THE START OF A BEAUTIFUL RELATIONSHIP.
ABOVE.
NOT MISSING A SHOT.
LOIS LANE.
TOO GOOD TO BE TRUE.
OLD MAN WHITE IS GONNA PLOTZ.
FRONT PAGE--OVER THE FOLD... YOU ARE MINE!
LAW AND ORDER, SUPERMAN... A PASSION WE SHARE. WE BOTH DESPISE THE AGENTS OF CHAOS.
OF TERROR.
LOOK NOW TO GOTHAM CITY, THEN...WHERE WE SHARE A COMMON ENEMY.
THE VIGILANTE. THE AGENT OF CHAOS. THE TERRORIST.
BATMAN.
I'VE HEARD ABOUT HIM. PLAYS IT ROUGH, THEY SAY...
...BUT GOTHAM'S A ROUGH TOWN.
ROUGH?
LET ME SHOW YOU SOME POLICE PHOTOS.
THEN YOU CAN SEE FOR YOURSELF HOW ROUGH HE PLAYS IT.
SHOW ME.
DON'T TRUST THIS MAN.
DON'T TRUST THIS MAN.

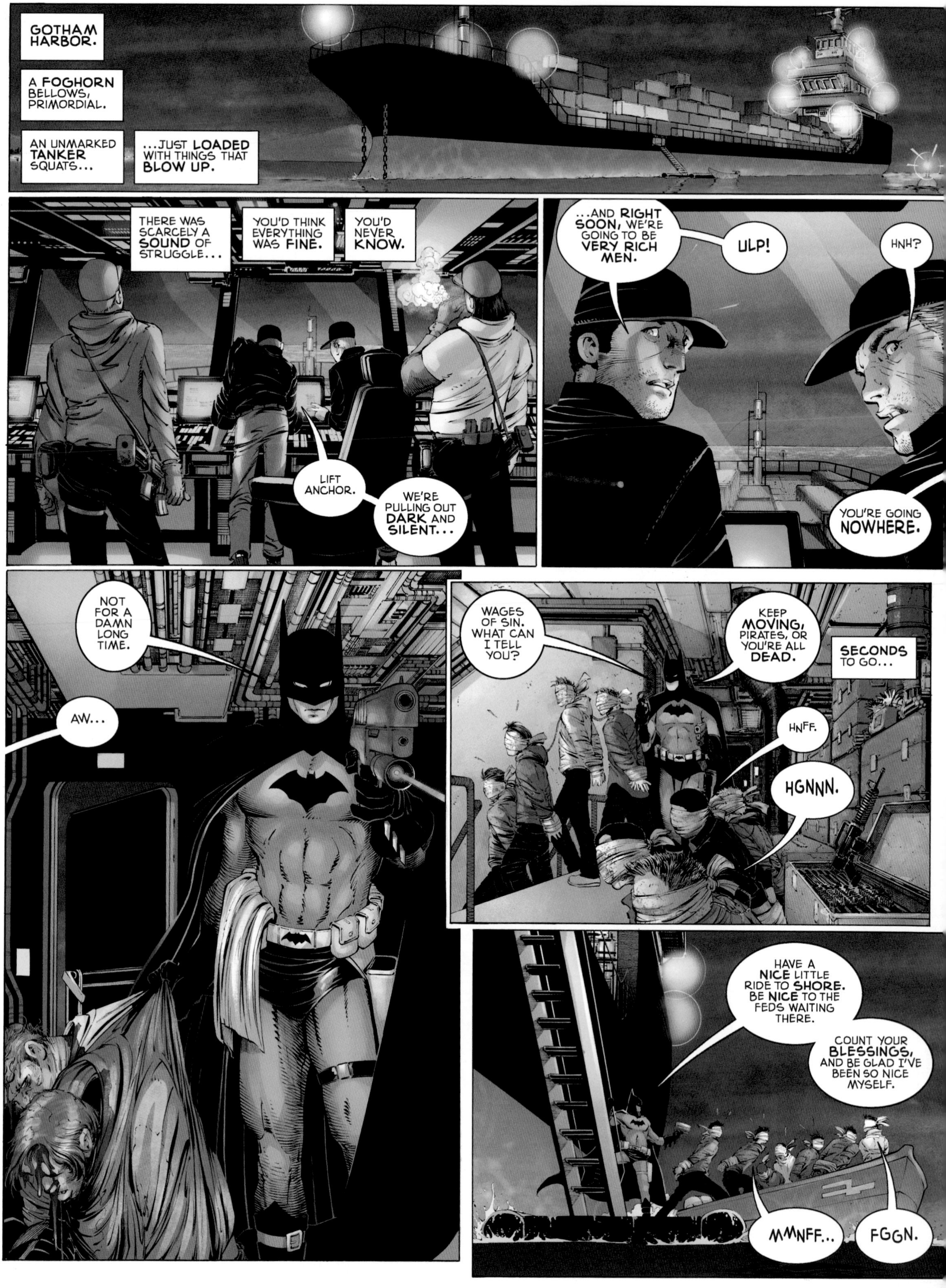
GOTHAM HARBOR.
A FOGHORN BELLOWS, PRIMORDIAL.
AN UNMARKED TANKER SQUATS...
...JUST LOADED WITH THINGS THAT BLOW UP.
THERE WAS SCARCELY A SOUND OF STRUGGLE...
YOU'D THINK EVERYTHING WAS FINE.
YOU'D NEVER KNOW.
LIFT ANCHOR.
WE'RE PULLING OUT DARK AND SILENT...
...AND RIGHT SOON, WE'RE GOING TO BE VERY RICH MEN.
ULP!
HNH?
YOU'RE GOING NOWHERE.
NOT FOR A DAMN LONG TIME.
AW...
WAGES OF SIN. WHAT CAN I TELL YOU?
KEEP MOVING, PIRATES, OR YOU'RE ALL DEAD.
SECONDS TO GO...
HNFF.
HGNNN.
HAVE A NICE LITTLE RIDE TO SHORE. BE NICE TO THE FEDS WAITING THERE.
COUNT YOUR BLESSINGS, AND BE GLAD I'VE BEEN SO NICE MYSELF.
MMNFF...
FGGN.

IT'S ALL SO WONDERFULLY QUIET, SO PERFECTLY GOTHAM...

...THE CONSTANT BLEATING OF MY CITY...THE CAR ALARMS CRYING...

...THE POLICE SIRENS RISING, THEN FALLING OFF, SO FAR AWAY...

...THE LAPPING WAVES...

...THE PIRATES' MUFFLED CURSES...

...ALL OF IT MUSIC TO MY EARS.

WHEN IT ALL GOES THIS SMOOTHLY...

...IT'S ALMOST LIKE PLAY.

I LOVE MY JOB.

I ALWAYS LOVE MY JOB.

AND LOOK THERE.

EVERYTHING'S JUST WHERE ALFRED DROPPED IT.

GOOD OLD ALFRED.

HE NEVER LETS ME DOWN.

745

SLAPPED THIS LITTLE DARLING TOGETHER IN MY WORKSHOP.

SHE CONVERTS SEA WATER STRAIGHT INTO ELECTRICAL POWER...

...GIVING ME AN OCEAN OF FUEL.

THE CONCEPT COULD HAVE APPLICATIONS.

THAT'S IF I EVER CARED TO SHARE IT.

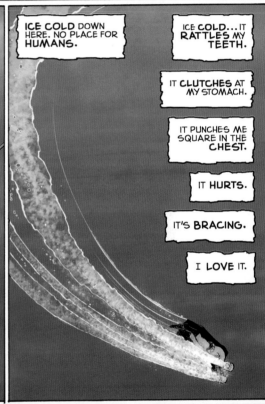

ICE COLD DOWN HERE. NO PLACE FOR HUMANS.

ICE COLD...IT RATTLES MY TEETH.

IT CLUTCHES AT MY STOMACH.

IT PUNCHES ME SQUARE IN THE CHEST.

IT HURTS.

IT'S BRACING.

I LOVE IT.

POOM POOM

POOM

SPOT ON TIME.

THE CHARGES GO UP.

...AND THIS OLD WHALE...

...SHE'S GOING NOWHERE.

IT'S THE PERFECT END...

...TO A PERFECT NIGHT.

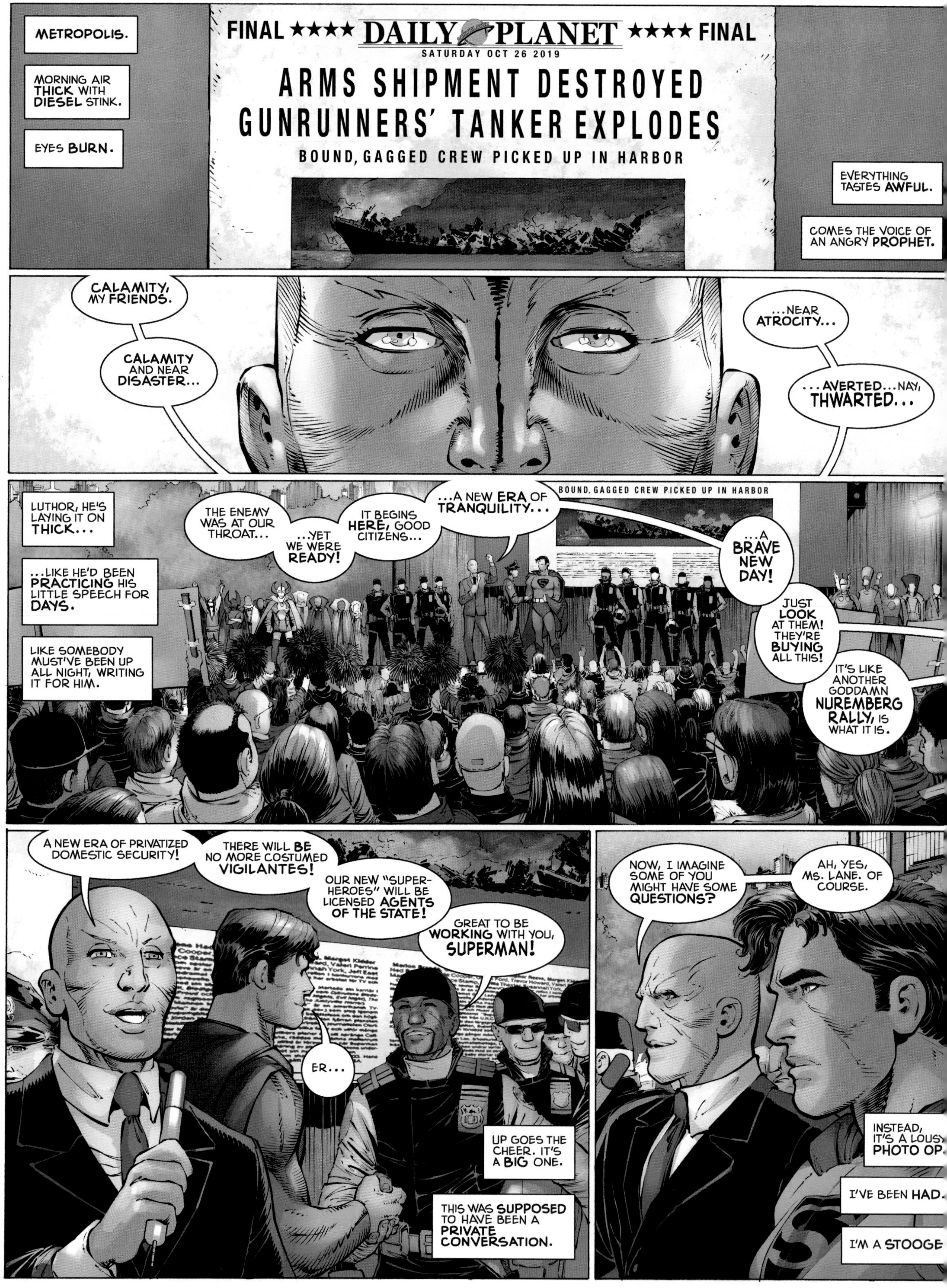
METROPOLIS.
MORNING AIR THICK WITH DIESEL STINK.
EYES BURN.
FINAL ★★★★ DAILY PLANET ★★★★ FINAL
SATURDAY OCT 26 2019
ARMS SHIPMENT DESTROYED
GUNRUNNERS' TANKER EXPLODES
BOUND, GAGGED CREW PICKED UP IN HARBOR
EVERYTHING TASTES AWFUL.
COMES THE VOICE OF AN ANGRY PROPHET.
CALAMITY, MY FRIENDS.
CALAMITY AND NEAR DISASTER...
...NEAR ATROCITY...
...AVERTED...NAY, THWARTED...
LUTHOR, HE'S LAYING IT ON THICK...
...LIKE HE'D BEEN PRACTICING HIS LITTLE SPEECH FOR DAYS.
LIKE SOMEBODY MUST'VE BEEN UP ALL NIGHT, WRITING IT FOR HIM.
THE ENEMY WAS AT OUR THROAT...
...YET WE WERE READY!
IT BEGINS HERE, GOOD CITIZENS...
...A NEW ERA OF TRANQUILITY...
BOUND, GAGGED CREW PICKED UP IN HARBOR
...A BRAVE NEW DAY!
JUST LOOK AT THEM! THEY'RE BUYING ALL THIS!
IT'S LIKE ANOTHER GODDAMN NUREMBERG RALLY, IS WHAT IT IS.
A NEW ERA OF PRIVATIZED DOMESTIC SECURITY!
THERE WILL BE NO MORE COSTUMED VIGILANTES!
OUR NEW "SUPER-HEROES" WILL BE LICENSED AGENTS OF THE STATE!
GREAT TO BE WORKING WITH YOU, SUPERMAN!
ER...
UP GOES THE CHEER. IT'S A BIG ONE.
THIS WAS SUPPOSED TO HAVE BEEN A PRIVATE CONVERSATION.
NOW, I IMAGINE SOME OF YOU MIGHT HAVE SOME QUESTIONS?
AH, YES, MS. LANE. OF COURSE.
INSTEAD, IT'S A LOUSY PHOTO OP.
I'VE BEEN HAD.
I'M A STOOGE.

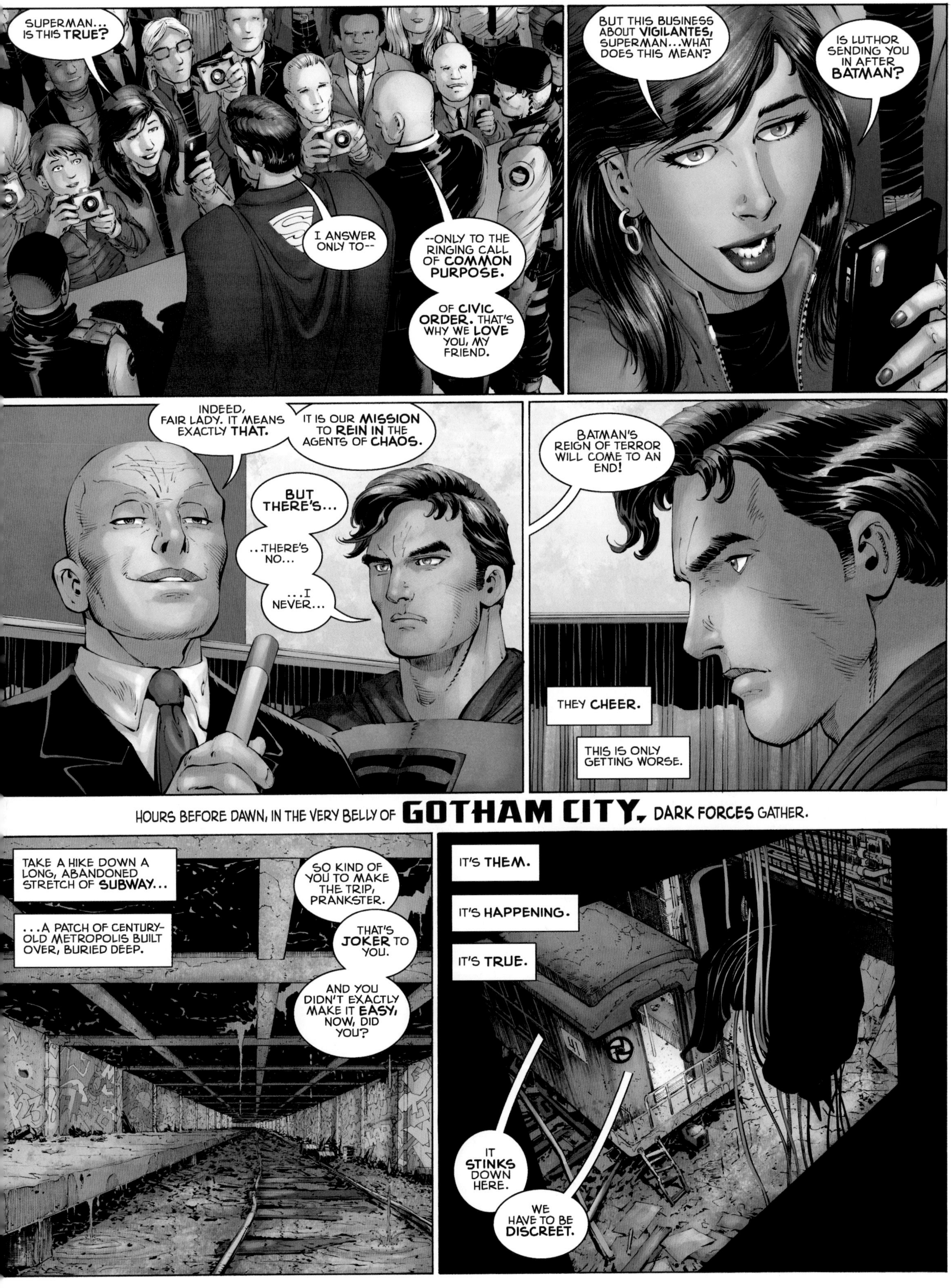
SUPERMAN... IS THIS TRUE?
I ANSWER ONLY TO--
--ONLY TO THE RINGING CALL OF COMMON PURPOSE.
OF CIVIC ORDER. THAT'S WHY WE LOVE YOU, MY FRIEND.
BUT THIS BUSINESS ABOUT VIGILANTES, SUPERMAN...WHAT DOES THIS MEAN?
IS LUTHOR SENDING YOU IN AFTER BATMAN?
INDEED, FAIR LADY. IT MEANS EXACTLY THAT.
IT IS OUR MISSION TO REIN IN THE AGENTS OF CHAOS.
BUT THERE'S...
...THERE'S NO...
...I NEVER...
BATMAN'S REIGN OF TERROR WILL COME TO AN END!
THEY CHEER.
THIS IS ONLY GETTING WORSE.
HOURS BEFORE DAWN, IN THE VERY BELLY OF GOTHAM CITY, DARK FORCES GATHER.
TAKE A HIKE DOWN A LONG, ABANDONED STRETCH OF SUBWAY...
...A PATCH OF CENTURY-OLD METROPOLIS BUILT OVER, BURIED DEEP.
SO KIND OF YOU TO MAKE THE TRIP, PRANKSTER.
THAT'S JOKER TO YOU.
AND YOU DIDN'T EXACTLY MAKE IT EASY, NOW, DID YOU?
IT'S THEM.
IT'S HAPPENING.
IT'S TRUE.
IT STINKS DOWN HERE.
WE HAVE TO BE DISCREET.

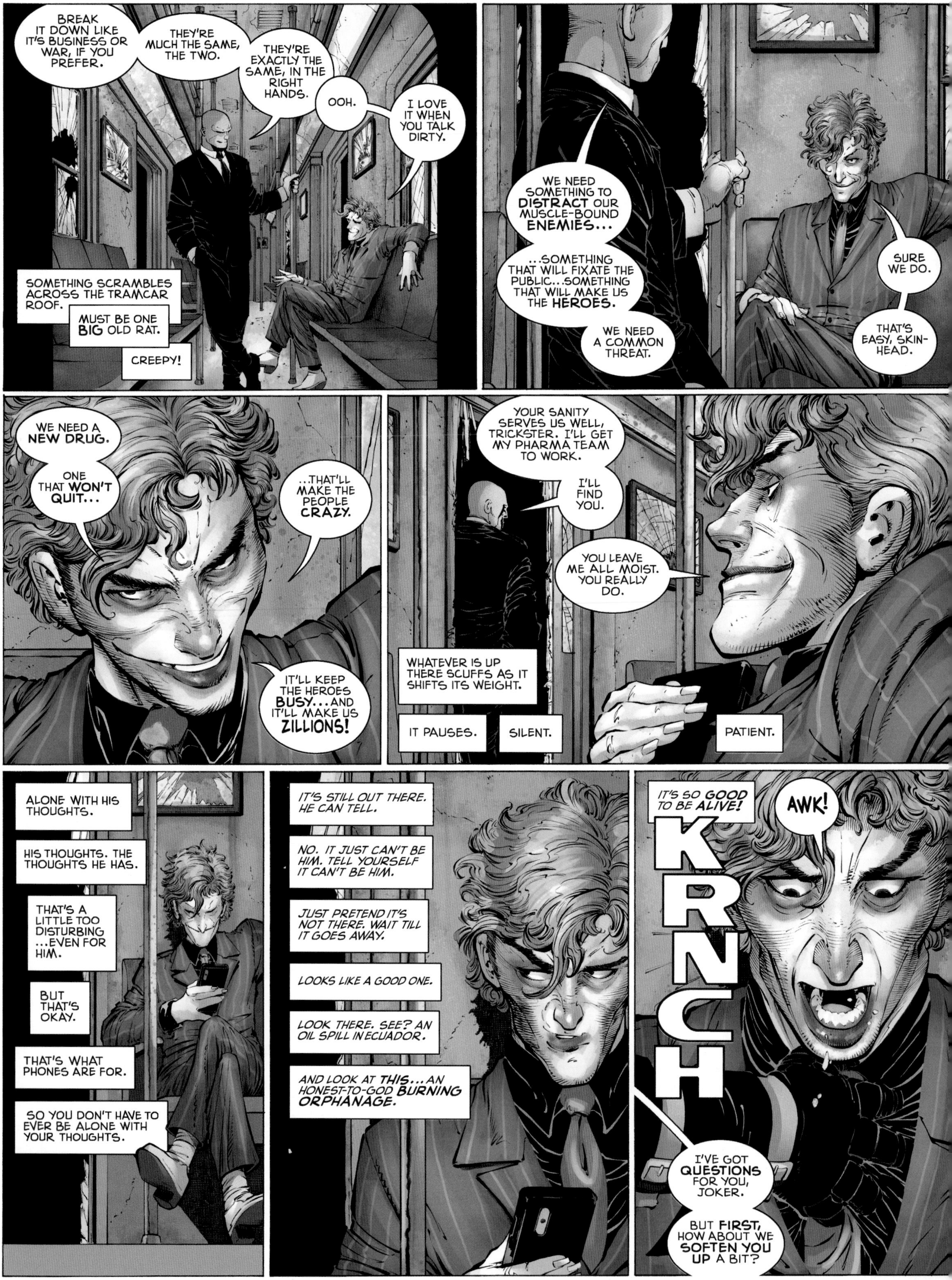
BREAK IT DOWN LIKE IT'S BUSINESS OR WAR, IF YOU PREFER.
THEY'RE MUCH THE SAME, THE TWO.
THEY'RE EXACTLY THE SAME, IN THE RIGHT HANDS.
OOH.
I LOVE IT WHEN YOU TALK DIRTY.
SOMETHING SCRAMBLES ACROSS THE TRAMCAR ROOF.
MUST BE ONE BIG OLD RAT.
CREEPY!
WE NEED SOMETHING TO DISTRACT OUR MUSCLE-BOUND ENEMIES...
...SOMETHING THAT WILL FIXATE THE PUBLIC...SOMETHING THAT WILL MAKE US THE HEROES.
WE NEED A COMMON THREAT.
SURE WE DO.
THAT'S EASY, SKIN-HEAD.
WE NEED A NEW DRUG.
ONE THAT WON'T QUIT...
...THAT'LL MAKE THE PEOPLE CRAZY.
IT'LL KEEP THE HEROES BUSY...AND IT'LL MAKE US ZILLIONS!
YOUR SANITY SERVES US WELL, TRICKSTER. I'LL GET MY PHARMA TEAM TO WORK.
I'LL FIND YOU.
YOU LEAVE ME ALL MOIST. YOU REALLY DO.
WHATEVER IS UP THERE SCUFFS AS IT SHIFTS ITS WEIGHT.
IT PAUSES.
SILENT.
PATIENT.
ALONE WITH HIS THOUGHTS.
HIS THOUGHTS. THE THOUGHTS HE HAS.
THAT'S A LITTLE TOO DISTURBING ...EVEN FOR HIM.
BUT THAT'S OKAY.
THAT'S WHAT PHONES ARE FOR.
SO YOU DON'T HAVE TO EVER BE ALONE WITH YOUR THOUGHTS.
IT'S STILL OUT THERE. HE CAN TELL.
NO. IT JUST CAN'T BE HIM. TELL YOURSELF IT CAN'T BE HIM.
JUST PRETEND IT'S NOT THERE. WAIT TILL IT GOES AWAY.
LOOKS LIKE A GOOD ONE.
LOOK THERE. SEE? AN OIL SPILL IN ECUADOR.
AND LOOK AT THIS...AN HONEST-TO-GOD BURNING ORPHANAGE.
IT'S SO GOOD TO BE ALIVE!
AWK!
KRNCH
I'VE GOT QUESTIONS FOR YOU, JOKER.
BUT FIRST, HOW ABOUT WE SOFTEN YOU UP A BIT?

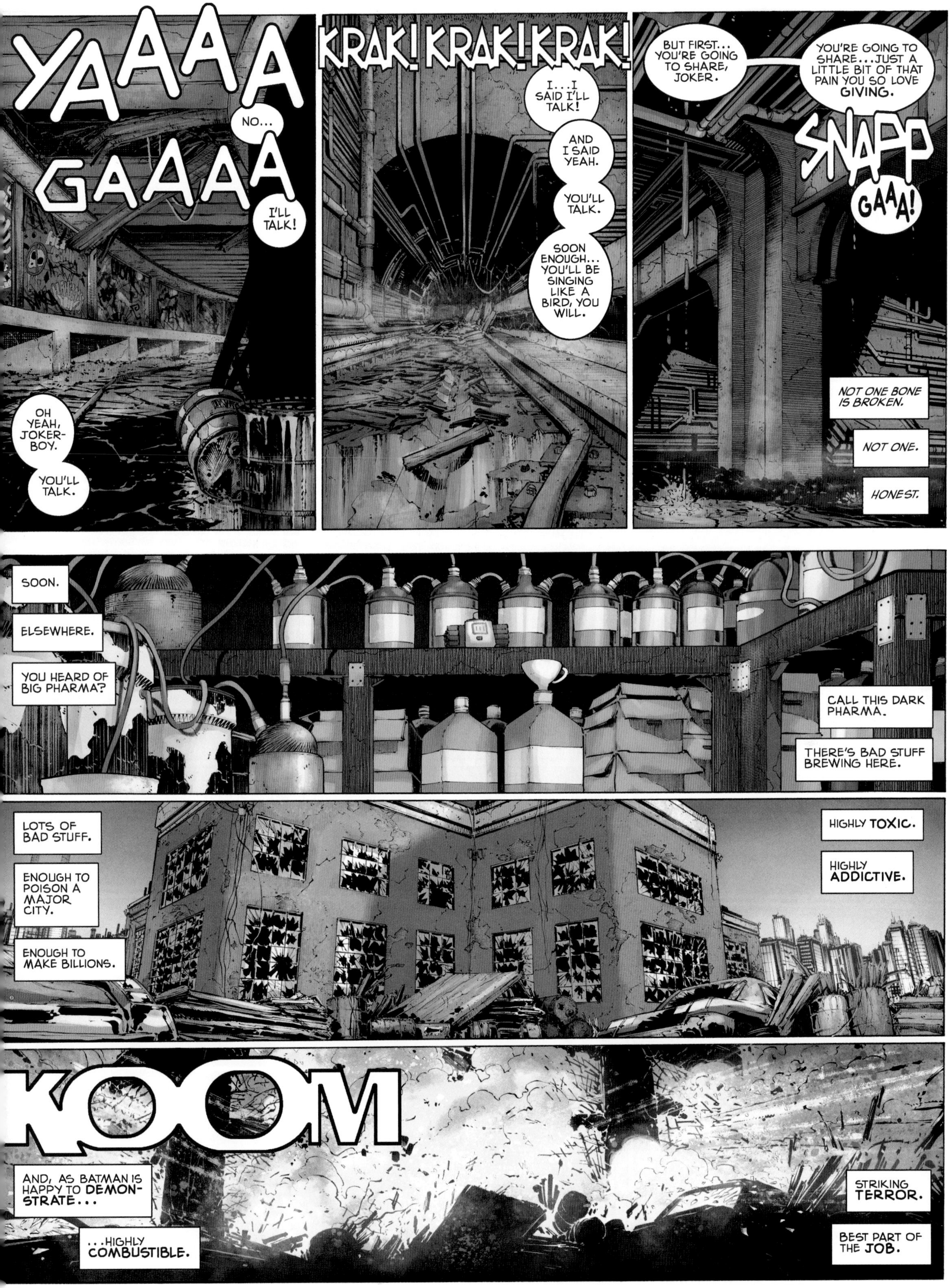
YAAAA
NO...
GAAAA
I'LL TALK!
OH YEAH, JOKER-BOY.
YOU'LL TALK.
KRAK! KRAK! KRAK!
I...I SAID I'LL TALK!
AND I SAID YEAH.
YOU'LL TALK.
SOON ENOUGH... YOU'LL BE SINGING LIKE A BIRD, YOU WILL.
BUT FIRST... YOU'RE GOING TO SHARE, JOKER.
YOU'RE GOING TO SHARE...JUST A LITTLE BIT OF THAT PAIN YOU SO LOVE GIVING.
SNAPP
GAAA!
NOT ONE BONE IS BROKEN.
NOT ONE.
HONEST.
SOON.
ELSEWHERE.
YOU HEARD OF BIG PHARMA?
CALL THIS DARK PHARMA.
THERE'S BAD STUFF BREWING HERE.
LOTS OF BAD STUFF.
ENOUGH TO POISON A MAJOR CITY.
ENOUGH TO MAKE BILLIONS.
HIGHLY TOXIC.
HIGHLY ADDICTIVE.
KOOOM
AND, AS BATMAN IS HAPPY TO DEMON-STRATE...
...HIGHLY COMBUSTIBLE.
STRIKING TERROR.
BEST PART OF THE JOB.

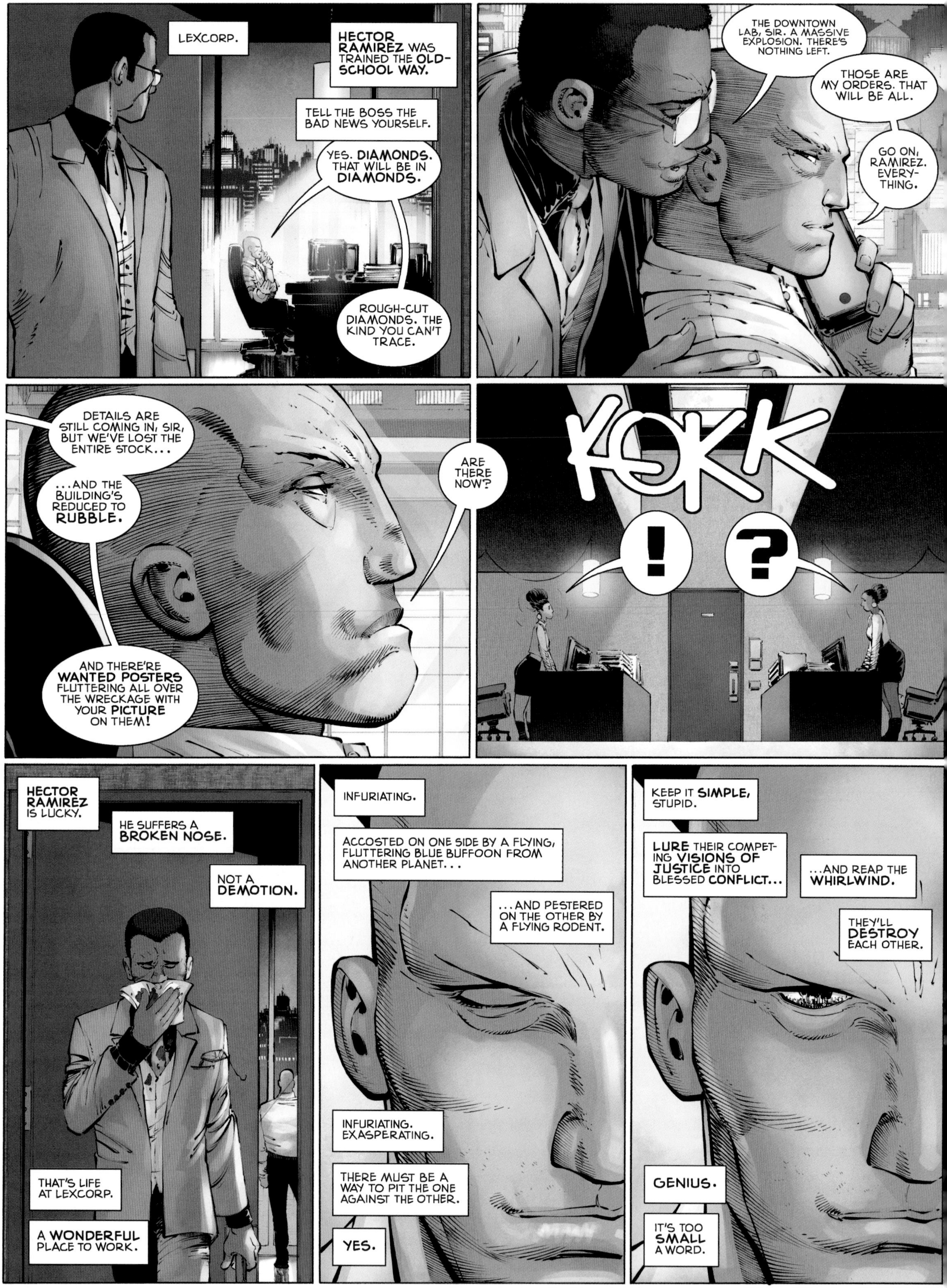

LEXCORP.
HECTOR RAMIREZ WAS TRAINED THE OLD-SCHOOL WAY.
TELL THE BOSS THE BAD NEWS YOURSELF.
YES. DIAMONDS. THAT WILL BE IN DIAMONDS.
ROUGH-CUT DIAMONDS. THE KIND YOU CAN'T TRACE.
THE DOWNTOWN LAB, SIR. A MASSIVE EXPLOSION. THERE'S NOTHING LEFT.
THOSE ARE MY ORDERS. THAT WILL BE ALL.
GO ON, RAMIREZ. EVERY-THING.
DETAILS ARE STILL COMING IN, SIR, BUT WE'VE LOST THE ENTIRE STOCK...
...AND THE BUILDING'S REDUCED TO RUBBLE.
ARE THERE NOW?
AND THERE'RE WANTED POSTERS FLUTTERING ALL OVER THE WRECKAGE WITH YOUR PICTURE ON THEM!
KOKK
!
?
HECTOR RAMIREZ IS LUCKY.
HE SUFFERS A BROKEN NOSE.
NOT A DEMOTION.
THAT'S LIFE AT LEXCORP.
A WONDERFUL PLACE TO WORK.
INFURIATING.
ACCOSTED ON ONE SIDE BY A FLYING, FLUTTERING BLUE BUFFOON FROM ANOTHER PLANET...
...AND PESTERED ON THE OTHER BY A FLYING RODENT.
INFURIATING. EXASPERATING.
THERE MUST BE A WAY TO PIT THE ONE AGAINST THE OTHER.
YES.
KEEP IT SIMPLE, STUPID.
LURE THEIR COMPETING VISIONS OF JUSTICE INTO BLESSED CONFLICT...
...AND REAP THE WHIRLWIND.
THEY'LL DESTROY EACH OTHER.
GENIUS.
IT'S TOO SMALL A WORD.

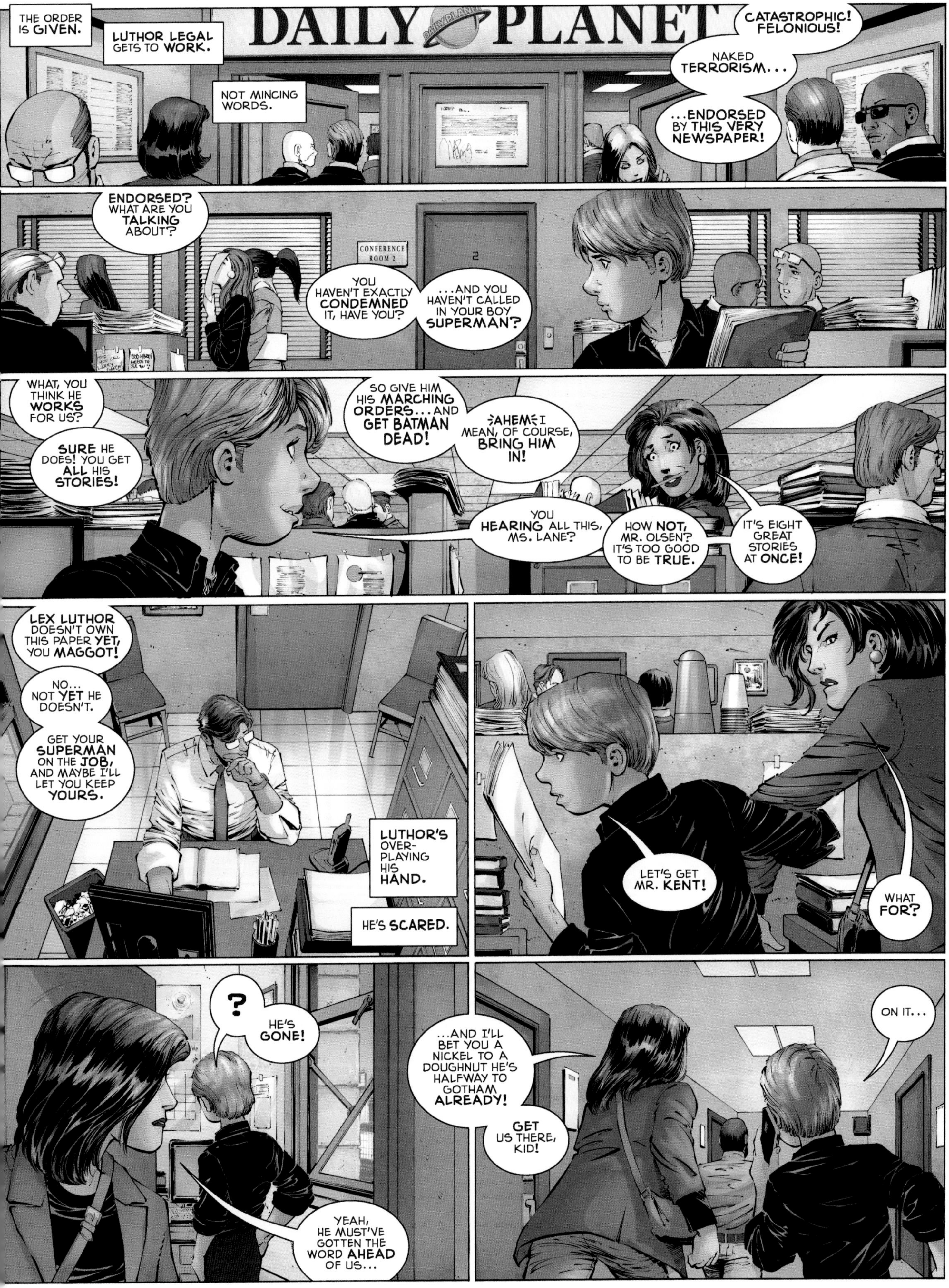

THE ORDER IS GIVEN.
LUTHOR LEGAL GETS TO WORK.
DAILY PLANET
NOT MINCING WORDS.
CATASTROPHIC! FELONIOUS!
NAKED TERRORISM...
...ENDORSED BY THIS VERY NEWSPAPER!
ENDORSED? WHAT ARE YOU TALKING ABOUT?
CONFERENCE ROOM 2
YOU HAVEN'T EXACTLY CONDEMNED IT, HAVE YOU?
...AND YOU HAVEN'T CALLED IN YOUR BOY SUPERMAN?
WHAT, YOU THINK HE WORKS FOR US?
SURE HE DOES! YOU GET ALL HIS STORIES!
SO GIVE HIM HIS MARCHING ORDERS...AND GET BATMAN DEAD!
AHEM I MEAN, OF COURSE, BRING HIM IN!
YOU HEARING ALL THIS, MS. LANE?
HOW NOT, MR. OLSEN? IT'S TOO GOOD TO BE TRUE.
IT'S EIGHT GREAT STORIES AT ONCE!
LEX LUTHOR DOESN'T OWN THIS PAPER YET, YOU MAGGOT!
NO... NOT YET HE DOESN'T.
GET YOUR SUPERMAN ON THE JOB, AND MAYBE I'LL LET YOU KEEP YOURS.
LUTHOR'S OVER-PLAYING HIS HAND.
HE'S SCARED.
LET'S GET MR. KENT!
WHAT FOR?
?
HE'S GONE!
YEAH, HE MUST'VE GOTTEN THE WORD AHEAD OF US...
...AND I'LL BET YOU A NICKEL TO A DOUGHNUT HE'S HALFWAY TO GOTHAM ALREADY!
GET US THERE, KID!
ON IT...

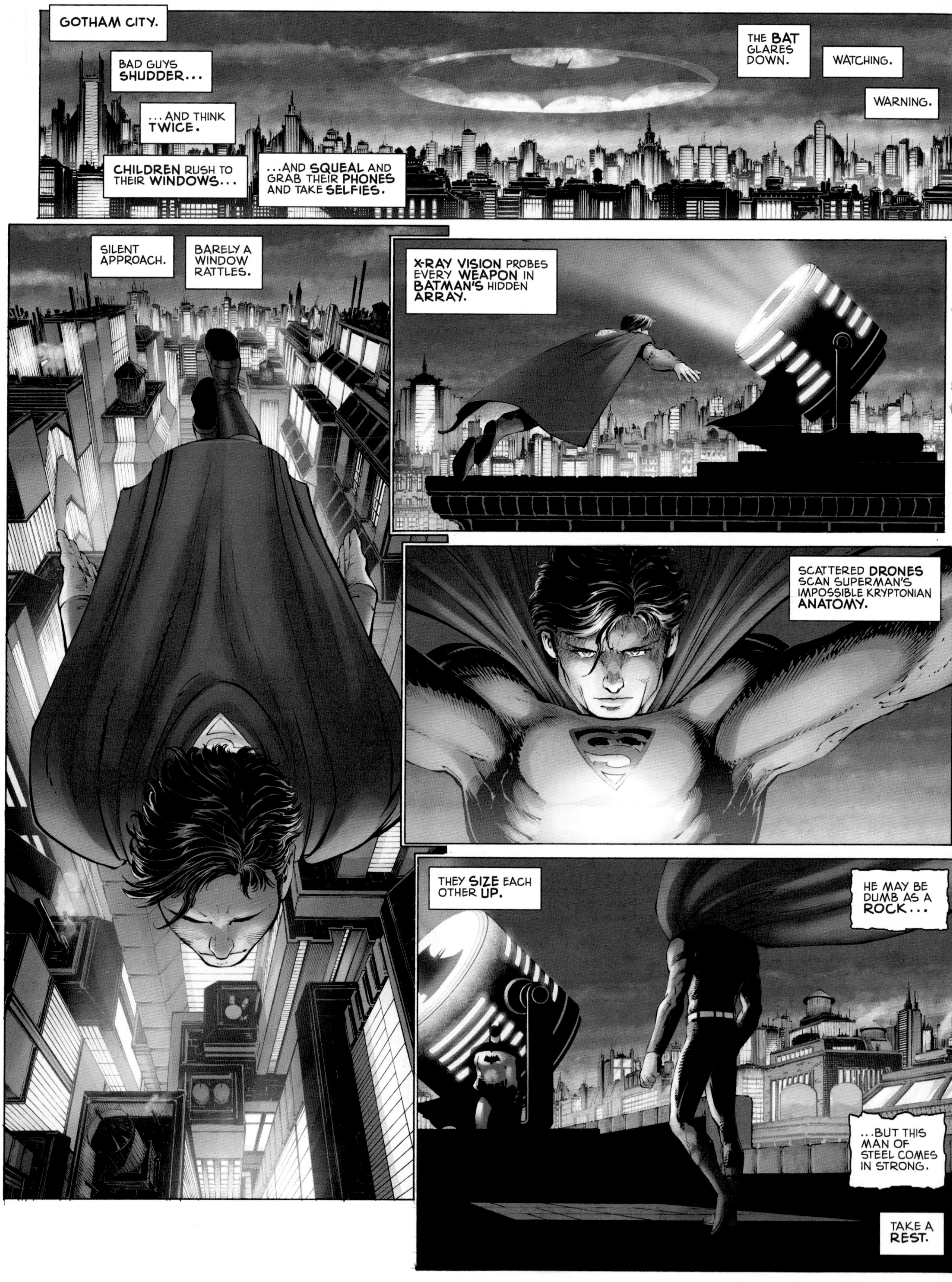
GOTHAM CITY.
BAD GUYS SHUDDER...
...AND THINK TWICE.
CHILDREN RUSH TO THEIR WINDOWS...
...AND SQUEAL AND GRAB THEIR PHONES AND TAKE SELFIES.
THE BAT GLARES DOWN.
WATCHING.
WARNING.
SILENT APPROACH.
BARELY A WINDOW RATTLES.
X-RAY VISION PROBES EVERY WEAPON IN BATMAN'S HIDDEN ARRAY.
SCATTERED DRONES SCAN SUPERMAN'S IMPOSSIBLE KRYPTONIAN ANATOMY.
THEY SIZE EACH OTHER UP.
HE MAY BE DUMB AS A ROCK...
...BUT THIS MAN OF STEEL COMES IN STRONG.
TAKE A REST.

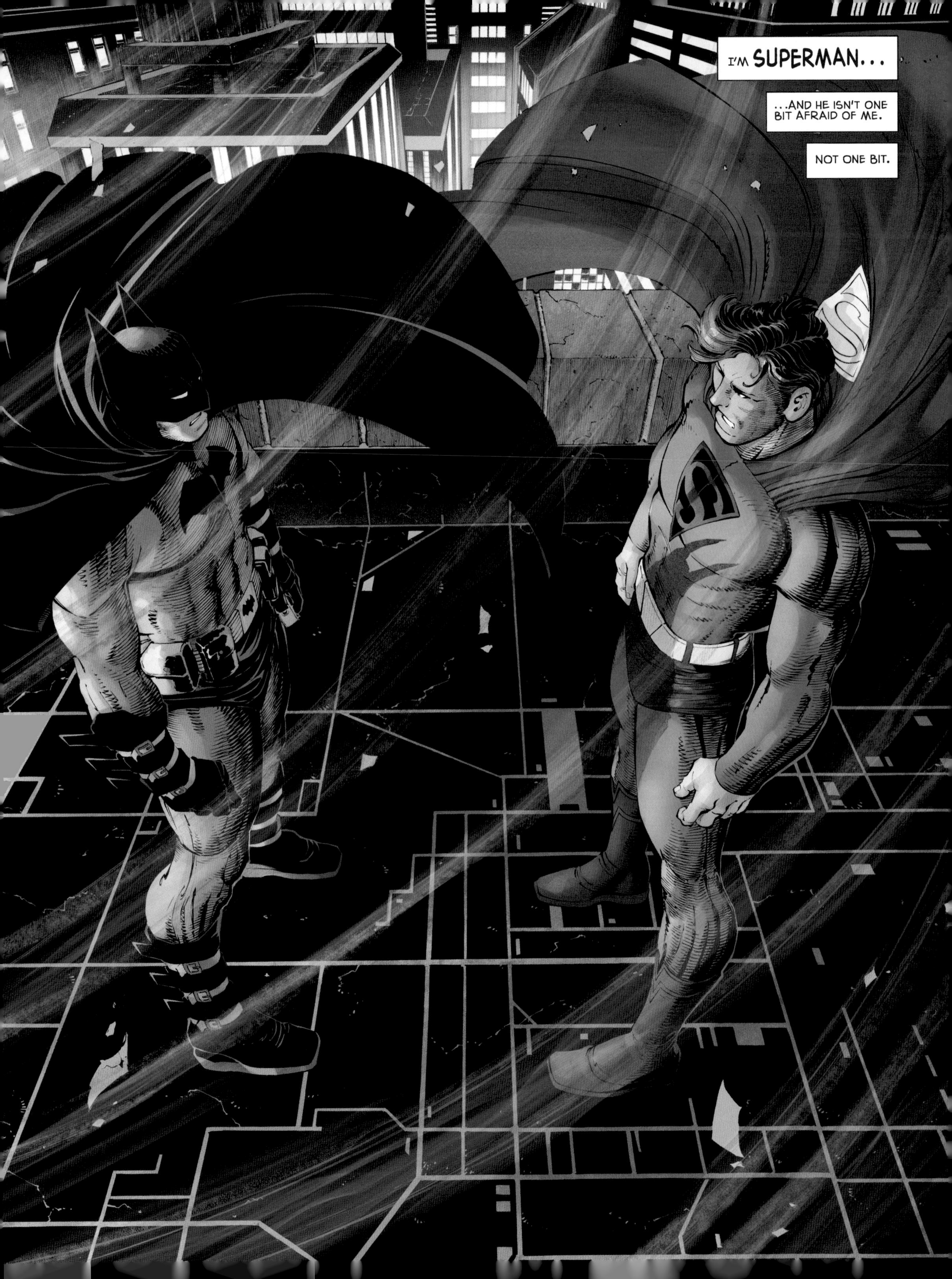
I'M SUPERMAN...
...AND HE ISN'T ONE BIT AFRAID OF ME.
NOT ONE BIT.

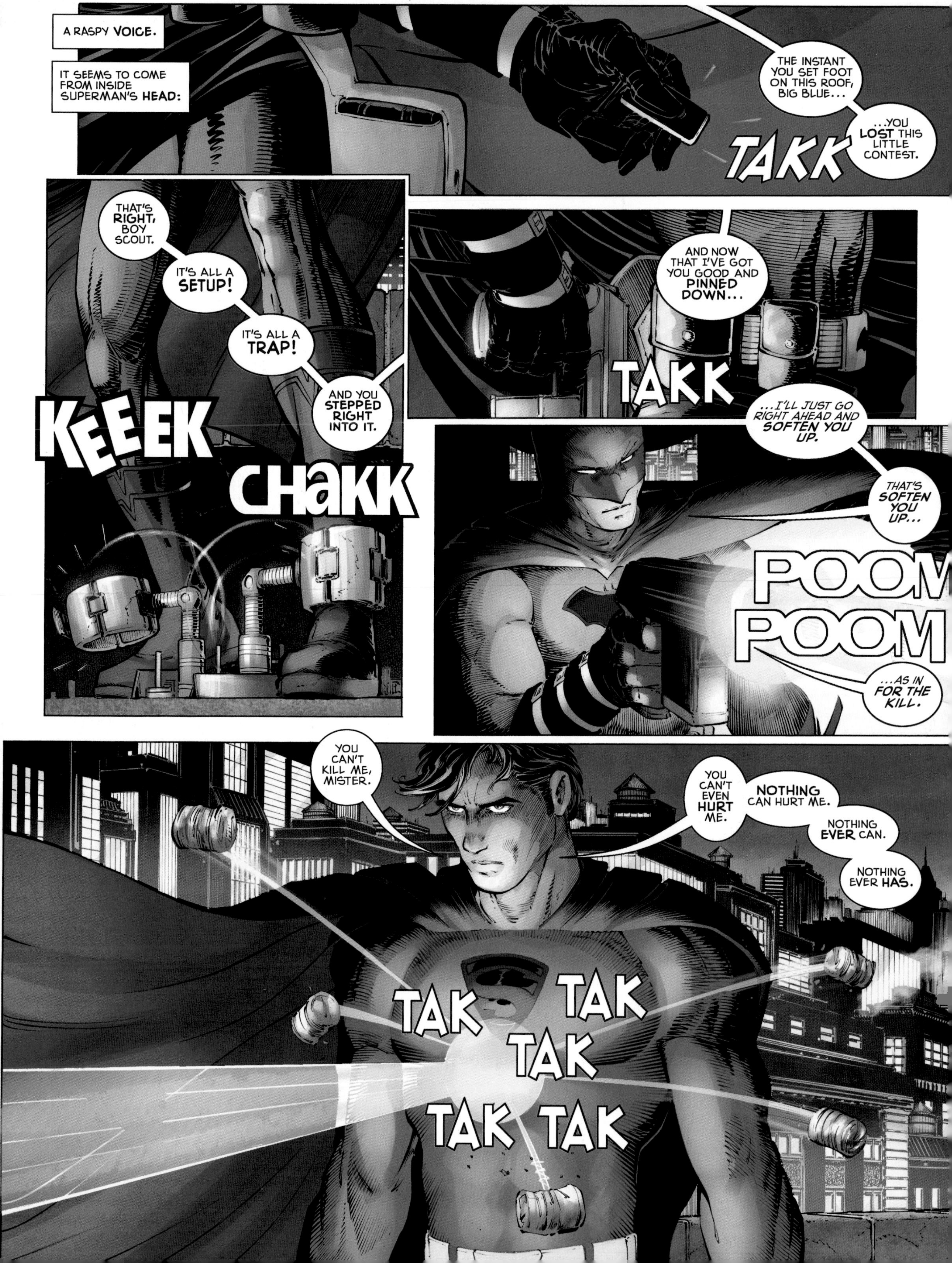
A RASPY VOICE.
IT SEEMS TO COME FROM INSIDE SUPERMAN'S HEAD:
THE INSTANT YOU SET FOOT ON THIS ROOF, BIG BLUE...
TAKK
...YOU LOST THIS LITTLE CONTEST.
THAT'S RIGHT, BOY SCOUT.
IT'S ALL A SETUP!
IT'S ALL A TRAP!
AND YOU STEPPED RIGHT INTO IT.
KEEEK
CHAKK
AND NOW THAT I'VE GOT YOU GOOD AND PINNED DOWN...
TAKK
...I'LL JUST GO RIGHT AHEAD AND SOFTEN YOU UP.
THAT'S SOFTEN YOU UP...
POOM
POOM
...AS IN FOR THE KILL.
YOU CAN'T KILL ME, MISTER.
YOU CAN'T EVEN HURT ME.
NOTHING CAN HURT ME.
NOTHING EVER CAN.
NOTHING EVER HAS.
TAK TAK
TAK
TAK TAK

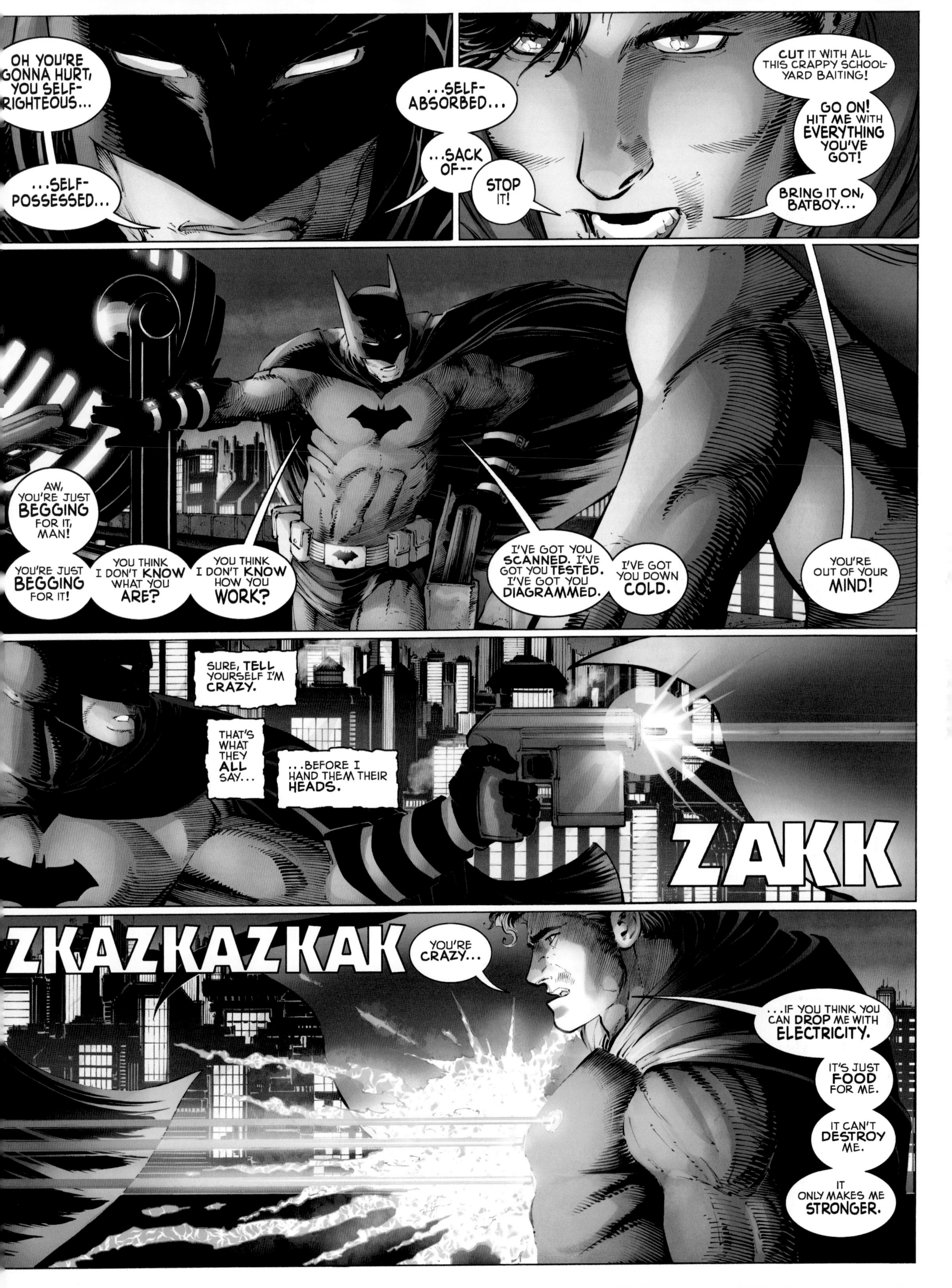

OH YOU'RE GONNA HURT, YOU SELF-RIGHTEOUS...
...SELF-POSSESSED...
...SELF-ABSORBED...
...SACK OF--
STOP IT!
CUT IT WITH ALL THIS CRAPPY SCHOOL-YARD BAITING!
GO ON! HIT ME WITH EVERYTHING YOU'VE GOT!
BRING IT ON, BATBOY...
YOU'RE OUT OF YOUR MIND!
AW, YOU'RE JUST BEGGING FOR IT, MAN!
YOU'RE JUST BEGGING FOR IT!
YOU THINK I DON'T KNOW WHAT YOU ARE?
YOU THINK I DON'T KNOW HOW YOU WORK?
I'VE GOT YOU SCANNED. I'VE GOT YOU TESTED. I'VE GOT YOU DIAGRAMMED.
I'VE GOT YOU DOWN COLD.
SURE, TELL YOURSELF I'M CRAZY.
THAT'S WHAT THEY ALL SAY...
...BEFORE I HAND THEM THEIR HEADS.
ZAKK
ZKAZKAZKAK
YOU'RE CRAZY...
...IF YOU THINK YOU CAN DROP ME WITH ELECTRICITY.
IT'S JUST FOOD FOR ME.
IT CAN'T DESTROY ME.
IT ONLY MAKES ME STRONGER.

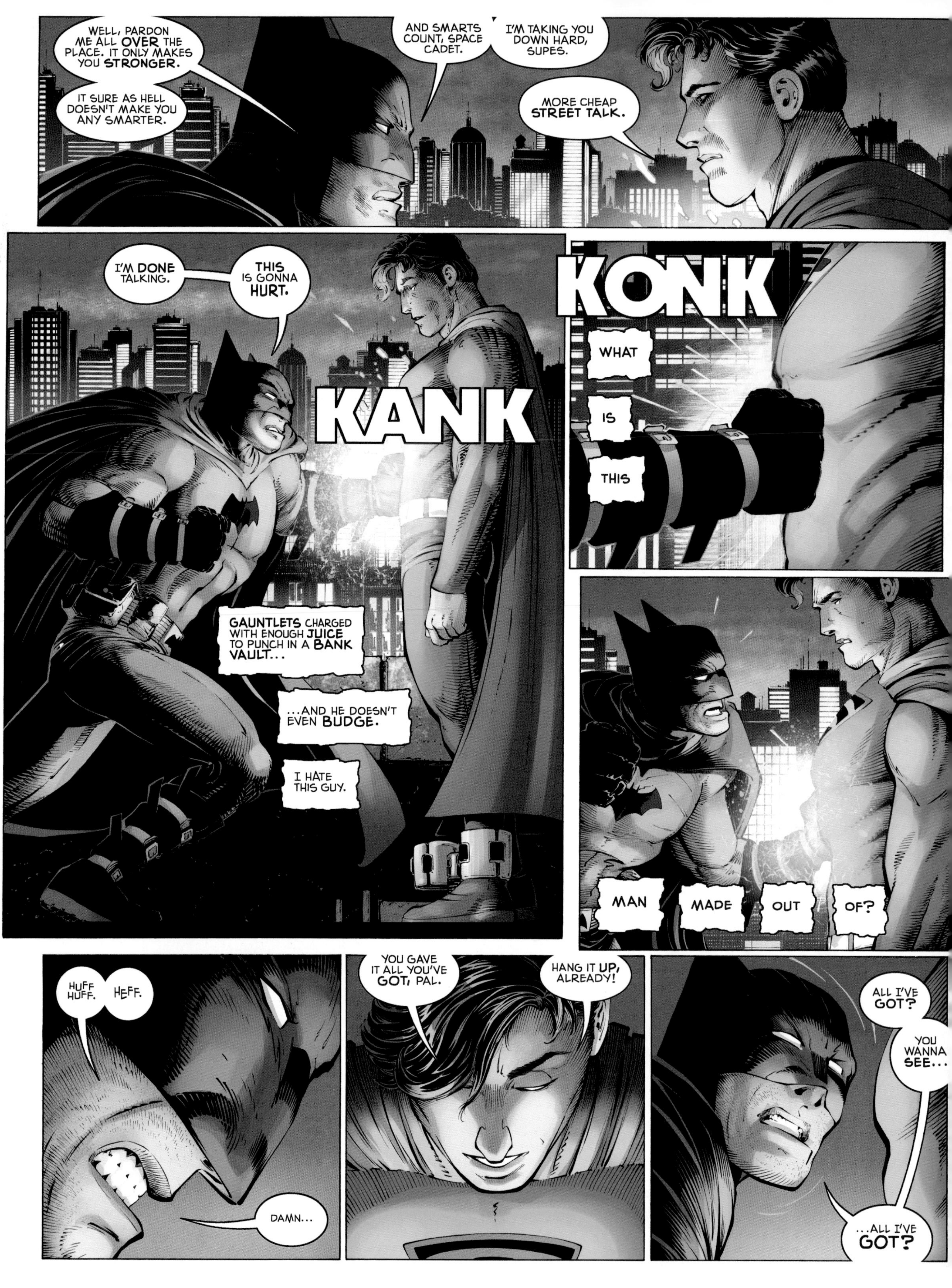
WELL, PARDON ME ALL OVER THE PLACE. IT ONLY MAKES YOU STRONGER.
IT SURE AS HELL DOESN'T MAKE YOU ANY SMARTER.
AND SMARTS COUNT, SPACE CADET.
I'M TAKING YOU DOWN HARD, SUPES.
MORE CHEAP STREET TALK.
I'M DONE TALKING.
THIS IS GONNA HURT.
KANK
GAUNTLETS CHARGED WITH ENOUGH JUICE TO PUNCH IN A BANK VAULT...
...AND HE DOESN'T EVEN BUDGE.
I HATE THIS GUY.
KONK
WHAT
IS
THIS
MAN
MADE
OUT
OF?
HUFF HUFF.
HEFF.
DAMN...
YOU GAVE IT ALL YOU'VE GOT, PAL.
HANG IT UP, ALREADY!
ALL I'VE GOT?
YOU WANNA SEE...
...ALL I'VE GOT?

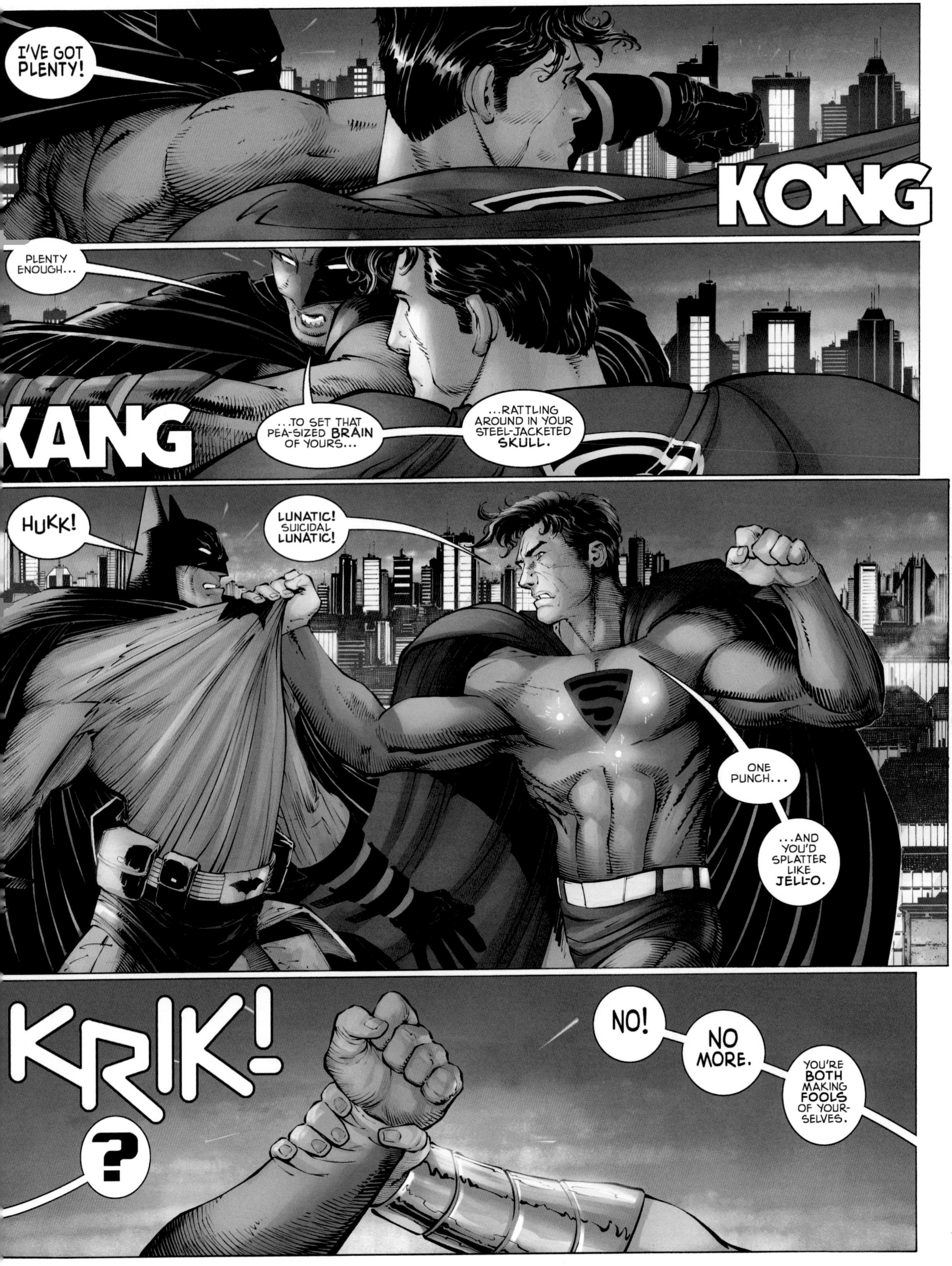
I'VE GOT PLENTY!
KONG
PLENTY ENOUGH...
KANG
...TO SET THAT PEA-SIZED BRAIN OF YOURS...
...RATTLING AROUND IN YOUR STEEL-JACKETED SKULL.
HUKK!
LUNATIC! SUICIDAL LUNATIC!
ONE PUNCH...
...AND YOU'D SPLATTER LIKE JELL-O.
KRIK!
?
NO!
NO MORE.
YOU'RE BOTH MAKING FOOLS OF YOUR-SELVES.

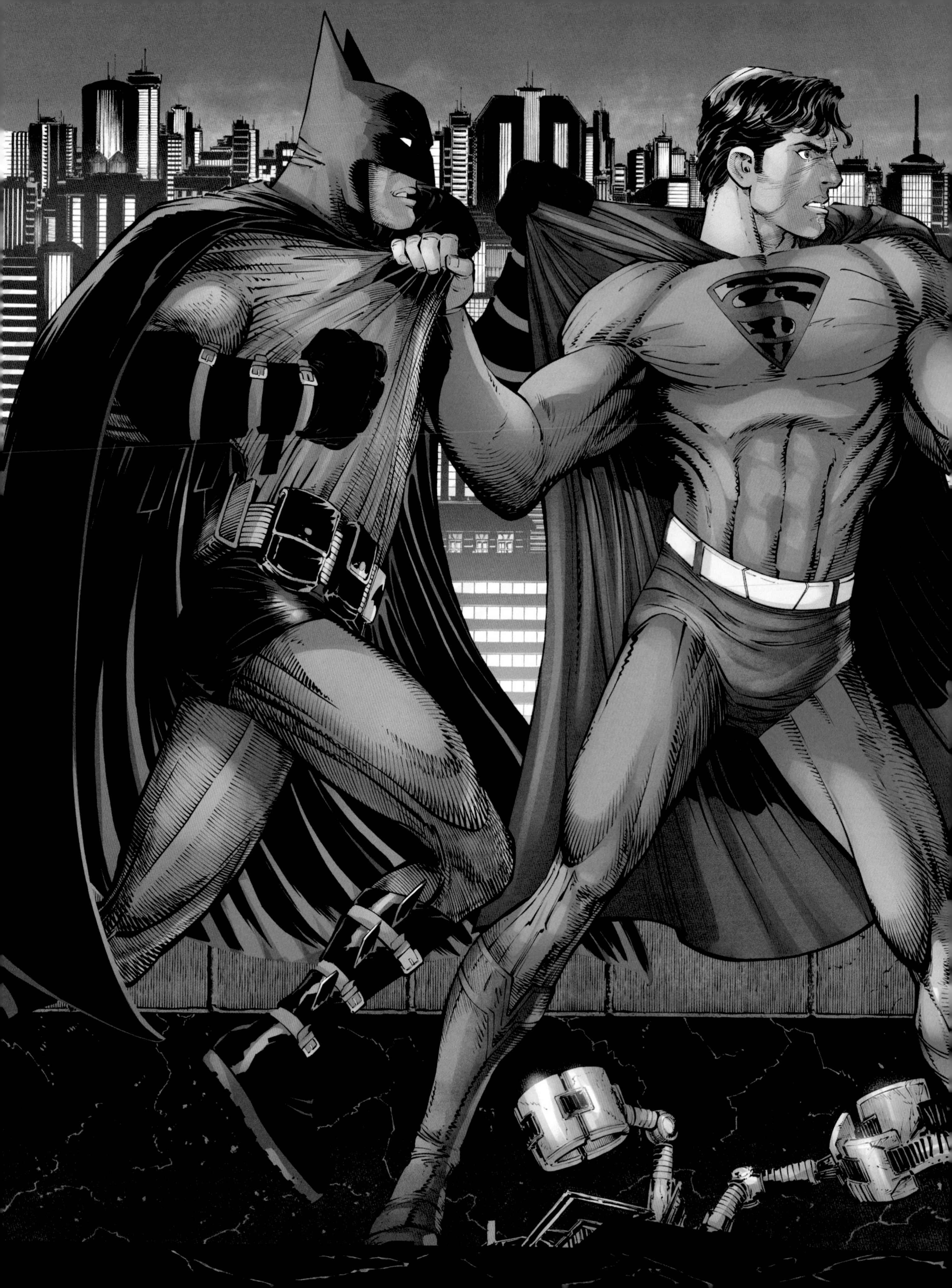

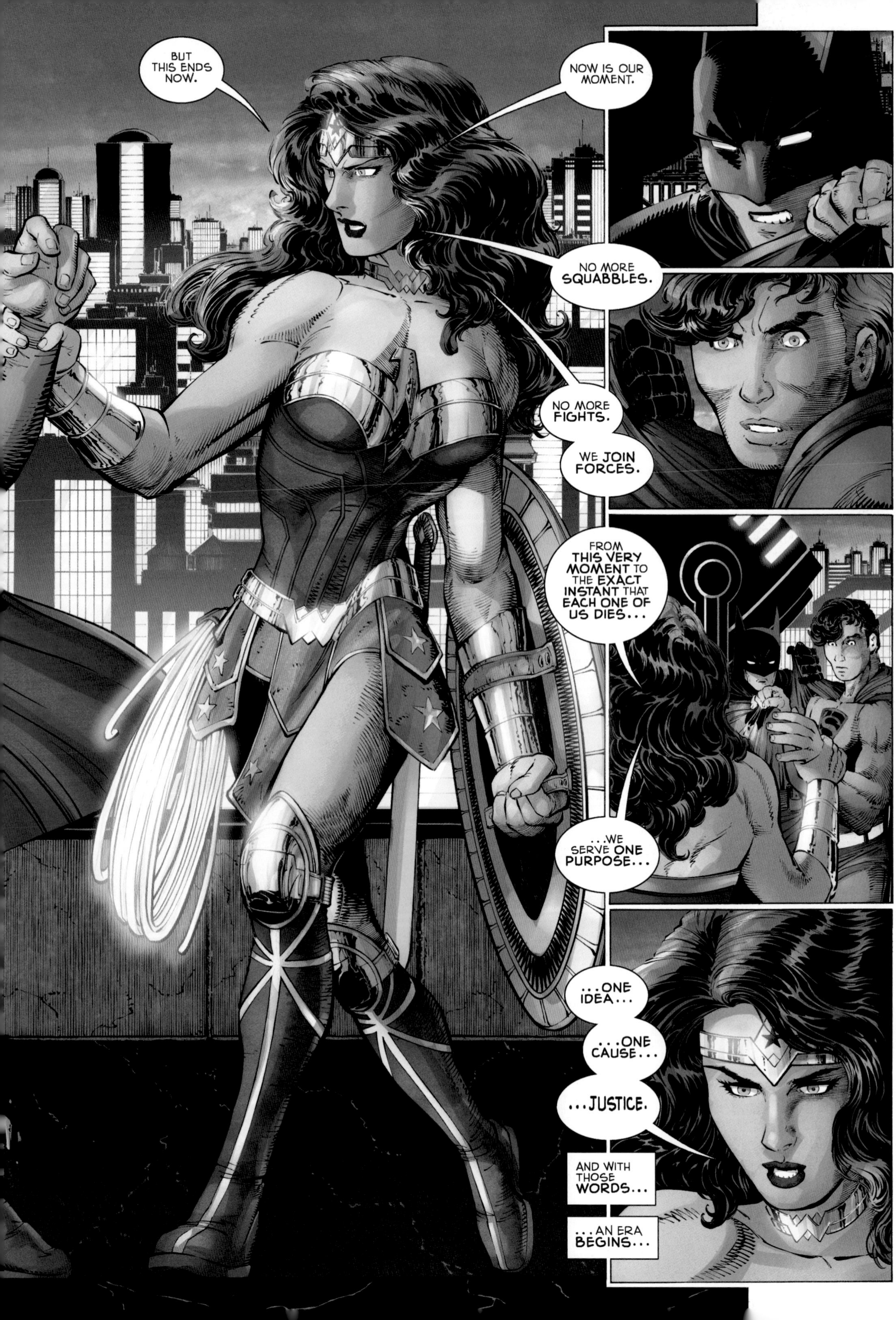
BUT THIS ENDS NOW.
NOW IS OUR MOMENT.
NO MORE SQUABBLES.
NO MORE FIGHTS.
WE JOIN FORCES.
FROM THIS VERY MOMENT TO THE EXACT INSTANT THAT EACH ONE OF US DIES...
...WE SERVE ONE PURPOSE...
...ONE IDEA...
...ONE CAUSE...
...JUSTICE.
AND WITH THOSE WORDS...
...AN ERA BEGINS...

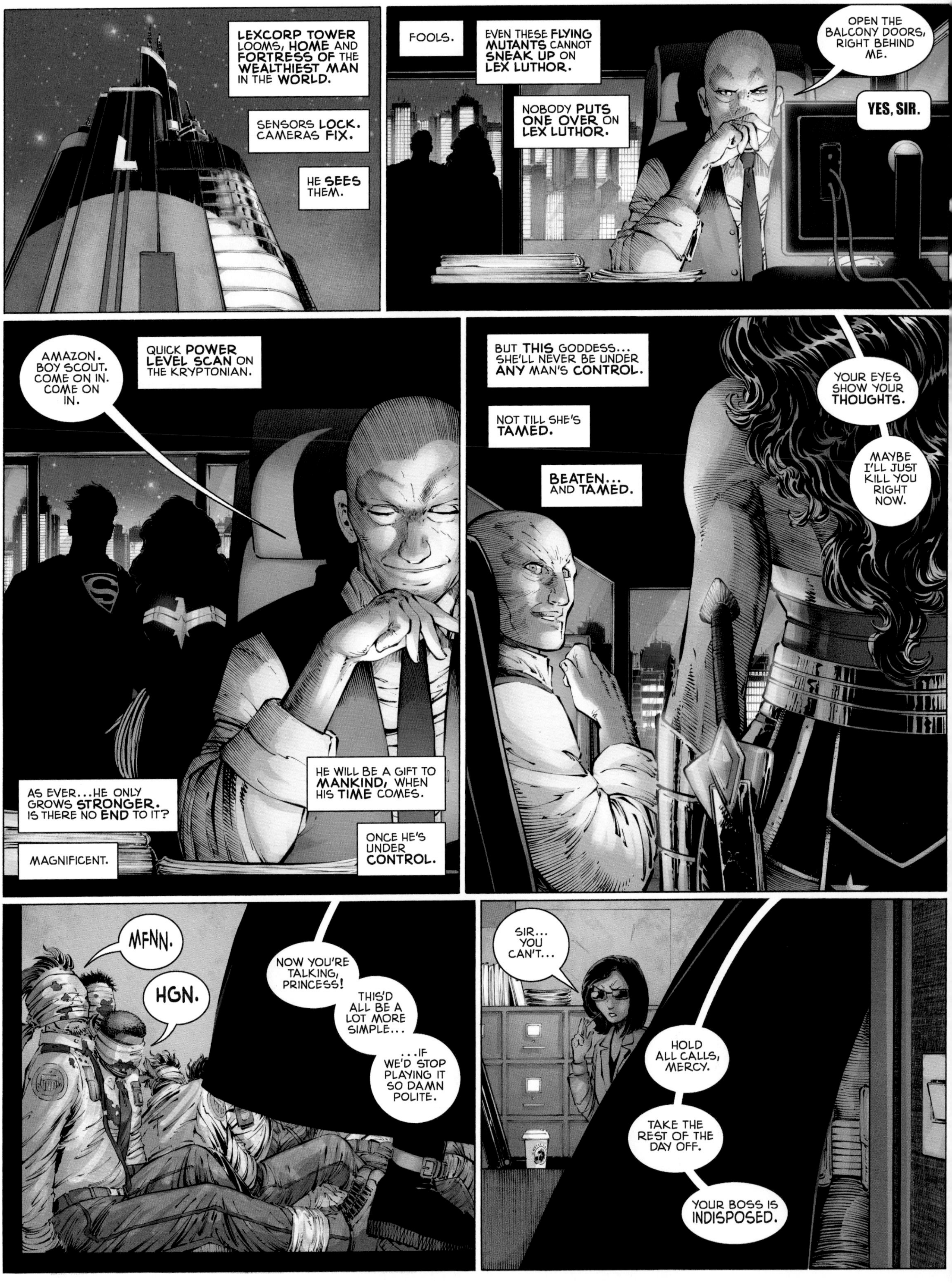
LEXCORP TOWER LOOMS, HOME AND FORTRESS OF THE WEALTHIEST MAN IN THE WORLD.
SENSORS LOCK. CAMERAS FIX.
HE SEES THEM.
FOOLS.
EVEN THESE FLYING MUTANTS CANNOT SNEAK UP ON LEX LUTHOR.
NOBODY PUTS ONE OVER ON LEX LUTHOR.
OPEN THE BALCONY DOORS, RIGHT BEHIND ME.
YES, SIR.
AMAZON. BOY SCOUT. COME ON IN. COME ON IN.
QUICK POWER LEVEL SCAN ON THE KRYPTONIAN.
AS EVER...HE ONLY GROWS STRONGER. IS THERE NO END TO IT?
MAGNIFICENT.
HE WILL BE A GIFT TO MANKIND, WHEN HIS TIME COMES.
ONCE HE'S UNDER CONTROL.
BUT THIS GODDESS... SHE'LL NEVER BE UNDER ANY MAN'S CONTROL.
NOT TILL SHE'S TAMED.
BEATEN... AND TAMED.
YOUR EYES SHOW YOUR THOUGHTS.
MAYBE I'LL JUST KILL YOU RIGHT NOW.
MFNN.
HGN.
NOW YOU'RE TALKING, PRINCESS!
THIS'D ALL BE A LOT MORE SIMPLE...
...IF WE'D STOP PLAYING IT SO DAMN POLITE.
SIR... YOU CAN'T...
HOLD ALL CALLS, MERCY.
TAKE THE REST OF THE DAY OFF.
YOUR BOSS IS INDISPOSED.

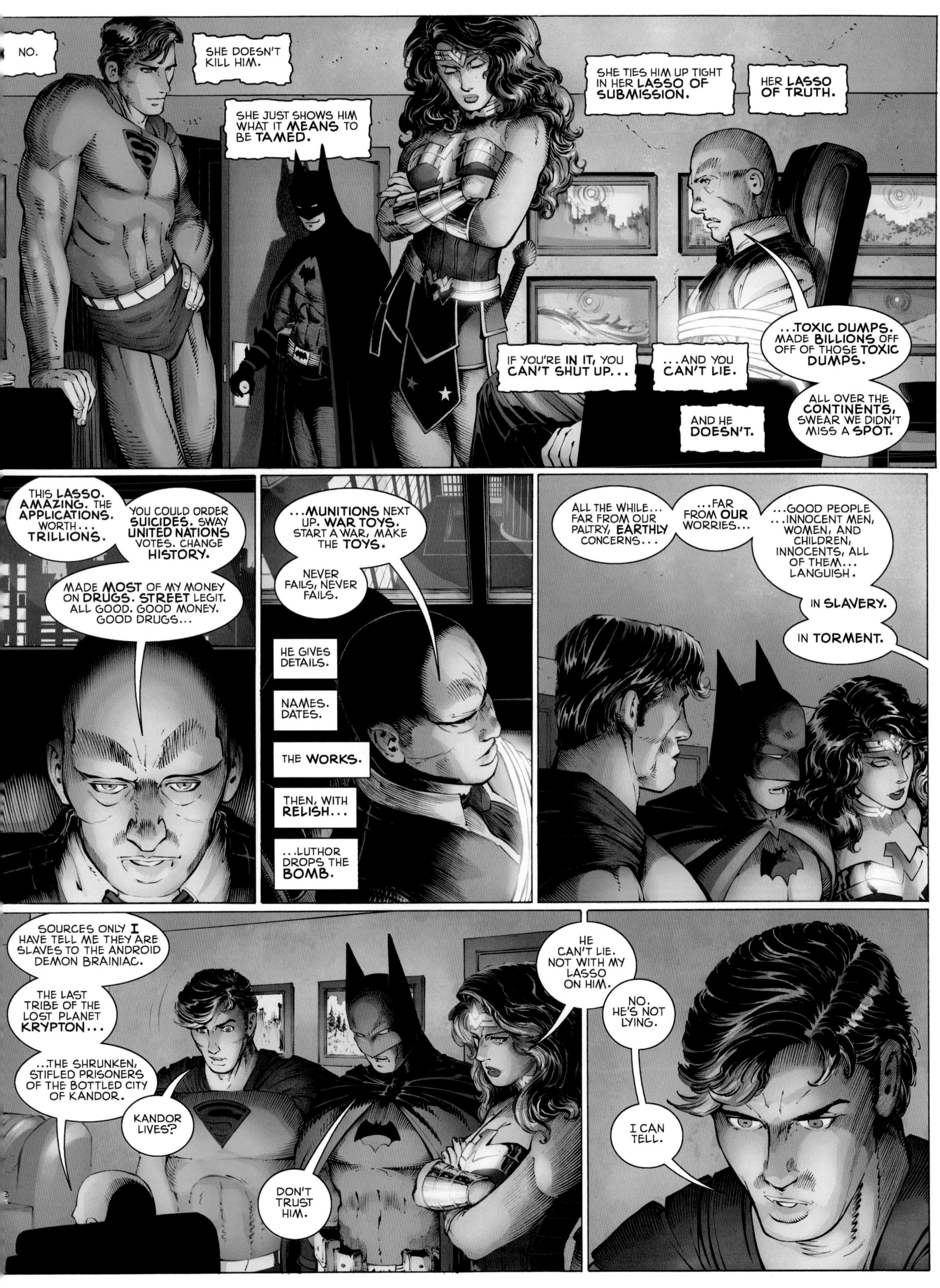
NO.
SHE DOESN'T KILL HIM.
SHE JUST SHOWS HIM WHAT IT MEANS TO BE TAMED.
SHE TIES HIM UP TIGHT IN HER LASSO OF SUBMISSION.
HER LASSO OF TRUTH.
IF YOU'RE IN IT, YOU CAN'T SHUT UP...
...AND YOU CAN'T LIE.
AND HE DOESN'T.
...TOXIC DUMPS. MADE BILLIONS OFF OFF OF THOSE TOXIC DUMPS.
ALL OVER THE CONTINENTS, SWEAR WE DIDN'T MISS A SPOT.
THIS LASSO. AMAZING. THE APPLICATIONS. WORTH... TRILLIONS.
YOU COULD ORDER SUICIDES. SWAY UNITED NATIONS VOTES. CHANGE HISTORY.
MADE MOST OF MY MONEY ON DRUGS. STREET LEGIT. ALL GOOD. GOOD MONEY. GOOD DRUGS...
...MUNITIONS NEXT UP. WAR TOYS. START A WAR, MAKE THE TOYS.
NEVER FAILS, NEVER FAILS.
HE GIVES DETAILS.
NAMES. DATES.
THE WORKS.
THEN, WITH RELISH...
...LUTHOR DROPS THE BOMB.
ALL THE WHILE... FAR FROM OUR PALTRY, EARTHLY CONCERNS...
...FAR FROM OUR WORRIES...
...GOOD PEOPLE ...INNOCENT MEN, WOMEN, AND CHILDREN, INNOCENTS, ALL OF THEM... LANGUISH.
IN SLAVERY.
IN TORMENT.
SOURCES ONLY I HAVE TELL ME THEY ARE SLAVES TO THE ANDROID DEMON BRAINIAC.
THE LAST TRIBE OF THE LOST PLANET KRYPTON...
...THE SHRUNKEN, STIFLED PRISONERS OF THE BOTTLED CITY OF KANDOR.
KANDOR LIVES?
DON'T TRUST HIM.
HE CAN'T LIE. NOT WITH MY LASSO ON HIM.
NO. HE'S NOT LYING.
I CAN TELL.

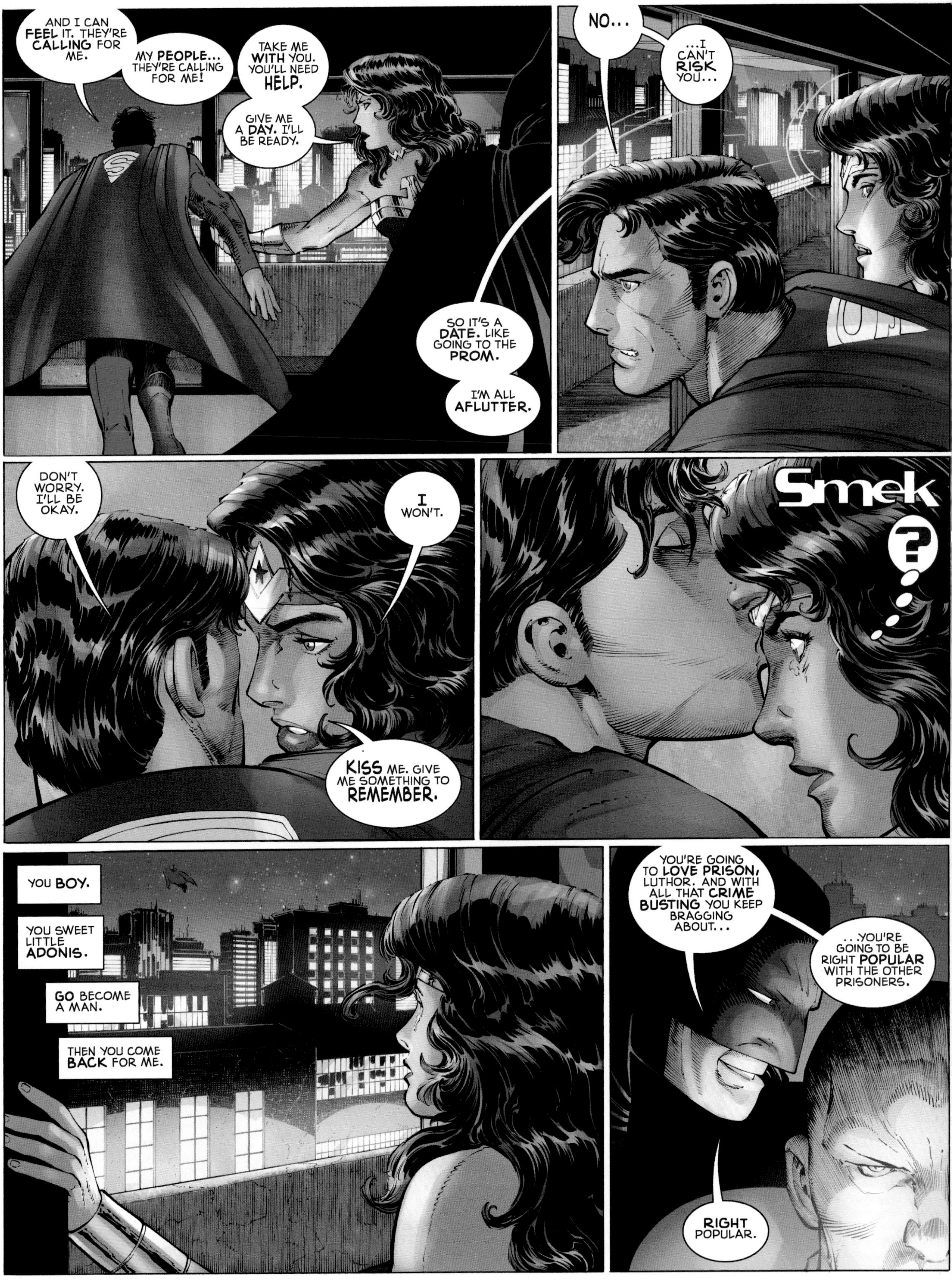
AND I CAN FEEL IT. THEY'RE CALLING FOR ME.
MY PEOPLE... THEY'RE CALLING FOR ME!
TAKE ME WITH YOU. YOU'LL NEED HELP.
GIVE ME A DAY. I'LL BE READY.
SO IT'S A DATE. LIKE GOING TO THE PROM.
I'M ALL AFLUTTER.
NO...
...I CAN'T RISK YOU...
DON'T WORRY. I'LL BE OKAY.
I WON'T.
KISS ME. GIVE ME SOMETHING TO REMEMBER.
Smek
?
YOU BOY.
YOU SWEET LITTLE ADONIS.
GO BECOME A MAN.
THEN YOU COME BACK FOR ME.
YOU'RE GOING TO LOVE PRISON, LUTHOR. AND WITH ALL THAT CRIME BUSTING YOU KEEP BRAGGING ABOUT...
...YOU'RE GOING TO BE RIGHT POPULAR WITH THE OTHER PRISONERS.
RIGHT POPULAR.

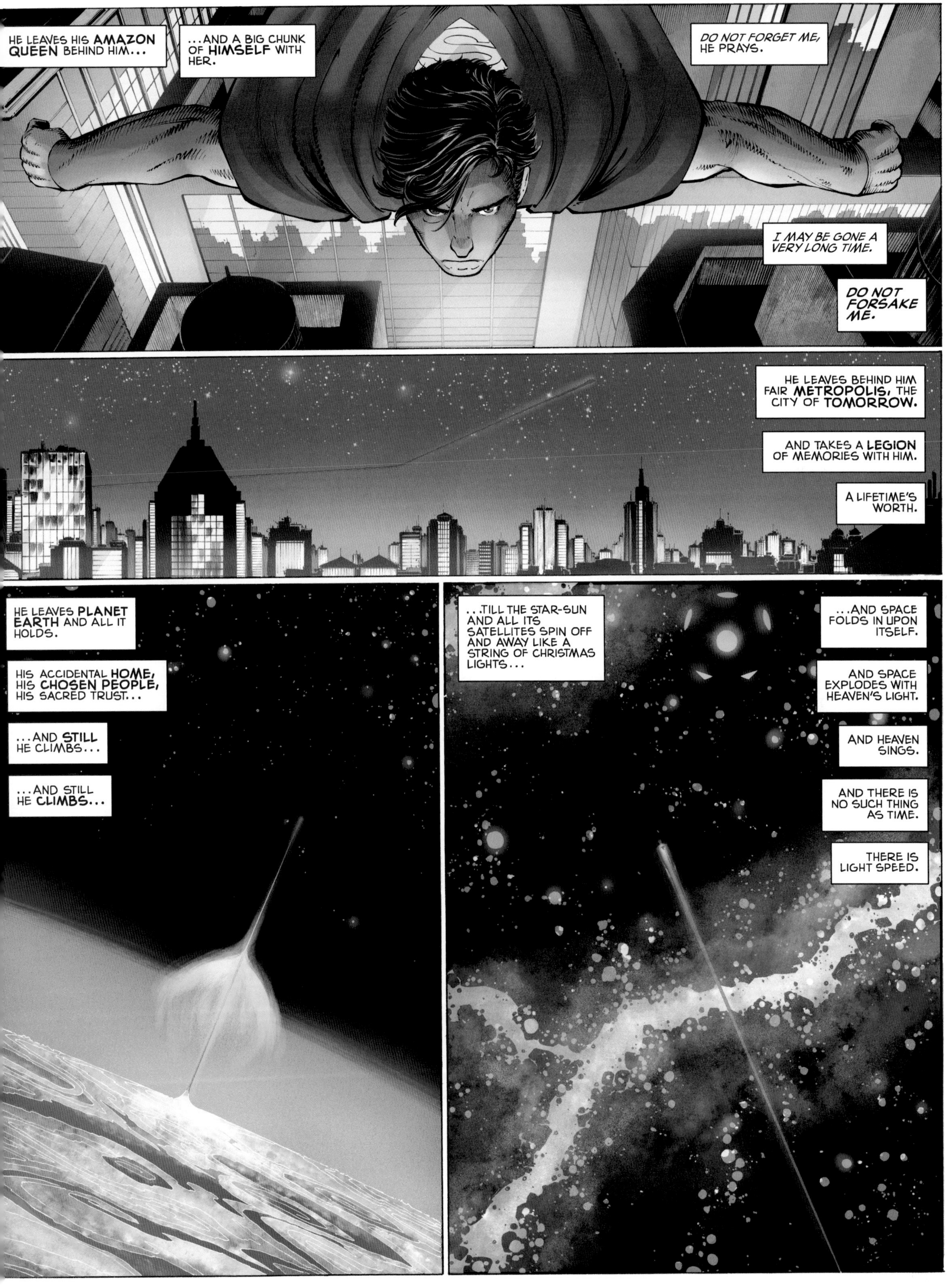
HE LEAVES HIS **AMAZON QUEEN** BEHIND HIM...
...AND A BIG CHUNK OF **HIMSELF** WITH HER.
DO NOT FORGET ME, HE PRAYS.
I MAY BE GONE A VERY LONG TIME.
DO NOT FORSAKE ME.
HE LEAVES BEHIND HIM FAIR **METROPOLIS,** THE CITY OF **TOMORROW.**
AND TAKES A **LEGION** OF MEMORIES WITH HIM.
A LIFETIME'S WORTH.
HE LEAVES **PLANET EARTH** AND ALL IT HOLDS.
HIS ACCIDENTAL **HOME,** HIS **CHOSEN PEOPLE,** HIS SACRED TRUST...
...AND **STILL** HE CLIMBS...
...AND STILL HE **CLIMBS...**
...TILL THE STAR-SUN AND ALL ITS SATELLITES SPIN OFF AND AWAY LIKE A STRING OF CHRISTMAS LIGHTS...
...AND SPACE FOLDS IN UPON ITSELF.
AND SPACE EXPLODES WITH HEAVEN'S LIGHT.
AND HEAVEN SINGS.
AND THERE IS NO SUCH THING AS TIME.
THERE IS LIGHT SPEED.

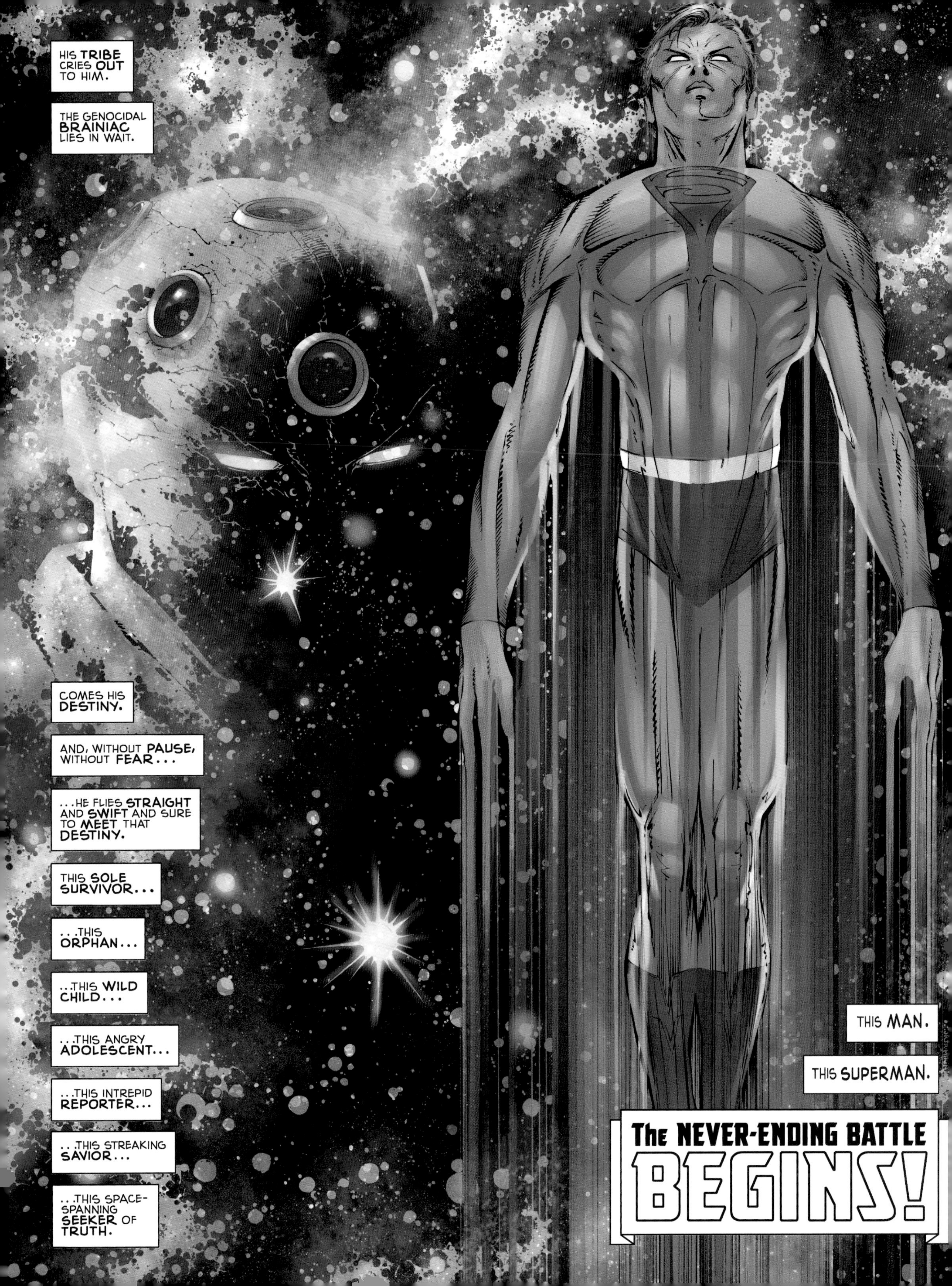
HIS TRIBE CRIES OUT TO HIM.
THE GENOCIDAL BRAINIAC LIES IN WAIT.
COMES HIS DESTINY.
AND, WITHOUT PAUSE, WITHOUT FEAR...
...HE FLIES STRAIGHT AND SWIFT AND SURE TO MEET THAT DESTINY.
THIS SOLE SURVIVOR...
...THIS ORPHAN...
...THIS WILD CHILD...
...THIS ANGRY ADOLESCENT...
...THIS INTREPID REPORTER...
...THIS STREAKING SAVIOR...
...THIS SPACE-SPANNING SEEKER OF TRUTH.
THIS MAN.
THIS SUPERMAN.
The NEVER-ENDING BATTLE BEGINS!

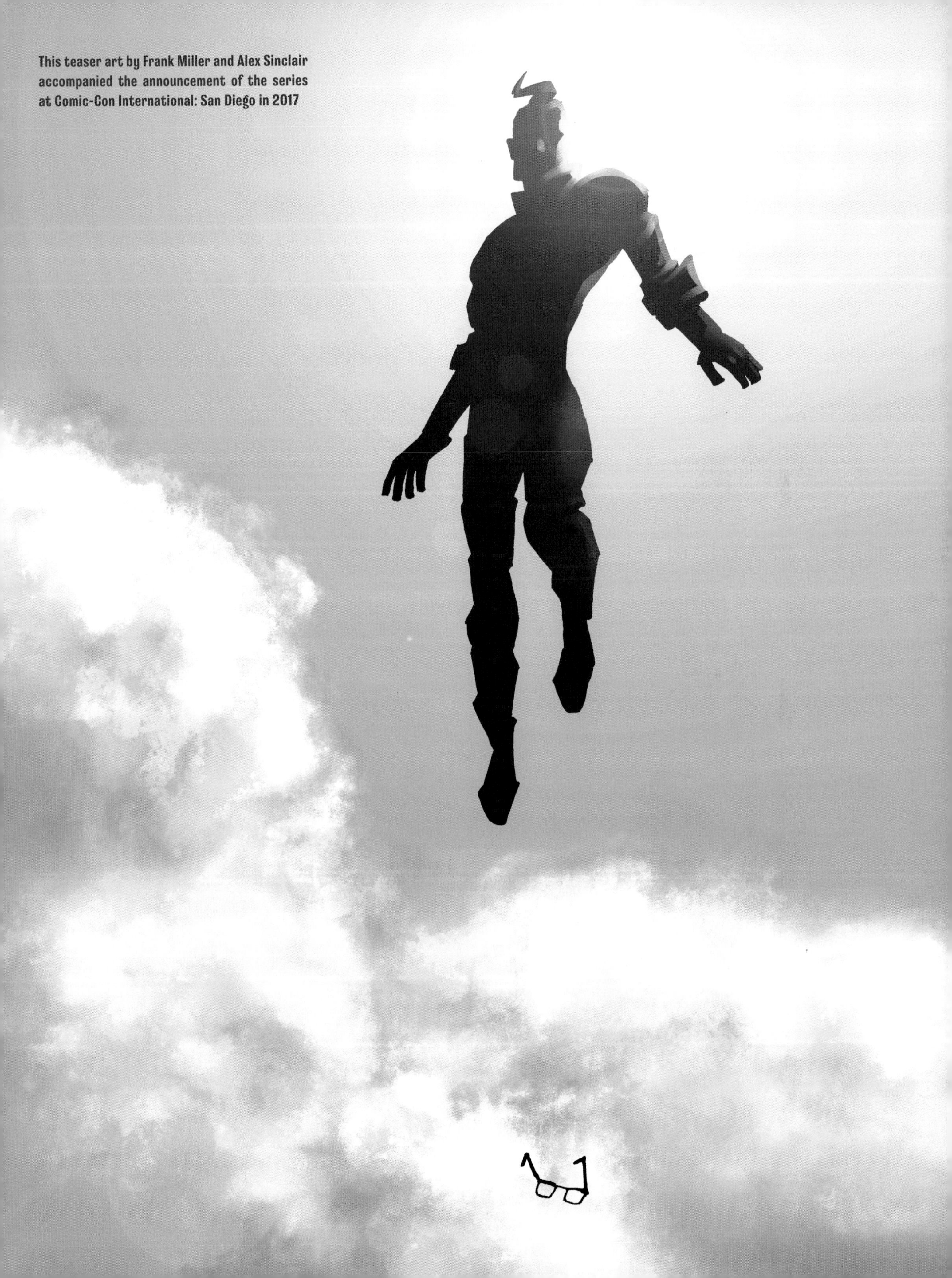

This teaser art by Frank Miller and Alex Sinclair accompanied the announcement of the series at Comic-Con International: San Diego in 2017

Variant cover art for Book One
by Frank Miller and Alex Sinclair

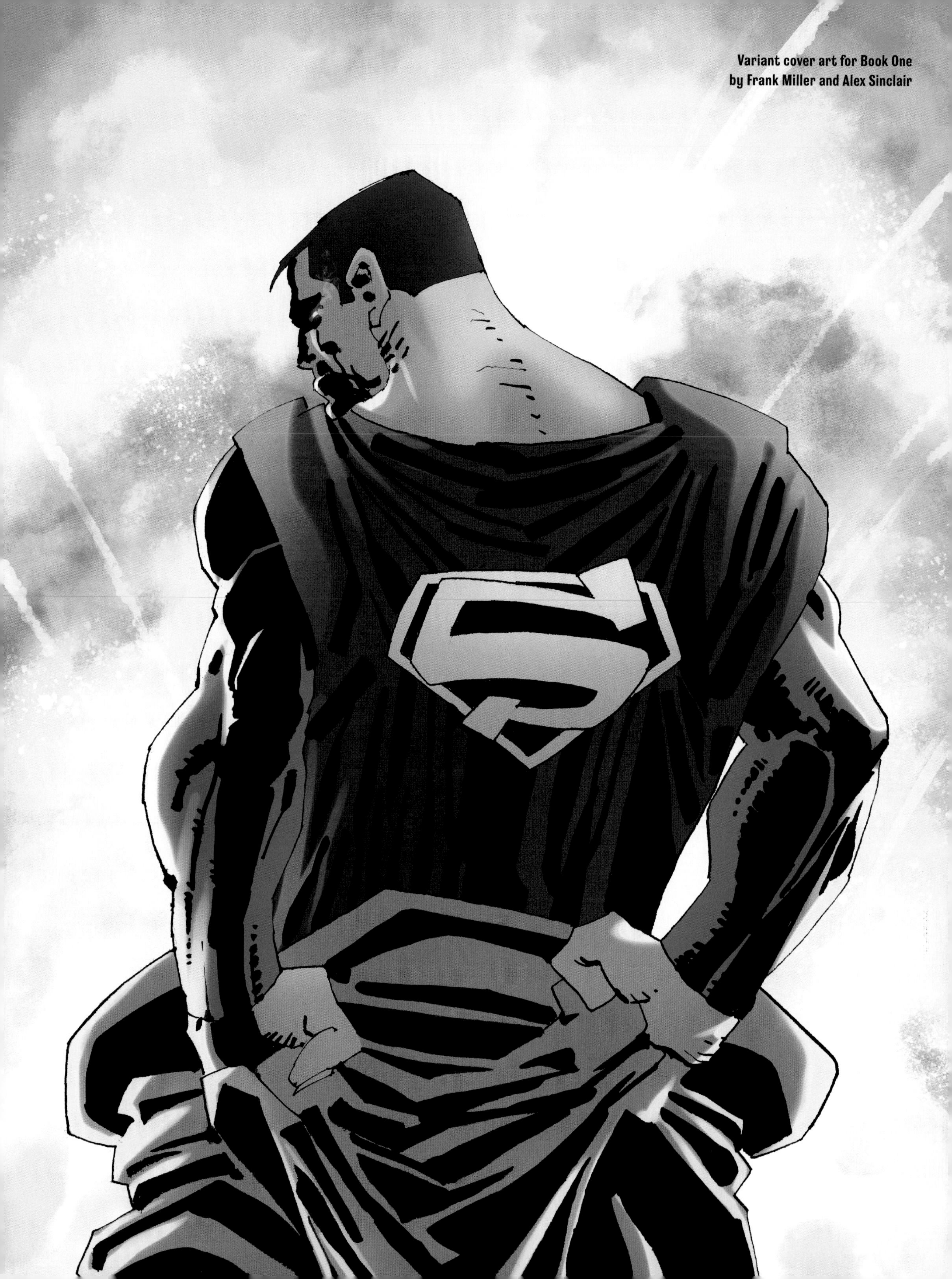

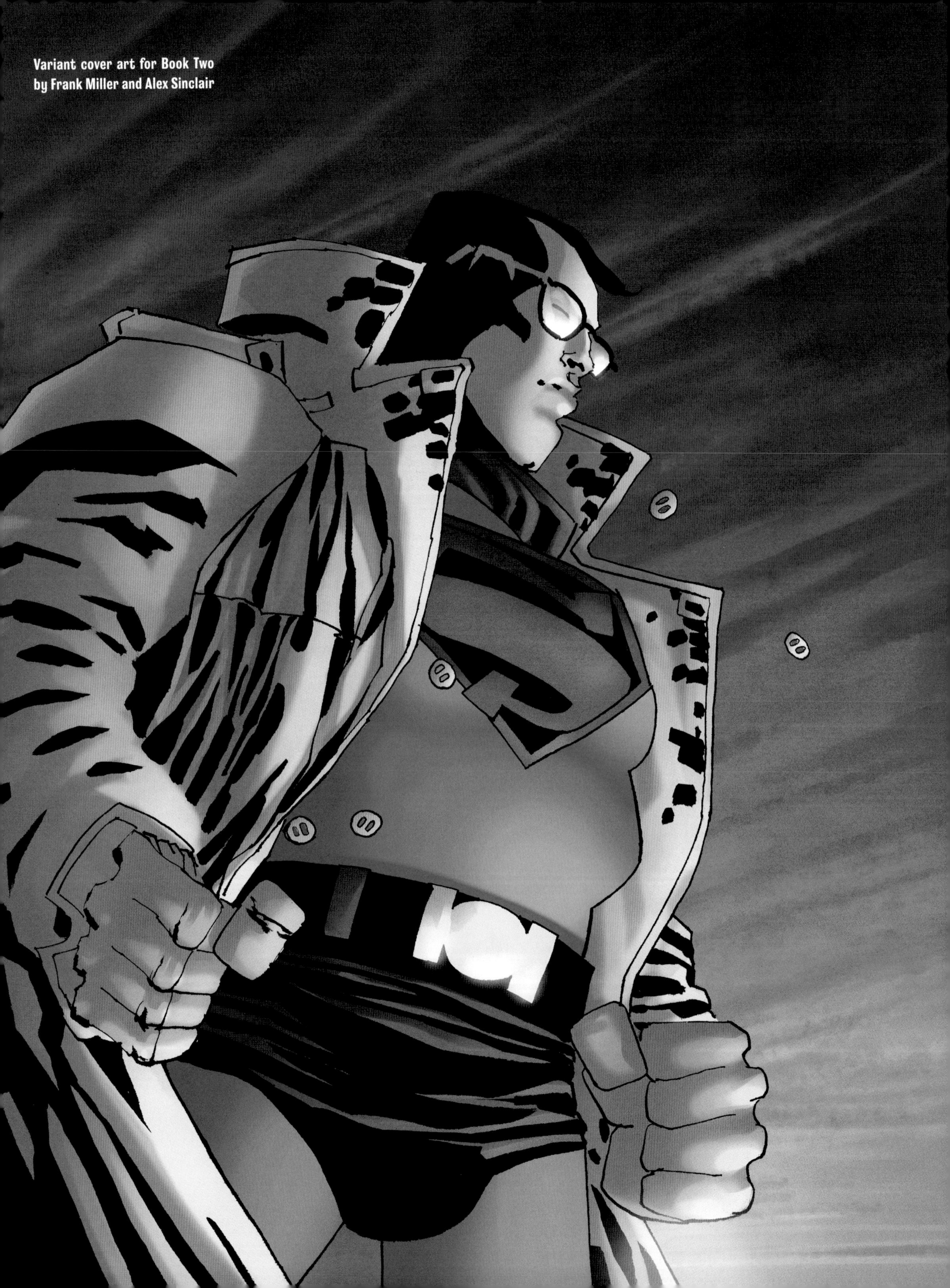

Variant cover art for Book Two
by Frank Miller and Alex Sinclair

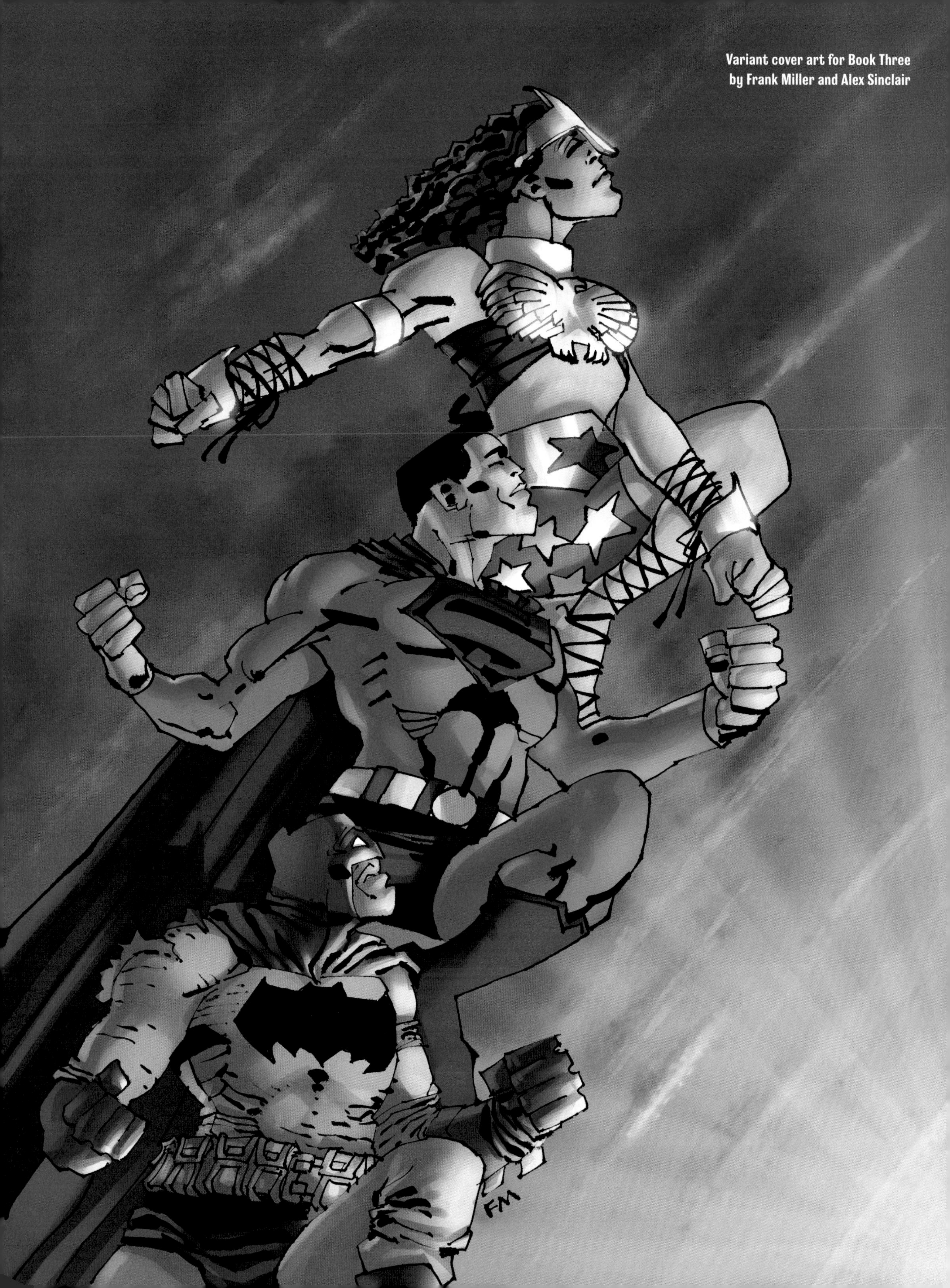

Variant cover art for Book Three
by Frank Miller and Alex Sinclair

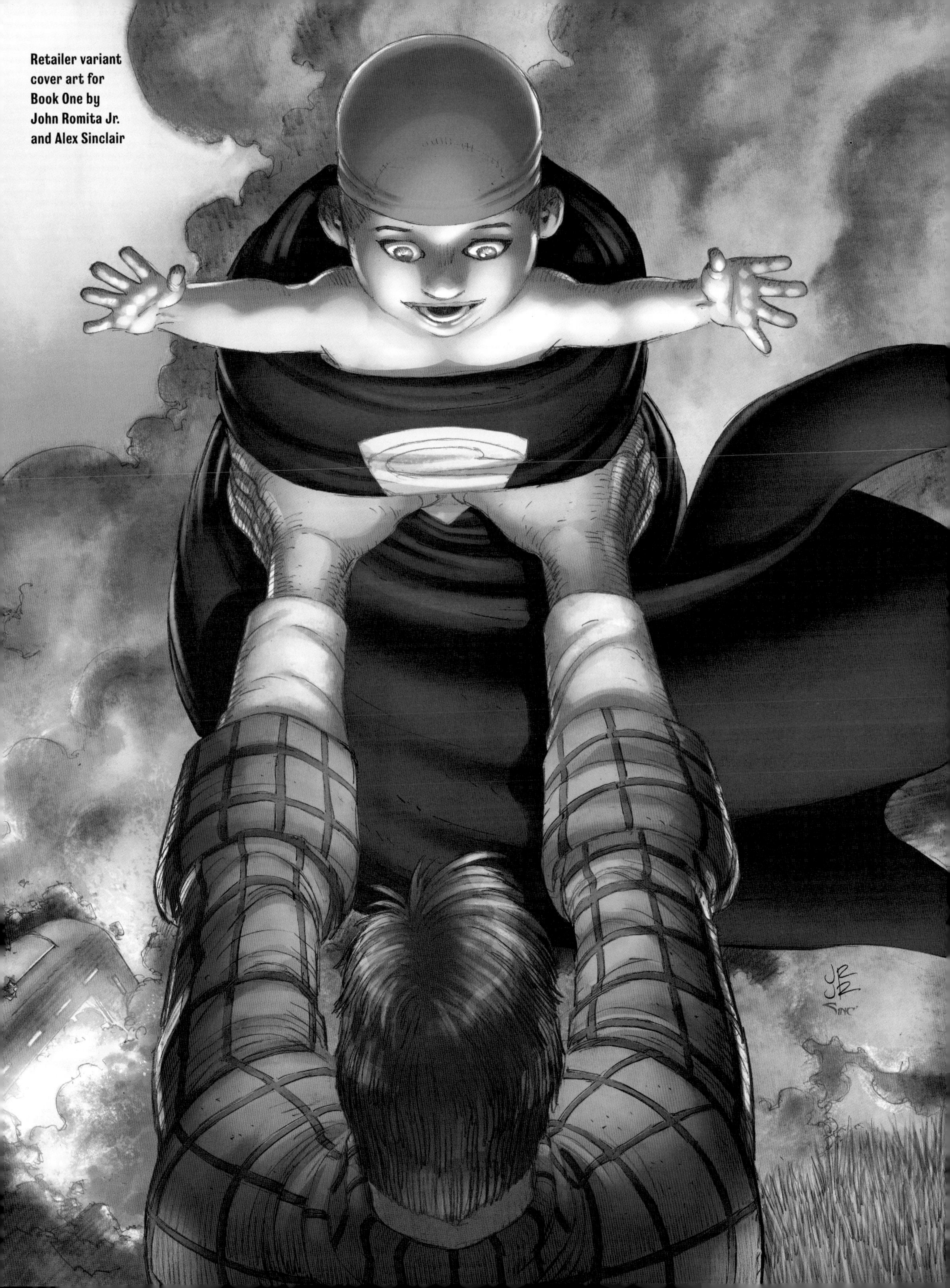

Retailer variant cover art for Book One by John Romita Jr. and Alex Sinclair

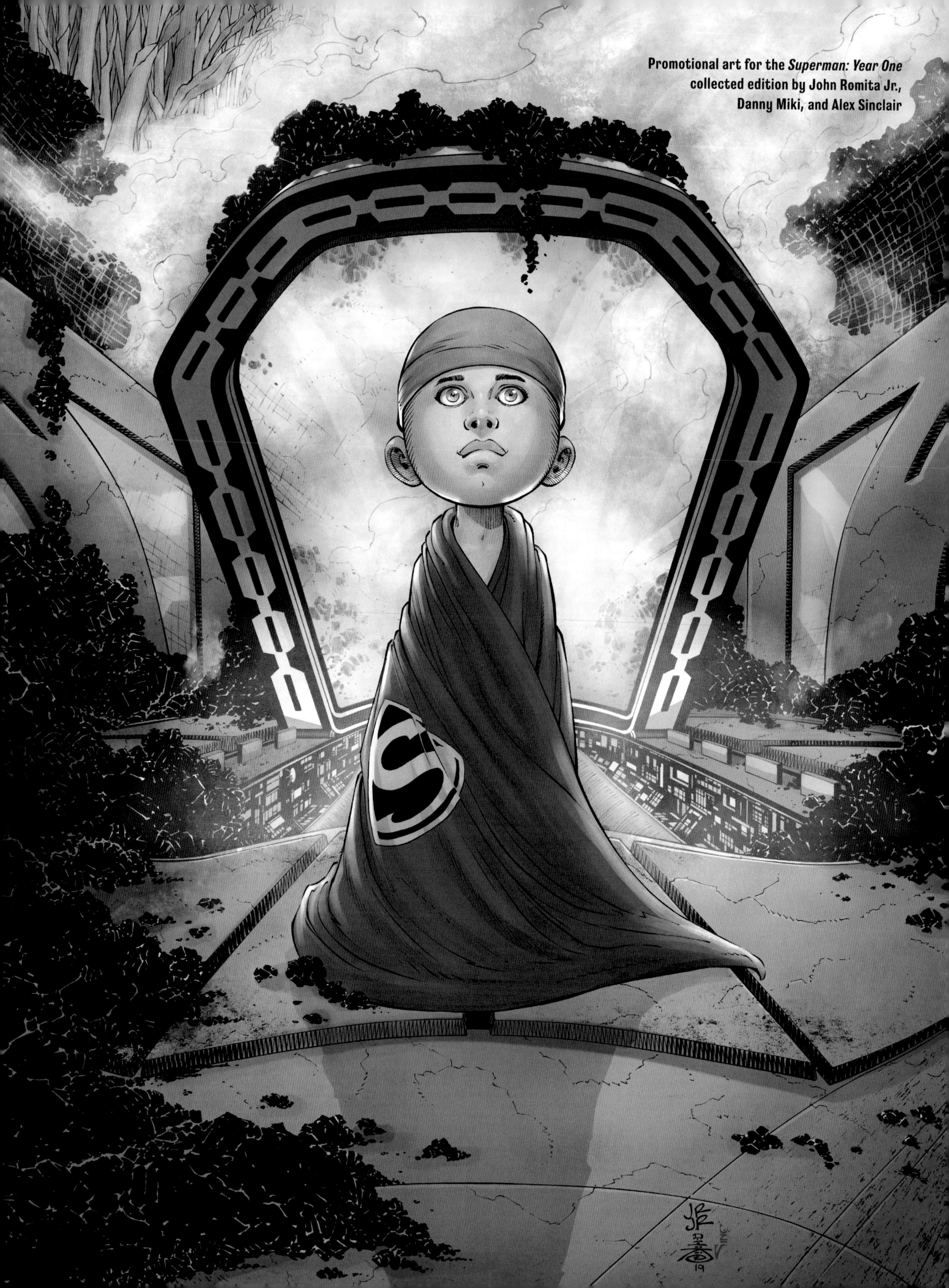

Promotional art for the *Superman: Year One* collected edition by John Romita Jr., Danny Miki, and Alex Sinclair

This page:
Cover sketches
by John Romita Jr.

Following pages:
Three unused covers
by John Romita Jr.
and Danny Miki

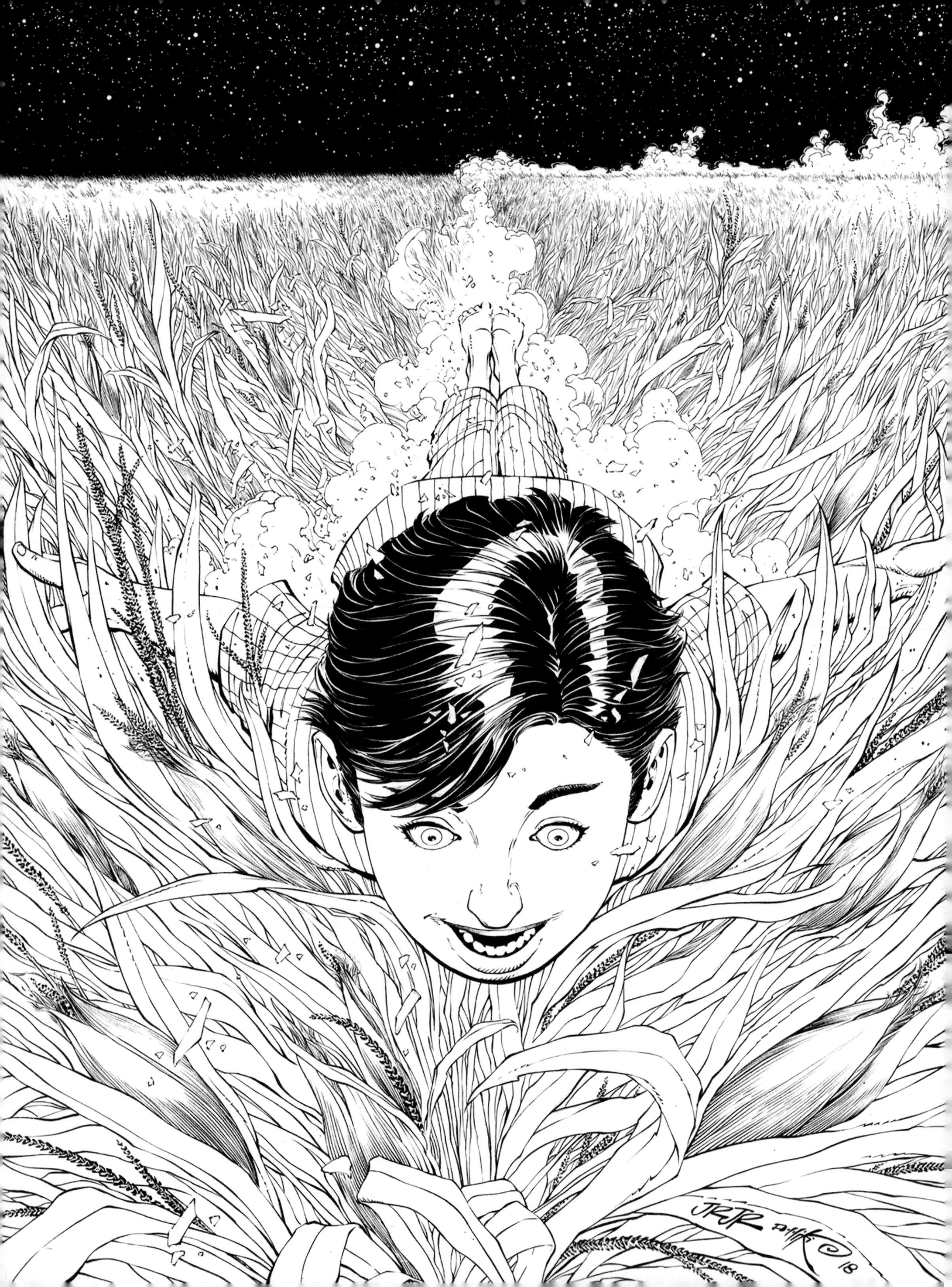

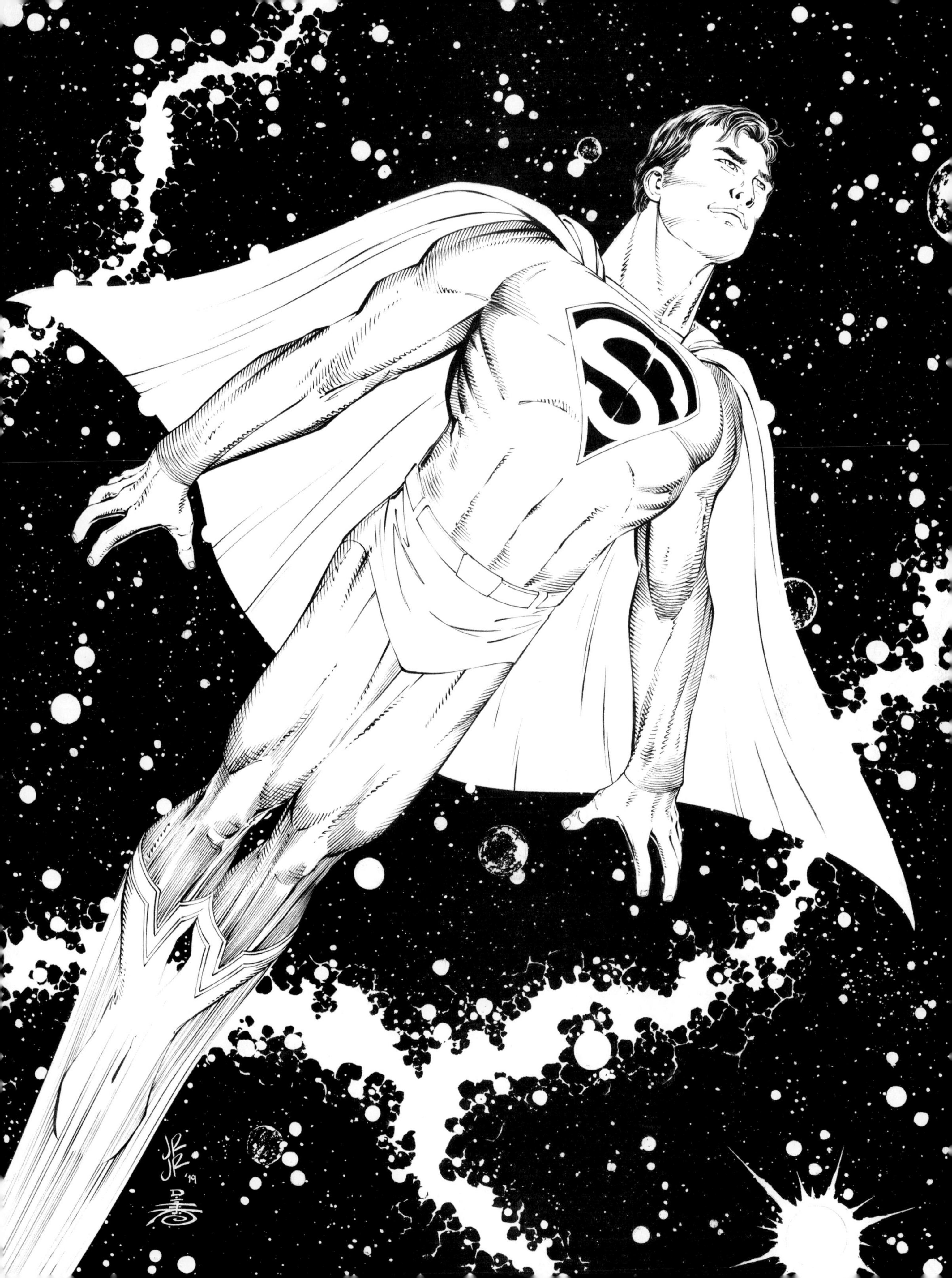

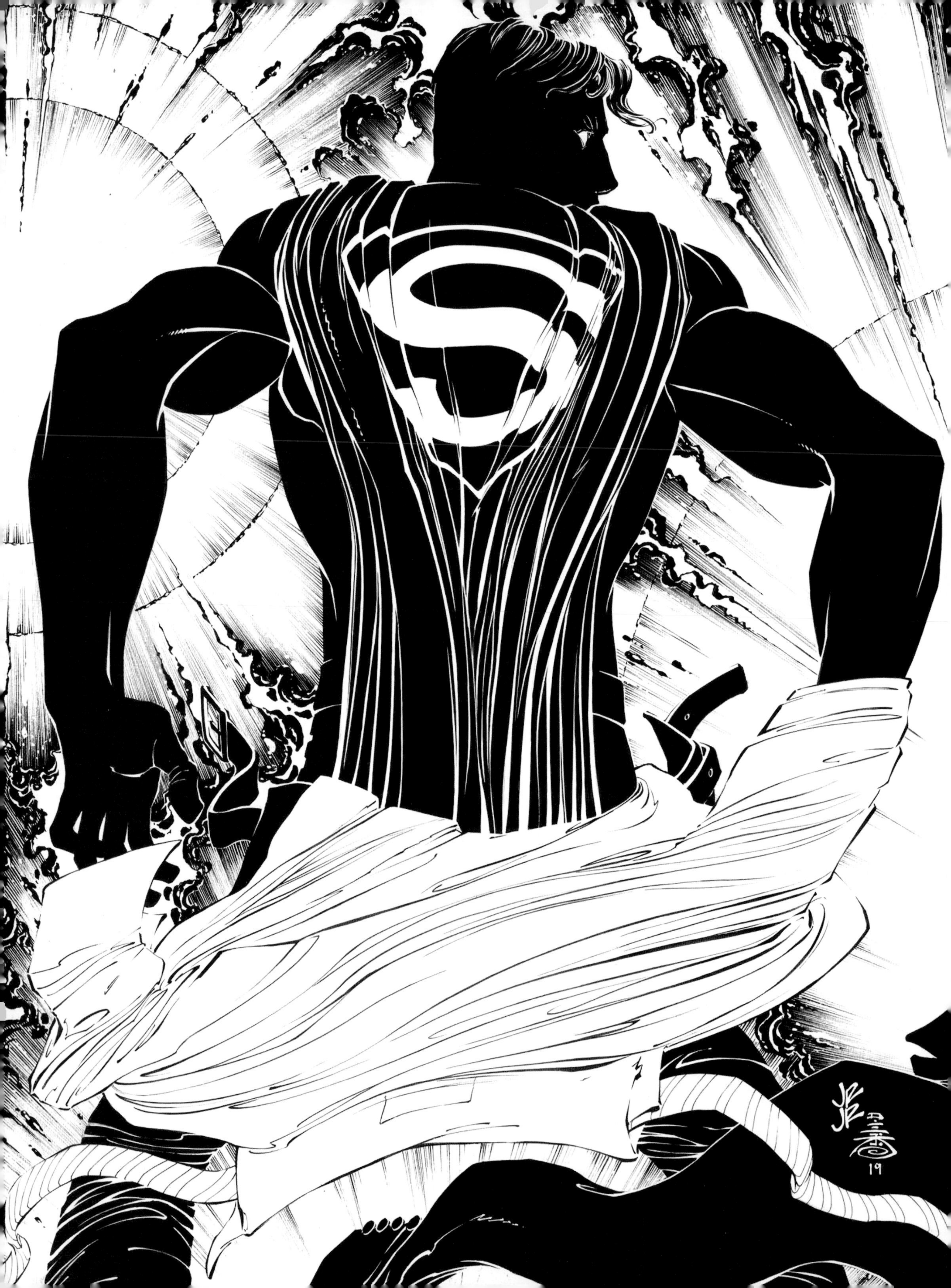

Early pencil tests by John Romita Jr.

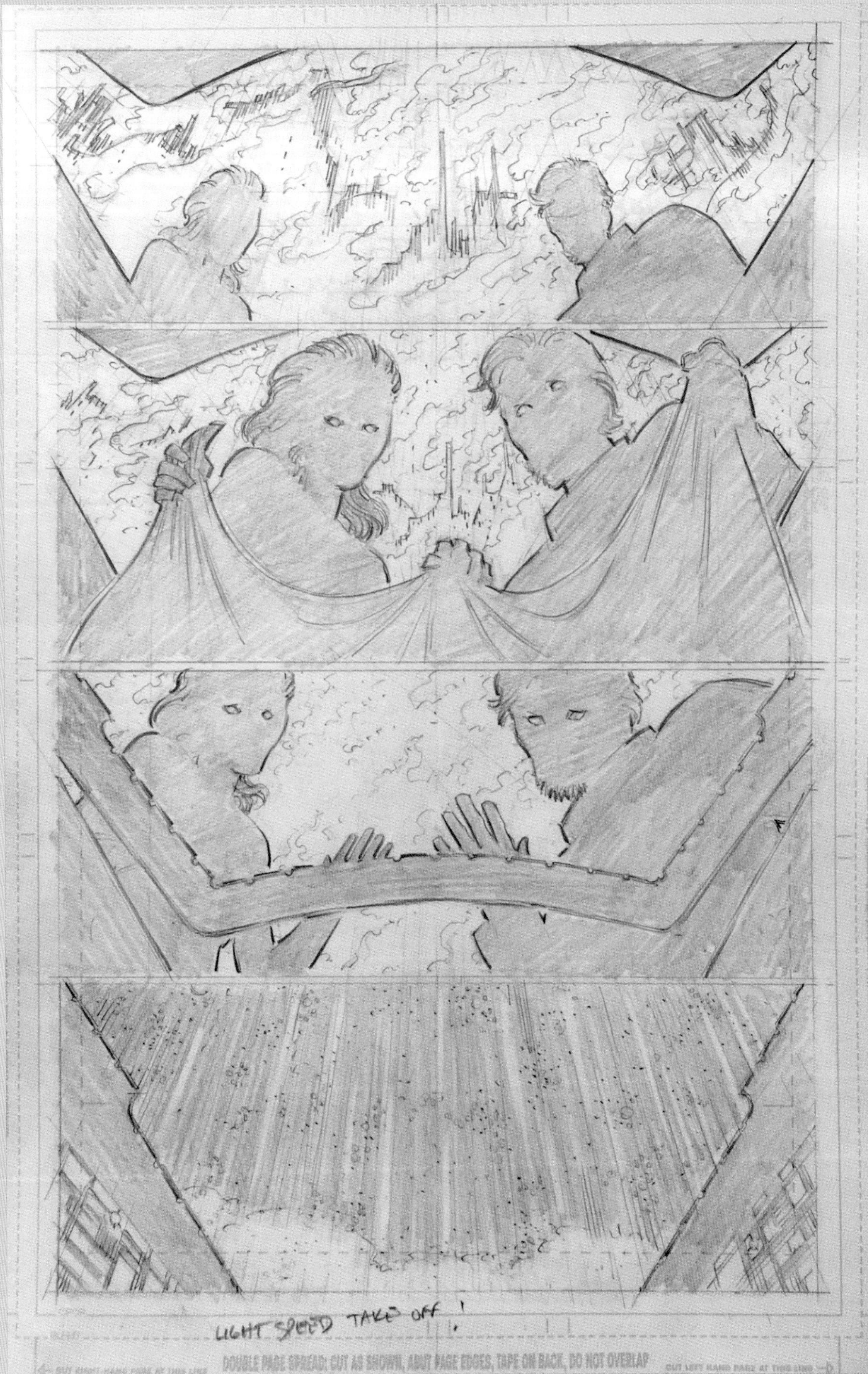
LIGHT SPEED TAKE OFF!
DOUBLE PAGE SPREAD: CUT AS SHOWN, ABUT PAGE EDGES, TAPE ON BACK, DO NOT OVERLAP
CUT LEFT HAND PAGE AT THIS LINE

Pencilled pages by John Romita Jr.

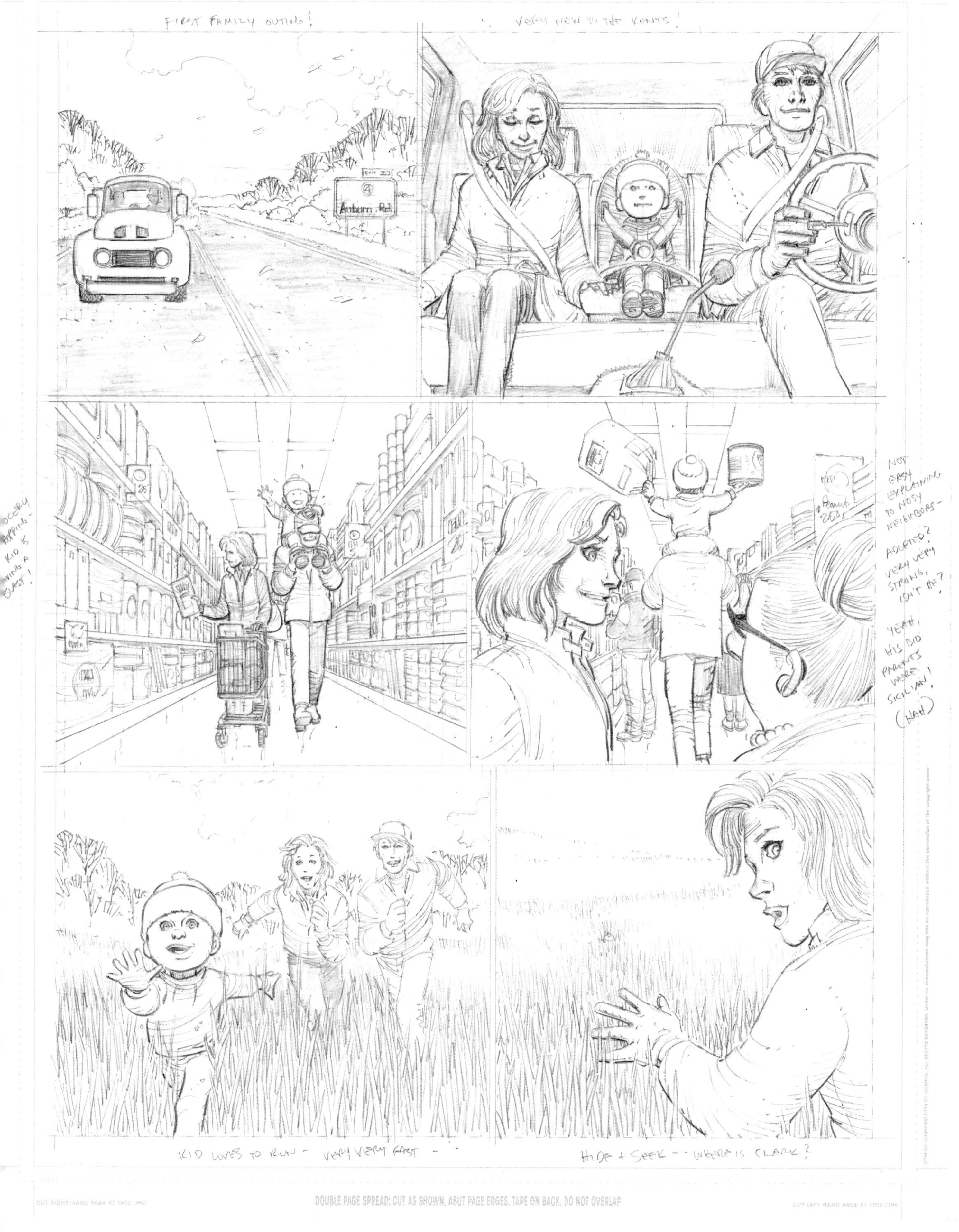
FIRST FAMILY OUTING!
VERY NEW TO THE KENTS!
Auburn Rd.
OCERY
PPING -
KID IS
VING A
BLAST!
NOT EASY EXPLAINING TO NOSY NEIGHBORS -
ADOPTED? VERY VERY STRONG, ISN'T HE?
YEAH, HIS BIO PARENTS WERE SICILIAN!
(NAH)
KID LOVES TO RUN - VERY VERY FAST -
HIDE + SEEK - - WHERE IS CLARK?
DOUBLE PAGE SPREAD: CUT AS SHOWN, ABUT PAGE EDGES, TAPE ON BACK, DO NOT OVERLAP

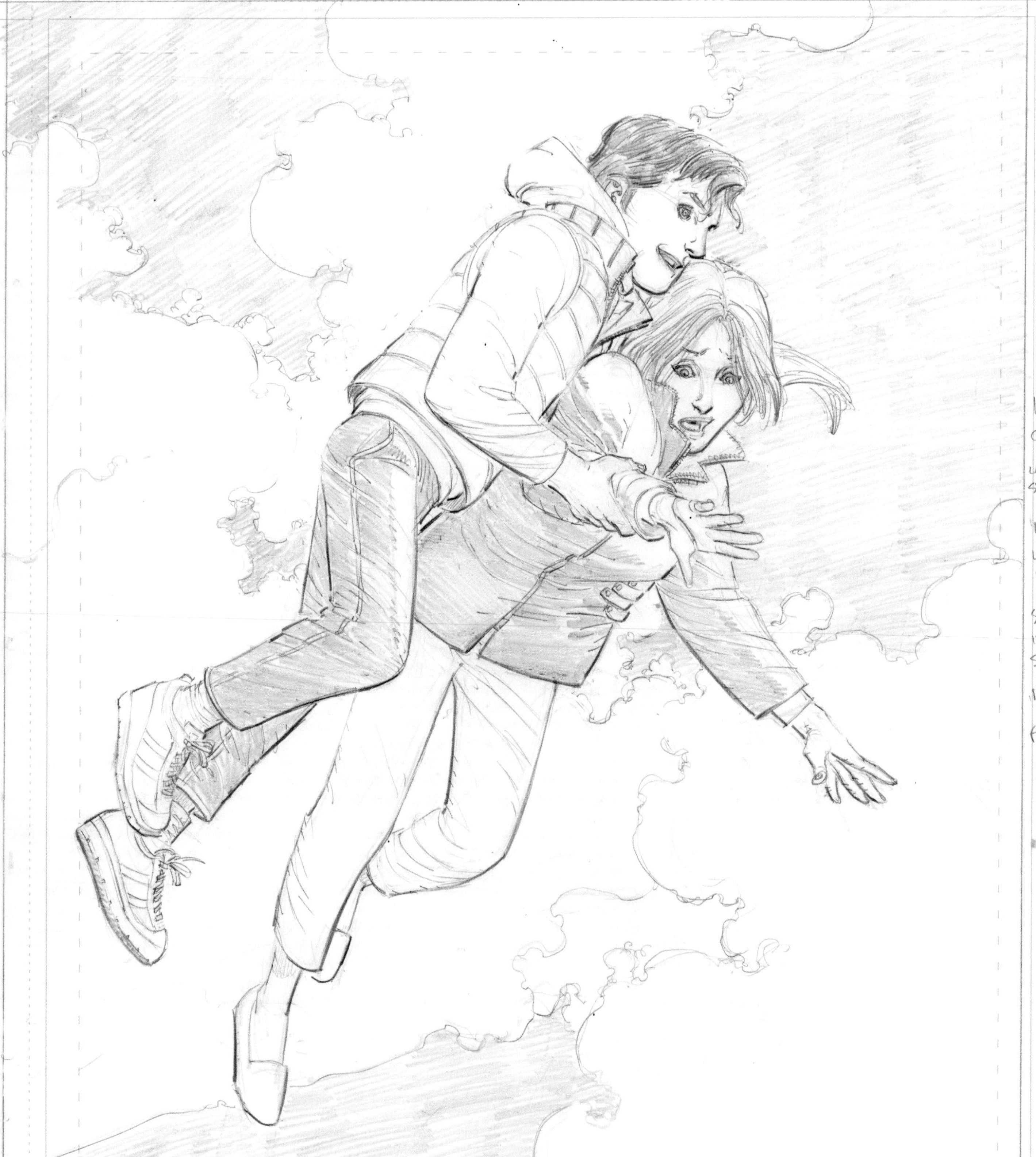

HOLY CRAP!

LANA STUNNED

IT'S A LONG STORY

SUFFICE IT TO SAY –

I'M NOT FROM THESE PARTS

PENCILLER JR INKER DANNY PAGE# 52
TITLE STRANGE VISITOR ISSUE # 1 MONTH

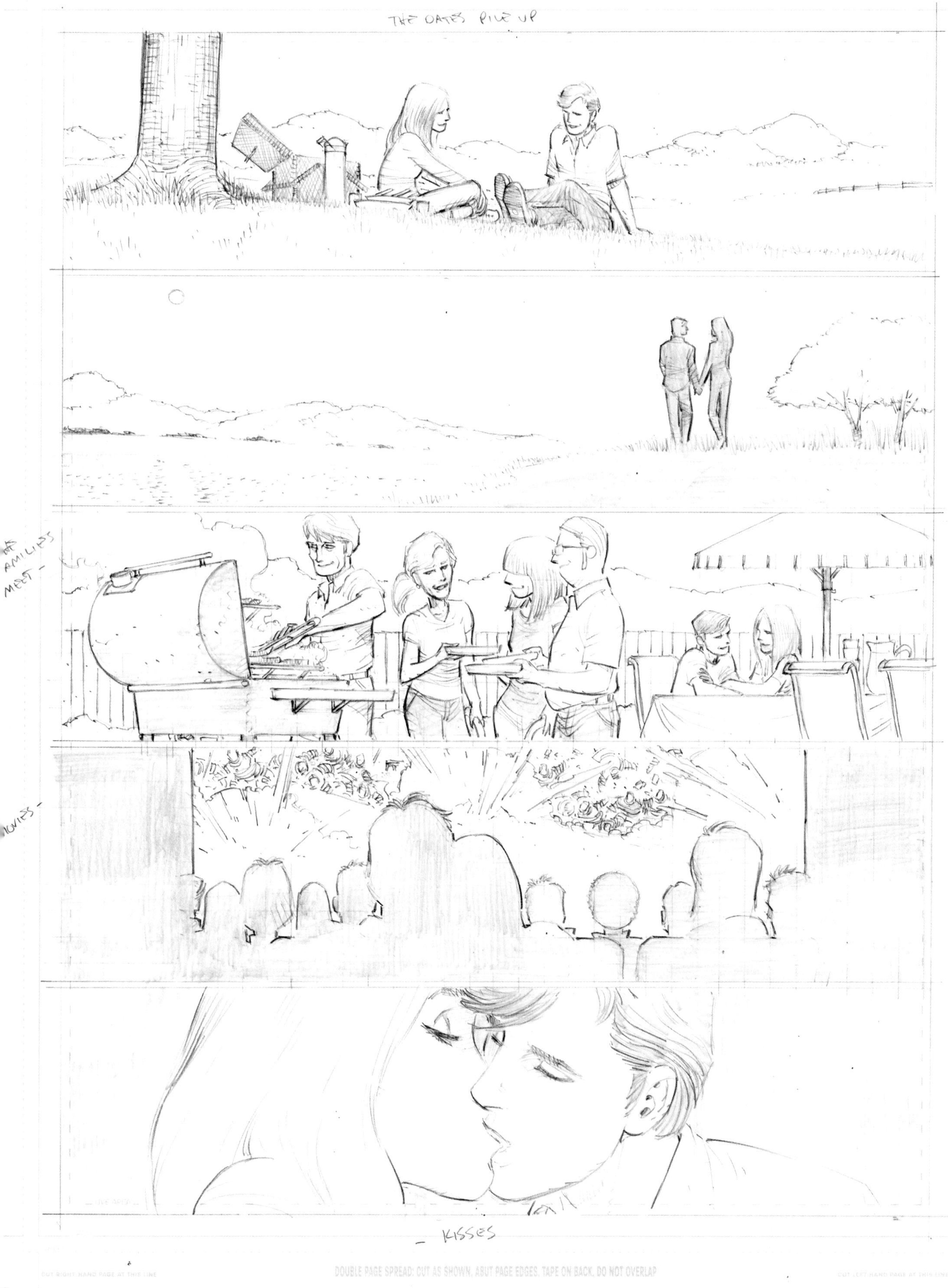

THE DATES PILE UP
AMILIES MEET -
OVIES -
- KISSES

DOUBLE PAGE SPREAD: CUT AS SHOWN, ABUT PAGE EDGES. TAPE ON BACK. DO NOT OVERLAP

PENCILLER JR INKER DANNY PAGE# 28
TITLE STRANGE VISITOR ISSUE # 2 MONTH

PIRATE SCREAMS - CLARK MOVES LIGHTNING FAST GRABS GRENADE - 7....6...

WRESTLES W/PIRATE PIRATE SCREAMS ..5... 4

KURTZ SVAES SEALS- KENT YOU ASSHOLE

KURTZ THINX CLARK + PIRATE ARE TOAST. CRAZY FOOL - GOTTA SPLIT OR-..

CLARK GETS GRENAD FREE ... 3

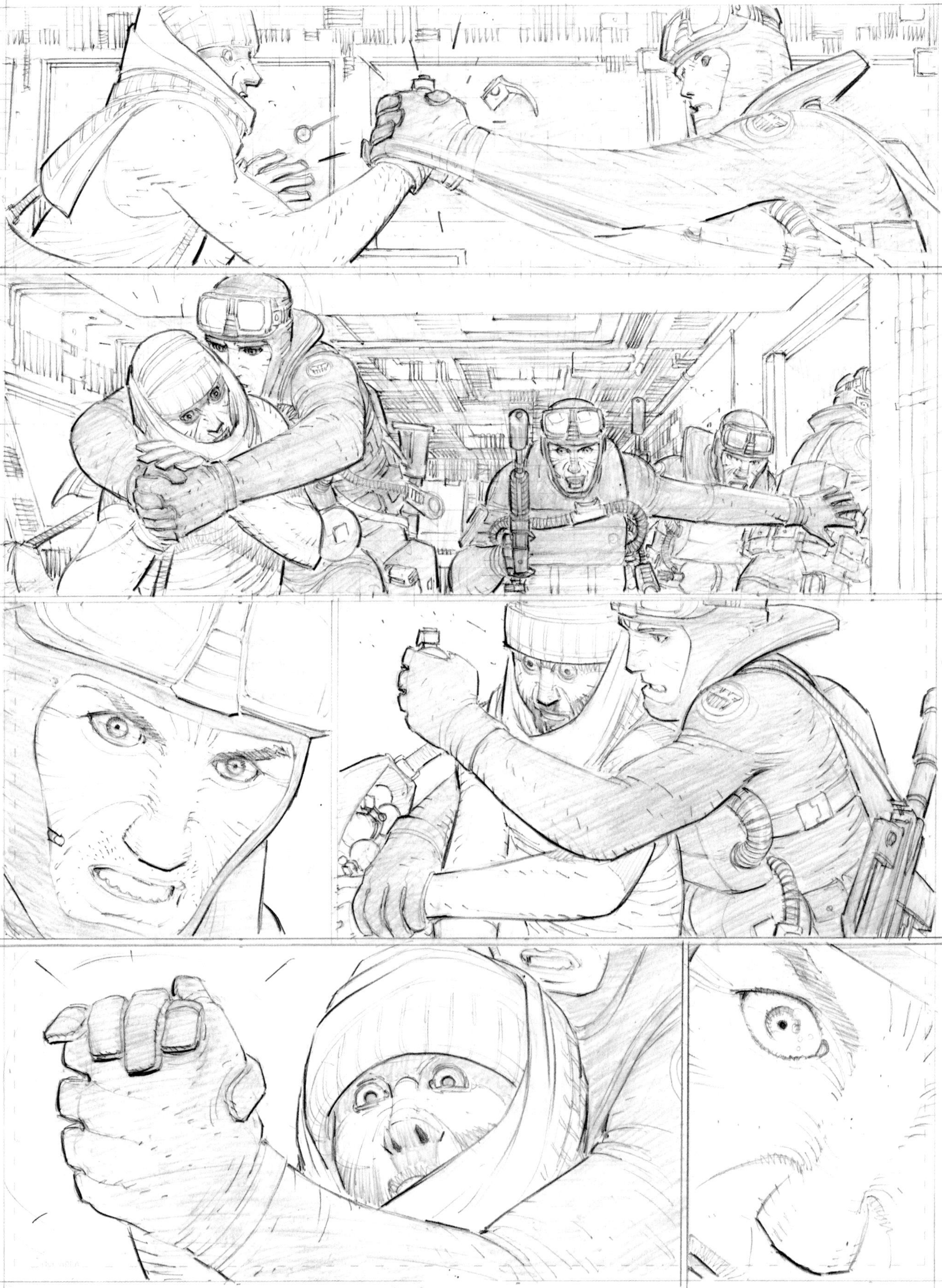

CLARK CLASPS HANDS OVER GRENADE - PIRATE SCREAMS --- 2 -- -..1 .. OH SHIT -

CUT RIGHT HAND PAGE AT THIS LINE DOUBLE PAGE SPREAD: CUT AS SHOWN, ABUT PAGE EDGES, TAPE ON BACK, DO NOT OVERLAP CUT LEFT HAND PAGE AT THIS LINE

PENCILLER JR INKER LANNY PAGE# 35
TITLE STRANGE VISITOR ISSUE # 2 MONTH

MER-FOLKS HANGING AROUND - LORI - PSYCHIC MESSAGE - I'M AT OUR SPOT -

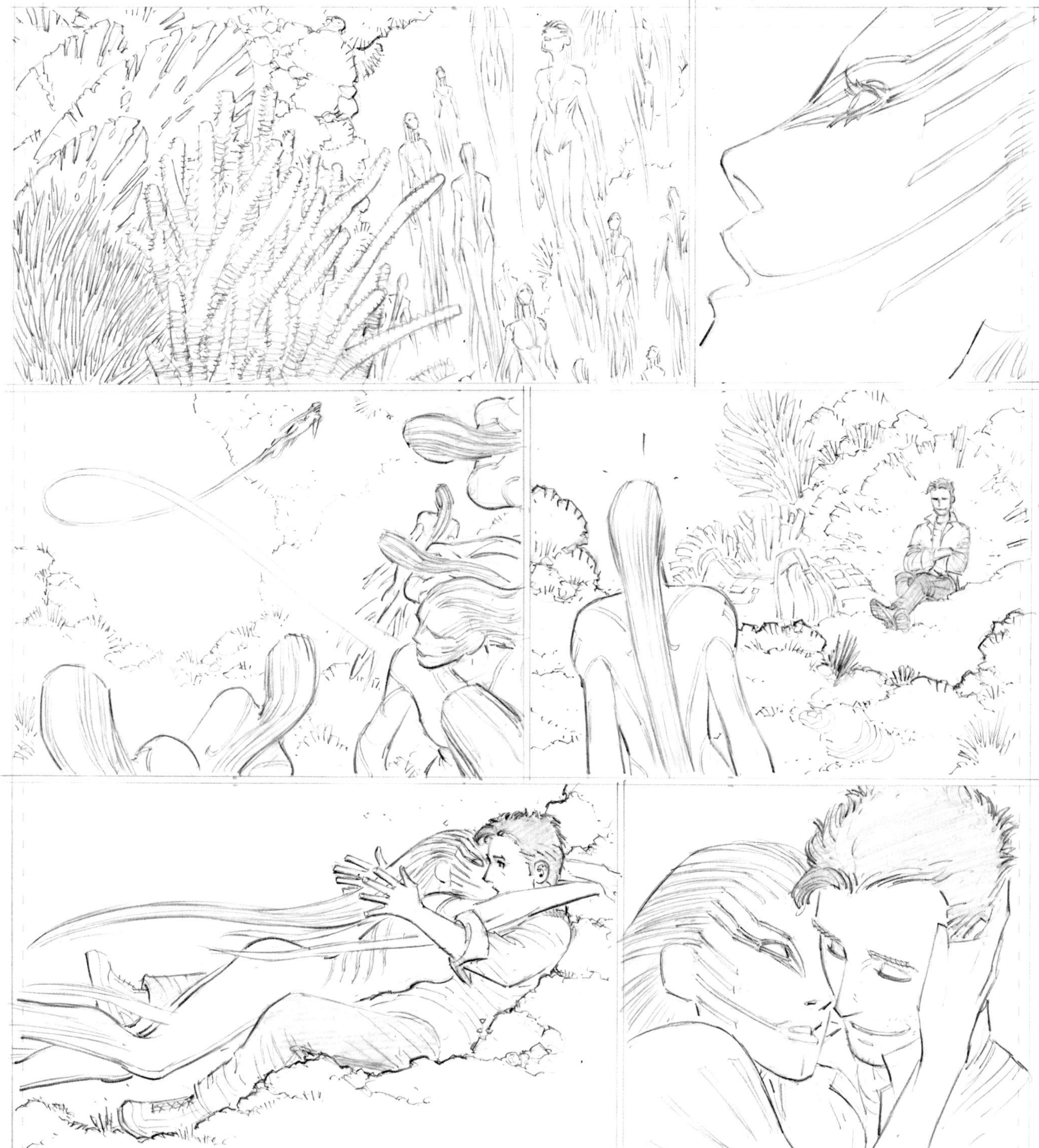

LIPS OFF.

UP - TO THEIR SPOT - SURPRISE!

ADORABLE -- I WANT YOU TO MEET THE FAMILY + --- DADDY -

CUT RIGHT-HAND PAGE AT THIS LINE DOUBLE PAGE SPREAD: CUT AS SHOWN, ABUT PAGE EDGES. TAPE ON BACK. DO NOT OVERLAP CUT LEFT-HAND PAGE AT THIS LINE

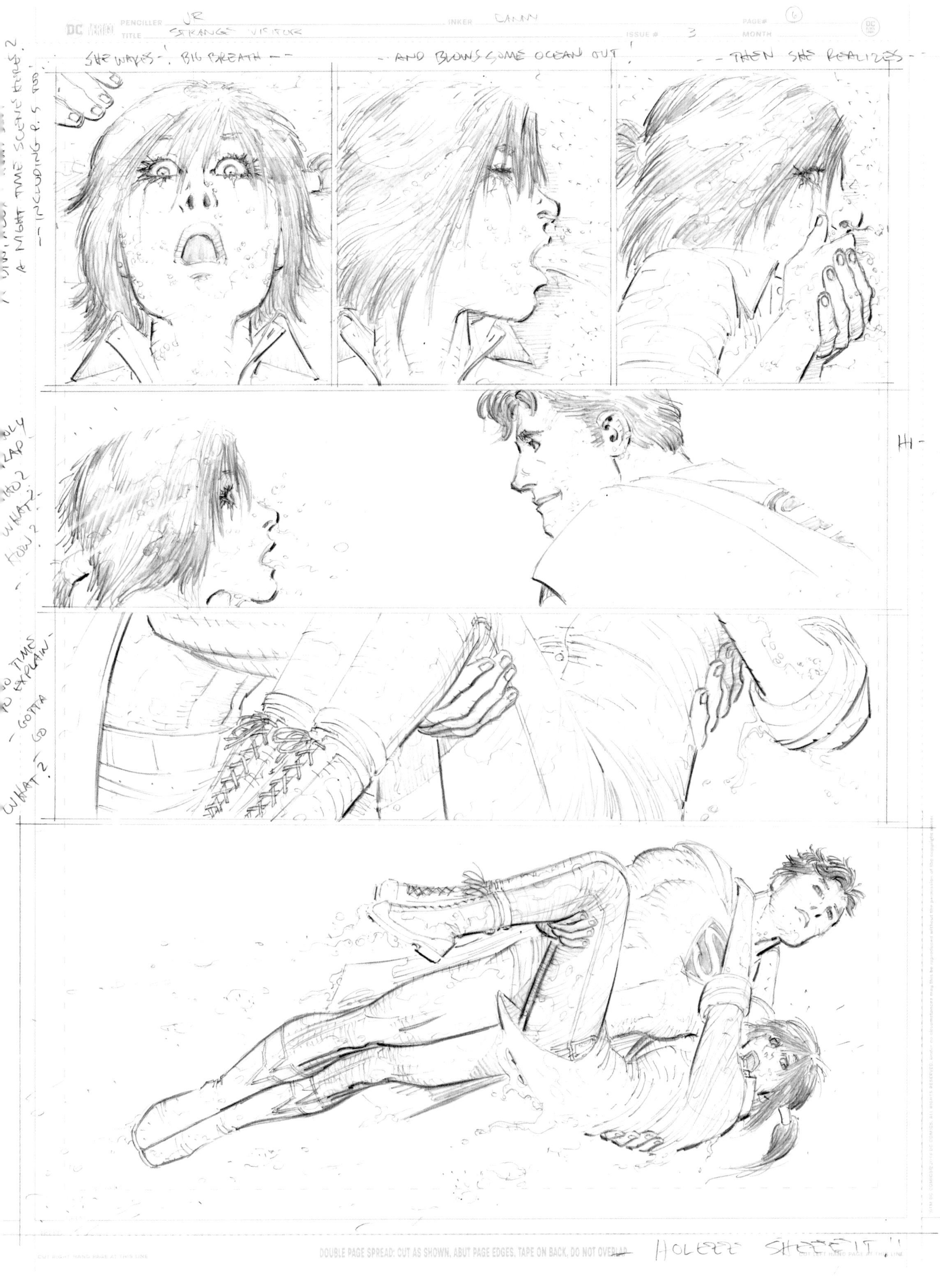
PENCILLER JR
INKER
PAGE# 6
TITLE STRANGE VISITOR
ISSUE # 3
MONTH
A NIGHT TIME SCENE HERE?
— INCLUDING P. 5 TOO
SHE WAKES! BIG BREATH —
— AND BLOWS SOME OCEAN OUT!
— THEN SHE REALIZES —
WHAT?
HOW?
HI —
TO EXPLAIN —
— GOTTA GO
WHAT?
DOUBLE PAGE SPREAD: CUT AS SHOWN, ABUT PAGE EDGES, TAPE ON BACK, DO NOT OVERLAP
HOLEEE SHEEEIT!!

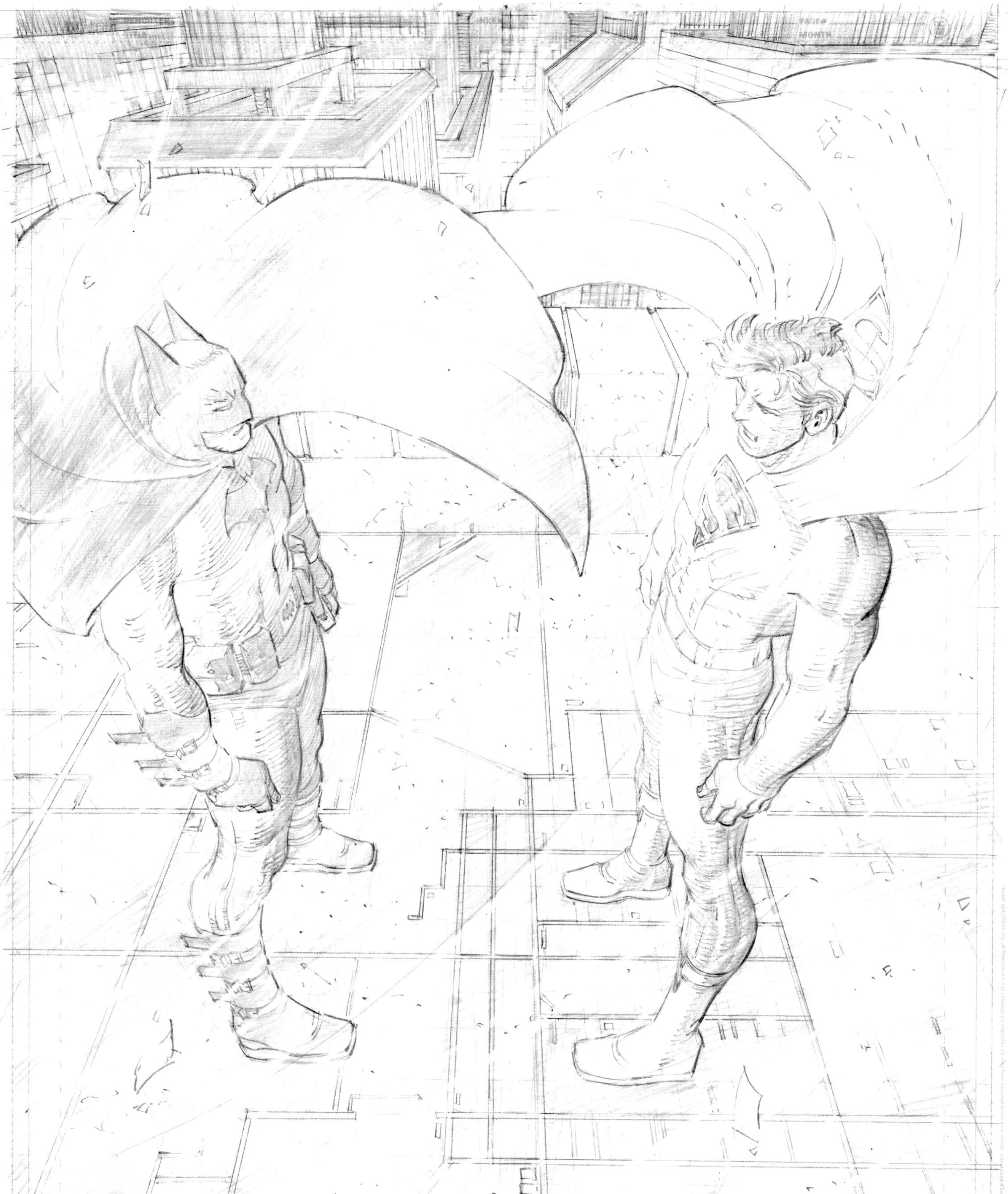

JR
STRANGE VISITOR

DANNY

#3

P. 53

DOUBLE PAGE SPREAD. CUT AS SHOWN. ABUT PAGE EDGES. TAPE ON BACK. DO NOT OVERLAP

Frank Miller

Frank Miller is regarded as one of the most influential and most-awarded professionals in the entertainment industry today, known for his intense, hard-boiled storytelling and gritty noir aesthetic across comics, graphic novels, and film. In 2019, Miller reteamed with artist John Romita Jr. for the highly anticipated *Superman: Year One*, a groundbreaking, definitive treatment of Superman's classic origin story released under DC's Black Label imprint.

Recently, Miller completed writing and illustrating *Xerxes: The Fall of the House of Darius and the Rise of Alexander*. Published by Dark Horse Comics, it's a five-issue companion epic to his award-winning series *300*.

Miller made his feature film directorial debut in 2005 with *Sin City*, the adaptation of his graphic novel, which he co-directed with Robert Rodriguez. The critically acclaimed film was nominated for a Palme d'Or at the 2005 Cannes Film Festival, won the Austin Film Critics Association's Austin Film Award, and garnered a Czech Lion nomination. In 2015, Miller and Rodriguez returned as co-directors of a sequel, *Sin City: A Dame to Kill For*, which reunited the duo with returning cast members as well as series newcomers Josh Brolin, Joseph Gordon-Levitt, Eva Green, and Lady Gaga, among others.

In 2007, Miller served as an executive producer on Zack Snyder's blockbuster *300*, based on the graphic novel written and illustrated by Miller and colored by Lynn Varley. The film went on to gross over $456 million worldwide in box office alone. In 2008, he wrote and directed his second feature, *The Spirit*, an action fantasy based on the Will Eisner comics series and starring Gabriel Macht, Eva Mendes, Sarah Paulson, Scarlett Johansson, and Samuel L. Jackson.

Miller became a professional comic book artist in his teens, working on a variety of assignments for major publishers including Gold Key, DC, and Marvel. He first drew attention to his work on two issues of Marvel's *Spectacular Spider-Man*, in a story that teamed the ever-popular arachnid with another popular character, Daredevil. Miller was then offered the regular pencilling slot on Daredevil's own book and, soon after, took over the writing chores on the title. Over the next several years, in collaboration with inker Klaus Janson, he created the ninja assassin-for-hire, Elektra.

In the early 1980s, Miller attracted further attention as one of the first comics freelancers who braved the field outside the comfortable world of company-owned characters with his creation of *Ronin*, a futuristic high-tech samurai pop adventure. It was the first of his several collaborations with Varley.

Since then, Miller has added a number of notable projects to his published works, including *Batman: The Dark Knight Returns*, with Janson and Varley; *Batman: The Dark Knight Strikes Again*, with Varley; *Batman: Year One*, illustrated by David Mazzucchelli and colored by Richmond Lewis; *Elektra: Assassin*, illustrated by Bill Sienkiewicz; *Elektra Lives Again*, with Varley; the award-winning Martha Washington miniseries *Give Me Liberty*, illustrated by Dave Gibbons; and *Hard Boiled*, illustrated by Geof Darrow. Recently Miller, alongside Brian Azzarello, completed DC's bestselling *Dark Knight III: The Master Race*, a nine-issue second sequel to The *Dark Knight Returns*.

The *Sin City* books have garnered numerous awards, including two Harvey Awards for Best Continuing Series in 1996 and Best Graphic Album of Original Work in 1998 and six Eisner Awards for Best Writer/Artist, Best Graphic Novel Reprint, Best Cartoonist, Best Cover Artist, Best Limited Series, and Best Short Story. In 2015, Miller was inducted into the Will Eisner Award Hall of Fame for his lifetime of contributions to the comics industry.

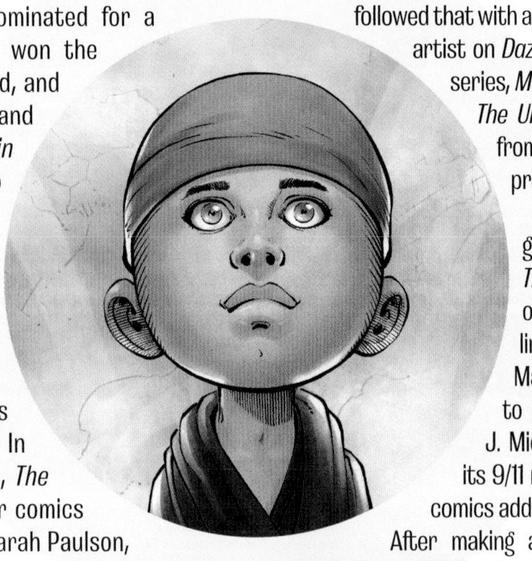

John Romita Jr.

John S. Romita, a.k.a. John Romita Jr., is one of the comic book industry's modern masters. The Eisner and Inkpot award-winning artist has worked on nearly every iconic hero in the Marvel and DC catalogs, and he also co-created the highest-selling creator-owned property ever published by Marvel: *Kick-Ass*.

Romita is the son of John Romita Sr., the former Marvel art director and legendary comics artist best known for his defining work on Spider-Man, and Virginia Romita, who worked at Marvel as a traffic manager. He made his first contribution to the world of comics in 1969 when, at the age of 13, he created the Prowler for his father to use in *The Amazing Spider-Man*. He began his professional career as a cover sketch artist for Marvel UK before making his prime-time debut with a backup story in *The Amazing Spider-Man Annual* #11 in 1977.

Romita landed his first regular series assignment with *Iron Man* in 1978, and he followed that with a run on *The Amazing Spider-Man*. He was the inaugural artist on *Dazzler*, and in 1982 he illustrated Marvel's first limited series, *Marvel Super Hero Contest of Champions*. He also drew *The Uncanny X-Men* from 1983 through 1986 [and again from 1993 through 1997], and between 1988 and 1990 he provided full pencils for *Daredevil*.

In 1993 Romita collaborated with Frank Miller on a graphic novel that became the miniseries *Daredevil: The Man without Fear*. He worked with Mark Millar on a run of *Wolverine* and with Neil Gaiman on the limited series *Eternals*, and he drew the core series for Marvel's bestselling *World War Hulk* event. His return to *The Amazing Spider-Man* with award-winning writer J. Michael Straczynski is especially well remembered for its 9/11 memorial issue, which was the first time mainstream comics addressed the attack and its aftermath.

After making an initial foray into the realm of creator-owned properties in 2004 with *The Gray Area* for Image, Romita reunited with Mark Millar in 2008 to create the *Kick-Ass* series, which was published under Marvel's Icon imprint. *Kick-Ass* became a top-five bestselling title, and its collected edition reached #1 on the *New York Times* graphic novel bestseller list. The title went on to be adapted into a series of major motion pictures, for which Romita served as a producer. He also directed an animated sequence in the first *Kick-Ass* film as well as consulting and providing visual development for the animated feature *Big Hero 6*. In addition, his contributions to comics culture overall have been acknowledged in the credits of *Avengers: Endgame*, *Captain Marvel*, *Avengers: Infinity War*, *Black Panther*, *Thor: Ragnarok*, and *Iron Man 2*, among others.

In 2014, after 36 consecutive years at the company, Romita left Marvel and signed an exclusive term agreement with DC—the biggest event of its kind since Jack Kirby switched teams in the 1970s. He immediately took over DC's flagship title *Superman* with writer Geoff Johns, followed by a collaboration with Scott Snyder on *All-Star Batman* and the co-creation [with Dan Abnett] of a new DC property, *The Silencer*. His work at DC has gone on to include numerous covers, the ongoing series *Suicide Squad*, and the acclaimed *Superman: Year One* with Frank Miller.

Following his departure from Marvel, Romita and Millar returned to *Kick-Ass* to relaunch the title at Image with the creation of a new female lead. Romita is also currently working on a new creator-owned property, *Shmuggy and Bimbo*, with comics legend Howard Chaykin, as well as developing several other film and media projects that have yet to be announced.

Romita is well-known within the industry for his charity work. In 2002 he undertook a 24-hour illustrating marathon to raise funds for cancer treatment, and in 2011 he contributed to a Guinness World Records comics-creation event in London to benefit the Yorkhill Children's Foundation. In 2012 he did another solo illustration marathon, continuously drawing for 48 hours in Las Vegas to support the Candlelighters Childhood Cancer Foundation of Nevada.

Influences on Romita's art from inside the world of comics include Romita Sr., Jack Kirby, and John Buscema. Outside influences include the Wyeth family painters and Charles Dana Gibson.

Danny Miki

Danny Miki started his career more than 24 years ago as an assistant on *The Uncanny X-Men* and *X-Men* before moving on to Image, where he helped to ink *Spawn, Curse of the Spawn,* and Greg Capullo's *Creech*. His most prominent work at Marvel was with David Finch on *Moon Knight,* as well as *The Avengers* and *The New Avengers*. Miki received a Harvey Award for Best Inker for his work with Neil Gaiman and John Romita Jr. on *Eternals*. His other projects include a Kevin Smith story for the *New York Times Magazine,* CD covers for the heavy metal bands Iced Earth and Demons and Wizards, and work for DC Comics, TMP, Wildstorm, and Top Cow. Miki is also the creator and owner of *Warcry, The Samurai Koimandos,* and *The Eduskaters*.

Alex Sinclair

Alex Sinclair has worked in the comic book industry as a colorist for 25 years. He has spent most of his career coloring for DC Comics and their many iconic characters. He has worked on many series, including *Batman, The Flash, Green Lantern, Justice League, Harley Quinn,* and *Wonder Woman*. His collaborations with Jim Lee and Scott Williams on *Batman: Hush,* as well as with Ivan Reis and Joe Prado on *Blackest Night,* earned him global recognition and multiple awards. Sinclair's current projects include *Harley Quinn, Superman,* and *Hawkman*. He lives in San Diego with his wife, Rebecca, and their four daughters: Grace, Blythe, Meredith, and Harley.

John Workman

John Workman started out in the world of advertising before breaking into comics in the early 1970s. From 1977 to 1984 he served as art director for the seminal comics anthology magazine *Heavy Metal,* for which he wrote, drew, edited, colored, designed, and lettered. He also has written and/or drawn for such publishers as DC, Marvel, Archie, Star*Reach, Image, Titan, and for *National Lampoon* and *Playboy,* but he is perhaps best known for his prolific work as a letterer for all those publishers and magazines and for his work in *TV Guide* and *Sports Illustrated*. His crisp, distinctive style and tight craftsmanship have helped him to forge long-standing partnerships with creators Walter Simonson (*Alien, The Mighty Thor, Orion, Star Slammers, Ragnarok*), John Paul Leon (*Wintermen, Mother Panic*), and Tommy Lee Edwards (*The Question, Turf, Mother Panic*), and he has partnered with a host of other collaborators over the course of his long and distinguished career. Workman also self-publishes his own comics, pamphlets, and posters through his Neonarcheos Publishing imprint.

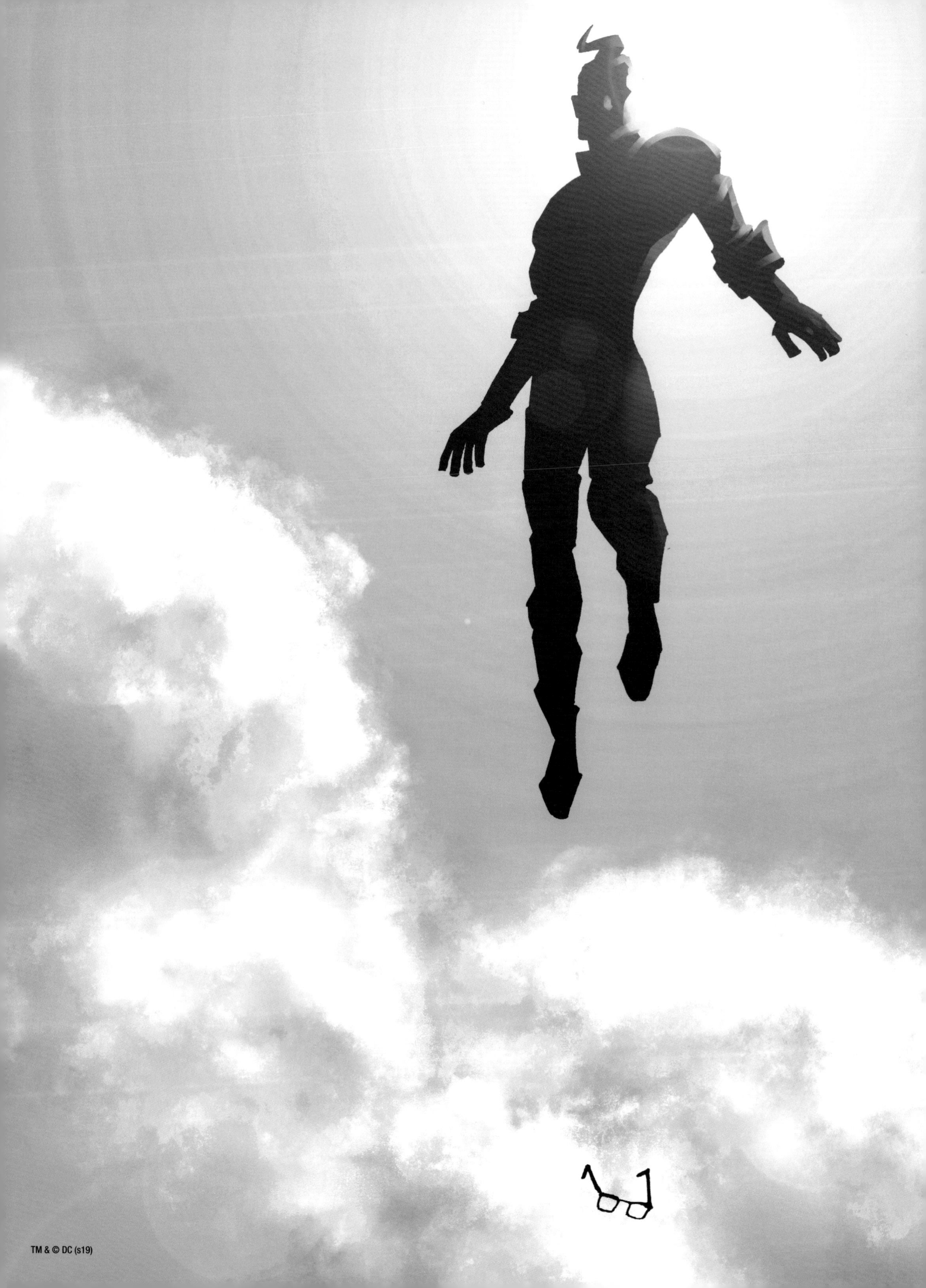